IGNATIUS OF LOYOLA

THE PSYCHOLOGY OF A SAINT

IGNATIUS OF LOYOLA

W. W. MEISSNER, S.J., M.D.

YALE UNIVERSITY PRESS   NEW HAVEN AND LONDON

Published with assistance from
the foundation established in
memory of Amasa Stone Mather
of the Class of 1907, Yale College.

Designed by Sonia L. Scanlon
Set in Trump type by
The Composing Room of Michigan, Inc.
Printed in the United States of America by
Vail-Ballou Press, Binghamton, New York.

Library of Congress
Cataloging-in-Publication Data
Meissner, W. W. (William W.), 1931–
Ignatius of Loyola : the psychology of a saint /
W. W. Meissner.
p. cm.
Includes bibliographical references and index.
ISBN 0-300-05156-5
1. Ignatius, of Loyola, Saint, 1491–1556—
Psychology.
2. Psychoanalysis and religion. I. Title.
BX4700.L7M54 1992
271'.5302—dc20
[B]   92-1270
CIP

A catalogue record for this book is available from
the British Library.

The paper in this book meets the guidelines
for permanence and durability of the Committee
on Production Guidelines for Book Longevity of
the Council on Library Resources.

10 9 8 7 6 5 4 3

CONTENTS

XIX

Mysticism: Psychoanalytic View 330

XX

Divine and/or Psychic Causality? 346

6

A PSYCHOANALYTIC PORTRAIT

XXI

Development and Conversion 361

XXII

The Personality of Ignatius 369

XXIII

The Spiritual Ascent 388

Appendix A

Letter from Ignatius to Archbishop Gian Pietro Carafa (1536) 401

Appendix B

Writings of Ignatius Concerning Holy Obedience 405

Appendix C

Letter from Ignatius to Sister Teresa Rejadella (18 June 1536) 417

Appendix D

On Sources and Versions of the *Spiritual Exercises* 422

PREFACE

When I began to gravitate toward the idea of undertaking this study, I thought it would be a formidable task, one that I hesitated to initiate and at many points found myself reluctant to pursue. Now that I have brought it to a conclusion, I have not changed my opinion—it was a formidable project. The task I set myself was to probe the mind and heart of one of the greatest saints to adorn the calendar of God's heroes. Ignatius of Loyola has assumed his place among the greatest figures in Western Christianity. He is known to history as the founder of the Society of Jesus ("the Jesuits"), as one of the greatest mystics in the history of the Church, and finally as one of the foremost figures in the Catholic Counter-Reformation. No small task!

Why would a psychoanalyst be interested in trying to understand the psychic life of this man? The psychoanalyst studies and tries to understand human behavior and motivation in any and all of its guises. He claims for himself that motto of Terence, "Nil humani me alienum puto." The complex personality of this great saint exercises an irresistible fascination for such a study. Moreover, it brings into focus significant questions about the complex interplay between human motivations and needs on one side, and religious experience and spiritual motivation on the other. Put in theological terms, the question has to do with how nature and grace were integrated in the life of this great saint.

An additional consideration is that this task has never, to my knowledge, been attempted before. Historians and biographers have not been idle in assembling, sorting, verifying, and assessing the facts of this fascinating and powerfully meaningful life. Biographies abound—good ones—that recount the events of his astonishing career and to a satisfying degree fix it in the perspective of the life, culture, and history of his times. I have set myself a different goal, one that is not possible without building on these impressive historical contributions, but one that also tries in a sense to go beyond them, or at least to explore a different path, parallel to the more well-worn historical and biographical tracks. No one has tried to enter that inner world of the saint that lies beyond the verifiable data of his life. The current endeavor seeks to look behind the façade, behind the events, behind the various accounts and documents, to try to discern the face of this man of God and what motivated his wondrous trajectory.

The question is whether it is possible to fulfill the task in any sense. It may be that it has never before been attempted because it cannot be done. I can do no better than Freud, who commented in his analysis of Leonardo, "If, in making these statements, I have provoked the criticism, even from friends of psychoanalysis and from those who are expert at it, that I have merely written a psychological novel, I shall reply that I am far from overestimating the certainty of these results" (1910, p. 134).

Ignatius was a charismatic leader who exercised a profound influence on the men of his time—not only those who shared his apostolic and spiritual vision, but many others who came to know the effects of his attractive, suasive, and forceful personality. He has also exercised a powerful influence through the ensuing centuries—on those who have chosen to follow his standard in the Society he founded, and on those who have been affected by his spiritual and religious teachings. Few men in the history of the world have touched the lives of their fellow men as profoundly and pervasively as Ignatius of Loyola. The prospect of exploring the inner psychic world of such a subject is irresistible. What propelled this fascinating and remarkable figure through the vicissitudes of his spiritual adventure toward his personal destiny and his place in history? As we shall see, probing into the life of Ignatius brings into dramatic relief questions regarding the motivation of spiritual experiences, the interplay of human psychology and religious experience, and the role of psychological factors in mystical experiences and states—among others.

Ignatius was one of the guiding spirits of my own life and career. Whatever spiritual substance and direction I have reflects my formative experiences in the course of my Jesuit training—all based directly on the teachings and spiritual guidance of Ignatius. The other dominant influence in my life—this one more intellectual than spiritual—has been Sigmund Freud, the guiding spirit of my career as a psychoanalyst. My path through life has been an effort to integrate these two disparate influences in some meaningful way—in both a personal and an intellectual sense. This exploration of the inner life of Ignatius may represent one phase of that enterprise. I can only remind my readers—and concur-

rently myself—that these two diverging yet interacting and intersect-
ing influences will be in play throughout what follows.

I would like to express my gratitude to the corps of Jesuit teachers,
spiritual guides, friends, peers, and mentors who have over the years
helped to shape my understanding of Ignatius and his spirituality. The
names of John Courtney Murray, Herbert Musurillo, George Kluber-
tanz, and Frank Keenan leap to mind; I regret that they will take satisfaction from their efforts only if reports of this work reverberate in the
heavenly kingdom. My debt to them is no less for that. Of others who
have lent a helping hand along the way, I would like to thank John
O'Malley, S.J., in particular for his reading of sections of the manuscript
and his suggestions for shoring up the historical references. My thanks
also to Daniel O'Connell, S.J., for a critical reading of an early draft. My
gratitude is due in equal measure to the many psychoanalytic mentors,
teachers, and friends who have helped me to clarify my thinking about
psychoanalysis and religion. My appreciation is owed to Elfriede Banz-
haf for her unfailing enthusiasm and energy in facilitating the preparation of this manuscript at every phase of its painful progression toward
realization. And last but not least, my thanks belong to Gladys Topkis
of Yale University Press, for her unfailing good humor and skill in helping to translate my poor efforts into readable English prose.

PSYCHOHISTORY, PSYCHOBIOGRAPHY, AND PSYCHOANALYSIS

INTRODUCTION

Whaen the psychoanalyst enters the world of history or biography, he enters a strange and alien territory, lacking all the familiar landmarks that he has habitually used to guide his explorations. While he normally deals with a living, talking, responding subject, he now confronts all the obscurities and opacities of the historical record. The immediacy of the psychoanalytic situation is replaced by the concealing veil of time and distance. Instead of the vitality and spontaneity of a patient's associations, he is met with the residues of history—faceless facts, dates, names, monuments, and the impenetrability of documents. One must conclude that this inherently perilous enterprise can be undertaken only at great risk.[1]

PSYCHOHISTORY

The alliance of psychoanalysis and psychohistory has never been an easy or comfortable one. Ever since William Langer's epoch-making presidential address to the American Historical Association, in which he challenged his fellow historians to seek a more psychologically meaningful basis for their studies of the motives and behaviors of historical subjects, the reaction among historians has been at best mixed, at worst hostile. Langer chastised his colleagues for their conservatism and pointed out that there was "still ample scope for penetration in depth. . . . I refer more specifically to the urgently needed deepening of our historical understanding through exploitation of the concepts and findings of modern psychology" (1958, p. 284). The most likely modern psychological approach for the task was psychoanalysis.

Some of Langer's colleagues found the challenge stimulating, even

exciting; others found it threatening, misguided, and fraught with problems and methodological issues of great complexity. After the introduction of psychological methods of any kind, could this hybrid approach
remain worthy of the name of history? And would the psychohistorical
approach generate any new knowledge?

Certainly the application of psychoanalysis to any context outside the
clinical is problematic. Freud himself was quick to sound a cautionary
note: "I would not say that an attempt of this kind to carry psychoanalysis over to the cultural community was absurd or doomed to be
fruitless. But we should have to be very cautious and not forget that, after
all, we are only dealing with analogies and that it is dangerous, not only
with men but also with concepts, to tear them from the sphere in which
they have originated and been evolved" (1930a, p. 144). The simple fact is
that psychoanalytic understanding and ideas best serve clinical experience; when they leave those fertile fields their certainty diminishes.

There are additional methodological incompatibilities. History tends
to be literal-minded, concentrating on facts that are concrete and verifiable by accepted methods. Psychoanalysis lives in the realm of metaphor, fantasy, and analogy. It focuses on meanings and motives rather
than facts—and meanings and motives are not always readily validated.
The psychohistorian is not immune to the demands of evidence and
proof, but because of the hidden nature of what he deals with, the proof
has a different cast than ordinary historical discourse. To take an example from my own past efforts (Minnich and Meissner 1978), one can
hypothesize that certain of Erasmus' attitudes and behaviors were
etiologically connected to the fact of his illegitimacy and associated
trauma. The causal links are nowhere immediate or evident. The proof
rests on a welter of facts, opinions, reactions, behaviors in various contexts, comments in letters and other writings. No single fact or connection will validate the hypothesis, but it begins to take on meaning and
consistency in the light of the total complex of facts, data, and their
integrating interpretations.

Freud faced a similar problem in trying to account for the validity of
dream interpretations. On the subject of dealing with the patient's resistance and doubts he commented:

One makes no attempt at shouting down this doubt by means of
one's authority or at reducing it by arguments. It must persist until it

is brought to an end in the further course of the analysis. The analyst, too, may himself retain a doubt of the same kind in some particular instances. What makes him certain in the end is precisely the complication of the problem before him, which is like the solution of a jig-saw puzzle. A coloured picture, pasted upon a thin sheet of wood and fitting exactly into a wooden frame, is cut into a large number of pieces of the most irregular and crooked shapes. If one succeeds in arranging the confused heap of fragments, each of which bears upon it an unintelligible piece of drawing, so that the picture acquires a meaning, so that there is no gap anywhere in the design and so that the whole fits into the frame—if all these conditions are fulfilled, then one knows that one has solved the puzzle and that there is no alternative solution. (1923, p. 116)

Solid ground for the historian's search for historical fact? No. Meaningful territory for the need to search out some psychological understanding? Possibly. The gestalt—the integration of parts into a meaningful whole—may or may not achieve coherence and provide meaning, but disproof is more complex than denying the validity of historical facts. It requires a piece by piece dismantling of the gestalt. When enough of the pieces have been removed, the hypothesis lacks the necessary support and so collapses. The degree to which this process is open to scrutiny depends on the specificity of the hypothesis, the validity of the relevant data, and the construction of the psychological argument through which they are integrated. The process, so conceived, is not unlike the psychoanalyst's approach to the history and meaning of his patient's life. The critical point here has been articulated by Bruce Mazlish:

In sum, psychohistorical inquiry helps us to understand the "meaning" of an event, but does not—in fact, cannot—offer us a simple causal explanation of it. It follows directly that history cannot be *reduced* to psychoanalytic explanation. . . . psychoanalysis adds to other explanations in history; it is no substitute for them. Because the psychohistorian focuses on aspects of the historical process that are different in nature and quality from the traditional focus of historical interest, his methods, his approach and his concepts are also different. The results should not stand in contradiction to the results of historical investigation; they may complement those findings and understandings, they may cast them in a somewhat different light, they may give rise to a more nuanced and variable interpretation, but they never can contradict established historical facts. Without such facts, the psychohistorical hypotheses are empty vessels without meaning and content. (1968, p. 232)

PSYCHOBIOGRAPHY

Turning to psychobiography, as a subdivision of psychohistory, brings us closer to the matter at hand. Biography lends itself somewhat more graciously and accommodatingly to the integration of a psychoanalytic perspective. Even Barzun concedes a place for psychological approaches in the realm of biography: "To take biography is convenient, despite the differences between biography and history, because psychology in its accepted meaning is the study of the mind; its utility to the historian is therefore most obvious when he is dealing with one individual, when he is a biographer" (1974, p. 7). And again: "The historical study of a person—biography—which has always called forth random psychological remarks, might be the true playground for a systematic tackling of the psyche" (pp. 33–34).

If there is legitimacy in the enterprise, there are also significant difficulties. None of the materials that history or biography offers can serve the psychobiographer without being shaped by his interpretation. His work consists in bringing to bear an interpretive schema, based on his clinical knowledge and experience and drawn from psychological theory—in this case psychoanalysis—to yield hypotheses that will add a significant dimension to the understanding of the subject's personality and behavior in the course of that individual's life. It is in the interplay between biographical fact and psychological interpretation that the pitfalls of this approach become apparent.

Problems arise in selecting data, arranging events into recognizable patterns, omitting or underemphasizing aspects that do not fit the putative hypothesis, proposing false connections, mistaking conjecture for historical fact, allowing one's own attitudes about the subject to contaminate or influence the process of judgment or interpretation. Keeping in mind that the psychobiographical approach cannot reach very far beyond the conjectural, there is an understandable impulse on the part of the investigator to find certainty and fact where none exists. Distorting factors can easily enter into the process, tending toward making the subject and his life fit the procrustean bed of psychoanalytically generated hypotheses. The subject is trimmed to fit the model rather than the model being designed to allow the subject the rich, full, complexity of his life (Mack 1971).

These difficulties are not unfamiliar to the psychoanalyst, who is confronted daily in his consulting room with a similar task—to fit the data coming from the patient into some recognizable pattern that will allow them both to better understand its meaning, with enough theoretical perspective to allow useful clinical work to be done. In that context, the patient never fits comfortably into any preexisting mold and by his very reality constantly reminds the analyst that he never will. The good psychobiographer must learn to live with ambiguity and uncertainty—and to settle for what he can get, even if that is no more than a loosely conjectural understanding of his subject.

The interpretive aspect of psychobiography carries its own inherent difficulties. As Mack has observed:

> The problems of unbalanced interpretation or overinterpretation of insufficient psychological and/or historical data are very great indeed. The available data may be insufficient from which to draw interpretive conclusions, may be unsuitable for interpretation except speculatively . . . or may equally well be interpreted differently with no confirmation or contradiction possible as in psychoanalytic treatment. Then too, there are the errors of interpretation that result from the biographer's limiting himself too much to internal psychological considerations with insufficient attention given to the period, cultural context, and other historical realities. (1971, p. 175)

In addition to these interpretive difficulties arising from data, the psychobiographer is burdened by certain attitudes and feelings about his subject that come from his own psychic makeup and inner life. This phenomenon is familiar to him in the form of countertransference[2]; it is an aspect of his clinical experience that he struggles with on intimate terms day in and day out. In the realm of psychobiography, it is involved in the choice to study and write about a particular subject as well as the measure the biographer takes of his subject as he learns more about him and begins to shape his view and understanding of the complex human phenomenon before him. Unrecognized and unmodulated countertransference distorts objectivity and impairs judgment throughout the process. Freud was well aware of this danger and took the trouble to warn future psychobiographers that their views of their subjects were in all likelihood contaminated by infantile needs and wishes. He wrote in his essay on Leonardo:

> To gratify this wish they obliterate the individual features of their subject's physiognomy; they smooth over the traces of his life's struggles with internal and external resistances, and they tolerate in him no vestige of human weakness and imperfection. They thus present us with what is in fact a cold, strange, ideal figure, instead of a human being to whom we might feel ourselves distantly related. That they should do this is regrettable, for they thereby sacrifice truth to an illusion, and for the sake of their infantile phantasies abandon the opportunity of penetrating the most fascinating secrets of human nature. (1910, p. 130)

Psychoanalytic interpreters have too often strayed from the confines imposed by uncertain data and tentative hypotheses, losing sight of the limitations in their formulations. The step between the recognition and definition of clinically identifiable patterns of behavior and motivation to interpretation of the behavior of an historical figure is slippery indeed. When the investigator identifies such a pattern, he too often leaps to the conclusion that his historical subject is another such case. The certainty of the conclusion may reflect a need to gain closure, or sheer intellectual arrogance. But the data are never hard and unequivocal— they are frequently mere guesses and speculations, often based on unreliable sources (Coles 1975).

And if the historical subject matches the clinical pattern in any significant degree, and this can be thoroughly demonstrated by reliable documentation, what does the discovery contribute to our understanding of the course of historically determinable events? To cite Langer's often-criticized study of Hitler (1972), what did Hitler's psychopathology have to do with his career and its disastrous results? Countless patients throughout the history of psychiatry have had similar mental aberrations but did not precipitate a world war and a program of genocide (Coles 1975). But one should not make the mistake of weighting the psychic hypothesis too heavily. Nor should one overstep the bounds of what a given hypothesis purports to explain. It seems reasonable to think that Hitler's paranoid grandiosity contributed to his attitudes about the Jews and his manic vision of the glorious thousand-year Reich. A Hitler lacking this dimension in his personality structure might have responded differently to the flow of events in the historical record—with what consequences we shall never know. The paranoid grandiosity is only one component among many complex determining factors.

One of the biographical pitfalls is the so-called genetic fallacy—explaining current behavior by appealing to its origins in the past, or what Erikson (1975) dubbed the "originological fallacy." In a trenchant footnote, Barzun (1974) disparages this aspect of the psychological approach: "Psychologizing may be defined as the practice of taking an utterance or an action not at its face value as an expression of straightforward desire or purpose, but as an involuntary symptom which, when properly interpreted, discloses a meaning hidden from the agent and from common observers. It is a form of the genetic fallacy." From a psychoanalytic perspective, symptomatic behaviors derive part of their motive power from psychologically meaningful events and experiences acquired in the course of development. Such originative connections achieve their most convincing validation in the course of psychoanalytic work. In the biographical context they remain no more than conjectural hypotheses that add texture to the historical picture. The possible role of Oedipal dynamics in Hitler's hatred of the Jews does not account for the Holocaust.

There is always danger in an attempt to determine states of mind or feeling that are not evident in the historical material. Genetic reconstructions are also risky, even when their plausibility is confirmed by clinical knowledge. The biographer is on safer ground when he starts with what is known about the background or development of his subject and applies it to its determinable consequences in later and historically relevant contexts. For example, the treatment Henry VIII received

at the hands of tutors and servants that vacillated between extravagant adulation and brutal discipline, and . . . the hypocrisy and self-serving nature of this adulation by what were in effect "paid foster parents," had the result that his upbringing did not offer the possibilities for forming permanent important relationships. All of these conditions fostered the development of Henry's pathological narcissism . . . so that a series of defeats and disappointments offended Henry's grandiose self-image, and caused the series of actions which led to the break with Catherine and with Rome, and to later events in Henry's career as well. (Shore 1972, as cited in Woods, 1974, p. 113)

I would add that the use of the word "caused" in this context must be understood in the qualified sense of psychic causality, as one determinant among many others, both psychic and nonpsychic.

The application of psychopathological models also brings its own burden. Lifton (1974) has noted the tension between the historical paradigm and the pathological paradigm. He cautions: "When this second paradigm dominates, psychopathology becomes a substitute for the psychohistorical interface. The psychopathological idiom for individual development (so prominent in the literature of psychoanalysis) becomes extended to the point where it serves as the idiom for history, or psychohistory. When this happens there is, once more, no history" (p. 26). The risk here seems to be primarily reductive—the psychological observer's need to see his subject in terms of the pathological models that are his stock-in-trade. The view through the psychopathological lens distorts and reduces by filtering out aspects of the subject's character and personality that are less than congruent with the model, even when it allows a clearer insight into the pathological aspects of the character. The appreciation for the subject that results from such an approach runs the risk of being forced to fit the pathological model—whether that is cast in specifically diagnostic terms or in terms of the conceptual formulations of a particular theory such as psychoanalysis.

THE PSYCHOANALYTIC APPROACH

The basic difficulties the psychoanalyst faces in this enterprise can be described as methodological and interpretive. The psychoanalytic method is intended for therapy with a patient lying on the couch, breathing, moving, associating freely, talking, thinking, developing resistances and transferences, and interacting with the analyst in the task of self-discovery and self-understanding. Analyst and patient seek that truth about the patient and his life that will set him free from the chains of his neurosis or characterological difficulties. In this arena of human experience, the analyst is trained and experienced to do his work.

What happens when the putative patient is dead—and nearly five centuries dead at that! The subject of investigation cannot talk, associate, resist, or do any of the things the analyst requires in order to do his job properly. Only the vestiges of a life are available—residues that conceal as much or more than they reveal. The myriad documents from the life of Ignatius have been collected, meticulously edited, and published as the massive *Monumenta Historica Societatis Jesu* (MHSJ), with the kind of care and devotion one would expect from the best of Jesuit scholarship.[3] Few biographers would complain about having all that valuable material gathered on one shelf in the library—a long shelf, but all in one place.

Were the task at hand simply biographical, one might well be satisfied with such a resource. But the psychoanalyst seeks not merely to establish and validate the facts of his subject's life, but to see beyond, into the heart and mind of the man. How is he to do that when his subject is dead and can be reached only through these lifeless and opaque remnants? Needless to say, he cannot even begin his attempt if the work of biography has not been done well.

Thanks to generations of outstanding Jesuit study and scholarship, the details of Ignatius' life are well established. There are the inevitable gaps and omissions that plague any biography or history—one always wants to know more—and there are many details that cannot be known with certainty, but the history has been established to the extent that it can be known. Even this much, however, provides only guideposts, for the work of psychobiography is necessarily more interpretive than historical, more concerned with hidden motives and meanings than with establishing and validating facts. Substantiating the claims of psychological interpretation requires a distinctly different method.

Most historians have come to recognize that the Rankean "Wie es eigentlich gewesen ist" (as it really was) represents an outmoded ideal never fully realized. The gaps must be filled even in the objective historical record. In this enterprise correspondence and coherence complement each other in the search for historical truth. The analyst's approach is less avowedly a posteriori than the biographer's and more self-consciously a priori in that he views the given historical data through the lens of his theory, seeking to gain some congruence between the emergent patterns of the data and the dictates of his the-oretical perspective. The problem is complicated by the nature of the data—remote, lifeless, faceless. None of them conveys any meaning, particularly any psychologically relevant meaning, without interpreta-tion. Even personal documents such as letters can conceal more than they reveal and must be read within a specific historical context and set of conditions that qualify their meaning. They are in a sense public documents, and the question of the audience intended by the author, consciously or unconsciously, beyond the immediate recipient, always lurks in the background. And in all such precipitates of the flow of a human life and experience there remains the issue of what is not said, not included, in a given document. Because the analyst's target in all this is not historical fact but personal meaning and motive, the conceal-ment factor looms very large indeed, since motives are by their nature largely concealed even from the subject himself. If we could resurrect him, he might tell us what he thinks his real motives were—much as analytic patients do in their analytic hours—but the account would be misleading and faulty—much as it is in a typical analytic exploration. The unconscious does not yield its secrets so easily.

THE IGNATIAN MATERIAL

When we turn to a consideration of the life of St. Ignatius of Loyola, all of these difficulties come into play. First, there is the material on which we might base our appraisal. Our man is not only dead but has been dead for going on four-and-a-half centuries. Our view through the murky mists of such a distant vista must be clouded and uncertain. But such temporal disparity is not necessarily disconcerting to the historian, de-pending on what sort of material remains. So, what is there to work on?

The material related to Ignatius' life and career is not inconsiderable. There are copious documents—his own writings and testimonies of various sorts offered by his first companions, his fellow Jesuits from those early years, many of whom worked and lived with him. His own writings include the *Spiritual Exercises*, a little book that is perhaps his main contribution to the Church and history, a distillation of his spir-itual teaching;[4] taken as expressions of Ignatius' deepest and most per-sonal insights and convictions, the *Exercises* are perhaps the most re-vealing and telling. Although there are uncertainties regarding the time and place of their composition, there is no doubt that they are the authentic work of Ignatius alone. The *Constitutions* of the Society of Jesus (MHSJ, MI series 3), the magnificent and magisterial legislation that has guided the fortunes of the Society over the centuries, has become the model for constitutions of religious orders of men and women the world over. The *Constitutions* were the fruit of intensive labor during the years of his Generalship. How much of the actual text is from Ignatius remains uncertain, since Polanco and perhaps others may have contributed. But there is nothing in the documents that was not studied and approved by Ignatius and does not reflect his mind and heart. But these *Constitutions* are formal legal documents that conceal more than they reveal about their author. Their tone is abstract and impersonal, and only by reading between the lines can we discern anything about the man who stands behind them.

There is also his *Spiritual Journal* (MHSJ, MI series 4, vol. 1) which records some of his spiritual and mystical experiences during the period in Rome. And finally there are detailed documents from the canonization process in which the life of Ignatius was examined and documented to establish his claim to sainthood.

Lastly there is the mountain of letters and instructions that Ignatius wrote or dictated during the course of his years as General (MHSJ, MI series 1). They number nearly seven thousand (Bertrand 1985),[5] addressed to fellow Jesuits, dealing with matters of governance in the Society, and to kings and queens, princes and princesses, and nobility of all ranks, to popes, bishops, cardinals, priests, and nuns, and to large numbers of lay people, including the poor and humble. But these too are exclusively public documents that, with rare exceptions, present a public persona—always tactful, devout, courtly in manner, and gracious in tone. In these letters we can recognize that the courtier, the diplomat, the noble hidalgo, qualified by blood, tradition, and training to move with ease among the highest levels of society and church, was still very much alive.

Even in Ignatius' lifetime, especially during his career in Rome as General of the Society of Jesus, the process of collecting and arranging material pertinent to his life had already begun. Especially instrumental in inaugurating this process was his faithful secretary, Juan de Polanco. Polanco collected his recollections of life with Ignatius in his *Chronicón* (Polanco 1894–1898) and occupied himself later in gathering narrative accounts from the first companions of Ignatius and others who had extensive dealings with him. These accounts, collected into the *Fontes Narrativi* (MHSJ, MI series 4), are of inestimable historical value, but their value for psychobiography is limited. They are highly personal accounts, based on memory with all its retrospective distortion, selection, and omission, and colored by the rampant idealizing transferences that seem to have affected many who had dealings with Ignatius.

The most valuable of such biographical accounts is that written by Gonsalvez da Camara, who persuaded Ignatius to tell him his story toward the end of his life. Assuming that da Camara was a faithful recorder, how much can we rely on an account that came from Ignatius' own lips? Because of its authenticity and because it is the best source we have, we shall have to rely on it as a primary source—but with a grain of salt. First, the *Autobiography* (MHSJ, MI series 4, vol. 1) was dictated years after the events, and we have no reason to believe that Ignatius' memory was any better than yours or mine. At many points he is honest enough to say that his recollection is shaky or uncertain, or that he simply does not remember—but there were undoubtedly many more instances when his memory may have been faulty but he was not aware of it. Next, we cannot be sure how much retrospective distortion entered into the account. One of the themes I will develop is that Ignatius' memory and the reconstruction of his own life history were in some part determined by an inner need to shape and maintain the identity of one who aspired to sainthood.[6]

Lastly, we can only guess at what was omitted from the account—either from this same motive, or simply because of poor memory, or even because of forces that repressed certain episodes as insignificant and prevented others from even coming to mind. There is no reason to conclude that Ignatius was trying to deceive or mislead—he is forthcoming about what he saw as his own imperfections and limitations—but he was human and did have an unconscious that could play as many and as effective tricks on him as on any of us. At certain points, he gives us little hints that would have provided rich fodder for the psychoanalyst, but he then quickly draws the veil over them.

The risks of the psychoanalytic method are particularly meaningful when the subject is a profoundly religious figure, a great saint and mystic. If the theologian allows that Ignatius was the recipient of great mystical graces and that the miraculous course of his inspired saintly career was the work of God's grace guiding and inspiring him at every step of the way, on this subject the psychoanalyst can say neither yea nor nay. That interpretation lies beyond the scope of his methodology and theory. The psychoanalyst is concerned only with those aspects of his subject that reflect basically human motivation and the connections of psychic meaning—whether or not the patterns of behavior have religious or spiritual meaning.

The psychoanalyst is in no position to deny or exclude any actions, effects, or purposes of God. He is simply not interested in them since his approach has nothing to say about them. He is interested in determining what can be learned about the motives and dynamic intrapsychic forces and conflicts that may have come into play at various points in the great saint's career. To this extent, the psychoanalytic approach is iconoclastic—necessarily and inherently so. As Ricoeur has commented:

It is difficult to pinpoint what is properly psychoanalytic in Freud's interpretation of religion. However, it is essential to put into sharp focus those elements of his interpretation that merit the consideration of both believers and unbelievers. There is a danger that believers may sidestep his radical questioning of religion, under the pretext that Freud is merely expressing the unbelief of scientism and his own agnosticism; but there is also the danger that unbelievers may confuse psychoanalysis with this unbelief and agnosticism. My working hypothesis . . . is that psychoanalysis is necessarily iconoclastic, regardless of the faith or nonfaith of the psychoanalyst, and that this "destruction" of religion can be the counterpart of a faith purified of all idolatry. Psychoanalysis as such cannot go beyond the necessity of iconoclasm. This necessity is open to a double possibility, that of faith and that of nonfaith, but the decision about these two possibilities does not rest with psychoanalysis. (1970, p. 230)

The same point has been made by Hans Küng:

And must God for that reason be merely a human wishful structure, an infantile illusion or even a purely neurotic delusion? As we have argued elsewhere against Feuerbach, a real God may certainly correspond to the wish for God. . . . It does not follow—as some theologians have mistakenly concluded—from man's profound desire for

God and eternal life that God exists and eternal life and happiness are real. But those atheists who think that what follows is the nonexistence of God and the unreality of eternal life are mistaken too. . . . Here, then, we have reached the crux of the problem, which is not at all difficult to understand and in the face of which any kind of projection theory, opium theory, or illusion theory momentarily loses its suggestive power. Perhaps this being of our longings and dreams does actually exist. Perhaps this being who promises us eternal bliss does exist. Not only the bliss of the baby at its mother's breast . . . but a quite different reality in the future which corresponds to the unconscious and conscious aspirations precisely of the mature, adult human being and to which the oldest, strongest, most urgent wishes of mankind are oriented, which can fulfill our longing for infinite happiness. Perhaps. Who knows? (1990, pp. 78–80)

Thus, while the approach in this study may be regarded as reductive, it is not intended to be reductionistic. It is reductive insofar as it brings into focus only certain aspects of Ignatius' life and personality—those that can be delineated and encompassed in strictly and specifically psychoanalytic terms. But the resulting account is not meant to be exclusive or to substitute for a more spiritual or theological reading. This issue will return more forcefully when we deal with Ignatius' ascetical and mystical life. If we come to see with more clarity the human side of Ignatius, his inner psychic needs and conflicts, his hopes and desires, and the forces that drove him to the extremes of spiritual devotion and the heights of mystical experience, I shall count the effort as worthwhile.

The psychoanalytic lens, therefore, is necessarily very selective in what it brings into focus. If a pattern of meaning and motivation discerned in the life of Ignatius can be explained in completely natural and human terms, in terms of psychoanalytic theory, what does that imply for the relevance of a more theologically attuned understanding? From the perspective of the methodological difficulties, the disparity in points of view poses a problem, since the accounts of the saint's life, and even the source materials themselves, have been contaminated by the hagiographic bias. All the early accounts and biographies are so colored by idealization and admiration for the extraordinary qualities of this spiritual giant that we lose sight of the man. The authors of these accounts were not interested in his inner psychological dimensions. One recent student of Ignatius' life has written: "But even when a judgment according to purely naturalistic principles does not lead to such a one-sided view, it requires little reflection to see that whenever the supernatural guidance of God's grace is perceived and acknowledged, greater justice is done to a saint and we receive a more comprehensive view of the reality than when only the natural conditions and forces are examined. Even a lack of psychological analysis may be admissible as long as one sees and correctly portrays the workings of God in the saint" (Becher, 1977, p. 70).

Nor is there any effort, as was the style of Ignatius' time, to see his career in any but the most spiritual and theological terms. Even the most definitive biographies in our own time, those by Dudon (1949) and Dalmases (1985), are cast along exclusively historico-biographic lines with no attempt to look within, to see the human and dynamic aspects of Ignatius' experience. For Dudon, interpretations take the form of the loftiest spiritual and theological considerations—the hand of God is everywhere. For Dalmases, the spiritual hand is not as heavy, but whatever minimal effort he makes to interpret, the result is much the same.

Even the most direct and valuable material we have, Ignatius' dictation of his reminiscences to da Camara at the end of his career, is open to the charge of retrospective distortion.[7] Certainly the aura of his personality strongly influenced those around him and inevitably influenced their views and recollections. Like many great men in history, Ignatius evoked powerful transferences from those who knew him.

That factor also plays a dominant role in the work of his biographers and is a potent source of distortion in his potential psychobiography. The psychoanalyst must keep to the path of strictly psychoanalytic interpretation and avoid the snare of hagiographic countertransference. I would insist in this connection that application of the psychoanalytic method intends no disrespect, nor does the inquiry diminish any of the significance and greatness of St. Ignatius. It provides little more than a partial portrait, limited in scope and implication, that should offer a unique perspective on this dynamic and complex figure. If we can achieve some clearer picture of his humanity, it should do no violence to his spirituality and his sanctity.

At this juncture, we would do well to pay attention to Freud's comments on the subject, made on the occasion of his receiving the Goethe

Prize. His remarks are as appropriate in the case of Ignatius as they were for Goethe:

> I am prepared for the reproach that we analysts have forfeited the right to place ourselves under the patronage of Goethe because we have offended against the respect due to him by trying to apply analysis to him himself: we have degraded the great man to the position of an object of analytic investigation. But I would dispute at once that any degradation is intended or implied by this.
>
> We all, who revere Goethe, put up, without too much protest, with the efforts of his biographers, who try to recreate his life from existing accounts and indications. But what can these biographies achieve for us? . . . And yet there is no doubt that such a biography does satisfy a powerful need in us. . . . People generally say that it is our desire to bring ourselves nearer to such a man in a human way as well. Let us grant this; it is, then, the need to acquire affective relations with such men, to add them to the fathers, teachers, exemplars whom we have known or whose influence we have already experienced, in the expectation that their personalities will be just as fine and admirable as those works of art of theirs which we possess.
>
> All the same, we may admit that there is still another motive-force at work. The biographer's justification also contains a confession. It is true that the biographer does not want to depose his hero, but he does want to bring him nearer to us. That means, however, reducing the distance that separates him from us; it still tends in effect towards degradation. And it is unavoidable that as we learn more about a great man's life we shall also hear of occasions on which he has in fact done no better than we, has in fact come near to us as a human being. Nevertheless, I think we may declare the efforts of biography to be legitimate. Our attitude to fathers and teachers is, after all, an ambivalent one since our reverence for them regularly conceals a component of hostile rebellion. That is a psychological fatality; it cannot be altered without forcible suppression of the truth and is bound to extend to our relations with the great men whose life histories we wish to investigate.
>
> When psycho-analysis puts itself at the service of biography, it naturally has the right to be treated no more harshly than the latter itself. Psycho-analysis can supply some information which cannot

be arrived at by other means, and can thus demonstrate new connecting threads in the "weaver's masterpiece" spread between the instinctual endowments, the experiences and the works of an artist. Since it is one of the principal functions of our thinking to master the material of the external world psychically, it seems to me that thanks are due to psycho-analysis if when it is applied to a great man, it contributes to the understanding of his great achievement (1930, pp. 210–212).

IÑIGO DE LOYOLA

1

ORIGINS

I

To the eye of history, the background and traditions of the family into which a historical figure is born have meaning only in terms of the sequence of political events. It is as significant to history that Philip of Macedonia had a son as that Henry VIII of England did not. In neither case is the historian concerned with the meaning of the event to the infant in question (or not in question, in Henry's case). To the psychobiographer, however, the event has meaning if not significant implications for the psychic development of the newborn subject and the shaping of his emerging personality.

Iñigo de Loyola entered a world dominated by forceful personalities, staunch family traditions and loyalties, and values and ideals that extended back to the furthest reaches of memory and legend. If there is one quality of the house of Loyola that strikes us with peculiar force, even across the centuries, it is pride and independence. It is often said that the Basques are a proud, even haughty, people. Guipúzcoa, the province of the Loyolas, maintains itself in splendid isolation behind the rugged Pyrenees. Dudon (1949) quotes a local historian of the sixteenth century to the effect that the name Guipúzcoa itself means "to terrify the enemy." Lope de Isonti tries to explain the warlike character of the Guipúzcoans: "Iron ore abounds in the country; the drinking water is charged with it, and the inhabitants have it in their veins: that is the whole secret of their energetic temper."[1] The Loyolas were one of the great families of Guipúzcoa, and if any family did more to shape the image of the Guipúzcoans as rugged and fiercely independent, history has not recorded it. All these influences played a part in shaping the personality and psychic structure of the child whose story we will pursue.

FAMILY HISTORY

Iñigo's father was Beltrán Yañez de Loyola, a descendant of a noble and ancient family. The Loyola name carries with it a somewhat pugnacious

3

association. One chronicler of the time commented: "The Loyolas were one of the most disastrous families our country had to endure, one of those Basque families that bore a code of arms over its main doorway, the better to justify the misdeeds that were the tissue and pattern of its life" (quoted in von Matt and Rahner, 1956, p. 3). Dudon (1949) reports that the family can be traced back at least to the thirteenth century. Dalmases (1985) extends the date back to the twelfth century in the person of Lope de Oñaz, lord of the manor house in the latter years of that century. Papers extant in the seventeenth century record the marriage of Inés de Loyola to Lope García de Oñaz in the thirteenth century. Alfonso XII of Castile presented the family with a coat of arms in 1331 to celebrate the fusion of these two ancient houses. The fourteen alternating bands of gold and red of the shield of Oñaz and a black cauldron suspended between two wolves against a field of silver served notice henceforth of the dignity and tradition of the house of Loyola.

The royal favors had been well earned. During the battle of Beotibar, on 19 September 1321, the troops of Guipúzcoa, the province in which the Loyola stronghold was located, and Castile met the combined forces of the French and the Navarrese in battle and roundly defeated them. A great deal of the credit for the victory fell to Juan Pérez de Loyola and his seven sons. The exploits of the sons of Pérez de Loyola are still celebrated in the legends of Guipúzcoa, and every year, on the feast of St. John the Baptist, the crowds come to the village of Iguerondo to dance and sing, in Castilian and Basque, in memory of the exploits of this famous band of brothers. If the victory of Beotibar accomplished little else, it served to consolidate the alliance between Guipúzcoa and the kings of Castile (Dalmases 1985).

The next generation of Loyolas, particularly Beltrán Ibáñez de Loyola, joined with the powerful Castilian nobles to fight against the Moors. The reconquest of the Iberian peninsula from the Moors created a kind of frontier. When any new territory was liberated, there would soon spring up an urban core centered around a castle surrounded by farms and villages. As Gies and Gies comment: "Such new communities strove to replace the violent swirl of warfare with order and stability, and to substitute for the masculine military presence the normal compound of civil society. Newcomers were encouraged by a variety of incentives to 'make smoke,' that is, to bring wives to found hearths and households" (1987, p. 152). Henry III, the young monarch who came to the throne in 1393, rewarded Don Beltrán for his many services both to himself and to his father. Basking in such favor, Beltrán was not content with the manor house of the Loyolas and determined to build himself a real castle, or at least a fortress.

It was not merely Beltrán's vanity that led him to this course. In these troubled times, the tragedy of anarchy and strife was carried out through most of the European continent. The Middle Ages was in its death throes. In England, the War of the Roses created an agony of desolation for more than thirty years and prepared the way for the Tudor dynasty. In France, the Armagnacs and the Burgundians stayed at each other's throats. In Germany and Italy, there was the turmoil of the robber barons and the unending fratricidal strife of republic against republic, house against house, brother against brother. In Castile, the weak and troubled reigns of John II (1406–1454) and Henry IV (1454–1474) set the stage for an upsurge in the aspirations of the nobility. The kingdom of Navarre was split by contending parties as well, and the Basque country could hardly remain an exception. Beltrán was not the only noble to beat his plowshares into swords and build a fortress around himself. A score and more of the noble families of the area did the same, and these fortresses became safe havens from which they could periodically venture forth to plunder their weaker neighbors and to contend with other claimants for hegemony over the surrounding hills and valleys. In time, these conflicting, often belligerent claims menaced the welfare of the kingdom, and King Henry IV was compelled to interfere; when he did so, it was with a strong hand.

Of these warring and plundering clans, the Loyolas were as bad as any. Beltrán had built his fortress in a valley between two medieval towns, Azpeitia and Azcoitia. The castle had impenetrable stone walls six feet thick and well-placed battlements. Azpeitia had grown up around the old church and monastery of the Templars, named after San Sebastián. The municipal charter issued by Ferdinand IV of Castile in 1310 granted all ecclesiastical rights and privileges to the lay authorities of the new town. However, Azpeitia fell under the canonical jurisdiction of the bishop of Pamplona in Navarre. The good bishop had declared war against secular patronage and was nominating priests of his own choosing to the benefice of San Sebastián.

Don Beltrán de Loyola found this a perfect opportunity to render further service to the crown of Castile. According to the town charter, if

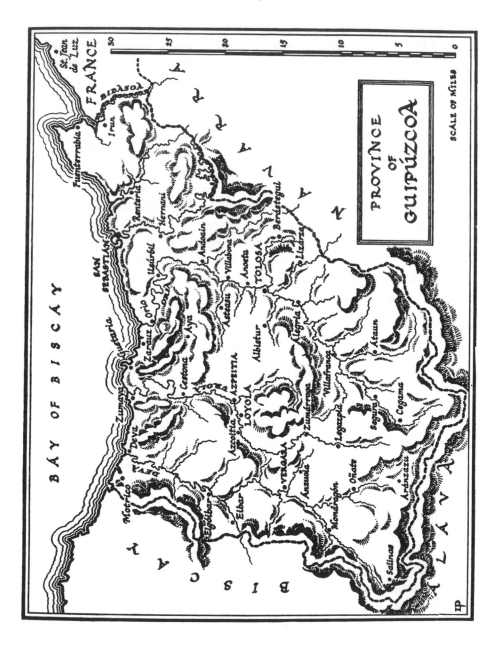

PROVINCE OF GUIPÚZCOA

Azpeitia were to relinquish its rights and ecclesiastical patronage, they would revert automatically to the crown. Beltrán launched an attack against the unfortunate clergy, even to the extent of doing them physical violence. As a reward, King John I (1379–1390) transferred to the Loyolas his own rights over San Sebastián. In 1387, by royal letters variously renewed and authenticated, the Loyolas became lords and patrons of the Church of San Sebastián of Azpeitia. It was a benefice that proved to be a source of countless difficulties, however, which lasted even until the time of Ignatius. Almost immediately the Bishop of Pamplona excommunicated Beltrán and his family and put Azpeitia under interdict. However, this was the time of the great schism; in 1394 the Avignon Pope, Benedict XIII (1394–1423), had set himself up as rival to the Roman Pope, Boniface IX (1389–1404). The Pamplonian bishops, along with the rest of the Spanish episcopacy, recognized the jurisdiction of Benedict XIII, so that when he issued a bull in 1414 confirming the rights and privileges of the Loyolas, the controversy was effectively put to rest (Leturia and Batllori 1956). Pressing their advantage, the Loyolas also claimed and secured jurisdiction over ten *ermitas*, small rural chapels scattered throughout the valley, that were dependent on the parish church of Azpeitia.

In 1456, Iñigo's grandfather, the testy and rebellious Don Juan Pérez, took up arms against the twin cities of Azpeitia and Azcoitia, which bordered his castle lands. His stronghold was conquered and the castle razed down to the second story. Juan Pérez himself was banished by the king in April 1457 to fight against the Moors in Andalusia and was charged with the support of an armed company. When his term of banishment was completed in 1461, the lord of Loyola was allowed to return to his home. He rebuilt the castle with brickwork, this time in the more graceful and delicate Mudejar style, reflecting a Moorish influence. The house still stands as he reconstructed it, a memorial to its ancient heritage and elegance.

Despite this episode, the Loyolas remained faithful to the house of Castile. In 1475, Don Juan Pérez and his son Beltrán, who would become Iñigo's father, swore an oath of fealty to the throne of Castile in the persons of Ferdinand and Isabella. Royal gifts and confirmation of the ancient privileges and rights of possession of the Loyolas preserved and extended the family heritage. One of these, the right of patronage of the parish church, was surrounded by controversy carried over from previous generations. Iñigo's father, Beltrán, had apparently sided with the king during another uprising by the inhabitants and had distinguished himself in the service of the Catholic kings during the occupation of Toro and the liberation of Bourgos in 1476, and later in the defense of Fuenterrabia against French incursion. These deeds of valor won him a charter of privileges in 1484 confirming his right of patronage over the church of Azpeitia (Dalmases 1985). This patronage was subsequently controverted and challenged on many fronts. There were trials before the Ordinary, trials in Rome, opposing verdicts, papal bulls, contracts signed and violated. But through it all, the Loyolas' right of patronage was maintained from generation to generation.

Few details are known of the family life in the castle of Loyola. The Loyolas were prosperous certainly—"This lord of Loyola is the most powerful among the lineage of Oñaz, both in revenues and wealth and relations, except for the lord of Lescano" (Dalmases 1985).[2] The revenue of the house of Loyola continued to be substantial even in the time of Ignatius.[3] The marriage contract between Beltrán Yáñez de Loyola and Marina Sánchez de Licona, dated and notarized on 13 July 1467, includes among Beltrán's holdings a foundry, seven farms, more land, and sheep.

Marina Sánchez de Licona, Iñigo's mother, was the daughter of Martín García de Licona, a gentleman and landowner of Azcoitia who was vested by royal order with the patronage of the church of that village which bordered on Azpeitia. The family was an ancient one. Marina's great-grandfather had settled at Ondarroa in 1414 and there built a house, the Torre Barria, which even today bears the escutcheon of the Liconas over its entrance. Her father had been royal counsel, a man held in high esteem. Through her mother's family, she was related to the counts of Oñate and to the dukes of Nájera. In 1459, Marina's father had purchased the property and later the ecclesiastical privileges of Azcoitia. When his daughter married in 1467, Martín gave her 1600 gold ducats of Aragonese mintage, a rich dowry that she carried with her to the newly reconstructed castle of Loyola.

The marriage was a fruitful one, even by the generous standards of the time. There were apparently thirteen children in all, if the testimony of the Azpeitian witnesses in Ignatius' canonization process of 1595 can be trusted. The order of birth and the names of the children are in doubt, since the registers of Azpeitia were burned in a fire in 1515. In addition to Iñigo, who was born some time in the summer or autumn, probably of 1491,[4] there were six sons and three daughters whose names could be recalled. Apparently Beltrán fathered three additional children out of wedlock, a boy and two girls.

Iñigo was born in the castle of the Loyolas and was baptized at Azpeitia with the name Iñigo López, after an eleventh-century Benedictine abbot. Soon after Iñigo's birth his mother died, and the child was put out to nurse with María de Garín, the young wife of the local blacksmith, who lived in a modest cottage scarcely a half mile from the castle. It was María who taught Iñigo his first prayers in her own Guipúzcoan tongue, and it was in the arms of this devoted nurse that he began to learn the virtues of love, devotion, and trust (Brodrick 1956). He was brought up with María's children, who were his boyhood playmates.[5]

PSYCHOANALYTIC IMPLICATIONS

These early events cause hardly a ripple in the historical record, but to the psychoanalytic eye, the early loss of a parent can cast a shadow across the entire life course of a child. The impact of maternal deprivation on young infants has been extensively documented. Spitz has examined its effects in producing anaclitic depressions, hospitalism, and even marasmus[6] in children (Spitz 1945, 1946, 1951, 1965). The effects can even be devastating on infants hospitalized for infantile diarrhea (Solnit 1970). In such cases, when maternal separation is relatively acute and short-term, providing a substitute for the lost maternal care may reverse the deleterious, possibly life-threatening consequences of maternal deprivation.

It is generally agreed that the process of mourning requires the capacity for tolerance of painful affects, the ability to meet repeated demands for reality testing in the face of powerful wishes, and other more developed ego functions that a young child may not have adequately established. In this view, preadolescent children do not mourn, or if they mourn it is in some partial and incomplete fashion (Wolfenstein 1966, 1969; Rochlin 1965; Fleming and Altschul 1963; Deutsch 1937). But the mourning process in children may follow a somewhat different path than in adults. While adults try to detach memories, hopes, and wishes from the dead object, in children the mourning process has the opposite goal, "to avoid the acceptance of the reality and emotional meaning of the death and to maintain in some internal form the relationship that has been ended in external reality" (Miller 1971). Typically, at the time of the loss there is little crying or expression of sadness; the child seems to go about his daily activities relatively unperturbed. Wolfenstein (1969) saw this as a denial, overt or unconscious, of the finality of the loss, thus allowing the hopeful fantasies of reunion and restitution to persist. At times the painful affect is replaced by elevations of mood, to deny the loss, as has been observed in hypomanic patients who had suffered parental losses in childhood (Lewin 1937). Such individuals tend to develop elaborate fantasies in which the lost parent is idealized. The parental image is no longer that of the parent as he was known in life but the glorified parent of early childhood who is now perpetuated in fantasy, most often unconscious fantasy (Miller 1971). Freud (1914) described such idealization as a process by which the object "without any alteration in its nature, is aggrandized and exalted in the subject's mind."

There are also long-term sequelae of this syndrome of loss-and-restitution (Rochlin 1965; Birtchnell et al. 1973). As Wolfenstein (1969) reports, some people are caught up in a lifelong effort to maintain the denial and rewrite the tragedy with a happier ending, acting out symbolic repetitions of the loss of the parent—as in attachment to idealized substitute figures or devotion to idealized causes—in an unsuccessful attempt to master the trauma of loss. The other important long-term consequence of such early loss is the powerful motif of identification with the dead parent. "Identification with the lost object is a feature of adult grief, but in children it is commoner and usually takes a more dramatic form. . . . Identification occurs irrespective of the sex of the parent lost. Such a reaction is probably an attempt to deny the loss. It is as though the child is saying, 'My father is alive because I am he'" (Birtchnell, 1969, pp. 7–8). The identification may also take the form of an identification with the state of death itself, reflecting an unconscious wish to achieve reunion with the lost parent.

These dynamic elements continue to play themselves out throughout the individual's adult life. Loss becomes inextricably bound with damage to self-esteem (Rochlin 1965). The need for restitution may become a dominating force in the patient's unconscious, may take the form of various unconsciously dictated enactments, and may impair the development of the child's capacity for object relationships.[7] In many cases there are also significant reactions, such as exacerbation of emotional or psychosomatic symptoms, on the anniversary of significant childhood losses (Pollock 1970; Mintz 1971). Psychiatric research in this area tends to confirm the association of early maternal deprivation through death, divorce, or separation with relatively severe forms of lifelong psychopathology[8] (Gregory 1985; Earle and Earle 1961; Bradley 1979), although there are some indications that the quality of home life and childrearing after the loss of the mother may also play a critical role in determining whether psychopathology will develop in adulthood (Breier et al. 1988; Krueger 1983).[9] We have no information about the quality of the mothering and nurturing experiences provided for Iñigo in those early years and thus cannot evaluate their impact.[10]

We can assume that the combination of the loss of his mother and exile from the castle of Loyola must have had great psychic impact on the infant who was to become the great saint and founder of the Society of Jesus. If this hypothesis is valid, the loss and separation would not have outwardly disturbed Iñigo, both because of denial and repression of the sense of loss and its associated pain and because in the late fifteenth century there was little sense of the special needs and vulnerabilities of children. The idea of childhood only began to take shape in the thirteenth century and did not come into common acceptance until well into the seventeenth century. It was only in the sixteenth century that the child began to become the center of the new, more closely knit nuclear family (Ariès 1962). Traces of medieval attitudes toward children persisted in Europe well into the nineteenth century. In late fifteenth-century Spain, children were regarded as little adults, but without the adult capacity to think and reason, until the magic age of seven. After that age it was assumed that they had more or less the same cognitive and emotional capacities as adults. Certainly by the time of puberty they were treated as and expected to act as adults. Prevailing cultural attitudes regarded childhood as no more than the first stage of life, with little to distinguish it qualitatively from later stages.

Iñigo's removal from the household may have been largely a practical matter. After Marina's death, there was no adult woman living in the castle of Loyola who could nurse and care for the infant. It was therefore expedient that he be put out to the first available woman on the estates who could provide for his needs. But if we give credence to the theory of parental loss, particularly maternal deprivation, the psychological sequelae could be expected to play themselves out through the ensuing years. The effect of the early loss of the woman who gave him birth may also have been complicated by Iñigo's subsequent separation from his nurse, when he was returned to his rightful place in the castle of Loyola.

From our vantage point, we can list some possible effects: a pervasive sense of loss and an underlying depression; an unsatisfied yearning for attachment and reunion with the lost mother that would affect his future relationships with women; idealization and aggrandizement of the repressed image of the lost mother; a powerful identification with the lost mother; a yearning for reunion with the mother in death and an attachment to and idealization of the state of death itself. Further exploration of these themes must wait for a later chapter, but we can be sure that they were not without significance.

THE EARLY YEARS

While little Iñigo was nursing at the breast of his substitute mother, an intrepid Genoese sailor under the commission of the crown of Castile had set out on a voyage of discovery across the Atlantic Ocean. The year 1492 saw the fall of Granada, the last of the Moorish strongholds, the expulsion of the Jews, along with the opening of the New World. Spain was on the verge of becoming the dominant power in European politics, and in the realm of the spirit, the great Cardinal Ximénes de Cisneros led a powerful movement of spiritual transformation and reform. Spain, along with the rest of Europe, was being roused from its medieval slumber to a new world of discovery and revolution. But the expulsion of the Moors from the West only increased the pressure they exerted on the eastern borders of Europe—a circumstance that would play a significant role in the future path of the youngest Loyola. It also meant that the attention and power of Emperor Charles V was absorbed by the Turkish question, leaving a vacuum for the flourishing of the Reformation. From 1494 on, the Italian wars had a devastating effect on the Italian peninsula and on the Church. In 1492, the infamous Borgia, Alexander VI, ascended the papal throne. In another half century his grandson, Francis Borgia, would enter Ignatius' Society and become its third General. But at the end of the fifteenth century, the Church was badly in need of reform from top to bottom. In 1491, when Iñigo was born, Luther was only eight years old and still a schoolboy at Mansfeld.

Iñigo's brothers were all but one soldiers and adventurers, true to the spirit of the Loyolas. Christopher Columbus had turned a new page in the history of mankind. The excitement and tumult of discovery and conquest could hardly have escaped the daring men of Loyola. In 1493, Juan Pérez, the oldest of Iñigo's brothers, set out to join the escort for a second voyage of Columbus, equipping a vessel complete with 85 armed men. Three years later, he fought in his own ship in the struggle with the French over the kingdom of Naples and died a hero's death. The next oldest, Martín García, fought in the wars of Navarre and road to the defense of Pamplona in 1521 at the head of a troop of fifty or so men. The third son, Beltrán, who remained a bachelor, also fought and died at Naples. Ochoa Pérez was in the service of Queen Juana in the Low Countries and Spain. Hernando set sail for the New World in 1510 and there met his death in the struggle with the Indians. Pero López, an exception to the military bent of the others, followed an ecclesiastical career and became rector of the church in Azpeitia in 1518.

When Juan Pérez, the oldest of Iñigo's brothers, died a hero's death in the conquest of Naples, the next oldest brother, Martín García, became heir to the estates of Loyola. In 1498 he married Magdalena de Araoz, a lady of noble birth, the daughter of Don Pedro Araoz, Inspector General of the forces of Fernandez de Cordoba, with whom the eldest of the Loyolas had fought and died. She had been a maid of honor to Queen Isabella and one of her favorites. On her wedding day the Queen gave her, among other precious gifts, a painting of the Annunciation. Magdalena brought the painting with her to Loyola and installed it in a special chapel she had constructed for it. Ignatius developed a special devotion to this picture. Rahner (1960) quotes Leturia (1949) who commented, "In the life of the author of the *Exercises*, Doña Magdalena's picture of our Lady had the first place, long before those of Olaz, Aránzazu and Montserrat" (p. 116). Her religious books, particularly the Spanish translation of Ludolph the Carthusian's *Life of Jesus* and Jacobus de Voragine's *Legends of the Saints* were to play a pivotal role in the conversion of the future saint. When the wounded soldier was borne to the refuge of Loyola, she it was who nursed the patient back to health and strength. Her kindness, tenderness, and religious devotion must have had an impact on Iñigo and may have played an important role in his conversion. When she arrived at Loyola Iñigo was seven years old and would certainly have been brought back to live with his family. Doña

Magdalena became the equivalent of a third mother for him, replacing the one he had lost and the one he had outgrown.

It is difficult to assess the circumstances that surrounded the early years of Iñigo de Loyola. But Christian faith and a chivalrous sense of honor seemed to have been a family inheritance. The wills of the Loyolas provide eloquent testimony to their Catholicism, which was as central to their lives as bravery in battle. The men had the custom in making out such documents of surrendering their souls to God, asking pardon for their sins, committing their salvation to the Blessed Virgin, and arranging for thirty Masses for the repose of their souls. There were always legacies for various pious works—particularly the rustic *ermitas* or *basilicas* that dotted the neighboring mountains. The Loyolas had the right of patronage over these sanctuaries and appointed caretakers and drew up rules for them.[11] The women of the family were no less pious. Several of them were remembered as guardians of basilicas and even as founders of convents.

Despite the rich religious traditions, the times were violent and morals were loose. And the Loyolas were substantial contributors to the temper of the time. Besides Beltrán's three or more illegitimate children, Martín García had three illegitimate daughters whose names are recorded in his will. Even Pero López, who died in 1529 as the parish priest of Azpeitia, left four children.

It is little wonder that the proud and passionate men of Loyola should have had their way with women. They were rich, attractive, and strong, and in a culture that placed high value on masculinity and sexual prowess, they were proud and vain enough to leave few of these cultural expectations unfulfilled. The life of the Loyolas was a rich amalgam of deep religious tradition, sincere piety, burning passion and lust, fierce pride, and an attitude of aristocracy and nobility.

We cannot doubt that this complex atmosphere left an indelible stamp on the young Iñigo. It is significant, of course, that Iñigo was the youngest of this sizable family group, born more than a quarter century after his parents had pronounced their marriage vows. His father was in his prime and in full possession of his titular rights and affluence. Marina was probably approaching the end of her fertile years. The castle of Loyola was a place full of the vitality of youth, and it remained intact until Juan Pérez set off for Naples.

Like his brother Pero López, young Iñigo was, in the course of things, destined for the clerical state. It is not very likely that he took to the idea very much. He was set to learn the rudiments of letters with the other young clerks of the parish, but learning and education were never highly prized by the Loyolas. They were landowners and men of action who needed only such education as required by their status and nobility. Iñigo's next-older brother, Pero López, was destined for the clerical state and was certainly able to read and write. Martín García kept his account books in mixed Castilian and Latin, but he was not at home in the classical idiom. It is also fairly certain that his was the language of the sword rather than the pen. To make their fortunes in the world, at Naples and in the Indies, Juan Pérez and Hernando needed little more than their name, a few florins, and a little daring. The growing Iñigo was unquestionably amply provided with these ideals and values to guide his ambitions.

Beltrán de Loyola died in 1507, when Iñigo was about sixteen years old. With the death of his father, the first period in his psychological development, centered within the solid granite walls of the castle of Loyola, came to an end.

IDENTIFICATIONS

The influence of the extraordinary climate of the times on the young Iñigo cannot be overestimated. High prerogatives were placed on the qualities that made a man both a gentleman and a soldier. Beltrán himself was the head of the house of Loyola, one of the *parientes mayores* or lords of the manor of Guipúzcoa. The feudal families of Guipúzcoa were divided into two parties, the Oñacinos and the Gamboinos. The violent and chronic rivalries between these factions bathed the countryside in blood. The house of Loyola stood at the head of the Oñacinos. Life in those violent times meant that a man had to have considerable skill in the use of arms and his sword at his side had to be ready to leap to his hand at the least provocation. Violence was ever prepared to meet violence, and the very stamp of a man's masculinity and repute lie in his sword as well as in his sexuality. Add to this the Loyolas' family reputation for courage and bravery that had to be upheld.

Beltrán de Loyola, warrior and leader, vigorous and vital in all his undertakings whether on the field of battle or in bed, presents in many ways a picture of a forceful personality. His influence on his growing son would also have been strong. We might conjecture that the identification of the boy Iñigo with his father was significant in its far-reaching impact on his emerging personality. The paternal figure is, after all, the primary model of mature masculinity. In the house of Loyola, embodying as it did all the characteristics of a strongly patriarchal culture, Beltrán de Loyola was master of all that transpired, not only within the castle walls, but on the farms and countryside he owned, and to a large extent in the whole of Guipúzcoa.

Identification with such a father figure meant that awareness of family position and tradition became part of Iñigo's orientation to life and reality. Military prowess and adventurous daring were highly valued, and that courage was part of the fiber of a man—a real man would never back away from a fight even when the odds were against him. Young Iñigo was instilled with the pride of the Loyolas, which called them to be leaders, heroes, extraordinary men. It must also be remembered this heritage included a profound, almost instinctive, religious faith. For Beltrán was a man of deep faith, and Catholicism was ingrained in the family tradition. Yet it was that peculiar brand of faith that could willingly shed blood in defense of religion and celebrate the victory with a night of unbridled lechery. While Beltrán himself was most likely the major source of identification for his youngest son, Iñigo's six older brothers would likely have reinforced his influence.

So by the time of Beltrán de Loyola's death, the passage from infancy to the brink of young manhood had already begun to shape the life and personality of Iñigo. He had been schooled in the rudiments of language, but like his father and most of his family he had little taste for letters or for learning. But he had also been schooled in the qualities and ideals and values that the name of Loyola embraced. And young as he was, he adopted those values as strongly as any of his brothers. He was a Loyola, proud of his family's traditions, eager to make his name before all the world as a soldier of courage and daring, filled with the mystique and romance of the Spanish hidalgo. His mind was replete with adolescent fantasies and dreams of bold and chivalrous deeds, romantic exploits, fame and fortune.

Because so much of this portrait is reconstructed from what we know of the traditions and reputation of the Loyolas and from what we know of Iñigo himself a little later on, it is necessary to fill the historical gap with some measure of conjecture. But one senses with Iñigo that one is dealing with an extraordinary personality. He was a man of extremes, not only in what he did or sought to do, but in his wishes and fantasies. It seems appropriate, therefore, that the portrait of Iñigo de Loyola, as he steps forth from the castle of Loyola, should be one of adolescent strengths and extremes, out of which would crystallize a strong and dynamic identity.

SATIN AND SWORD

II

ARÉVALO

As the years passed and Iñigo grew to young manhood, inevitably the question of his future was raised. He had originally been destined for the clerical state, and subsequently had gone through a rudimentary clerical education. It is likely that he had already received the tonsure. It was clear, however, that this developing hidalgo was too full of life and fire, of ideas of romance and gallantry, for a peaceful ecclesiastical position.[1]

At the same time, he was not old enough to seek his own fortune in the world. He was therefore sent to Arévalo to join the household of Juan Velázquez de Cuéllar, majordomo of Queen Isabella and treasurer-general of Castile. This was by no means an unusual move; it was customary for the sons and daughters of the nobility to be sent to other aristocratic households, the boys to be trained as knights and the girls to learn the necessary social graces (Gies and Gies 1987). Juan Velázquez was related by marriage to the Liconas, Iñigo's mother's family. He had invited Beltrán, sometime between 1504 and 1507,[2] to send him one of his sons, offering to maintain the boy in his home and to act as his patron at court. The choice fell on Iñigo, who was then between thirteen and sixteen years of age. When young Iñigo left his family to become part of the household of Velázquez, he moved from an atmosphere of nobility and substance into one of great wealth and royal magnificence.[3] Velázquez was a gentleman and a noble in the finest traditions of old Spain. He is described as an "intelligent, virtuous, generous and Christian man; of fine appearance and of scrupulous conscience. He governed, as over his own domain, the fortresses of Arévalo and Madrigal, and dealt so kindly toward the inhabitants . . . that in 'Old Castile' there were no villages that were better treated" (Dalmases, 1985, p. 36). He was a good soldier, an able administrator, and stood in high favor at court, both during the reign of the Catholic kings and subsequently during that of Queen Juana (the Mad) and the Archduke Philip. He was

18

also a religious benefactor, having founded the convent and hospital of the Poor Clares in Arévalo. Moreover his wife, María, was a confidante of Germaine de Foix, who married Ferdinand of Aragon after the death of Isabella in 1504.

When Beltrán died, not long after Iñigo's departure from home, the kindly Velázquez took a paternal interest in the boy, out of his long friendship with Iñigo's own father. Under the direction of the cultured Velázquez, the lad flourished and learned many things that were to stand him in good stead in the years ahead. He developed a love of music that stayed with him all his life. His manners became polished and elegant, as befitted a page in the royal court. He learned to deal with the powerful and highly placed in both royal and ecclesiastical circles (Dalmases 1985).[4] His penmanship took on some of the firmness and style typical of the Renaissance. He remarked in later years that he had become "quite a fair writer" (Ortiz et al., 1918, p. 35).[5] He once even composed a poem, as was the fashion among young gallants. But his literary pretensions were limited at best. His ambitions had a more active bent—fencing, riding, dancing, gambling, and the intrigues of courtly romance.

At the palace of Arévalo, his companions were no longer the simple, rugged lads of Azpeitia but men of noble birth like himself, pages to the court of the king of Castile, men born to wealth, position, and power. He became a member of a household where culture, intelligence, courtly etiquette, and luxurious living flourished. But most important was the figure of Iñigo's patron. The kindly Velázquez was also a man of no mean accomplishment. His position alone bespeaks his great gifts, and together with a generous salting of political shrewdness, made for success in the intricacies of court intrigue. Velázquez was a man of the world.

It seems likely that Iñigo responded to Velázquez's fatherly interest. His experience in his new home must have been a congenial and rewarding one. Forty years later, as General of the newly founded order of the Jesuits, he requested the Licentiate Mercado to extend to one of Velázquez's grandsons his "humble regards, as from one formerly inferior to him, and still so, and to his father; and to his entire family, of which he now has such fond memories and will continue to have in Our Lord" (Epistolae, I, 705). One can picture the young Loyola, recently deprived of father and home and shaken by the rapid changes in his life, being received by Velázquez with kindness and warmth.

ADOLESCENT DEVELOPMENT

At this impressionable age, Iñigo entered upon a new phase of his life, with a whole new set of influences and identifications. The new influences were a function of the new setting, so very different from the simple family life at Loyola. The new identifications were a function of Iñigo's own inner growth.

For the shift from Azpeitia to Arévalo marked Iñigo's entrance upon that stage of life when he would begin to put away the things of his childhood and take up the things of his manhood. There was a laying aside, after a fashion, of old patterns of behavior and ways of adapting, a shedding of old identifications, and an assumption of new roles and new identifications. Erikson remarks of this period in the life cycle that "these new identifications are no longer characterized by the playfulness of childhood and the experimental zest of childhood: with dire urgency they force the young individual into choices and decisions which will, with increasing immediacy, lead to a more final self-definition, to irreversible role patterns, and thus to commitment 'for life'" (1959, pp. 110–111).

One senses an element of violence in Iñigo's entrance to this decisive phase. Adolescence can be a period of violent rebellion in any case, but the external circumstances of his life presumably provided their share of upheaval. There was the physical uprooting, of course, and on top of that one cannot underestimate the impact of Beltrán de Loyola's death on young Iñigo. The father, after all, represents to his children the model or image of masculinity, by way of identification for sons, by way of adaptation to masculinity for daughters. If the father is inadequate or weak or distant, the identification of his sons must suffer. That is to say, it must become something other, or it must seek its meaning elsewhere. If the father is hyperadequate, domineering, or repressive, his presence provokes "the ambivalent interplay of rivalry with the father, admiration for him, and fear of him which puts such a heavy burden of guilt and inferiority on all spontaneous initiative and on all phantasy" (Erikson, 1958, p. 123).

We know very little of the relations between Beltrán de Loyola and his sons, but we have already seen evidence that the sons turned out to be an adventurous lot. Whatever influence Beltrán had, it seems likely that it was far from repressive or prohibitive and must have been a positive one

that fostered strong identifications in his sons. The loss of this supporting relationship must have disrupted both the internal and external
worlds of young Iñigo. It brought to a climax and closed the door on the
first formative period in his life and plunged him into a crisis of identity.

But older identifications were deeply embedded. Even psychologically,
change is never completely change; a new situation retains the semblance of the past, the residues of prior experience. Pride, high ideals,
and a nascent masculinity had become Iñigo's by right of birth and
family tradition, of course, but more significantly by reason of the
deeply meaningful identification between father and son. Values and
traditions are meaningless to the growing child unless and until they
become actual and realized, as functioning dimensions of his own point
of view, his way of behaving, his attitudes and feelings, in his strong
identification with the respected and admired figures who themselves
embody those traditions. Identification is thus not only a mechanism of
adaptation and personalization; it also transmits social norms and cultural heritage.

Out of this amalgam of childhood experiences that Iñigo carried with
him to Arévalo and the host of new impressions and new identifications
he found there, Iñigo was to fashion an identity. We cannot, unfortunately, say more of this crucial period in Iñigo's development, but we
have some idea of the result. Between the time the young boy first came
to Arévalo and 1515, the hesitancy and shyness of youth changed
through a period of adolescent fantasies of romance and gallantry,
through the schooling in arms and courtly ways, into the self-assurance,
even daring, of the young Loyola.

THE ROMANCE OF CHIVALRY

Iñigo was drawn into the literature of the Spanish Renaissance, with its
tales of amorous intrigue and ideals of chivalry and courtly love. He
drank it all in—for better or worse. He remarks in his autobiography
that "his mind was filled with the adventures of Amadís of Gaul and
such books" (Vita 17).

The *Amadís*, a prototype of the literature of the time, attained a remarkable popularity in the Spanish peninsula. The revised *Amadís*,
published in 1508 (probably the edition Iñigo read) reflected, to a re-

markable degree, the spirit of the age. Brodrick describes it in the following terms:

> Amadis is the type of the perfect knight, the mirror of valour and courtesy, the pattern of loyal vassals and of constant lovers, the shield and support of the weak and necessitous, the strong arm at the service of the moral order and justice. Even his shortcomings, which are not great, do but show him without clouding the splendour of his admirable virtues. He is sincerely devout, an honest lover even if he weeps too much, brave without cruelty or boastfulness, always courteous and considerate, faithful and unshakable in friendship and love. To the qualities of the heroes of the *Chansons de Geste* he brings a tenderness, a delicacy of feeling, a gracious humanity which are entirely new. It is these that gave his book so great an educational and social value. It became the manual of the finished caballero, the epopee of faithful lovers, the code of honour which moulded many generations. Even in its superficialities and frivolities, it remained throughout the sixteenth century the textbook of polite deportment, the oracle of elegant conversation, the repertory of good manners and of gallantry in forms of address. (1956, p. 40)

The king, Amadís, and his lady, Oriana, are Catholic to the core; they assist in works of piety and devotion and go to confession to have their sins absolved. But alongside these religious observances, the central theme is the constant and noble passion of the couple. In this regard, the book is a compendium of all the qualities of romantic chivalry—the exaltation of the feminine, the emphasis on love and passion, the cult of chivalry, and a certain degree of moral laxity. All this was quite characteristic of the world in which Iñigo was growing to manhood. Staunch Catholic faith and sexual license stood side by side. Even the clergy were far from above reproach.

THE COURTIER

The picture that emerges of Iñigo's life at this time is a colorful one. Polanco tells us: "Like all the young men who live at court and dream of military exploits, he was rather free in affairs of the heart, in games of chance and in matters of honor" (Polanco, FN II, cited in Ravier, 1987, p. 55). Ribadeneyra, Iñigo's first biographer, describes him as a "gay and vain youth." Alonso de Montalvo, who was a page in the Velázquez household along with Iñigo, confirmed that Iñigo's main aspiration in those days was a military career. Iñigo was becoming a man of the world—his world—ambitious, proud, self-confident, fearing no danger, with sword at hand, and with a head filled with notions of romantic chivalry and libidinous adventure. By his own admission, "Up to his twenty-sixth year he was a man given over to the vanities of the world, and took special delight in the exercise of arms, with a great and vain desire of winning glory" (Vita 1).

Dudon says of Iñigo that he was "very careful of his personal appearance, anxious to please the fair sex, daring in affairs of gallantry, punctilious about his honor, he feared nothing. Holding cheap his own life and that of others, he was ready for all exploits" (1949, p. 21). This son of the Loyolas was first of all a man of arms, courageous and loyal. Beyond that he was a gallant, a libertine whose morals were questionable but whose *machismo* was never in doubt.

There was a dark side to this portrait. The extant records of the magistrate of Azpeitia indicate that court proceedings were brought against Iñigo and Pero López in 1515. The surviving documents do not indicate the exact nature of the crime, but it was undoubtedly serious and, in view of the involvement of Pero López, quite possibly related to the scandalous litigation over the local parish. The Franciscans had been sent to found a new convent and direct the parish, and it was feared that the exemptions of the friars would diminish tithes and limit the jurisdiction of the parish. The rivalry was complicated by antagonism between the pastor and the Loyola family. The pastor wanted his nephew to succeed him as rector, while the Loyolas, who enjoyed the prerogatives of patronage, had decided that the office should go to Pero López. The rector's nephew was violently slain in 1519. There is no evidence that the Loyolas were involved in the murder or that the earlier indictment of 1515 was related to any fatality.

Whatever the charge, there seems little doubt that Iñigo was guilty. The crimes were said to be "very grave, because committed at night, with full deliberation and premeditation" (Dudon, 1949, p. 21). Iñigo and his brother claimed clerical immunity. For Pero López, this was not a problem, but for Iñigo it was. According to the statutes of 1449, he should have been entered on the register of tonsured clerics in the diocese of Pamplona, but he was not. Further, clerics were required to wear the tonsure and clerical garb, which Iñigo had never worn. The documents comment on Iñigo: "He is in the habit of going round in cuirass and coat of mail, wears his hair long to the shoulder, and walks about in a two-colored, slashed doublet with a bright cap: no one has ever seen him in clerical attire" (von Matt and Rahner, 1956, p. 11). The affair was settled through the protection of Velázquez and the influence of the Loyolas on the court in Pamplona. There is no record of a sentence, and whatever the outcome, it did not prevent Pero López from continuing as pastor of Azpeitia.

Another unsavory episode has come to light regarding the escapades of the young hidalgo. Apparently a serious rivalry arose between Iñigo and another courtier, Francisco de Oya, over the affections of an unknown woman. Francisco let it be known that he was out for Iñigo's scalp and intended not only to wound him but do away with him. Iñigo seems to have bribed a young woman, who told him of Francisco's plot. He took the matter straight to the king in 1518, requesting the right to bear arms and to have two bodyguards for self-protection. On 10 November 1519, Charles I gave him the royal permission to bear arms for one year and to hire one bodyguard. Apparently the threat continued for some time, for these concessions were renewed on March 5 of the following year (Martin 1975).

The atmosphere of the court was not conducive to a life of virtue. Isabella made serious efforts to reform the morals of the court, but without lasting effect. Montesino, the Franciscan poet and favorite of Queen Isabella, has left us a ballad depicting the corruption of the court:

This palace you see, ladies and men of wealth, know it is a lair of snakes that overcomes virtue and exhausts all ages. So leave its precincts scaly with sluggish rust, for its ugly environs more surely kill consciences than does poison. Do not bear as hirelings the cross only out of interest, distinguished in garb, rich in income, and your soul in rags!

He goes straight to Hell who crosses himself externally if he looks to gain and not to the straight judgment that awaits. And the ladies of the court in perils skilled, who through vain hopes have not their honor whole and have dead souls. If they would consider well the purpose of the banquets and gallants, I know well that their feet would run as they do in festive gardens to the Cross and to your concerns. . . . But alas, for never the dregs of the sinful world do you leave until old age or in danger of pregnancy: deadly sin! (Quoted in Leturia, 1949, p. 171)

Father Laynez remarks that Iñigo was "tempted and overcome by the lusts of the flesh" (FN I, 76). And Polanco adds: "Though he was attached to the faith, he lived nowise in conformity with it and did not avoid sin. Rather he was much addicted to gambling and dissolute in his dealings with women, contentious and keen about using his sword" (cited in Brodrick, 1956, p. 45). The source of these impressions could only have been confidences from Ignatius himself.

Iñigo had moments of trial and torment at Arévalo as well. Ribadeneyra records a curious episode: "He contracted a rather serious infection of his nose, of a kind that hardly anyone could tolerate the foul odor that it emitted. For a while he longed to withdraw into the desert and conceal himself in inaccessible solitude away from the eyes of men so that he wouldn't have to suffer their holding their noses and turning away in disgust rather than out of any desire or purpose of serving God" (FN II, 326). He desperately sought relief from physicians, but to no avail. He shut himself up in his room and treated the nose with his own remedy of cold water douches. Eventually, the swelling diminished and the odor disappeared. No longer disfigured and repulsive, he could once again take his place in the courtly gambols and amorous intrigues. We can easily imagine the mortification and humiliation the young gallant must have suffered. But we also catch a fleeting glimpse of his characteristically fierce independence and determination.

Whatever one might think of this dashing young hidalgo, it is apparent that he was a child of his age and reflected the values and spirit of Catholic Spain at the beginning of the sixteenth century. The boy who had set forth from the castle of Loyola in 1507 had become a man. It is easy to catalog the extrinsic influences on the course of his development, but it is more difficult to grasp the inner forces that made Iñigo de Loyola what he was.

CHARACTER STRUCTURE

Even as the portrait emerges from the dim pages of history, there are clinical reverberations for the psychoanalytic observer. The picture of the brash young courtier is permeated with signs of phallic narcissism.[6] The narcissistic strain provides the cast of his personality organization, but it also carries with it certain lines of cleavage or vulnerabilities that portend future difficulties.

The phallic narcissistic personality demonstrates a constellation of characteristics that include exhibitionism, pride in prowess, and often counterphobic competitiveness and a willingness to take risks or court danger in the service of self-display. Such individuals are frequently quite self-centered but invariably have an intense need for approval and especially admiration from others. One often finds an arrogance or contempt for others that is basically defensive and masks underlying feelings of inadequacy or inferiority.

This inner sense of inferiority often stems from a sense of shame derived from an underlying identification with a weak father figure— which is compensated for by the arrogant, assertive, aggressively competitive, often hypermasculine and self-glorifying façade—or from a never quite adequate response to the demands, expectations, and standards set by an idealized and feared father figure. In other words, the unconscious shame derived from the fear of castration by an aggressive and hypermasculine father is continually denied by phallic assertiveness. This may even be accompanied by feelings of omnipotence and invulnerability that allow such individuals to take risks continually, believing that some miraculous fate or good luck will carry them through. At the same time, their strength of will, determination, and often ruthless drive to overcome all obstacles and conquer all dangers gives them the appearance of strength of character and resourcefulness.

In the light of this profile, which Iñigo seems to fit quite well, we are forced to reconsider our argument. We have postulated that a major contributing factor in the shaping of Iñigo's identity was his identification with his strong-willed and aggressive father. Does this identification not speak of strength rather than narcissistic vulnerability? The answer must, of course, be yes and no. Beltrán himself fits the portrait of phallic narcissism all too well; in fact, the pattern seems endemic to all the Loyolas. Moreover, it was sanctioned and reinforced by the culture as well as by family history and traditions. In fact, given Spanish history and the turmoil of the times, phallic narcissistic propensities might well have been the preferred means for getting on in the world.

Whatever the external influences, an individual's character structure carries inherent vulnerabilities. The identification of young Iñigo with his forceful father embraced the elements of his father's personality. We learn from clinical experience that, when such internalizations take place on defensive or drive-determined bases,[7] the individual assimilates not only positive and constructive aspects but also less desirable and less mature qualities as well. In addition, elements may be assimilated on a quite unconscious level—both for the subject who internalizes and for the object of the internalization. We can argue, then, that both the sense of unconscious inner vulnerability and defenses against it were inherent in the character structure of Beltrán and were passed on to his sons in varying patterns by way of internalization. The history and traditions of the Loyolas, extending back to the earliest legends, to the "band of brothers" and the battle of Beotibar, are a paean to phallic narcissism. We will see shortly what these apparent narcissistic vulnerabilities may have meant for the youngest Loyola.

CRISIS

Soon after the trial of Iñigo and Pero López at Pamplona on 23 January 1516, King Ferdinand of Castile died, with Juan Velázquez at his side. From that moment the fortunes of Velázquez took a turn for the worse. Ferdinand had appointed his Flemish-born grandson, Charles, regent of Castile in place of his deranged mother, Juana. On her death Charles, who was no more than sixteen at the time and knew nothing of Spain, its language, or its customs, succeeded to the throne of Castile. One of his first acts was to change the arrangements for the widowed Queen Germaine's pension. He directed from Flanders that the pension left to the queen from the revenue of Naples should be transferred to certain Castilian towns, some of which were governed by Juan Velázquez. In consequence, the towns, with their lands and jurisdiction, were to be handed over in seignory to the queen for her residence. Juan Velázquez was to retain his office but would now govern in the queen's name. The decree in effect dismembered the royal patrimony of Castile, of which the towns in question were a part, and violated the rights of the towns, which had possessed the privilege of non-alienation from the Castilian crown since the days of Ferdinand IV (1295–1312). This was a highly prized privilege for which they were ready to fight. Cardinal Ximénez de Cisneros, the regent, tried to get young Charles to change his mind; but meanwhile he insisted that Velázquez obey the order. Velázquez and the council of Arévalo declared that the law and the royal patrimony were exempt from the orders of a distant and ill-informed young king. Charles finally did reverse the orders in 1520—but in 1516 he insisted that they be carried out.

Cisneros acted quickly. He removed Velázquez from his post. The old noble organized an armed resistance and prepared a formidable fortification of Arévalo. But diplomatic maneuvers averted the necessity of armed conflict, and the old soldier had to yield. He retired to Madrid, heavily in debt, saddened by the recent death of his oldest son, hated by Queen Germaine for his stand at Arévalo, and deprived of all favor and influence at court. He died on 12 August 1517.

And what of Loyola during this contest? Alonso de Montalvo, his comrade in the service of Velázquez, vouched for Iñigo's loyalty to his patron. The witness is not very reliable, but Iñigo's ties to Velázquez were too strong for us to imagine that he would not remain loyal. He did so, however, at the cost of his ambition. He had become disenchanted with life at court and yearned for the life of the soldier, for the opportunity to display his prowess in battle and to gain fame and renown. It so happened that Cisneros in 1516 was organizing *La Gente de la Ordenanza*, the first permanent army of the Crown. Iñigo's loyalty to Velázquez meant that he would have to forgo this opportunity to serve.[8]

With Velázquez's death, Iñigo's world fell apart. Velázquez's widow provided him with five hundred escudos and two horses and advised him to seek out the duke of Nájera, to whom Iñigo was related. Iñigo headed for Pamplona, the capital of Navarre. This time he went forth not as a timid, impressionable adolescent but as a young man of arms, bearing a proud name, sure of his own strength and courage.

PAMPLONA

III

As Iñigo rode toward Pamplona, he headed into a phase of his life in which the course of political events would play a decisive role. It was to be one of those fascinating episodes in which history and personality seem inextricably intertwined.

Pamplona was the capital of the kingdom of Navarre, one of the pivotal points in the dynastic contention between the French Valois and the Spanish Hapsburgs for European hegemony and in the struggles among contending factions in the Spanish peninsula. It was a strategic gateway, for the roads from Navarre ran straight to Saragossa in Aragon and to Burgos in Castile. The crisis might not have been so severe if Navarre were a united kingdom, but it was not. The rival factions of the Agramonts and the Beaumonts had threatened the unity of the kingdom and opposed the authority of the crown for nearly a century. Ferdinand had annexed it by force in 1512, sending an armed force headed by the duke of Alba under the pretext of a supposed Franco-Navarrese invasion of Castile, and in 1515 arranged for its definitive incorporation in the territory of Castile.

The story unfolded against the backdrop of the dynastic struggle between the French Valois and the Spanish Hapsburgs for European hegemony. On the French side, Charles VIII, the last of the Valois, annexed Naples in 1495, but soon had to retreat in the face of the Holy League, an alliance of Hapsburg, Spanish, papal, and Italian power. The subsequent history of shifting alliances and struggles left a stalemate. When Francis I came to the throne, he immediately annexed Milan and sought to extend French power even further. The rest of his reign (until 1547) was consumed by wars between France and Spain. Charles had succeeded to the Spanish throne in 1516 as Charles I after the death of Ferdinand. On his election to the imperial throne in 1519, he became Emperor Charles V.

By the time Iñigo arrived at the duke's court in Pamplona, Navarre was

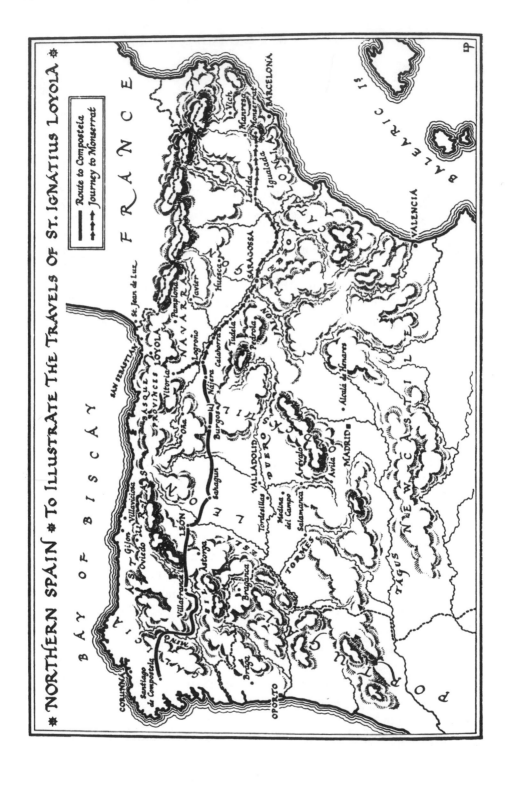

✳ NORTHERN SPAIN ✳ TO ILLUSTRATE THE TRAVELS OF ST. IGNATIUS LOYOLA ✳

Route to Compostela
Journey to Monserrat

part of the kingdom of Castile. Antonio Manrique de Lara, the duke of Nájera, had been chosen viceroy, despite the opposition of Iñigo Fernández de Velasco, the powerful constable of Castile, stemming from the ancient feud between the Oñacinos and Gamboinos, noted above. Velasco was regarded as chief of the Gamboinos, and the duke of Nájera was head of the Oñacinos. The Loyolas, of course, were one of the leading houses of the Oñacinos. In Navarre, the Agramonts were the ancient allies of the Gamboinos, as were the Beaumonts of the Oñacinos.

THE MAN-AT-ARMS

The son of the Loyolas was a most welcome addition to the duke's company and was on intimate terms with the viceroy's family from 1517 on. When the grandees of Castile assembled at Valladolid in 1518, Iñigo would have been among the men-at-arms in the splendid retinue of the duke. Some years later, in 1552, Ignatius would have occasion to write to the viceroy's son of the "favors and affection for which he was under obligation to his [the viceroy's son's] forebears" (Epistolae IV, 385; letter of 28 August 1552).

Francisco Manrique, the duke's brother and later bishop of Salamanca, has given us an eyewitness account of the young hidalgo in action. Apparently, Iñigo was making his way along one of the streets of the town alone when a group of men, either because they were Agramonts or perhaps just offended by the proud bearing of the duke's new courtier, suddenly tried to "push him against the wall." Francisco, some forty years later, recalled that Iñigo reacted immediately. "He drew his sword and chased them down the street. If someone had not restrained him, either he would have killed one of them, or they would have killed him" (Scripta I, 566). This Loyola was evidently not a man to be trifled with.

Iñigo's first activities in Navarre after he arrived in June of 1517 were not military. Charles arrived in September, and the duke and his household, very likely including Iñigo, were present at the new king's oath-taking. Iñigo's brother Martín García was also there, since he requested and obtained from Charles, with the duke's recommendation, confirmation of the honors and patronage of the house of Loyola.

In May 1520, an uprising began in Toledo as a protest by old Castilian communities against the "foreign" influences on Charles' government,

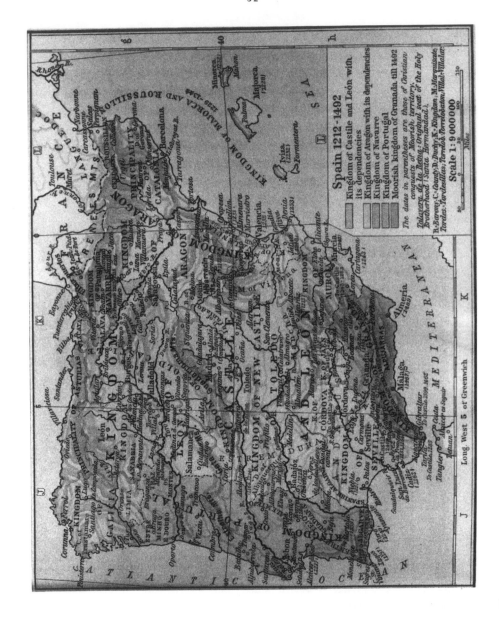

Spain 1212-1492

Kingdom of Castile and León with its dependencies

Kingdom of Aragon with its dependencies

Kingdom of Navarre

Kingdom of Portugal

Moorish kingdom of Granada till 1492

The dates in parentheses are those of Christian conquests of Moorish territory.
B.: Barony; C.: County; D.: Duchy; K.: Kingdom; M.: Marquisate;
P.: Original seat of the Holy Brotherhood (Santa Hermandad).
Tordes.: Tordesillas; Torrelob.: Torrelobaton; Villal.: Villalar.

Scale 1: 9000000

particularly his preference for the interests of the empire over those of the kingdom. The Spanish were particularly angered by the honors and dignities the young king heaped on Flemish entrepreneurs. The resentment became a rebellion. The "Comuneros" uprising, as it was called, involved a number of the nobility, but many more remained loyal to Charles. It was a revolt essentially against foreign influences that were eroding traditional rights and privileges and stripping the country of its wealth and shipping it abroad. The junta of Tordesillas on 20 October 1520 demanded that the king reside in Castile and that he bring no "Flemings, Frenchmen, nor natives of any other country" with him (cited in Elliott, 1977, p. 150). The revolt gradually fragmented into contending factions and turned into a movement of social protest against the aristocracy and nobility. The Comuneros forces were finally crushed at Villalar on 23 April 1521 and the leaders executed, but Charles had learned his lesson and avoided further infringement on traditional rights.

In the revolt of the Comuneros, Francis I of France, Spain's traditional enemy, supported the rebels and took the opportunity to invade Navarre. When the revolt reached Nájera, the duke swiftly marched to the site from Pamplona at the head of some royal troops and men of his own company and entered the city by force. And although he tried to prevent plunder, the city was nonetheless sacked. Iñigo was among the first to force his way into the town, fighting with reckless abandon. Polanco tells us, "He displayed his great and generous spirit as one of the duke of Nájera's nobles. When Nájera was taken and sacked, though he might have taken much booty, he deemed it unworthy and would have none of it" (Leturia, 1949, p. 61).

In the early stages of the uprising, the revolt of the count of Salvatierra at Alava was put down by the duke's son in April 1521. A second disturbance broke out in Guipúzcoa over the appointment of a governor. Most of the towns refused to accept the appointed candidate, and civil war soon erupted. The duke of Nájera, alarmed because the united support of Guipúzcoa was essential to the military security of Navarre, decided to intervene, sending envoys to conduct negotiations. Iñigo was one of these emissaries. The talks had hardly begun when one faction seized some messengers of the other, and hostilities were renewed with even greater violence. The viceroy again sent representatives to seek an agreement, and again Iñigo played a prominent role. Polanco tells us,

"On several occasions he proved himself a man of great prudence and ingenuity in worldly affairs, especially in settling disputes. He was particularly successful in this when the Viceroy of Navarre sent him to settle a serious conflict in the Province of Guipúzcoa. By his tact he brought about an agreement that was satisfactory to all parties" (FN I, 156; cited in Dalmases, 1985, pp. 36–38). Iñigo was further entrusted with promulgating and enforcing the decrees. He was in Guipúzcoa a month later when the French invasion began, and he had to rush to Pamplona with the auxiliary troops of the province.

THE BATTLE FOR PAMPLONA

The revolt of the Comuneros gave Francis I the opportunity he was looking for. He had been on more or less friendly terms with Charles until 1519, when Charles outmaneuvered him in the competition for the coveted imperial crown. King Charles I of Spain was one thing, but Emperor Charles V of the Holy Roman Empire was quite another. Francis saw a chance to strike at the heart of Castile through a vulnerable Navarre. There is good evidence that there was some "understanding" between the Comuneros and Francis I. The viceroy's position was critical. Two years before, he had had an army of ten thousand men, which had made the French think twice. The duke's repeated requests to Charles for reinforcements to aid in the defense of the kingdom were in vain. Now, he could rely only on his own company, some auxiliaries, and a small band of disgruntled royal troops.

The situation was desperate. The viceroy left Pamplona for Segovia, but before his departure he had armed the citadel with nineteen large cannons and some smaller pieces and laid in a supply of food and munitions. He then stationed about a thousand militia in the city under Francis de Beaumont and finally ordered Iñigo de Loyola to bring whatever help he could from Guipúzcoa. Iñigo managed to deliver a sizable force before the French arrived.

As Iñigo's troops drew up before the walls of the city, the inhabitants, presumably resentful of the soldiery and perhaps fearful of the destruction of the city, vociferously opposed its presence. The city council demanded that the entire military and civil administration be turned over to them. Beaumont and his men refused. The troops of the Loyolas, led by Iñigo and Martín, negotiated from outside the walls for entry.

When no agreement was reached, Martín became enraged and rode off with his troops. Iñigo remained and, with a handful of volunteers, entered the city at a gallop and rode into the citadel, where they put themselves at the disposition of the commandant.

Meanwhile, a French army of over twelve thousand men, equipped with heavy artillery, had drawn up outside the gates. Beaumont was preparing to abandon the city. His force was too small to oppose the French, and he could not trust the people of Pamplona. The city council, fearing the power of such an overwhelming force and the devastating French cannon, sent a deputation to the French commander, André de Foix, with the terms of capitulation. The French accepted the terms, entered the capital city of Navarre, and called on the troops in the citadel to surrender. Herrera, the commandant of the troops in the citadel, had also apparently opted for surrender in the face of overwhelming odds. But Iñigo, Polanco records, "refused to follow for he was ashamed lest departure be regarded as flight, but put himself at the head of those willing to defend the fortress along with its garrison" (FN I, 155). Defeatism was in the air within the citadel, but not in the lion heart of Loyola. Ignatius himself tells us what happened:

> He was in a fortress which the French were attacking, and although the others were of the opinion that they should surrender on terms of having their lives spared, as they clearly saw there was no possibility of a defense, he gave so many reasons to the governor that he persuaded him to carry on the defense against the judgment of the officers, who found some strength in his spirit and courage. On the day on which they expected the attack to take place, he made his confession to one of his companions in arms. (Vita 1)

Iñigo was prepared to fight to the death. An eyewitness account states that the bombardment lasted for six hours. The garrison's cannon gave a good account of itself in the duel with the French artillery, easily the best in Europe. The French losses were considerable. But finally, a part of the wall crumbled, and the gates were breached. Iñigo was at the point of attack, sword in hand, when, as he recalled later, "a cannon ball struck him in the leg, crushing its bones and because it passed between his legs it also seriously wounded the other" (Vita 1). When he fell, the resistance fell with him, and the fortress of Pamplona surrendered.

The French were at first successful but soon met stiffer resistance.

Francis I was finally defeated and captured in the battle of Pavia in 1525 and was forced to sign the Treaty of Madrid by which he abandoned his claims on Italy and his designs on Spain.

Ignatius' autobiography merely notes that after the battle of Pamplona the French "took possession and treated the wounded man with great kindliness and courtesy" (Vita 2). Polanco's account adds that the chivalrous Iñigo responded to this compassion. "While he was being cared for at Pamplona by the doctors in the French camp, he gave them affectionately and generously whatever gifts he could. On one he bestowed his shield, on another his dagger, and still another his corselet" (FN I, 156). After nearly two weeks of care and rest, it was decided to transport him to his own country, to the castle of Loyola. He was carried in a litter and after several weeks arrived at Loyola wounded and weakened. Thus the service of Iñigo de Loyola in the company of the viceroy of Navarre came to an end.

THE NOBLE HIDALGO

The picture that emerges of him during these years is a striking one in many ways. He was proud and idealistic, an able and courageous soldier who would not back off from a fight, even when the odds were against him, whether in a street encounter or the defense of a fortress. Yet he refused to take booty from a helpless town, and he could respond to the chivalry of his enemies with generosity and charm. He was a man to whom difficult diplomatic assignments could be entrusted. The successful settlement of the Guipúzcoan affair must have required considerable tact and sagacity, for the roots of the bitter dispute ran deep, and Guipúzcoans were more inclined to fight than to negotiate. The viceroy had undoubtedly recognized Iñigo's extraordinary gifts and put them to good use. And the siege at Pamplona demonstrates vividly that he was a leader, able to inspire men to acts of courage in the face of adversity.

Iñigo had become a man. More to the point, he had become Iñigo de Loyola. If we ask ourselves what kind of man could have done what Iñigo did, we can only conclude that he had to be a man of noble ideals, a stalwart courtier of a certain self-assurance, of strength of conviction and character. When the cannonball at Pamplona literally knocked his legs out from under him, Iñigo was about thirty years of age, a seasoned soldier, courtier, gentleman—in short, quite a successful man of the world.

The part of his life we have been discussing is dispatched by Ignatius with the comment: "Up to his twenty-sixth year, he was a man given over to the vanities of the world, and took a special delight in the exercise of arms, with a great and vain desire of winning glory" (Vita 1).[1] With this simple statement, Ignatius the saint draws a veil over the face of Iñigo de Loyola. We shall have to look more closely at what lies behind the veil, to discern the psychological significance of what can be seen there for the understanding of Ignatius' complex personality.

The meeting between Iñigo and the French cannonball was one of those remarkable events in which the course of history reaches into the lives of men and seems to steer them toward an unseen but determined destiny. In a sense, the French artillery put an end to Iñigo de Loyola. Iñigo was never more fully himself, never more fully exploiting his own resources than in the siege of Pamplona. In those moments, sword in hand, he achieved an acme of personal courage in the heat of battle, facing the onslaught of superior forces and the desperate certainty of defeat. It was in this moment that he was struck down. If the man Iñigo de Loyola survived, the identity of Iñigo was never to be the same.

PERSONALITY AND IDEALS

We have followed Iñigo through the formative years of his childhood, through the shaping influences of his early adolescence, through the crisis of identity formation, and into the consolidation of that identity into its adult realization. The boy gave way to the dashing and daring young hidalgo, and the young hidalgo became the skillful and courageous soldier and promising statesman. Our concern has been with Iñigo's origins only in the derivative sense that it is possible to discern a pattern in Iñigo's maturation. We are not concerned, however, with the specifics of the generative influences that lay behind this intriguing identity.

Our concern is rather with psychology—penetrating the vicissitudes to which the identity is subject as it grows to self-possession and realization and as it meets the demands of inner crisis and evolution. Consequently, we must direct our attention to the relation between the personality of Iñigo and his inner balance of strengths and weaknesses.

This approach lays a foundation for a further inquiry into the evolution of the structure and functioning of his personality from the rough and ready soldier into the saint. There is no question that there is a direct line of continuity. We must seek to understand the polarities of this evolution and the depth and meaning of the process that led from one to the other.

Since Iñigo was a product of his culture and his time, the features that stand out in his personality are those that were characteristically valued by the code of chivalry (Wickham 1954)—prowess in self-defense and in the arts of war; loyalty, generosity, courtesy, and the pursuit of glory; fierce pride and unquestionable courage. While these values permeated the culture and literature Iñigo had known in the days of his court apprenticeship, we cannot presume that the permeating influence of his environment completely explains the relevance of the aspects of Iñigo's own personality. Any culture, including sixteenth-century Spain, carries a multiplicity of values of which the individual internalizes some subset. Yet chivalric values, with their peculiar appeal and intensity for Iñigo, were not only ideals that defined his behavioral tendencies but wishes that dominated his inner life of fantasy and desire. He admits to us that, during the enforced idleness of his convalescence, his fantasies were taken up with matters of romantic chivalry and heroic deeds (Vita 6). In this fantasy world, Iñigo must have seen himself in the image of Amadís of Gaul, the hero of Montalvo's popular book, which he had so eagerly devoured.

It should be noted that these romantic fantasies had a strong in- stinctual, predominantly genital component. His fantasies and be- havior were permeated by a heterosexual and libidinal factor. But we shall consider these drives and impulses in the context of a functioning personality, as components of a dynamic and emergent identity. It is enough, for the moment, to recognize that the fantasies were primarily genital in level of psychosexual organization and that they were cultur- ally conditioned.

In his summation of the first three decades of his life, Ignatius men- tions the exercise of arms and the desire to win glory as defining charac- teristics (Vita 1). Prowess in the use of dagger, sword, buckler, and cross- bow, good horsemanship, and related skills were essential components of the young Loyola's sense of identity. Of course, there was already an image born of chivalrous ideals and early identifications and nourished by youthful fantasy. Later prowess in arms served both to activate such fantasies and to progressively define an emergent identity. It is woven not only out of self-awareness but also out of perceptions of the self projected by others in the course of social interactions; in Erikson's phrase, identity is compounded out of "self-realization coupled with a mutual recognition" (1959, p. 114). Further, identity formation involves the fashioning of a role and function within the community. The development of such a competence and its reciprocal recognition by the community are significant parts of the process by which identity evolves.

If we look at the adolescent Iñigo in the court of Velázquez, we can presume an antecedent desire to translate his fantasies into reality. After all, the young pages at the court were more or less playing games in their jousts and bouts. But at the same time, these boyish enterprises were not idle. In Renaissance Spain a young gallant's life might easily hang on his skill with the sword. Even in these training exercises, we can see the first interplay between prowess and recognition of prowess, between self-recognition and mutual recognition, which contributed to a growing structure that defined the emerging Loyola as a man of arms. One might say that Iñigo was cut out to be a soldier, and in a sense he was. But his view of himself as a man of arms had to be fashioned out of countless events in which success in combat both gratified his existing wishes and shaped his concept of himself as a man possessing these skills. Pari passu with this inner progression of self-definition, he would have become known among his fellows as a skillful swordsman, and this would have bolstered his perception of himself as such. Moreover, a series of interactions would have either tested this prowess or put it to use, both of which would have further reinforced this aspect of development.

THE EGO IDEAL

The other salient characteristic of Iñigo that Ignatius recalled was the young man's "great and vain desire of winning glory" (Vita 1). The glory was spelled out in terms of the chivalric ideal: military glory won in the service of his king in great victories and valorous deeds. But beyond this, it expresses an ambition, a consuming wish that mirrors Iñigo's fantasy about himself. This idealized self-image cast in the mold of chivalrous heroics was Iñigo's ego ideal or ideal self.

Another element of the chivalric model that we can discern in Iñigo is fidelity. His staunch loyalty to the fallen Velázquez, even when it meant the sacrifice of his own desires and ambitions, and his fierce loyalty to the cause of the duke of Nájera are striking. According to the chivalric code that Iñigo had so successfully internalized, devotion to a lord to whom one had sworn fidelity was a primary quality of the soldier and nobleman (Wickham 1954). In a sense, Iñigo's loyalty was as much to his own ego ideal as it was to the persons and causes to which he pledged himself. Just as it would not allow certain crude desires to enter his consciousness, that ideal would not allow him to abandon any cause to which he was pledged. Such fidelity and commitment to persons, causes, and institutions contributes to the creation of a specific identity through involvement with the community. The direction of such involvements is determined, in part at least, by the ego ideal. We cannot conceive of young Iñigo's pledging himself to any enterprise that did not satisfy the requirements of his ideal, although its terms may not always have been unselfish or just or charitable. By the same token, the fierce intensity with which Iñigo clung to his ideal gives us some sense of its importance both for the maintenance of his own narcissistic integrity and equilibrium and for reinforcement of his sense of himself. It is the ego that executes such control and mobilizes psychic resources to meet the demands of action.

The trustworthiness implicit in fidelity indicates in turn a basic trust in oneself and a correlative trust in others and establishes a sense of confidence in one's own critical evaluation and judgment. These basic dimensions of ego strength underlie the capacity for decisive action that stands out as a dominant quality of Iñigo the soldier and captain. They also represent fundamental residues of the resolution of a primary psychosocial crisis, the crisis of basic trust. The quality of fidelity, which emerges in the adolescent period, forms a "cornerstone of identity" (in Erikson's phrase) in the sense that it represents a fundamental and decisive sense of trust in an emerging identity.

Our attention is likewise called to Iñigo's gallant generosity. His bestowal of all his worldly possessions, meager as they were, on his captors in return for their kindness to him was a chivalrous gesture. Montaigne (1958) has remarked that the name of liberality has the sound of liberty.

Such liberty bespeaks a certain freedom from attachment to objects[2] as well as a fundamental liberty to make that commitment to another which is implied in the giving of a gift. The chivalric code demanded generosity not only in giving one's possessions but also in denying oneself profit at the expense of others. Iñigo's refusal of plunder from the conquered town of Nájera was unique. Taking advantage of the people of the town for his own benefit did not fit with his idealized self-image as a soldier of honor.

The ego ideal of Iñigo serves as a point of conjunction for much of the psychology of his development. It ties together the early primary libidinal relations and identifications with his parents, especially with the virile figure of his father, the imaginative impact of the romantic literature that gave concrete shape to his fantasies, and the formative impact of cultural expectations and norms. We have by no means exhausted the elements represented in these fantasies, for the ideal image they project conveys a major portion of the complex psychology of Iñigo de Loyola. Yet, in some sense, this whole inquiry is an exploration of elements of this same ideal. The desire to win glory, a major theme in this ideal, is a motif that forms one of the lines of continuity between the swashbuckling Iñigo and the saintly Ignatius.

PSYCHOPATHOLOGY

As we have previously noted Iñigo's ego ideal included the chivalric values that contributed to the strength of his character as well as strains of pathological narcissism. If the heroic events of the siege of Pamplona demonstrate Iñigo's unusual strength of character, they also tell us much about his potential weakness. His refusal to capitulate, even in the face of overwhelming odds, seems foolhardy, if not suicidal. Yet death held no terrors for him. The impossible situation brought no rational acceptance of defeat, no compromise, but only stirred him to greater efforts. Such behavior can only be spurred by fantasies of invincibility that reflect underlying elements of grandiosity and omnipotence.

The pathology here is that of phallic narcissism. Such personality structures do not often experience regressive crises, but under the appropriate stress, regression can be severe. In cases of war neurosis, some individuals suffered little fear or anxiety prior to the traumatic event but subsequently seemed incapable of regaining pre-trauma levels of functioning. The severe anxiety of the assault on the individual's self-esteem, which had been based on a view of himself as fearless and capable of withstanding any amount of stress or danger, would have destroyed that image and created an impediment to its reconstitution or effective treatment (Meissner 1979). Iñigo's injury at the battle of Pamplona was just such a traumatic event.

Coloring this complex identity was the impact of his noble family tradition on Iñigo's psychology, undoubtedly mediated by his strong identification with his father, himself the embodiment of this heritage. The family's refusal to have its rights or honor brought into question was unmistakable. These values were distilled into that precipitate of parental identifications within the ego, the ego ideal.

Pride and vanity accompany pathological narcissism, and Iñigo de Loyola, the strutting peacock with his gay colors and jaunty plume, presents a picture of all three: proud, vain, and narcissistic. Yet pride can exist on a continuum and, in fact, a moderate degree of displacement of libido is required for self-esteem and ultimately a positive sense of identity. But the very notion of pride carries with it the possibility of excess. The ego ideal can be too highly valued. A surfeit of pride places the self and its ideal above all other considerations, regardless of the rights and needs of others. It takes the form of egoism which erects a façade of self-sufficiency and pseudo-strength, so radically opposed to real ego-strength and identity. Such excessive "ego-interests" are usually preconscious and are often difficult to bring to consciousness because of their closeness to underlying wishes and instinctually motivated desires (Hartmann 1964).

In the developing personality, psychic potential is normally channeled into the synthetic construction of an identity. If these forces are diverted into the elaboration of an egoistic and hypertrophied ego ideal, the evolution of identity suffers. Pride then becomes a mechanism to compensate for an inadequate sense of identity; it becomes a "lasting and characterologically significant aspect of a personality" (Hartmann and Loewenstein 1962). The pride of the Loyolas, which often bridged into vanity, was an almost necessary complement and consequence of the ego ideal that formed a central part of Iñigo's personality. In this lay both his strength and his weakness.

All this reached a thunderous climax in the dramatic siege of Pamplona. The dazzling light that was Iñigo de Loyola was snuffed out and was not to be rekindled. As the litter bore the wounded soldier on the painful miles to the castle of Loyola, Iñigo was carried into a new and decisive phase of his life. Perhaps it is better to say that he was carried into a new life. It was somehow fitting that the very house that first gave him life should be the place to give him the new life that lay before him.

CONFLICT AND CONVERSION

IV

Once arrived at the castle of Loyola, Iñigo entered on a severely trying series of events. The hardship of the journey had done his broken leg no good. The surgeons, after consultation, decided that the leg should be operated on again and the bones reset. Thirty years later, he recalled this surgery: "Again he went through this butchery, in which as in all the others that he had suffered he uttered no word, nor gave any sign of pain other than clenching his fists" (Vita 2). We must remind ourselves that this was several centuries before the introduction of surgical anesthesia.

After the surgery, his condition grew worse, he lost appetite, and he was told that if he showed no improvement, he could expect to die. He made his confession and received the last sacraments. But the hardy Basque was not finished yet. His condition improved on the feast of Saints Peter and Paul, and within a few days he was judged to be out of danger of death (Vita 3). Iñigo later attributed this recovery to his devotion to St. Peter.

But the ordeal was not yet over. The healing of this second fracture was not very successful. He recalled: "When the bones knit, one below the knee remained astride another which caused a shortening of the leg. The bones so raised caused a protuberance that was not pleasant to the sight. The sick man was not able to put up with this because he had made up his mind to seek his fortune in the world. He thought the protuberance was going to be unsightly and asked the surgeons whether it could not be cut away. They told him that it could be cut away, but that the pain would be greater than all he had already suffered, because it was now healed and it would take some time to cut it off. He determined, nevertheless, to undergo this martyrdom to gratify his own inclinations. His elder brother was quite alarmed and declared that he himself would not have the courage to undergo such pain. But the wounded man put up with it with his usual patience" (Vita 4).

This remarkable episode suggests the resources Iñigo could bring to the service of his ego ideal, which includes a bodily component. The deformity would not fit the image of a handsome soldier, especially when the fashion of the day, particularly the tight-fitting cavalier's boots, would reveal the deformity so readily. His willingness to undergo the torment of surgery is a measure of the extent to which the ego ideal dominated his life and behavior. But it also provides a glimpse of the fundamental strength of Iñigo, his courage, unflinching determination, and capacity to endure hardship and suffering to attain a goal he had set himself. He was the same Iñigo whether he was facing the overwhelming odds of the battlefield or the torment of the surgeon's knife. When the cosmetic surgery was finished, a combination of medicaments and painful stretching was employed to prevent the shortening of the affected leg. He later commented that this caused him many days of martyrdom (Vita 5). The convalescence was long and painful, and since he was unable to stand on the leg, he was forced to remain in bed.

CONVERSION EXPERIENCE

His health was otherwise good, and he looked for some means of diverting himself. He asked for some of the romances he favored, but in the unlettered environs of Loyola none could be found. His sister-in-law, Magdalena, could offer him only the four-volume *Life of Jesus* by the Carthusian Ludolph of Saxony and a volume by Jacobus de Voragine of the lives of the saints, commonly called the *Flos Sanctorum*, which had been in circulation on the Iberian peninsula since about 1480 (Vita 5; Dudon 1949; see also Leturia 1936). The preface to the *Flos Sanctorum* by the translator, the Cistercian Fray Gauberto Vagad, would have fed Iñigo's fantasies. De Guibert commented on these works:

> Vagad dwelt on the lofty achievements of those whom he names "the knights of God" and on the splendid works of the holy founders whose religious and civilizing influence he recalled to memory. Thus he opened before Ignatius' eyes unsuspected horizons of glorious service. But above all Fray Gauberto clearly set forth, in the center of these admirable men, "the eternal Prince, Christ Jesus," as the incomparable Chief whose "ever victorious flag" these knights of God were following. The *Flos Sanctorum* opened the way into Christ's marvelous life and Passion, and Montesino's translation of Ludolph

presented Ignatius with long explanations and meditations about them. (1964, p. 26)

What followed was a most crucial phase in the transformation of Iñigo de Loyola. We can best follow the account in his own words.

By the frequent reading of these books he conceived some affection for what he found there narrated. Pausing in his reading, he gave himself up to thinking over what he had read. At other times he dwelt on the things of the world which formerly had occupied his thoughts. . . . Nevertheless, our Lord came to his assistance, for He saw to it that these thoughts were succeeded by others which sprang from the things he was reading. In reading the Life of our Lord and the Lives of the Saints, he paused to think and reason with himself. "Suppose that I should do what St. Francis did, what St. Dominic did?" He thus let his thoughts run over many things that seemed good to him, always putting before himself things that were difficult and important which seemed to him easy to accomplish when he proposed them. But all his thought was to tell himself "St. Dominic did this, therefore, I must do it. St. Francis did this, therefore, I must do it". These thoughts also lasted a good while. And then other things taking their place, the worldly thoughts above mentioned came upon him and remained a long time with him. This succession of diverse thoughts was of long duration, and they were either of worldly achievements which he desired to accomplish, or those of God which took hold of his imagination to such an extent, that worn out with the struggle, he turned them all aside and gave his attention to other things. (Vita 6, 7)

He then adds some reflections which give us a glimpse of the later Ignatius, who had crystallized his own interior struggles in his rules for discernment[1]. Even so, the introspectionist comes through to us.

There was, however, this difference. When he was thinking of the things of the world he was filled with delight, but when afterwards he dismissed them from weariness, he was dry and dissatisfied. And when he thought of going barefoot to Jerusalem and of eating nothing but herbs and performing the other rigors he saw that the saints had performed, he was consoled, not only when he entertained these thoughts, but even after dismissing them he remained cheerful and satisfied. But he paid no attention to this, nor did he stop to weigh the difference until one day his eyes were opened a little and he began to wonder at the difference and to reflect on it, learning from experience that one kind of thoughts left him sad and the other cheerful. Thus, step by step, he came to recognize the difference between the two spirits that moved him, the one being from the evil spirit, the other from God. (Vita 8)

Besides the analytic tone of this account, which is in itself quite note-worthy, it may be well to remark in passing that Ignatius' reference to the movement of the good and evil spirits was representative of a common medieval position. Ignatius remarks in his *Spiritual Exercises*, "I presuppose that there are three kinds of thoughts in my mind, namely: one which is strictly my own, and arises wholly from my own free will; two others which come from without, the one from the good spirit, and the other from the evil one" (Puhl, 1963, p. 18). In our own day, we would express such ideas in psychological terms rather than the mythologi-cally flavored medieval perspective (Meissner 1963; Boyle 1983).
But let us return to Ignatius' account.

He acquired no little light from this reading and began to think more seriously of his past life and the great need he had of doing penance for it. It was during this reading that these desires of imitating the saints came to him, but with no further thought of circumstances than of promising to do with God's grace what they had done. What he desired most of all to do, as soon as he was restored to health, was to go to Jerusalem, as above stated, undertaking all the discipline and abstinences which a generous soul on fire with the love of God is wont to desire. (Vita 9)

His absorption in reading the spiritual books at hand seemed to grow by the day. He could not restrain himself from discussing this new enthusiasm with family members. He even took to copying passages from the life of Christ or those of the saints—the words of Christ were inscribed in red, those of the Blessed Mother in blue, formed in the courtly hand he had learned so well at Arévalo. The rest of his time was given over to prayer and contemplation. As he recalled, "Part of his time he spent in writing, part in prayer. It was his greatest consolation to gaze upon the heavens and the stars which he often did, and for long stretches at a time, because when doing so he felt within himself a powerful urge to be serving Our Lord. He gave much time to thinking about his resolve, desiring to be entirely well so that he could begin his journey" (Vita 11).

This brief autobiographical account is essentially all that is known about the series of events that brought about the remarkable transformation of Iñigo de Loyola, the proud and gallant hidalgo, into a man filled with the desire to serve God and to imitate the saintly warriors whose heroic deeds he had been reading. He would retreat to the desert and live on herbs like the holy hermits. He would turn his back on the world and its pleasures and devote himself to fasts, flagellations, and penances, like God's heroes. He first thought of committing himself to a life of solitude, silence, and prayer among the monks of Cuevas. Then he felt the urge to wander as a poor pilgrim through the world, begging for his sustenance and bearing the contempt of men. His model would be Il Poverello,[2] to whom God had spoken: "Francis, take the bitter things for sweet and despise thyself, if thou really desirest to know me."

THE PSYCHOLOGY OF CONVERSION

To find the inner meaning that can illuminate the psychological significance of this intriguing series of events, we may take the experience as a conversion of sorts. The conversion phenomenon has long been a subject of psychological and psychiatric interest. Writing at the turn of the century, William James summarized much of what was then known and thought about religious conversion. James describes the preexisting symptoms—"a sense of incompleteness and imperfections; brooding, depression, morbid introspection, and sense of sin; anxiety about the hereafter; distress over doubts, and the like." He adds:

> And the result is the same—a happy relief and objectivity, as the confidence in self gets greater through the adjustment of the faculties to the wider outlook. In spontaneous religious awakening, apart from revivalistic examples, and in the ordinary storm and stress and moulting-time of adolescence, we may also meet with mystical experiences, astonishing subjects by their suddenness, just as in revivalistic conversion. (1902, p. 167)

James was elaborating on the previous work of Starbuck (1903), who compared the phenomenon of religious conversion to the more gradual process of psychological change and growth into a broader spiritual perspective, which he felt was characteristic in adolescent development. It was this adolescent conversion that marked the child's passage from the smaller universe of childhood to the wider intellectual and spiritual perspectives of adult life.

James emphasized the contrasting elements in the mental state of the potential subject of conversion. The first element is the sense of sinfulness or inadequacy, which dominates the individual's consciousness and from which he seeks escape. The second element is the positive ideal for which the individual yearns and toward which he struggles. In the ordinary cases, the motif of escape from sinfulness rather than striving toward an ideal is paramount, almost becoming an obsession. James comments:

> A man's conscious wit and will, so far as they strain towards the ideal, are aiming at something only dimly and inaccurately imagined. Yet all the while the forces of mere organic ripening within him are going on towards their own prefigured results, and his conscious strainings are letting loose subconscious allies behind the scenes, which in their way work towards rearrangement; and the rearrangement towards which all these deeper forces tend is pretty surely definite, and definitely different from what he consciously conceives and determines. It may consequently be actually interfered with (jammed, as it were, like the lost word when we seek too energetically to recall it), by his voluntary efforts slanting from the true direction. (1902, pp. 174–175)

Later contributions to the psychological study of conversion have tended to emphasize the psychopathological aspects, particularly the connection with depression. Ducasse (1953) emphasized that an underlying conflict, pressure for commitment, guilt and fear seem to be necessary factors involved in religious conversion. Individuals experiencing conversion often felt an inner conviction of sinfulness and failure and a sense of profound incapacity to live up to the demands made by religious and ethical commitments. This readily turned into a tormenting fear of damnation and death or expressed itself in the form of depression, brooding, and endless self-examination.

Coe (1916) extended the hints offered by James in his reference to forces working toward rearrangement at a more or less subconscious level, postulating that self-realization was an important aspect of the conversion experience. Usually the convert feels that his basic sense of himself has been profoundly changed and that he is not an active agent in this alteration; it has somehow been worked upon him. In this connection, Coe saw the need to submit to a higher authority as a basic characteristic of the convert's personality. Noting that most conversion experiences were found in adolescence, he also postulated a connection between conversion and the vicissitudes of adolescent sexuality. In Coe's view, "conversion is a step in the creation of a self—the actual coming-to-be of a self" (p. 171).

But it is important to suggest some immediate qualifications. Erikson, following William James, regards religious conversion as a phenomenon of youth, as involved in the need for ideological commitment. Erikson remarks: "Ideologies offer to the members of this age group overly simplified and yet determined answers to exactly those vague inner states and those urgent questions which arise in consequence of identity conflict" (1958, p. 42).

But Iñigo de Loyola was not an adolescent; he was a grown man whose ego functioned at a mature level. His identity was strong and dynamic, with extraordinary qualities that distinguished him as a courageous soldier, a leader, and a not unskilled diplomat, a man trained in letters and etiquette, who moved at ease in the highest circles and had won the respect and trust of important and influential members of the ruling class. Yet, it remains obvious that something significant had happened to the identity of Iñigo.

Christensen (1963) has reported on the conversion experience of twenty-two men who were treated in intensive psychotherapy, all of whom were professionally engaged in some form of religious occupation. These patients all had a sufficient degree of psychopathology to warrant psychiatric treatment, although only two of them were diagnosed as psychotic. Caution is required in extrapolating from such a patient population, since selective factors may be operating that relate to the underlying psychopathology rather than to the religious conversion itself. However, the study does illuminate certain aspects of the conversion experience.

To begin with, in all these individuals, an unconscious conflict was identifiable relating to distorted identifications, depreciated self-image, and psychosexual pathology. Secondly, all these individuals were still in the adolescent phase of development at the time of the experience. And finally, all of them had experienced a fundamentalist religious belief as a part of their early environment and psychic experience. But such predisposing factors are not sufficient to account for the conversion experiences. "There must be a current force which 'lights the fuse,' so to speak, and which culminates in the 'explosion' of the religious conversion experience" (Christensen, 1963, p. 211). Frequently, such conversion occurs when the individual attends an intense religious gathering, such as a revival meeting or a church retreat. Such meetings are usually devoted to soul-searching and frequently emphasize emotion-laden themes such as the sinfulness of man, the worthlessness of his existence, and his utter dependence on God. These experiences often intensify guilty conflicts and underlying depressive tendencies.

The religious conversion experience itself is regarded as a form of transitory, acute, hallucinatory reaction, set in the framework of the individual's religious beliefs. This belief system reflects the individual's unconscious conflicts, while at the same time it supports a structurally weak ego. On the conscious level, it can intensify guilt and anxiety. It may also bring about a solution to the underlying conflicts, which is sometimes successful, sometimes not. In any case, the religious conversion experience can be regarded as an attempt to reintegrate the ego (see Boisen 1936).

The conversion experience is also associated with certain phenomena that appear regressive in character. In these cases, there seems to be a relaxation of the synthetic capacity of the ego, resulting in internal dissociation and fragmentation that are connected with a sense of estrangement. The onset of the subjective experience of estrangement heralds the initial disintegration of the ego and is often associated with a sense of confusion regarding the self and its identity (Conn 1986). The fragmented aspects of the self-organization which are dissociated from integration with the individual's sense of self are usually dealt with defensively—more often than not, by projection. At times the process of disintegration extends even to the individual's body image and perceptual capacity. His perceptions of his own body or of external objects will no longer seem familiar and real and will be experienced as alien. If the confusion increases and the disintegration continues, the person becomes unable to distinguish "self" from "nonself." This dedifferentiation of the self and objects is connected with the acutely confused state seen in the preconversion process; it is usually halted by the conversion experience.

Prior to the actual conversion experience, there is a period during which the individual is caught up in both conscious and unconscious conflict. At its peak intensity, when the conflict threatens the ego with disintegration, there is a tendency for the individual to stop trying to resolve the conflict actively and consciously. Christensen (1963) notes that this giving-up is related to earlier behavior patterns in which the child was forced to conform to parental demands, especially to those of the mother. The giving-up phenomenon tends to occur immediately before or concurrently with the sense of divine presence. This may be regarded as a projective phenomenon, but an important aspect is that it can inspire guilt feelings if its assumed dictates are not followed. The guilt may be atoned by acts of expiation or submission.

In Christensen's subjects, when the sense of divine presence was a part of the religious conversion experience, the clarity of the experience tended to vary. Some individuals experienced it as a kind of influence, while for others it was the feeling of a distinct other person close by. Inevitably, the sense of psychic presence was related to the individual's concept of God. Christensen felt that the projection involved in the experience of divine presence was related to the defensive projection of the mental representation of the mother. Thus, the surrender and submission to the will of God has as one of its psychic equivalents the child's submission to the demands of the mother. Auditory hallucinations may be a part of this experience of psychic presence and are usually interpreted by the convert as the voice of God.

Further exploration relates the auditory hallucination to unconscious conflicts and particularly to fears of abandonment. With the feeling of submission and the sense of acceptance and conformity to the divine will, there is a sense of sudden understanding accompanied by elation. The auditory and sometimes visual hallucinations may form a part of this complex experience. The result is a feeling of change in the individual's sense of self, or in his sense of himself in relation to some other important person (Conn 1986). Moreover, the change is experienced passively, as happening to him, rather than actively, as brought about by his own agency, and is associated with a sense of presence.

Christensen (1963) describes four possible solutions to the regressive crisis involved in the conversion experience. In the first case, the conflicts on both unconscious and conscious levels are sufficiently resolved so that they can be meaningfully integrated with the functioning ego. The resulting synthesis and solution are compatible with current reality experience and are brought within the adaptive control of the ego. The result is a sense of completeness or totality, as well as a sense of deep understanding within oneself. Energies previously bound up in conflict may then become available for more creative, productive, and adaptive use by the ego. For such individuals, the conversion experience becomes a process of growth toward greater personal and spiritual maturity.

However, in most cases of conversion the strength of the ego often seems insufficient to integrate the underlying conflicts, as though the suppression of more conscious conflicts allows them to gain strength from association with the unconscious conflict and thus become a source of deep psychic threat. Such elements may be responded to by a variety of ego defense mechanisms, the result often taking the form of a kind of symbolic representation which expresses the mystical nature of the religious beliefs. While this does not resolve the conflict in any sense, it does alleviate anxiety, thus creating a sense of relief and some understanding. The sense of completeness and integration is felt as belonging to an object outside the self—specifically God, the symbol of psychic presence. Consequently, the psychic energy remains to that extent bound in terms of continuing repression and defense and is not freed for more adaptive functions of the ego. The religious belief system in such cases serves to maintain the repressive barriers and support the ego insofar as any challenge to the belief system will be perceived as a threat and must be opposed.

In cases where the ego lacks sufficient strength to deal with the underlying conflicts, the result is often a disintegration of the ego. Reality testing is lost and the individual becomes confused, self-object differentiation is lost and the person becomes acutely disoriented. In the effort to allay the intense and overwhelming anxiety and to maintain some sense of self-organization, the person resorts to a fantastic and psychotic symbolic solution in the form of a religious delusion. In cases of outright psychosis, this may take the form of assuming another, fictitious identity, usually that of some well-known religious figure. The assumption of such an identity may serve as a nucleus around which subsequent reintegration can take place. The individual may function in terms of this substitute identity until he is able to gain some reintegration in more realistic terms. When this happens, the delusional system is surrendered. If it does not happen, the psychotic process continues, and the delusion may become chronic.

The sudden breakthrough or flash of illumination so commonly experienced in conversion has been found in a variety of ruminative states (Frosch 1977). Similar experiences include the emergence of sudden insights in psychotherapy, the feeling of discovery, revelation, or illumination and realization. In this context as in religious conversion, there is a sense of sudden breakthrough, which is often preceded by a period of confusion, stress, anxiety, and disorientation. There may also be a physical or psychological withdrawal from reality. This period of uncertainty and confusion is interrupted by a sudden revelation, which brings a feeling of clarity, an understanding of the revelation or truth, a seeing of the light with an accompanying sense of conviction and certainty, which gives the insight a powerful impact and guiding influence on the course of the individual's life. In Moloney's (1954) view, the experience of the revelation is frequently accompanied by the sense of lightness and exultation and may be associated externally with sudden flashes of light, loud explosions, and thundering noise. The outcome is often a radical transformation of the internal structure of the personality, which results in a profound alteration of identity (Conn 1986).

IÑIGO'S CONVERSION—A PSYCHOANALYTIC VIEW

Returning to Iñigo's conversion experience, it seems clear that the impact of the cannonball at Pamplona set in motion a series of events that were to have far-reaching consequences. In the castle of Loyola, Iñigo experienced the first stages of conversion, which characteristically had the quality of sudden illumination or revelation. But it seems clear that this episode was only the first in a long conversion process that led him, step by difficult step, away from the home of his ancestors and the tradition and loyalties of the house of Loyola to the cave of Manresa and its bitter spiritual and psychic struggle.

I will take up that part of the story in the next chapter; here we focus on the events that took place during Iñigo's painful convalescence. As William James (1902) and others have observed, the more or less acute and climactic experience of religious conversion is frequently accompanied by a long, arduous process that brings about a gradual restructuring of the individual's personality. The process set in motion in Iñigo's soul would work itself out only after months and years of continuing conflict.

To begin with, the narcissistic grandiosity and omnipotence so prominent in his character were shattered at Pamplona. That cannonball crushed not only the bones of his leg, but also his ideals, ambitions, and dreams of glory. After all, for this sword-swinging hidalgo, phallic activity and a sense of counterphobic invincibility and omnipotence had formed a considerable part of his character structure. The weeks of pain, passivity, and dependence his convalescence required must have activated those basic anxieties his defenses had so effectively contained. Basic to this underlying core of anxiety had to be the threat of castration, intensified by the trauma of physical injury and broken bones.

We can add to this the intense narcissistic cathexis of his body image, which suffered the traumatic deformity of his leg. How could he maintain the image of a handsome, dashing hero with a misshapen leg and an obvious limp? The motifs of castration and defectiveness here blend with the narcissistic strains of diminished self-worth and the countering of exhibitionistic wishes and impulses in the sense of shame. The power of this need for psychic well-being is manifest in his willingness to undergo further surgery, however painful, in the hope of overcoming this impediment. Understandably, then, as he lay on his bed in pain, Iñigo's mind would have been searching for substitutes for the shattered ideals, ambitions, and values that had been so central to his sense of himself.

It is clear that in the early phases of his convalescence, the ego ideal that had served as a major focus of the psychological life of Iñigo was still intact and quite functional. His insistence on cosmetic surgery at exquisite cost seems utterly unintelligible without an appeal to some such powerfully determining normative image. But the deformity of his limbs not only constituted a hindrance to the realization of his chivalric ideal but was unassimilable to his body image. The deformation must have mobilized deep-seated anxieties stemming from the insult to Iñigo's basic self-concept.

If we adjust the focus of the psychoanalytic lens ever so slightly, it becomes clear that we are dealing here also with the dynamics of loss and restitution.³ The loss is cast in terms of the traumatic assault on his body image and the associated narcissistic vanity with regard to appearance and physical prowess. He could no longer carry the image of the handsome and dashing courtier, nor could he remain the skilled man of arms. The strong narcissistic investments in the code of honor, valor, and glory were stripped away; thus the desires, ambitions, and ideals that had dominated his life to this point had to be mourned so that the losses could be effectively resolved and his energies remobilized in the service of restitution. Freud (1917) regarded mourning as a normal and transient response to the loss of a loved object. The grief reaction and the process of mourning allow the subject ultimately to accept and to come to terms with the loss and to integrate it in such a way that he is free to enter into other relationships. The process of loss and restitution applies to other contexts as well—the loss of work or career investments, for example, which might involve narcissistic gratifications and the fulfillment of ego ideals. Iñigo's loss called for a restitutive process that would salvage the remnants of his shattered narcissism and create new investments and new ideals that would respond to his powerful narcissistic needs. Iñigo's narcissism was profoundly damaged by a traumatic castrative experience, creating a psychic demand for restoration of the narcissistic loss and for the creation of a new set of ideals and a sense of an ideal self that would heal these wounds and allow for a meaningful and self-sustaining reintegration of his personality.

At this point his imagination was captured by the heroic tales of the saints and the life of Christ. He tells us in his autobiography how he became fascinated by these tales of saintly heroism and how he alternated between the remnants of his former narcissism, the vanity and worldly deeds of glory, particularly those he might have performed in the service of his royal lady, and the more spiritual heroics he found in his reading. The residues of shattered narcissism were beginning to be shaped to a new form and a new meaning.

In this process, the elements of a typical conversion experience began to assert themselves. As he read the accounts of the lives of the saints, he began to think more seriously of his own past life, his sinfulness, and the need to atone for it. He began to think of the ways in which he might imitate the lives of the saints by doing various penances and fasts, even making a pilgrimage to Jerusalem.⁴

At this juncture, an incident occurred that seems to have been the central event in Iñigo's early conversion experience.

One night, as he lay awake, he saw clearly the likeness of our Lady with the Holy Child Jesus, at the sight of which he received most abundant consolation for a considerable interval of time. He felt so great a disgust with his past life, especially with its offenses of the flesh, that he thought all such images which had formerly occupied his mind were wiped out. And from that hour until August of 1553, when this is being written, he never again consented to the least suggestion of the flesh. The effect would seem to indicate that the vision was from God, although he never ventured to affirm it positively or claim that it was anything more than he had said it was. But his brother and other members of the family easily recognized the change that had taken place in the interior of his soul from what they saw in his outward manner. (Vita 10)

The vision provides considerable food for psychoanalytic thought. During the period of Iñigo's convalescence, his brother Martín, the master of Loyola, had been away on the campaign against the French, and Martín's wife, Magdalena, cared for the sick man. Ignatius was to speak of the same Magdalena years later when he confessed to one of his novices that a picture of our Lady in his prayerbook reminded him so much of her beauty that he had to cover the picture in order that his intense affection and passion for her might not be aroused. Is it possible, then, that in his weakened and tormented condition Iñigo might have been erotically stimulated by the tender and intimate ministrations of the beautiful Magdalena? We can recall here an observation of Freud:

In young men egoistic and ambitious wishes come to the fore clearly enough alongside of erotic ones. But we will not lay stress on the opposition between the two trends; we would rather emphasize the fact that they are often united. Just as, in many altar-pieces, the portrait of the donor is to be seen in a corner of the picture, so, in the majority of ambitious fantasies, we can discover in some corner or other the lady for whom the creator of the fantasy performs all his heroic deeds and at whose feet all his triumphs are laid. (1908, p. 147)

Just as the saint of later years in his devotions had replaced the picture of the Blessed Mother with the face of Magdalena, in this central conversion experience could the bedridden soldier have substituted the vision of our Lady for the loved and desired Magdalena? We might also remember that the Blessed Mother was the dominant image of chaste perfection in Iñigo's culture.[5] The possibility raises the fascinating and deeper question of Iñigo's relationship with women—a subject that we reserve for separate discussion.

In the present context, it seems safe to say that Magdalena was a most significant participant in the drama that unfolded around the fallen warrior. We remember that Iñigo had lost his own mother at a very early age and had subsequently been nursed and raised by the loving and motherly María de Garín. When Magdalena came to the castle of Loyola as Martín's bride, Iñigo would have been about seven years of age. She became for all practical purposes his mother through the years of his latency development and on into adolescence.

We have already commented on the powerful identification of the young Iñigo with his powerful father. This phallic narcissistic identification—a major line of defense against the underlying castration anxiety that must have been aroused in his relationship with this commanding figure—was undermined by the symbolic castration of Iñigo's wound and his convalescence. Lombillo (1973) has argued that, as the identification with the father was undermined, the identification with the maternal elements began to assert themselves through the conversion experience. In this sense, the idealized aspects of Iñigo's lost mother were projected onto Magdalena, whose pious influence led him increasingly toward identification with the saints.

The saintly heroes embodied maternal qualities of suffering, resignation, penance, self-denial, and ascetic resignation, qualities that were set over against the phallic striving, aggressiveness, and ambition for glory connected with Iñigo's identification with his father. However, the wish to imitate the saints was contaminated by aspects of the earlier paternal configuration, particularly with regard to the competitive wish to outdo the saints in heroic deeds. The themes of phallic conquest are reflected in his desire for penance and ascetic heroics, in his plans for a pilgrimage to Jerusalem, and in the spiritual ambition that seems to characterize his thinking.

A recurring question concerns the extent to which Iñigo, throughout his fascinating life's journey, was able to disengage himself from the deep-seated introjections that arose from his profound attachments to pious mother-substitutes, on the one hand, and from the powerful and forceful influence of his aggressive and phallically narcissistic father, on the other.

We can conjecture, then, that the vision of our Lady with the child Jesus was the reflection of Iñigo's idealized image of his own mother as well as that of Magdalena, toward whom his unconscious libidinal impulses had been stirred. We might suggest as well that in his fantasy Iñigo saw himself as the baby Jesus, who could be cared for, loved by, and who in turn could possess his idealized mother. The wishful regression to a preoedipal state would avoid the destructive consequences of the potential oedipal conflict. Regression to a state of blissful union with the idealized mother also denies any incestuous longings that might carry the stamp of a more mature and differentiated sexuality.

The regressive wishful fantasy is followed by the imposition of a powerful repressive barrier, outlawing all sexual (incestuous) wishes. Such a barrier can be taken here as a sign of a new and powerful narcissistically invested ego ideal. When Freud (1914) began to discuss narcissism, he connected it with the mechanism of repression. He observed that an individual would repress instinctual impulses and wishes only if they were in conflict with his ethical ideas and ideals. Such ideals in fact seem to be a prerequisite for repression. Freud spoke of the "self-respect of the ego." Repression flows from the self-respect of the ego in the sense that impulses give rise to anxiety as a signal of danger insofar as they violate an ideal that the individual has set up in himself and by which he measures himself. Any content that would not be consistent with and acceptable to the ideal thus becomes repressed. While Ignatius presents this repressive reaction in its totality, the psychologist will ponder whether or not there was room for the return of the repressed and how much this turning away from sexuality and the disavowal of its influence represented outright repression as opposed to sublimation.

Our first interest is in trying to understand the psychological transformation taking place in Iñigo. His was not an identity crisis in the psychosocial sense defined by Erikson, for his identity was already well-established. Moreover, the transformation was not a sudden or climactic event, but a slow process that began during his convalescence, was subjected to its definitive reconstruction in the cave of Manresa, and finally came to fruition in the extraordinary career of Ignatius. We have already examined some aspects of the development of Iñigo's ego and the emergence of his personal identity. Just as that development represented a continuing process of epigenetic development[6] and incremental synthesis, so the process of transformation we examine here took place in stages that progressively added their contribution to the emergence of Ignatius the saint and religious leader.

In the first phase of his convalescence we are confronted with the same Iñigo—vain, ambitious, proud, courageous. The transformation is inaugurated in the long phase of recuperation from his painful operation. With plenty of time to indulge in romantic and heroic fantasies, his thoughts drifted frequently to the inspiring deeds of the saints. Since he was born and raised in an atmosphere of deep religious belief and a profoundly Catholic culture in which the saints are revered as great heroes of God, Iñigo fantasied himself doing similar deeds. But his mind was still in conflict over these contending ideals—the romantic-heroic and the spiritual—along with their corresponding values, beliefs, and codes of conduct.

THE PILGRIM'S WAY

By February 1522, Iñigo's legs had finally healed, and he felt ready to leave his ancestral home to seek his spiritual fortune. His brother Martín García tried to dissuade him, but Iñigo remained firm (Vita 12). Under the pretext of a visit to his former commander, he set out with his brother Pero López and a couple of attendants for Navarrete, where the duke of Nájera was in residence. His actual objective was the shrine of our Lady at Montserrat. He was elegantly and appropriately garbed for such a mission. The brothers stopped first at Oñate, to visit their sister. Iñigo persuaded Pero López to pass the night in vigil at the shrine of Aranzazu. Later, he would recall to a friend: "As he left his homeland to go to Montserrat, he was more afraid of being overcome by the sin of the flesh than by any other burden; it had occasioned him many a struggle and defeat. Consequently, he made a vow of Chastity to Our Blessed Lady and entreated her to take him under her protection and patronage" (von Matt and Rahner, 1956, p. 28).

Leaving his brother and sister in Oñate, Iñigo dismissed the two attendants and rode on to Navarrete alone. The duke wanted to reward Iñigo by putting him in charge of one of his properties, but Iñigo again remained firm in his resolve and left Navarrete (Dalmases 1985). He recounts an episode that tells something of his state of mind as he rode toward Montserrat:

An experience befell him on the way which it would be good to recount. It will help to an understanding of how our Lord dealt with his soul who, although still blind, had a great desire to serve Him to the best of his knowledge, and was set on performing great penances, not so much with an idea of satisfying for his sins, as to placate and please God. Then, when he remembered to do some penance which the saints had performed, he resolved to do the same and even more. All his consolation was in these thoughts. He never took a spiritual view of anything, nor even knew the meaning of humility, or charity, or patience, or discretion as a rule and measure of these virtues. His whole purpose was to perform these great, external works, for so had acted the saints for God's glory, without thought of any more particular circumstance. Well then, as he went on his way, he came upon a Moor riding a mule. They both fell to talking, and the conversation turned on our Lady. The Moor admitted that the Virgin had conceived without man's aid, but could not believe that she remained a virgin after once having given birth, and for this opinion submitted the natural reasons which occurred to him. For all the arguments which the pilgrim gave against this opinion, he could not refute it. The Moor then took the lead with such haste that he was soon lost to view, and left the pilgrim with his own thoughts of what had taken place. There gave rise to emotions that brought on a feeling of discontent in his soul, as he thought that he had failed in his duty. This in turn led to indignation against the Moor, as he thought that he had done very ill to allow a Moor to say such things against our Lady, and that he was obliged to defend her honor. Hence a desire arose to go in search of the Moor and give him a taste of his dagger for what he had said. This battle of desires lasted for some time with the pilgrim quite doubtful at the end as to what he ought to do. The Moor, who had gone on ahead, had said that he was going to a place, which was on the same highway, a little further on, but a little to the side of the highway. The royal highway, however, did not pass through the place. . . .

Tired out from this examination as to what it would be good for him to do, and not being able to come to any clear decision, he thought of letting the mule decide, and gave her a free rein up to the spot where the road divided. If the mule took the road that led to the village, he would search out the Moor and give him a taste of his dagger. If she did not take the village road, but continued on the royal highway, he would leave him in peace. This he did. But it was our Lord's will that, although the village was only thirty or forty steps away, and the road to it broad and even, the mule took the royal highway and passed by the village road. (Vita 14, 15, 16)

This reaction resembles that of a chivalrous knight who feels that he must fight to defend the honor of his queen. Iñigo was still very much a proud hidalgo. But if we contrast this incident with the occasion on which he was pushed against the wall and then chased his antagonists, sword in hand, the change is striking. In the earlier incident he did not hesitate to express his anger in action. The impulse to fight was, we might say, ego-syntonic.[7] But in the later instance, anger produced conflict which prevented its translation into action. The code of the chivalrous Iñigo urged action with the dagger, but the code of the pilgrim would not permit this course. The value system of the earlier phallic narcissistic ego ideal, which would have allowed immediate retaliatory action, had been complemented by another, opposing set of values. It is interesting that at this stage Iñigo could not resolve the conflict. His solution seems clever, but we have the feeling that, if the mule had decided otherwise, the impassioned Iñigo might well have given the unfortunate Moor a taste of his dagger.

It is also curious that the argument was about sexuality. The Moor had cast aspersions on the virginity of the idealized Mother, who had become the sublimated vessel for Iñigo's repressed and conflicted libidinal impulses. The impulse to kill him who would sully and make sexual the idealized Mother can hardly elude the implications of oedipal determinants and origins. The oedipal struggle is cast against repressed incestuous wishes that are projected onto the Moor, who can then be effectively punished and destroyed as the bearer of such dangerous sentiments. We are forced to conclude that, however repressed, Iñigo's sexual wishes remained a vital force in his psychic economy and a source of continuing conflict.

It is also striking that Ignatius identifies himself at this stage of his career as "the pilgrim." The designation is apt, since a pilgrim is first of all one who is going to some religious destination and who, moreover, is doing penance for his past life. He had told us already that he "began to think more seriously of his past life and the great need he had of doing penance for it" (Vita 9). This undoubtedly reflects the extent to which his ego had assimilated the new set of values and the degree to which he had gained an awareness of the imperfection and inadequacy of the value system that had previously guided his life.

But the chivalric ideal still carried a significant influence, as it would to the end of his pilgrimage. As he rode his mule toward the hills of Montserrat, he still wore the rich clothes of the gentleman, but also carried a little portrait of the Mother of Sorrows,[8] his last legacy from the house of Loyola. Progress was slow, and he spent the nights in inns along the road, lashing himself with the discipline until he bled and praying for forgiveness. When he finally reached Igualada, at the foot of Montserrat, he had traveled 368 miles from the castle of Loyola. In addition to the fine clothes, he still wore the familiar sword and dagger at his waist. His pack carried little more than a change of linen, scissors to trim his hair and nails, and the large notebooks in which he had written extracts from the *Vita Christi* and his own prayerful reflections. In Igualada he bought the garb and accoutrements of the pilgrim—a garment of hemp-linen, a rope-girdle, a staff, a water gourd, and a pair of rope sandals.

The mule soon carried him to the doors of the famous monastery of Montserrat on 21 March 1522 (Codina 1938), the feast of St. Benedict, always a day of great celebration at the monastery. Thousands of pilgrims would throng to the place on such days from all over Europe. It was Iñigo's intention to put his past sinful life behind him once and for all and to turn his face toward Jerusalem, where he hoped the patronage of our Blessed Lady would guide him.

A decade before Iñigo's arrival at Montserrat, a French priest named Jean Chanon had come to the monastery. Chanon would remain there for fifty-six years and become one of its most saintly members. His spiritual outlook had been formed by the great abbot of Montserrat, Garcia Ximénez de Cisneros, a cousin of the famous cardinal regent. Cisneros had come to Montserrat from Valladolid in 1492 with the mission of reforming the monastery. He had compiled for the instruction of the monks a work entitled *Ejercitatorio de la vida espiritual*.

Iñigo examined his conscience for the next three days and undoubtedly was given a copy of Cisneros' *Ejercitatorio* for his edification, which he might well have carried with him on his departure. He then sought out Chanon and presented him with a list of all the sins of his past life. Seeking to divest himself of his rich possessions, he gave the expensive clothes to a poor beggar at the monastery door. The mule was a more difficult matter. He offered it to the abbot, who refused it on the grounds that Iñigo might have second thoughts and regret giving up such a fine animal should he decide to return to the world. However, Chanon was able to persuade his superior to accept the worthy mule, who after all had saved the life of an impertinent Moor.

On the evening of the Annunciation, Iñigo made his general confession and received absolution from Chanon. The sword and dagger that had hung so menacingly from his waist he hung on the grille of the chapel of Our Lady that adjoined the body of the church as ex-votos, as was the common custom among pilgrims. Having exchanged the rich garb of the gentleman for the rough sackcloth robe and hemp girdle of the pilgrim, he took his stand before the altar of our Lady, lit by a hundred lamps of silver and gold,[9] and passed the night in knightly vigil. He gives us his account of the event.

> Alternating between kneeling and standing, with his pilgrim's staff in his hand, he thus spent the whole night. At daybreak he left, and to avoid being recognized, he took, not the highway that led straight to Barcelona where he would meet many who knew him and honored him, but byways by which he came to a small town called Manresa, where he decided to spend a few days in the hospital and to make a few notes in his book which he carried very carefully with him and which brought him many consolations.
>
> By the time he had covered about three miles from Montserrat, he was overtaken by a man who came after him in great haste to ask whether he had given some clothing to a poor man, as the poor man said he had. Answering that he had given the clothes, tears of compassion started from his eyes, compassion for the poor man to whom he had given his clothing, compassion for him because he had been suspected of stealing them. But no matter how much he tried to avoid esteem, he could not be long in Manresa before the people were saying great things about him, a report having got abroad from what happened at Montserrat.

It was not long before they were saying more than was true, that he had given up a large income, and such things. (Vita 18)

He was, as it were, a knight of Christ, consecrating himself in the night-long watch of arms. He emerged from the vigil as a new knight of the spiritual order, wearing a suit of spiritual armor. The gallant Amadís had found his spiritual lord and service.

THE PILGRIM YEARS

2

MANRESA

V

At daybreak the pilgrim left the chapel of our Lady of Montserrat and, clad in his rough garb, made his way to the town of Manresa. He put up in the little hospital of Santa Lucía outside the town and earned his bed by working in the hospital. He begged food in town. He had intended to stay in Manresa only a few days and then move on to Barcelona, where he could catch a merchant vessel headed for Jerusalem. As it turned out, he remained in Manresa from March 1522 until February 1523. These were to be the most important months in the entire life of Iñigo de Loyola.

Manresa was a town of some two thousand inhabitants, nestled on the banks of the Cardoner. During the rest of his sojourn there Iñigo lived in a small cell in the priory of the Dominicans (Dudon 1949). At times, especially when illness got the better of him, he stayed in the houses of charitable benefactors—Señor Ferrer, Señor Amigant, and others (Dalmases 1985). But his prayers and penances were carried out in a cave overlooking the valley of the Cardoner. The experiences of the pilgrim in the cave of Manresa were so profound and so extraordinary that at first they seem to defy psychological understanding.

IN THE CAVE

He began by severe and intensive penances. He ate no meat, drank no wine, although both were offered him. On Sundays he did not fast, and he drank the little wine that was given him. Because he had been fastidious about caring for his hair, of which he was quite proud, he made up his mind to neglect it and let it grow wild, without combing or cutting it or covering it either day or night. For the same reason, he allowed his fingernails and toenails to grow (Vita 19).

In punishing every aspect of his person and behavior that had once been a source of satisfaction to him the pilgrim was following the principle of *agere contra*. He would describe it later: "Hence, that the Crea-

69

tor and Lord may work with greater certainty in His creature, if the soul chance to be inordinately attached or inclined to anything, it is very proper that it rouse itself by the exertion of all its powers to desire the opposite of that to which it is wrongly attached" (Exercises 16).

One would be tempted to regard this neglect of personal appearance as a breakdown in self-esteem and a disruption of socially acceptable forms of behavior. But in the pilgrim's case, this strange conduct, rather than representing a regressive phenomenon, suggests that he was entering into a struggle with powerful inner drives. He was setting about to destroy the old ego ideal and its associated values by attacking the image at any point where narcissism was evident, specifically his love of elegance and worldly honors and his boundless desire for glory. His inclinations to charm and attract the fair sex would also have a place on this list (Wilkens 1978). Psychodynamically, this process represents a mobilization of ego resources and a direction of the ego to exercise control over such libidinal or narcissistic investments. Because he once took pride in his fine hair, for example, this slice of narcissism had to be brought under control and into conformity with the spiritual value system he was assimilating.[1]

The pilgrim's effort was intensified by the very strength of these narcissistic and libidinal attachments and compounded by his weak understanding of spiritual principles. But we have seen already that his ego was capable of heroic efforts. He was coming to grips with himself in a profound and meaningful sense, reconciling ingrained patterns with new beliefs, drawing on tremendous resources of ego energy and strength. The goal was nothing short of complete ego control.

Throughout this period, he continued to exercise himself in this manner. He begged his food in the streets of the town and deprived himself of sleep in his prayer vigils. He became known among the townsfolk as the "Holy Man" who had become Christ's fool. His fasts and penances were so severe that his health suffered. On several occasions he was deathly ill. It was also in these days that he developed the painful biliary colic that troubled him the rest of his life. Some of the pious women of Manresa, among them Inés Pascual, who was to have a special place in the pilgrim's story, nursed him back to health. They were nicknamed the "Iñiquas" on account of their connection to the strange man of God, with his unkempt appearance, his straggly hair and unclipped nails. As winter came on, these friends persuaded him to accept and wear a rough cloak and a cap and shoes.

THE MANY-EYED SERPENT

The rigor of Iñigo's ascetic practices, particularly the lack of nutrition and sleep, may well have induced states of altered consciousness in which regressive hallucinatory experiences would have been likely. He recalls:

> It often happened to him in broad daylight to see something in the air close to him, which gave him great consolation because it was very beautiful. He could not make out very clearly what the thing was, but somehow it appeared to have the form of a serpent. It was bright with objects that shone like eyes, although they were not eyes. He found great delight and consolation in looking at this thing, and the more he saw it the greater grew his consolation. When it disappeared, it left him displeased. (Vita 19)

The experience was strange and disconcerting, and Iñigo did not know what to make of it. He finally decided that the apparition was the devil (Vita 31), but nonetheless it continued to appear occasionally for a period of fifteen years, until he went to Rome. It is tempting to put this apparition in an archetypal context, where the serpent would represent the unconscious libido, the symbolism expressing phallic erotic conflicts (Jung 1956). "Snake dreams," Jung has commented, "always indicate a discrepancy between the attitude of the conscious mind and instinct, the snake being a personification of the threatening aspect of that conflict" (p. 396). We can recall the vision of our Lady holding the Christ Child during his convalescence at Loyola, a vision that was followed by a powerful repression of his libidinal impulses. If Iñigo's effort succeeded, it would have excluded sexual impulses from the conscious mind, but not from the unconscious. The repression was made possible by the transformation of his spiritual value system. We can be sure that the repression of sexual libido was no easy matter, as libidinous elements were so prominent in his fantasies and romantic exploits. But Iñigo the invalid, and later the pilgrim, rejected these desires with as much vigor as he later used against the residues of his own narcissism.

The serpent that appeared to him in such curious fashion at Manresa may be regarded as the resurgence of these same repressed elements from the depths of the unconscious—"the return of the repressed" (Freud, 1915, p. 154). It is interesting that this manifestation of the unconscious was presented in a symbolic form of such great beauty and that it elicited pleasure and consolation. To protect itself, the pilgrim's ego could admit this threatening content only in a highly symbolic and transformed manner. The symbol assimilates an unconscious content, thus in a sense reducing the inner conflict between ego and id. The conscious system of the ego perceives such a confluence as pleasurable because it results in a reduction of inner tension arising from the struggle to bring the impulses of the id into conformity with ego objectives and values. The struggle the pilgrim had begun in the cave was one that reached into the depths of his unconscious. In the tremendous exhaustion of psychic energies, the rigid repression of the ego permitted the resurgence of unconscious elements. The relaxation of this continuing conflict was experienced as consolation.

The emergence of the beautiful serpent was also symptomatic of the deep-seated alteration that was taking place. The most profoundly difficult experience a man can undertake is to probe and assimilate his own unconscious. By mobilizing his ego energies in an attack on object-cathexis[2] and narcissism, the pilgrim set about destroying those agencies that had stabilized his ego-adaptation. The systematic destruction of the ego ideal, at least as a functioning system, had far-reaching effects. It stirred and activated the depths of libido. If the pilgrim was to emerge psychologically intact, the ego ideal had to be reconstructed in terms of a more realistic, ego-derivative, and spiritual value system, and a new integration had to be achieved between the ego and the dynamic forces of the id.

The evolution of such vivid symbolic imagery therefore represents the resurgence of unconscious contents on the one hand, and a form of regression of the ego, which has been termed "regression in the service of the ego" (Kris 1952) on the other. The ego requires the capacity to tolerate a certain amount of regression in order to adapt adequately, specifically to achieve productivity and creativity in art and science. The artistic ego requires the ability to assimilate unconscious contents in such a way that these elements are permitted conscious expression in symbolic form. The symbol, therefore, functions as a mechanism for the translation of unconscious elements, which can be consciously expressed as a dream, a fantasy, an idea, a hunch, or a vision. In whatever form it appears, it makes itself felt as excitement, joy, consolation, or a sensation akin to intoxication. The assimilation to the ego of unconscious energies likewise serves to vitalize and reinforce the ego.

REGRESSIVE CRISIS

But the pilgrim's way was filled with inner torment. The vision of the serpent was followed by a period of severe regressive crisis. He writes:

Up to this time he had continued in the same interior state of great and undisturbed joy, without any knowledge of the inner things of the soul. Throughout the days when this vision [the serpent] lasted, or a little before it began, for it went on for many days, there occurred to him a rather disturbing thought which troubled him by representing to him the difficulty of the life he was leading, as though he heard a voice within him saying: "How can you stand a life like this for the seventy years you have yet to live?" But this he answered also interiorly with great strength, feeling that it was the voice of the enemy: "You poor creature! Can you promise me even one hour of life?" In this way he overcame the temptation and remained at peace.

This is the first temptation that came to him after what has been said above. It happened while he was entering the church in which he heard high mass daily and in which he found great spiritual comfort. As a rule he read the passion during the Mass, always preserving his serenity of soul. But soon after the temptation just now related, he began to experience great changes in his soul. Sometimes his distaste was so great that he found no relish in any of the prayers he recited, or in hearing Mass, or in any kind of prayer he made. At other times, everything was just the contrary, and so suddenly, that he seemed to have got rid of the sadness and desolation pretty much as one removes a cloak from the shoulders of another. Here he began to marvel at these changes which he had never before experienced, saying to himself: "What new kind of life is this that we are now beginning?" At this time he still spoke occasionally with a few spiritual persons who had some regard for him and liked to talk with him. For although he had no knowledge of spiritual things, he showed much fervor in his talk and a great desire to go forward in the service of God. (Vita 20, 21)

From July through October of 1522, he suffered a severe depression, which he described as "darkness of soul, turmoil of spirit, inclination to what is low and earthly, restlessness rising from many disturbances and temptations which led to want of faith, want of hope, want of love. The soul is wholly slothful, tepid, sad, and separated, as it were, from its Creator and Lord" (Exercises 317).

Hartmann (1964) has remarked that a healthy person must have the capacity to suffer and be depressed. There comes a point in ego-adaptation, in fact, where depression has a constructive function. The rapid alternation of depression or, as the pilgrim would say, "desolation," and consolation must have reflected the ego's continuing effort to reconcile the discharge of intrapsychic energies with the system of values the pilgrim's ego had accepted. In Freud's (1917) classic analysis of depression, the essential mechanism is the turning against the ego of the sadistic impulses of the superego.

We have already spoken of the ego's conflicts with libidinal impulses. But this constitutes only one aspect of the ego's struggle to establish control over and integration of psychic forces. The superego enjoys a certain autonomy, and where the superego has a harsh and severe code that is transgressed, it can direct its rage against the ego. The pilgrim's ego was caught up in just such an onslaught, which was very likely triggered by its attempts to subdue the inherent narcissism of the superego. It is as though all of the hostile and sadistic elements in the personality were entrenched in the superego and had turned against the ego (Freud 1923).

The onslaught of the superego is also at the root of obsessive symptoms. The pilgrim goes on to tell us:

But at this time he had much to suffer from scruples.[3] Although the general confession he had made at Montserrat had been entirely written out and made carefully enough, there still remained some things which from time to time he thought he had not confessed. This caused him a good deal of worry, for even though he had confessed it, his mind was never at rest. He began, therefore, to look for some spiritual man who would cure him of his scruples, but without success. Finally, a doctor of the Cathedral Church, a very spiritual man who preached there, told him one day in confession to write out all he could remember. He did so. But after confessing it his scruples returned, each time becoming more minute, so that he became quite upset, and although he knew that these scruples were doing him much harm and that it would be good to be rid of them, he could not shake them off. Sometimes he thought the cure would be for the confessor to tell him in the name of Jesus Christ never to mention anything of the past, and he wished that his confessor would so direct him, but he did not dare tell the confessor so. But without his having said a word to him, his confessor told him not to confess anything of his past life unless it was something absolutely clear. As he thought that everything was quite clear, this direction was of no use to him and he remained always with his trouble.

At this time he was in a small room which the Dominicans had given him in their monastery, where he continued with his seven hours of prayer on his knees, rising faithfully every midnight, and performing all the other exercises already mentioned. But none of them provided him with a cure for his scruples, although it was now some months that they had been afflicting him. (Vita 22, 23)

These obsessive symptoms represent the ego-dystonic demands of the superego. The punitive demands and expected punishments that lie behind such scrupulous obsessions, are possibly the result of a "super-ego regression" to more instinctual levels. It reflects primitive destructive impulses deflected from the unconscious. The ego, of course, must defend itself from this punitive attack. For the pilgrim, the destructive and punitive inroads of the superego constituted a major battlefield.

The intensity of these destructive impulses is suggested by the continuation of the pilgrim's account:

While these thoughts were tormenting him, he was frequently seized with the temptation to throw himself into an excavation close to his room and adjacent to the place where he did his praying. But, knowing that it was a sin to do away with himself, he cried again: "Lord, I will do nothing to offend you," frequently repeating these words. . . . Here he recalled the story of a saint who, to obtain from God something he much desired, went many days without eating until he got what he wanted. Giving a good deal of thought to this fact, he finally made up his mind to do the same thing, telling himself that he would neither eat nor drink until God did something for him, or he saw that death was approaching. For, if he saw himself reduced to the extremity of having to die if he did not eat, in that case he would ask for bread and food (as though in that extremity, he could either ask for it or even eat it).

He resorted to this one Sunday after having received communion, and went through the whole week without putting a morsel of food into his mouth. He omitted none of his ordinary exercises, even going to the divine office and praying on his knees from midnight on and so forth. But on the following Sunday, which was his confession day, as he was accustomed to be very detailed with his confessor, he told him also that he had eaten nothing that week. The confessor bade him give up this abstinence, and although he was still strong, he obeyed his confessor and that day and the next found himself delivered from his scruples. But on the third day, which was Tuesday, while he was praying, he began to recall his sins, and so went on thinking of his past sins, one after the other, as though one grew out of another, until he felt that it was his bounden duty to confess them once again. As a sequel to these thoughts, he was seized with a disgust of the life he was leading and a desire to be done with it. It was our Lord's way of awakening him, as it were, from sleep. As he now had some experience of the different spirits from the lessons he had received from God, he began to look about for the way in which that spirit had been able to take possession of him.

He therefore made up his mind, which had become very clear on the matter, never to confess his past sins again, and from that day on he remained free of those scruples, holding it a certainty that our Lord in His mercy had liberated him. (Vita 24, 25)

The pilgrim was thus driven by the destructive forces of his superego to the brink of suicide. The destructive impulses unleashed in this process were derived from the basic aggression which had once been effectively sublimated by Iñigo's ego ideal and had been satisfied by direction to external objects. We must remember that the heroics of the man of arms and the drive to fight to the death at Pamplona carried a powerful complement of aggression that took a form entirely consonant with the demands of his ego ideal. As that ideal was gradually replaced and transformed into another set of values, the aggressive impulses were no longer permitted external expression. The destructive force of this aggression turned against the ego. Freud (1923) has observed: "It is remarkable that the more a man checks his aggressiveness towards the exterior, the more severe—that is, aggressive—he becomes in his ego ideal . . . the more a man controls his aggressiveness, the more intense becomes his ideal's inclination to aggressiveness against his ego" (p. 54).

The psychological and spiritual crisis through which Iñigo de Loyola passed in Manresa was an extension of the conversion process begun on his sickbed at the castle of Loyola. The hypothesis we have been following here is that the strong, courageous, and fearless identity the young Iñigo had shaped, in the image of the chivalrous knight who feared no danger and sought glory and conquest on all sides, whether libidinal or aggressive, was formed around a phallic, narcissistic core that left him vulnerable to certain kinds of regressive stress. The core element in the pathological narcissistic organization of his personality lies in the ego-ideal, in which the residues of archaic, narcissistic grandiosity and omnipotence were firmly embedded. The residues of earlier archaic narcissistic structures left him with a certain narcissistic vulnerability that carried with it the potentiality for regressive crisis.

We have argued that the physical trauma he suffered at Pamplona and the subsequent convalescence, enforced helplessness, and painful dependence, as well as the intolerable resulting deformity, severely attacked his underlying narcissism, with far-reaching consequences. In the cave at Manresa, these narcissistic vulnerabilities and their inherent regressive potential came to full realization. He struggled to overcome his depression by obsessive ruminations and by mobilizing hypomanic defenses. At times the depression would suddenly lift, and he would find his taste for spiritual things renewed.

We might infer that the intense and prolonged periods of meditation and seclusion to which the pilgrim subjected himself produced a corresponding reduction of environmental stimulus. This would imply a narrowing of the field of consciousness and withdrawal from contact with people. Normally, conscious experience requires an optimal range and patterning[4] of external stimuli in order to preserve normal cognitive functioning. In terms of the formulation provided by Rapaport (1951, 1958), the continued autonomy of the ego in relation to the id or to the environment depends on an appropriate degree of "stimulus nutriment." Stimulation from the external world helps bolster the ego's autonomy in relation to the inner world, while stimuli arising from the inner world of the drives or other psychic structures guarantee the autonomy of the ego from environmental influences. During his ascetic practices, the pilgrim severely limited external stimuli, thus diminishing his autonomy from internal, drive-related influences. The resulting regression lowered repressive barriers and thus increased the level of stimulation derived from internal sources, particularly those having to do with instinctual impulses and unconscious fantasies. The increased availability and influence of these previously repressed, unconscious influences contributed to a variety of conversion experiences.

The shift in levels of autonomous functioning of the ego is reflected in the modification of certain ego functions such as reality perception. For example, the pilgrim experienced visual illusions, reflecting less autonomous visual functioning that produced a more intensified and less organized sensory experience. In this respect, the images the pilgrim describes are reminiscent of reports by cataract patients, whose initial visual experiences after successful surgery do not as yet have the integration and autonomous organization of normal visual experience. The loss of this autonomy and structure of normal perception could have allowed for the phenomenon of "sensory translation" (Deikman 1966), through which psychic actions such as conflict, repression, and problem-solving are perceived through relatively unstructured experiences of light, color, movement, sound, and so on. By the same token, a regressive de-automatization[5] of the reality function might transfer the sense of reality of objects to more abstract psychic or religious entities.

In his bouts of depression, his scruples, and his suicidal impulses, the pilgrim's ego felt the wrath of the superego. But more significant for our present interests is the manner in which he overcame these symptoms. As far as we can make out from these sketchy accounts, the pilgrim set about mobilizing the resources of his ego to bring his appetites under control. Whatever the physiological effects of these ascetical practices, however they may have contributed to the weakening of his functional ego autonomy in the short run, in the long run the resilient strengths of his embattled ego seem to have won out. The effort of self-mastery brought his life and patterns of behavior closer to the spiritual values he had espoused. What is significant is not the ultimate course of action but the fact that his ego was able to achieve a deeper insight and to proceed to the organization and direction of its energies, and finally to a course of action.

THE ROLE OF THE CONFESSOR

Iñigo was not unaided in this titanic struggle with the forces within him. Undoubtedly, the father-confessor to whom the pilgrim turned in his hour of torment played a crucial and highly influential role. This Dominican priest (for he must have been one of the members of the Dominican monastery where the pilgrim stayed) remains nameless and faceless to the eyes of history, but he undoubtedly served his function well. Confronted by the pilgrim's depressive torments, suicidal impulses, and seemingly endless obsessional ruminations, the good father would have been severely challenged even had he possessed all the skills and knowledge of an experienced psychoanalyst.

As the case turned out, he managed to do well enough under the circumstances. He offered advice and directions to his troubled penitent, probably serving in many ways as an auxiliary ego, assisting the pilgrim to discern more carefully, to integrate, and master his overwhelming anxiety. In the midst of the pilgrim's scrupulous torment and depression, the confessor served as a wise teacher who helped him discern what was real from what was fantastic, teaching him that there was a difference between the impulses and graces that came from God and the temptations and delusions that arise from the influence of the devil. By his advice and even the use of his confessorial authority, he also served the important function of softening the severity of the pilgrim's superego. And finally, he must have served as a sort of idealized object whom the troubled pilgrim could trust and whose authority he would accept as leading him closer to God. In short, the confessor seems to have provided an effective object relationship that served to sustain the troubled pilgrim in his spiritual agony and also served as a firm, accepting, supporting, and spiritually uplifting model for identification.

If we think of this significant relationship, coming at such a crucial point in the development of the pilgrim's spirituality, as a kind of religious transference, we can assume that in the course of the conversion process Iñigo must have experienced a revival of rather infantile impulses originally directed toward the parents. These impulses were then projected into a religious context, and the confessor became, in effect, the good father to whom the infantile yearnings in the depths of Iñigo's heart responded with a sense of attachment, devotion, and humble submission. Ignatius himself tells us that "he obeyed his confessor, and that day and the next found himself delivered from his scruples" (Vita 25). This turn of events carries all the marks of the well-known transference cure.

MYSTICAL EXPERIENCES

But there is much more to be learned from the pilgrim's account. He completes the story of Manresa in these words:

At this time God treated him just as a schoolmaster treats a little boy when he teaches him. This perhaps was because of his rough and uncultivated understanding, or because of the firm will God Himself had given him in His service. But he clearly saw and always had seen that God dealt with him like this. Rather, he thought that any doubt about it would be an offense against His Divine Majesty. Something of this can be gathered from the five following points.

First. He had a great devotion to the Most Holy Trinity, and thus daily prayed to the Three Persons distinctly. While he was also praying to the Most Holy Trinity, the objection occurred to him as to how he could say four prayers to the Trinity. But this thought gave him little or no trouble, as being something of only slight importance. One day while he was reciting the Hours of Our Lady on the steps of the same monastery, his understanding began to be elevated as though he saw the Holy Trinity under the figure of three keys. This was accompanied with so many tears and so much sobbing that he could not control himself. That morning he accompanied a procession which left the monastery and was not able to restrain his tears until dinner time. Nor afterwards could he stop talking about the Most Holy Trinity. He made use of many different comparisons and experienced great joy and consolation. The result was that all through his life this great impression has remained with him, to feel great devotion when he prays to the Most Holy Trinity.

Second. Another time there was represented to his understanding with great spiritual delight the manner in which God had created the world. It had the appearance of something white out of which rays were coming, and it was out of this that God made light. But he did not know how to explain these things, nor did he remember well the spiritual illumination which at that time God impressed upon his soul.

Third. At Manresa also, where he remained almost a year, after he began to feel God's consolations and saw the fruit produced in the souls with whom he dealt, he gave up those outward extremes he formerly adopted, and trimmed his nails and hair. One day, in this town, when he was hearing Mass in the church of the monastery already mentioned, during the elevation he saw with the inner eyes of the soul something like white rays that came from above. Although he cannot explain this after so long a time, yet what he clearly saw with his understanding was how Jesus Christ our Lord is present in the most holy sacrament.

Fourth. When he was at prayer, he often and for a long time saw with the inner eyes the humanity of Christ. The shape which appeared to him was like a white body, not very large or very small, but he saw no distinction of members. He often saw this in Manresa. If he were to say twenty, or even forty times, he would not venture to say that it was an untruth. He saw it another time when he was in Jerusalem, and still another when he was on the road near Padua. He has also seen Our Lady in like form, without distinction of parts. These things which he saw gave him at the time great strength, and were always a striking confirmation of his faith, so much so that he has often thought to himself that if there were no Scriptures to teach us these matters of faith, he was determined to die for them, merely because of what he had seen.

Fifth. Once out of devotion he was going to a church which was about a mile distant from Manresa, and which I think was called St. Paul. The road ran along close to the river. Moving along intent on his devotion, he sat down for a moment with his face towards the river which there ran deep. As he sat, the eyes of his understanding began to open. He beheld no vision, but he saw and understood many things, spiritual as well as those concerning faith and learning. This took place with so great an illumination that these things appeared to be something altogether new. He cannot point out the particulars of what he then understood, although they were many, except that he received a great illumination in his understanding. This was so great that in the whole course of his past life right up to his sixty-second year, if he were to gather all the helps he had received from God, and everything he knew, and add them together, he does not think that they would equal all that he received at that one time.

After this had lasted for some time he went to kneel at a nearby cross to give thanks to God, where again appeared that vision which he had often seen and which he had never understood, that is, the object described above, which he thought very beautiful and which seemed to have many eyes. But he noticed that as it stood before the cross it did not have that beautiful color as heretofore, and he understood very clearly, with a strong assent of his will, that it was the evil one. Later it often appeared to him for a long time, but he drove it away with the pilgrim's staff he held in his hand and a gesture of contempt. (Vita 27–31)[6]

The remarkable events recorded in this account reflect the intensity of the psychological effects being wrought in the pilgrim's soul. There were illuminations that deepened his understanding and conviction of the most profound spiritual realities. There were also striking apparitions, but we note that these were purified symbols, images of brightness and light. The Trinity appears as three keys, the humanity of Jesus as a white body, and these images carry with them feelings of overwhelming consolation, joy, and strength. We are dealing here with mystical experiences of the highest order. But it is plain, in terms of our discussion to this point, that the desperate inner conflict was being won by the ego. Unconscious elements have been successfully assimilated to the conscious sphere of ego-activity, and this assimilation has enriched and reinforced the ego and its functioning. The images that dominate the pilgrim's imagination are the archetypes of ego-consciousness. The relation between the images associated with the creation of light and the symbolic representation of the emergence of consciousness is striking (Neumann 1954).

PSYCHOANALYTIC REFLECTION

In our earlier discussion of conversion experience, we saw that on both an unconscious and a conscious level the underlying conflicts can be sufficiently resolved to allow for meaningful integration with the subject's functional and reality-adapted ego. The synthesis and resolution of conflicts, then, not only are compatible with the current sense of reality but also give rise to a sense of completeness and a deepened understanding or illumination, which can have an enhancing, elevating, and even expansive effect on the convert's self-awareness. In such individuals, the conversion process represents a reshaping of the organization of the self and its core elements, giving rise to a newly integrated identity, most often cast in a religious or spiritual framework.

Christensen (1963), however, argues that the more frequent and likely resolution is one in which the underlying conflicts are not fully synthesized and integrated. The residual conflicts may be repressed to some degree and are dealt with by a variety of defense mechanisms. One result may be the transformation of psychic experience into a kind of symbolic representation in the form of a variety of mystical experiences.

In the case of the pilgrim of Manresa, the difficult psychic crisis he endured undoubtedly brought about a regressive state, marked by severe suicidal depression, a loss of ego boundaries in which the capacity to differentiate self and object was undermined, and acute identity diffusion. As the conversion process continued, the resolution allowed for the shaping of a new identity, now cast specifically in religious and spiritual terms.

From a psychoanalytic perspective, however, the resolution does not appear complete and the underlying conflicts do not seem fully resolved and thus continue to exercise their derivative influence. Supporting this view are the mystical experiences Iñigo describes, including a variety of hallucinations along with ruminative states, which issued eventually into internal experiences of deep understanding and illumination. Some of the hallucinatory experiences he ascribed to the influence of the good spirit, some, like the dragon of the many eyes, finally to the evil spirit.

There can be no doubt of the profound and meaningful character of these revelations and illuminations. The vision of the Holy Trinity under the image of the keys was so moving that, he tells us, "all through his life this great impression has remained with him, to feel great devotion when he prays to the most Holy Trinity" (Vita 28). Again, "These things which he saw gave him at the time great strength, and were always a striking confirmation of his faith, so much so that he has often thought to himself that if there were no Scriptures to teach us these matters of faith, he was determined to die for them, merely because of what he had seen" (Vita 29). And of the great illumination on the banks of the Cardoner, he observed: "This was so great that in the whole course of his past life right up to his sixty-second year, if he were to gather all the helps he had received from God, and everything he knew, and add them together, he does not think that they would equal all that he received at that one time" (Vita 30).

In a sense, the process that had begun on the bed of convalescence was extended and deepened in the cave of Manresa. At Loyola, Iñigo had undergone an experience which could best be summarized under the rubric of a deepening and broadening of his value orientation. That value-system was highly cathected with libidinal and aggressive elements, permeated with a sublimated set of romanticized masculine sexual ideals, and shot through with highly narcissistic elements. At Loyola Iñigo became aware of and sensitive to another dimension of reality, the spiritual dimension, which from his childhood had remained a significant, but not determining, element in his colorful milieu. During the reflections of his convalescence, this aspect of reality emerged from the background as new and significant. Iñigo gave the values implicit in his new spiritual awareness a tentative acceptance, which grew quickly into an internalized and operative value system.

The response to this widened perception and deepened value orientation was to cast off the identity of Iñigo de Loyola. The fine clothes and the sword and dagger were put aside, and with them the identity of Iñigo. In its place, there appeared the rough cloth and staff of the pilgrim. It does not seem accurate to say that Iñigo put on the identity of the pilgrim. It was not that easy. The guise of the pilgrim was more of a transition, a quest for identity.

Perhaps instinctively, the pilgrim must have sensed the profound change that was taking place. He sensed the need to retire and face the labor of transformation, the need for a kind of disengagement. Erikson (1950) has drawn attention to the psychosocial moratorium necessary for identity formation. The usual adolescent moratorium takes place during the course of normal development; something analogous may have been necessary for the pilgrim. But he was no adolescent passing through an identity crisis, but a mature man who had achieved a strong, dynamic sense of self.

Yet a new system of values put that previous identity into a state of crisis; the pilgrim had to work his way through a transvaluation of identity, a transformation of the value-system and ideals that form the core of the sense of identity. That transvaluation required, in a sense, an internal reorganization and resynthesis of the structure of the pilgrim's psyche. The primary agency of that reconstruction was the pilgrim's ego. The primary target was the superego, particularly those narcissistic elements that constituted a major component of the superego and its ego ideal. Under the force of this attack, the superego and the old ego ideal began to fragment. This was followed by a kind of superego regression, attended by the unleashing of hostile, destructive, and punitive impulses against the ego. The fragmentation of superego likewise relaxed the grip of the ego's repression on unconscious libidinal energies. The ego was consequently under severe attack from two directions, from both the superego and the id.

This crisis of inner revolution had to be worked through. The ego was the only psychic agency capable of establishing the necessary control over these divergent psychological forces and carrying out the necessary reconstruction and synthesis. The pilgrim was in fact wrestling with an angel of God. We have seen its desperate character and the depths to which it reached. The transvaluation of the identity of Iñigo de Loyola was an almost total transformation.

If the moratorium at Manresa had in fact produced a new personality, the lines of continuity between Iñigo the courageous man of arms and the emerging personality of the pilgrim were all too clear. If the superego had been reconstructed, it nonetheless retained some of its old characteristics, but these were assimilated into a totally new system of spiritual values. They were purged of some of the old narcissistic involvements, at least the pathological phallic narcissism of the proud and noble hidalgo, and transformed—indeed, transvaluated.

In some profound sense, the transvaluation of identity that transformed Iñigo de Loyola into Ignatius was a process of evolution. Both because of the effects produced and because of the mechanisms of transvaluation, it does not seem accurate to envision this process as the elimination of an old identity and its replacement with a new one. The identity of Iñigo was not destroyed; it was transformed. The effort of transformation and transvaluation was not a reflection of ego-regression or collapse. These were transitory phenomena. Rather, it was a reflection of the extension and mobilization of ego resources. The ego of Iñigo de Loyola matured to a new level of functioning and effectiveness. Rather than an exchange of identities, there was an enrichment of the ego which achieved a fuller realization of its own potentiality and a higher level of internal organization and synthesis. In a sense, then, the transforming experience of Iñigo made him more fully, more authentically himself.

THE SPIRITUAL EXERCISES

VI

The months the pilgrim spent at Manresa proved to be the decisive period of his remarkable conversion. Through the dim mists of history, we are able to catch glimpses of what must have transpired. The pilgrim himself gives us only occasional hints, and even his autobiography, dictated to the faithful Gonsalvez da Camara many years later, does more to pique our curiosity than to satisfy it.

Yet we know that from the earliest days of his conversion Iñigo kept notebooks, one of which he used to record citations from the lives of Christ and the saints, but another that carried more personal observations on his experiences. It seems that this notebook was with him at Manresa, and we have evidence to suggest that those notes served as the basis for what we now know as Ignatius' *Spiritual Exercises*.[1]

The *Spiritual Exercises* is one of the most influential works in Western civilization. It became a guide for spiritual renewal in the Roman church during the entire Counter-Reformation and has been a primary influence in the spiritual life of the church ever since, particularly through the efforts of Ignatius' followers in the Society of Jesus. It remains a powerful influence and is the basis for much of the contemporary retreat movement.

The unique quality of this small volume is evident from the very first. It is not a book *on* spirituality; it is, rather, a book *of* spirituality. It contains a series of practical directives—methods of examining one's conscience, engaging in prayer of various kinds, deliberating or making life choices, and meditating. This program of spiritual development, if you will, is interspersed with outlines and directives for various meditations and contemplations. It proposes no spiritual doctrine but rather offers a pragmatic program of prayerful spiritual exercises, a systematic outline and methodology of Christian spirituality. It is in no sense a book that is simply to be read; rather, it is a book to be put into practice (De Guibert 1964).

THE WINDOW OF THE SOUL

The *Exercises* provide us with a unique window into the soul of Ignatius at the time of some of the most profound and meaningful experiences of his life. Although the material in the *Exercises* is sparse and not directly revelatory in any psychological sense, there are two aspects of the *Exercises* that seem to me to offer a basis for a psychological understanding of their author. The first is the method the pilgrim uses in his little work, which may tell us something about the use of such methods in Ignatius' experience, both in Manresa and in the course of his later spiritual development. The second aspect concerns the content of particular meditations. I propose to approach the text of the *Spiritual Exercises* as an expression of Ignatius' inner psychic world—on the assumption that this central document of the Ignatian experience was a manifestation of his own psychic experience and reflects in some degree his internal world of dynamic and unconscious fantasy.[2]

When one opens Ignatius' *Spiritual Exercises*, one sets foot in a world of spiritual combat. It is a world in which the forces of goodness and truth labor to establish the kingdom of God, and the forces of evil and falsehood struggle against them to destroy that kingdom. Images of the battlefield are never far from the mind of Iñigo de Loyola. For him, it is on the basis of self-denial that the kingdom of God can be established, and it is man's deep-seated unwillingness to overcome his unruly desires that is his greatest tragedy. Without victory over self, there can be no rationality, no belief, no salvation. If man does not rule his passions, he is inevitably ruled by them. A Christian who shrinks from the task of self-denial at the same time denies the example and teaching of Christ and refuses to follow in his footsteps. The lesson of the saints is also a lesson of self-denial. In their lives and in their preaching they teach the victory over self-indulgence. They reject worldly honors and passions; their lives are a war without truce against pride, honors, and riches which destroy the soul by drawing it away from Christ and God.

UNION WITH CHRIST

The motifs of union with Christ, self-immolation, and absorption into the body of Christ as the vehicle for achieving eternal salvation are articulated from the very beginning. One opens to the first page and reads the beautiful prayer "Anima Christi":

Soul of Christ, sanctify me.
Body of Christ, save me.
Blood of Christ, inebriate me.
Water from the side of Christ, wash me.
Passion of Christ, strengthen me.
O good Jesus, hear me;
Within thy wounds hide me;
Suffer me not to be separated from thee;
From the malignant enemy defend me;
In the hour of my death call me,
And bid me come to thee,
That with thy saints I may praise thee
Forever and ever. Amen.[3]

The sense of utter devotion is unmistakable. Union with Christ, service to the divine Master, and total dedication and commitment of self are the keys to spiritual growth and salvation. The prayer, although addressed to Christ, Lord, Master, and Savior, nonetheless has a maternal quality. The imagery of protection, being enfolded within the sacred wounds, recalls associations to a fantasy of reunion with the lost mother—damaged in the delivery of her last child, perhaps even to the point of death. Might we not hear in this prayer echoes from the depths of Ignatius' heart—the long-repressed longing to rejoin the mother who was torn away from him by death, perhaps even death brought about by giving him life? Can we presume to interpret the water as amniotic, or the wounds as the bloody consequence of a delivery that threatened, if it did not terminate, his mother's life? Can we discern the unconscious fantasy that Iñigo himself was the murderer who by his birth brought death to his mother?

THE ENEMY

Another important note sounded in this text is that union with Christ serves to defend against the power of the "malignant enemy." The theme of combat against this spiritual enemy is a dominant leitmotif in the *Exercises* that pervades the consciousness of this hidalgo turned saint. This ever-present and menacing force is referred to as "the enemy of human nature" [paragraphs 7, 10, 135, 136], "the enemy" [8, 12, 140, 217, 314], "enemies" [96, 196], and "the evil spirit" [315].[4]

The most vivid portrait of the enemy comes in the second week in the famous meditation on the Two Standards [136–148], contrasting the standard of the evil one with that of Christ. The portrait is sketched in three points:

First Point. The first point is to imagine as if the chief of all the enemy seated himself in that great field of Babylon, as in a great chair of fire and smoke, in shape horrible and terrifying.

Second Point. The second, to consider how he issues a summons to innumerable demons and how he scatters them, some to one city and others to another, and so through all the world, not omitting any provinces, places, states, nor any person in particular. . . .

Third Point. The third, to consider the discourse which he makes them, and how he tells them to cast out nets and chains; that they have first to tempt with a longing for riches—as he is accustomed to do in most cases—that men may more easily come to vain honor of the world, and then to vast pride. So that the first step shall be that of riches; the second, that of honor; the third, that of pride; and from these three steps he draws on to all the other vices. [140–142]

Keeping in mind that these are the words of a man of the sixteenth century, we can regard these references as a personalized and culturally derived projection reflecting inner conflicts between spiritual ideals and the destructive wishes that continued to torment him. Ignatius had to struggle against these desires and their consequences all through his life, but they caused a particularly wrenching agony in the cave of Manresa. The enemy was never far from his conscious experience.

These conflictual desires and wishes, or "disordered tendencies" [1], are more generally referred to as "inordinate affections." Inordinate affections are emotional attachments (Iparraquirre 1955) that have escaped effective control and do not fit with the system of ideals and spiritual values that are at the heart of the ego ideal. In one of the early annotations, Ignatius refers to a beginner in the spiritual combat as "a person who has not been versed in spiritual things, and is tempted grossly and openly—having, for example, suggested to him obstacles to going on in the service of God our Lord, such as labors, shame and fear for the honor of the world" [9]. The description, I would submit, passes for a portrait of the ambivalent Iñigo as he struggled to find his spiritual footing. In his autobiography, he describes himself in similar terms:

"Up to this time he had continued in the same interior state of great and undisturbed joy, without any knowledge of the inner things of the soul. . . . there occurred to him a rather disturbing thought which troubled him by representing to him the difficulty of the life he was leading, as though he heard a voice within him saying: 'How can you stand a life like this for the seventy years you have yet to live?'" (Vita 20). The mention of "shame and fear for the honor of the world" speaks to the narcissism so close to the heart of his personality organization.

THE IGNATIAN CREDO

The great statement of the Ignatian credo comes at the beginning of the First Week in the Principle and Foundation. It reads:

> Man is created to praise, reverence, and serve God our Lord, and by this means to save his soul.
>
> And the other things on the face of the earth are created for man and that they may help him in prosecuting the end for which he is created.
>
> From this it follows that man is to use them as much as they help him on to his end, and ought to rid himself of them so far as they hinder him as to it.
>
> For this it is necessary to make ourselves indifferent to all created things in all that is allowed to the choice of our free will and is not prohibited to it; so that, on our part, we want not health rather than sickness, riches rather than poverty, honor rather than dishonor, long rather than short life, and so in all the rest; desiring and choosing only what is most conducive for us to the end for which we are created. [23]

This is as direct and condensed an expression of Ignatius' ego ideal as I have found. It expresses a profound and meaningful Christian view of man's purpose and his place in God's salvific plan. It also serves as the basic postulate for the rest of the Ignatian program of spiritual exercises. It enunciates an ideal of profound indifference that encompasses the entire created order: nothing is to be allowed to stand between man and his divinely appointed destiny.

Ignatius provides a catalog of the special targets for such studied indifference, which can be read as having personal relevance—health versus sickness, riches versus poverty, honor versus dishonor, long versus short life. We can add to them the list of temptations by which the enemy draws men into sin and vice—first riches, then honor, and last pride [142]. We remember not only Ignatius' vanity of physical appearance (after all, he endured the torment of the surgery on his leg out of a basically narcissistic need to maintain his handsome and dashing figure!), but his strength and physical prowess as well. We remember that he was born and raised in an atmosphere of wealth and power. We know the ardent desire that burned in his heart for the acclamation of the world. These intense desires received the brunt of his ascetic efforts. He starved and punished his body until it became emaciated, weak, and sickly; he turned himself into a poor pilgrim, divesting himself of all the trappings of wealth and position to follow his Lord in abject poverty; and he made every effort to avoid the honors of the world as a curse and burden. He wished only to serve his fellow men and his Lord. "Take, Lord, and receive all my liberty, my memory, my intellect, and all my will—all that I have and possess. Thou gavest it to me: to Thee, Lord. I return it! All is Thine, dispose of it according to all Thy will. Give me Thy love and grace, for this is enough for me" [234]—such was his prayer.

THE FIRST WEEK

The exercises of the first week [21–90] dwell on the enormity of sin and the terrors of hell. These meditations offer us a unique window into the guilt-ridden inner world of the pilgrim. He sees himself as a "soul imprisoned in this corruptible body, and all the compound in this valley, as exiled among brute beasts: I say all the compound of soul and body" [47]. His intention is "to ask shame and confusion at myself, seeing how many have been damned for only one mortal sin, and how many times I deserved to be condemned forever for my so many sins" [48] and "to make me more ashamed and confound me more, bringing into comparison with the one sin of the Angels my so many sins, and reflecting, while they for one sin were cast into Hell, how often I have deserved it for so many" [50]. And again, in the meditation on personal sin, we hear: "The first Point is the statement of the sins; that is to say, to bring to memory all the sins of life, looking from year to year, or from period to period. . . . The second to weight the sins, looking at the foulness and the malice which any mortal sin committed has in it, even supposing it were not forbidden" [56–57]. These reflections lead to a colloquy with the Blessed Mother "that she may get me grace from Her Son and Lord for three things: first, that I may feel an interior knowledge of my sins, and hatred of them; second, that I may feel the disorder of my actions, so that, hating them, I may correct myself and put myself in order; third, to ask knowledge of the world, in order that, hating it, I may put away from me worldly and vain things" [63].

These images of sinfulness and inner evil certainly have theological underpinnings. But we might wonder whether the themes of guilt and shame enunciated here do not also reflect multiple levels of sinfulness in the levels of psychic integration within Ignatius. Personal sins there were, both sexual and aggressive, but might there not have been behind the profound and pervasive sense of sinfulness a deeper seated sense of himself as evil, the one who brought destruction to his mother—a murderer from the beginning. That primal crime demanded justice through punishment, an unending demand that could never be satisfied. The primal murder stained his soul and could never be erased, no matter how unrelenting and severe his self-punishments. To this burden could be added the weight of a sinful life of lust, murderous rage, and narcissistic desire for self-glorification and grandiose ambition.

Mingled with these guilt-ridden exercises is Ignatius' imaginative vision of hell. In the meditation on hell, the composition of place aims "to see with the sight of the imagination the length, breadth, and depth of Hell" [65]. In this vision, he seeks an "interior sense of pain which the damned suffer, in order that, if, through my faults, I should forget the love of the Eternal Lord, at least the fear of the pains may help me not to come into sin" [65]. He vividly details "the souls as in bodies of fire" [66], the "wailings, howlings, cries, blasphemies against Christ our Lord and against all His Saints" [67], the putrid smell of sulfur, and the taste of "bitter things, like tears, sadness and the worm of conscience" [69].

In developing these themes, Ignatius reveals some of the dark imagery that inhabited his mind. We should note the dominance of aggressive and destructive themes on the level of unconscious fantasy. There is little doubt that his accounts reflect the culturally reinforced spiritual and ascetic conventions of the day, but this context does not diminish the psychic impact of such images on Ignatius' mind. Cultural influences join with intrapsychic factors that absorb, respond to, and assimilate such peripheral influences into a pattern that reflects the dynamic and unconscious components operating within the individual psyche. These theologically impregnated images took on personal reference and implication for Ignatius. They became the vehicle for transformed aggressive drive derivatives that were channeled through his more severely judgmental and punitive superego—the guilt that plagued his soul and the harsh images that crowded his mind reflect the punitive force of his superego-driven imagination.

CONSCIENCE

These same dynamic forces lie behind the obsessional, almost compulsive practices that played a dominant part in his own spiritual career and that he proposed to any who undertook the Spiritual Exercises. A glance at his recommendations for the particular examen[5] [24–31], the general examination of conscience [32–43], and the general confession[6] [44] conveys a sense of the detailed and programmed character of his efforts to ease the torment stemming from his relentlessly punitive superego. The language is frequently that of battle, struggle, and conquest, as for example, in his discussion of ways of overcoming sinful impulses or thoughts:

> First Way. A thought of committing a mortal sin, which thought I resist immediately and it remains conquered. [33]
> Second Way. The second way of meriting is: When that same bad thought comes to me and I resist it, and it returns to me again and again, and I always resist, until it is conquered. [34]

The first method is a sort of psychic knockout punch—we are reminded of his repressive banishment of all impure temptations after the vision at Loyola. The second way resembles a bout of many rounds that is won only after numerous attempts, by a decision as it were. The image calls our attention to Ignatius' lifelong struggle with his disordered desires, which became a preoccupation and focus for endless examinations, sorrow, confession, and self-demeaning protestations.

We know that the obsessional aspects of Ignatius' character made him vulnerable to symptomatic self-doubting and shame—the components of a pathological scrupulosity. The fruit of his own struggles with this dilemma was distilled into his rules for dealing with scruples[7]—linked immediately to the persuasions of the enemy [345–351]. However vulnerable he might have been to such severely neurotic symptoms, we must also respect the psychological acumen with which he was able to examine his own experience and make some telling and astute observations.

In the rules he distinguishes erroneous judgments from scruples—in the first the subject decides that something is sinful that is not (for example, accidentally stepping on crossed straws). The phenomenon of scruples is more complex:

> After I have stepped on that cross, or after I have thought or said or done some other thing, there comes to me a thought from without that I have sinned, and on the other hand it appears to me that I have not sinned; still I feel disturbances in this; that is to say, in as much as I doubt and in as much as I do not doubt.
>
> That is a real scruple and temptation which the enemy sets. [347]

The description captures the ambivalence and obsessional doubting at the heart of scrupulosity. Ignatius notes that true scrupulosity may have a positive effect on spiritual progress since it draws the soul farther away from sin [348].

Other notes in the *Exercises* also reflect aspects of Ignatius' own experience of scrupulosity. He says: "The enemy looks much if a soul is gross or delicate, and if it is delicate, he tries to make it more delicate in the extreme, to disturb and embarrass it more. For instance, if he sees that a soul does not consent to either mortal sin or venial or any appearance of deliberate sin, then the enemy, when he cannot make it fall into a thing that appears sin, aims at making it make out sin where there is not sin, as in a word or very small thought" [349]. Should we not hear this as reflecting his torments of delicate conscience in the cave of Manresa? And in the opposite case: "If the soul is gross, the enemy tries to make it more gross; for instance, if before it made no account of venial sins, he will try to have it make little account of mortal sins, and if before it made some account, he will try to have it now make much less or none" [349]. These were in fact the circumstances of the preconversion Iñigo.

THE SECOND WEEK

The great meditations of the Second Week [91–189] draw us closer to the images of gallant chivalry that played an elemental role in the psychic life of the young Iñigo and probably of the mature Ignatius. To further the soul's progress along the path of increasing identification with Christ and to bring the Christian values into clearer focus, Ignatius proposes a series of meditations that have become classic. The first of these, the meditation on Christ the King and the meditation on the Two Standards, set the stage for the spiritual struggle to follow, even as the ideas embedded in them provided the framework within which Iñigo carried on his own spiritual conquest. First, there is the call of the temporal king:

First Point. The first Point is, to put before me a human king chosen by God our Lord, whom all Christian princes and men reverence and obey.

Second Point. The second, to look how this king speaks to all his people, saying: "It is my will to conquer all the land of unbelievers. Therefore, whoever would like to come with me is to be content to eat as I, and also to drink and dress, etc., as I: likewise he is to labor like me in the day and watch in the night, etc., that so afterwards he may have part with me in the victory, as he has had it in the labors" [92–93].

Such a king deserves the noblest and devoted service, so that anyone who would not respond generously would be nothing less than a "mean-spirited knight."

The image of the temporal king is then transferred to Christ:

First Point. And as to the first Point, if we consider such a call of the temporal King to his subjects, how much more worthy of consideration is it to see Christ our Lord, King eternal, and before Him all the entire world, which and each one in particular He calls, and says: "It is My will to conquer all the world and all enemies and so to enter into the glory of My Father; therefore, whoever would like to come with Me is to labor with Me, that following Me in the pain, he may also follow Me in the glory.

Second Point. The second, to consider that all those who have judgment and reason will offer their entire selves to the labor.

Third Point. The third, those who will want to be more devoted and signalize themselves in all service of their King Eternal and universal Lord, not only will offer their persons to the labor, but even, acting against their own sensuality and against their carnal and worldly

love, will make offerings of greater value and greater importance.
[96–98]

The imagery reverberates with echoes of the courtly life and Iñigo's adolescence, the magnificence and splendor of the royal trappings, as well as his reverence for and devotion to old Velázquez and even the duke of Nájera—and beyond them, in the chain of associations, to his father, Beltrán. Clearly the imagery of soldierly conduct, chivalrous service, and dedication to the service of his appointed king never left the heart of Iñigo de Loyola.[8]

THE IMITATION OF CHRIST

Part of the transformation that Iñigo passed through at Manresa had to do with a reshaping of his personal values—the guideposts for the spiritual life that opened before him. This refashioning of the basic values that constituted his ego ideal I have called a "transvaluation."[9] The model for this transvaluation is the person of Christ, the exemplar of spiritual maturity. Ignatius expresses his objective in a number of ways: "to imitate Thee [Christ] in bearing all insults and reproaches," [98] "to follow and better imitate our Lord," [109] "and for grace to imitate Him," [139] "in bearing reproaches and insults, the better to imitate Him in these" [147]. The basic mechanism Ignatius calls on to implement spiritual growth is identification with the person of Christ. This is expressed in conscious terms in the language of imitation (recall that Ignatius was especially devoted to the *Imitatio Christi*), but this behavioral level is sustained and complemented by unconscious internalization and identification. The person of Christ is proposed as a kind of ideal to which the ego is drawn by increasing admiration and love. At the very beginning of the second week, Ignatius tells the exercitant (one going through the program of the Exercises) to seek "for interior knowledge of the Lord, Who for me has become man, that I may more love and follow Him" [104].

The content of this meditation brings us back to an earlier day when the young hidalgo was caught up in visions of glory and heroic deeds in his king's service as the intrepid and valorous knight-errant whose sword was ever ready to serve its master. For Iñigo de Loyola such loyalty could not be cast in modest terms; it had to be writ large in terms of heroic sacrifice and the courageous confrontation and conquest of even the greatest dangers and threats. Only such a spirit could have led him to face overwhelming odds with such reckless daring and courage.

If such had been the nature of his labors for his temporal king, we should not be surprised to find a similar quality in his service to a heavenly king. The same Iñigo who defiantly faced the the French at Pamplona for the glory of Castile later entered into a deathly struggle with the forces within at the cave of Manresa. For that triumph in the name of Jesus Christ, no labor was too great, no pain too intense, no sacrifice beyond his reach. The ideals of conquest and glory had been transformed and sublimated and recast in a spiritual mold: the pilgrim saw himself as a warrior of God and of Christ. The warfare was not of this world, and the weapons and tactics were decidedly different. But the same desire for struggle, conquest, and glory burned in his soul as had been there from the first. The words of the meditation can be read as Ignatius' own: "It is My will to conquer all the world and all enemies and so to enter into the glory of My Father; therefore, whoever would like to come with Me is to labor with Me, that following Me in the pain, he may also follow Me in the glory" [96].

The second meditation is that on the Two Standards:

First Point. The first Point is to imagine as if the chief of all the enemy seated himself in that great field of Babylon, as in a great chair of fire and smoke, in shape horrible and terrifying.

Second Point. The second, to consider how he issues a summons to innumerable demons and how he scatters them, some to one city and others to another, and so through all the world, not omitting any provinces, places, states, nor any person in particular.

Third Point. The third, to consider the discourse which he makes them, and how he tells them to cast out nets and chains; that they have first to tempt with a longing for riches—as he is accustomed to do in most cases—that men may more easily come to vain honor of the world, and then to vast pride. So that the first step shall be that of riches; the second, that of honor; the third, that of pride; and from these three steps he draws on to all the other vices.

So, on the contrary, one has to imagine as to the supreme and true Captain, Who is Christ the Lord.

First Point. The first Point is to consider how Christ our Lord puts himself in a great field of that region of Jerusalem, in lowly place, beautiful and attractive.

Second Point. The second, to consider how the Lord of all the world chooses so many persons—Apostles, Disciples, etc.—and sends them through all the world spreading His sacred doctrine through all states and conditions of persons.

Third Point. The third, to consider the discourse which Christ our Lord makes to all His servants and friends whom He sends on this expedition, recommending them to want to help all, by bringing them first to the highest spiritual poverty, and—if His Divine Majesty would be served and would want to choose them—no less to actual poverty; the second is to be contumely and contempt; because from these two things humility follows.

So that there are to be three steps; the first, poverty against riches; the second, contumely or contempt against worldly honor; the third, humility against pride. And from these three steps let them induce to all the other virtues. [140–146]

Once again, the words of the meditation enable us to catch a glimpse of the old Iñigo, the soldier of honor and high ideals, guided by fidelity to his lord. It suggests that the old ego ideal has not perished, that there is something of the old Iñigo in the new Ignatius. But the very imagery of the chivalric ideal is transformed and elevated; no longer is the ideal of any lord in question, it is the ideal of service through humility and suffering in the name of Christ that is now proposed. We can think of no better way to conceptualize this transformation than in terms of the transvaluation of identity.

We have some indication of the weight that Ignatius would place on these meditations in later years. De Guibert (1964) quotes Manareo, one of the early members of the Society of Jesus, to the effect that Ignatius "applied himself chiefly to two exercises, namely, those of the two standards and of the king, thus preparing himself for the war against the infernal enemy and the world" (p. 118). Similarly, Nadal, writing in 1544, emphasizes that Ignatius showed particular devotion to these same two exercises and felt that the objectives contained in these meditations were also to be the goals of the Society he founded. De Guibert adds that these texts seem to confirm the importance and influence of the *Flos Sanctorum* in Iñigo's conversion experience.[10] Undoubtedly, they also reflect the spirit and frame of mind that influenced him at that time.

The meditation on the Two Standards particularly indicates the essentials of the Ignatian approach. Ignatius' thinking, from beginning to end of the *Exercises* and his own life, is dominated by commitment to service, here the service of God under the banner of Christ. The lines of battle are clearly drawn; the enemy is known and identified. He is the devil, the tempter of men, who uses every device, exploits every weakness, and loses no opportunity to attack and destroy the souls of men. No man is secure from his ambushes. His subtlety and trickery are such that he often deceives men into doing evil in the name of good. He is a liar and a murderer, as he has been from the very first. Constant vigilance is mandatory, therefore, along with an unwavering resolution to do the opposite of what the evil one proposes. Only along this path lies the promise of wisdom, virtue, and salvation.

The battle is thus joined, but the followers of Christ have a superior force on their side. The arm of the Lord is not shortened, and his greater desire and power to save men overcomes any resource the demon can employ to destroy them. The enemy attacks the weaknesses of love of riches, care for the vain honor of the world, and finally pride. "And from these three steps," Ignatius tells us, "he draws on to all the other vices" [142]. The discourse of Christ spells out the battle plan for countering these maneuvers of the enemy. Against the desire of riches, the soldier of Christ seeks spiritual or even actual poverty, should that be God's will. Against ambition and the desire for worldly glory, he seeks humiliation and contempt. And finally, against the threat of pride, he seeks humility.

SELF-PORTRAIT

The influence of Iñigo's own experience is unmistakable here. It is as though in the portrait of the victim of the devil's machinations he was depicting himself before he was struck down by the French cannonball. Certainly, the young Iñigo was not lacking in intense, consuming ambition and the willingness to sacrifice all in the search for worldly acclaim. We know little directly of his cupidity, but we do know that the lords of Loyola were wealthy and powerful by the standards of the time. But we can guess that the desire for riches was secondary in the hidalgo's mind, overwhelmed as it was by his intense ambition and quest for military glory.

The meditation also suggests the basis for the pilgrim's approach in the transformed, spiritual conquest. Here the primary values and ideals that had governed his preconversion life now became the object of specific and unrelenting attack. Every vestige of worldly desire, ambition, the yearning for glory and recognition, and particularly pride—at once his family heritage and his own dominating passion—had to be rooted out and cast aside. In psychoanalytic terms, it seems clear that the spiritual program of the pilgrim was nothing less than an assault on his own narcissism and self-love, which he saw as the impediment to his spiritual growth and conquest.

The subsequent meditation, also casting light on Ignatius' state of mind, deals with the Three Classes of Men [149–157]. It is uncertain whether this was part of the material gathered at Manresa; it may have been added subsequently. As Ignatius presents the three classes, each class of men is faced with a conflict between the desire to save their souls and inordinate attachment to money or other material goods. The money obviously represents any excessive attachment. We can read these descriptions as snapshots of stages in his own spiritual growth. The first class of men would like to rid themselves of this excessive attachment but take no steps to do so. This is a defective solution insofar as the person is unable to pass beyond mere desire to any kind of resolution and action. The second class would also like to rid themselves of their affection, and they take some ineffective steps to do this. This solution is also defective in that the individual resolves the conflict by adopting a substitute attachment, one that offers less resistance than the conflictual attachment. These weak and inadequate solutions are presumably those that Ignatius himself pursued in much of his preconversion life.

Only the solution of the third class is adequate. This class want to rid themselves of the attachment, but want so to rid themselves of it that they have even no liking for it, to keep the thing acquired or not to keep it, but only want to want it or not want it according as God our Lord will put in their will and as will appear to them better for the service and praise of his Divine Majesty; and meanwhile they want to reckon that they quit it all in attachment, forcing themselves not to want that or any other thing, unless only the service of God our Lord move them: so that the desire of being better able to serve God our Lord moves them to take the thing or leave it. [155]

This is the solution toward which the *Exercises* aim, and which Ignatius himself had achieved through his arduous spiritual discipline and ascetic self-denial.

HUMILITY

Insofar as pride and narcissistic grandiosity hold such a central place in our reconstruction of the personality of Iñigo de Loyola, it is hardly surprising that the opposite virtue, humility, should become a central facet of Iñigo's postconversion spiritual outlook. In fact, Ignatius' meditation on humility [164–168] is a pivotal point in the whole program of the *Exercises*. Spiritual commentators generally regard the so-called third degree of humility as the pinnacle of Ignatian spirituality (De Guibert 1964).

First Humility. The first manner of Humility is necessary for eternal salvation; namely, that I so lower and so humble myself, as much as is possible to me, that in everything I obey the law of God, so that, even if they made me lord of all the created things in this world, nor for my own temporal life, I would not be in deliberation about breaking a commandment, whether Divine or human, which binds me under mortal sin.

Second Humility. The second is more perfect Humility than the first; namely, if I find myself at such a stage that I do not want, and feel no inclination to have riches rather than poverty, to want honor rather than dishonor, to desire a long rather than a short life—the service of God our Lord and the salvation of my soul being equal; and so not for all creation, nor because they would take away my life, would I be in deliberation about committing a venial sin.

Third Humility. The third is the most perfect Humility; namely, when—including the first and second, and the praise and glory of the Divine Majesty being equal—in order to imitate and be more actually like Christ our Lord, I want and choose poverty with Christ, poor rather than riches, opprobrium with Christ replete with it rather than honors; and to desire to be rated as worthless and a fool for Christ, Who, first was held as such, rather than wise or prudent in this world. [165–167]

The Ignatian principle of agere contra, fundamental to Ignatian asceticism and spirituality, here reaches its apogee. Its application is part of the approach to overcoming inordinate attachments that stand in the way of spiritual growth. In the *Spiritual Exercises* he wrote: "For this—namely, that the Creator and Lord may work more surely in His creature—it is very expedient, if it happens that the soul is attached or inclined to a thing inordinately, that one should move himself, putting forth all his strength, to come to the contrary of what he is strongly drawn to" [15]. The primary vulnerabilities of human nature, which we have already noted were evident in the preconversion Iñigo, are here again put under attack by the embracing of their opposites. In the third degree of humility, the desire for riches is countered by the wish to be poor, excessive ambition and the desire for worldly honors are countered by the wish for opprobrium, and the wish to be respected and praised in worldly terms is countered by the wish to be thought worthless and a fool for Christ's sake. These values dictated Ignatius' spiritual ascent, but they also underline the conflicting vulnerabilities that plagued his journey, particularly those that pertain to his narcissistic conflicts. These dynamics were embedded in the heart and mind of Ignatius from his earliest years, and they remained permanent fixtures of his psychic landscape until the moment of his death.

One might argue that the second degree of humility is sufficient for meaningful spiritual development. Ignatius is not satisfied with this but must go even further. This ultimate degree of humility presses the principle of the imitation and identification with Christ to its limit, a stripping from the self of all narcissistic trappings, all honor and admiration the world can deliver. Acceptance of and commitment to spiritual values that run counter to those of the world achieve their greatest realization.

PSYCHOANALYTIC CONSIDERATIONS

The ascetic tactic of the Ignatian agere contra raises some interesting psychoanalytic questions, especially since this seems without doubt to have been the repeated strategy of the saint himself. In psychoanalytic terms there are certain risks in the general approach of rooting out inordinate attachments and vices by practicing the opposing virtue. We can translate the process of agere contra into terms of drive and defense.[11] An attempt to regulate libidinal desires, for example, by the mechanics of agere contra would seem to repress or suppress such impulses and rule them out of court—at least out of the court of conscious access. Internal psychic management of such impulses, as well as external behavioral adaptations—ascetic practices either denying or disciplining such desires of the flesh—would seem necessarily to have a strong defensive cast. In the cave of Manresa, Iñigo set about a program of fasts, sleepless nights, vigils, penitential practices like flagellations and inflicting pain—standard practices in the lore of ascetic spirituality—as punitive attacks on the body as the seat and source of physical desire and pleasure. The enjoyment of eating was to be countered by the denial of food through fasting. The gratification of the senses was to be punished and denied through inflicting pain.

One can question how effective such practices may really be. Does the oppositional practice really root out the inordinate desire? Or does it merely drive the desire out of conscious awareness, only to disguise it and displace it into unconscious fantasies and their possible derivatives? If this is the case, increasing psychic tension may be created—the tension of drive versus defense—that calls for an ever-higher level of defensive organization and relatively pathological degrees of compromise formation.[12] In addition, the effort to resolve pride by resorting to humility may only drive the narcissistic impulses underground, so that they find equivalent satisfaction in the exercise of a humility that can make one feel unconsciously superior to the rest of men—who have not achieved such a high degree of humility!

We have reason to wonder what may have been the effect of such practices on the disposition of conflicts and compromises in the inner life of Ignatius. The techniques he proposes in the *Exercises* for implementing the agere contra have an obsessional quality. Repeated, frequent, and detailed examinations of conscience are recommended. We are reminded of Iñigo's own scrupulous torments, and the fact that these obsessional practices remained a primary feature of his spiritual teaching and activity to the end of his life. The unremitting pressure of unresolved drive derivatives calls for heightened defensive control and continued obsessional vigilance.

Ignatius was motivated in large part by guilt. From the postconversion perspective, there was much to be guilty about: his libidinous desires and amorous adventures; his flamboyant aggression that kept sword and dagger at hand for any adventure. We remember the troubling murder at Azpeitia, the numerous sword fights; any opposition or insult would call forth an aggressive response that would hardly balk at inflicting injury, even death. There was also the overweening pride and ambition. And, as I have already suggested, there was the ineradicable guilt of having possibly contributed to his mother's death.

Against these guilt-laden impulses, desires, and ventures, which he now saw as sinful and hateful, the pilgrim launched his grim attack. The ascetic onslaught against every facet of his former life and behavior rode on a current of guilt and shame. The guilt was a reflection of the turning of superego aggression against the self; the shame came from the narcissistically based failure to live up to the demands of his newly acquired ideals in his postconversion life.

The terms of Freud's equation relating internal and external aggression seem to bear themselves out in the pilgrim's turning of his immense aggression against himself. Freud had suggested that the more its external expression is denied and inhibited, the greater would be the internally directed aggression. The outcome for the pilgrim was an overwhelming sense of guilt and the sadistic, destructive assault of the superego—reflected particularly in his pathological scrupulosity, his intensely self-punitive ascetic practices, and especially his suicidal impulses.

One might be tempted to say that this was essentially masochism, in which the pilgrim's sadistic and destructive impulses had been transformed into a punitive and guilt-inducing attack on himself. Undoubtedly, this transformation of instinctual derivatives was part of the picture. However, we must also consider that the pilgrim's ascetic effort took place in the context of a highly specific value system and in relation to a powerful and newly formed ego ideal. In addition, Iñigo de Loyola was a child of the Catholic culture of sixteenth-century Spain, both in his role as sword-swinging, amorous courtier and hidalgo, and in his role as penitential ascetic.

NARCISSISM

The values that the pilgrim embraced and espoused were therefore by no means idiosyncratic or deviational but were embodiments of the culturally endorsed heroic ideals. They provided models to which narcissistic strivings could be inexorably drawn and in terms of which narcissistic needs could be most meaningfully satisfied. The cultural context in which value systems and the ego ideal are formed assumes considerable importance in evaluating these elements of personality integration. The superego, including the ego ideal, is the primary repository of environmental influences, particularly those aspects internalized in the form of guiding principles and norms for individual conduct and communal involvement. The inherent values and ideals that guided Iñigo's attitudes and behavior both before and after his conversion reflected the fundamental values and ideals of his culture. Moreover, they were supported and reinforced by social acknowledgment and acceptance.

In both of his embodiments of culturally endorsed ideals—as the fearless and loyal soldier and the saintly ascetic—the dynamics of narcissism were displayed in dramatic and telling ways. The narcissism of the preconversion phase was, by current psychoanalytic standards, pathological in organization and operation. Embracing the ascetic ideal, however, did not overcome or resolve narcissism in any sense; rather, it translated it into terms of the spiritual ideal to which the pilgrim turned in his conversion and in the related crisis of Manresa. Whereas the narcissism of the soldier was connected with the ideals of selfless and loyal service to his king and refused to accept defeat even in the face of impossible odds, the narcissism of the saint found its realization in the service of a heavenly king, a service that knew no limits of pain, penance, and sacrifice in the work of advancing the spiritual kingdom. In both cases, narcissism was reinforced by the sense of special union and favor in service of his lord—one an earthly leader, the other a divinely omnipotent leader. This theme will be further explored in considering Ignatius' mystical gifts.[13]

PROJECTION

We also note projective elements written into the *Exercises*. The identity of the enemy, as we have seen, is clearly the devil and his minions on their mission of destruction. The exact psychological mechanisms are difficult to pinpoint in this context because Iñigo's allusions were common among the spiritual writers of his day and reflect a long-standing Christian usage. That tradition tends to personify the devil as an actual spiritual force, going about like a roaring lion seeking to devour men's souls and to lead them into temptation, then into a variety of sins, and finally to damnation.

Despite this traditional rhetoric, I would argue that projective mechanisms are also at work in this depiction of the spiritual struggle. What is in question is not merely a culturally endorsed style of spiritual discourse but a personalized realization of determinate projective mechanisms. The impulses that were so central in the psychology of the preconversion sinner are now internally denied, then externalized and attributed to the evil one, the prince of darkness. The enemy becomes the embodiment of the repentant sinner's deepest desires and impulses. This inner conflict, the burden of guilt attached both consciously and unconsciously to the sinner's own wishes for riches and worldly power, for the honor and esteem of men, is deprived of its internal power and is attributed to the hated and feared enemy.

The projective resolution is all the more effective in that it is supported by the traditions of Catholic spirituality in Spain and the theological doctrine, carried down through the centuries, regarding the devil and his wiles. Projections that find such a culturally adaptive niche can often be cognitively sustained, and may even serve important adaptive ends, whereas the delusional projections of the psychotic, which tend to be idiosyncratic and culturally deviant, do not.

TRANSFORMATION OF IDENTITY

The *Spiritual Exercises* make it clear that the pilgrim of Manresa passed through a spiritual crisis that involved a radical restructuring of his personality. Out of this regressive crisis, with its concomitant dissolution of psychic structures and the weakening of repressive barriers, a new identity emerged. The transformation, as we have noted, does not rule out a powerful and decisive continuity between the character of the dashing and daring hidalgo and the later ascetic and mystic. The dynamic forces at work in his personality, particularly the narcissistic components, persisted. But the transformation nonetheless involved a radical alteration through the exchange of value systems and the integration of the pilgrim's ego ideal. The alteration was not limited to these aspects, however. The changes that accompanied this remarkable transformation also found their way into the organization of his superego, with a marked increase in the powerful guilt dynamic and the internalizing of aggression. Remarkable changes must have occurred in his ego as well—replacing the impulsive intolerance for opposition or frustration with long-suffering, quiet determination, and fortitude—much of this distilled into his remarkable capacity for discernment.

If the spirit of the proud hidalgo reverberates at all, it is in the fanatical determination with which the pilgrim stormed the castle of virtue. He brought to this spiritual struggle and conquest the same spirit of undaunted courage and fierce determination that had set him apart from his fellow soldiers. Once he had set his mind to the goal, nothing would stand in his way—not an enemy army, the legions of the devil, or his own human vulnerability and weakness. That ruthless fanaticism was a quality that greater wisdom and experience would teach him to modify. But in the first flush of his spiritual campaign, moderation was not part of his code. The struggle was one of life and death for him, calling for an all-out assault meant to sweep the enemy from the field and to inflict a final and irrevocable defeat.

The reshaping of identity that the pilgrim sought in the cave of Manresa was distilled into the practices of the *Spiritual Exercises*. He proposed to his followers and to those whom he directed in the Exercises the same end—a restructuring of the self, of one's sense of self, one's identity, in terms of total commitment to God's will and to unstinting enlisting in His service. The entire corpus of the *Exercises* is organized and directed to this end. It proposes nothing less than a restructuring of one's life, one's ideals and values, one's goals and hopes, and the commitment of that life to the service of the King of Kings.

THE PILGRIM

VII

FAREWELL TO MANRESA

Iñigo's final days at Manresa were not comfortable. During the winter of 1522 he fell severely ill. His friends and acquaintances were so concerned for his health that they insisted on putting him up at the house of one of the local gentry. Again the local matrons took care of him, nursed him back to health, and insisted that he dress decently.

Iñigo's heart was restless, and he had determined on a clear path that he felt he had to follow. He therefore said his farewells to our Lady of Villadordis, in whose shrine he had passed so many prayerful hours, and to our Lady of Montserrat in order to place his projected journey to Jerusalem under the protection of the Black Virgin (Dudon 1949) and at last turned his face toward Jerusalem.

In mid-February 1523 he headed for Barcelona and the home of Inés Pascual, who had befriended him in Manresa. He took only a few books and spiritual notes in his knapsack and traveled on foot, together with Inés' brother Pujol and a few others. Once in Barcelona, he resisted efforts to provide him with help or a companion who might make his journey easier or more enjoyable. Iñigo was not setting out on a pleasure trip but on a pilgrimage—to walk in the footsteps of his Lord. He wanted only God as his companion. He had to wait about twenty days before he could secure passage to Italy. During his stay, he continued to live as he had at Manresa, begging his food, visiting churches, and praying. He had booked passage on a small brig, but his friend Isabel Roser urged him to seek out a larger vessel. The advice was well taken; the ill-fated brig sank soon after it left port (von Matt and Rahner 1956; Brodrick 1956). He finally persuaded the captain of a merchant vessel to give him free passage, on condition that he bring his own supply of biscuits (Vita 35).

He could not escape his scrupulosity, and agonized over whether his taking these provisions reflected a lack of trust in God's providence. He finally turned to his confessor to resolve his obsessional doubts. The confessor advised that he beg for his provisions and take those along.

We also detect strains of his unresolved narcissism. He was preoccupied with keeping his noble origins secret so that he could maintain the façade of the humble beggar of Christ. Ignatius recalls: "As he was begging from a lady, she asked him where he intended to go. At first he hesitated to tell her, but finally said that he was going to Italy and Rome, not daring to say any more. . . . The reason that he did not dare to say that he was going to Jerusalem was his fear of vainglory; this fear so plagued him that he never dared to say from what country he came, nor who his family was" (Vita 36). We can infer that the strains of grandiosity and exhibitionism continued to conflict with his newly formed spiritual ideals.

ON TO JERUSALEM

Leaving behind the extra alms he had collected, he boarded the ship with only the required biscuits in mid-March 1523 and with the help of a strong wind soon landed in Gaeta, about seventy-five miles south of Rome. It was a period when the plague was relatively active in Italy, and the Turkish threat hung over the land. Spanish soldiers were everywhere. Walking was painful for Iñigo because of his leg, but he nevertheless pressed on to Rome in the company of several other travelers, including a mother and daughter from the ship. The trip was not uneventful. One night at an inn, Iñigo was roused from sleep by the screams of the women, who had been accosted by soldiers. Iñigo's outrage could not be restrained and he confronted the culprits, dressing them down in proper fashion—echoes of the old commanding officer. So fierce was his onslaught that the shame-faced men withdrew in confusion and guilt. Beneath the worn and tattered cloak of this humble pilgrim, do we catch a glimpse of the chivalrous knight, the ferocious soldier whose rapier leapt to his hand at the slightest provocation? Is it any wonder that rough-hewn soldiers should recoil before his rage? This display is all the more remarkable in that his health and strength were not the best.

The journey had further difficulties. At one town, probably Fondi (see Dudon 1949 and Tylenda 1985), they could not gain entrance and had to sleep in a damp church.[1] The rest of the company moved on the next day, but Iñigo was too ill to travel. He was able to gain entrance to the city and help for his weakness by imploring the aid of a noblewoman who happened to come by.[2] Once again, a woman's help furthered the pilgrim on his course.

When he finally arrived in Rome, on Palm Sunday, Iñigo found lodging in the Spanish hospice in the Piazza Navone and turned his efforts to gaining papal permission for his pilgrimage. The reigning pontiff was Adrian VI, formerly mentor to Charles V and later regent of Castile after Cisneros. Access to the Pope by way of the Spanish colony in Rome was not difficult, so the pilgrim received the apostolic blessing and permission to continue on to Jerusalem (Leturia and Batllori 1956). He set off for Venice soon after Easter. Many pointed out to him the folly of trying to travel to Jerusalem without money. He yielded to these prudent cautions to the extent of taking a few ducats along to defray the cost of passage. But his scruples reasserted themselves:

He had taken them [the ducats] because of the fear with which others inspired him of not being able to get to Jerusalem otherwise. But two days after leaving Rome he began to realize that accepting this money meant that he was losing the confidence he had had, and he worried much for having taken the ducats and thought it would be good to get rid of them. Finally, he made up his mind to distribute them generously among those who presented themselves, who were usually poor. He did so in such a way that when he reached Venice all he had left was a little change which was necessary for that night. (Vita 40)

As he struggled on his painful leg along the weary road to Venice, Iñigo had little on his mind but to follow in his master's footsteps in the Holy Land. If he knew anything of the turmoil around him, he paid little attention to it.

And turmoil there was. Rhodes had fallen to the Turks that December, and the Turkish Janissaries were looking to lay siege to Rome. The Pope's efforts to reconcile the emperor and the king of France were in vain. The Holy Land was still in the hands of unbelievers. Within Europe itself, the storm of the Lutheran revolt was tearing the fabric of the Church apart. Within months, Pope Adrian would lie on his death bed, and Rome would face the prospect of the sacking of the city. Renaissance Rome was tottering, and even the rising columns of the new basilica of St. Peter's could not prevent her collapse.

Iñigo's journey to Venice was fraught with difficulty. His pallor made people think he might have the plague, so that he was obliged to sleep in the open fields. Sleeping in the fields before the barred gates of Padua, he had a consoling vision of Our Lord. He finally reached the quay of San Marco in May, after four weeks of painful walking. Trusting in God, he made no effort to provide for himself and slept in the Piazza San Marco (Vita 41; Dudon 1949).

He recalled:

> He did not care to go to the house of the Ambassador of the Emperor, nor to make any special effort to find something with which to get along. He had a deep certainty in his soul that God must give him the means of getting to Jerusalem, and this gave him such confidence that no reasons or fears suggested by others were enough to make him doubt.
>
> One day a rich Spaniard met him and asked him what he was doing and where he wanted to go. Learning his intention, he took him home for dinner, and kept him there for several days until arrangements were made for his departure. From his Manresa days the pilgrim had this custom that when he ate with anyone, he never spoke at table, unless to answer briefly; but he listened to the conversation and made note of some things, from which he later took occasion to speak of God. When the meal was over this is what he did. (Vita 41–42)[3]

The contact proved advantageous. His host took him to the newly elected doge, who issued orders for the pilgrim's free passage to the Holy Land. But because of the fall of Rhodes, there were not enough passengers for the usual pilgrim ship to sail. Instead the passengers were assigned to two merchant vessels. The smaller ship, with thirteen pilgrims aboard, set sail in the middle of June, and the larger vessel, the *Negrona*, with Iñigo and seven other pilgrims on board, left on 14 July 1523. His companions on the voyage included the governor of Cyprus, who was en route to his post, a group of Spaniards, including Diego Manes, commander of the Order of St. John, and some Swiss.[4] Just before sailing, Iñigo came down with a fever. He was treated with purgatives and counseled by the doctor not to continue his journey. This advice made little impression on Iñigo, who vomited his way out of the port of Venice and finally began to improve (Vita 43).

As if the rigors of the voyage were not enough, the chivalrous fervor of the former hidalgo might have made matters worse. Some maidservants traveling in the governor's entourage attracted the attention of the sailors. Iñigo took exception to some "indecencies" that passed between them and made his opinions known. His Spanish companions warned him that the crew had already threatened to put him off on a deserted island if he didn't mind his own business, and he curbed his outrage (Vita 43–44; Dudon 1949).

After a month at sea, the *Negrona* docked safely at Famagusta, Cyprus, where the governor disembarked. The plan was for the ship to continue on to Beirut, from whence the pilgrims could make their way overland to Jerusalem. But the plague was then raging in Beirut, so Ragazzoni, the ship's captain, aborted the voyage. The pilgrims had to disembark and make their way to Salinas (modern Larnaca) where they met the other, tardy, pilgrim ship. The captain, Jacopo Alberto, had determined that he would go no further with only thirteen pilgrims on board, but the arrival of the additional eight and the fees they were willing to pay for passage apparently changed his mind. The revenues were sufficient for him to allow Iñigo free passage. They set sail on 19 August and came within view of Jaffa by the twenty-second. A storm kept them from landing, however, until 25 August (Vita 44; Tylenda 1985).

"Throughout this time," Iñigo recalled, "our Lord appeared to him very often, which gave him much strength and consolation; but he thought that he saw something that was large and round, as though it were of gold. This kept appearing to him from the time he left Cyprus until they reached Jaffa" (Vita 44).

THE HOLY LAND

The situation in the Holy Land was precarious, to say the least; pilgrims risked a number of threats. The Turkish soldiers and officers who guarded the city entrances were often tough and greedy, demanding large sums of money from the easily exploited travelers; and yet payment did not guarantee good treatment. Pilgrims were also at the mercy of other robbers and vagabonds and frequently fell victim to the plague and other illnesses. As was the custom, the captain notified the Franciscans, who were in charge of the holy places, that the party had arrived, and safe conduct and a Turkish escort to Jerusalem were set up. With these arrangements completed, the pilgrims were finally able to leave the ship on 31 August. They made their way to the Holy City, and at the first sighting of the city walls Iñigo felt deep consolation and joy. As the pilgrims visited the holy places, he again and again experienced a deep sense of spiritual fulfillment and peace.

But after a few days, a contingent of Turkish cavalry arrived in the city. The governor of Jerusalem advised the pilgrims to stay off the city streets to avoid any incidents, and accordingly they spent the last week of their stay in relative seclusion. This must have been frustrating for Iñigo, since he had other ideas. He tells us the story:

It was his firm determination to remain in Jerusalem, perpetually visiting the holy places. But in addition to this devotion, he also proposed to be of help to souls. For this purpose he brought letters of recommendation to the Guardian [the superior of the Franciscans], which he gave to him, telling him of his intention to remain there to satisfy his devotion. But he said nothing of his desire to benefit souls, for this he had told to no one, while he had often spoken freely of the first part of his plan. The Guardian told him that he did not see how he could remain, since the house was in such need that it could not support the friars, and it was for this reason that they had determined on sending some of the friars to the west with the pilgrims. The pilgrim answered that he wanted nothing from the house, but only someone to hear him when he came to confession. At this the Guardian told him that they might be able to arrange things, but that he should wait until the provincial came, who was the chief superior of the Order and was at the time in Bethlehem.

The pilgrim remained satisfied with this promise, and set about writing letters to some spiritual persons in Barcelona. Having written one, he was at work on the second on the eve of the departure of the pilgrims when he was summoned to the provincial and the Guardian, the former of whom had returned. The provincial addressed him kindly and told him that he had learned of his good intention to remain in the holy places, and had given the matter careful thought. From the experience he had of others, he thought that it would not be wise. Many, he said, had entertained a like desire, some of whom had been taken prisoner, others died, and that his Order had been later obliged to ransom those who had been taken captive. For this reason, he should get ready to leave the next day with the other pilgrims. His answer was that he had made up his mind to stay, and was determined to let no reason prevent him from sticking to his resolve, giving him honestly to understand that although the provincial did not agree with him, if it was not a matter that obliged him under pain of sin, he would not give up his purpose out of any fear. To this the provincial replied that they had authority from the Apostolic See to dismiss or retain, and to excommunicate anyone who refused to obey. In his case they judged that he should not remain. (Vita 45–46)

The account is striking insofar as it tells us something of the intense devotion Iñigo experienced and the fierce determination with which he pursued his aims. The driving force was undoubtedly the wish to follow in the Lord's footsteps, not merely in the geographic locale of Christ's earthly life but to imitate the very pattern and mode of that life in its intimate details. His near fanaticism would brook no interference and count no cost too great to achieve its aims—even the threat of prison and death.

Confronted with Iñigo's determined resistance, the provincial offered to show Iñigo the papal bulls confirming his authority to excommunicate anyone who did not abide by his decision. Realizing that he had no choice, Iñigo bowed to the ruling of the Pope. He resigned himself with the thought that "it was not our Lord's will that he remain there in those holy places" (Vita 47). We can surmise that obedience to legitimate authority was highly valued by this onetime military commander, but we should also note that his submission was not altogether unmitigated.

If Iñigo was to obey on one front, his unbridled devotion would lead him to rebel and risk on another. He was seized with a powerful impulse to visit once again the places where Our Lord had walked and prayed, especially the Mount of Olives. He slipped out unnoticed and without a Turkish guide made his way to the Mount of the Ascension. He managed to bribe the guards with a pocket knife and, kneeling on the ground, prayed with a sense of deep consolation. He then hurried to Bethany, where the Palm Sunday procession into Jerusalem had begun. Then, fretting that he had not noted the exact position of Our Lord's feet when he ascended into heaven, he rushed back to the mount, again bribed the guards with some trinkets, and found the rock with the supposed impression of Christ's feet. Satisfied, he returned to the city.

By this time, the Franciscans had discovered his absence and were beside themselves, searching for him everywhere. Finally one of the servants saw him descending the mount, seized him, and dragged him back to the monastery. It hardly mattered to Iñigo, who was in a rapture. He recalled, "He had great consolation from our Lord Who he thought he saw above him all along the way. This consolation lasted in great abundance till they reached the monastery" (Vita 47–48; Dudon 1949).

The quality of the pilgrim's devotion and behavior was simpleminded and almost fanatical. He was at this point relatively uneducated and theologically naive. It was enough for him that he was in the Holy Land and in the Holy City. Like other pilgrims of his day, he was not troubled by the uncertainty regarding the exact location of the events of our Lord's life or by the fact that the impression of the Savior's feet on the supposed rock of ascension was undoubtedly apocryphal.[5] There was no room for hesitation, critical appraisal and judgment, or any suggestion of doubt about these matters. He was transported by the fervor and devotion of the moment, even to the extent of seeing the figure of Christ guiding his way.

RETURN

And so the weary band of pilgrims began the painful journey homeward. The Turkish escort threatened them with blows and imprisonment, demanded ransom money and gifts, and locked them in an infested dungeon, where several of them became seriously ill. At Jaffa, the shipmaster, Francisco, managed to bargain their way out on 2 October. They were without provisions since these had been pillaged and sold by the sailors. They were becalmed and lost direction on the sea, and one passenger died. They finally reached Cyprus on 14 October.

Negotiations for passage to Venice were difficult. The shipowners were asking fifteen ducats per head. Iñigo had no money, so his companions tried to persuade the owners to take him aboard for nothing. They refused, and other shipmasters were no more accommodating. Finally the pilgrims were able to contact the governor through a Franciscan friar at the convent of St. John de Montfort, and he persuaded one of the shipmasters to lower the price of passage—and to allow Iñigo free passage. They set sail on 1 November (Dudon 1949).

About the second day out, they ran into a terrible storm that forced them back to Salinas, on Cyprus. They set sail again on 12 November, were driven off course by a violent headwind, and reached Rhodes on 20 November. Because of the weather, they could not set out again until 27 November. Another fierce squall battered the ship. The pilgrims prayed together and made vows to St. Roch, fearing that they were doomed to a watery grave. They struggled into a small Cretan port on 12 December. That winter was one of the most severe in the Mediterranean in living memory. The rest of the voyage they had to endure winter storms, heavy snow, and a hurricane that tore the mainsail. Through it all the vessel struggled on and finally made port at Parenzo. There they switched to a light bark that carried them to Venice, where they landed on 12 January, three and a half months after they had left Jaffa (Dudon 1949).

The journey to Jerusalem tells us something of the mettle of this man. The fanatical determination with which he set himself on the course that he divined to be God's will for him echoes the relentless determination of the fierce hidalgo who would brave overwhelming odds and certain death in the service of his master. Once Iñigo had decided on his course, nothing would deter him from it—not poverty, sickness, raging seas, hurricanes, Turkish marauders, or Franciscan provincials. Only when confronted with papal authority would he back down and accept the denial of his wish as reflecting God's will for him. Rather a stubborn man, certainly a determined and courageous one. We might even think that his behavior was foolhardy, impractical, irrational. Would any reasonable man have undertaken the dangers and torments he endured in the service of such an unworldly vision? Iñigo de Loyola was a man of extremes, if nothing else.

The pilgrim must have been relieved to get his feet on dry land again, but it was winter and he was not well equipped to withstand the cold. His tattered trousers covered only half his legs, and his torn and threadbare coat was far too small. A compassionate gentleman gave him a piece of cloth that he could wrap around his chest to keep out the bitter cold (Vita 50).

But a new plan was taking shape in the mind of the shivering pilgrim. The Jerusalem trip had been a disappointment, and his cherished dream of working there for the good of souls seemed remote. He began to think of other ways in which he might fulfill God's will and serve men and wondered if perhaps his ability to bring souls to God was compromised by his lack of schooling and theological training. If he educated himself, he might be able to do more in the service of his king. He determined to return to Barcelona to begin his studies (Vita 50).

The walk across Venetia and Lombardy was fraught with peril. He had given away the few remaining coins in his possession to beggars in the cathedral of Ferrara. On the road to Genoa, he encountered a party of Spanish militia who advised him to stay off the main road to avoid marauding French troops, who were contesting the claims of Francesco Sforza, who was supported by the Spanish forces of Charles V against those of Francis I, to control the duchy of Milan. Iñigo rarely accepted sound advice and went on his way. Not surprisingly, he fell into the hands of the French, who took him for a spy and subjected him to an interrogation. He wisely played the fool until the French captain in exasperation freed him. He was soon recaptured by some Spaniards, but this time he had the good fortune to encounter an officer who knew something of Guipúzcoa and let him go.[6]

Part of the reason for Iñigo's difficulties was that Lombardy was the scene of continuing struggle between the Spanish and French for the hegemony of Europe. At the time the French had invaded northern Italy and were doing battle against the Spanish instead of joining forces against the Turks. Andrea Doria with his Genoese fleet had sided with the French. The Spanish forces were encamped at Milan and Pavia, and the French held the ground of the Italian side of Ticino. The struggle was a continuation of the war in which Iñigo himself had been a participant in the battle of Pamplona. The suspicious French troops and possibly even the Spanish might have regarded him as a spy, particularly when he refused to take the road the Spanish soldiers had advised. When he was seized by another group of Spaniards, he was subjected to the kind of questioning and examination that was typically administered in such cases. Obviously Iñigo was clever enough to play dumb, and the Spanish captain simply thought that he was not worth bothering with. The pilgrim finally arrived safely in Barcelona toward the end of February 1524. He then faced the next phase of his mission to serve God and help souls.

THE STUDENT YEARS

3

BARCELONA, ALCALÁ,
AND SALAMANCA

VIII

Months of reflection on the difficulties and disappointments of his Jerusalem sojourn had persuaded Iñigo that he would have to acquire the skills of language and learning if he were to have any influence over his fellowmen. Or so it seemed. On his return to Barcelona, he contacted his good friend Isabel Roser, who supported his plans and even put him in touch with Jerónimo Ardevol, a pious man who had earned a master of arts degree from the University of Barcelona and was at the time one of the regents of the university. Ardevol generously offered to teach Iñigo grammar, not in the general public courses offered to young boys, but as a special student in his own home.

This was without doubt an opportunity that suited Iñigo's needs well. It would have been much more difficult for him, at thirty-one, to sit in the benches with schoolboys.[1] But Iñigo was still torn between his decision to study and the continuing urges toward prayer and devotional exercises. He had a powerful wish to return to Manresa, his spiritual home in a sense, where he could renew his fervor and dedication, particularly with the help of his friend and confessor, Fra Bernardine, in the Cistercian monastery of San Pablo (Vita 54).[2] He decided to go to Manresa but promised Isabel and Ardevol that if he did not find what he was seeking there he would come back to Barcelona and take up their offer. On his arrival at Manresa, he discovered that the good friar had died. He returned to Barcelona and set about the task of learning grammar (Vita 54).

Along with Ardevol's private instruction he enrolled in the Estudio General and applied himself as well as he could.[3] But he ran into difficulties almost immediately. He began to feel the tension between the demands of his prayer life and the need to spend long hours on his studies. His account gives us a sense of the quality of Iñigo's ego functioning and the spiritual vantage point he had acquired at Manresa and through the formulation of his rules for the discernment of spirits. He recounted:

> When he began to learn by heart, as has to be done in the beginning of grammar, he received new light on spiritual things and new delights. So strong were these delights that he could memorize nothing, nor could he get rid of them however much he tried.
>
> Thinking this over at various times, he said to himself: "Even when I go to prayer or attend Mass these lights do not come to me so vividly." Thus, step by step he came to recognize that it was a temptation. After making his meditation, he went to the Church of Santa María del Mar, near the house of his teacher, having asked him to have the kindness to hear him for a moment in the church. Seated there, the pilgrim gave his teacher a faithful account of what had taken place in his soul, and how little progress he had made until then for the reason already mentioned. And he made a promise to his master, with the words: "I promise you never to fail to attend your class these two years, as long as I can find bread and water for my support here in Barcelona." He made this promise with such effect that he never again suffered from those temptations. (Vita 54–55)

The touches here are typically Ignatian: the prayerful discernment, the seeking of guidance, and, once the matter has become clear, a firm resolution and determination that banishes all ambiguity and ambivalence. The sequence of events suggests his lingering ambivalence—his return to Manresa seeking spiritual renewal, the distracting temptations that reflect some reluctance to devote himself to the program of studies. Once the decision had been made, however, he stuck to it. But he could not do without penances of some kind: "The stomach pains which he had suffered in Manresa and were the cause of his taking to shoes, left him, and he felt well enough in that regard from the time he left Barcelona for Jerusalem. For this reason, while he was still at his studies in Barcelona the desire returned of resuming his past penances, and he began by making a hole in the sole of his shoes, which widened little by little until by the time the cold of winter arrived, nothing remained of the shoes but the uppers" (Vita 55).

It is also characteristic that he sought assistance in sorting out his dilemma from his teacher. And once again, as with his scrupulous obsessions at Manresa, contact with a father figure seems to have done the trick—transference magic at work. Once the decision was reached the ambivalence seemed to disappear—at least outwardly. This is a typical Ignatian pattern and an aspect of his spiritual doctrine that encourages seeking spiritual succor from others and turning to a trustworthy mentor for help in reaching decisions or clarifying uncertainties. In spiritual matters especially, he continually sought to open his heart and mind to a confessor or spiritual guide and often responded to the help he received as though it came from God. We can also note how, having reached a point of spiritual discernment, and having clarified for himself the nature of this temptation, he declares it to be once and for all banished. This is similar to declaring the end of all temptations of the flesh—a powerful and defensive suppression of desires and impulses. The banishment of his spiritual desires seems, in the present instance, to be in the service of the ego.

ASCETIC PRACTICE

During his stay in Barcelona, he lived with Inés Pascual and her family above the little store they ran. Iñigo still begged his food in the streets and continued his life of prayer, penance, and study. It was not long before the well-to-do ladies of Barcelona came to know him and loaded him with food and money when he came to their doors begging. The pilgrim would carry these goods back to his garret cell and sort out the best, which he distributed to the sick and the poor, who would gather at the door of the Pascual house. Inés took charge of the distribution, and Iñigo took food and money to the sick. Once again, a woman helped him to carry out his mission.

He seemed never to tire of trying to do good—catechizing children, visiting the sick, reconciling enemies. One day he heard loud voices coming from a house as he passed on the street; he rushed inside and found two brothers quarreling over their inheritance. One was in the process of trying to hang himself. Iñigo cut him down and prayed over the unconscious figure. As the man opened his eyes, Iñigo urged him to seek forgiveness and confess to a priest.

There were also times when Iñigo had to pay for his zeal. In the wake of his efforts to reform a local convent, which had developed the scandalous custom of permitting male visitors, the vengeful suitors had some ruffians beat him severely. Some passersby brought him back to the Pascual house, bruised and bloody. Inés and her friends nursed him back to health, but he had to remain in bed for nearly two months. He complained little but experienced transports of love for his crucified Lord, who had been beaten and bruised for the sins of men (Dudon 1949).

During his stay with the Pascuals, Iñigo continued his saintly ways. When his confessor told him to get rid of the hair shirt and take his meals with the Pascual family, he found ways to continue his mortifications. At meals he ate little, spending his time discoursing fervently on Our Lord. In his little room there hung a picture of the Last Supper; when he gazed at it he would often fall into a rapture, later returning to his senses as though nothing had happened.[4] He shared the room with young Juan Pascual, who feigned sleep in order to witness the saint's nightly prayers, penances, and ecstatic devotion. Dudon recounts in his otherwise sober history:

> This life of complete self-renouncement, this forgiveness of injuries, this seeking after the effects of poverty, this zeal for souls, this angelic modesty, struck the whole house with admiration. All looked upon Iñigo as a great saint. The supernatural favors with which God loaded His servant appeared quite natural to Inés Pascual. They frequently saw Iñigo lifted from the earth while he prayed, his face all aglow as though transfigured. They heard him foretell the future. He foretold Juan's life in all its particulars, his marriage, his large family, his reverses of fortune, all his trials. (1949, p. 101)

Hagiography? Miracles? Mystical experiences? Wishful thinking? What is the reality in the telling? Do these fantastic images convey a truth beyond their literal meaning?

Throughout his studies, Iñigo had ample opportunity to reflect on the future course of his ministry. He was able to put some finishing touches on his *Spiritual Exercises* and to further clarify his thinking about the future. He vacillated between joining some religious congregation and maintaining his freedom to travel throughout the world and do good on his own. But it became increasingly clear to him that his work for souls could have only limited impact as long as he tried to carry it out single-handedly. The greater good required companions who would join him in this work. He wrote, "Here in Barcelona arose the desire to bring together a handful of men in a fraternity, men who might be, as it were, the trumpeters of Jesus Christ" (von Matt and Rahner, 1956, p. 50). His efforts actually attracted three young men, Juan d'Arteaga, López Cáceres, and Calixto de Sa, to whom he gave the Spiritual Exercises and shared his enthusiasm for returning to the Holy Land (Dalmases 1985).

Wilkens (1978) also comments on the contrast between the tenacity Iñigo showed in his apostolic efforts, even braving severe personal injury, and the self-effacement and humility he displayed in almost every other context, never speaking unless spoken to, never imposing on others, never making known his noble birth and position. He would follow in the footsteps of his Master, particularly insofar as it led along paths of humiliation, degradation, and painful suffering; at the same time he regarded himself as a worthless sinner and presented himself to the eyes of men as a humble penitent and servant.

ALCALÁ

Iñigo spent two years in Barcelona, praying, fasting, doing penances, and studying. Finally, Ardevol advised him that it was time to move on to the university. With his usual prudence, Iñigo sought a second opinion from a doctor of theology who, after questioning him, gave him the same advice. And so he left Barcelona and made the long trek—about four hundred miles—on foot with his companions to Alcalá. The university there had been founded in 1508 by the great Cardinal Ximénes de Cisneros with the encouragement and support of the Spanish crown. In a few short years the university had taken on a considerable luster and was reputed to be one of the foremost seats of learning in Europe. Iñigo, arriving in the city after a long and weary journey, followed his usual program. He tells us:

> When he arrived at Alcalá, he began to beg and live on alms. One day, after he had been living this way some ten or twelve days, a cleric and some others who were in his company, seeing him thus begging, began to laugh at him and insult him, as they usually do to those who being hale and hearty take to begging. At this moment the superintendent of the new hospital of "Antezana," passed by, and feeling sorry for him, called him and took him to the hospital, where he gave him a room and all that he needed. (Vita 56)

Despite the distinction of the university and its faculty, Iñigo did not approach his studies systematically. He did not matriculate at any college and apparently did not even have a director for his study. He tells us that he studied the logic of de Soto, the natural philosophy of Albert the Great, the theology of the Master of the Sentences (Peter Lombard), and a hodgepodge of other disciplines. He seemed impatient to learn and scurried haphazardly through dialectics, physics, and courses in theology—as if simply listening to lectures on these subjects was sufficient to gain all the knowledge he needed for his mission (Vita 57; Dudon 1949).

APOSTOLIC EFFORTS

Along with this immersion in studies, Iñigo continued his apostolic mission unabated. It seems that he brought the three companions from Barcelona with him to assist in his charitable works. It also seems that he had his usual success in locating benefactors to support and help him in his work. He tells us:

As soon as he arrived in Alcalá, he made the acquaintance of Don Diego de Guia [Eguia], who was living with his brother, and in the printing business and comfortably well off. They helped him with their alms to support the poor, and maintained three companions of the pilgrim in their house. Once when he came to ask alms, Don Diego told him that he had no money, but he opened a chest in which there were various things, bedspreads of various colors, some candelabra, and such things, all of which he wrapped in a sheet, and gave to the pilgrim, who lifted them to his shoulders and went off to bring succor to his poor. (Vita 57)

Dudon (1949) tells us about a meeting with a fellow countryman from Azpeitia, Juan Martín Sáenz de Goyas, a wealthy man who had known Iñigo at Loyola and thought he recognized him among the students in the university. He followed him hoping to make sure that it was in fact Iñigo and saw him enter a small house and leave again quickly. Martín also entered the house, where he found a poor widow. He asked for the name of the man who had just left. The widow did not know but said that he came every day bringing alms. Martín told her to tell Iñigo that if he needed anything—money, a horse—Martín would see that he got it. When the widow told Iñigo, he reportedly said, "I am very thankful to you, and God will reward you; but I cannot come here any more."

Martín finally did meet Iñigo and actually carried a letter from Iñigo to his family at Loyola. One gets the impression that the pilgrim wanted to dissociate himself from all connections with the past and was even embarrassed by meeting an old friend who would have known of his noble family.

Nor was he above admonishing his fellow students for their scandalous behavior. He confronted one aristocratic profligate, who was at first angered that a perfect stranger should reproach him in his own house. But Iñigo's manner was so firm and winning that the dissolute young man asked him to stay for dinner and when it was time for Iñigo to leave offered to send him home on a mule with an escort of torchbearing servants (Dudon 1949).

Iñigo contacted many students at the university, some of whom sought to join the band he was gathering around him. The fifth member to join was a Frenchman, Jean de Reynalde. The group now donned long cassocks and caps of rough wool and gradually became known in the city as the Graycoats. As Iñigo's notoriety spread, people from all walks of life and all levels of society began to gather around him. Rumor spread that this barefoot man in the gray cassock was actually a noble knight who had an exceptional gift for teaching spiritual matters. Many came out of curiosity. Iñigo instructed these hungering souls of the things of God and even led them through the Spiritual Exercises. But he learned that his message would find a better audience if he spoke of what his listeners needed to hear rather than what filled his heart. His skills as a preacher were limited, but in intimate conversation or discussion in small groups, the force of his personality found more ample play (Clancy 1978). He tended to use familiar forms of address, even with nobility, and was not averse to exploiting a dinner invitation to draw his companions into a discussion about spiritual matters (Vita 65; Dalmases 1985).

THE PALE OF SUSPICION

But with notoriety came suspicion. As the reputation of the Graycoats increased, rumors of their extraordinary life style and teaching reached the inquisitors in Toledo. Suspicions arose that they were illuminati (*alumbrados*), a worrisome accusation since the Inquisition had condemned some forty-eight propositions of the alumbrados the preceding

September of 1526. This was after all the period of the Reformation, which posed a severe challenge to the integrity of the Church. Who were these strange preachers—followers of Luther? of Erasmus? members of some heretical sect?

In Spain, the illuminati were a heretical sect of considerable importance. They espoused a form of sixteenth-century gnosticism, believing in direct illumination from the Holy Spirit; thus they did not consider themselves subject to the same norms for sanctification as the rest of the Church. They seem to have been a sort of throwback to earlier medieval movements like the Albigensians, the Waldensians, and the Beghards and Beguines.[5] The sect's teachers appeared in a good number of cities and caused concern to the Inquisition for more than a century (Brodrick 1956). The ecclesiastical records at Alcalá reveal that there had been trials of the alumbrados even a few years before Iñigo had come to the university. The possibility that such heretical teachings were arising once again at Alcalá would undoubtedly have alarmed the guardians of the faith.

Iñigo himself recounts his first informal encounter with the Inquisition:

> As mentioned above, there was much talk through the country of the things that were happening in Alcalá, each one telling a different story. Reports reached the Inquisition at Toledo, some members of which came to Alcalá. The pilgrim was warned by their host that they were calling the companions the sack-wearers, or, I believe, the illuminati, and that they were going to make hash of them. They began at once to make enquiry and investigate his manner of life, and finally returned to Toledo without summoning him, although they had come for that sole purpose. (Vita 58)

Some time later, Iñigo was not so lucky. Two inquisitors came from Toledo to conduct the trial along with Juan Rodriquez de Figueroa, the representative of the archbishop of Toledo. The enquiry, held in the episcopal palace in Alcalá on 19 November 1526, was Iñigo's first actual brush with the Inquisition, and its resolution took a curious turn. He tells us:

> They left the trial to the Vicar Figueroa, who is now with the Emperor. After a few days he called them, and told them that an enquiry

and investigation into their manner of life had been made by the Inquisitors, and that no error had been found in their teaching or in their lives, and that therefore they could go on as they had been without any interference. But as they were not religious, it did not seem good for them to be wearing the same habit. It would be good, and they so directed, if two (pointing to the pilgrim and Arteaga) dyed their clothing black, and the other two (Calixto and Cáceres) brown. Juanico, who was French, was allowed to remain as he was. (Vita 58)

Iñigo was content to accept this decision, but was not slow to press his case:

The pilgrim promised to follow his instructions. "But, I do not know," he observed, "what use there is in these investigations. Just a few days ago a certain priest refused to give communion to one of us, because he received every week, and they have even made it difficult for me.[6] We should like to know whether we have been found in some heresy." "No," answered Figueroa, "for if they had they would burn you!" "They would burn you too," rejoined the pilgrim, "if they found you in heresy." They dyed their clothing as they were commanded, and for about fifteen or twenty days Figueroa commanded the pilgrim not to go barefoot but to wear his shoes. This he did, as he found it easy to obey in matters of this kind when he was given a command. (Vita 59)

Dudon (1949) notes that Figueroa was so moved by the pilgrim's devotion when he spoke of communion that he allowed Iñigo and his companions to receive the sacrament and experienced such consolation in administering it that he even invited them to dinner.

But the suspicions of the Inquisitors were not completely allayed. That December of 1526 Iñigo and his group were warned to stop their secret meetings—apparently referring to the Spiritual Exercises. Evidently the visits of pious women to the hospital where Iñigo was staying also aroused suspicions. Iñigo recalled:

Four months later [in March 1527], the same Figueroa held another investigation concerning them. Besides the ordinary charges, I believe there was another occasion of a married woman of some importance who had a special devotion for the pilgrim. To prevent herself being recognized, she came veiled, as is the custom in Alcalá de

Henares, between [servants carrying] two lights, to the hospital. On entering, she removed her veil and went to the pilgrim's room. But they did nothing this time, nor even after the trial did they call him or say anything to him. (Vita 59)

Figueroa questioned some of the women about what went on during these seemingly clandestine meetings. They told of Iñigo's teachings from the *Spiritual Exercises*—and this seemed to put the matter at rest for the time being.

PRISON

It was not long, however, before the pilgrim was in hot water again. On Good Friday, 19 April 1527, he was again summoned by the Inquisition. He recalled:

After another four months, when he was established in a small house outside the hospital, an officer of the law stood at his door and called him: "Come with me a moment." He brought him to the jail and told him not to leave until other arrangements were made. This was in summer, and as his movements in the jail were not much restricted, many people came to visit him, and he accomplished as much as he would have had he been free in the teaching of catechism and giving the Exercises. He never consulted a lawyer or attorney, although many offers were made to him. He remembers especially Teresa de Cardenas, who sent someone to visit him who made many offers of obtaining his release. But he accepted nothing, always answering with the words, "He for Whose love I came here will release me when it seems good to Him."

He was eighteen days in custody without any examination or knowing why. At the end of this time, Figueroa came to the prison, and questioned him on many points, including this, whether he had commanded the sabbath to be observed.[7]

He also asked him whether he was acquainted with two women, mother and daughter. He said that he was. And whether he had known of their departure before they actually left. This he denied under oath. The Vicar then laid his hand on the pilgrim's shoulder with every sign of joy and told him: "That is the reason for your being here." Among the many people who followed the pilgrim's talks, there was a mother and a daughter, both widows, the daughter very young and beautiful.[8]

They had made great progress in the spiritual life, especially the daughter. Although they were of noble birth, they had made a pilgrimage on foot to the veil of Veronica at Jaén, by themselves, but I don't know whether they begged their way. This started a great deal of talk in Alcalá, and Doctor Ciruelo, who had some responsibility over them, thought it was the prisoner who had induced them to make the pilgrimage, and so had him arrested. As the prisoner heard what the Vicar told him, he asked: "Would you like me to enlarge a little on this matter?" He answered, "Yes." "Well, then, you ought to know," said the prisoner, "that these two women had often insisted with me that they wanted to go through the whole world, serving the poor now in one hospital, now in another. I have always withdrawn them from such a resolve, since the daughter is so young and so beautiful, and so on, and I told them that when they wanted to visit the poor they could do so in Alcalá, and bear the Blessed Sacrament company." At the end of the conversation, Figueroa took his leave with his notary who had taken everything down in writing.[9]

At this time, Calixto was in Segovia, and learning of this imprisonment, he came at once, although but recently recovered from a serious illness, and bore him company in his prison. But the prisoner told him that it would be better to go and present himself to the Vicar. The Vicar [Figueroa] received him kindly, and told him that he would send him to the prison since it was necessary for them to be there until the women returned, to see whether they confirmed the statements made. Calixto remained in the prison a few days only, as the pilgrim saw that he was doing himself more harm because of the poor state of his health, since he was not yet quite fully recovered. With the help of a doctor who was a good friend of his, he had Calixto released.

The pilgrim had remained forty-two days in confinement, at the end of which the devout ladies having returned, the notary came to the prison to read the sentence that set him free, but required him to dress as the other students and forbade him to speak on matters of faith for four years, that is, until they had studied more, since they had not knowledge of philosophy and theology. The truth is that the pilgrim was the most learned of them all, but what he knew was without a solid foundation. Whenever they examined him this was the first statement he usually made.

After this sentence, he did not clearly see what he should do; for apparently they had shut the door to his helping souls, and for no other reason than that he had not studied. Finally he made up his mind to go to Archbishop Fonseca [of Toledo] and put his case in his hands. He left Alcalá and found the Archbishop in Valladolid, gave him a faithful account of what had happened, and told him that although he was not in his jurisdiction, nor obliged to abide by the sentence, he would act according to the Archbishop's orders. . . . The Archbishop gave him a cordial reception, and when he understood that he wished to change to Salamanca, said that in Salamanca he also had a college and friends, all of which he placed at his disposal, and gave orders that four gold crowns be given him as he left. (Vita 60–63)

Iñigo's mission in Alcalá was finished. He had ten days to obtain new clothes, and he was forbidden under pain of excommunication to do any teaching or preaching. He and his companions turned toward Salamanca.

THE ALUMBRADOS

The issue of possible relations with alumbrados was to resurface at various points in Ignatius' career and he was always at pains to dissociate himself from them.[10] But the matter was not so simple. Study of the archives of the Inquisition in Madrid shows that of the forty or so names connected with Ignatius at Alcalá, several seem to have had connections with the illuminist movement during those same years. Perhaps one of the most significant was Diego de Eguia, who had early on befriended Iñigo and provided him with generous alms. He would later join Ignatius in Venice and become a devoted member of the Society of Jesus. His brother Miguel, a printer for the University of Alcalá, was tried by the Inquisition of Toledo for Lutheran and illuminist heresies in the 1530s. Diego is mentioned in several trials of illuminists as a friend and associate of many of the leaders of the movement. Whether Iñigo knew that so many of his adherents were associated with members of the alumbrados remains an open question. Certainly it seems safe to conclude that among the illuminati a number must have found something attractive in the spiritual teaching of the pilgrim. The Inquisitors would surely have been interested in these associations (Longhurst 1957; de Vries 1971). The ecstasies and fainting spells among Iñigo's female adherents[11] may also have contributed to their suspicions. Iñigo's lack of learning and the fact that he drew his teaching from his own experience, not from books, was also an issue since the illuminists relied on their experience of the Spirit speaking within them rather than on the reading of scripture or theology (de Vries 1971).

SALAMANCA

The University of Salamanca was then at the height of its glory as one of the leading centers of learning in Europe, with many distinguished professors. The four companions went on ahead and took lodgings in an inn. Iñigo joined them in July 1527. Since Salamanca was outside the jurisdiction of the archbishop of Toledo, Iñigo and his companions set about teaching catechism to the children and preaching to their elders.

The timing of Iñigo's adventure in Salamanca could not have been worse. Violent arguments over the teachings of Erasmus and the doctrines of northern humanism had engulfed the city. The Inquisition was at that very time holding sessions in Salamanca to deal with these aberrations. The companions arrived without causing a stir, but the calm lasted less than two weeks. Iñigo tells us the story:

In Salamanca he confessed at St. Stephen's to a friar of St. Dominic. One day, after he had been there some ten or twelve days, his confessor said to him: "The fathers of the house would like to talk with you." "In God's name," he answered.

"Well, then," said the confessor, "it would be good for you to come and have dinner with us on Sunday. But I warn you of one thing: they will ask you many questions." On Sunday he came with Calixto, and after dinner, the subprior, in the absence of the prior, together with the confessor, and I think another friar, went with them to a chapel where the subprior[12] began pleasantly enough to tell him what good reports he had heard of his life and practices—that he went about preaching like the apostles, and that he would be glad to know something more in detail of what he had heard. He began by asking him what studies he had made, and the pilgrim answered: "Of us all, it is I who have studied the most." He then gave him a clear account of the little he had studied and the poor foundation he had.

"Well, then, what is it you preach?" "We do not preach," replied the pilgrim, "but we speak familiarly of spiritual things with a few, as one does after dinner, with those who invite us." "But," asked the friar, "what are the things of God you speak about; that is what we should like to know." "We speak," answered the pilgrim, "sometimes of one virtue, sometimes of another, to praise it; sometimes of one vice, sometimes of another, to condemn it." "You are not educated," observed the friar, "and you speak of virtues and vices? No one can speak of these things except in two ways, either because he has studied, or through the Holy Spirit. You have not studied; therefore, you speak through the Holy Spirit." The pilgrim kept cool at this, as this method of arguing did not meet with his approval. After a moment's silence, he said that there was no need of going further into the matter. But the friar was urgent. "Even now, when there are so many errors of Erasmus about, and of others which have misled the world, you don't want to explain what you mean?"

"Father, I will not say more than what I have said, unless it be before my superiors who can oblige me to." Before this the friar has asked why Calixto had dressed as he did. He wore a short cloak, a broad hat on his head and carried a pilgrim's staff in his hand, and shoes that reached halfway up his leg. As he was very tall it made him appear deformed. The pilgrim related that they had been jailed in Alcalá, and had been commanded to dress as students. The hat he wore because of the excessive heat had been given to him by a poor priest. Here the friar said as though through clenched teeth, "Charitas incipit a se ipsa"—Charity begins at home. But coming back to our story, the subprior being able to get no further word from the pilgrim, said: "Well, remain here; we can easily see to it that you tell us all." The friars themselves departed with considerable haste. The pilgrim first asked whether they should remain there in the chapel, or whether they would prefer some other place. The superior told them to remain in the chapel. Straightaway the friars saw to the locking of all the doors, and they opened negotiations, it seemed, with the judges. The two of them were meanwhile three days in the monastery without a word being said to them of justice. They took their meals with the friars in their refectory. Their room was nearly always full of friars who came to see them, and the pilgrims talked to them about the things they usually talked about. The result was that there was something of a difference of opinion among them, many showing themselves well disposed towards them.

At the end of three days a notary came and took them off to jail. They were not confined below with evildoers, but in a higher room, which because it was old and unoccupied was very dirty. They put them both in chains, attached to the foot of each of them, the chain then being fastened to a post in the middle of the building. The chain was from ten to thirteen palms long, so that when one wished to move anywhere the other had to go along with him. All that night they lay awake. The next day when news of their imprisonment got abroad in the city, people sent to the prison what they both needed for proper sleeping, and supplied all their needs abundantly. Many kept coming to see them, and the pilgrim continued his practice of speaking of God and so forth. The Bachelor Frías came to examine them separately, and the pilgrim turned over to him all his papers, which were the Exercises, for examination. He asked them whether they had any companions, and he told them yes, and where they were, and they went after them at once, at the bidding of the Bachelor, and brought in Cáceres and Arteaga, but left Juanico, who later became a friar. But they did not place them above with the two, but below with the common criminals. Here too he preferred not to have a lawyer or attorney.

A few days later, they were summoned before four judges, the three doctors Sanctisidoro, Paravinhas, and Frías, and the fourth the Bachelor Frías.[13] By this time they had all seen the Exercises. They put many questions to him, not only about the Exercises, but on theology; for example, on the Trinity and the Blessed Sacrament, asking in what sense he understood these articles. First he made a short introduction, but being commanded by the judges to go on, he spoke in such a way that they had no fault to find. The Bachelor Frías, who in similar circumstances had always shown himself to be more severe than the others, proposed something that had to do with canon law. He was required to give an answer to all questions, and did so by always saying that he did not know what the doctors said about such things. Then they bade him explain the first commandment as he usually explained it. He began to do so and continued at such length and said so much about the first commandment that they had no desire to ask him more. Before this, however, when they were talking of the Exercises, they insisted much on one point alone which is at the beginning of the Exercises, and concerns when a thought may be a venial sin and when it may be mortal. Their difficulty was that he, being without training, should determine a point like that. He answered that they should determine whether the answer were correct or not. If it were not correct, condemn it. The end of it all was that they went off without having condemned anything.

Among the many who came to the prison to talk to him, there was a certain Don Francisco de Mendoza, who is now Cardinal of Burgos. He came with the Bachelor Frías, and to his question as to how he felt in prison and whether he found the time heavy on his hands, he answered: "I will answer you as I answered a woman today who spoke words of compassion at seeing me a prisoner. I told her: 'In this you show that you do not desire to be a prisoner for the love of God. Why does prison seem so great an evil to you? I will tell you that there are not bars enough or chains enough in Salamanca but I would desire more for God's love.' " It happened at this time that the prisoners of the jail made their escape; but not the two companions who were there confined. When they were found there in the morning with the doors wide open, and the jail empty of prisoners, the fact gave edification to all and caused a good deal of talk in the city. As a result, they were given for prison an entire palace which stood nearby.

After being in prison for twenty-two days they were called to hear their sentence. No error was found either in their life or in their teaching, and so they were allowed to continue as they had been doing, teaching catechism and speaking of the things of God, provided that they never defined what was mortal and what was venial sin, until they had studied four years longer. When the sentence was read, the judges gave signs of great affection, as though they wished to see it accepted. The pilgrim said that he would do all that the sentence required of him, but that he would not accept it, because without condemning him on any point, they closed his mouth to prevent his helping his neighbor in what he could. No matter how much the Doctor Frías, who showed great friendliness, urged the matter, the pilgrim said that as long as he was in the jurisdiction of Salamanca he would do as the sentence bade him. They were at once released from custody. But after commending the matter to God, he began to think of what his course would be. He found great difficulty in remaining in Salamanca, because this prohibition against defining mortal and venial sin seemed to close the door to his helping souls. (Vita 64–70)

Clearly the shadow of the alumbrados had once again fallen across Iñigo's path. The prior's questioning had as its major focus to determine whether the preaching of this unusual group was based on learning or on divine illumination. Iñigo managed to avoid the trap, but once again he was faced with the familiar verdict—there was nothing heretical in his spiritual teaching, but he was forbidden to teach without obtaining further credentials. If he was to carry on his mission, he would have to obtain a degree in theology. But where, and how?

ON TO PARIS

The best place to study theology was the University of Paris. But it would be difficult for a Spaniard, given the hostilities between the French and the Spanish and the recent history of wars and bloodshed. At the same time, Iñigo was in a quandary:

When the pilgrim was debating in Barcelona as to whether he should study and how far, his whole object was whether after he had studied he should enter religion, or whether he should go on as he had been going through the world. When thoughts of entering religion came to him, the desire also came of entering an Order that had become relaxed and was in need of reform. He thought that he would thus have more to suffer, and at the same time God would perhaps come to their help, and give him likewise a deep confidence which would enable him to bear patiently the contumely and the insults that would be heaped upon him. Well, all through the time of his incarceration at Salamanca, he was never without the same desires of helping souls, and to study to this end and to gather together a few who felt as he did and hold those he had gathered. Once he had made up his mind to go to Paris, he agreed with them that they would wait for him where they were, while he would go and see whether there was some way in which they could all carry on their studies.

Many important persons did what they could to keep him from

going, but they could get nowhere with him. Before they were fifteen or twenty days out of prison, he left by himself, taking a few books along on a donkey. When he arrived at Barcelona, all who knew him tried to dissuade him from passing over to France because of hostilities. They recounted many instances of atrocities, even going so far as to say that the French roasted Spaniards on spits. But he saw no reason for being afraid. (Vita 71–72)

So in September 1527 Iñigo made his way toward Paris. His route took him past Montserrat to Barcelona, a distance of over five-hundred-fifty miles. Laconic as always about worldly matters, he tells us little about the trip, but in view of his deformed leg, the long journey, like others before and after, must have been torture. But we hear not a word from him. He stayed in Barcelona about ten weeks, visiting friends who had helped him in his efforts—especially Inés Pascual, who had been like a mother to him. He had to listen again to all the warnings about a Spaniard's trying his luck in the midst of hostile Frenchmen, but to no avail. When he finally took his leave, Inés and her son Juan accompanied him a few miles along the road and then bid him a tearful farewell. The pilgrim set his determined face toward Paris.

In all these adventures, we are struck by the wily skill, the diplomacy, and the unbending determination Iñigo displayed. We can see reflections of the old courtier and diplomat in his dealings with the Inquisition. His stance is respectful and dutiful, but not yielding in his conviction or independence. When the verdict is against him he bows to the voice of authority, but his obedience extends no further than the nearest limits of its jurisdiction. Even with powerful ecclesiastical figures, he is deferential, but only to a point—beyond that he defends his position and belief with as much vigor as on the battlements of Pamplona. This Iñigo was his own man, determined on his own course, and stubbornly defying anyone, friend or foe, powerful or humble, who might stand in his way. Was it his own proud, narcissistically invested spirit that drove him on, as the psychoanalyst might think, or was it the guiding spirit of his Lord, whom he sought so determinedly to serve and follow?

PARIS

IX

Iñigo made the long journey from Barcelona to Paris, nearly seven hundred miles, on foot, arriving on 2 February 1528. He wrote Inés Pascual, "Favoured by the weather and in perfect health, by the grace and goodness of God our Lord, I arrived in this city of Paris, where I shall continue my studies until it please the Lord to ordain otherwise, on the second day of February" (Epistolae I, 74; also in Rahner, 1960, p. 180).

The University of Paris that Iñigo entered was a far cry from the institutions he had known in Spain. The Sorbonne was older, larger, and more international in composition and flavor. It was the center of theology in Europe, embracing close to sixty colleges, grouped into four "nations." The Spaniards, despite the political situation of the time, were included in the "Nation of France." In 1528, the university was torn not only by the continuing struggle between the French and Spanish for hegemony of Europe but by the conflicts engendered by the Reformation. Luther had already been condemned by Leo X in 1520; the Diet of Worms, which marked his definitive rupture with the church, was in 1521; and by 1525 his heretical works were available in Paris.

Iñigo decided to return to the study of grammar, and so matriculated at the Collège de Montaigue, where he remained for about a year. Montaigue was a grim place—Rabelais' considered opinion was that galley slaves and imprisoned murderers had a better lot than the poor students of Montaigue.[1] But Iñigo, the noble courtier and man of arms, submitted himself at the age of thirty-seven to these inhumane conditions. His circumstances were not improved by his giving all the money he had to an impoverished Spaniard, who then absconded with it. He recalled:

> On his arrival at Paris he was given twenty-five scudi by a merchant on a draft from Barcelona. This he gave for safekeeping to one of the Spaniards at that inn, who went through it in a short time, and had nothing with which to pay him back. Thus when Lent was over and the pilgrim had no money left, he himself having met his expenses

and the other having spent it as already narrated, he was reduced to begging, and had to leave the house in which he had been living.

He was taken in at the hospital of St. James, just beyond the church of the Innocents. This caused great inconvenience with his studies, because the hospital was a long distance from Montagu, and it was necessary to be home at the stroke of the Ave Maria to find the doors open, and not to leave in the morning before daylight. This made it difficult for him to be present at his lectures. There was another handicap: he had to beg alms to support himself. It was now some five years since he had had any stomach pains, and he began to undertake greater penances and abstinences. (Vita 73–74)

He had to find some solution that would allow him to survive and also apply himself to his studies. "Spending some time in this hospital and beggar's life, and seeing that he was making little advance in his studies, he began to think about what he ought to do. Noticing that there were some who served other regents in the colleges, and still had time for study, he decided to look for an employer" (Vita 74). But the search was unsuccessful. Finally one of the Spanish friars advised him to try his luck in Flanders. A number of wealthy Spanish merchants lived there, and in the space of two months he could easily collect enough alms to support himself for the rest of the year. The idea appealed to Iñigo. In Bruges he found his way to the door of Gonzalvo de Aguilera, a Christian gentleman of considerable means. Iñigo repeated this pilgrimage from 1528 until 1530. He also had the good fortune to find a generous benefactor in Antwerp, the Spanish merchant Juan de Cuellar, who began sending him regular bank drafts so that he would not have to continue his arduous journeys seeking money. Iñigo even made his way to London in 1531, where he reaped a rich harvest.[2] In effect, from 1531 on, Iñigo was on a secure footing financially, even to the point of being able to render assistance to other poor students.

VIVES

Polanco adds a tantalizing detail to Iñigo's visit to Bruges. He was invited to dine at the home of the celebrated Spanish humanist and reformer Juan Luis Vives. In his studies, Iñigo may well have had the opportunity to peruse Vives' *Exercitatio Latinae Linguae,* a book of

Latin dialogues written for schoolboys. In his own day, Vives had sat at the benches in Montaigue, where he had had to endure the table reading of Jacopone de Voragine's *Legenda Aurea*—one of the books that had been instrumental in Iñigo's conversion during his convalescence at Loyola. Whatever Iñigo's passion for the *Legenda*, Vives did not think much of it and treated its hagiographic excesses with disdain. The dinner must not have been altogether an exchange of charming pleasantries. Polanco tells us:

> I must not omit to mention that when Ignatius was in Bruges he was invited to dinner by Luis Vives. Others also were present on the occasion and, it being Lent, the conversation came round to the subject of Lenten fare. Luis appeared to think that it was not much of a mortification because the foods permitted could be quite tasty and appetizing, especially if spices were used in their preparation as is commonly done in Flanders. Ignatius, thinking that such a way of speaking went counter to the Church's traditions, took up Luis Vives with spirit. "You and others," he said, "who can dine sumptuously will not, perhaps, find in this abstinence much help towards the end intended by the Church, but men and women in general, whose interests the Church must primarily consult, are not so nicely fed but that they have in the law of abstinence an opportunity of chastising the body and performing a work of penance." He came out with many other arguments to the same effect. As for Luis Vives, he considered Ignatius to be a saintly man and one likely to be the founder of some religious order, as his intimate friend Dr. Maluenda afterwards related. But Ignatius himself, not at all liking Luis' view as unfavorable to the Church's laws of fasting and abstinence, began to have doubts about the spirit that moved him, and subsequently forbade the reading of his books in our Society, even those that contained nothing objectionable, in the same way as he forbade the reading of Erasmus (FN I, 466).[3]

SAINTE BARBE

Iñigo entered into his studies with determination in the fall of 1529. The helter-skelter approach of the earlier days was replaced by serious and systematically organized study. He returned to the school benches to learn the basics of Latin with boys of nine and ten, and he kept at that task until the autumn of 1529. That October he was able to enroll in the Collège de Sainte Barbe and pay his own way. The director was a Portuguese, Diego de Gouvea. The college had a reputation for strict discipline, opposition to humanistic innovations, and the high quality of its professors.

Iñigo's determination to follow through on his plan and to seek his Master's service involved considerable sacrifice and a spartan discipline. There were also important compromises. He began to realize that his effort to lead a beggar's life did not allow him to properly engage in the work before him. Something had to give, and the course of learning he had set himself was of greater moment and implication than the exercise of Christ-like poverty. Studying required adequate nourishment, sufficient sleep, warm clothing, and reasonably comfortable quarters. The fanaticism of this dogged pilgrim was capable, after all, of yielding in the face of expediency and practicality.

If it seems that Iñigo's devotion to his studies left no room for the exercise of his spiritual ministry, apparently the work for the good of souls did not in fact abate to any great degree. He took every opportunity for spiritual conversation and for giving the Spiritual Exercises to a select few. Three students in particular responded to his inspiration—Pedro de Peralta, studying for his Masters, Juan Castro, then teaching at the Sorbonne, and Amador de Elduayén, a Guipúzcoan like Iñigo, who was also a student at Sainte Barbe. Their enthusiastic following in the pilgrim's footsteps—giving away their possessions, begging, ministering to the poor, and so on—created a considerable stir.

Suspicions and accusations were heaped on the pilgrim's head for diverting these respectable students from their responsibilities in the university. Some of these difficulties were stirred up by Iñigo's vision of establishing a group that would devote itself to the service of Christ. The first companions were the small group he gathered around him in Alcalá, who followed him to Salamanca where they continued their charitable efforts together. He tried to keep in contact with them, but fate drew them apart. He therefore began to seek out new companions who might join him on his mission. The sight of these men giving all their possessions to the poor and begging in the streets offended the Spanish students, who came in force to set things straight. Apparently an agreement was reached that averted serious harm, but the incident did not pass unnoticed. Gouvea accused Iñigo of unduly influencing the young student Amador, turning him into a "madman," and "made up his mind, so he said, that the first time the pilgrim appeared at Sainte Barbe he would give him a drubbing as a seducer of the students" (Vita 78). As it turned out, Iñigo was not chastised but was actually praised publicly to the assembled students—not without, one would guess, Iñigo's agreement to exercise his mission with more moderation (FN II, 383–384; Dudon 1949; Ravier 1987).

Actually Iñigo would not have cut a very impressive figure at this time. Aged about forty, he was a former man of arms who had been forced out of service by his war wound, which left him with a deformed leg and a noticeable limp. His life after his unceremonious discharge had been that of a derelict and beggar. His plans were hardly decisive or specific, he seemed to have little ambition for a career in any worldly sense, and his drift seemed to be toward the priesthood but nothing more. He was desperately poor, not physically strong, and often sickly, troubled by recurrent abdominal pains. Moreover, he had been brought before the Inquisition on several occasions as well as having been the object of suspicion and even persecution by university authorities. Not someone to excite the enthusiasm of devoted followers, one would think!

TURNING THE OTHER CHEEK

In the midst of all this, Iñigo carried on his saintly ways. You may remember the wayward Spaniard who had made off with Iñigo's money when he first came to Paris. Iñigo not only turns the other cheek but finds a way to repay evil with good.

The Spaniard whom he had as one of his first companions, who had squandered his money without recompensing him, left for Spain by way of Rouen. While awaiting passage at Rouen, he fell sick. From a letter, the pilgrim heard of his falling sick and conceived the desire of going to visit and help him, thinking also that in this union of souls, he might induce him to leave the world and give himself entirely to the service of God.

In order to obtain this he wanted to make the twenty-eight leagues between Paris and Rouen barefoot and fasting from food and drink. While he was recommending this adventure in prayer, he was seized with a great fear, until he went to the church of St. Dominic and there determined to go as was said, when all the fear of tempting God passed away.

But on the next day, the morning of his departure, as he was getting up early, he was seized with so great a fear that he could hardly get his clothes on. In this conflict of emotion he left the house and indeed the city before daybreak. It continued with him as far as Argenteuil, which is a walled town a few miles from Paris on the way to Rouen, where the vesture of our Lord is said to be preserved. He passed by this town in the grip of that spiritual struggle, and as he began to climb a hill the dread began to slip from him and in its place came so great a joy and spiritual consolation, that he began to cry out through the fields and to talk with God. That night he spent with a poor beggar in a hospital, after having covered fourteen leagues. The next night he spent in a straw hut, and the third day he reached Rouen. All this time he had taken nothing in the way of food or drink and had walked barefoot, as he had planned. At Rouen he comforted the sick man, helped him board a ship bound for Spain, and gave him letters of introduction to his companions at Salamanca, viz., Calixto, Cáceres and Arteaga. (Vita 79)

The mention of the old companions makes us wonder about their fates. Iñigo had remained in correspondence with them after leaving Salamanca. Young Reynalde had become a friar even before Iñigo had left. Iñigo tried to arrange for Calixto to join him in Paris. Through the good offices of Doña Leonora de Mascarenhas, he tried to arrange for a royal scholarship for him to study in Paris. Doña Leonora gave Calixto a mule and money to make application at the Portuguese court. Instead he shipped out to the West Indies or Mexico, where he made his fortune, finally settling in Salamanca a rich man. Cáceres settled in Segovia, his native city, where he seems to have led a dissolute life—quite different from his time with the pilgrim. Arteaga seems to have had a more respectable career but came to an unfortunate end. "Having fallen ill, he happened to have two glasses of water for his refreshment in his room. One of the glasses contained water which the doctor had ordered, the other a corrosive sublimate, very poisonous, which being given him by mistake ended his life" (Vita 80). Without the inspiring presence of the pilgrim, these first companions seem to have cooled their fervor and turned to more worldly paths. The initial attempt to form a group of like-minded workers for the Lord as well as the first efforts in Paris came to naught.

Iñigo's description of the mission to Rouen sparks the psychoanalyst's curiosity. He describes a series of relatively intense emotional states: the fears and dread give way to joy and consolation. The psychoanalyst would suspect some underlying conflict that was expressing itself in these symptoms, and Iñigo himself refers to a spiritual struggle. Wilkens (1978), following Ribadeneyra's lead (FN IV, 762–764), focuses on the conflict of motives that prompted him to undertake this difficult apostolic journey. Was his impulse to assist the wayward thief born out of the pure love of God or was it some form of revenge in the guise of doing good? The fellow had played a dirty trick on Iñigo, leaving him without any money. The pre-Pamplona Iñigo might well have pursued the villain and made him pay for his crime. Even after Pamplona, after all, this warrior-knight was ready to go after a hapless Moor for speaking ill of our Lady. To the possibility that this was an instance of aggression wearing the mask of mercy, Ribadeneyra, of course, would answer with a resounding no; the psychoanalyst would reply quite possibly yes.

I suggest that the basic conflict here is between the murderous and vengeful wishes that reflect aggressive and narcissistic aspects of Iñigo's character and the more spiritual motives that counsel forgiveness, mercy, and charity. Iñigo could not easily resolve these contending urges. The situation was compounded by the physiological imbalance of his lack of food and drink. Why were such severe penances called for—was it to redress the impulses to angry retaliation welling up within him, triggering a paroxysm of guilt? Perhaps. The visit to the church of St. Dominic would have tipped the balance in favor of the more Christian virtues, but the conflict was renewed when he awoke the next day. The return of spiritual joy and consolation, which may have signaled resolution of his conflict, took place in the confines of Argenteuil, the location of the holy vesture with its associations to the suffering Christ. He was able to reconnect with the humility and tolerance of suffering and outrage of the crucified Christ and so might have renewed his commitment to these virtues. The conflict is overcome and the aggressive and vengeful impulses defended against by a reconfirmed identification with the humiliated, suffering, and forgiving Christ. The crisis is resolved by consolidation and reinforcement of the ego ideal that provided the guiding spirit of Iñigo's religious life—a kind of manic defense in the interest of regaining narcissistic equilibrium. So Ribadeneyra was not far from the mark—he simply omitted the conflict that helps us to understand the obvious symptoms.

CONFLICTS AND SYMPTOMS

No sooner had Iñigo returned to Paris than he found himself once more in trouble with the Inquisition. The issue was again his dealings with Peralta and Castro. Diego de Gouveia, the principal of the college, had threatened to subject Iñigo to the *sala* ("the hall"), a humiliating procedure in which the culprit was stripped to the waist and flogged in the presence of the assembled students of the college. But Iñigo, by this time an old hand at this game, went directly to the Inquisitor, one Master Matthew Ory, a Dominican friar. He presented his case and urged the good friar to get the whole business over with so that he could get on with his studies. The Inquisitor had little to say except that he had been told about Iñigo's activities, and that was that (Dalmases 1985).

Iñigo wanted to keep his band of followers together while he continued his study, but almost immediately the old temptation of Barcelona reasserted itself: his spiritual devotions and thoughts were so distracting that they interfered with his study. The Ignatian solution is now familiar—a conversation with his professor and a promise to stay the course:

> Just as he began the lectures of his course, so also began once more the same temptations that beset him when he studied grammar in Barcelona. Whenever he attended lectures he could not, for the multitude of spiritual ideas that came upon him, fix his attention upon the lecture. Seeing that he was thus making little headway in his studies, he went to his teacher and gave his word that he would not fail to attend the whole course, if only he could find enough bread and water to keep himself alive.
>
> After making this promise, all these devotions which were so untimely ceased and he went on with his studies in peace. (Vita 82)

Iñigo's language is that of the spiritual rhetoric of his day; the psychoanalyst would speak of conflicts rather than temptations. What conflicts might be embedded here? We have seen that Iñigo seemed to have difficulties whenever anything drew him away from the idealized path of almost literal imitation of the impoverished life of Christ. The relative indulgence of traveling on a ship to the Holy Land, having money to buy food and anything but the humblest of clothing were sources of discomfort and anxiety for him. They seemed to him to violate his commitment to serve Christ. The prospect of giving up his penitential and ascetic practices had not yet been accepted and integrated with his sense of mission and commitment. As before, he seems unable to resolve the conflict without an appeal to an external authority who can give him permission to contradict his vow to follow in his Master's footsteps. Why is this a matter of conflict? Perhaps because the attributes of the proud hidalgo, with his flair for fine clothing and stylish living, were still alive within him; these impulses and desires remained troubling sources of "temptation" and required unrelenting suppression and chastisement.

The *Autobiography* recounts another example of symptom formation from this period. Iñigo recalled:

> In the meantime, while they were talking, a friar approached Doctor Fragus[4] to ask him to be good enough to help him find a house, because in that in which he lodged there had been many deaths which it was thought had been caused by the plague, because at that time the plague had begun to spread in Paris. Doctor Fragus and the pilgrim wanted to visit that house under the guidance of a woman who was very skilled in diagnosing the disease. She went into the house and said that it was plague-stricken. The pilgrim also entered, found a sick man there, comforted him, laying his hand on the man's sore. After a few words of comfort and encouragement, he left by himself. His hand began to pain, and he thought that he had caught the plague. So strong did this fancy become that he could not control it, and he ended by thrusting his hand into his mouth, moving his fingers about, and telling himself: "If you have the plague in your hand, you'll also have it in your mouth." This done his imagination quieted down and the pain in his hand left him.
>
> But when he returned to the College of Sainte Barbe where he had lodgings and where he attended lectures, the inmates would not allow him to enter when they learned that he had gone into the

plague-ridden house, and fled from him. He was thus obliged to spend several days outside. (Vita 83–84)

The episode is of considerable psychological interest. It reminds us that the plague—in one form or another, not always bubonic—had devastated Europe for the preceding several centuries and persisted until well into the eighteenth century—we remember that Mozart may have been a victim. So the diagnosis of plague was enough to strike terror in the heart of any man or woman of the time. This particular plague had begun about 1531 and reached its peak in the summer of 1533, when institutions closed and many fled the city. The pilgrim's motives were born out of his deep sense of charity and the wish to imitate his Lord and Master's ministry to the sick. The pain in his hand seems to represent an example of hysterical symptomatology, some unresolved bit of psychic conflict displaced to the body and expressed as a physical symptom. Common examples are hysterical paralyses reflecting an underlying conflict about performing some act or actions, or hysterical blindness based on a conflict about looking at something or things—or even conflicts about acting or seeing as such. What might have been Iñigo's unresolved conflict that found expression through this physical symptom?

The account conveys a sense of his capacity for psychological observation: he realizes that his imagination has gotten the better of him, but his manner of dealing with his conflict and anxiety borders on the self-destructive. If his imagination was correct—namely, that he had contracted the plague by touching the victim—his action would seem suicidal. The dominant motive must have been fear—that was, after all, the common reaction of his fellow students, who would not even let him back in the college. But fear was a despicable emotion for the one-time hidalgo. Was this not the Iñigo who stood on the ramparts of Pamplona and courageously faced the overwhelming force of the French when everyone around him counseled surrender? The counterphobic defensive capacity was part of his psychological makeup, and was apparently again called into play in the face of his underlying fear and vulnerability.

Iñigo's apostolic efforts continued apace. Besides the three Spaniards, he gathered other students around him. They met on Sundays at the Carthusian convent, where they went to confession, received communion, and conversed at length about spiritual subjects. But these meetings conflicted with the weekly disputations at the college, where attendance was lagging, so Master Peña cautioned Iñigo not to continue his divisive practice. The warning did not have its intended effect, so Peña took the case to the principal of Sainte Barbe, the same Gouveia who had previously threatened Iñigo with the odious sala. Once again he decided on the same punishment. When Iñigo got word of this, he confronted Gouveia and explained the problem. When the time came for the punishment to be exacted, to the surprise and edification of all, the principal fell to his knees at Iñigo's feet and begged his pardon. The relationship between them remained warm and cordial for many years (Dalmases 1985).

MASTER IGNATIUS

In the meantime, he carried on his work as a student. His matriculation at Sainte Barbe in the fall of 1529 marked a step forward in his intellectual progression. He began the study of scholastic philosophy under the direction of Peña, immersing himself in the study of Aristotle and the commentators for the next few years. He received his bachelor's degree in January 1532. In this connection his name appears for the first time in the records of the University Rectorate as "Ignatius of Loyola." The Paris experience had transformed Iñigo into Ignatius. On 13 March 1533, after a rigorous examination, he received the licentiate in philosophy, and finally after a lengthy delay was vested with the degree of master of philosophy in March 1535. The parchment placed in his hand read: "Our dear and worthy Master Ignatius de Loyola from the diocese of Pamplona has passed searching examinations and merited the degree of Master in the world-famed Faculty of Arts of Paris with distinction and honour. In witness whereto we have affixed our great seal to this parchment." Iñigo was now once and for all Master Ignatius.

His continual mortification, fasting, and failure to eat properly had an increasingly deleterious effect on his system. "Every two weeks he had stomach pains which lasted a good hour and brought on a fever. Once the pains lasted some sixteen or seventeen hours. By this time, however, he had finished the course in philosophy, and had studied theology for several years and gathered about him a number of companions. From then on the ailment continued to increase, and all the remedies they tried proved unavailing" (Vita 84).[5] It may have been poor health but possibly also his financial situation that forced him to postpone taking the degree. The expenses for testimonial letters, gifts, and banquets involved in the licentiate had wiped out his funds. He was forced to borrow and beg. He wrote to Inés Pascual that he was "at the end of his rope" and asked if she could mobilize his benefactresses in Barcelona to come to his aid (Dudon 1949).

SAVING SOULS

With his master's degree out of the way, Ignatius could devote himself with renewed energy to his apostolic efforts. During the period of intense study, he had more or less refrained from these endeavors, with the result that people left him alone. One day Dr. Fragus remarked on how peaceful life had become for the pilgrim; Iñigo replied, "It is because I do not speak to anyone of the things of God, but once the course is finished the old life will return" (Vita 82).

He would go to great lengths to recall wayward souls to the path of virtue. One account tells of a student who was carrying on with a prostitute. All Ignatius' appeals and arguments went for naught, so he devised a dramatic strategy. He knew that the fellow would pass over a certain bridge on his way to meet his lady. One winter night Iñigo waited by the bridge until the man approached, then waded into the icy water up to his neck. As the sinner made his way across the bridge, a voice from the depths cried out: "Go, unhappy man, and enjoy your filthy pleasures, while I stay here doing penance for you, if perchance I may avert from you the just vengeance of God." The poor student fled in shame—and, as the story goes, reformed his way of life from then on (FN II, 356).[6]

Another tale tells of a priest whose corrupt way of life was a great scandal. Ignatius tried every means of persuasion but without effect. Then one Sunday morning, Ignatius boldly walked in, found the man in bed, and begged that he hear his confession. Resenting the intrusion, the priest acquiesced, and Ignatius knelt by the bed and tearfully poured out the tale of his youthful sins and the worldliness of the first thirty years of his life. The priest was so moved that he repented, reformed his life, and afterwards became a distinguished member of the Society of Jesus.

And again, there was the game of billiards. This had to do with a certain doctor of theology whom Ignatius had targeted for a better life. He found the doctor one day playing billiards. Challenged to a game, Ignatius answered that he had never played but would take up the challenge on one condition: if he lost he would put himself at the doctor's disposal to do whatever he wished for a period of thirty days, and if he won the doctor would be obliged to do the same for him. With a laugh the doctor took up his cue, but the wily Basque began to play like a demon—as though he never did anything else in his life, as one witness recalled. Ignatius won hands down, and the doctor was required to make the Spiritual Exercises.[7]

By the time Ignatius took his master's degree, he was already at work on theology with the Dominican fathers of the Rue Saint-Jacques, an establishment known since the Middle Ages for training future teachers of theology. In the few preceding years, the *Summa* of the great Dominican Thomas Aquinas had come to replace the older *Sentences* of Peter Lombard as the cornerstone of theological study. Ignatius continued some eighteen months in this effort and was forced to interrupt it without benefit of a degree in theology. However, the years in Paris, from 1528 to 1535, were a period of intense learning and spiritual development. Laynez, who knew him well during this time, recalled: "Although he was faced with more obstacles to study than others, nevertheless he applied himself with such diligence, that he profited, ceteris paribus, as much and more than his contemporaries, as can be seen from his public examinations and from his disputes with his fellow-students" (Scripta I, 139; cited in Dudon, 1949, p. 145).

COMPANIONS IN CHRIST

When Iñigo entered the College of Sainte Barbe, he moved into crowded quarters with three others. The oldest was his teacher, Juan de Peña, then a professor in the college; the others were Peter Faber, a Savoyard, and Francis Xavier, a Navarrese, who had roomed together for several years.[8] Faber had already passed his exams for the licentiate, and Xavier had taken a doctor's biretta and was then Regent of Philosophy in the College of Beauvais. As soon as Iñigo moved in, it was agreed that Xavier would serve as his tutor in philosophy, but most of the work fell to Faber, who soon came under the charismatic influence of the pilgrim. Faber was uncertain about his future career, at times even thinking of joining a monastery. Finally, early in 1534, Iñigo persuaded him to make the Spiritual Exercises. The month of prayer, penance, and spiritual reflection turned the mild, gentle Savoyard into a saint.

Xavier—proud and ambitious—was another matter. His was a mixture that Iñigo could well understand. Xavier was born to a noble family, and dreams of greatness had not escaped him even after his family's resources were decimated in the wars of Navarre. Xavier hoped to become a famous professor, perhaps a counselor of princes as his father had been, even perhaps restoring the kingdom of Navarre. Dreams of glory—even a touch grandiose perhaps. In 1533, two recent graduates of the University of Alcalá arrived in Paris, Diego Laynez and Alfonso Salmerón.[9] They had known Iñigo at Alcalá and contacted him almost as soon as they had arrived. They too became companions and promptly followed Faber in the Spiritual Exercises. Soon after, a young student from León, Nicólas Bobadilla, who had studied at Vallodolid and Alcalá, joined the group and went through the Spiritual Exercises.[10] The last of the companions in Paris was Simón Rodriguez, who had come to Paris on one of the royal scholarships from John III of Portugal in 1527.[11] He also lived at Sainte Barbe and probably joined the group soon after Laynez and Salmerón.

Under Ignatius' guidance in the course of the Spiritual Exercises, each of them arrived at a common resolution—to consecrate themselves to the service of God and to labor for the salvation of souls. The dream that had burned brightly in the heart of Iñigo all these years was beginning to come to fruition. Uppermost in his mind was the wish to minister to unbelievers, but most particularly to return to Palestine and to dedicate himself there to the conversion of the infidel. During 1534, the companions debated their options and decided that when their studies were completed, they would vow themselves to evangelical poverty, chastity, and to labor for the kingdom of God in Jerusalem. If this last prospect proved impossible, they would put themselves at the disposal of the Supreme Pontiff to determine their destiny. They had no thought at the time of founding a religious order, even of forming a stable group.

They determined to take these vows on the Feast of the Assumption. They met on the morning of 15 August 1534, in the little chapel dedicated to the martyrdom of St. Denis on Montmartre. Faber, who had been ordained that May, celebrated the Mass, and the other six companions pronounced their vows and received communion. Their hearts were full of joy and determination. From this point on they began to live a sort of common life together, and they resolved to renew their vows on the same feast day as long as they were together in Paris. In 1535, after Ignatius' departure, they were joined by Claude Le Jay, a countryman of Faber, and in 1536 by Paschase Broet and Jean Codure (Dalmases 1985).12

OLD GHOSTS

As these developments were taking place, Ignatius was having more difficulties with his health, particularly the stomach pains. More drastic remedies seemed to be required. The doctors urged a change of climate, perhaps some of his native air. He agreed to return to Azpeitia to try to regain his health and in the course of the journey bring some news of his Spanish companions to their families. But an old ghost rose up to haunt him once again:

> This was the year 1535, and according to their agreement the companions were to leave Paris in 1537, the feast of the Conversion of St. Paul (January 25th). But because of the war, they were forced to anticipate that date, and left in November of 1536. But just as he was about to leave, the pilgrim heard that an accusation had been lodged against him with the Inquisitor, and a process begun. Knowing this, and seeing that he had not been summoned, he went in person to the Inquisitor and told him what he had learned, that he was about to leave for Spain, and that he had associates. For this reason he asked him to pass sentence. The Inquisitor said that it was true there had been an accusation, but that he did not see that there was anything of importance in it. He only wanted to see what he had written in the Exercises. When he saw them, he praised them highly, and asked the pilgrim to leave him a copy. This he did. Nevertheless, the pilgrim insisted that his case be brought to trial and that sentence be passed. But, as the Inquisitor seemed unwilling to do this, the pilgrim brought a public notary and witnesses to the Inquisitor's house and received formal testimony of the whole affair. (Vita 86)

In the shifting currents of the Reformation, the Inquisition was alert to the least suspicion of heresy.13 Ignatius' Spiritual Exercises were a convenient target. The pattern of events is by this time familiar. The old accusations were undoubtedly brought against him, and this time the pilgrim responded in much the same fashion as he dealt with similar situations once before in Paris and before that in Salamanca. On this occasion, however, he demanded that the favorable judgment of the Inquisitor be formally notarized in the presence of witnesses. He hoped that the charges and suspicions that had dogged his heels could be laid to rest once and for all.

FROM IÑIGO TO IGNATIUS

I noted the first appearance of the name "Ignatius" on his master's diploma, but the shift from the usual "Iñigo" deserves some comment. In the official register of the University of Paris for 1535, the name of the new Master of Arts is listed as "Dominus Ignatius de Loyola, dioecesis Pampilonensis." The first time he signed this name was in August 1537, in a letter to Pietro Contarini in Venice.[14] The final salutation reads "Tuus in Domino frater, Ignatius." For the next few years, until 1542, he signed letters in Spanish "Iñigo" and those in Latin "Ignatius." After 1542, "Ignatius" becomes the prevailing usage, and "Iñigo" disappears (Dalmases 1985).[15]

This gradual evolution in name may have reflected a humanist trend to latinize names, although Ignatius was not really the proper translation of Iñigo. Brodrick (1956) conjectures that the selection of the name Ignatius may have had to do with Iñigo's devotion to the great martyr saint of the second century, Ignatius of Antioch. Iñigo was undoubtedly deeply impressed by the heroic tale of the great saint that he read in the Golden Legend, while convalescing at Loyola from his wounds. He subsequently developed a deep devotion to the martyr-saint; he wrote to Francis Borgia, Duke of Gandia, who had fallen ill on the saint's feast day:

> As to your lordship's recent illness, I learned from a letter received at the same time of your recovery. I find, therefore, no occasion for regret. I should rather rejoice, I think, supposing that the experience has not been without some spiritual benefit. But seeing that this visitation and profit began on the feast day of the glorious St. Ignatius, I find more reason for rejoicing in our Lord, under the persuasion that your lordship will grow in devotion to the name of this blessed

saint, to whom I have, or at least wish that I had, a very special reverence and devotion in our Lord. (Epistolae I, 529; translated in Young, 1959, Letter 176, p. 138)

We can imagine that somewhere in the heart of Ignatius there burned a deep desire to emulate the courageous martyr and serve his crucified Lord, even in martyrdom. The fanatical quality of this devotion was evident—for example, when the fear of death by plague forced him to plunge the suspect hand into his mouth. The same fanatical drive forced him to leap to the parapet of Pamplona to meet the oncoming cannonball. The name Ignatius was overburdened with implication and motivation. Iñigo was the name that carried with it all the burdens of the past, of family ties and traditions, of sinful lusts and murderous rages, of vainglory, ambition, the intrigues of courts and the heroism of battle. It was a name born of the world. Ignatius had a different ring to it—a ring of devotion, saintly dedication, self-sacrifice of heroic proportions, and a new and glorious mission of the service of Christ. Perhaps behind the change in names lies the meditation on the two kingdoms from the Exercises. Assuming the name Ignatius meant fashioning a new identity, the identity of the dedicated follower of Christ, the courageous warrior of God who will face all dangers, count no sacrifice too great, no challenge too daunting, no battle too difficult, in order that the kingdom of God be extended to embrace the whole world and bring all men within its fold. The shift in names reflects the transformation of Iñigo de Loyola into Ignatius of Rome.

In the beginning of April 1535, Ignatius yielded to the urging of his companions and doctors and set off for Spain. They bought a small horse to ease his journey. Leaving the band of brothers in Faber's charge, Ignatius turned toward the Basque country where his pilgrimage had begun. The plan was for the rest of the group to leave Paris in January 1537, meet Ignatius in Venice, and from there embark for Jerusalem.

AZPEITIA

X

I gnatius covered the five-hundred-fifty miles from Paris to Azpeitia in a month. After crossing the border of Guipúzcoa, he took the back roads rather than the royal highway. He was resolved to avoid his ancestral home and take up residence in the local hospital like a poor beggar. As luck would have it, he was recognized by a former soldier from his command at Navarre, who scurried to the castle of Loyola with the news. As Ignatius made his way toward the hospital, he ran into a pair of armed men who had been sent to find him by his brother Martín García. The priests of the parish, undoubtedly commissioned by Martín, met him soon after and tried to persuade him to come to Loyola, but to no avail. He kept on his way, now attended by this retinue, until he reached the little Hospital of the Magdalena, located outside the town, on the evening of 30 April 1535.

For the first time since he had mounted his mule and turned his back on the castle of Loyola in 1522, Ignatius cast his eyes on the country of his birth. He had distanced himself from his family and had had no communication with them for fully a decade. Apparently, after all the years of silence, Martín García, who had by then become the lord of Loyola, located him in Paris and wrote to find out what had befallen him. We do not have Martín's letter, but it seems to have contained a series of questions reproaching Ignatius for his abandonment of his family. Martín seems also to have sought Ignatius' advice about his son's education. We do have Ignatius' reply, which deals with questions of situating his nephew at Paris in a business-like fashion. He then delivers a sermon justifying his divinely inspired mission and turns to lecturing his brother on the responsibilities of a man of wealth to use his resources for the benefit of the poor and needy for the love of Christ.[1]

The tone of this letter is cold and distant. Could there have been some latent ambivalence in the youngest son, who had been disinherited or, more properly, had disinherited himself, toward the older brother who had assumed the place of the father? Was this another reflection of that penitential superego whose religious fervor allowed no room for affection or sentimental attachment to any but a divine object? Is it reasonable to infer that the pull of attachment and loyalty was still too strong to allow any weakening of the defenses against them? We know by now Ignatius' capacity for the use of reaction formation—the agere contra of the *Spiritual Exercises*.

Certainly in later years, when Ignatius had established himself in Rome as General of the Society, his attitude toward his family seems to have softened somewhat—as is attested by the only other letter he wrote to his brother, a letter that Martín never saw since he died in 1538, a year before it was written. There were only three other letters addressed to the house of Loyola—two (in 1540 and 1542) to his nephew, who took Martín's place as the master of Loyola (Epistolae I, 165–167, 188–190), and one to his sister Magdalena in 1541 (Epistolae I, 170–171).

We can wonder with what mixed emotions the master of Paris approached the little town and the rolling hills he had known as a child and the forbidding walls of the castle of Loyola where he had grown up, suffered the pain of his wounded leg and recuperation, and experienced the powerful emotions of his religious conversion. As he drew closer to the place where he had begun both his earthly life and his life with God, whatever he felt must have moved him deeply.

APOSTOLIC WORK

Once he had established himself in the hospital, he quickly turned his attention to the work of converting sinners and spreading God's kingdom. He became for a time the Apostle of Azpeitia (Dalmases 1985). He tells us: "In this hospital he began to talk on divine things with many who came there to visit him, and by God's grace gathered no little fruit. As soon as he arrived, he made up his mind to teach the catechism daily to the children. But his brother made strenuous objection to this, declaring that nobody would come. The pilgrim answered that one would be enough. But after he began, many came faithfully to hear him, even his brother" (Vita 88).

Apparently his routine was much the same as the one he had followed previously in his apostolic efforts. He lived in the hospital, begged food and alms at the doors of relatives and neighbors, and carried his gains back to the hospital to feed and clothe the poor and sick. Martín García must have been appalled at the sight of one of his noble house behaving in such fashion. But he was no match for Ignatius—all his pleading and arguing fell on deaf ears. Whatever Martín's objections, we can guess that Ignatius must have sensed a hunger in his countrymen for his sort of fervent preaching and teaching of the faith. Even Martín must have recognized that something significant was happening.

But there was more to his mission. He found obvious abuses that cried out for reform. As he recalled:

> For example, regarding gambling, he saw to it that regulations were made and enforced by those who were responsible for the administration of justice. There was also another abuse. In that country young girls went bareheaded and never wore anything on their heads until after they were married.[2] But there were many who became concubines of priests and other men, and remained faithful to them as though they were their wives. This became so common that these mistresses had not the least shame in saying that they had covered their heads for so and so, and they were commonly known and acknowledged as such.
>
> This custom gave rise to many evils. The pilgrim persuaded the governor to make a law that all those who had covered their heads for anyone but their lawful husbands, should be publicly punished. Thus a beginning was made in the removal of this abuse. He saw to it that some provision was officially and regularly made for the poor, and that the bells were rung thrice in the day, at the time of the angelus, morning, noon and evening, and that the people should pray as they do in Rome. (Vita 88–89)

Ignatius must have been an object of curiosity for the citizens of Azpeitia—the youngest son of the great house of Loyola, the hero of Pamplona, who had gone off mysteriously to be a beggar and holy man and who now returned, a master of the University of Paris, but living a life of abject poverty in the hospital, begging in the streets, and preaching the word of God like a prophet. If curiosity brought them to look and hear, something more profound captured their hearts and drew them back. The little chapel of the hospital was soon too small to hold them all, so Ignatius preached in the open air. On Sundays and feast days he ascended the pulpit in the parish church. On one occasion, there was such a crowd that he was forced to climb a plum tree so that he could be seen and heard.

His zeal was inexhaustible; he spared himself no pain or trouble to bring the word of God to any who would listen. He preached endlessly and was always available to all who came to see him seeking help, advice, or counsel. The word spread quickly that there was a saint at the Hospital of the Magdalena in Azpeitia, and they flooded the little monastery—climbing walls and trees, crowding into every corner of the monastery garden to hear the words of the man of God. And after the sermons, many came to him privately to finish the work of reconciliation.

In attacking the problem of the concubines, Ignatius combined the zeal of his preaching with action, enlisting the help of the town corregidor, the chief administrator. Despite the long-standing nature of the practice, they found an old ordinance issued by Ferdinand and Isabella in 1484 that had set up strict censures of fines and banishment for these offenses. But Ignatius sought more than observance of the law; he strove for conversion in the depths of the soul. He preached daily on the commandments, especially against impurity and blasphemy. Several women of scandalous reputation were converted. Some went on a pilgrimage of penance to Rome. He made every effort to bring the wayward bachelors who carried on these practices back to the path of virtue and a new life (Dudon 1949; Brieskorn 1980).

FAMILY SCANDALS

Matters closer to his own family also required attention. At the time of his departure from Loyola in 1522, Ignatius had persuaded his brother Martín to make a peaceful settlement between the rector of the parish church and the convent of the Isabelitas. The issue involved the rights of the Loyolas as patrons of the convent, which had been hotly contested by the rector, Juan de Anchieta. The controversy had even broken out in armed conflict which resulted in the death of the rector's nephew.[3] The convent had been founded in 1497 by one of Ignatius' cousins, María López de Emparán, but it was in difficulty from its inception. Since it was so close to the parish church, jurisdictional disputes arose between the parish clergy and the church patron on one side and the nuns of the convent of the Immaculate Conception (the "Isabelitas") on the other (Brieskorn 1980).

Some of the events had been scandalous. Anchieta, a celebrated court musician before he became pastor of the little church, had specified in his will that he be buried in the convent church. At his death on 30 July 1523, Andrés de Loyola, Ignatius' nephew, and the rest of the clergy seized the body to bury it in the parish rather than in the convent. At Ignatius' urging, Martín García decided to put an end to this shameful affair. Some of the Loyolas had actually taken the case to Rome to be tried before the Rota, the ecclesiastical court, but apparently had used false assertions to deceive the Rota and gain a verdict in their favor. Subsequent efforts at reconciliation had come to naught.

Even before Ignatius' arrival, Martín García had drawn up a peace plan and had ordered his representative in Rome to stop all juridical action. Ignatius may or may not have had a hand in these negotiations, but soon after his arrival he could add his signature to the official document that put an end to a bitter quarrel that had lasted over thirty years. On 18 May 1535, all the clergy and religious of Azpeitia gathered with Martín García, Ignatius, and the local notary to sign the agreement that set the conditions governing the monastery chapel. The agreement received apostolic confirmation by Paul III in 1539. For the religious and people of Azpeitia it was a "blessed day" (Dudon, 1949, pp. 163–164; Dalmases, 1985, pp. 133–134; Brieskorn 1980).

OTHER WORKS OF REFORM

On other fronts, Ignatius helped to settle a quarrel between the local clergy and the poor Franciscan nuns; he dealt with abuses of gambling and begging; he formally renounced his inheritance and rights to the ancestral estate of the Loyolas and persuaded Martín García to use it as an endowment for the local church, and he persuaded the clergy to ring the bells of the parish church and the hermitages every day at morning, noon, and evening as a reminder for those in mortal sin to repent.

Ignatius continued to live as a beggar at the hospital and carried on his work for the poor. He persisted in his penitential practices. Witnesses recalled his fasting, the hairshirt he wore at all times, the metal chain with sharp points with which he girded himself, the lacerations and festering wounds on his shoulders from the self-inflicted scourgings. All his endeavors, tirelessly pursued, along with the relentless austerities, took their toll. We know only that he had to be hospitalized and that his illness was severe enough to incapacitate him for several weeks.

In addition, Ignatius turned his zeal toward reformation of the clergy, who had wandered from the paths of virtue. Ignatius' father, Beltrán, had set up benefices for the local clergy, but in later years the competition for these benefices had grown intense. With such assured support, the holders seemed gradually to fall away from the conduct demanded of their state. When the town council, under the leadership of Martín García, took remedial action, it came to light that Anchieta and his successor as rector, Ignatius' brother Pero López, had been living scandalously. The benefices included tithes and stole fees, which were divided among the recipients. There were also fourteen chaplains who had no support but the alms they received in return for their ministries. Unfortunately their greed outstripped their zeal for souls. They were lax in their duties, often could not be found when needed, rarely if ever preached, and almost never recited the canonical hours. They were largely indifferent to religious matters and spent their time in idle pursuits and various vices.

Ignatius would hardly tolerate this state of affairs. During his illness, he continued his efforts to reform the local clergy. The result was a pledge of the beneficiaries to divide the income from the stole fees equally between the beneficiaries and the chaplains. In the same year, 1535, a number of clerics confessed to the unjust possession of certain benefices. For example, Andrés de Loyola, admitted that he had retained an earlier benefice along with the rectorship of the parish and that he had not met his obligations under it. Andrés declared the benefice vacant and requested that his uncle Martín García dispose of it properly. Martín himself had abused his power as patron and by giving a benefice to his son Pérez de Loyola in 1527, a chaplaincy to his illegitimate son Gil de Oñaz in 1529 and another benefice to Oñaz in 1531. These and other transactions were undoubtedly targeted by Ignatius.

Ignatius had a significant impact and brought about genuine progress. In the canonization process of 1595, witnesses testified to his remarkable reform of the Azpcitian clergy, especially in moral matters. The notary Juan de Aquamendi left an account of his work in the register of the Hospital San Martín commemorating for posterity the extraordinary experience of this apostle and his effects on the people of Azpeitia:

"God, our Lord, has, therefore, shown the town of Azpeitia a great mercy, as well to the members of this family in giving them so great a man, and in giving to Himself such a servant of His Divine Goodness." Ignatius himself bears testimony to his concern for genuine reform in his letter to his nephew Beltrán on 20 September 1539, on Beltrán's becoming head of the house of Loyola. Ignatius wrote: "I am persuaded in God our Lord, that the Divine Majesty has preserved you to this day and has given you authority, principally to reform the clergy of Azpeitia and preserve peace among them. To do this will be to show them a genuine love, while to neglect it would be to love them unworthily and to do them harm. Once again, I beg of you for the love and reverence of God our Lord, give this matter your whole attention. Remember how often this was the subject of our conversations at the time of my visit to Azpeitia" (Epistolae I, 148–151; cited in Dudon, 1949, p. 169).

DEPARTURE

As soon as he recovered his strength, he decided that it was time to be on his way, "to accomplish the tasks laid upon him by his companions, and to set out without a penny. His brother took this very ill, as he was ashamed to see him thus traveling on foot and at evening. The pilgrim was willing to yield to him on this point, and ride a horse to the confines of the province accompanied by his brother and his relatives" (Vita 89). But he would allow his family to go no further. He refused all assistance, turned his back on Guipúzcoa, and took the road to Pamplona, on foot, penniless, and alone.

But he did not forget the good friends and neighbors of Azpeitia. Some years later, he wrote an almost affectionate letter to them from Rome, recalling his visit among them and the spiritual renewal they had experienced. He encouraged them to continue on the ways of spiritual profit and growth, especially the practice of frequent Communion.[4]

Ignatius' contacts with his family thereafter were, as I have suggested, sparse. Any sense of attachment or affection is distilled into additional spiritual wishes and prayers. In his final letter to his brother Martín, which arrived almost three months after Martín's death, Ignatius writes:

Happy they who in this life prepare themselves for the judgment and salvation by His Divine Majesty. For His love and reverence I beg of you not to put off setting your conscience aright. Your soul will thus be without uneasiness in that moment of extreme and ultimate need. My greetings and best wishes to all. Let all those who wish to have word of us and to benefit their consciences consider this letter as addressed to them. I close, asking God our Lord, by His infinite and supreme goodness to give us all His abundant grace to know His most holy will and perfectly to fulfill it.

Last Christmas Day, in the Church of St. Mary Major, in the chapel which preserves the manger in which the Child Jesus was laid, with His help and grace I said my first Mass. I earnestly desire and beg of you by the love and reverence of His Divine Majesty that we remember each other in our prayers. Let us not lose sight of the fact that we are at the very end of our days and about to give a strict account of our lives. (Epistolae I, 145–147 [Letter 19]; in Young, 1959, pp. 38–39)

Ignatius' subsequent letter to his nephew Beltrán, after urging him to persist in the reformation of the clergy, seeks the assistance of the new master of Loyola in the work of the Society.[5] The humble saint was not above pressuring his relatives or anyone else who could advance his cause.

We have only one other indication of the nature of Ignatius' relations with his family. Years later, in 1552, Ignatius had occasion to write to the duke of Nájera, Juan Esteban Manrique de Lara, at the request of his family to intercede on behalf of his niece Laurentia de Oñaz in favor of her proposed marriage to one of the duke's relatives. The marriage never came about, but it provided Ignatius with an opportunity to re-establish contact with a house with which he once had close ties: it was in the service of his father, the previous duke of Nájera that he had fought the French and suffered his shattering wound. Responding to a letter from the duke, he wrote:

Yesterday Don John de Guevara gave me a letter of yours dated January 22. I will not delay to excuse the want of care on my part in answering. It has been my practice, as it is with all those who have left the world for Christ our Lord, to forget as much as possible the things of the world in order to be more mindful of those of heaven, and to make all the less account of merely human courtesies as we make more of those things which pertain to God's service. But if an opportunity had offered itself of serving your lordship to God's glory, I would not have failed you, insofar as my poverty and my profession would allow, and would have shown you the affection which I owe to you personally and to the family of your lordship in return for the favors and affection by which your predecessors have laid me under obligation. So in my poor prayers, my only opportunity of serving you, I have commended you, and with God's grace will continue to commend, your lordship personally and all your affairs to God our Creator and Lord. May your lordship and all your house always experience His very special protection and grace, to the glory of His Divine Majesty.

Regarding the matter of the marriage of which your lordship writes, it is of such a nature and so alien to my least profession that I feel that any interference on my part would be out of place. It is in fact ten or eleven years since I have written to anyone in the house of Loyola. I felt that, once I had left home and the world for Christ, I should not in any way look upon it again as belonging to me. And yet, if your lordship thinks that it would be to God's greater glory that this union between the two houses take place, and that it will be for their good in view of the end we ought to desire, I think it would be proper to write to the lord of Ozaeta and to Martín García Loyola, my nephews, to have a conference with your lordship, and that you personally deal with them about the marriage. I believe that these two can speak for the family, as I have spoken to Don John at length about it. (Epistolae IV, 385–386 [Letter 2816]; in Young, 1959, pp. 266–267)

It is the old courtier who speaks here, with all the deference and courtly graces—the art of the vassal addressing his lord. He had not forgotten old habits and manners (Bertrand 1985). Yet, just as clearly, he had distanced himself from the house of Loyola. Ignatius had joined the family of Christ.

1. The manor house of Loyola, the lower portion in masonry from the end of the fourteenth century; the upper in brickwork from 1461. The exterior has remained unchanged. The building has a more or less square shape, with each side measuring roughly fifty feet.

2. Altar of the castle chapel at Loyola. In the center the Flemish picture of the Annunciation that had belonged to Queen Isabella. At right and left, Saints Catherine of Siena and Catherine of Alexandria. Above, a late Gothic Pietà.

3. The castle of Arévalo. Situated on a hill on the northern outskirts of the city, the castle was connected by a subterranean passage with the fortress church of St. Peter, which is no longer standing.

4. The old city walls of the fortress of Pamplona. Above the walls rises the Barbazana chapel, built by Bishop Arnauld de Barbazan after 1317. It belongs to the beautiful cloister that is attached to the cathedral.

5. The Infanta Catherina, painted by the Portuguese artist Carvalho, as St. Catherine. The painting is in the Prado, Madrid.

6. High above the monastery rise massive spires of rock, among which in Iñigo's time were twelve hermitages, almost impossible to reach. On the highest spire stood the hermitage of the good thief, Dismas, which Iñigo the pilgrim loved to visit.

7. The companions vow themselves to poverty and chastity in the little chapel of St. Denis on Montmartre. Faber celebrated the Mass and holds the host before Ignatius kneeling at his feet. Painting by K. Baumeister, Munich, 1881.

8. The vision of Ignatius at La Storta on the way to Rome. The painting is from the Collegium St. Michael, Freiburg. Christ says to Ignatius, "I will be propitious to you in Rome."

9. Drawings of Ignatius' first companions, from the Archivum Romanum Societatus Jesu, Rome. From left to right, first row: Laynez, Xavier, Faber; second row: Bobadilla, Rodriguez, Salmerón; third row: Broët, Codure, Le Jay; fourth row: de Hocez.

10. This seventeenth-century painting commemorating the approval of the Society by Pope Paul III hangs in the sacristy of the Gesù. It is "in memory of Pope Paul III."

11. Portrait of Ignatius by Jacopino del Conte, one of Ignatius' penitents who painted the portrait from the death mask on the day Ignatius died. Contemporaries were not satisfied with the result.

12. Portrait of Ignatius by Sánchez Coello, court painter to Philip II of Spain. Ribadeneyra commissioned the painting in 1583, again from death masks. The result seemed more satisfactory to those who had known Ignatius. The painting was destroyed during the Spanish Civil War.

13. The General's seal. The first three letters of the Holy Name, "I. H. S.," have, since Ignatius' time, been the seal and emblem of the Society of Jesus.

14. Ignatius at work on the Constitutions. The painting is by Jusepe de Ribera from around the time of Ignatius' beatification in 1609.

15. The Infanta Juana of Spain (1535–73), widow of the heir apparent of Portugal, regent of Spain. Portrait by Antonio Moro.

16. Margaret of Austria (1522–86), duchess of Parma, natural daughter of
Charles V. Portrait by Antonio Moro.

17. Eleanora de Medici (1517?–86), duchess of Florence and consort of Duke Cosimo I.

18. The death of Ignatius. This Spanish painting, probably by Carducho from the time of the beatification, hangs in the Farnese Chapel in Rome.

19. The death mask. The photograph is of the head, formed in plaster on the basis of the original wax mask. It is preserved in the Curia of the Society of Jesus in Rome.

20. This silver statue of Ignatius stands in the basilica at Loyola. It was modeled in Rome by the sculptor Francisco de Vergara the younger in 1741. Ignatius' finger points to the legend that was the guiding motif of his life—"Ad majorem Dei gloriam"—to the greater glory of God!

THE GENERAL

4

THE BAND OF BROTHERS

XI

Leaving Guipúzcoa behind, Ignatius turned to the next stage of his mission in Spain—to visit the families of his comrades in Paris and bring them news of their loved ones. His first goal was the house of Xavier in Navarre. This leg of his journey carried him past the walls of Pamplona, where fourteen years before the fatal cannonball had put an end to his military career. What thoughts and feelings must have crowded his mind as he made his way along that road!

But he could not tarry. He carried a letter from Francis Xavier to his family. The Xaviers had fallen on bad times because they had remained faithful to the French claimants to the throne of Navarre and so had not endeared themselves to Charles V. Ignatius must have been warmly received, but he was eager to continue his journey. After a brief rest he turned south to Almazan, bringing letters to the family of Laynez. Then he moved on to Siguenza, where he may have stopped to deliver a letter from Laynez to an old professor. Next, in Toledo, he contacted Salmerón's relatives. At each stop he was a welcome guest, and money for his journey and his mission was urged upon him. But he would accept nothing, holding firmly to his conviction that divine providence would take care of his needs.

Then he crossed the peninsula and made his way to Valencia, where he sought out Juan de Castro, the student he had counseled at Paris and who had been the occasion for the near riot at the College of Sainte Barbe. Castro had become a Carthusian, and Ignatius stayed with the good monks for eight days. His next objective was Genoa. The monks tried to dissuade him from this course, for the pirate Barbarossa was terrorizing the Mediterranean. Ignatius nevertheless boarded ship and, despite a heavy storm that almost wrecked the vessel, arrived in Genoa in mid-November.

If the sea had treated him roughly, apparently the dry land was no better. He recalls:

On his arrival in Genoa, he took the road to Bologna, along which he had much to suffer, especially once when he lost his way and began to walk along a river bank. The river was deep and the road high, getting narrower the higher it went.

Finally, it got so narrow that he could neither go forward nor turn back. So, he began to crawl on hands and knees and went on thus for some time with great fear, because every time he moved he thought that he would fall into the river.

This indeed was the greatest of all physical efforts he had ever made. But he reached the end at last. Just as he was about to enter Bologna he slipped from a little wooden bridge and found himself as he rose covered with mud and filth. The bystanders, of whom there were many, had a good laugh at him. (Vita 91)

He goes on to tell us: "From his entrance into Bologna he began to ask alms, but did not get even a single quatrino, although he covered the whole city. He stayed in Bologna some of the time ill, but afterwards went on to Venice using always the same method of travel" (Vita 91).

This brief account conceals more than it reveals. On his arrival in Bologna he made his way to the Spanish college at the University of Bologna, where he was welcomed and given warm clothes and a place to stay. He was eager to continue his theological education and hoped that he would be able to do so at the famous university among his younger countrymen in the Spanish college. It was the beginning of the scholastic year, and enough assistance had arrived from his friend Isabel Roser to make this project possible. But his health, weakened by so many austerities and privations, failed him. In mid-December, he fell ill, plagued by chills and fever and the return of the bedeviling abdominal pains. By the end of December, he had recovered sufficiently to make his way to Venice, where he would wait for his companions from Paris to join him for the projected journey to the Holy Land.

VENICE

He arrived in Venice at the end of 1535 and spent the whole of the following year alone. He devoted the time to theological study and to prayer, penances, and apostolic efforts, usually in the form of the Spiritual Exercises. His influence began to reach important circles. Some, however, like the Bachelor Diego de Hocez, were suspicious of Ignatius' teaching and thought it possibly heretical. This may have been the source of a number of Ignatius' future difficulties, but even Hocez finally yielded to the pilgrim's persuasions, made the Exercises, and became a devoted follower.[1]

The goodwill and generosity of his benefactors followed Ignatius to Venice and made life as comfortable as it ever had been. Isabel Roser sent twelve scudi with a promise of more to enable him to continue his work. He wrote to another benefactor, Jaime Cazador, an archdeacon and future bishop of Barcelona, "I have been living in great style in Venice for a month and a half now, very much improved in health and enjoying the company and the home of a learned and excellent man. Indeed, I think that nowhere else in this country could I find circumstances more favorable" (cited in Brodrick, 1956, p. 321). Cazador hoped that Ignatius would return to Barcelona to preach; Ignatius replied, "I should certainly like to do so when I have finished my studies, some time between the Lent of this year and the next. It is my hope not to let another year go by without bringing the word of God to Spain. And I shall begin with Barcelona, for there is no other place in the world to which I am so obliged and indebted" (cited in Dudon, 1949, p. 180). At this point in his career, theological learning took priority.

The "learned and excellent man" who served as Ignatius' host was probably Andrea Lippomani, the prior of La Sanctissima Trinita in Venice (Martini 1949). He provided the pilgrim with a comfortable place to stay, and the generosity of various other benefactors enabled Ignatius to gather a few essential books with which to continue his study. Lippomani very likely had a good theological library that he would have put at the pilgrim's disposal as well.

Once again, as at Alcalá, Salamanca, and Paris, suspicion fell on Ignatius' teaching and on the contents of the Exercises. He does not elaborate on this episode: "In Venice also another persecution was begun against the pilgrim. There were many who said that his likeness had been burned in Spain and in Paris. Matters came to such a pass that a trial was held and sentence rendered in favor of the pilgrim" (Vita 93). Little is known about these accusations or the trial. The opposition of Cardinal Gian Pietro Carafa—the former bishop of Chieti, founder of the Theatines, and later to be elected Pope Paul IV—may have been involved as a result of the anxieties and doubts of Hocez. Carafa became one of Ignatius' adversaries during his stay in Venice and later in Rome. The papal legate ordered an investigation which was duly carried out.

Whatever the accusations, a complete acquittal on all charges was pronounced by the pilgrim's friend Gaspard de Doctis on 13 October 1537
(Wilkens 1978; Tylenda 1985).

THE COMPANIONS

At the beginning of 1537, the original six companions, their number
augmented to nine by the addition of Claude Le Jay in 1535 and Paschase
Broet and Jean Codure in the following year, finally arrived in Venice.
They had planned to leave Paris at the beginning of 1538, but the erup-
tion of hostilities between Francis I and Charles V caused them to
accelerate their plans; they started out on 15 November 1536. The departure was fraught with great anxiety, and many advised them not to
go. Instead of heading south through France, since hostilities had
broken out in Provence and Savoy, they detoured through Lorraine and
Germany and across the Swiss Alps—a longer but safer route through
neutral territories. They sold their meager possessions and had just
enough to cover their expenses on the way to Venice.

Their safe arrival in Venice on 8 January 1537 was the occasion of great
joy for them all. Ignatius presented Diego de Hocez and the two Eguia
brothers as new recruits. After celebrating their reunion, they decided
to wait in Venice until travel to Jerusalem was possible, and in the
meantime to devote themselves to the needs of the poor and sick. Five
companions went to the Hospital of Sts. John and Paul, the other five to
the Hospital of the Incurables. Ignatius continued to live at Lippomani's
and spent much time in prayer and conversation with his companions.

One item on the agenda was to seek a blessing from the Pope for the
pilgrimage to Jerusalem. Ignatius tells us: "After two or three months
they all went to Rome to get the Pope's blessing before setting out on
their journey to Jerusalem. The pilgrim did not go with them, because of
Doctor Ortiz and the Theatine Cardinal [Carafa] who had just been
created" (Vita 93). The fact that Ignatius refrained from going to Rome
because of his difficulties with Carafa is telling and brings us back to
this persistent tension that plagued Ignatius in these early years.

A MISCALCULATION

The Theatines had been established in Rome in 1524 by the Venetian
Gaetano di Tiene. He and his followers performed such heroic works of

charity during the plague of 1524 that his portrait was installed at the main entrance of the Hospital of the Incurables. He and Ignatius may have crossed paths during Ignatius' stay in Venice, but this cannot be substantiated. They did finally meet in Rome in 1545. It is very likely that Ignatius and Carafa, Tiene's successor as prelate, had actually met in Venice during those years. According to Ribadeneyra, they were on familiar terms.

In any case, Ignatius wrote a letter to the Theatine prelate some time in 1536, prior to the arrival of his companions.[2] In his innocent zeal, Ignatius badly misjudged his man and made an unfortunate blunder. To begin with, Carafa hated Spaniards, probably because of the abuse he had suffered at the hands of Charles V's soldiery during the sack of Rome in 1527 and the abuse suffered by his family in the Barons' Revolt of 1528. Carafa had resigned his bishopric and dedicated himself to a life of evangelical poverty. Ignatius, concerned by what seemed to be the decline in fervor among the Theatines, wrote in a spirit of mingled frankness, sincerity, humility, and boldness that the aging cardinal must have received as impertinence, coming from an unknown upstart and a Spaniard at that. Ignatius wrote as the devout religious reformer. We recall that in his ruminations about what path of life to follow, one of his fantasies was to join some religious order badly in need of reform, so that he could bring the wayward religious back to the path of Christ. In the letter he urged Carafa to keep the bonds of his community intact, criticized Carafa for his elegant dress and comfortable lifestyle, setting a poor example for his followers, and finally chastised the bishop for the Theatine practice of accepting benefices and alms without committing themselves to any specific works for the benefit of souls. They did not beg, preach, or practice the corporal works of mercy—how could they expect any support from the faithful? The result was that some of their priests lacked the bare necessities of life.

Carafa, who was raised to the cardinalate shortly thereafter, in December 1536, was in his way a holy man, but stubborn, impetuous, rather rigid, and impatient with all opposition. Who was this impertinent Spaniard to set himself in judgment over *his* order? The rupture between the two men was clear, and the consequences would be felt later on in Rome (Dudon 1949; Bottereau 1975).

Despite Ignatius' attempts at humility and self-effacement, the letter must have offended the cardinal. Ignatius must have felt that one of the rules of the order was ill-suited to highly commercial Venice. The rule counseled the members of the order to possess nothing, not even to seek alms from the faithful or accept Mass stipends.[3] They could only accept freely offered donations. This was hardly a problem under Tiene, who encouraged preaching and works of charity. The faithful responded with generous appreciation. But under Carafa, who tended to be overbearing, ruthless in his austerities, and who forbade his subjects to preach or to perform the corporal works of mercy, support gradually diminished, with the result that the order fell into dire straits and the faithful were increasingly alienated. Ignatius, eager to see the valuable work of these holy men expanded, and probably also piqued by Carafa's apparent failure to do anything about it, must have felt disturbed by this state of affairs. For all his good intentions, Ignatius earned little but Carafa's hostility—and it was not opportune to have such a powerful figure, a future Pope, as an enemy (Brodrick 1956).

The tension between these two reformers has remained an enigma for historians.[4] Was Ignatius' letter, however imprudent and undiplomatic, really the cause? Carafa, born in 1476, was Ignatius' senior, and after the sack of Rome in 1527 had settled with his followers in Venice. He had been a cofounder with Tiene of the Theatines and served as their first superior. His program sought the reform of ecclesiastical authority and the hierarchy, strict discipline of the clergy, rigorous suppression of all heresy, and reform of religious orders. His memorial to Pope Clement VII recommended the creation of a new order under obedience to the Pope and charged with the defense of the Church against heretics. His view of religious life was archconservative, so that any new order would have to follow strictly traditional lines. Any religious who did not live in cloister would be excluded from pastoral activities.

The differences between Carafa and Ignatius in mind-set and approach are striking. But when Ignatius arrived in Venice in January 1536, he was no more than an itinerant cleric begging his bread in the streets of a city torn between supposed heretics and those who feared them. The shadow of the Inquisition fell heavily on Ignatius, and the usual suspicions surfaced again in Venice. This may have colored Carafa's view of Ignatius and his companions. The ill-begotten letter could hardly have improved Ignatius' relations with the cardinal and future Pope. Hocez may have played a role in stirring up Carafa's antagonism. He would have been in a position to relate to Carafa the rumors and suspicions that swirled around Ignatius and his companions. Hocez's decision to join Ignatius' Society would not, after all, have sat well with the Cardinal. Twenty years later, the cardinal and the General would have occasion to cross swords once again: Carafa obtained a papal indult for a noble Roman family to force their son out of the Jesuit novitiate, whereupon Ignatius secured the withdrawal of the indult.

TOWARD ROME

So during Lent of 1537 the band of brothers set out for Rome without their leader to seek the blessing of the Holy Father on their projected journey and ask his permission to receive holy orders. They arrived on Palm Sunday after a difficult journey and started their usual begging. Some wealthy Spaniards soon provided for them and arranged lodging at the Hospital of San Giacomo. Armed with letters from Ignatius, they sought out Dr. Pedro Ortiz, who was Charles V's proctor in Rome and had represented Catherine of Aragon's interests in the face of Henry VIII's efforts to gain a papal divorce. Ortiz, who had known Ignatius in Paris, gave them a cordial welcome and arranged an audience with Pope Paul III, who requested that they hold a theological discussion he and his other guests could listen to during dinner. The Iñiguists, as they were called, must have impressed him with their learning, for he responded by blessing their pilgrimage and presenting them with a gift of thirty-three gold crowns. Not to be outdone, the other dignitaries added the princely sum of one-hundred-fifty ducats. Further, the Pope granted them permission to be ordained without the payment of patrimony or benefice, wherever or whenever they wished, either on three successive feasts or Sundays. They could not have asked for more. They returned to Venice to share the good news with Ignatius (Dudon 1949; Ravier 1987).

At last, their hearts and minds turned toward Jerusalem. But fate and history were against them. Because Venice had allied with Charles V in the war against the Turks, no ship sailed for the East that year. According to the vow at Montmartre,[5] they had agreed on 8 January 1538 as a target date. If they had not found a way to the Holy Land by then, they were sworn to put themselves at the service of the Pope to fulfill whatever mission he might impose on them. So they remained at Venice, hoping against hope, working in the hospitals, and preparing themselves for ordination to the priesthood. They renewed their vows of perpetual poverty and chastity before the papal legate Geronimo Verallo and soon after, on June 10, received minor orders. The major orders followed: subdiaconate on June 15; diaconate on June 17; and holy orders on June 24.

The joy of these events was marred by the continuing uncertainty of their Jerusalem mission. As hopes dimmed, the companions decided to diversify their efforts. They broke up into groups of two or three, each going to a different town. Xavier and Salmerón went to Monselice; Le Jay and Rodriguez to Bassano; Broet and Bobadilla to Verona; and Hocez and Codure to Treviso. Ignatius recalls:

> It fell to the pilgrim to go with Faber and Laynez to Vicenza. There they found a house outside the city limits, which had neither door nor window, where they slept on a little straw they brought with them. Two of the three went twice daily to ask alms, and brought back so little that they could hardly subsist. Usually they ate a little toasted bread when they had it, prepared by the one whose lot it was to remain at home. In this manner they spent forty days intent on nothing but their prayers.
>
> After the forty days, Master John Codure arrived, and the four of them decided to preach. They went to four different piazzas on the same day and at the same hour, and began to preach, first by shouting out to the people and waving their hats at them. This style of preaching started a great deal of talk in the city; many were moved to devotion and supplied their physical needs with greater abundance. (Vita 94–95)

There the companions continued their life of prayer and penance, the rigors of which had put Xavier and Rodriguez in the hospital. For Ignatius, the time at the house, part of an abandoned monastery called San Pietro in Vivarolo, was a time of renewed graces and mystical experiences. He recalls: "While he was in Vicenza he had many supernatural visions and much ordinary consolation, just the opposite of what he experienced in Paris. These consolations were specially given while he was preparing for ordination in Venice and getting ready to say his first Mass" (Vita 95).[6] In all his journeys he had great supernatural visitations of the kind he used to have when he was at Manresa (Vita 95). His clairvoyance was at times striking: "While he was in Vicenza, he learned that one of his companions who was staying at Bassano [Rodriguez] was sick and at death's door. He himself at the time was ill with a fever. Nevertheless, he started off and walked so fast that Faber, his companion, could not keep up with him. In that journey he was given the certainty by God, and so told Faber, that the companion would not die of that illness. When the pilgrim arrived at Bassano, the sick man was much consoled and soon got well" (Vita 95).

THE COMPANY OF JESUS

After this period of prayer and penance, at about the beginning of September 1537, Ignatius called the companions together in Vincenza. Once reunited, they could celebrate their first masses together. All possibility of the Jerusalem trip had faded. By the end of 1536, the Turks had established themselves on the coast of Dalmatia, and the Pope was forced to begin constructing defenses for the Papal states. Paul III had committed himself by treaty to join forces with Charles V, and considerable effort was being expended to resolve the differences between Charles and the king of France so that they could ally themselves in the pending war against the sultan. There was even talk of a crusade. By 1537 matters had become more desperate. The Pope led public prayers and penances amid fears of an invasion. In July the Turks landed at Otranto and soon declared war on Venice and Corfu. In September the Venetian islands fell. By October Hungary was under siege, and the King of the Romans was defeated. The Holy League against the Crescent was formed and provided an unstable alliance against the threat from the East. Venice sent no pilgrim ship that year and the next; clearly it was no time for pilgrimages to the Holy Land (Dudon 1949).

The companions reached the conclusion that they had to separate once more. This time Ignatius, Laynez, and Faber would go to Rome, Codure and Hocez to Padua, Broet and Salmerón to Siena, Xavier and Bobadilla to Bologna, Le Jay and Rodriguez to Ferrara. Thus they invaded Italy to conquer it for Christ. And what were they to say when people asked them who they were? The answer came from Ignatius: "We shall answer that we are of the Company of Jesus." The band of brothers had become the Company of Jesus.

It was November 1537 when Ignatius and his companions made their way toward Rome.[7] A few miles outside the city walls, at the crossroads of La Storta, they entered a little shrine, and there Ignatius experienced one of the most powerful and influential mystical illuminations of his life. In a vision, he beheld the divine Father with Christ carrying his cross; both regarded him with love. The Father said to the Son, "I wish that Thou take him for Thy servant." Then Christ said to Ignatius, "I wish that you be My servant." The Father then added, "And I will be propitious to you at Rome." Ignatius had no idea of the meaning of this vision, which time and history were to reveal. He confided to Laynez his fear that they might be crucified at Rome, perhaps like the apostle Peter before him. I will discuss this profound experience later, in the context of his other mystical visions,[8] but without doubt this illumination must have filled the pilgrim's heart with joy, courage, and trepidation (Dudon 1949; Dalmases 1985).

As the companions entered the Eternal City, Catholic Europe was in turmoil and tension. Henry VIII had divorced Catherine of Aragon, married and executed Anne Boleyn, passed the Act of Supremacy, and removed Thomas More's head and beard. Spain and France were still at each other's throats, this time over the duchy of Milan. The Inquisition was established in Portugal. The Farnese Pope Paul III was on the papal throne. Germany was in the throes of the Lutheran revolt. Only a decade before, Rome had suffered the ignominy and horror of the sack by Charles' mercenaries, and the Pope himself had been held captive. Saint Peter's would not be completed for another half century. Michelangelo was still at work on the Sistine Chapel.

The Pope lost no time in putting the young theologians to work, assigning Laynez and Faber to teach in the College of Sapienza. The goodwill of Paul III was supplemented by Ignatius' own influence on important persons. Dr. Ortiz retired with Ignatius to make the Spiritual Exercises and emerged from the month-long retreat a transformed man; if age and position had not prevented him, he would very likely have joined the group of Iñiguists. He remained thereafter a powerful friend and protector. Others who made the Spiritual Exercises included Francis Estrada and Cardinal Gaspar Contarini. This favorable reception in Rome made it possible for the Iñiguists to assemble there at the end of Lent 1538 in a little house put at their disposal.

CONTROVERSY

In view of the surrounding political upheaval, the Pope had told Ignatius that Rome would have to be his Jerusalem. So the Iñiguists set to work, preaching, hearing confessions, and teaching catechism. As so often before in Ignatius' apostolic ministry, suspicions of heresy were raised and presented one of the fiercest trials Ignatius had yet to face. The monk Mainadri di Saluzzo had gained a considerable reputation as a preacher, and during Lent large crowds came to hear his sermons. The Iñiguists were increasingly disturbed by the rashness of his preaching and the theological errors he propounded. When their cautions to their friends and their efforts to get Saluzzo to correct his teaching accomplished nothing, they began to set matters straight in their own sermons. Saluzzo's supporters took offense at this and denounced Ignatius and his companions as heretics.

The difficulties were compounded by the activity of Miguel Landivar. Landivar had known the Iñiguists in Paris and had even sought to join them in Venice. His rejection by Ignatius had inflicted a bitter and deep narcissistic wound that left him yearning for revenge. He began to spread rumors around Rome to the effect that Ignatius was an escaped convict, a braggart, and a conniver and had formed his congregation without knowledge or support from the Holy See, and so on. As the calumnies mounted, the position of the Iñiguists became increasingly precarious. Even the dean of the Sacred College was suspicious of Ignatius. Something had to be done.

With evidence in hand, Ignatius went directly to the governor of Rome, who called Landivar to account. Landivar was convicted of falsehood and banished from the city. But Ignatius was not satisfied. He demanded that the Spanish priests who had been most vocal in their support of Saluzzo be confronted and their accusations challenged. When the priests appeared before the governor, they retracted their charges against Ignatius. Realizing the potential harm to his apostolic work from such allegations, Ignatius pressed on, demanding letters of approbation from the bishops in all dioceses where his men had worked. Then he sought an official declaration from Paul III. In a long interview at the papal villa at Frascati he reviewed his difficulties with the Inquisition and other false challenges to his mission at Alcalá, Salamanca, Paris, and Venice. The Pope evidently saw the importance of extending his protection to these struggling apostles, and he ordered the charges to be dropped and the whole affair brought to an end. Ignatius requested that a thorough investigation be made of his life and works: if anything was found out of order, he would correct it; if all was in order, should he not be supported by His Holiness?

Meanwhile, like ghosts from the past, many of Ignatius' former ac-
cusers happened to be in Rome and came forward to defend and support
him. Figueroa, the inquisitor at Alcalá, was there, along with Gaspard de
Doctis from Venice and Matthew Ory from Paris.[9] A number of bishops
sent letters of praise and support. When the governor, Conversini, finally gave his judgment, the outcome was beyond doubt. The official
pronouncement of 18 November 1538 declared the rumors and charges
against Ignatius and his men groundless and false and went further,
praising their teaching and good works, including official approbation of
the *Spiritual Exercises* (Dudon 1949).

THE BIRTH OF A RELIGIOUS ORDER

When they gathered at Easter 1539, Ignatius and his companions, according to Polanco, quite clearly "had no plan to form a congregation,
nor any other form of religious order, but they wanted to dedicate themselves to the service of God and to that of the Apostolic See, from the
moment that they discovered that they could not go to Jerusalem" (FN I,
204).[10] Quite possibly the idea arose from the Pope's suggestions that
they carry on their work in Italy and forget the Jerusalem plan. We know
how fervently and tenaciously Ignatius had held on to this hope, ever
since he had been forced to leave the Holy Land the first time. The idea
that Providence intended his apostolate to be in Italy would not have
been easy for him to accept.

The first intimations of the idea of establishing an order seem to come
from the deliberations of the companions during Lent of 1539, as the
minutes of their meetings attest. The issues were clear. First, if the Pope
was to send them on missions to various places—he had already commissioned two of their number to go to Siena—did this mean that their
group was to be broken up, or should they bind themselves together in
some form of common body or union? They resolved to form themselves into an official body, if it could be done with papal approval. Their
conclusion took the following form:

God in his mercy graciously willed to assemble and to unite us,
although we were weak and strangers to each other by virtue of na-
tionality and mind. It is not up to us to break up that which God has
united, but we must rather affirm and stabilize this unity by drawing

closer into a single body, each having responsibility and understanding of the other; for courage itself when it is concentrated has more vigor and strength to accomplish all sorts of good but difficult deeds than when it is divided. (cited in Ravier, 1987, p. 84)

The next question was more difficult—whether to bind themselves to a superior by a vow of obedience. Ignatius had served as a leader of sorts since they first joined forces in 1534. Should they now go further? Days of prayer and concerted discussion brought them gradually to realize that they would have to commit themselves to Rome, to the continuation of their apostolate, and would have to carry on these deliberations as best they could. After the eight difficult months it had taken to beat back the attacks of their calumniators, they could not now retreat from the battlefield.

After lengthy and careful deliberations, they finally agreed on 3 May 1539 that they should undertake a vow of obedience to the Pope; that they should place themselves under a religious superior;[11] that they should travel anywhere in the world the Pope sent them; that their mission should be to teach the commandments and Christian doctrine; that they had a special mission to teach catechism to children; and finally that the determination of the work of each one should be left to the superior. In the ensuing three months, other details of the new order were worked out and distilled into a formula to be submitted to the Pope for approval. This slender document, probably drawn up by Ignatius, has become known to history as the *Deliberatio primorum patrum*— the "Deliberation of the first fathers." It would become the basis of the "Formula of the Institute," which provides the essence of the Constitutions of the Jesuit order.[12]

One of the questions that has long been debated is the nature of Ignatius' role in these deliberations. Toner (1974, p. 180) puts the issue in these terms: "The question is this: Did Ignatius come to the deliberation intending to search along with the others, not yet knowing whether God's will was for the companions to take a vow of obedience and form a religious order; or did he come with an assured vision of where God was leading them, seeking to enlighten the others, not to search?" The second view would seem to have arisen from a more spiritualized hagiographic tradition in which Ignatius' footsteps would have been guided all along by the hand of the Lord; in this view, his mystical illuminations, especially the illumination at the Cardoner, would have included the mission to found the Society of Jesus.[13] The first position brings the process closer to human psychology. Toner, after careful study, concludes that there is no evidence to support the second view and that Ignatius seems to have been as much in the dark as to the outcome of the deliberations as any of his companions. At the same time, Ignatius was the acknowledged leader of this band of brothers, so it is likely that the others would have listened to his opinions with considerable respect (Orsy 1973).

The precious document was turned over to Cardinal Contarini for presentation to the Holy Father. After several months of careful examination, the formula was judged to be pious and holy and worthy of papal approval. With papal blessing, orders were given to prepare the bull of approbation. But the Roman Curia has always lived up to the best of bureaucratic ideals, and this instance was no exception: the process consumed the entire following year. Cardinal Ghinucci was asked to draw up the papal bull, but he had difficulty with some of its provisions— particularly the abolition of choir and the suppression of certain traditional mortifications, especially the lack of penances imposed by rule. To him they smelled of Lutheran corruptions. He also objected to the vow of obedience to the Pope as superfluous. The Pope was caught between the support of Contarini on the one side and the opposition of Ghinucci on the other. To resolve the dilemma, he appointed Bartolomeo Guidiccioni as judge. The choice was not propitious for the Iñiguists; Guidiccioni was an excellent man of intelligence and good judgment, but he was strongly opposed to the creation of any new religious orders. He was even on record as thinking that any existing orders beyond the Benedictines, Cistercians, Franciscans, and Dominicans should be eliminated.

Ignatius, not one to sit by passively, set to work to bring to bear every possible influence to impress Guidiccioni with the merits and good works of the companions. Testimonials and letters of approbation poured in from bishops, cardinals, and kings. But Guidiccioni was hard to budge. He could not deny the quality of the formula and the evident fruit of the apostolic labors of these men, but he concluded that solemn approbation from the Pope was not necessary and that they should be satisfied with mere verbal endorsement. He transmitted this conclusion to the Pope in February 1540.

Undaunted, Ignatius turned to prayer, trusting more in the influence of God than men. He promised that his companions would say three thousand masses directed to one goal: to change the attitude of Cardinal Guidiccioni. Ignatius had emblazoned in his mind and heart the promise of La Storta, "I will be propitious to you at Rome." Finally, the prayers were answered; Guidiccioni yielded. On March 22, Bobadilla could write that the influence of Cardinal d'Este had persuaded the Pope to act in their favor. But if the winds had shifted, the issue was still not resolved. The Pope appointed a commission to determine the matter once and for all. A compromise was reached: the number of the professed in the new order was to be limited to sixty. With this agreement, the bull *Regimini Militantis Ecclesiae* was signed by the Pope in the Palace of St. Mark on 27 September 1540. The new order had become a reality. The band of brothers had been transformed into the Society of Jesus (Dudon 1949; Ravier 1987).

ELECTION OF THE GENERAL

The members of the new order were charged with setting up rules governing their religious life. Ignatius, Laynez, Le Jay, Broet, Salmeron, and Codure began deliberations on 4 March 1541. The forty-nine points were drawn up by Ignatius and Codure, then discussed and approved by all. The weightiest matter was the election of the first General of the Society. The companions gathered toward the middle of Lent 1541 to resolve this issue. Bobadilla, Faber, Rodriguez, and Xavier could not be present and sent written ballots. After three days of prayers and reflection, a vote was taken and all the ballots sealed in a box. After an additional three days, the votes were examined. To no one's surprise, all the votes were cast for Ignatius. The date was 9 April 1541.

But Ignatius would not accept the decision. He protested that he preferred to obey rather than command, that his past sins precluded him from accepting the offer, that he who was unable to govern himself was not fit to govern others. He could accept only if it was absolutely clear that it was God's will that he do so. He begged them to reconsider the matter for four more days, beseeching our Lord to help them in making a better choice. The others yielded to his request and after four days of prayer voted again. The result was the same. Still unconvinced, Ignatius sought the help of his confessor, a Franciscan of the Observance,[14] Father Theodore. After three days of a painful review of his past life and a general confession, he begged Father Theodore for a decision. The good priest replied that to refuse the office of General would be to resist the grace of the Holy Spirit. Ignatius was shaken but still unconvinced. He asked the confessor to pray over the matter for three days and then put his opinion in writing. After three days, the letter arrived with the same verdict. Only then did Ignatius yield and accept the position, on April 20. The companions then agreed that on the Friday after Easter, they would make a pilgrimage to the seven churches of Rome and end by pronouncing their vows of religion at St. Paul Outside-the-Walls on 22 April 1542 (Ravier 1987).[15]

The picture of Ignatius that emerges from these events is reminiscent of the resourceful diplomat and man of action in the days before Pamplona. But we know that this side of him had never been lost, and that when circumstances required he could summon up those qualities to meet the challenge. This had been the case every time he had been under suspicion or had his mission or teachings questioned. In these situations he was no isolated, withdrawn ascetic but a man of action and resolve. He knew what he wanted and commandeered every resource to accomplish it. Whether the challenge came from vicious calumniators who sought to destroy his work and discredit him and his followers or from the Roman bureaucracy balking at the revolutionary and radical proposals contained in his concept of a new religious order, Ignatius was not the man to wait passively and acceptingly. The same spirit of courageous confrontation and of unwillingness to surrender that had flared on the battlements at Pamplona now carried the crusade to victorious conquest in Rome.

The religious viewpoint finds it easy to see the hand of God in all this—the promise of La Storta was being fulfilled. The psychologist and psychoanalyst remain somewhat more skeptical. To what extent and in what sense do these events reflect dynamic forces at work in the heart of Ignatius? To what extent do they reflect the realization of the wishes, hopes, desires, and ambitions of this intrepid hidalgo—the knight of God? Was it all part of his personal crusade rather than a divinely inspired and guided mission?

As he took the final steps on the path to Rome, he had much to fear. He had enemies in Rome—he had been afraid to appear there when his companions came seeking the Pope's approval for the projected trip to

Jerusalem. He even entertained fantasies of crucifixion. Perhaps the fears had something to do with his own hopes and ambitions, which at the same time drew him toward Rome. It was as though his whole career had been a preparation for his Roman mission, and yet he held back from it in trepidation. Had the vision at La Storta been a form of hallucinatory wish-fulfillment? Some of his anxieties may have found their way into the account he gave da Camara many years later:

> Arriving at Rome, he observed to his companions that he noticed that all the windows were closed, meaning by that that they would have to suffer many contradictions. He also said: "We must walk very carefully and hold no conversations with women, unless they are well known." What happened to Master Francis is very pertinent here. At Rome he heard a woman's confession and visited her occasionally to talk about her spiritual life. She was later found to be pregnant. But it pleased God that the responsible party was caught. The same thing happened to John Codure whose spiritual daughter was caught with a man. (Vita 97)

The process of the election of the General is psychologically interesting as well. As we watch Ignatius back off, delay, and maneuver to escape the apparent sentence passed on him by his brothers, were we watching an exercise in saintly humility, seeking every available means to escape any preferment, any recognition by his fellow men? Possibly. But might we also have been witnessing an exercise in conflict, ambivalence, or the struggle with narcissistic residues in the form of conflicts over ambition and omnipotence? In the vacuum of certainty, it falls to the theologian to propose the aspects of saintliness and humility permeated by grace. It falls to the psychoanalyst to play devil's advocate and propose the venal and psychologically meaningful aspects of the human drama of this peculiar behavior.

Might Ignatius have been ambivalent about assuming the role of General? There can be little doubt that the responsibility was potentially awesome, especially if the Society were to grow in numbers and influence. The General would inevitably become a powerful and important figure. Ignatius had surrendered his youthful ambitions of power and glory—or had he? As a young man, he had dreamed of conquest, military glory, fame, success. When those hopes were shattered at Pamplona, he had put in their place other dreams—this time of self-conquest, self-denial, and the glory of saintly sacrifice. It may be of no little significance that the office to which he had been elected was that of General—a military designation of a position of power and command. Was Ignatius torn between his denied and repressed wishes for power and influence on the one side and the desire for saintly self-denial and humble service on the other?

And what of the narcissism that seems to surface again and again in the character of Ignatius? He has told us many times that he continues to struggle with sinful and worldly desires. Perhaps the narcissistic wishes were too pervasive, too insistent. On the road to Rome, in an ecstasy of wish-fulfillment, God the Father and Christ the Son appeared to him in his hour of doubt and anxious fear, to reassure him that they would support and sustain him in Rome. What greater testimony to the fulfillment of his spiritual ego ideal? What better sign of divine favor and selection, the nearly unalloyed gratification of narcissistic impulses and desires, than to receive such divine favor? The narcissistic elements here are overpowering—sublimated, spiritualized, even transcendental—but narcissistic nonetheless. Could it be that the wish to be chosen as a spiritual hero, the vessel of divine grace and blessing, still occupied a corner of his soul? Were these the sinful and worldly inclinations that he struggled with throughout his life? Consideration of Ignatius' career as General may shed further light on these questions.

THE GENERAL

XII

Hardly had the ink on the papal documents dried and the crucial election of the General been accomplished when Ignatius and his companions moved into a little house near the church of Santa Maria della Strada. The house was small and dilapidated, but it provided space where they could carry on their apostolic works. The chapel and some additional houses were given to them, so that gradually the place evolved into the center of the Society of Jesus in Rome. It housed the little room where Ignatius was to live for the next fifteen years, where he organized and directed the Society, where he wrote the Constitutions, and where he was to die. The pilgrim had found a place to rest. "In fact," as Ravier puts it, Ignatius "would scarcely ever leave this place during the fifteen years of his generalship, but from the heart of his little room, he would follow the flight of his sons on the roads of the world, he would inspire them in their missionary zeal, sustain them in their battles. There, success and failure, sorrows and joys, good news and bad would blend; hundreds of companions would pass through there to be trained or to work" (1987, p. 11).

Ignatius became the director of an apostolic and intellectual venture that spanned the globe and involved him in details too numerous to count. The mission of the Society was to go to any corner of the world where the Vicar of Christ might send them. The house of La Strada became the headquarters for all the Society's endeavors, including the training of novices under the supervision of Ignatius.[1]

The original companions began to disperse. Bobadilla continued his missionary work in Italy and later in Germany. Faber went first to Germany and later to Spain. Le Jay replaced him in Germany. Xavier and Rodriguez were in Portugal waiting for passage to India, but the king, John III, wanted them to stay in Portugal to establish colleges. Ignatius brought the matter to the Pope for a decision, and the Pope deferred to the king. Ignatius then proposed a compromise: one would go, the other stay. The king agreed, so Xavier boarded ship for India and Rodriguez stayed in Portugal. Ignatius sent several groups to Paris in the vain hope of establishing a college of the Society there. The Pope ordered Broet and Salmerón as papal nuncios to Ireland—the ends of the earth. This prompted Ignatius' first instruction, one of many.[2]

GOVERNING

As the years passed, the work of the Society grew by leaps and bounds. Its efforts to establish missionary beachheads and colleges in all parts of the globe, and the dealings with the papal court, with kings, bishops, and nobility of all ranks, and with Christians of all walks of life and all levels of society reflected the scope and complexity of the mission (Bertrand 1985).

Ignatius became more and more absorbed in the details of governing this unwieldy organism. The training and spiritual direction of the novices demanded a great deal of his attention. Increasingly his efforts were taken up by the essential task of writing the Constitutions, which were to be the guiding norms for the Society and would form his legacy for generations to come.

It must have become clear, not only to Ignatius but to others, that the burden was too heavy and the task too complex for one man to handle. His health had not been robust for many years, and under the burdens of his office it grew worse. Something had to be done. In March 1547, Juan de Polanco was appointed secretary of the Society. Ignatius could not have made a better choice. Polanco turned out to be a superb administrator and organizer, and as secretary he remained unobtrusive but extremely effective. He was gifted with intelligence and sensitivity, a capacity for work, and a remarkable ability to understand the mind and heart of Ignatius, and to make his efforts complement those of Ignatius in an extraordinary and effective manner. They would work closely together until Ignatius' death.

Polanco immediately started reorganizing the vast correspondence that Ignatius carried on with companions throughout the world. The task took years to complete. Polanco classified the material required for the writing of the Constitutions. He also devoted his efforts to organizing archives for the Society; it was on this material that he based his own *Chronicón*, an invaluable account of the early years of the Society under Ignatius.

Polanco's assistance undoubtedly lifted much of the burden from Ignatius' shoulders. But the weight that remained was considerable. Ignatius had thoughts of resigning—he may have hinted as much in a letter to Laynez. His health would have been reason enough. But, all in all, his performance was extraordinary. Ravier (1987) comments:

> Ignatius' relationship with the entire Society was astonishing. Undoubtedly, because of distances and postal delays, certain things escaped him, but even in these cases he instinctively grasped the situation. One after the other he established the indispensable canonical structures—too slowly for the wishes of some people. He encouraged those responsible to provide better training of recruits and called some Fathers or Brothers to him in Rome to complete their first novitiate which had been too summary. He was concerned about the quality of obedience: as he had done with the companions in Paris, he tested the obedience of the companions in Rome upon the occasion of the upcoming departure of ten among them to Sicily; published several documents on perfect obedience; he stopped using almost contradictory variations in the exercise of his authority because he took into account the mental or physical health of individuals. Certain of his contemporaries were themselves disconcerted by this. (p. 144)

FATHER GENERAL

The more we come to know of Ignatius' work as General, the more remarkable is the picture we gain of his personality and character. He was beyond question charismatic—he attracted men to his cause and edified and inspired them. His character was Basque to the core—headstrong, obstinate, passionate, stern, taciturn, but even so, at times charming and playful. He was a man of great gifts and obvious limitations. He could be stern and demanding at one moment and kind and gracious at the next—and the transition was often abrupt, leaving his listeners confused and puzzled. As the Society grew, he was confronted by relationships with figures in political and ecclesiastical authority, by matters of finances, diplomacy, and difficult negotiations that called the skills of the old courtier into play in many ways. The whole was pervaded by his spiritual presence—his devotion, his single-mindedness to do God's work, his unfailing charity, and his almost total self-abnegation.[3]

Ignatius was revered as a saint by those around him, but his manner was simple and unpretentious. He wished to be called by his first name; in the house he was Iñigo. At table he chatted familiarly but ate sparingly and slowly, so as to finish with the others. He exercised special—almost maternal—concern for those who were ill or depressed. Despite the financial burden, he insisted on buying a villa in the country for the community's recreation. He seems to have been supportive and reassuring to his novices. To one young novice troubled by feelings of guilt and unworthiness, he recounted the sins of his youth, weeping all the while. He tailored the regimen to the individual needs of his subjects. One novice from a noble family found manual work in public humiliating, so Ignatius put him to work inside the house. Ribadeneyra, later to be his first biographer, impishly imitated the limp behind his back. Ignatius found out and told the miscreant to choose his own penance. The young wag suggested a day off for everyone in the house, and so it was. There was kindness and consideration along with obdurate severity.

His companions, to a man, remarked on his magnanimity, his spiritual goodness, and his persistence in important causes. Nadal particularly remarked on his "excelente grandeza de alma y una vehemente apetencia del honor y de la gloria," excellent greatness of soul and a vehement desire for honor and glory (FN II, 62; my translation). It seems that his companions were not blind to the narcissistic aspects of Ignatius' character. They were also deeply impressed by his self-possession and the prudent reflection in everything he did, seemingly regulating all his actions by the twin criteria of spiritual discernment (of which he had become a master) and the service of God (Nicolau 1957).

His unwavering determination, once he had decided on a course of action, was legendary. His fortitude and persistence in the face of adversity were accompanied by indomitable energy (Nicolau 1957). Ribadeneyra recalls one episode:

In November of the year 1552, Ignatius set out on a journey . . . On the morning of the day fixed for their departure, it was raining in torrents. Father Polanco said to Ignatius that it would perhaps be more advisable to put off their departure till the morrow, so that he might not come to harm because of the pouring rain. But our Father answered: 'We leave at once. For thirty years I have never let myself be put off by rain or wind, or by any inclemency of the weather, from beginning punctually at the appointed time any work in the service of God our Lord.' So they set out at the hour appointed. (FN II, 414; cited in Rahner, 1960, pp. 139–140)

On one occasion he sat in the waiting room of one of the cardinals for fourteen hours, until finally the cardinal received him (FN IV, 899; cited in Becher 1977).

His disposition seems to have been generally amiable and courteous, but he could also be harsh and uncompromising. Many of those who worked most closely with him felt the sting of his lash—Laynez, Nadal, Polanco, even da Camara. Polanco complained that in the nine years he served as Ignatius' secretary he scarcely heard a good word. Nadal was often so harshly rebuked that he could hardly keep from crying; Laynez was to moan to Ribadeneyra, "What have I done against the Society that this saint treats me this way?" (FN III, 690).

His desire to win souls for God was a consuming passion. He wrote to Jacqueline de Croy that God, "to whom all things, even our inmost hearts, are known, knows what desires of the salvation and progress of souls he has given to me" (Epistolae II, 303; cited in Rahner, 1960, p. 160). As he led one of the courtesans of Rome to the House of St. Martha, someone might point out that the conversion was unlikely to last and was hardly worth the effort. He was likely to reply: "And if with all my trouble and care I could persuade only one single person to refrain from sin for one night for the sake of my Lord Jesus Christ, then I would stop at nothing that for this time at least she might not offend God—even if I knew that she would afterwards fall back into her old vice" (Scripta I, 355–356; cited in Wulf 1977).

His apostolic passion was matched by a genius for the direction of souls, and he was widely consulted by the powerful and the humble. He knew how to console, how to encourage, how to read the hearts of those who came to him. People found him to be serious, attentive, kind, his words few but carefully chosen and penetrating always the noble knight, the man of breeding and courtly manners, bearing himself with dignity and respect for his fellows, and great reserve (Wulf 1977). De-

spite this detachment, men were drawn to him irresistibly. As Ribadeneyra wrote, "Our father possessed to a high degree the art of winning
the affection and trust of those who associated with him, and thus of
leading them to God" (Scripta I, 461). He had a gift for spiritual conversation that inspired and consoled others. Nadal's comments are typical:

> As he was inflamed with love for his neighbor and was outstanding
> in regard to the discernment of spirits and moral prudence, he so
> adapted himself to those with whom he conversed by the brevity and
> kindness of his words and caused them to be so well-disposed toward
> him that he evoked amazing movements of soul in them. He had
> such insight into them that he almost seemed to enter into their
> mind and heart. He spoke in such a manner that no one could with-
> stand his words. Furthermore, a mysterious, divine power and light
> appeared to shine forth from his countenance, which much en-
> kindled the love of spiritual things in those who looked upon him
> (Epistolae Nadal IV, 662).[4]

THE PORTUGUESE CRISIS

He moved from crisis to crisis—struggling to preserve the Society and
its mission intact in the face of pressures on many sides. The events in
Portugal would absorb his attention for most of 1552 and into 1553.
Early efforts to establish the Society in Portugal had enjoyed great success, partly because of the favorable disposition of King John III, who
generously supported the works of the Society, and because of the enormous influence of Simón Rodriguez who founded several colleges and
accomplished other works. For reasons which are obscure, deviations
soon developed from the pattern of religious life Ignatius had laid down
for the Society. The variations followed two extremes: excessive prayer
and penances ("holy follies") on the one hand, and too much attention
to physical comfort on the other. Ignatius' insistence on obedience was
at risk.

The situation had reached the point at which some Portuguese
Jesuits had begun to attract followers and gained considerable influence at the Portuguese court. A movement arose to form a separate
religious order and withdraw from the Society and obedience to Ignatius. One source of the difficulty had been Rodriguez, who seemed to
prefer his own counsel to Ignatius'. Near the end of 1551 Ignatius

decided to remove him from office as provincial of Portugal and send him to Aragon, where he would have less influence. Rodriguez refused to go and remained in Portugal. There was a flurry of orders and counter-orders, letters that never arrived or arrived too late, miscommunications, and orders and decisions that were never implemented. For a time Ignatius did not even know who the provincial of the Portuguese province was. He had named Michael de Torres to the post at the beginning of 1552, but Aragon still had no provincial, and Rodriguez never arrived there. Confusion reigned! The group at Coimbra were shocked and confused, friends of the Society were disedified, and rumors circulated that the Society in Portugal was being dissolved. John III, ever a friend of the Society, tried to bolster the order by appointing a Jesuit to be his confessor. This also proved abortive. Departures and dismissals from the Society followed, to the consternation of many, especially when some of those dismissed continued their apostolic work to good effect. Ignatius was finally able to pour some oil on these waters by recalling Torres, but the agitation continued for well over a year. He also recalled da Camara from Portugal to get some sense of what was going on there. The whole affair was painful and difficult, particularly the behavior of Rodriguez, Ignatius' old companion, whom he was forced to recall and subject to ecclesiastical discipline. As Ravier (1987) comments:

> The balance sheet of the crises, departures and dismissals was not encouraging. In July, one hundred five companions remained in Portugal. The dissidents dreamed of founding a new Society. The King dissuaded them. For Ignatius, the refusals and equivocations of Símon Rodriguez were very painful: he was torn between his friendship for his former companion of the early days and what he thought to be his duty as Superior General. Should he expel Símon Rodriguez from the Society? (p. 178)

Rodriguez arrived in Rome on 10 October 1552. At his trial the following February the court imposed a series of penances which Ignatius dispensed. Rodriguez submitted at first, then rejected the decision as unjust. He finally appealed to Cardinal Carpi, the protector of the Society, for exemption from his vow of obedience. The affair came to naught and he remained in the Society, thus saving Ignatius the pain and embarrassment of dismissing him.

Historians have not been kind to Rodriguez. Dudon comments: "This man is not an insolent rebel, strutting about and blowing his trumpet to rally his friends against his leader. But he is shockingly disobedient all the same. With his humble and gentle words, he sticks to what he wants; and to cover his resistances, he does not lack quibbles or suspicious moves or a sort of shameless daring" (1949, p. 344). Brodrick writes: "Father Simón went on being the big man at court and the adored man at Coimbra. His Jesuit subjects loved him intensely, partly because he deserved to be loved, and partly for the less noble reason that he allowed them to do pretty well as they listed. It all went to his head, never a very wise head, and he gradually came to think and act almost in independence of St. Ignatius" (1940, pp. 242–243).

For Dalmases (1985), probably quite correctly, the issue was obedience, so dear to the heart of Ignatius. Rodriguez had his problems, but the rift between Ignatius' central government and one of his subordinate administrators, also an early companion, was central. The fundamental role of Ignatian obedience had not really been established—the authority of the founders, Rodriguez among them, had not been fully explicated, and the principle was not yet in place in any institutional sense (Endean 1987). The threat to Ignatius may have been more in his own anxieties over the questioning of his authority. His vision of the structure of the Society and the essential role of unquestioning obedience would have been challenged by Rodriguez's relative independence. We might conjecture that, in addition, Ignatius was getting a bit of his own medicine; at least in his persistence and his independent mind, Rodriguez was not that far from offering a mirror to the saint.[5]

Other serious matters continued to plague Ignatius: a problem with the mission to Ethiopia, the troublesome decree of the theology faculty at the University of Paris, the position of the newly professed, the severe poverty of the Roman missions bordering on starvation and bankruptcy, suspicions and attacks against the Spiritual Exercises in Spain, the question of succession to the office of General—and on and on.

CARAFA

One of the most difficult crises confronted Ignatius in 1555. In March Pope Julius III died, and on April 9 Cardinal Cervini ascended the papal throne as Marcellus II. His choice must have brought a sigh of relief to

Ignatius since Cervini was a good friend and favorably disposed to the Society. The first blow came with Marcellus' sudden death on May 1. The second blow fell with even more force when, on May 23, Gian Pietro Carafa was elected as Pope Paul IV. The news rocked Ignatius. Da Camara reported that "after he saw a message that the Theatine Cardinal had been elected Pope he underwent a noticeable change as well as alteration of expression . . . ; all the bones of his body shook" (FN I, 582–583). Nadal reported that Carafa had thrown his weight against the approval of the Society by Paul III (Scripta IV, 706). Fortunately Ignatius had been able to gain Paul III's approval of his Society before Carafa's influence had been strongly established in Rome. Now the enemy Ignatius dreaded most had been elected Pope. Ignatius' letter criticizing Carafa and the Theatines came back to haunt him. Subsequently, he had on two occasions refused offers of merger with the Theatines, actions that could not have pleased the cardinal. In addition, Carafa was well known to disapprove of several aspects of the Society's Constitutions.

The new Pope had been described as stubborn, harsh, impetuous, and impatient of all opposition. Loyola was equally determined, if somewhat less volatile. The mixture was potentially explosive. Yet Carafa's dislike for the Spaniard was not absolute; their confrontation went beyond the clash of their personalities to basic principles: perspectives on Church reform and their respective visions of the spiritual renewal of Christendom (Quinn 1981). Quinn contrasts these visions:

> The Theatine Rule is directed toward the establishment of a model community, a light to shine before men. Prayer is to be observed twice daily in each cell; fasts are to be "observed most conscientiously"; the Office—"both night and day parts"—to be chanted in choir; no priest is to leave the community alone and the community itself, mindful of God's providence, will refrain from the self-corrupting process of soliciting financial support and will live "by the gifts of the faithful freely offered." An order purified in head and members, they will stand as an example to the world and the Church of a renewed and perfect Christian community. (1981, pp. 396–397)

And of the Ignatian vision:

> Loyola, now with "the responsibility of authority," is not interested in creating spiritual models but in an order that seeks out the world

in "actual accomplishment and meaningful service." The tradition of the cloister, however reformed and oriented toward works of mercy, is irrelevant to Loyola's design, to his direction that the Society will have no limits, going where the Pope sends them whether "to the Turks or to the New World or the Lutherans or to others be they infidel or faithful." Loyola's charge is to the formation of an "état de mission," a radical departure from the restrictions of tradition, that makes the liturgical punctiliousness of the Theatines mere encumbrance. (p. 397)

Ignatius seemed to flourish in the penumbra of respectability. His ministry to the prostitutes of Rome was considered scandalous by many and was publicly condemned. This and other of Ignatius' activities did not sit well with the conservative cardinal and certainly did not conform to his view of what was proper for religious. Carafa's eighty-year-old sister, Beatrice, threw one of the Jesuits out of her house for fear he might ruin her reputation. As Paul IV, Carafa made his views quite explicit in a blast he leveled at Ignatius' successor, Laynez, in August 1558. The old man gave the new Jesuit General kneeling before him a tongue-lashing, inveighing against the appointment of the General for life, and even more harshly against the refusal to sing choir. Carafa made many efforts toward modifying the Rule of the Society in the direction of the Theatine Rule, which he had authored in 1526. Carafa's assuming the papal tiara must have sounded the knell of doom to the mind of Ignatius—the archenemy, the main opponent and critic of his own religious vision and organization, had assumed the fullness of ecclesiastical authority.

Ecclesiastical politics were in the background as well. When Ignatius and his companions arrived in Italy, they were welcomed by a circle of influential and devout persons, the "Catholic evangelicals," centered around the figure of Cardinal Gaspar Contarini. The members, including Vittoria Colonna, Reginald Pole, and possibly even Michelangelo, were instrumental in assisting the struggling Iñiguists in the performance of their mission. Michelangelo offered to participate in the building of the great Church of the Gesu for the Jesuits without any remuneration (Epistolae Nadal I, 284), and Contarini even made the Spiritual Exercises with Ignatius. At the Vatican, Contarini led a group

of reformers of the papal court and had been one of the important influences pressuring Paul III to issue the bull *Regimini Militantis Ecclesiae*
in 1540 establishing the Society of Jesus. Not surprisingly, the arch-
opponent of the reformers was Carafa. He saw Contarini and his group
as soft on heresy and felt that reform of the Curia was a betrayal of the
Church.

Contarini's death in 1542 set the stage for Carafa's vendetta. He persuaded Paul III to establish the Holy Office under his direction, charged
with protecting faith and morals; efforts to reform the Church from
within were turned into attacks on the heretics without. By the time he
became Paul IV, Carafa had become fanatical. He launched the attack on
Contarini's group with vehemence, even throwing one bishop, Giovanni Morone, into prison. Had Pole not returned to England as papal
legate, he would have had to stand trial for heresy. Carafa refused to
allow the Council of Trent to continue and created the infamous Index
of Forbidden Books (O'Malley 1982). We do not know what Ignatius'
relations with the Contarini group were, but his sentiments and loyalties were with them—a fact that would have set him in opposition to
the intransigent and heresy-obsessed new Pope.

The effects on the Roman and German colleges were severe. Pope
Julius III had supported these institutions and even sought to provide
stable revenues for the Roman college. Unfortunately these arrangements had not been completed at his death. Paul IV saw to it that
nothing came of the plan. The straitened conditions forced Ignatius to
order the rectors of the colleges to accept externe students, but this was
not enough. He had to send a hundred companions out of Rome, leaving
only about one hundred and fifty to feed. The companions elsewhere
had to abandon their works to beg alms for the support of the Roman
houses.

Perhaps even more damaging, the election of Paul IV revived old accusations against the Society. It was well known that the order was not in
favor with the Pope, and in this climate long-smoldering animus against
the Society burst into flame. Certain Dominicans in Spain began to
preach openly against the Society. The decree from the theology faculty
at Paris condemning teachings of the Society had considerable repercus-
sions outside France. Ignatius' answer, as in so many previous crises,
was to collect the testimonies of kings, princes, cardinals, and bishops

who knew the work of the Society firsthand and could bear witness to the good results of his sons' efforts.

Despite these financial hardships and political difficulties, the apostolic work of the Society prospered; La Strada, the Roman college, and the German college all flourished. Young candidates eagerly filled places in the novitiate as soon as they became available (Ravier 1987).

As time went on, the relations between Ignatius and Paul IV seemed to settle into a more tolerant pattern. Ignatius did what he could to placate the Pope without compromising the work of the Society. For example, as a conciliatory gesture Ignatius introduced choral chant to the chapel of La Strada. For his part, the Pope seemed more respectful and encouraging of the work of the Society—although he continued to disapprove of certain aspects of the Society and had not abandoned his intentions of changing the Constitutions. But he seems to have tried not to interfere with Ignatius' work, at least while he was still alive. There were papal favors as well. Paul granted the Roman college the right to confer its own degrees and entrusted several important missions to members of the Society. He often confided in Laynez and Bobadilla with whom he maintained a close relationship (Ravier 1987).

THE GENERAL AT WORK

One of the most striking aspects of Ignatius' career as General was his immense correspondence. The letters and instructions, written in the years from 1524 to 1556, number nearly seven thousand documents,[6] and give us a fairly accurate picture of the General at work. Ribadeneyra described the painstaking care with which Ignatius carried on this correspondence, especially in the many letters to important personages about matters of significance. Every letter was written and rewritten, pored over with great care and thought, every word examined. He often crossed out and corrected sections, even making several copies. He regarded the time and effort spent in this work as well worthwhile (FN II, 494). The letters show him as constantly bending every effort to instruct, organize, and consolidate the work of the Society in the far corners of the globe. He seems indefatigable, despite his chronic illness and the many hours he spent in mystical absorption. He was anxious, even obsessed with passing on to his sons the spirit of prayer and sacrifice that had been won through the grace of God with such pain and fortitude in a lifetime of prayer and penance. In his letters he exhorted, encouraged, inspired, directed, scolded, and punished.

How to assess Ignatius' career as General? Of praise and admiration there was no lack, especially among the early biographers.[7] Ravier (1987) lists the accomplishments of Ignatius' tenure as General:

1. At Ignatius' death, the Society was established, instituted and confirmed by papal authority.

2. The Society had been granted the highest privileges for the exercise of its ministries.

3. Ignatius had written and promulgated the *Constitutions* containing the rules and regulations guiding the administration of the Society and the implementation of its various functions.

4. The Society spanned the globe, and contained many members of outstanding virtue and ability. . . .

5. Ignatius was able to witness the good effects of his efforts and the works of his sons in establishing God's kingdom and especially in the struggle of the Counter-Reformation.

6. The Society enjoyed an excellent reputation and the respect of Popes, bishops, the laity, kings, and secular princes.

7. The Society had established many houses and colleges throughout the world, many of which boasted advanced faculties of philosophy and theology (pp. 265–266).[8]

The record is impressive, if not brilliant. Beyond the external achievements, there was also a measure of charisma. The psychic world in which Ignatius lived and worked was never far removed from the cave of Manresa and the spirit of the *Exercises*, which permeated every aspect of his life and thought. There was a spirit of vitality and mission—the sense that God was using Ignatius and the Society as an instrument to restore the spirit of the primitive church to the world. As Ravier puts it: "The arm of God—the *Dextera Excelsi*, or the *Verbi Dei energia* to use the language of Polanco—was perceptible to the whole generation of companions. They had a very strong feeling of disproportion between acts and effects, especially the spiritual effects of their acts: between what they did and the results of what they did, the power of God intervened. A very apostolic, very Pauline feeling: it was in weakness that the force of the spirit was revealed" (1987, p. 322). It was as though the charisma—the energia—of Ignatius had been communicated to his companions, so that the rich rewards of their labors became for them a sign of divine favor. Ignatius found it necessary from time to time to curb the understandable spiritual pride of some of his sons.

A SELF-PORTRAIT

Ignatius himself provides a vivid idealized portrait, in the *Constitutions*, of the character and spiritual stature he thought any future General of the Society should possess. The description is embodied in ten points:

1. In regard to the qualities which are desirable in the superior general, the first is that he should be closely united with God our Lord and intimate with Him in prayer and all his actions, that from God, the fountain of all good, the general may so much the better obtain for the whole body of the Society a large share of His gifts and graces, and also great power and efficacy for all the means which will be used for the help of souls.

2. The second quality is that he should be a person whose example in the practice of all virtues is a help to the other members of the Society. Charity should be especially resplendent in him, toward all his fellowmen and above all toward the members of the Society; and genuine humility too should shine forth, that these characteristics may make him highly lovable to God our Lord and to men.

3. He ought also to be independent of all passions, by his keeping them controlled and mortified, so that in his interior they may not disturb the judgment of his intellect and in his exterior he may be so composed, particularly so self-controlled when speaking, that no one, whether a member of the Society who should regard him as a mirror and model, or an extern, may observe in him any thing or word which does not edify him.

4. However, he should know how to mingle rectitude and necessary severity with kindness and gentleness to such an extent that he neither allows himself to swerve from what he judges to be more pleasing to God our Lord nor ceases to have proper sympathy for his sons. Thus although they are being reprimanded or punished, they will recognize that in what he does he is proceeding rightly in our Lord and with charity, even though it is against their liking according to the lower man.

5. Magnanimity and fortitude of soul are likewise highly necessary for him to bear the weaknesses of many, to initiate great undertakings in the service of God our Lord, and to persevere in them with constancy when it is called for, without losing courage in the face of the contradictions (even though they come from persons of high rank and power) and without allowing himself to be moved by their entreaties or threats from what reason and the divine service require. He should be superior to all eventualities, without letting himself be exalted by those which succeed or depressed by those which go poorly, being altogether ready to receive death, if necessary, for the good of the Society in the service of Jesus Christ, God and our Lord.

6. The third quality is that he ought to be endowed with great understanding and judgment, in order that this talent may not fail him either in the speculative or the practical matters which may arise. And although learning is highly necessary for one who will have so many learned men in his charge, still more necessary is prudence along with experience in spiritual and interior matters, that he may be able to discern the various spirits and to give counsel and remedies to so many who will have spiritual necessities. He also needs discretion in exterior matters and a manner of handling such diverse affairs as well as of conversing with such various persons from within and without the Society.

7. The fourth quality, one highly necessary for the execution of business, is that he should be vigilant and solicitous to undertake enterprises as well as energetic in carrying them through to their completion and perfection, rather than careless and remiss in such a way that he leaves them begun but not finished.

8. The fifth quality has reference to the body. In regard to health, appearance, and age, on the one hand account should be taken of propriety and prestige, and on the other hand of the physical energies which his charge requires, that in it he may be able to fulfill his office to the glory of God our Lord.

9. The sixth quality pertains to extrinsic endowments. Among these, preference ought to be given to those which help more toward edification and the service of God in such a charge. Examples are generally found in reputation, high esteem, and whatever else aids toward prestige with those within and without.

10. Finally, he ought to be one of those who are most outstanding in

every virtue, most deserving in the Society, and known as such for a considerable time. If any of the aforementioned qualities should be wanting, there should at least be no lack of great probity and love for the Society, nor of good judgment accompanied by sound learning. For in regard to other things, the aids which he will have . . . could through God's help and favor supply to a great extent for many deficiencies. (Constitutions 723–735)

This passage has long been regarded as a self-portrait, whether consciously or unconsciously created. His biographer da Camara wrote in 1555: "How often I observed that in his whole manner of proceeding, the Father observes with exactitude all the rules of the Exercises. Thus he appears to have planted these rules in his own soul and then to have drawn them from his own interior acts. The same thing can be said of Gerson [i.e., of the *Imitation of Christ*], to such an extent that to converse with the Father seems to be nothing else than to read John Gerson put into practice. I must remember to write down many instances from which this universal statement can be drawn. The same thing is true of the Constitutions, especially of the chapter in which he portrays the General, in whose case he seems to have portrayed his own self" (FN I, 656).[9] The question remains as to how far we can go in accepting this description as an unself-conscious self-revelation rather than an idealized model. Clearly any prospective General would have to be a paragon of all virtues and psychic strengths.

Ignatius' basic methods of governing are reflected in the Constitutions, as we shall see. A primary principle was the centrality of the vow of obedience to the Pope whose voice was the voice of God. And where the Pope gave him a free hand, Ignatius responded to requests from bishops, cardinals, and princes who had been benefactors of the Society and to whom he owed a debt of gratitude. Beyond that, his ears were attuned to any situation of spiritual need or human misery. As Ravier (1987) notes, "The voice of misery was for him the Voice of God" (p. 330).

In addition to the papal will, the principles of discernment that Ignatius had evolved at Manresa were constant guidelines. Requests from bishops and princes, factual circumstances, friends and enemies, favorable and unfavorable situations, all had to be weighed and finally discerned in the light of his interpretation of God's will. The manner in which he dealt with persecutions and calumnies is telling. When the theology faculty at Paris passed its decree, many urged Ignatius to institute a countersuit; but Ignatius chose a course he felt was more in keeping with divine intentions: he assembled testimonials to the good works of the Society to answer the attack. Nor was he slow to receive four of the Parisian doctors at La Strada in December 1555.

SHORTCOMINGS

Yet the record is not unblemished; Ignatius had failures and disappointments along with successes. From the beginning, he tried to establish the Society in Paris, a place that had such personal meaning for him and historical significance for the Society, but after fifteen years of effort, he had nothing to show for it. Nor could he establish a beachhead in England, even after the coronation of Mary Tudor. He also never gave up on the idea of a mission to the Holy Land. He backed the plan of Peter de Zarate, a knight of the Holy Sepulcher, who had founded an "archconfraternity of the Holy Sepulcher," with the support and endorsement of the Pope and many cardinals, for the purpose of venerating the holy places and recovering the Holy Land by war against the infidels. The plan called for establishing colleges of the Society in Jerusalem, Constantinople, and Cyprus. But Ignatius' old desire to live and work in the places where Christ had walked was not to be fulfilled. These colleges were never more than figments of his wishful imagination set down on paper.

An aspect of Ignatius' administration that would disconcert his supporters was his financial management. He was chronically up to his ears in debt; he had to learn the bitter lesson that the poverty, which can free the spirit in individual terms, can become a severe problem for a community and an institution. Many of the houses of the Society had no stable revenue but were dependent on the good will of individual cardinals, bishops, or princes. The financial situation of La Strada itself hinged on the generosity of one Pietro Codacio. His death in December 1549 was a near disaster for the house. The Roman College was opened in January 1551 with the support of Francis Borgia, then duke of Gandia. The arrangement worked as long as Francis had control of his resources, but when he renounced them to enter the Society, his successor did not maintain the promised revenues and this heavy debt had to be assumed by La Strada. The German College was founded in 1552 with the promise of support from the king of the Romans, Ferdinand I, and some cardinals. They soon found it convenient to ignore their promises. Promises of help from Julius III were aborted by his death, and subsequently the good intentions of Paul IV were frustrated by the drain on the papal treasury from the war with Spain. From 1551 to 1556 the Roman houses were constantly in debt, and Ignatius had to exploit the Society's every resource to beg money for their support. Not the recommended model for fiscal responsibility and prudence.

This was undoubtedly another dimension of the increasing tension between the religious ideals of the pilgrim and the practical functions and obligations of the superior General. He had struggled arduously to overcome all attachments to money and creature comforts. But he could not expect his men, especially the younger scholastics, to persevere in pursuit of the advanced degrees and higher learning so essential to the work of the Society without sufficient support. More to the point, he had to provide for a growing number of communities and for the many novices who were flocking to the Society. All this required funds—and not just a pittance. We can recall that the issue of evangelical poverty was one of his criticisms of the Theatines in the infamous letter to Gian Pietro Carafa in 1536. In the decade following that letter, Ignatius had come to see that money and financial resources were essential means for achieving apostolic goals—the touchstone of reality (Bertrand 1985).

MANNER OF GOVERNING

Ignatius retained a somewhat simplistic ideal, derived from the spirit of the first fathers, that he tried to impose on his growing Society. It was a zealous ideal, filled with magnanimity, generosity, and zeal for souls. His harshness often came into play in his efforts to mold the Society according to this image when the material was not sufficiently pliant to suit him. His idealism and rather rigid expectations did not always serve him well in dealing with the emotional difficulties and weaknesses of others, particularly around the question of admitting or even readmitting candidates to the Society. Ravier (1987) comments: "We should acknowledge that he needed some time to realize that not all candidates for the Society had his strength of character nor the dynamism of his

grace. To the extent that one can discern an evolution in his ars guber-
nandi it is toward a more indulgent appreciation of human fragility, of
'the weakness of many' which takes place. Was it without a certain
regret of thus seeing the idea devalued which he was creating of the
'companion of Jesus Christ'? Must we not necessarily perceive a certain
disenchantment in this avowal offered at the end of his life: 'If he
wished,' reports Polanco, 'to live longer, it would be to prove himself
more severe in admissions into the Society'" (p. 339).

His inclination was at first to freely admit to the Society all who
expressed a desire to follow Christ. But even in 1542, two-thirds of those
admitted would leave. With time he grew more exacting. In 1555 he
dismissed a dozen scholastics from the Roman College. In the same year
Don Teotonio, brother of the duke of Braganza, was sent packing; he had
been an exemplary religious since his admission in 1547 but set himself
against Ignatius with regard to the removal of Rodriguez from Lisbon.
Ignatius' firmness and patience had little effect. Finally Teotonio applied for dismissal. Ignatius wrote the duke: "Permit me to assure your
illustrious Lordship, that we have had a special desire to aid Don Teotonio in finding peace, and to help him behave as is becoming a true
religious and servant of God; the more so, since his family's position
obliges him to signalize himself more than others in all that concerns
our Institute, should he wish to remain with us. But after having tried
according to the knowledge our Lord vouchsafed us we find that we have
not succeeded in our purpose. We can only pray the divine goodness that
Don Teotonio direct his life in the service of our Lord in some other
way" (Epistolae IX, 547–548; cited in Dudon, 1949, pp. 333–334).

While not slow to resort to the extreme measure of dismissal, Ignatius
would usually consult with others and give much time to prayer over
the matter before he acted. Once his mind was made up, he moved
quickly and resolutely to execute the decision. After a candidate had
been admitted, Ignatius watched over his progress with great care and
consideration. He spared no expense to care for the sick; although he
often seemed to be obsessed by the demands of poverty, he often re-
proved ministers or procurators who tended to be less than generous
with their subjects.

Ignatius was firm in carrying out his decisions. His deliberations were
guided by the experience of the election and the discernment of spirits

in the Exercises.[10] Once the decision had been made, it became for Ignatius the will of God, and could not be altered without grave and urgent reasons. Da Camara offers us a description of the process:

Our Father [Ignatius] is accustomed to being so firm in things which he undertakes, that this steadfastness amazes everyone. Here are the reasons that come to my mind. First is that he carefully considers each matter before deciding it. Second, he prays very much on this subject and is illuminated by God. Third, he makes no particular decision without hearing the opinion of those who are competent in the matter, and he asks them for the majority of circumstances with the sole exception of those of which he has full cognizance. He was accustomed also, very often, when he did not have full knowledge of the matter, to postpone it and to let some general opinions on the topic suffice for the moment. (Memorial, p. 205, n. 282b; cited in Ravier, 1987, p. 341)

Simón Rodriguez alluded to this in 1553 when he remarked to da Camara, "You must realize that Father Ignatius is a kindly man and of much virtue, but he is a Basque, and once he has taken something to heart . . ." Cardinal Carpi, the protector of the Society, made the same point in commenting on Ignatius' decisions, "He has already driven in the nail" (Dalmases, 1985, p. 26).

These aspects convey a sense of Ignatius' public performance as General. We would also like to catch some glimpse of his personal relationships. Ravier (1987) discusses these in relation to the first companions, the professed fathers of the Society, other Jesuits, and laymen. The first companions were his original followers, whom he regarded as cofounders of the Society. He turned to them first when difficult tasks needed to be undertaken and counted on their resourcefulness and virtue as he would on his own. He entrusted to them the most demanding and important missions—Xavier to the Indies, Faber to many corners of Europe, Broet to Paris—and when he sent them forth, he was confident of their capacity to exercise prudence and wisdom under God's guiding influence. As Ravier (1987) comments: "So they enjoyed everywhere great prestige: they were, in the eyes of all and especially in the eyes of Ignatius, the companions of the 'early hours,' those on whom the Holy Spirit had breathed, those who had lived a unique, novel adventure, the ideal of Paris, Venice, and Rome" (p. 346). This made it all the more difficult to deal with the disruptions caused by Bobadilla or to treat the rebellious and contentious Rodriguez with the respect and love due a true companion during the Portuguese crisis.

The professed were regarded as the highest rank in the Society, men who realized the best qualities envisioned by the founders and who were marked by special gifts of nature and learning. Ignatius looked on the professed, who took a special fourth vow of obedience to the Holy Father, as men of mission, especially prepared to carry out the most difficult of apostolic efforts, men of maturity who could take the place of the founding fathers and were prepared to go to any place and undertake any responsibility for the good of the Society and the Church.

The creation of this special rank opened the door to rivalry and ambition from the beginning. Both Bobadilla and Rodriguez were reluctant and delayed making their professions, Bobadilla until October 1541 and Rodriguez until December 1544—and then only at Ignatius' request. As always, preferment brings its inevitable weight of narcissistic investment, intensified by the selectivity of the honor. At the time of Ignatius' death, fewer than forty out of nearly one thousand members of the order were professed. Most of these held positions as superiors or provincials,[11] and a few, like Canisius, were advanced to profession on the basis of exceptional virtue and learning. Another group were missionaries destined for particularly difficult or dangerous missions—such as Ethiopia, the Indies, Bohemia, or Brazil. Ignatius also had additional missionaries advanced to full profession in situations of crisis to strengthen and confirm the place of the Society in these perilous regions.

The rest of the members of the Society were allied with the General by ties of obedience. The members had all responded to the call of Christ to a life of self-sacrifice and service. Ignatius was particularly concerned about whom to admit to the Society and laid special emphasis on the capacity to undertake the difficult work of the Society and on the candidate's free choice in committing himself to the Society for life. Candidates were admitted only after a long and careful examination and trials that put their devotion and motivation to the test. Ignatius was ever available to help candidates by his prayers and often lengthy conversations and offered every spiritual help he could devise when they might be tempted.

The picture is somewhat different with regard to those who transgressed in some manner. His judgment was often harsh, and he was quick to impose severe penances. We can recall the intensity of his own penances and self-mortifications during the early years of his conversion that he had to learn to modify for apostolic purposes. But da Camara's *Memorial* reeks of severity and harshness that seems excessive and punitive. These extremes were not unopposed—Viola, the superior in Genoa, did not want to implement them, Adriani in Rome objected that they were incompatible with the Nordic temperament, and Jay and Lanoye claimed the same for the Germans. Despite these objections, Ignatius insisted that he did not impose such penances for their own sake but sought repentance and reform. And he spared no one—Polanco, later his secretary, and his old companion Laynez were subjected to this treatment. Yet he did not always deal with transgressors harshly; he could be kind and fatherly—an inconsistency that confused and attracted many of his followers. Da Camara expressed this feeling: "One totally remarkable fact is the way in which our Father, in matters which seem identical, uses totally opposite methods, like great severity with one and great gentleness with another; and one sees immediately by the result that the remedy he used was the best, though we had not previously recognized that. However, he was always rather inclined toward love; even more, it seems total love and through that he was universally loved by all and one will find no one in the Society who does not have a very great love for him and does not consider himself much loved by him" (Memorial, n. 86–87; cited in Ravier, 1987, p. 356).

One might be tempted to regard these accounts as suspect because of the inherent need to whitewash the portrait of the founder and spiritual hero—and there may be some of that here. But there may also be a kernel of truth. We have had ample occasion to note Ignatius' psychological insight, especially his capacity to empathize with the interior movements of the souls of his charges—notably with those whom he directed in the Spiritual Exercises. The same capacity undoubtedly played a role in his dealings with his companions and novices.

Then there were those who were dismissed from the Society or left as a matter of personal choice. There was a high rate of turnover— apparently customary for the times (Dudon 1949). Ignatius had a hair-trigger intolerance for certain kinds of behavior. He would dismiss novices in the middle of the night, and da Camara reports his saying that he would not spend a single night under the same roof with anyone in mortal sin (Memorial, n. 396, cited in Ravier 1987). But with other cases he could be patient, waiting for repentance to develop, sending the transgressor on a pilgrimage of repentance or putting him to work in the hospitals. And though he protested that not enough candidates were dismissed, he would at times accept returning candidates (Ravier 1987). The decisions were always personal and tailored to the circumstances. When dismissal was called for, Ignatius wanted it done with love and concern for the spiritual well-being of the one dismissed—as in the case of Don Teotonio. His directions in the Constitutions read:

> For the satisfaction of the one dismissed, three other things ought to be observed. One, pertaining to the exterior, is that as far as possible he should leave the house without shame or dishonor and take with him what is his.
>
> Another thing, pertaining to the interior, is to try to send him away with as much love and charity for the house and as much consoled in our Lord as is possible.
>
> Another, pertaining to the circumstances of his person, is to try to give him direction whereby he may find another good means to serve God in religious life or outside it, according to what seems more conformed to His divine will. This is done by aiding the person through counsel and prayers and through whatever in charity may appear best. . . .
>
> Another is that they [members of the Society] should not remain disaffected or with a bad opinion in his regard, as far as this is possible. Rather, they should have compassion for him and love him in Christ and recommend him in their prayers to the Divine Majesty, that God may deign to guide him and have mercy on him. (Constitutions 223, 225, 226, 229)

The last fifteen years of Ignatius' life were spent mostly within the confines of the modest house of La Strada. At the same time, the Society he founded and governed was growing by leaps and bounds and had become a vital force in Christendom, both in Europe and in the far-flung missionary lands of the globe. At the center of this vast organization sat Ignatius, guiding, directing, exhorting, counseling, and above all praying. Ravier (1987) describes the scene: "It is a simple man who lives here; there is a tiny room where he works and sleeps; he takes his meals in a neighboring room, very often he has as guests a few companions from whom he likes to get advice on current concerns, or, more rarely, 'people from outside'; whoever the guests may be, the meal is frugal; a third room serves him as a chapel: here he celebrates Mass or merely attends, according to the physician's orders; in the fourth room sleeps the Brother who is at his service. A modest life, poor without outward glamor, without pretense, and monotonous" (p. 377).

His most noteworthy characteristic was his life of prayer. It was prayer of intense devotion, of mystical intensity—prayer for the work of the Society, for the missions he and his companions were undertaking for the glory of God, for strength and courage for his sons to persevere in the difficult paths they had chosen, that his decisions and choices would be governed by God's will and the good of God's children. He took upon himself the onerous task of shaping the Society according to the spirit that had prevailed among the first companions before 1539. His mode of governing, his method of instructing and training the novices, the tasks and apostolic missions he undertook, the endless stream of letters and instructions—all were directed to keeping this spirit alive as the Society grew and became more diverse and complex.

CHARISMATIC LEADERSHIP

These details raise the question of the charisma of Ignatius as a religious leader. We must take into account the presence of intense positive and idealizing transference reactions, but this realization only leads to the further question of what it was about Ignatius' personality that elicited such powerful responses. The issue reaches beyond Ignatius' personal charismatic qualities to the leader-follower interaction. This consideration reflects a major shift in the study of charisma. Max Weber's (1947) definition of charismatic authority emphasized the compelling forcefulness of the leader's personality—"a certain quality of an individual personality by virtue of which he is set apart from ordinary men and treated as endowed with supernatural, superhuman, or at least specifically exceptional powers or qualities. These are such as are not accessible to the ordinary person, but are regarded as of divine origin or as exemplary, and on the basis of them, the individual concerned is treated as a leader" (pp. 358–359). Or, as Zaleznik (1984) notes, "Charisma refers to any combination of unusual qualities in an individual which are attractive to others and result in special attachments, if not devotion, to his leadership" (p. 114).

Others have found both paternal and maternal characteristics in charismatic leaders, who can inspire love and awe, offer hope for salvation and deliverance from distress, and deal with subordinates with tenderness and harshness. As Abse and Ulman (1977) observe, "The charismatic leader is both intimidating and encouraging, and he may alternate rapidly between these two ways of dealing with people. . . . The man of action's genius for leadership is a two-faced thing, as the close associates of any great leader can often testify" (p. 41).

More recent work on charismatic leadership has broadened the focus to include the leader-follower interaction (Abse and Ulman 1977; Wilner 1984; Post 1986). Wilner (1984), for example, defines charismatic leadership as a relationship characterized by the followers' perception of the leader as in some fashion superhuman, their blind acceptance of the leader's statements, their unconditional compliance with his directives, and their unqualified emotional support of his cause.

One view of charismatic leader-follower relationships emphasizes the essentially narcissistic basis of the interaction (Post 1986; Kets de Vries and Miller 1985). Deficits in narcissistic development can result in two kinds of personalities; the ideal-hungry type constantly seeks an idealized object, attachment to which can salvage his damaged narcissism, while the mirror-hungry type needs a constant flow of admiration and acceptance in order to satisfy narcissistic needs. One view of charismatic leadership is that a charismatic marriage is effected when the mirror-hungry leader satisfies his ideal-hungry followers' narcissistic need for an ideal to follow, and the followers contribute their nurturing and sustaining admiration and compliance to maintaining the narcissistic balance in the leader (Post 1986).

Individuals with narcissistic dispositions, based on their need for power and prestige, are often drawn into leadership positions (Kohut 1971; Kernberg 1979). There is little question that the young Iñigo's narcissism was salted with the mirror-hungry component—we need only recall his vanity over his appearance. He was stamped as a hero, a leader, and he seemed willing to suffer any pain, undergo any risk, even the threat of death, to serve that ideal. In his role as General, the narcissistic strains were more muted and ambivalent. There is no doubt that he exercised a powerful charismatic attraction on his followers, especially the band of brothers who founded the Society under his leadership. But later, in the house at La Strada, he was regarded as the saint, the father, and his word was law, his every utterance regarded as if divine, or nearly so, in origin. To what extent did this adulation and reverential awe, which come through so impressively even over the centuries, reflect the ideal-hungry narcissistic need of his followers?

In their study of the narcissism in charismatic leaders, Kets de Vries and Miller (1985) describe three leadership styles: reactive, self-deceptive, and constructive. The reactive leader is the most pathological: his grandiosity and exhibitionism select the most sycophantic and solicitous followers, he rejects arguments contrary to his opinions, he willingly exploits or manipulates others for his advantage or enhancement, he lacks empathy for and ignores the needs of peers and subordinates, he takes little by way of information or advice before reaching his decisions, his actions tend to be bold and extreme owing to his grandiosity and rejection of any possibility of failure, and if any failure or reversal ensues he finds ways to cast the blame on subordinates or outside enemies.

Self-deceptive leaders, in contrast, are more likely to be concerned about their subordinates and their needs, more likely to listen to their input, but they are also insecure, hypersensitive to criticism, and have a strong need to be accepted and approved. They may be more concerned with finding threats in the environment of the group, and their need for approval and fear of failure often prompts active scanning to detect and neutralize possible threats. Their approach is more transactional than transforming and tends to be perfectionist, procrastinating, and conservative.

On the healthier end of the spectrum, constructive leaders tend to have more balanced relationships with subordinates, marked by more mutual respect and concern. They are confidant of their abilities and are more task- and goal-oriented, without an excessive need to extract admiration from their followers. They tend to be good listeners, accepting the contributions of subordinates, but assuming responsibility for decisions and consequences themselves. When they take a stand they tend to stick to it with determination. They can inspire others to share in a common cause and to transcend self-interest. Their independence and vision can often energize followers to undertake ambitious and challenging projects. Decision-making tends to be flexible, mutual, and characterized by a capacity for delegation.

How might we fix Ignatius in this spectrum? Certain aspects of his style of governing were reactive, certain aspects constructive, some even self-deceptive. Ignatius had many of the attributes of the constructive leader—he combined a capacity for transformative and inspirational leadership with an ability to interact with his followers in transactional terms that was remarkable (Kets de Vries and Miller 1985). In some respects, he also fits the reparative form of narcissistic leadership, in which followers reach a level of idealization that allows them to join in the grandiosity of the leader (Volkan 1988). Part of Ignatius' inspiration was his vision of the Society as carrying out the mission of Christ to defend and extend his kingdom throughout the world. His followers were caught up in this powerful and idealized crusade.

But reactive traits cannot be ignored. It is not always clear that he was attuned to the needs and best interests of his subordinates—the mission of the Society and the will of God took precedence. He was at times rigid and uncompromising, unaware of any objections or reactions in others, but at other times he could be exquisitely sensitive and responsive to the needs of his followers. If he at times took counsel from others before making a decision, he tended to close the door once the decision was made. At times the door may have been closed prematurely. The occasions when he entertained no compromise in his harsh treatment of some candidates to the Society or in his attitudes toward obedience may offer some testimony to the underlying grandiosity that supported his religious vision and convictions.

We should not overlook the fact that Ignatius was able, in a quite remarkable way, to institutionalize his religious inspiration. Ignatius' highly personal and individualized vision, which he experienced as divine in origin, and his sense of connection with a transcendent or immanent divine source is typical of charismatic religious leaders (Barnes 1978). His task, to translate this inner vision into a common inspiration and program of action, was the major achievement of his years as General. He accomplished this task by placing the *Exercises* at the center of his spiritual teaching. This program was further extended by his writing of the Constitutions, which gave a stable and explicit form to his vision for the Society. Then came the years of unflagging

effort to organize, direct, and promote the work of the Society throughout the world, to articulate the vision and the mission to his followers,
so that through them and through the Society the apparatus would be
set in place to continue for centuries the work he had begun. Ignatius
saw his leadership as intended by God for the future accomplishment of
God's purposes and the glory of His kingdom on earth.

EXTERNAL APOSTOLIC WORKS

When Ignatius did venture beyond La Strada, it was usually to preserve
the missionary work of the Society in Rome—a charge that he and his
companions had been given by His Holiness in 1538. The first objects of
his zeal and charity were the abandoned street children of Rome, victims of wars, famines, and epidemics that ravaged the papal states.
Carafa had begun efforts to help these children, and Ignatius had taken
up the cause almost as soon as he arrived in Rome. With papal assistance, he and others managed to create a confraternity for these orphans.

The problem of prejudice against the Jews in Rome also came to his
attention. They were despised and generally confined to ghettos. Ignatius felt compassion for these unfortunate souls—the race from which
his beloved Savior had come. But, true to the times, Ignatius directed
his efforts to catechizing and converting the Jews to Christianity from
1541 on. He welcomed many to La Strada and used his influence to get
statutes passed to benefit these new converts. The time was propitious;
thanks to Paul III's efforts, the papal brief *Cupientes judaeos* in 1542
made such conversions easier, for example, by providing that the new
converts did not have to renounce their patrimony. The traffic at La
Strada became so heavy that a separate house had to be rented for catechumens. The mission to the Jews in Rome and Moslems in their own
lands might be looked at somewhat askance today, but in the anti-
Semitic climate of sixteenth-century Rome, Ignatius' attitude and efforts were most charitable. One might wonder how lasting these multiple conversions were, given the fact that conversion might have offered
many an escape from prejudice and outright persecution. In any case,
Ignatius' liberality in the circumstances was well intended (Ravier
1987).

A more telling enterprise was Ignatius' work with the prostitutes of

Rome who were, even more than today, not only a moral and spiritual problem but also a severe social problem. They came from all parts of Europe and had made Rome the capital of European prostitution. If they accepted conversion or reformation, they were confronted with the problem of where to live and how to support themselves. Many of these women no doubt felt and to an extent were trapped in their life of sexual slavery. Marriage was for most of them no more than a remote possibility—the chances for a girl without dowry or property were not very good. Any possibility of shelter in the local monasteries was often contingent on the woman's intention to enter the religious life. Ignatius attacked the problem head-on. He set up a shelter for women who wished to escape from the life of prostitution, regardless of whether they were single or married or whether or not they had any wish to enter religious life. Thus the House of St. Martha came into being. Supporting it was another matter, for alms and donations were slow in coming. Again Ignatius provided a radical solution—he ordered Codacio to sell some of the ancient Roman marbles that had been unearthed during the excavation for the church of La Strada. In addition, he ordered a hundred gold pieces to be donated to the House of St. Martha. The gesture was all the more generous in that the community at the time was severely strapped for funds. As was the custom, a confraternity was established in 1543 by papal bull, the Society of St. Mary of Grace, and Ignatius continued to support it both spiritually and materially, even though it added considerably to the indebtedness of the professed house[12] (Dalmases 1985).

Not surprisingly, this ministry of Ignatius' was not universally admired. Some were outraged that religious men should devote themselves to the welfare of fallen women. There were other complications. A highly placed papal official, Mathias de San Cassiano, was a good friend of the Society, but when his mistress was converted he reacted with rage, even dragging Father Diego de Equia from the confessional in the chapel of St. Martha. He turned his rage against Ignatius with the vilest insults and calumnies. Such was his influence that the fathers could not dare to appear in public or exercise their ministry. Ignatius brought the matter to the attention of Paul III, who ordered a trial. Mathias tried to cover the matter over, but Ignatius, as was his wont, demanded a public hearing to vindicate himself and his work. Although the governor hesitated to sign a condemnation against the Master of the

Pontifical Post, Ignatius demanded justice. A formal verdict was issued imposing silence on Mathias and vindicating the Society (Ravier 1987; Dudon 1949).

Another focus of Ignatius' zeal were the young girls who lived in the houses of courtesans and who were put to prostitution at an early age. Beginning in 1546, Ignatius wanted to establish a house under papal auspices in which these girls could be settled and reared. The outcome was the monastery of Santa Catarina della Rosa and the confraternity set up to sponsor and direct it. The papal bull supporting it did not appear until after Ignatius' death, but he and his companions continued to carry on this mission regardless (Ravier 1987; Dalmases 1985).

To our contemporary eyes, other apostolic efforts of the intrepid General were less edifying. He worked to have the papal bull *Cum infirmitas* of Innocent III reinstituted, requiring physicians to see to it that patients confessed or were baptized before the doctors attended to their physical condition. The physicians protested violently, but Ignatius persisted, demanding that the question be submitted for ecclesiastical judgment. He got the support he wanted, although some clerics were uncomfortable with the terms of the decree. Ignatius made every effort to obtain the approval of the Sacred Penitentiary.[13] He succeeded on 30 May 1543. The religious rigidity behind this effort betrays certain less favorable aspects of Ignatius' character, but he does not stand alone in the defendant's box. This decree was first promulgated in 1215 and was still grounds for excommunication in 1725 under Benedict XIII. Ignatius was a creature of his times!

Equally disturbing was his support for establishing the Inquisition in Rome and the papal states. As Ravier (1987) notes, this by no means implies that Ignatius approved of the practices of the Inquisition without reserve. After all, he had had his own difficulties with the Inquisition along the way. And when John III of Portugal tried to turn the Portuguese Inquisition over to the Society, Ignatius put off the decision as long as possible and finally accepted the king's proposal with great reservations and regret. The original purpose had been to thwart the advance of Lutheranism in Italy. Cardinal Carafa had pressured Paul III to establish the Roman Inquisition. Ignatius also urged other cardinals to support the project and persuade the Pope to approve it in 1542. Ignatius was moved by his fear of the spread of heretical doctrines (Dalmases 1985). One can only say that in this matter, as with his seemingly benign attitudes toward the Jews and his almost incomprehensible attitudes toward the care of the sick, Ignatius was immersed in the prejudices and misapprehensions of the age. Even saints are human.

ASSESSMENT

What conclusions can we draw from this portrait of Ignatius in his role as Superior General of the Society of Jesus? Certainly the picture that emerges is a far cry from the fanatic intensity and impracticality of the pilgrim years. The project of establishing a religious order and integrating it within the structure and mission of the Church meant that Ignatius had to abandon his rebellion against and rejection of the conventions of society in order to turn toward a more acceptable behavior. One can detect a kind of Hegelian progression—from the thesis of courtly gallantry and military glory, to the radical antithesis of poverty and humble self-degradation, to the synthesis of a more formal religious structure and the manner of life of La Strada. An understanding of the man Ignatius must enable us to grasp the significance and interconnection of these phases.

Our immediate focus falls on the role of Ignatius as administrator of a newly formed and burgeoning organization. His decisions and directions were crucial for setting his sons on a path that would guarantee the continued existence of the Society—hardly secure in many places where it had been established—and facilitate God's work. Tensions permeated every aspect of the attempt. Ignatius constantly sought divine guidance through prayer and discernment, but in human terms the burden rested on his shoulders. There were no rules, no guidelines, no precedents. He had only his own prudence and worldly wisdom to guide him. He clung desperately, stubbornly, to his religious ideals—to poverty even though the service of God required large sums of money and resources to educate students, support houses and communities, and fund various missionary and apostolic enterprises. He valued education and urged his followers to absorb the most advanced thinking of the times, yet even the most learned were bound to the task of teaching catechism to little children. His Society gained favor, privileges, and power among the most powerful lords and churchmen, yet he insisted on humility and obedience as the hallmark of his sons in imitation of the ideal of the humble Christ who suffered and was humiliated. Whatever success and privilege came their way, the members of the Society were always and everywhere to regard themselves as the *instrumentum Dei*.

Ravier (1987) poses the crucial question regarding the continuity or discontinuity between the image of the pilgrim and that of the General:

> Was it really the same man who here roamed at random, asking on the "Way" the thrill of long prayers, the joy of providential encounters, and then immobilized himself into a punctilious administrator —the same man who asserted himself on every occasion, enamored of total Christian freedom and then legislated, created rules and even minutely detailed regulations, and distributed penances—also the same man who formerly quarreled openly with money, its property, its litigation, its security, and then changed into a man of business, filled his correspondence with requests, questions of inheritance, of "stable revenues" to assure the colleges? One could multiply the contrasts, if not the contradictions. (p. 393)

There is no question that his demeanor was saintly and cast an aura of holiness and charisma that impressed those who knew him. But the picture is far from consistent. The man who turned his back on worldly power and glory to choose a path of abject humility and self-effacement found himself in a position of great power and influence, not only within the Society but vis-à-vis the outside world as well. One would guess that the internal conflicts had by no means found resolution. One can catch only a fleeting glimpse of his uneven and conflicted superego, shifting unpredictably and precipitously from rigidity to tolerance, from harshness and severity to gentleness and kindness, from humble tolerance to authoritarian peremptoriness—often with a rapidity that confused and confounded his contemporaries. One might conclude that the possession and exercise of power was a conflictual issue that he never adequately resolved, to the end of his life.

ATTEMPT TO RESIGN

One incident in particular reveals this lingering uncertainty. In January 1551 the Spanish version of the *Constitutions* was finished and Ignatius summoned a number of the professed to Rome to discuss it. The meeting lasted until the end of the month. On January 30, Ignatius presented the fathers with a sealed envelope containing the following letter:

1. At different times throughout these months and years I have given this matter free and undisturbed thought, and I will state, in the presence of my Creator and Lord, who is also my eternal judge, what I take to be the balanced results of this reflection, to the greater praise and glory of the Divine Majesty.

2. Regarding calmly and with a sense of reality what I see in myself, as a result of my many sins, imperfections, and infirmities of body and soul, I have often and at different times come to the conclusion that I really do not possess (in fact, I infinitely lack) the gifts required for the proper discharge of the office which the Society itself has laid on me.

3. I have a great desire in our Lord that this matter be taken under consideration, and that another who is better, or not so bad, take over the office of governing the Society which is now mine.

4. I desire that such a person be chosen and given this office.

5. And not only does my desire persist, but I think with good reason that this office should be given, not only to one who would perform it better, or not so poorly, but to one who would have at least equal success.

6. Considering all this, in the name of the Father, and of the Son, and of the Holy Spirit, my one and only God and Creator, I lay down and renounce simply and absolutely the office which I hold, and beg and beseech in our Lord with all my heart, both the professed and those who wish to join them, to be pleased to accept this resignation which is made with so much sincerity before His Divine Majesty.

7. If those who are to accept and pass judgment on this petition to God's greater glory detect any inconsistency in it, I beg of them for God's love and reverence to commend it to His Divine Majesty, so that in all things His most holy will be done to His greater glory and to the greater general good of souls and of the whole Society, understanding everything for the greater praise and eternal glory of God. (Epistolae III, 303–304; also in Tylenda, 1985, pp. 38–39)

No doubt a bombshell to the assembled fathers! With the exception of Father Andres de Oviedo, who thought that whatever Ignatius wished should be done, they voted unanimously to reject Ignatius' request.

The move was far from capricious. Toward the end of 1550 Ignatius' health had deteriorated to the point that he and the brethren thought he was on his deathbed. Prudence dictated that a healthier and less moribund specimen be placed in such a responsible position. But the fathers declared that no one else should hold the office of General as long as Ignatius was still breathing. The layers of determination are no doubt multiple, but Ignatius' reluctant manner mirrors his response to his original election. Underlying conflicts over having and exercising power and authority, which may have further implications in our consideration of his views on obedience,[14] doubtless played a part. In any case, Ignatius accepted the decision without complaint, and the next day immersed himself once again in the arduous tasks of his office—a labor not to be interrupted until his death five years later.

Overall, the psychological observer cannot fail to be impressed, not only by the immensity and effectiveness of the undertaking, but by the extraordinary capacities of the man Ignatius. The continued exercise of judgment, wisdom, and prudence at such a sustained level for so many years is all the more impressive. He was a man of exceptional resourcefulness, great ego strength, and remarkable determination. It is not that Ignatius' work and experience did not reflect the vicissitudes of conflict and defense, but that despite these difficulties he was able to accomplish so much and to maintain such a high level of performance.

THE CONSTITUTIONS

XIII

When Pope Paul III established the Society of Jesus as a canonical order, the bull already contained a rough outline of regulations governing the order, derived from the deliberations of Ignatius and his companions in 1539. The so-called *Formula*, based on the *Prima Societatis Jesu Instituti Summa*, was included with some modifications in the papal bulls *Regimini Militantis Ecclesiae* of 1540, establishing the Society, and *Exposcit Debitum* of 1550, confirming it. The bulls also established the right of the order to draw up constitutions by which it was to be governed and directed.[1]

On 4 March 1541, Ignatius and his companions divided the material into forty-nine points. Even though this revision was provisional, Ignatius regarded it as having the force of law and promulgated the articles in a letter to Laynez (Epistolae I, 246–247; in Young, 1959, pp. 67–68). But this only brought Ignatius to the threshold of what might well be his most important work. The rapid growth of the Society and the signs of papal favor made it mandatory that the Constitutions be written. The companions had imposed this burden on Ignatius and Codure, but Codure died on 29 August 1541 and Ignatius had to struggle with this monumental labor on his own. Very likely, he was occupied (indeed preoccupied) with it from 1543 on. It was a long and difficult labor, made all the more complex by his many other obligations as General and by his continued ill health (Dudon 1949).

As early as 1542, certain decisions had to be made, particularly regarding poverty and the endowment of colleges. Pietro Codazzo's gift of the church of La Strada raised the question of whether the church could possess property independently of the Jesuit community. The answer was at first the traditional one observed by mendicant orders—that it could—but this did not satisfy Ignatius. He continued to struggle with the matter, studying the rules of other religious institutes and seeking divine inspiration in prayer. The Spiritual Diary of 1544–1545 records his fervent effort to resolve the issue of the poverty appropriate for the professed houses of the Society.

POLANCO'S CONTRIBUTION

By the end of 1546, the first section of the Constitutions, the Examen Generale, dealing with the admission of candidates to the Society, was completed (Aldama 1973). The work had gone slowly, partly because of Ignatius' plodding style and the care he took over each detail, but also presumably because of the other demands on his time. The situation changed in 1547 when Polanco became Ignatius' secretary. As Rahner writes: "With his finely trained theological mind and lucid legal temperament, he was the born secretary. He prepared rough drafts, copied extracts from the rules of Orders from Benedict to Dominic, understood how to adapt himself with sensitive modesty to his master, to whom he was entirely devoted, and saw that Ignatius had time for writing undisturbed." Polanco was to prove his worth over the following quarter century as secretary to the first three Generals of the Society and, after the death of Francis Borgia in 1572, as its Vicar General.

When Polanco arrived in Rome, he was confronted with a formidable task. First he had to put the haphazard notes that Ignatius had been collecting since 1544 into manageable order, consulting Ignatius frequently on points that were unclear or poorly formulated. Next he set about gathering and organizing the legislation of other religious orders as a resource for Ignatius' further reflections on what might be incorporated into the Constitutions of the Society. Then the papal documents regarding the Society had to be assembled and systematized. Through all this, Polanco continually made notes and summaries and presented doubts and suggestions to Ignatius for consideration (Aldama 1973).

THE FIRST DRAFT

By August 1548, enough progress had been made for Ignatius to call a meeting of the professed fathers in 1550. The flood of correspondence between Rome and the provinces brought questions, problems, and suggestions about matters pertaining to the vows, the ministries, and issues of poverty and obedience. He and Polanco had managed to pull together a provisional draft by the end of 1550. The meeting of the professed fathers lasted from the beginning of November 1550 until the beginning of February 1551. There were a good many criticisms: Bobadilla thought the draft was too long and that there should be a summary that would be easier to assimilate. Laynez and others objected that divesting oneself of all possessions before profession was unfair and risky, and they thought it would be better for the Pope rather than the General to decide if and when to send religious to foreign countries. Salmerón objected to some points pertaining to the vows.

Despite these reservations, the fathers voted their overall approval of the draft provided by Ignatius and Polanco. At this point Ignatius tried to resign as General,[2] but the good fathers insisted that he continue. Ignatius accepted what he came to regard as God's will. But he was not yet satisfied with the version of the Constitutions that his companions had approved, known as text A. He continued testing its provisions, gathering fresh data and impressions, rewriting, and clarifying. Nadal brought back observations and criticisms from Sicily, Spain, and Portugal; Ignatius and Polanco would examine them closely, consider their relevance, and make whatever modifications might be called for. The resulting text, known as text B, reflects the efforts of Ignatius and Polanco to refine and perfect the document. The task continued until Ignatius' death (Aldama 1973; Ganss 1970).

But communication of the Constitutions to the rest of the Society could not wait. In December 1551 Ignatius decided that the text the fathers had approved (text A) should be promulgated. The plan was that Nadal would carry the printed version to each locale and there would declare the Constitutions and facilitate putting them into practice insofar as possible. He began in Sicily and then went to Spain, Portugal, Germany, Austria, and Italy. The reception in the provinces was complicated by local difficulties and divergences. Ignatius had wanted his Constitutions to become not a lifeless document but a living and meaningful guide. But he had to rely increasingly on those he commissioned to promulgate it—for the most part Nadal, but also Laynez and Ribadeneyra (Ravier 1987).

THE HAND OF IGNATIUS

No doubt Ignatius needed the help he got from Polanco and also Nadal. It is probably safe to say that without their assistance the work might never have been completed. In October 1547 Polanco had written to Spain: "One responsibility has cost our Father a great deal of time. It is his work on the Constitutions, which with God's grace will keep our Society in good estate and greatly advance it. It is necessary work, but it demands a large amount of time and is laborious" (von Matt and Rahner, 1956, p. 88). Ignatius undoubtedly put his unique stamp on the Constitutions. Essential points had already been decided before his collaborators came into the picture, and even after 1551 the manuscripts bear the unmistakable marks of Ignatius' revisions. The last word throughout was his, and there is no question that writing the Constitutions became his major preoccupation. Nadal was fond of quoting Ignatius' comment: "I have asked God to grant me three graces before I die, in the first place the confirmation of the Society of Jesus by the Holy See, secondly a similar approval of the *Spiritual Exercises,* and thirdly that I might be able to write down the Constitutions" (cited in von Matt and Rahner, 1956, p. 89).

Ignatius had founded not only a new order but a new kind of order, distinctly different from the Franciscans, the Dominicans, the Benedictines, and others. The prevailing style of religious life included the wearing of identifying habits, performance of the office in choir, observance of feasts and penances imposed by rule, and so on. Ignatius abandoned these traditional practices, prolonged the trial period of the novitiate, postponed the solemn vows to the end of a long and rigorous course of training, and instituted the practice of the account of conscience.[3] The habit, choir, austerities of rule, acceptance of ecclesiastical benefices, and the capitular system[4] were all abolished. Ignatius' work has become the model for the constitutions of many religious groups that came into being subsequently. Through the Constitutions, more than any other single work, Ignatius placed his mark on the history of the Church.

At his death in 1556, the text of the Constitutions was in manuscript form—essentially four separate treatises: the General Examen, the explanations entitled Declarations on the Examen, the text of the Constitutions proper, and the explanatory Declarations on the Constitutions. This autograph manuscript edition, text B, received final approval and confirmation from the Society's First General Congregation assembled in 1558 to elect Ignatius' successor as General (Ganss 1970).[5]

Our interest in this enormous effort is here confined to what the document tells us about the personality and character of Ignatius himself. The task is not made easier by the style of the Constitutions. They are legal documents, regulations meant to govern the organization and works of the Society for all time. They are to that extent without emotion, personal reflection, nuance, or suggestion about the man who poured his life's blood and even dying breath into them. We are forced to read between the lines to discern something of Ignatius the man.

The first point to note is that the guiding spirit throughout is the *Spiritual Exercises* (Leturia 1941). The powerful spiritual insight Ignatius gained at Manresa had never left him, and now, three decades later, after the years of pilgrimage and study, and even his ongoing experience as the General of the Society, the same inspiration seems to come to fruition in his writing of the Constitutions. The same spirit of submission to God's will, prayerful devotion to the advancement of God's kingdom, humble acceptance of God's graces, and self-sacrifice that comes through so vividly in the Exercises appears in the pages of the Constitutions—now transformed into prescriptions, directions, rules, and guiding norms.

What has changed is the man Ignatius, mellowed and made wise by his years of experience. He is no longer the fanatical extremist with a burning desire to take the kingdom of heaven by storm. The tone is measured, prudent, holding up ideals and lofty ambitions while at the same time urging moderation. He had ruined his health and destroyed his body in his impatient and immoderate zeal for self-abnegation and severe penances; he did not wish his sons to make the same mistake and render themselves less, rather than more, fit for God's work. The same progression can be seen in his directions regarding poverty, which strive for balance between the ideals of evangelical poverty and the practical needs of supporting large houses and many laborers in the vineyards. He had to feed his men, maintain the houses where they lived and worked, support the novices and others still in training, foot the bill for advanced degrees in the great universities, keep the doors of the colleges open, and so on. The ideals and practices of the pilgrim years had to give way to more prudent arrangements and procedures.

The same emphasis can be seen in the two portraits of the General in the last part of the Constitutions (723–735).[6] The longest part of this description is a highly idealized catalog of the qualities that should be possessed by any prospective General. If the portrait in some sense represents Ignatius himself, where would another such be found? Fortunately, at the end of this paean to virtue, Ignatius adds a more sober and reassuring note: "If any of the aforementioned qualities should be wanting, there should at least be no lack of great probity and of love for the Society, nor of good judgment accompanied by sound learning. For in regard to other things, the aids which he will have . . . could through God's help and favor supply to a great extent for many deficiencies" (Constitutions 735). As Ravier comments, "These gifts are all human gifts, or at least can be merely human gifts. And they are only qualified in the most temperate way: no longer the superlatives, but this estimable 'ordinariness' in which common mortals participate!" (1987, p. 470).

OBEDIENCE

Many aspects of the Constitutions may yield further access to the man Ignatius—his views on the admission of candidates, on poverty, on prayer, on the apostolic mission of the Society, on charity, and so on. But the one that promises the richest yield is his view on obedience.

Ignatius' thinking about obedience began to take shape in the course of creating the Society. Obedience and submission to God's will had been a prominent theme since the days at Manresa. Later, when the companions of Paris had banded together, the idea of submission to the authority of the Pope was central in their considerations. And in the discussions of March–June 1539, which culminated in the *Deliberatio primorum patrum*, one of the central questions was whether they should commit themselves to one of their number under a vow of obedience. The decision "to obey one among us" did not come easily— the deliberation consumed several weeks (Ravier, 1987, pp. 84–89, 369–374). The outcome undoubtedly reflected Ignatius' opinion but was wholeheartedly endorsed by the companions.

After his election to the office of General, Ignatius was not slow to promulgate his views on obedience.[7] In August 1542, he wrote to Giovanni Battista Viola, who was having difficulties with his studies in Paris and had imprudently ignored Ignatius' advice:

I received your letter but I fail to understand it. In two different places you speak of obedience. In the first you say that you are ready to obey me, and in the second you say: "Because I would rather die than fail in obedience, I submit to the judgment of your reverence." Now, it seems to me that obedience seeks to be blind, and is blind in two ways: in the first it belongs to the inferior to submit his understanding, when there is no question of sin, and to do what is commanded of him; in the second it is also the inferior's duty, once the superior commands or has commanded something, to represent to the superior whatever considerations or disadvantages may occur to him, and to do so humbly and simply, without any attempt to draw the superior to either side, so that afterwards he can follow, with peace of mind, the way pointed out to him or commanded. (Epistolae I, 228–229 [Letter 52]; in Tylenda, 1985, p. 4)

Again in 1550, Ignatius ordered that a directive be delivered to all the Jesuit houses in Rome on the subject of obedience. He makes it clear that the obedience he expected from his sons was to be prompt and unquestioning—blind obedience. The text is Polanco's.

Our reverend Father Master Ignatius wishes for God's greater glory and the greater spiritual progress of all of Ours (as he has already partly declared in other ordinances), that in the future, when his reverence or father minister summons anyone, whether he be a priest or not, or the subminister calls one who is not a priest, they should all answer the call at once, as though it was the voice of Christ our Lord, and practice this obedience in the name of His Divine Majesty. In this way obedience should be blind and prompt. If one is at prayer, he should leave his prayer. If he hears the voice of his superior, or rather the voice of Christ our Lord, when he is writing and has begun a letter, say A or B, he should not wait to finish it.

In like manner, if he happens to be with anyone at all, even a prelate (supposing he owes him no obedience), he should come if he is called by any of his superiors. Should one be called who happens to be taking some bodily refreshments of any kind, whether he be at table or in bed, or busy with an invalid, serving a drink or a medicine, or engaged in a service which could not be interrupted without harm to the patient, such as helping to bleed him, or should he be going to confession or about to receive Communion, or hearing the confessions of others, if a priest, in all such cases he should send word to the superior and ask whether he wishes him to leave his meal, his bed, or whatever else it may happen to be. (Epistolae III, 156 [Letter 1326]; in Tylenda, 1985, pp. 36–37)

Other communications about obedience stemmed from the persistent problems in Portugal. Ignatius had appointed Father Diego Miro in place of the troublesome Rodriguez. But this only gave rise to further tensions. Where Rodriguez had been mild in manner and relaxed in his governance, Miro was strict and demanding. Some of Rodriguez's adherents refused to obey the new provincial. Ignatius had sent Miguel de Torres to implement the transition, but Torres' reports disturbed Ignatius, who could not tolerate such disobedience. Ignatius wrote a stern letter to Miro[8] expressing an uncompromising demand for complete, unquestioning submission to the orders of superiors. Ignatius' terms are harsh—those who will not submit themselves to the superior as if to Christ himself are to be expelled or delivered to Rome, where they will have to deal with Ignatius himself.

The situation in Portugal plagued Ignatius for several years. His aside at the end of this letter seems to suggest his annoyance with these continuing difficulties. Part of the blame lay with Rodriguez, whose lax manner of governing tended to create favorites and foster intense devotion in his followers, and to inspire equally intense sentiments among his opponents. All this upset Ignatius, who saw his Portuguese sons straying from the path of virtue that he envisioned for his Society.

Ignatius' efforts to rekindle the spirit of obedience in the divided province met with little success. In January 1553 da Camara described the sad state of affairs and begged Ignatius to address the members of the province on the subject of obedience. Ignatius did so in March. In the letter, drafted with the help of Polanco, Ignatius achieves a magisterial and classic pronouncement on the subject of holy obedience. This letter (which appears in Appendix B) stands as the most developed statement of Ignatius' views on the vow of religious obedience. His understanding of the virtue, essentially unchanged throughout his career, was the view that was incorporated in the somewhat lapidary and legalistic formulae of the Constitutions.[9]

This text of the Constitutions on obedience, essentially completed by 1550, provides a distillation of Ignatius' thinking on the subject, later expounded in the letter to Portugal. In these passages as in other aspects of his spiritual teaching, the Ignatian inspiration harkens back to the

Exercises and their roots in the Manresa experience. The context here derives from the meditations on the Two Standards and the Three Degrees of Humility. The field of battle is that of the kingdom of Christ versus that of the Devil, waging war for men's souls and the establishing of God's Kingdom. The good soldier surrenders himself in total self-abnegation and humility to the will and commission of Christ, the ideal and loving leader.

Ignatius' vision reverberates with echoes of the illuminations on the banks of the Cardoner and at La Storta. Ignatius saw himself and his company as engaged in a struggle to achieve God's redemptive plan, to follow Christ and the earthly representation of his Vicar the Pope and all who derive jurisdiction from this authority down to the lowest superior in the Society. He envisioned a company of dedicated soldiers, ready with prompt and unquestioning obedience to pursue any task or mission set before them by the Vicar of Christ. Obedience was thus the essential principle of unity, action, and coordination. The authority to command such obedience came directly from God, so that the least command of the superior was synonymous with the will of God. The command of the superior, then, was given *in loco Christi*, in the place of Christ.[10]

Ignatius' approach, drawn from his military background and experience, is the spirit of command and obedience characteristic of Iñigo the warrior. He was, we can presume, a courageous leader who demanded unquestioning obedience and tolerated no insubordination in his men. The military objective was all-important and overruled any obstacles. This was the spirit and determination that led him to the ramparts of Pamplona.

Part of Ignatius' rigor may also have been due to a diffuse crisis over both obedience and poverty throughout the Society. Ravier (1987) noted the increasing split between Ignatius the spiritual director and Ignatius the administrator, especially after 1552, when the Portuguese scandal broke. But Ignatius' view of obedience was not unlike that of Xavier from his post on the other side of the world. They both took a fairly severe position in matters of obedience. But then it could be said that they were cut from the same cloth. There seems to be little question, however, that the situation in Portugal had tried Ignatius' patience and prudence to the breaking point and that he located the difficulty in the failure of holy obedience.

PSYCHOANALYTIC PERSPECTIVE

To the psychological eye, Ignatius' repeated and unremitting emphasis on the centrality of obedience plays rather oddly alongside the pattern of his own life and career. Ignatius throughout his life remained rather headstrong, determined to follow his own course without much regard for the wishes and expectations of those around him, and in good hagiographic style, his biographers have cast this independence and strong will in a spiritually positive light—that in following his own idiosyncratic path he was merely following the directives of the Holy Spirit guiding him toward his divinely inspired destiny. This may well have been the case. Ignatius seems to have possessed an unerring sense of the guidance of divine providence in all that pertained to obedience, that whatever the superior commanded under holy obedience—in loco Christi—was guaranteed by divine influence (Blet 1956). But from a psychoanalytic perspective, we cannot be sure.

Divine guidance aside, we are left with a psychological paradox. The spiritual mentor and Superior General who so avidly counseled absolute, immediate, unquestioning, perfect, and blind obedience was not noteworthy for obedience in his own career. He was not following the laws and mores of his home country when he got into trouble as a rambunctious youth; it was not compliance with the decisions of his commanders that made him defy the French when the commander of the garrison at Pamplona was prepared to surrender; nor was he responsive to the needs and wishes of his family when he turned his back on the castle of Loyola to seek his destiny as a beggar of Christ. Time and again he defied the expectations of superiors, mentors, and officials of both church and realm, insisting on his own approach, his own inspiration, his own view of things. He refused to submit to the wishes of the superior of the Franciscans in Jerusalem, insisting on doing things his own way until the poor friar had to invoke the power and authority of the Holy See. In his repeated confrontations with the Inquisition, he proved rather a brazen, contentious, almost defiant defender of his views and practices. One might guess that this less-than-compliant attitude may have contributed to the suspicions and reactionary posturing of the judges.

Perhaps most striking, when Ignatius was deciding what manner of religious order he would found, he again struck out on an independent course. He would follow none of the prescribed and approved models of religious community extant in the church. His order was to be different, unique, special. From this perspective, his counsel to the Portuguese scholastics at Coimbra is ironic: "It is a great delusion in those whose understanding has been darkened by self-love, to think that there is any obedience in the subject who tries to draw the superior to what he wishes. Listen to Saint Bernard, who had much experience in this matter. 'Whoever endeavors either openly or covertly to have his spiritual father enjoin him what he himself desires, deceives himself if he flatters himself as a true follower of obedience. For in that he does not obey his superior, but rather the superior obeys him'" (Tylenda, 1985, p. 7).[11]

Ignatius flagrantly contradicted this advice on countless occasions in the course of gaining papal approval for his vision of a new religious order. If there were ever a case of bending the superior to one's own wishes, of drawing him into obeying one's own views and desires rather than submitting in unquestioning obedience to the wishes and directives of the superior, Ignatius' behavior would be hard to beat. From the perspective of five hundred years of history, we can salute this rebellious quality as salutary and providential. We can allow ourselves to believe that God was using the unique qualities of this saintly warrior to achieve great wonders for the church and for the advancement of his kingdom on earth.

This consideration does not eliminate the paradox, but it prompts a question that may illuminate the psychological sources: can these observations be taken to suggest an underlying unconscious conflict over authority in Ignatius? To what extent do Ignatius' attitudes toward authority and particularly his view of obedience reflect unresolved conflictual and authoritarian aspects of his own personality?

THE AUTHORITARIAN CHARACTER

Our understanding of the authoritarian personality arises out of post-World War II studies of anti-Semitism and ethnocentrism. The major work in this area was the massive study that culminated in *The Authoritarian Personality* (Adorno et al. 1950). This study uncovered a consistent profile of personality characteristics: authoritarian individuals tended to adhere rigidly to conventional and generally accepted values; they tended to be uncritically submissive to whatever moral authorities existed in the group to which they belonged, authorities whom they frequently idealized; they tended to turn their aggression against anyone violating or rejecting the values they espoused, so that their attitudes were often harsh, condemnatory, and punitive; they tended to be tough-minded rather than tender-minded, so that they usually rejected the subjective or imaginative approach to things; their thinking tended to superstition and stereotypes, often in the form of belief in more or less mystical determinants of individual fate and a tendency to think in rigid categories; they were frequently preoccupied with power and control, emphasized issues of power and submission in regard to authority, and identified with powerful figures; their attitudes were often hostile and cynical, tending to view the world as dangerous and threatening and projecting strong negative emotions to the outside; and finally sexual fantasies were a source of excessive concern (Adorno et al. 1950; Meissner 1971).

AUTHORITY CONFLICTS

A case can be made for locating some of these characteristics within Ignatius' personality. Ignatius certainly adhered to conventional values of his time, especially the religious values that so strongly dominated his culture. He was, with the exceptions noted above, respectful and submissive to authority, both ecclesiastical and civil; the regime he instituted in the Society, however, was far from totalitarian. He was capable of delegating authority and more often than not deferred to the judgment of local superiors, who could understand the circumstances of a given case much better than he could. As Bertrand (1985) has observed about all Ignatius' writings on obedience: "The circumstances that motivated the *Letter on Obedience*, and all the other letters dealing with this subject as well, are always the same. It is never a question of defending the central power, but of rousing or sustaining the peripheral power, either in local terms or at the level of great nations. This is a constant without exception—at least during Ignatius' lifetime" (p. 77).[12]

His attitude toward church authorities, the Popes and bishops, was in some respects submissive and idealizing, but not without a degree of manipulation and "managing" on his part. One would hardly place Ignatius among the tender-minded; his approach was usually pragmatic and concrete, except for his mystical experience, which was exquisitely tender and affective. His mystical inclination was broad and deep, and the wish to submit himself totally and without reserve to the power and direction of the divine will was uncompromising and complete. His view of the world as threatening tended to focus on the spiritual realm, where he saw dangers on all sides—a fantasy of the evil one carrying on his diabolical campaign for the destruction of the Church and pious souls. Finally, we have noted the role of sexuality in Ignatius' emotional life: the powerful repressive barriers he was forced to erect against any sexual impulses, and the displacement and sublimation of his libidinal inclinations into apostolic and even mystical paths.

These considerations draw us back to Ignatius' *Spiritual Exercises*, particularly to the Rules for Thinking with the Church (Exercises 352–370). These rules were composed sometime in 1539–1541, possibly to buffer his newborn Society from suspicions of heresy or even to counter the threats of the fanatical adherents of Carafa. In any case, the rules must be read as reflecting the mind of Ignatius as he assumed the reigns of government of the Society. The authoritarian elements are unmistakable. The first rule reads: "All judgment laid aside, we ought to have our mind ready and prompt to obey, in all, the true Spouse of Christ our Lord, which is our holy Mother the Church Hierarchical" (Exercises 352). Again, in rule nine: "Finally, to praise all precepts of the Church, keeping the mind prompt to find reasons in their defence and in no manner against them" (Exercises 361). Complete submission of intellect and judgment is recommended in rule thirteen: "To be right in everything, we ought always to hold that the white which I see, is black, if the Hierarchical Church so decides it, believing that between Christ our Lord, the Bridegroom, and the Church, His Bride, there is the same Spirit which governs and directs us for the salvation of our souls. Because by the same Spirit and our Lord Who gave the ten Commandments, our holy Mother the Church is directed and governed" (Exercises 365). The rest of the rules are concerned with opposing all questioning, doubting, or criticism of the Church and its practices.

Whatever their theological prudence in the context of the heretic-baiting and fanatic counter-Reformational dynamics that flourished in Rome and elsewhere, these rules breathe a spirit of authoritarian control and the suppression of freedom of thought or expression. They share the spirit of Ignatius' letters and directives concerning absolute and blind obedience. They must be considered expressions of Ignatius' own authoritarian characteristics and conflicts.

Freedom is threatening because it allows for unpredictability; it cannot be controlled. The tendency of the authoritarian disposition is to suppress freedom—in the name of any other noble investment—but unequivocally to suppress freedom. In whatever guise, authority concerns itself with achieving a balance between the demands of order and the demands of freedom. While authoritarians may find themselves driven to an emphasis on control that sacrifices freedom, libertarians may surge to the opposite extreme of complete license to the detriment of order. Functional authority operates somewhere between the extremes. There is no one point on the continuum at which maximal freedom is guaranteed along with order. There is an optimal point, however, for each authority relation operating within the distinctive requirements for order and commitments to individual freedom that characterizes the group (Meissner 1971). In Ignatius' dealings with the Portuguese problem, his task was not merely bringing dissident and recalcitrant followers back into line, but in allowing the degree of freedom that permits initiative and self-actualization in undertaking and carrying through apostolic works, while keeping in place the prescriptions of obedience that serve the purposes of coordination and sustaining of the works and directions of the Society as a whole. He was forced to ease the reins when the Portuguese provincial was too strict and severe, and to tighten his grip when faced with rebelliousness and recalcitrance.

To a certain degree, freedom was threatening in the mind of Ignatius, and he sought to regulate the risks of his own inner freedom by obsessive devices, constant self-examination and accusation, self-denial, and repression of all inordinate desires. He imposed on himself, both psychically and externally, a routine that minimized spontaneity. He sought in his Constitutions to impose a similar order on the inner and outer lives of his sons. Viewed in authoritarian terms, these efforts might constitute an elaborate form of what Fromm (1947) called the "escape from freedom." A primary mechanism of escape from freedom is surrendering one's independence and fusing oneself with something external in order to acquire the strength one lacks. This is most commonly found in strivings for submission or domination, the normal counterparts of neurotic sadomasochism. The masochist often shows a marked dependence on powers outside himself—other people, institutions, even nature or God. The connection between such masochistic propensities and the authoritarian personality was noted by Charmé (1983), who comments:

> The masochist is willing to sacrifice all individual decisions, responsibility, or interests and to find meaning, direction, and protection by submitting to some larger power. He identifies with a person, group, cause, nation, or religion which defines the meaning of his life and offers the prestige and strength he lacks as an individual. This form of masochism is associated with the authoritarian personalities found in both fascist and religious movements. The appeal of many religious "cults" is based on a similar process. In most cases the cult member willingly sacrifices all signs of individuality in thought and personality in exchange for the security and power offered by the group in general and the leader in particular. (p. 229)

To this formulation, we can add Fromm's comment: "The feature common to all authoritarian thinking is the conviction that life is determined by forces outside of man's own self, his interest, his wishes. The only possible happiness lies in the submission to these forces. The powerlessness of man is the leitmotif of masochistic philosophy. . . . To suffer without complaining is his highest virtue—not the courage of trying to end suffering or at least diminish it. Not to change fate, but to submit to it, is the heroism of the authoritarian character" (1947, pp. 194–195). Sadistic tendencies may be found hand-in-hand with masochistic ones, often in the same personality. They involve wishes to make others dependent on oneself, to have absolute power over others, to rule others in such a way to exploit and use them, to see or make others suffer. These tendencies are usually less conscious and are often covered over by reaction formations and rationalizations of excessive concern for and goodness toward others. "I rule you because I know what is best for you."

The question here is whether and to what extent Ignatius' appeal to absolute authority and his insistence on perfect and blind obedience reflect the underlying authoritarian structure of his personality and the sadomasochistic drive determinants it implies. In my view, Ignatius would certainly not fit the full-blown picture of the perverse authoritarian Fromm describes. To Fromm, the strength and power of the sadist depend on the submission of weak subjects. Where such sadism wears the face of love, it must be remembered that the sadist does not dominate the lives of others because he loves them; he loves them only because he can dominate them. The very essence of the sadistic drive is the pleasure derived from complete domination over the other. The paradox of such sadomasochistic propensities is that the need for power is rooted not in strength, but in weakness. It is an expression of the individual's inability to stand alone and of his need for others to sustain him. As Fromm (1947) points out, power can mean either domination, the power over others, or potency, the power to make and do. "Far from being identical, these two qualities are mutually exclusive. Impotence, using the term not only with regard to the sexual sphere but to all spheres of human potentialities, results in the sadistic striving for domination; to the extent to which an individual is potent, that is, able to realize his potentialities on the basis of freedom and integrity of his self, he does not need to dominate and is lacking the lust for power. Power, in the sense of domination, is the perversion of potency, just as sexual sadism is the perversion of sexual love" (p. 184).

Fromm refers to this sadomasochistic type of personality as the "authoritarian character" on the grounds that it is consistently characterized by its attitude toward authority. Briefly, the authoritarian character admires authority and tends to submit to it, while simultaneously wishing to be an authority and have others submit to him. When the authority relationship is benevolent, the authority serves also as an object for identification. Fromm uses the example of the teacher who nourishes the growth of the student by the exercise of his authority. Authority in this type of relationship tends to dissolve insofar as the student gradually approaches the knowledge of the teacher. In an authoritarian relationship, however, the authority is inhibiting and is, therefore, either hated or, by way or repression and reaction formation, overly admired. The hatred or overestimation tends to increase as the relationship becomes more intense.

It is characteristic of the authoritarian character to see himself as governed by fate, rationalized as destiny, natural law, duty, or the will of God. The essential factor is that there be a higher power to which he can only submit. The authoritarian does not lack courage, activity, or belief. But the root of his existence in powerlessness transforms these characteristics. Activity becomes action in the name of something higher than himself. To suffer is the highest virtue. His heroism is to submit to fate, not to change it. His belief is rooted in doubt and compensates for it.

Related to the authoritarian factor is Ignatius' conflicts over aggression. His preconversion personality was marked by aggressiveness, and it seems fairly clear that the management of these impulses remained a serious problem for him after his conversion, in his efforts to follow in the footsteps of the passive, suffering, and nonaggressive Christ. We have speculated over the degree to which his efforts to deal with his inherently aggressive impulses took the form of punitive penances and self-torment, driven by a harsh and judgmental superego. Moreover, his mystical experience may also have ridden on a defensive denial of aggression. Conflict over aggression implies a developmental defect in the formation of mechanisms for dealing effectively with aggressive feelings. Aggressive feelings are poorly controlled, and the sense of mastery over them is inhibited. When the mental apparatus has reached such a state of evolution that it can utilize the energic potentialities of aggression for more constructive purposes, the conflict is minimized. Psychoanalysts speak of this as neutralization of aggressive drives. When the development of this capacity is impaired, however, neutralization is limited, and the aggressive drives retain their primitive and hostile character, threatening the integrity of the ego. The frailer the ego, the more menacing is aggression. Control is, therefore, a matter of deep concern, whether it be the inner control of destructive forces or the outer control of angry impulses. It is no surprise, therefore, that authoritarian individuals are preoccupied with control and power. The often unconscious activation of aggressive impulses is reflected in the generalized hostility, suspicion, distrust, and cynicism they often display. By projection of these impulses they come to view their environment as riddled with dangers and hostile threats and the people around them as threatening, hurtful, dangerous, and untrustworthy.

Because the effort to deal with aggression strains the inner resources of the individual, he seeks support and reinforcement by identifying with the sources of power around him. It is as though by psychic alliance with the sources of power in his environment he is able to bolster his own wavering inner sense of control. His submission to the moral authorities in his milieu tends to be rigid and uncritical. If he wields authority, he does so insecurely and is threatened by anything that may undermine his control and the absoluteness of his power. His anxiety is alleviated by unquestioning submission from his subordinates. If a subordinate should question his authority, or even worse take initiative independently of it, his control is weakened and his power challenged. None of this need be present to his conscious mind, but it may well lie hidden in the deeper recesses of his unconscious thought. His authoritarian behavior is then rationalized on some other grounds, while the real motives, rooted in the conflicts over inner aggressive impulses, are untouched. Nonetheless, the anxiety implicit in any threat to his control drives him to embrace the elements that support that control. He therefore clings to conventional values and becomes punitive toward those who violate them; his thinking is constrained into more or less rigid categories and stereotyped concepts.

It is hard to escape the impression that Ignatius fits the authoritarian mold to some degree. The question is how much. These authoritarian trends appear to have played a strong role in his psychic make-up and were to an extent distilled into the formulas of the Constitutions. But they were tempered significantly by other elements in Ignatius' complex personality and his practical genius as an administrator. As his letters and directives make clear, he relied greatly on the judgment and prudence of his subordinates, particularly when the problems existed far from Rome and when he had no direct knowledge of the situation. The authoritarian strain was also tempered by Ignatius' capacity for drawing men to him in a spirit of devotion and companionship. The love and generosity that pervade his writings and seem to have been an important part of his everyday dealings with his fellow Jesuits may have gone a long way toward moderating the severity and obsessive perfectionism revealed in his more authoritarian utterances. We have some inkling of this from the reports of da Camara. In his *Memorial*, he tells us, "Our Father strongly deplored and punished the lack of obedience not only in essential matters, . . . but also in every other matter" (Memorial, n. 3; cited in Ravier, 1987, p. 373). But he strikes certain other notes that suggest that Ignatius was slow to appeal to obedience and much preferred to call upon the mature judgment and good will of men he could trust: "Our Father was accustomed, in all that he could have others do with gentleness and without recourse to obedience, not to let obedience intervene; on the contrary, when he could have someone do something, not because the person had seen the wish of His Reverence, but because the individual did it of his own free will—that pleased

Ignatius much more than if the individual did something because he had realized Ignatius' wish but without anyone's telling him to do so—that pleased him more than to have to give the order, finally, for the same reason, [it pleased Ignatius more] when the matter was ordered without its being under pain of obedience" (Memorial, n. 262; cited in Ravier 1987).

We have good reason to wonder whether in his strong statements on obedience—for example, in his letter to Father Miro on the dismissal of disobedient subjects[13]—Ignatius was not responding to the impulse to erect a kind of authoritarian system of governance within the Society. In such a system, the more authoritarian the tendencies of those participating, the more evolved the social defense system becomes. The superior becomes punitively aggressive toward his inferior, and the inferior becomes masochistically submissive to this superior. Thus the pattern and structure of the system derive from and in a sense depend on the interaction of authoritarian intrapsychic forces. However we balance these various elements, and however we understand their interplay in Ignatius' complex personality, we cannot forget that, if he manifested masochistic and submissively authoritarian attitudes, this was nonetheless the same Ignatius who tangled with the Inquisition and stalwartly argued his case, the same Ignatius who founded a group of which he was the guiding spirit, the leader, and until the end of his life the primary authority.

WOMEN

XIV

Women play an important role in the saint's life experience, from the beginnings at the castle of Loyola to the very end of his saintly journey. It is safe to say that, had it not been for the assistance of important women at critical points in the early history of the Society of Jesus, that organization may have met a far different fate.

Ignatius was born a nobleman and raised a chivalrous courtier, and his dealings with women from all walks of life were always marked by concern, respectful warmth, tact, circumspection, and seemingly endless charity. From the days of his conversion on, he manifested a noteworthy dedication to the spiritual welfare of the women who crossed his path. He took special concern to preach to women in his pilgrim years; he devoted himself to the spiritual direction of many troubled feminine souls and undertook, often with near heroic efforts, the reformation of convents. And in Rome, the apostolic endeavors closest to his heart were the care of the poor women and prostitutes of the city.

Even more, Ignatius exuded a charm and a power of attraction that drew women to him. Huonder (1932) writes that "in spite of this reserve [in spiritual direction] and his powerful, masculine style—indeed, because of them—but above all on account of his virtues, pious women felt strongly drawn towards Ignatius" (p. 297). In a psychoanalytic context we would more readily speak of transference and wonder what aspects of Ignatius' personality would elicit such attachment from his female adherents. But we also know that the attachment and devotion were not limited to the opposite sex—the same was true of many of his sons in the Society. As Rahner (1960) comments: "This saint is indeed never merely the soldier of God, the imperious general, the unapproachable man. His companions who knew him best always remarked on the 'motherly' strain in him, his cheerfulness and the smiling radiance of his countenance. For them he was simply the 'Father,' just because he could be so motherly—the eternally insoluble paradox of the saint" (p. 5).

The women of Ignatius' world may thus have sensed in him a fatherly strength and a motherly solicitude that generated trust and confidence. These transferential dispositions were undoubtedly carried along on a current of sublimated sexuality—heterosexual in the case of his female adherents, homosexual for his male followers. We can argue that the powerful sexual urges that had been so abruptly and ruthlessly suppressed at the time of his conversion continued to exercise their influence and that one of the important channels of this sublimated expression was to be found in Ignatius' dealings with women and in his apostolic efforts on their spiritual behalf.

THE WOMEN OF LOYOLA

This story cannot be told without returning to the very beginning. The fact that Iñigo's mother died shortly after his birth and that he was put out to be nursed by the blacksmith's wife, María de Garín, whose cottage was located less than a half mile from the castle (Brodrick 1956), may have had lifelong implications. María became, in effect, a second and substitute mother. But it is also worth noting that the blacksmith's hut was close quarters with little or no personal privacy. The conditions regarding separation of the sexes, nudity, sleeping arrangements, and the dangers of primal scene exposure would have put little Iñigo in a state of high sexual stimulation, intensifying his oedipal desires and the corresponding level of libidinal conflict, oedipal guilt, and castration anxiety.[1]

It is not clear how long Iñigo lived with the blacksmith's family. We know he had returned to live in the castle by the time Magdalena de Araoz arrived at Loyola as the wife of Martín García when Iñigo was seven years old. There can be little doubt that Magdalena's influence on Iñigo was profound and meaningful. It was she who for all practical purposes took over the task of raising the youngest of the Loyolas. She brought with her all the refinement, taste, and pious devotion of the court of Isabella the Catholic. When the wounded soldier was borne to the refuge of Loyola it was she who nursed him back to health and strength. Her kindness, tenderness, and religious devotion (as well as her books, notably the Spanish translation of Ludolph the Carthusian's *Life of Jesus* and Jacobus de Voragine's *Legends of the Saints*) must have had an impact on Iñigo and may have played an important role in his conversion. There is reason to think that there was more than charity and sisterly affection in their relationship. Rahner (1960) notes this more libidinal dimension: "Magdalena's care for her brother-in-law not only brought him bodily recovery but also gave a decisive impulse to his inner conversion. The impression that his sister-in-law made on him is made clear to us by a little incident related many years later. Ignatius once told a Belgian novice that a picture of our Lady, before which he was wont to recite the Hours of the Blessed Virgin, reminded him so much by its beauty of his sister-in-law Magdalena that it disturbed him in his devotions, and he forthwith stuck a piece of paper over the face" (p. 116).

Is it possible that, in the intimate and regressive context of his invalidism and the nursing care administered by the beautiful Magdalena, Iñigo's libidinal desires for his sister-in-law were stirred to such an extent that they had to be repressed with all the psychic force at his command? The vehicle for this radical defense was a vision of our Lady—the same as in the picture that was so much the representation of Magdalena's spiritual presence in the castle of Loyola. Does it surprise us that Magdalena's books should become a source of intense devotion for the crippled convert? Could it be that one of the determinants of Ignatius' persistent and profound devotion to our Lady was his libidinal attraction to Magdalena?[2]

ROMANCE

As we have seen,[3] in his adolescent and early adult years Iñigo was something of a sexual libertine—living up to the expectations of his culture and time. He was caught up in the sexualized dreams of the romantic chivalry that was such a prevalent part of the courtly life of the hidalgo.

One reflection of this libidinal surge was his infatuation with Doña Catherina,[4] the lovely younger sister of Charles V and later wife of John III of Portugal. Iñigo probably first saw her during his visit to the court in Valladolid. She was born at Torquemada in 1507, the daughter of Philip the Fair and Juana the Mad. After her father's death she endured a melancholy childhood in the gloomy castle of Tordesillas, where her mother led a life of isolation and depression. When young King Charles first journeyed to Spain, he visited his mother, the mad queen, at Tordesillas and was shocked by the miserable situation in which his eleven-year-old sister was living. Juana forced her to wear a rough dress of gray wool and a cap. She was not allowed out of the castle and could only watch the ships on the river and other children at play through a window.

Charles hatched a plot to free the young princess. On the night of 12 March 1518 he abducted her from the castle. Two hundred armed men escorted her to Valladolid. There, clothed in royal garments, she watched knights jousting in her honor. Her arrival at court made a great impression, particularly on Iñigo. But her freedom was short-lived. Back in Tordesillas Juana was in a rage and refused to eat until the princess was returned. Catherina was doomed to another six years of imprisonment. She finally escaped by marrying John III of Portugal in 1524.

At the time of her abduction, Iñigo was an officer in the retinue of the duke of Nájera. No doubt he had visited Tordesillas more than once in the entourage of Velázquez, when King Ferdinand and his consort, Germaine de Foix, visited his insane daughter, Juana. But whether Iñigo had first seen the lovely princess on his visit with Velázquez or later in Valladolid, she became the object for his romantic visions of gallant chivalry. It was she he dreamed of on his bed of pain at Loyola. As he recalled to da Camara:

> Of the many vain things that presented themselves to him, one took such possession of his heart that without realizing it he could spend two, three, or even four hours on end thinking of it, fancying what he would have to do in the service of a certain lady, of the means he would take to reach the country where she was living, of the verses, the promises he would make her, the deeds of gallantry he would do in her service. He was so enamored with all this that he did not see how impossible it would all be, because the lady was of no ordinary rank; neither countess, nor duchess, but of a nobility much higher than any of these. (Vita 6)

CONVERSION

This libidinal and romantic enthrallment came to an end with Iñigo's conversion experience—or so he tells us. The vision of our Lady was accompanied by the near total repression of all sexual impulses and temptations. We know that such repressive barriers are difficult to maintain, and the psychoanalytic eye scans for displacements and derivatives of these thwarted and denied instinctual drives. One path for this sublimated diversion came in the form of the vision of our Lady— the maternal woman toward whom he could turn all his libidinal desires and there find the spiritually sanctioned satisfaction of these urges and the realization of his new-formed ego ideal that became the dominant motif of his conversion. These repressed forces seem to have been at work in his conversion experience and emerged in a lifelong intense devotion to the Blessed Mother. My speculation is that Iñigo derived much of the required motivational force from unresolved needs and wishes for reunion with the lost mother or mothers of his childhood—perhaps under pressure of the libidinal stimulus provided by the healing ministration of the lovely Magdalena to the weakened and regressed soldier in his enforced passivity and dependence.[5] I am suggesting here a layering of displacements that reaches back through a sequence of mother figures to the lost mother of infancy.

THE PILGRIM YEARS

This background of conflict, repression, and defense brings to the fore the issue of the extent to which repressed and displaced libidinal elements might have come into play in Iñigo's apostolic efforts—in his preaching and teaching, and particularly in his efforts to engage women in the Spiritual Exercises.

Iñigo drew pious and good-hearted women to him from the very beginning of his ministry. He was limping painfully from the mountain of Montserrat toward Manresa in 1522 when he met Inés Pascual for the first time. We know something of the event from the deposition of her son Juan at the beatification process many years later. Juan recalled:

[While] my mother was coming back from a visit to the Holy House of Our Lady of Monserrat with two of her kinsmen . . . and three women. . . . she met a young man dressed as a pilgrim, of low stature, with a pale face and reddish hair, whose manner was so grave and modest that he hardly raised his eyes from the ground; and he limped with the right foot. The man asked my mother if there was in the neighborhood a hospice in which he might lodge for a few days. Being struck by the noble yet friendly air of the pilgrim, she looked at him more closely and felt moved to piety and devotion. She answered that the nearest hospice was three miles away and that she herself was going thither and if he were willing, she would be of use and service to him, to the best of her ability. The pilgrim was pleased with my mother's offer and decided to follow her. (cited in Rahner, 1960, pp. 173–174)

So Iñigo found his first benefactress. On his first day in the hospice of Santa Lucía, the good widow sent him a boiled fowl for supper. Before long other women from the town had taken an interest in him, and soon after that ladies from the local aristocracy came to hear and help him. It was in the house of Angela de Amigant that he was nursed back to health from his first serious illness at Manresa. Once again he fell ill, probably as a result of his undue austerities, and again the women of the town came to his aid and by devoted nursing brought him back to health.[6]

His spiritual conversations with the pious ladies of Manresa, however spiritual and well intentioned, seem to have roused suspicions and slanderous accusations. Dudon (1949) hints that Iñigo was urged to leave by Inés and her brother, the canon Pujol, because of the trouble that these conversations stirred up. There is little to go on here, and Iñigo himself does not mention it, emphasizing instead his wish to follow his destiny in Jerusalem. But we have to wonder what might have given rise to such suspicions. Might there have been something subtly, unconsciously libidinal in these involvements that affected these good women and provoked innuendoes of something erotic? Might the currents of repressed sexuality have played a part unbeknown to the naive but sincere pilgrim, whose only thought was for the good of souls? There seems little doubt that the field of interaction was rife with positive transference, which we know is libidinal in origin. We have all the more reason to be suspicious in that later in Alcalá, Ignatius' ministry to women would run into similar difficulties.

We recall that Iñigo was brought to trial by the Inquisition in Alcalá under suspicion of teaching heresy—perhaps another version of the alumbrados' doctrine or even a form of Protestant heresy that was infiltrating the university. Iñigo and his companions were also accused of other improprieties. Among the many who flocked to hear him teach was a number of women and young girls. One of the nurses from the hospital testified that the women were usually veiled, and no suspicion attached to them initially. But the constant comings and goings of these women provoked new denunciations. Some of them were summoned before the court to give an account of what went on in these meetings. They could testify only to Iñigo's teachings based on the Spiritual Exercises—certainly not a matter of capital punishment.

But toward the end of Lent 1527, a certain event added fuel to the fire and set tongues wagging. The widow María del Vado and her daughter Luisa, members of the group that had gathered around Ignatius, had gone on a pilgrimage to some shrines of our Lady and had disappeared . . . One Doctor Ciruelo, a distinguished lecturer in the university, took this opportunity to raise charges against Iñigo before Figueroa, the judge of the court. Figueroa quickly sent the police to bring Iñigo in for questioning.[7] Once again the women were summoned to give depositions regarding Iñigo's teaching, with the same results as before. But one salient fact stood out: some of these women experienced attacks of severe depression and melancholy, even seizures and epileptic fits. One in particular, possibly María de la Flor, had led a life of loose morals and experienced quite severe episodes. Figueroa questioned Iñigo about these fainting fits and nervous attacks. Iñigo's answer was that, as far as he could see, these women were all reforming their lives and that these nervous manifestations were the work of the devil. He encouraged the women to persevere firmly in their efforts and thought that the attacks would soon cease. These episodes, he felt, were not unlike his own experiences at Manresa. Figueroa seemed satisfied, but Iñigo remained under suspicion until the two missing women returned from their journey to exonerate Iñigo (Dudon 1949).[8]

We can easily recognize in these events hysterical phenomena in part induced by the interaction with Iñigo. Wilkens (1978) notes that the affected women were either widows or adolescents of about sixteen or seventeen years of age—the married women were not affected. The sexual origin of such hysterical attacks was thoroughly analyzed by Freud early in his career. In such cases, repressed sexual wishes find their disguised expression in various symptoms, including fainting fits and so-called hysterical seizures. I would suggest that Iñigo was engaging these women in an intimate, deeply personal, and trusting interaction. These women were drawn to reveal their innermost wishes, hopes, failures, sins—sexual and otherwise—to this relatively young, noble, sympathetic, and undoubtedly attractive holy man.[9] Transference is rampant here—transference which is positive, idealizing, libidinal if not erotic, intense, hysterical, and sexually stimulating. According to psychoanalytic theory, this form of intense, emotionally laden involvement reflects infantile levels of libidinal attachment to the parent of the opposite sex—the positive oedipal attachment. Ignatius, then, became for these women the displaced object of infantile libidinal attachment originally directed to the father figure. The religious context of this exchange—an additional aura of holiness, trust, and idealization—completes the picture.

If our hypothesis is valid, Iñigo's unresolved, repressed, yet still active libidinal impulses would contribute his own unconscious determinants to the libidinal charge of this intense situation. There is reason to wonder how fragile was the line of discrimination that separated these saintly apostles from their more libertine fellow students in the minds of some of these women. In the case of María de la Flor, whose loose morals had made her the bed companion of many students, did she see the handsome hidalgo in much the same terms? Her symptoms were picked out as most dramatic, and we would be hard pressed to think that her interaction with Iñigo was entirely devoid of sexual overtones. We can only conclude, on the basis of these considerations, that the young preacher had much to learn, especially with respect to tempering his apostolic fervor, and that the implicit aura of inhibited and repressed sexuality might well have given friends and relatives of these women, as well as the Inquisition's examiners, reason for concern.

There seems little doubt that throughout his career Ignatius had a special effect on women and exercised an unusual attraction on them. Isabel Roser, who first saw him teaching catechism to little children, was drawn to him by an almost mystical appeal. A similar case was that of Leanora Zapila, who encountered the pilgrim walking along the street and observed the difference between the appearance of his face and his miserable dress. As Dudon (1949)[10] tells the story:

She decided that there was a young man of gentle birth, and in her indignation she addressed him in a tone of reprimand: "You must be lost to all sense of shame to go through the world like that. Go home to your parents, from whom, I am sure, you have run away to lead a life of adventure like a child of the streets." Iñigo answered humbly: "I thank you for your kind advice: you are quite right, I am a lost child, and a great sinner." When Leonora Zapila heard these words, she was moved to the depth of her soul by the modesty with which they were spoken, and she hastened to give the pilgrim alms and provisions for his journey. (p. 72)

Other women of Barcelona were eager to help the pilgrim in his efforts to beg for the poor and to accumulate provisions for his journey to Palestine. He gathered a little group of spiritual followers who collected money and food for him that they brought daily to the hospital.

During his second stay in Barcelona, after his adventures in the Holy Land, he lived with the family of Inés Pascual, who had been so helpful at Manresa. Many women of the better families of Barcelona were willing to assist him, so that when he came begging they were quick to ply him with food and money that he could carry off to his sick patients and starving poor. And when Iñigo's zeal got him beaten to a pulp for his troubles,[11] it was Inés who nursed him back to health. When he could no longer meet his expenses for the licentiate at Paris, it was Inés to whom he turned for help, begging her to enlist the faithful women who had supported him in Barcelona (Epistolae I, 90–92 [Letter 5]).[12]

MINISTERING TO WOMEN

Perhaps the greatest portion of Ignatius' apostolic work, from his earliest efforts at preaching, were directed toward women. Pious women gathered around him even at Manresa, as well as in Barcelona and Alcalá. Again and again in the course of his career he was occupied with the spiritual direction of nuns and the reform of convent life. Often he paid the price in wagging tongues and inquisitorial suspicions. He had to learn to temper his apostolic enthusiasm with prudence. Late in life, he sent fatherly advice to the Society in Portugal:

I would not have any dealing with young women of the common people, except in church or in an open place. On the one hand, they are light-headed, and whether there be foundation for it or not, it frequently happens that such dealings give rise to evil talk. Such females are in general more inclined to be giddy and inconstant in

God's service. After their devotions are over, they not infrequently turn, sometimes to the flesh, sometimes to fatigue. For this reason many allowances have to be made as to their corporal needs.

If I had to deal with women in matters spiritual, it would be with women of birth against whom no breath of evil rumor could arise. Above all, I would not talk with any woman behind closed doors or in remote places. In this way I would avoid all criticism or suspicion.

In all spiritual associations I should try to make one step of progress safely, and prefer this to making a hundred by putting myself in danger, or to advance another at the cost of the serious difference of opinion with him, although I might have been right. A scandal, whether it has foundation or not, does us more harm and neutralizes more than half the progress which God our Lord accomplishes through us, especially in times and places such as these. (MI I, xii, 676–678, Appendix VI, [Letter 12]; in Young, 1959, p. 442)

By the time he arrived in Salamanca, after the debacle in Alcalá, his approach had changed. His plans had gelled and his eyes were turned toward Paris, where his purpose was to study and learn. But the fates— or their psychic equivalents—drew him inexorably back to the spiritual care of women. In Azpeitia, he attacked the practice of concubinage among priests vigorously and brought about the conversion of many prostitutes—to the wonder of all. And when he finally entered Rome, his oft-repeated warning to his companions was: "We must keep watch over ourselves and never enter into spiritual conversations with women, unless they be ladies of noble rank." Despite his caution, he could not stop the noble ladies of Rome from flocking to his cause and he channeled their energies into the care of the poor, orphans, and the women of the streets (Rahner, 1960).[13]

QUEEN CATHERINA OF PORTUGAL

In his years as General of the Society of Jesus, Ignatius had extensive contact and correspondence with the great and noble families of Europe, especially the house of Hapsburg. His voluminous exchange of letters with Philip of Spain extends from 1545 until Ignatius' death in 1556.[14] Yet it was primarily through his friendship with the Hapsburg women that he gained privileged access to the imperial court. One of these correspondents was Queen Catherina of Portugal, the erstwhile prisoner of the dark castle of Tordesillas, who as Infanta had captured the heart of young Iñigo de Loyola.

Fate seems to have intertwined the histories of Ignatius and the Infanta Catherina. In the revolt of the Comuneros, the rebels seized the castle at Tordesillas with the intent of holding Queen Juana and the princess for political ransom. Within a few months, the royal troops had recaptured it and soon after inflicted a decisive defeat on the uprising. At this juncture, the duke of Nájera had pulled together his forces for the protection of Navarre. The defense of Pamplona, in which Iñigo was so severely wounded, was part of the campaign to free the royal women held captive at Tordesillas. Because the situation remained so tenuous, plans were even made in 1522 to remove them to Arévalo. All this transpired while Iñigo was recuperating in the castle of Loyola.

The Infanta's fate brought her to Portugal, where she married John III in 1524. The new queen received news of Ignatius and his new order with enthusiasm—doubtless she remembered the dashing young courtier. She received Simón Rodriguez and later Francis Xavier on his way to India. A lively correspondence arose between the queen in Lisbon and the General in Rome. The royal couple were of great assistance in promoting missionary efforts in the East (China, India, Japan), and Catherina herself had a Jesuit confessor and made the Spiritual Exercises. Her interest in and support of the Society made the difficulties in Portugal all the more painful and embarrassing for Ignatius, for he was eager to maintain his good relations with the queen. She was devoted to the collecting of relics and Ignatius occupied himself from 1551 until March 1552 with collecting the bones of saints and, with the blessing of Pope Julius III, sent them to the queen. Ignatius' anxieties are reflected in his letter to Catherina:

> When he was here in Rome last year, Master Simón [Rodriguez] took some trouble to procure leave from His Holiness to bring away some relics for Your Majesty and the Prince; and although His Holiness willingly gave leave, as Master Simón left Rome, this favour did not actually take effect. As, therefore, this seemed to me to be a matter in which Your Majesties would be served to the glory of God our Lord, I begged the Pope once again to give this permission, and, having received it, I myself, with others of this house, went to bring away all

that could be had. Your Majesty may dispose of all as it seems to you best in our Lord, for the Prince's Highness will be satisfied, as to the share that falls to him, with the division that Your Majesty makes, according to the intention of His Holiness.

I shall not write at greater length, nor shall I offer my person and those of this humble Society again, for the continual service of Your Majesty in our Lord, for it is now so many years since we have considered ourselves, as is most fitting, and as Your Majesties, I believe, consider us, a thing entirely yours in this Lord of ours. May his infinite and sovereign goodness deign to give us all his abundant grace so that we may always know his most holy will and perfectly fulfill it. (Rahner, 1960, pp. 49–50)

The queen, for her part, remained a devoted and faithful follower of Ignatius and his Society. Even after his death—she outlived him by two decades—she continued to support the Society and show her gratitude for Ignatius' favors and for the help his sons had provided for her unfortunate, mad mother. Later, death and madness would bring misery to her family. As Rahner (1960) comments, "The knight of Loyola's fair princess became one of the tragic figures of the House of Hapsburg" (p. 50).

PRINCESS JUANA OF SPAIN

The case of the Princess Juana of Spain is of special interest since she is the only woman who became a permanent member of the Society of Jesus. She was born in 1535, the daughter of Charles V and his short-lived wife Isabel of Portugal. When the Jesuit Father Araoz, who was to have such an impact on her life, preached to the court at Valladolid in 1540, Juana was just a toddler. At eight, she was a talented and gifted child who understood Latin and had mastered several musical instruments. She was betrothed to John Emmanuel, the sickly heir to the throne of Portugal. Much of her contact with the Society came through Leonora Mascarenhas, whom we will meet later. Two of her ladies-in-waiting were the daughters of Francis Borgia, so that when he entered the Society the bonds between Juana and the Society were tightly drawn. After her marriage, Borgia stayed with the princess for several months and converted her court into a convent of sorts.

Tragedy soon struck. Juana's husband died, and within a few weeks she gave birth to a son, Sebastián, who would inherit his grandmother's insanity.[15] Juana soon left Portugal and returned to Valladolid. In 1554, her father, the emperor, appointed her regent of Spain during Philip's absence due to his ill-fated marriage to Mary Tudor. This circumstance was a boon to Ignatius and his Society since both Philip and Juana had been most generous in their support of the Society. The regency lasted five years, and Juana proved herself a capable ruler, intelligent and strong willed. She led an almost monastic life and harbored a secret wish to renounce the world and retire to a convent. Borgia was her confidant and close adviser. She gradually conceived the idea of becoming a member of the new Society of Jesus, probably deeply influenced by Borgia and Araoz. Araoz was particularly enthusiastic about the idea of a female branch of the Society. Borgia broke the news of the princess' decision in 1554. We can imagine Ignatius' shock and consternation. In October he called a conference of professed fathers. Refusal was impossible, but at the same time, at nineteen the young widow would still be subject to the demands of Hapsburg matrimonial policy and could not allow any permanent obligations, such as religious vows, to interfere with a future remarriage. The decision was somewhat Solomonic—she would be admitted to the Society with the vows of a scholastic, a form devised by Ignatius, by which the recipient would bind himself to permanent poverty, chastity, and obedience, but the Society would retain the right to release him or her from such vows for reasonable cause. The solution got Ignatius out of an embarrassing trap—he would not have to refuse the princess, yet the acceptance could be revoked if necessary.

The arrangements were formalized in secret. Once a member of the Society, the regent lost no time in wading into controversy in defense of her order. She put down the persecution of the Society in Saragossa, caustically put the archbishop in his place, and defended the Jesuits against the vitriolic attacks of the great Dominican Melchior Cano. Her "jesuitical practices" stirred up resistance and opposition at court. Fortunately Borgia was able to influence her father Emperor Charles and her uncle King John of Portugal to take a favorable position regarding the Society. Nor was Ignatius slow to exploit his advantage. The Jesuit princess was deeply involved in a host of his enterprises, both large and small, including support of the Roman College, the founding of a college at Valladolid, support of the Louvain foundation (Ignatius' attempt to establish a college in the University), and reform of Spanish nunneries. In 1555, Polanco could write: "The Princess Regent of Spain has such an affection for the Society that one can think of no other person of high or low degree who has more. She shows it by favouring our cause in every way, and this she does with quite especial love and with sincere confidence in the fathers of this Society" (cited in Rahner, 1960, p. 60).

But all was not sweetness and light. The princess became increasingly dependent on Borgia and Araoz for counsel and assistance, gradually drawing them more deeply into the affairs of court. To Ignatius, these developments imperiled the apostolic freedom and independence of the Society. He tried to recall his men but met the resistance of an emperor's daughter. He would not recall Borgia or Araoz without the regent's consent—she responded with expressions of gratitude and ordered both of them to stay put. Ignatius, for whom holy obedience was such a central part of his vision of the Society and its work for God, could do little to restrain and direct this pious, loving, yet headstrong and imperious woman. Until he lay on his death bed, he could not escape the presumptuous and imperious demands of his loving and devoted follower (Rahner 1960).

MARGARET OF AUSTRIA

The relationship between Ignatius and another Hapsburg princess, Margaret of Austria, was another saga complicated by personality and politics. The illegitimate daughter of Charles V, she later became regent of the Netherlands in 1559 and was of immense help to the Society in Flanders. She was strong-willed and domineering, proud and difficult to deal with, and often played the part of the misunderstood and mistreated woman.

Ignatius had his work cut out for him. Margaret's governance of the Netherlands was prudent and skillful, and no doubt Ignatius had a considerable hand in this through the years of his spiritual direction from which she profited greatly. In 1538, at the age of sixteen, she was forced by her father to marry Ottavio Farnese, grandson of the then-reigning Pope Paul III. She soon became one of Ignatius' penitents and involved herself actively in his efforts for the moral reform of Rome.

The marriage was disastrous, and Charles wrote demanding that she submit in wifely obedience. Margaret's replies were by no means compliant, and so scandal loomed. The political and religious heads of Christendom were about to clash over the marital discord of two of their illegitimate offspring. Suddenly Margaret backed off—probably due to the influence of several Jesuits, most notably Jean Codure, who had been appointed her confessor at the request of the Pope. Codure's mission was a sort of "taming of the shrew."

After Codure's untimely death in 1541, Ignatius took over the task; he had to make weekly visits to Margaret's palace, the Palazzo Madama, where he undertook the spiritual direction of the court ladies. The collaboration between Ignatius and the Madama would last for several years. Her support was instrumental in founding the house of catechumens; she was one of the primary sponsors of the House of St. Martha. Her friendship was a great help to him in maintaining good relations with the Spanish ambassador, the emperor, and even the Pope.

DUCHESS ELEANORA OF FLORENCE

With an eye to reforming Florence, after Rome the most important city of Italy, Ignatius directed his efforts to establish a college there. The opportunity presented itself through the good offices of the Duchess Eleanora, wife of Duke Cosimo. She was from a noble Spanish family to which the dukes of Alba also belonged. As the daughter of Spanish grandees—her father Don Pedro de Toledo was viceroy of Naples from 1532 to 1553—she knew her way in the world of wealth and aristocracy, the world from which Ignatius himself had come. In 1549 she purchased the Pitti Palace and the Boboli Gardens for a ducal residence and turned it into the intellectual center of the city. She gave Florentine politics a Spanish and Hapsburg direction, much to the satisfaction of Charles V.

For Ignatius, she proved to be one of his most difficult aristocratic correspondents. She was imperious, secretive, and overly conscious of and sensitive about her dignity—a combination that called for the greatest adherence to etiquette and great tact. Rahner (1960) cites a contemporary description of her: "The duchess was virtually never seen to go on foot, so proud was she. Nor did she let herself be seen on horseback; but she generally appeared publicly in a litter, as if in a reliquary; that is to say, one half of the litter was open, and in the other half she could be seen. It was a marvelous thing to behold such a proud woman. She was never seen to visit churches or other holy places, as her high station demanded—even if it were only for the sake of good example" (p. 94). Her spiritual life presented its problems as well. The confessors Ignatius sent her had a hard time of it.

In 1546 Ignatius sent the newly ordained Juan de Polanco to Florence,
and the overzealous Polanco decided that the ducal court needed reforming. He sent a somewhat imprudent memo to the duchess admonishing her to keep a less splendid court. Ignatius reprimanded the young
man and recalled him to Rome. He was replaced by the more circumspect Laynez in 1547. Laynez became increasingly indispensable to the
duchess and at first had great influence over her. He tried to advance
the idea of founding a college in Florence. The duke was cool, and the
enthusiasm of the duchess seemed to wane rather than wax. In 1550
a visit from Duke Francis Borgia (already secretly a Jesuit) had the
same purpose. Ignatius orchestrated the process in minute detail from
Rome—paying particular attention to how the fathers and scholastics
comported themselves in the duchess' presence. The plan for establishing the college finally came to fruition in 1552, but the foundation was
quite modest. The Jesuits carried on their work in extreme poverty. The
duke was unrelenting, but Eleanora seemed troubled by the course of
events. Nonetheless, she squandered more on her gambling habit than
on the foundation of the Jesuit college.

All this set the stage for the tragicomedy that was to follow. A young
member of this impoverished community was Tarquinio, a scholastic
from Rome whom Ignatius had spirited to Florence to protect him from
interference with his vocation by his outraged and disappointed father.
The father, a man of some influence, presented his complaint to Duke
Cosimo. The duke arranged to lure the young scholastic into the Pitti
Palace, where he was stripped of his cassock and forced to don military
garb. But he stood firm against his father's threats and refused to return
to Rome. The duchess took the side of the aggrieved father, pleading
with Ignatius for a compromise—the young man should remain in the
Society but continue his studies in Rome so that he could be near his
father. Ignatius' dilemma was clear—the favor of the duchess or the
vocation of the novice. He responded with a piece of spiritual diplomacy
that preserved what he wanted without damage to his cause:

My Lady in our Lord,
  By a letter from Your Grace of the sixteenth of this month, I see
what is asked and required of me in respect of Tarquinio, scholastic of
our Society, and I do not doubt that Your Grace's piety and tender
heart will have sympathized with Master Cesare Rainaldi, his father

according to the flesh, which he has shown he loves in his son more than the spirit or spiritual profit, since he is using very great diligence to turn him aside from the way in which God our Lord had set him for his service; and the wish he now expresses of his being moved to Rome might very well be with that intention. Therefore, since I respect (as I should do) Your Grace's letter and since it gives me some opportunity of assuring myself of the young man's constancy and also of obtaining fulfillment of certain promises which his father made us, I shall do what you want about Tarquinio, provided that he has the courage to come, and trust that God our Lord will give him strength. I would beg Your Grace in matters of this kind not to interpose your authority lightly, for it might be the cause of some soul's leaving God's service and being lost for ever. That, I know, is very far from Your Grace's holy intention. It is, indeed, better not to give way to the importunity of those who treat matters without much fear or love of God even in things which bring no little burden to one's conscience, and since I and our whole Society are Your Grace's, it has seemed to me that I ought not to refrain from giving this advice, as one who sincerely desires in Your Grace the service of God our Lord, with his supreme and eternal gifts. (Rahner, 1960, pp. 97–98)

Ignatius had won that round.

Meanwhile, the duchess made an even more imperious claim on Laynez. Ignatius again found himself in a difficult corner—he did not think that Laynez, who was needed desperately for work in other parts of Italy, should be put at the exclusive service of the duchess. The obstinate Eleanora regarded any attempt to recall her confessor as a serious affront. The proposals put forth then reversed, the permissions granted then retracted, the imperiousness and sensitivity of the duchess, all almost drove the poor General to his wit's end. The duchess had a trump card—"If Father Laynez does not come back soon, it will be the end of the whole college."

By the summer of 1554, Ignatius had sufficiently loosened Laynez's ties to Florence to be able to send him to Germany at the Pope's request to act as theological adviser to Cardinal Morone at the Diet of Augsburg. The importance of that mission overruled the anxieties of the duchess. She was, however, adamant. Ignatius was caught between the duchess and the Pope. He decided to take a firm stand with Eleanora:

From a letter from Your Grace dated January 21st, I have gathered that it would be to your service if Master Laynez might be prevented from going to Germany—and this because of certain fruit to God's service which might come from his preaching and contact with souls if he remained where he is, and particularly because Your Grace (whom we all so rightly desire to serve in our Lord) shows that it would please you not a little, I should be very glad in that same Lord of ours if all that Your Grace asks for God's greater glory could be done.

It is true, however, that the Pope himself personally appointed Master Laynez and another of our Society to accompany the Cardinal Legate and the embassy it was decided to send to the German Diet, and, in addition to the fact that that mission is of such a nature that in it the very great and universal good of religion is aimed at, for it will help to bring back that nation to the Catholic Church, we cannot and ought not to refuse obedience to the Vicar of Christ our Lord; it is therefore necessary to accept the order given to us. (Rahner, 1960, p. 100)

The duchess, not to be so easily deterred, wrote to the Pope and several cardinals. The Pope and Ignatius stood firm, but in the end she had her way. On the day the legation arrived at Augsburg, the Pope died and the mission was recalled. Laynez returned to Florence, where he remained until Paul IV was elected to the papal throne. The new Pope gave Ignatius an excuse to bring Laynez back to Rome, where the Pope insisted on retaining him. The duchess was deeply affronted and angered. Ignatius tried to placate her and sent a substitute, Father Diego de Guzman. She resisted, but soon mollified her anger. Ignatius' courtly diplomacy and Guzman's charm soon made the new confessor as indispensable as Laynez had been. Guzman had his hands full—the duchess continued her excessive gambling and neglected the suffering Jesuits in the college. The permanent foundation for the college was never endowed.

TERESA REJADELLA

From the earliest days of his ascetic career, Ignatius devoted a great deal of effort to the reform of convents. He began in Barcelona, where a special target was the Benedictine convent of Santa Clara. One of the good sisters in this convent was Teresa Rejadella, daughter of a noble Catalan family. The regimen of the convent had grown lax, but a small group of nuns, led by Sister Teresa, was determined to bring about canonical and spiritual reform. Teresa met Iñigo and placed herself under his spiritual direction. Their efforts to reform the convent continued until her death in 1552. Out of their correspondence comes one of the finest of Ignatius' spiritual letters—a kind of summary and commentary on the Spiritual Exercises.[16] Teresa had written in June 1536 begging for his spiritual advice. His reply expressed his fatherly concern and presented a compendium of his basic spiritual ideas. The wiles and temptations of the enemy are described—first doubts, then vainglory, and finally false humility. The remedies are the familiar ones—detachment, indifference, and humility. Central to spiritual progress is the discernment of spirits by which the devout soul can make its precarious way between the temptations of the lax conscience to deny or minimize the seriousness of sin and the temptations of the delicate conscience to find sin and doubt where there is none, to distinguish the sorts of consolation and desolation that come from the evil spirit and those that come from the spirit of God.

The nun and the pilgrim would never meet again, but the conversation continued by way of letters between Rome and Barcelona. A recurring issue was the convent reform in which Teresa was so deeply embroiled. She would often complain when Ignatius failed to respond to one of her letters. Meanwhile, the canonical situation in the convent grew more complex and difficult. The little band of zealots was staging a revolt, insisting on frequent communion (at Ignatius' urging) to the dismay of the rest of the good sisters. In 1546 a new abbess was elected through the influence of her aristocratic relatives. Teresa and her cohorts refused in conscience to show her religious obedience. Father Araoz, the Jesuit provincial, was involved in consultations; he conveyed the details of the situation to Ignatius and suggested that one solution was to put Teresa's band under obedience to the Jesuits. Teresa was in collusion with Isabel Roser, and Isabel became the energetic advocate for Teresa's reforms and the Jesuit connection.

Ignatius was again placed in a difficult and embarrassing position. Prince Philip of Spain and several of the bishops were pressuring him to address the serious problem of the reform of Catalan nunneries generally. Ignatius set to work. Every influential connection was brought into play. He was firm about his apostolic commitment to the reform of the nunneries and equally clear that there could be no question of admitting nuns into the Society. He finally wrote to Teresa in rather strong terms:

By the letters I have received from Barcelona from various persons I see how God our Lord visits them with trials, giving them no little occasion to exercise the virtues which his divine goodness has instilled in them, and to show the solidity of those virtues, for in difficult matters (of which I see there are many in your affairs) an opportunity is given us of true spiritual profit. May it please Jesus Christ, who did and suffered so much for all of us, to give us abundant grace, so that whatever there is to suffer may be suffered fruitfully for his holy love and all that needs remedying may be remedied in the way most pleasing to his divine goodness.

This I hold for certain that what you are now thinking of is not according to the mind of God; for, although in our Society, as one of the many obligations which it holds especially dear in our Lord, there is the wholehearted will to console and serve you in conformity with our profession, the authority of the Vicar of Christ has closed the door against our taking on any government or superintendence of religious, a thing which the Society begged for from the beginning. This is because it is judged that it would be for the greater service of God our Lord that we should have as few ties as possible in order to be able to go wherever obedience to the Sovereign Pontiff and the needs of our neighbours may call us. This remedy then I do not think would be pleasing to God our Lord in any way and I hope in his infinite goodness that some other more suitable way will be found to arrive at what you and all of us desire in our Lord, his peace and special consolation. (Rahner, 1960, p. 355)

Teresa did not give up so easily; several more letters arrived in Rome imploring Ignatius to change his mind. The case of Santa Clara had become celebrated by this time. The abbess and the reformers were at war, and the religious life of the convent was a shambles. Efforts were made to reorganize the convent according to Franciscan rules since no help was forthcoming from the Jesuits. This plan failed too. Lawyers were called in and the case dragged on in royal and ecclesiastic courts for years. Finally an accommodation was made to continue the convent under Benedictine rule. Ignatius continued his spiritual support, but his view was that as long as the convent was under Benedictine jurisdiction, no real reform was possible without religious obedience—a familiar Ignatian theme. In the end all the planning and struggling came to naught; the convent remained unreformed until long after both Teresa and Ignatius had gone to their rewards.

LEONORA DE MASCARENHAS

The figure of Leonora de Mascarenhas surfaces repeatedly in the narrative of Ignatius' adventures. It was to her he turned to influence the king of Portugal to provide a scholarship for his follower Calixto at the University of Paris.

On the birth of Prince Philip of Spain, his father, Charles V, appointed Leonora his governess. She and Iñigo may have met at about that time, possibly during his imprisonment at Alcalá in 1527. They met again in Madrid in 1535, when Ignatius visited her on his way to see the families of his Spanish companions. The pilgrim had undoubtedly made a deep impression on Leonora, and he found in her a like-minded soul. When Charles' wife Isabel died, Leonora became like a substitute mother for the royal brood. From her intimacy with the royal family, she was able to do Ignatius and his followers much good. She also became a close friend and confidante of Peter Faber in 1541 and wrote to him often. She told Faber, "I would with readiness choose the life of perfection, that is, follow you and Ignatius, if I were a man. But I am only a woman, a sinner making no progress in virtue, and so I may not join you in meditating and speaking about holy things, much less those that concern the Company of Ignatius" (cited in Dudon, 1949, pp. 418–419).

In any case, Leonora was one of Ignatius' most loyal supporters. Her influential position at the royal court in both Valladolid and Madrid enabled her to do a good many favors for the fledgling Society Ignatius had founded. Rahner (1960) cites a contemporary biography of her:[17] "She did all in her power to assist Ignatius in founding the Society of Jesus. She was heartily devoted to him and gave him alms all her life; she helped the Jesuits in their first beginnings, when difficulties were always to be expected, and gave them the house in which the college of this city of Madrid was first opened" (p. 417).

When young Philip married the Infanta María of Portugal in 1543, life changed for Leonora. The marriage, promoted by Hapsburg political ambitions, resulted in the birth of Don Carlos, who inherited the madness of his great-grandmother Juana. María died within a few days of giving birth, even before Charles V could be notified that he had a grandson. The distraught father again turned to Leonora and entrusted the infant to her care with the words, "My son has lost his mother; now you must be a mother to him. For my sake, treat him as your own" (Dudon, 1949, pp. 418–419). Faber and Araoz kept Ignatius abreast of these developments.

In the midst of these troubles, Leonora besieged Ignatius with a series of requests for dispensations and other favors. To all this Ignatius maintained a patient, kindly, forbearing, and solicitous demeanor. For his part, he was not above exploiting his leverage with the woman who stood in such an influential position at court. He enlisted her aid in the reform of the Catalan convents, in the difficulties stemming from the hostility of the Archbishop Siliceo of Toledo against the Society. Although the letters from Ignatius' later years have disappeared, we know that he maintained contact with the royal governess. In 1552 communications through Francis Borgia dealt with postponing Leonora's entrance in a convent. Instead of the cloistered life, she organized several important charities, especially to benefit prostitutes and poor women. The correspondence must have lapsed in subsequent years, since she complained that Ignatius had stopped writing her. By this time Ignatius was in his last months of life. Two final letters arrived when he was nearly on his deathbed, and he answered them in his own hand. He could not forget the woman who had helped him and been so loyal to his cause for so many difficult years. Part of the letter reads:

I received on the same day, at the end of April, two letters from Your Ladyship dated November and December. From them I see clearly how deeply you stand written in my soul, from the day we first became acquainted in our Lord, and the very deep love and charity we have for each other in his divine Majesty. This, I hope in God's goodness, will always last both on your side and on mine, and will continually increase.

As to the difficulties of your station and your physical sufferings, I have done what you so earnestly recommended to me, namely that I should have recourse to God our Lord in prayer, that he may show you how you can serve him better. You add that I should write you my opinion and advise you what you ought to do. Accordingly, speaking in the presence of God our Lord, I will tell you what I feel within me in his divine Majesty, as if I were in Your Ladyship's place. I should, then, remain firm and steadfast in the same condition and estate in which His Highness had left me until he should ordain some other thing for me; and for this, and for what is most to God's glory, I should write him telling him everything, namely, my desires, my sicknesses and all other things that might occur to me in this connection. If you do this, beyond any doubt, I think that His Highness, looking at the matter all round, will clearly come to see whatever is most for God's glory, and you will be comforted and at peace in our Lord. (Rahner, 1960, p. 430)

ISABEL ROSER

One of the most interesting and trying of Ignatius' dealings with women concerned Isabel Roser, who had befriended the poor beggar in the streets of Barcelona and remained his devoted follower ever after. She had put him in touch with Jerome Ardevol to study grammar and supported him during these early years of study.

Isabel, from the noble Catalan family of Ferrer, had married the wealthy merchant Juan Roser and lived in a beautiful house across from the church of San Yusto y Pastor. The Rosers were among the most influential families of Barcelona. The marriage was childless, and in his later years Juan became blind. Isabel had helped Iñigo to realize his dream of traveling to Jerusalem and after his return continued to help him in many ways. After his departure for Paris, she was the leader of the group of noblewomen who contributed to his support. That generosity became all the more necessary and valued as Iñigo gathered companions around him. It was by no means easy for her to be continually dunning her friends for money, especially when her own resources were stretched. Rahner notes, "She suffered from nervous disorders; calumny abounded; probably, indeed, her relations with Ignatius formed the subject of pious gossip in the town. So it came about that many letters and complaints which have not been preserved accompanied the money to Paris" (Rahner, 1960, p. 263).

One letter of sympathy and consolation came from Ignatius on 10 November 1532. It expresses quite vividly the depth of his concern for Isabel's trials and tribulations, both physical and mental, as well as for the jealousy and accusations she endured, partly because of her devotion to and close connection with Ignatius himself.[18] But Ignatius goes on to drive home his argument with a story that has its own interest. His letter continues:

The friars of St. Francis often used to come to a certain house and as their conversation was very pious and holy, a girl, already growing up, who was in the house, grew extremely fond of that monastery and house of St. Francis—so much so that she one day dressed as a boy and went to the monastery to ask the Guardian to give her [i.e., the boy] the habit for he had a great desire to serve, not only God our Lord and the holy Master Francis, but all the religious of that house. He spoke so persuasively that they gave him the habit forthwith, and he remained in the monastery leading a very collected life full of consolation. Now it happened that one night he and another of his companions stayed in a certain house, with leave of their superior, as they were on a journey. There happened to be a girl in this house and she fell in love with the good friar, or rather, the devil entered into this girl, and she determined to go in to the good friar as he was sleeping, that he might sin with her. As the friar awoke and drove her from the room, she became so filled with anger that she immediately sought ways and means by which she could cause all the annoyance possible to the good friar, so much so that a few days later the wicked girl went to speak to the Guardian demanding justice—saying that she was pregnant by a good friar of his house, and other things. The Guardian, because the matter was so much talked of in that city, took the friar and put him in the street at the gates of his monastery, bound, that all might see the justice that was being done. He remained like that for many days, rejoicing at the abuse, revilements and insulting words, which he heard referring to his person. He did not justify himself to anyone, but discoursed with his Creator and Lord within his soul, since he was offered the material of so much merit before his divine Majesty. After a certain time had thus elapsed during which he was thus a spectacle to all, when people saw that his patience was so great, they asked the Guardian to forgive him all the past and take him again into his affections and his house. The Guardian, already moved to pity, took him back and the good friar spent many years in that house until the will of God in his regard was accomplished. After he died, when they undressed him for burial, they discovered that he was a woman and not a man, and consequently that very great calumny was lifted from him. Thus all the friars marvelled and praised his innocence and holiness more than they had blamed his supposed guilt. Many of them even now remember more clearly this friar or nun than any of those who lived a long time in their house.

Thus I should prefer to look more to one point in which I had failed than at all the ill that was spoken of me. (Rahner, 1960, pp. 266–7)

The manifest point of this story has to do with acceptance of the calumnies of the world, but a psychoanalytic interpretation looks beyond the manifest content to the latent levels of meaning. The latent content is explicitly sexual, more precisely about gender confusion and deception. Do we hear in this story faint echoes of inner sexual conflicts in the chaste man of God? Does the account of sexual attraction, rejection, and rage have anything to do with the concealed and implicit aspects of the relationship between Ignatius and his loving, giving, yet complaining and importuning benefactress? Was Ignatius revealing some sense of his unacceptable irritation or ambivalence with regard to Isabel's neediness and neurotic demands?

To take another tack, the theme of sexual ambiguity is striking. Is Ignatius expressing in this displaced metaphor his own sense of gender ambiguity? We can recall at this point that the culturally enforced masculinity was established by the phallic properties of Spanish machismo, so that his style of spiritual nonviolence was more feminine than masculine. These dimensions of his own psychic structure were connected to underlying identifications—on one side with the phallic narcissistic image of his father, on the other side with the pious, gentle, self-effacing, and suffering image of his mother. The masculine pattern had been repressed and denied, the feminine pattern dictated his post-conversion course. But the phallic and narcissistic aspects of his character had by no means been left behind, nor had the libidinal currents been totally obliterated. The implication of the story, after all, is that masculine sexuality is evil and to be punished, while feminine is to be valued and praised as holy and blameless.

The support and cloying attachment of the good matron of Barcelona followed him from Paris to Bologna and Venice. But as Ignatius' vision shifted from Jerusalem to Rome, his life took a different course; founding and guiding his fledgling Society left him little time to write letters of consolation and support to Barcelona. Isabel was peeved and complaining. Finally, on 19 December 1538, he wrote a long, detailed letter describing the vicissitudes of his enterprise in Rome.

Meanwhile Isabel's husband's health grew worse, and she herself was afflicted by illness. When Don Juan Roser died on 8 November 1541, the widow turned to spiritual matters with increased energy. Her first thought was to join her friend Teresa Rejadella in the convent of Santa Clara, but the situation in the convent was too unsettled. Isabel turned her efforts to monastic reform in Barcelona and Catalonia. Antonio Araoz, who had come to Barcelona in October 1539, went to Rome to be ordained and professed, then in February 1542 returned to Barcelona. He carried with him a letter from Ignatius recommending him to Isabel and trying to straighten out some misunderstandings about convent reform. A month later Faber visited Barcelona and held long conversations with Isabel, which were dutifully reported to Ignatius. She was concocting plans for coming to Rome with generous donations and putting herself at Ignatius' service.

While Faber was skeptical, Araoz was enthusiastic and developed a close relationship with Isabel. Ignatius was obviously uneasy and ambivalent about Isabel's desires. He asked whether she and Araoz had discerned whether the idea was from the good or the evil spirit, obviously a question that bothered Ignatius himself. (In the story the devil had infected the young woman who wanted to sleep with the female friar. And remember that the whole story was about a woman who became a member of a male religious order.)

But Ignatius' temporizing was too late. Isabel was already settling her affairs and divesting herself of her properties. Preparations for the journey were made—Isabel and her close friend Isabel de Josa were coming to Rome. In a long letter to Ignatius on 1 October 1542, she announced: "I am making plans to withdraw to Santa Clara to [Sister] Rejadella's little cell and this I have told my brother, so that he will not be surprised at the household goods being sold. I shall stay in that monastery until God our Lord shall have provided a good opportunity for the journey, with your permission and blessing, as I have written you, for otherwise I have come to no final decision, because I do not want some enemy of quietude to drag me away to what suits my own will and is not with Your Reverence's leave and the obedience due to your person as a servant of Christ our Lord. Then, however small the difficulties might be which hindered my project, it would seem to me that my presumption in going away without leave had been the cause of them" (Rahner, 1960, pp. 278–79).

Thus far Ignatius had been outmaneuvered. Ignatius then recalled Araoz and Diego de Eguia from Barcelona, warning them not to travel with Isabel. When Isabel heard of this move, she sped from her country house back to Barcelona and there exerted herself to have the fathers returned. Even the Emperor Charles was drawn into the matter. Letters landed like mortar shells around poor Ignatius. One of Isabel's went as follows:

Very dear Father: These few days I have written you four or five letters. I have already kept you informed of the departure of Father Araoz and Don Diego. They have now been in Palamos twelve days for, to comply with obedience, they went before I wished, for I realize the great loss they are to this city; in truth it is so great that it cannot be written about. May God forgive you for having taken them away from here, just when they were getting known and the people were going to them, some for confession, some for the Exercises, some for advice. The fruit that was produced was so great, both in the orders of nuns and among secular persons of both high and low degree, that I think that, if they had been here for some time more, it might have been possible for this city, whose need is so great, to have been said to be Christian. Now those who remain, both those beginning a Christian life and those who are established in it, feel their absence so much they every day come here lamenting over the great loss their departure makes. I do not dare tell you what my own feelings are, except that now I feel widowed anew, to find myself so deprived of company that was more angelic than human.

I hope in God our Lord that you will remember that we are all near neighbours and that some persons of quality will write to His Holiness asking him to send them back again, because since they are known here, people are very much devoted to them.

For the love of God our Lord, help us rather than hinder us, and give them back to Barcelona. (Rahner, 1960, pp. 281–282)

The devotion of this aging widow, who was willing to sacrifice so much to travel the hard miles to Rome to see her beloved Ignatius once more before her death, could not fail to touch Ignatius deeply. By April 1543, Isabel had set sail for Rome with her lady-in-waiting and a friend. Before long they stood before the door of La Strada. The meeting was recounted by a nun who heard it from Isabel herself. "When Father Ignatius saw Isabel, he was highly astonished, put his hands to his head and said: 'God save me, Roser, are you here? Who brought you?' And she answered: 'God and you, Father.'"[19]

Apparently once she arrived, Ignatius could not do enough for Isabel. As Rahner (1960) recounts: "From Genoa arrived a whole shipload of chests and boxes, in charge of one of her servants. The ladies were at first lodged in a private house, and the lay-brother Esteban de Eguia, Father Diego's brother, had to wait on them. This was no small matter for the elderly and highborn Eguia, who out of humility had wished to be only a lay-brother. In a report dated May 3rd, 1547, when all was over, we read: 'Esteban de Eguia, that nobly born old man, had the duty of looking after her night and day, and he continued in this service for two years. He had to wait upon her, accompany her to church, even to sweep out her apartments, and help her into the saddle whenever she had a mind to go riding.' Everything was done for Sister Roser" (pp. 282–83).

The problem for Ignatius was what to do with these high-born women. Fortuitously, he was taken up at the time with the foundation of the House of St. Martha; on 16 February 1543, Paul III had signed the papal bull establishing the confraternity to run it. Isabel's help was invaluable, especially when the patronage of some of her friends could be enlisted in the cause. Isabel herself lived in the House of St. Martha, acting as a sort of self-appointed mother superior, and was soon joined by other ladies of good will. So far, so good.

But Isabel had other things on her mind. The question was not long in coming—what form would her admittance to the Society and her religious vows take? Ignatius was able to bob and weave for the next two years, but Isabel would not be put off. She applied to the Pope for permission to take vows and for a papal order forcing Ignatius to accept them. These were granted just before Christmas 1545. Ignatius was troubled— to say the least. He wrote to Rodriguez in Portugal recounting the problems he was having with Isabel and her companions. She was rich and used to having her own way, and nervous and hysterical as she was, she was not suitable for a life of poverty and obedience.

Ignatius' objections were brushed aside by the onslaught—she summoned every resource to achieve her goal. By Christmas Eve, she had bequeathed the rest of her property to the Society. Ignatius bobbed again, renounced the gift the very next day and restored it to her, at least for the time being. But Ignatius' hand was forced. On Christmas Day 1545, three women knelt before the altar in the little church of Santa Maria della Strada in the presence of Ignatius and pronounced the vows of poverty, chastity, and obedience he had drawn up for them. They were Lucrezia di Bradine, Francisca Cruyllas (Isabel's lady-in-waiting), and Isabel Roser. Isabel had gotten her way; the foundation was laid for an order of female Jesuits.

This turn of events has puzzled historians. Dalmases (1985) points out that Ignatius and his companions had not foreseen that they would have to deal with female Jesuits when they organized the Society. Others point out that there is no reason to think that female Jesuits would have been any more of an innovation than the appointment of local superiors, given the temper of the times. As Endean (1987) notes, in 1545 the Society was still a small group struggling to find its way, without benefit of legislation or a permanent secretary. Moreover, the Pope was more immediately involved in its everyday decisions. In this light, the decision may not seem so strange, but it does give us a better sense of the extent to which Ignatius was driven by forces and influences over which he had little control.

Despite his misgivings, Ignatius' own sense of gratitude and obedience to the Pope and Isabel's determination did him in. Isabel was triumphant. But this was only the first act of the piece. The second act took the form of a "comic battle" (Rahner, 1960, p. 287). Within weeks Ignatius' worst fears began to be realized. Nadal was scandalized by the fact that Sister Isabel took her food from the fathers' kitchen. He would later complain how the three women kept all the Jesuits in Rome busy. Certainly Isabel, with the best intentions, imposed herself on the ailing General as his nurse, but he could not escape her continual litany of complaints, scruples, and neurotic anxieties. He strove patiently to comfort her, but even saints have their limits. He had had enough of Isabel—in addition to the fact that she had, without permission, brought her two nephews to Rome to find wives. Feathers were ruffled and Ignatius had all he could do to smooth things over. But enough was enough. He presented his problem to Paul III in April, and the Pope, who had previously ordered Ignatius to accept the vows of the women, now gave his permission for the vows to be rescinded.

Not wishing to seem excessive or harsh, Ignatius vacillated. Nor was Isabel happy, hinting that she would soon return to Barcelona—as a Jesuitess, of course. In the summer Ignatius again presented the case to the Pope for a final decision. Armed with papal approval, Ignatius moved into battle. The parties met in the house of Leonor Osorio, the Spanish ambassadress. The atmosphere was tense. The nephews demanded money, and Isabel produced a list of all the gifts she had given the Society in Barcelona and Rome. Ignatius, knowing his adversaries well, produced his own list proving that in fact Isabel was financially in debt to the Society. The session lasted for hours, but Ignatius did not budge. Tears, hysterical outbursts, even bribery—Isabel promised two hundred ducats for St. Martha's if Ignatius would yield—made no difference.

The next day Ignatius drafted the letter of renunciation that Nadal had to present to Isabel. It read:

To Isabel Roser, venerable Lady, my mother and sister in Jesus Christ.

It is true that for God's greater glory I should like to satisfy your good desires and have you under the bond of obedience, as up to now you have been for some time. In that way I should be able to exercise the care necessary for the sure salvation and greater perfection of your soul. Nevertheless, since I do not find within my power the strength I desire for this because of my continual infirmities and the being occupied in matters for which I have a primary obligation to God our Lord or to his Vicar on earth, and, moreover, since according to my conscience, it is not fitting for this little Society to have special charge of women bound to us by vows of obedience, as six months ago now I explained at length to His Holiness, it has seemed to me for God's greater glory that I should withdraw and separate myself from this care of having you as a spiritual daughter under obedience, having you rather as a good and pious mother, as you have been to me for several years now for the greater glory of God our Lord. Accordingly, for the greater service, praise and glory of his eternal goodness, as much as I can (always excepting all higher authority) I hand you over to the most prudent judgment, ordinance and will of the Sovereign Pontiff so that your soul may be tranquil and comforted in all things to God's greater glory.

Ignatius
In Rome, October 1st, 1546

(Rahner, 1960, pp. 288–289)

Isabel, for her part, was not at all receptive to the decision. Nadal had to read it to her aloud in the presence of witnesses four times in succession. Indignant and ailing, she moved out of the House of St. Martha to stay with a fellow countryman where she became the center of opposition to Ignatius. Her vows were commuted to a vow of obedience to the ordinary of the diocese.

But she had no intention of accepting defeat. Her tears and complaints found a hearing in Cardinal Carpi and others, so that before long the matter was brought before an ecclesiastical court. Ignatius was accused of being a hypocrite and a thief who was only out to steal Isabel's fortune.[20]

Isabel lost that round too and had to sign a formal statement to the effect that all her gifts to the Society had been made freely. Ignatius was master of the field and lost no time in concluding the issue. In May 1547 he petitioned Paul III to free the Society for all time from the spiritual direction of any women who might want to place themselves under obedience to any priest of the Society of Jesus. He also saw to it that this provision was written into the Constitutions.

After the dust had settled, peace returned and the spiritual relationship between the two combatants was re-established. As she was departing for Barcelona, Isabel made a long and sincere confession to Ignatius. When she reached Barcelona, she wrote him a touching letter:

Most reverend and virtuous Father,
    May the love and charity of Jesus Christ our Lord be in our souls.
    Considering my great wretchedness, my imperfections and my lack of all things, I did not venture to dare to write to Your Paternity. Yet since I am so much in your debt for the very many spiritual benefits received from Your Paternity and from all others in your house, and for the many labours and much toil and fatigue you have suffered and

undergone for me, I beg you for reverence of the Passion of Jesus Christ our Lord, and by his precious blood, to forgive me, and thus in this letter I humbly ask your pardon, confessing my imperfection and my wretchedness, not knowing how to draw profit from the virtue of humility and patience. Rather do I confess my lack of mortification, and when I once more considered all that had happened, I came near to losing courage. The mercy and goodness of God our Lord, however, is so great that he has not regarded my sins and weaknesses, rather like a most loving Father he has guarded me and brought me to this city to care for small orphans, for those we now have in the house are twenty-nine, not counting those that have been placed in service, and through the lack of the necessary formalities for the bull and indults there is no one to care for them except Mosen Caselles. May our Lord grant them someone to concern himself with them for in truth they need this very much.

May our Lord fill you with his grace, and although I do not deserve that Your Paternity should remember me in your Masses and prayers, your charity will [I know] extend to this. Thus I beg this of you and I ask the same of your sons for, although I am such a wretched sinner, I do not forget to pray to God, whenever I see him in the hands of the priest, for Your Paternity and those of your house, and I bear you all no less love and affection than formerly. God our Lord is my witness of this. I conclude kissing Your Paternity's hands and praying God's Majesty that he would let us live and die in his holy love and service.

> Your Paternity's unworthy and useless servant,
> Widow Isabel Roser
> From Barcelona, December 10th, 1547

(Rahner, 1960, pp. 290–291)

She continued in her last years to be a true spiritual daughter of Ignatius. She founded an orphanage for poor children and in 1550, entered the Franciscan convent of Holy Jerusalem at Barcelona, where she found the peace and joy she had been seeking.

The whole business had scarred Ignatius. The issue of admitting women to the Society surfaced again on several occasions. Some of these women were inspired by the example of Isabel. In November 1546, Father Miguel Torres carried with him to Spain a detailed memorandum that read in part:

As far as we can judge in our Lord, what really matters is to keep the Society free to move unhampered in order to meet essential demands, and we must not tie ourselves down to unessential things. Moreover we must, if we wish to progress along the way of the Lord, think first of ourselves and look after ourselves. For although we are not worthy to loose the shoestrings of the blessed St. Francis and St. Dominic, yet we observe how their orders are much burdened and troubled by the constant complaints of their houses of nuns— indeed, we see this daily at the Roman curia. Therefore we have formed the opinion that in the future our Society might be involved in such disputes and scandals, if we were to undertake the spiritual direction of women and accept their obedience. Even with regard to the three women whose direction we have undertaken at the special command of His Holiness, we hope soon to gain the favour of being freed from them again. (Rahner, 1960, p. 308)

THE SPIRITUAL HIDALGO

It is difficult to know what to make of these adventures, but certainly they cannot be understood in isolation from Ignatius' more general attitudes toward women. Ignatius devoted himself with quite exceptional tenacity to the spiritual well-being of women from many walks of life and social conditions—from the highest strata of royalty to the poor and disadvantaged women of the streets of Rome. He inspired intense devotion and attachment in his female followers, a problem that had bedeviled him in the early years when his efforts to preach to women and discourse with them about spiritual matters drew suspicions and accusations on his head. The arena and the mission were different in Rome, but we can wonder whether the substance was any different. We can conjecture that behind the spiritual façade the currents of libidinal attachment were active in the sublimated love that drew these women to the spiritual hidalgo—a love and eroticized attachment that was denied and repressed on both sides but remained a troubling component that neither the women nor Ignatius could effectively eliminate. I would hazard the hypothesis that it was this unconscious aspect of his relations with women that reasserted itself in his spiritual dealings and created the distortions that so troubled him and that he found so difficult to manage.

Yet if the motivating forces in Ignatius' various involvements with women were based in part on libidinal drives, a hypothesis of repression and sublimation, based on a simple model of drive modulation and defense, does not suffice. Beyond the libidinal lies a more infantile level that was caught up in the vicissitudes of conflict and fixation, determined by the dynamics of loss and restitution, that permeate in subtle and unconscious fashion all Ignatius' relationships with women. Throughout his spiritual journey, important women were at his side—starting with his nursing mother in the peasant's cottage, the lovely Magdalena, whose presence permeated his adolescent and young adult years, including the complex psychic revolution that took place around his conversion, the dutiful women who gathered around at Manresa to help, succor, support, and nurse him back to health when he fell ill from his excessive austerities. They were there, in effect, to "mother" him.

My hypothesis is that Ignatius' ambiguities, ambivalences, and vacillations in his more troublesome dealings with these substitute mothers resulted from his inability to resolve the unconscious, peremptory infantile needs that bound him to his lost biological mother, seeking ever to confirm and sustain the ties to these necessary mother figures that satisfied deeply unconscious yearning for maternal sustenance. This maternal stratum is part of the libidinal connection and interconnection that bound him to the women who became his spiritual daughters and, no less pressingly and urgently, bound them to him as the source and sustaining strength for their spiritual lives.

DEATH

XV

Ignatius had faced death many times. By the time he encountered it for the last time, he had accomplished his life's work and had scaled the spiritual heights. Death was a welcome release and brought with it the rewards for his life of devoted service, struggle, and sacrifice. Death came to the little room in La Strada as a welcome guest.

But Ignatius' brushes with death earlier in life were hardly so serene. He had faced death on the battlements of Pamplona with defiant denial and almost counterphobic bravado. The French cannon that struck him down brought him to death's door. After his injury, did the experience of hovering on the brink of death, in such pain for all those weeks, perhaps contribute to his conversion? Not at all unlikely, I should think. Then there were the terrifying storms and the threats of shipwreck on his voyages to and from Jerusalem. And even when the elements were calm and peaceful, the countryside and the towns through which he had walked during most of his life were rampant with disease—especially the plague that was still the scourge of the continent. Death walks hand-in-hand with life, but in Ignatius' time it was a much more immediate and formidable companion.

If Ignatius had suffered the threat of death from the external forces of man and nature, the threat also came from within. There was first of all the thoughts of suicide that arose during the profoundly shaking crisis at Manresa. If one accepts the hypothesis that the suicidal impulse is buried deep within the unconscious of every man, that it is part of the human condition that we all struggle to keep repressed, then that impulse burst upon Ignatius at a point of regressive vulnerability. What happened to it afterwards? What more devious and displaced expression did it find in the mind and heart of Ignatius? Could it be that the severity of his penances, the life-threatening extremes of his fasting, and the generally unrelenting destructiveness he unleashed on his own body were all substitute expressions of his repressed suicidal impulses?[1] The possibility cannot be ignored.

These self-imposed rigors were in large measure responsible for the sad state of his health. The long fasts, the severe penances that often took the form of corporal assaults, undermined his health and ate into his physical reserves so that he had to deal continually with pain, weakness, and disability. His right leg, crippled at Pamplona and later by the rehabilitative attempts at Loyola, was a source of considerable pain and discomfort, especially on his long journeys, a good part of them on foot. And from the beginning of his austerities at Manresa he had suffered stomach pains.

His companions commented on the change in his health after Manresa. Laynez said that the man who "had been before robust and of a strong constitution, underwent a complete change in his body" (FN I, 78; cited in Dalmases, 1985, p. 287). And Ribadeneyra added: "At first he was of great physical strength and robust health, but he wore himself out by his fasts and excessive penance, from which he came to suffer various ailments and very severe pains of the stomach, caused by his great abstinence during the first years" (FN IV, 111; cited in Dalmases, 1985, p. 287). The most striking example of this was the swoon at Villadordis, when Ignatius was found unconscious after he collapsed following eight days of total fasting. The effects of his penitential excesses remained with him through the rest of his life in the form of almost chronic relapses. He fell ill in Paris, where the doctors could do no better than recommend a return to his native climate. At Azpeitia he fell ill again. His health would not allow him to stay in Barcelona, where he hoped to continue his studies, but forced him to move to Venice.

In Rome his condition did not improve. On 2 January 1539, Paul III dispensed him from reading the office for reasons of poor health, specifically exhaustion and pains in his abdomen (Dudon 1949). The pains in his stomach were sharp, frequent, exhausting, and often accompanied by fever. When he became gravely ill in 1550, he offered his resignation to his companions—partly because he felt his health would not allow him to continue to bear the burdens of his office. He recovered to a degree after that, but his course was up and down, and his health and strength were never good. June and July of 1554 were particularly bad. He spent the month of June 1554 in bed, and any attempt to get back to his routine only produced another collapse. Throughout his strength was feeble at best.

FINAL ILLNESS

Polanco's letters after 1548 frequently mention the poor state of Ignatius' health. On 2 April 1556, he wrote that Ignatius had failed considerably (FN XI, 284). Thinking that a sojourn in the country might help, Ignatius spent some time in July at the villa the Society had recently purchased on the Aventine. He seemed improved for a few days. But the improvement did not last long, and by July 24 he was back at La Strada. No one thought he was in danger of dying. His illness had been so severe and debilitating for so long that his doctors felt this was simply more of the same. They were not in fact paying very close attention, especially since others in the house, particularly Laynez, were gravely ill.

But Ignatius himself seems to have sensed that the end was near. On July 29 he asked Polanco to have Father Baltasar Torres, a physician, visit him. Torres and Ignatius' regular physician, Dr. Alessandro Petroni, were at his bedside daily. The next afternoon he again summoned Polanco. Dalmases (1985) recounts the conversation:

> After sending the infirmarian out of the room he told Polanco it would be fitting for him to go to the Vatican to inform His Holiness that "he was near the end and almost without hope of temporal life, and that he humbly begged from His Holiness his blessings for himself and for Master Lainez, who also was in danger." Polanco replied to him that the physicians saw no particularly alarming symptoms in his illness and that he himself hoped that God would preserve him for some years more. He asked Ignatius: "Do you really feel as ill as that?" Ignatius' answer was: "I am so ill that nothing remains for me except to expire." Polanco then promised the Father that he would fulfill his desire, but he asked him if it would suffice to do it on the next day. The reason was that on Thursdays the mail went out for Spain, via Genoa, and he had still some letters to dispatch. Ignatius replied: "I would be pleased more today than tomorrow, or, the sooner the better. But do what you think best in the matter. I leave myself entirely in your hands." (p. 294)

Polanco consulted Dr. Petroni, who did not think Ignatius was in danger, so Polanco decided to wait till the next day. At dawn, however, they found Ignatius failing badly. A desperate search was made for Pedro Riera, Ignatius' confessor, but he could not be found. Polanco rushed to the Vatican and despite the early hour was received by the Pope and was given the papal blessing. He rushed back to the house only to find that Ignatius had expired.

CODA

His death was ordinary. He died without the last sacraments; he had received his last communion two days before. The papal blessing that meant so much to him arrived too late. Polanco saw these circumstances of Ignatius' death in the light of his humility. He wrote:

> Although he was sure that he was about to die . . . he did not wish to summon us in order to give us his blessing, or to name a successor, or even a vicar, or to close the Constitutions, or to give any other such manifestation, such as some servants of God often do in such circumstances. Rather, just as he thought so humbly of himself and did not desire the Society's confidence to be placed in any being other than God our Lord, he passed from this world in the common manner and perhaps he had in a fitting way obtained this favor from God, whose glory alone he desired, that there should not be any striking signs in his death. (FN I, 767–768; cited in Dalmases, 1985, p. 296)

A medical footnote concerning the cause of Ignatius' death and the nature of his chronic illness is in order. On the day of Ignatius' death, an autopsy was performed by Dr. Realdo Colombo, a renowned surgeon from Cremona, in fact the successor in the chair of anatomy to the famous Vesalius, who had been the physician for Charles V and Philip II. The results of the autopsy were published three years later, in 1559. Colombo wrote: "With my own hands I have extracted almost innumerable gallstones of various colours, found in the kidneys, the lungs, the liver, and the portal vein . . . of the venerable Egnacio, Founder of the Congregation of Jesus" (FN I, 769; cited in Dalmases, 1985, p. 288). We can conclude that the diagnosis of Ignatius' chronic stomach ailment was biliary colic and that the stones had eroded into several organs and must have been the source of considerable pain,[2] and without analgesics or adequate medical care. Anyone who has had the experience of biliary colic knows what kind of pain Ignatius suffered through most of his life.

Ignatius was buried in the Church of the Gesu in Rome. Above his tomb was raised a magnificent baroque altar adorned by a splendid silver statue of the saint. The monument, completed in 1587, soon became a shrine to which the faithful flocked to beg the intercession of the man who had spent himself so selflessly on earth on their behalf. Canonization moved ahead rapidly. The process of examining his life and his virtues was set in motion in 1595, and on 27 July 1609 he was beatified. On 12 March 1622 he was raised to the honors of the altar and canonized as a saint of the Catholic Church. His companion in canonization was the same Francis Xavier who had been his soul mate in the student days in Paris and was his most valued fellow worker in the harvest fields of the kingdom.[3]

This brings to a close our account of the remarkable career and life of this extraordinary human being and saint. We are left then to ponder the meaning of this powerful narrative, particularly what understanding of his spiritual life and his profound mystical experiences it offers us in the more human and mundane terms of psychoanalytic explanation.

MYSTICAL AND SPIRITUAL LIFE

5

THE MYSTIC

XVI

Ignatius was without doubt one of the great mystics in the history of the Christian church, ranking with Francis of Assisi, John of the Cross, and Teresa of Avila. Ignatius' mystical journey led him to the heights of mystical experience that spiritual writers describe as infused contemplation. Theologians distinguish between acquired contemplation and infused contemplation, which requires extraordinary grace from God to achieve. As Egan comments:

> According to the mystical tradition, mystical prayer in the strict sense, or infused contemplation, cannot be attained through one's own efforts, even efforts aided by ordinary grace. This prayer requires God's special activity. God gives the person something new: the explicit awareness that God is present and that the person clings lovingly to Him. By actual experience the person becomes directly and immediately aware of God's loving, purifying, enlightening, and unifying presence. The person realizes that something *totally* new is occurring. (1987, pp. 23–24)

The characteristics of this state include the experience of God's presence in a form of knowing that is at once general and obscure yet rich and satisfying; the experience of love penetrates and dominates the soul as though the mystic is under the complete control of God—he is totally unable to arouse, elicit, prolong, or renew these experiences or even predict their beginning or end; and he finds it impossible to express these experiences in language or otherwise to convey to his fellowmen what they are like (De Guibert 1964).

Contemporary witnesses confirm the impression of Ignatius' intense contemplative life. Nadal, who knew Ignatius intimately during the Roman years, reported that he was able "to see and contemplate in all things, actions, and conversations the presence of God and the love of spiritual things, to remain a contemplative even in the midst of action," and that he experienced "continual recollection, to the point that it was necessary for him to seek diversions and to apply himself to some other pursuit" (De Guibert, 1964, p. 45). Ribadeneyra reported hearing Ignatius say that "as far as he could judge, it would not be possible for him to live without consolation, that is, without experiencing in himself something that was not and could not be a part of himself, but depended entirely on God." The catalog of infused mystical gifts found in Ignatius' writings include tears, spiritual relish and peace, intense consolation, elevation of mind and divine illuminations, spiritual understandings and visitations, visions, interior and exterior locutions, intense feelings of love, touches, consolations without previous cause, interior joy and attraction to heavenly things, quiet repose of the soul in his Creator and Lord, interior knowledge and divine inspirations (Young 1958).[1]

In addition to habitual recollection, that is keeping his mind focused in God and living in the presence of God, there were more intense experiences. At prayer or at Mass, his reaction could become so powerful that at times strong physical symptoms overwhelmed him. Nadal noted, "At Mass, he received great consolations and an extreme sensitivity to divine things. At times he was even obliged to omit saying Mass, for the disturbance was so strong that it weakened and damaged his bodily strength and his health." With regard to the recitation of the Divine Office, a daily obligation of priests, "because of the abundance of spiritual consolations, of interior feelings, and of tears, he felt so great a difficulty that he had to spend the greater part of the day in its recitation, and . . . his health and physical strength suffered considerably" (De Guibert, 1964, p. 46; see also Rahner 1977).

Laynez offered a description of Ignatius' nightly prayer:

At night he would go up on the roof of the house, with the sky there up above him. He would sit there quietly, absolutely quietly. He would take his hat off and look up for a long time at the sky. Then he would fall on his knees, bowing profoundly to God. Then he would sit on a little bench because the weakness of his body did not allow him to take any other position. He would stay there bareheaded and without moving. And the tears would begin to flow down his cheeks like a stream, but so quietly and so gently that you heard not a sob nor a sigh nor the least possible movement of his body. (FN IV, 746–749)

Iñigo was introduced to the mystical life by his vision of the Blessed Virgin and her divine son during his convalescence at the castle of

Loyola. But it was at Manresa that decisive events transformed him into a mystic in an authentic sense. Rahner (1953) describes the experience at Manresa as "God's mystical invasion into the soul of Iñigo, conquering all opposition, linking together all Iñigo's previous spiritual experiences, yet at the same time sovereignly transcending them with the object of making him, as he acknowledges in his autobiography, 'a new soldier of Christ, a man of the Church' " (p. 47). Ignatius himself recalled that the visions at Manresa "gave him such a great and lasting strengthening of faith that even if there were no Scripture to teach him these things of faith, he would be ready to die for the faith merely because of what he had seen at that time. . . . These illuminations were so great that all these things seemed new to him, and he received such insights and was so enlightened that he felt himself almost a new man" (Vita 29, cited in Ravier, 1987, p. 413).

Iñigo's mystical life developed as he made his way toward Rome. Even though there were periods in which he was forced to mitigate the intensity of his ascetical practices and prayer—for example, while he was caught up in his studies in Paris—the current of infused graces seems to have continued unabated. His prayer may have been lessened, but it lost none of its intensity and sense of union with God. Once the work of intellectual preparation was behind him, divine grace once again inundated his soul. He wrote: "During his sojourn at Vincenza, it was the reverse of what had happened in Paris, the pilgrim had many spiritual visions, numerous and almost continuous consolations. During all these trips, and especially at Venice, when he got ready to receive priestly ordination and prepared himself to say Mass, he received great supernatural visits, similar to those which he had constantly had at Manresa" (Vita 95). The experiences of Manresa provided a foundation upon which the great structure of his mystical life was erected. That identity was to be shaped and molded through years of pilgrimage and study, so that finally he would scale the heights of sanctity and mystical experience (Rahner 1968). But it was during the Roman years, after the founding of the Society of Jesus and his assumption of duties as the first Father General, that Ignatius' mystical life reached its apogee.

SOURCES

The primary sources for the study of Ignatius' mystical life are the *Exercises,* his *Autobiography,* and finally his *Spiritual Diary.* The *Ex-*

ercises reveal the methodology of his spirituality; it was apparently Ignatius' continual application of the techniques discovered at Manresa and incorporated in this manual of spirituality that provided the core of his own ascetical practice as well as the model for the spiritual formation of his followers. The autobiography provides accounts of some of his more meaningful and influential mystical experiences, particularly some of the more important visions and illuminations.[2]

Most revealing are the pages of his *Spiritual Diary* that have been preserved. These fragments consist of two copybooks written in Ignatius' hand. The first, covering the period 2 February to 12 March 1544, is composed of rather extensive notes from Ignatius' long deliberation on poverty in the Society. The second copybook, covering the period 13 March 1544 to 27 February 1545, contains cryptic entries with thoughts indicated by no more than abbreviations or algebraic signs.

There is little question not just that these notes were intended for Ignatius only and not for anyone else's eyes but that he attached great importance to them and made considerable use of them in his own prayer life (De Guibert 1964; Haas 1977). They are probably only part of extensive notes that Ignatius made but kept very much to himself. He refused to let even Gonzalves da Camara, to whom he communicated his autobiography, see any of them (Young 1958). Toward the end of his life, he was careful to destroy most of these notes; the few pages that remain were discovered in his desk drawer after his death. As Haas (1977) comments: "In the *Diary*, . . . Ignatius lays completely bare the mystery of his intimacy with God. Consequently, no other document offers us a more penetrating insight into the magnificent world of faith that was the inner life of Ignatius" (p. 165). The importance he attached to these jottings is suggested by his framing of certain lines as being especially important, passages which he transcribed elsewhere. One use he made of these pages was to place them on the altar when he said Mass to beg God for new illumination about his deliberations (Haas 1977).

That the *Diary* reveals the depths of true mystical infused contemplation seems beyond question. It is also important to remember that there is an intrinsic connection between the *Exercises* and the diary. As De Guibert has written:

> While the *Exercises*, whatever may be the mystical horizons they open up and the adaptations of which they are capable, are in their

very text first of all a book of supernatural asceticism, a method of personal effort to submit to the action of grace, the *Journal* [*Diary*] places us from the beginning on the mystical level in the strictest sense of the word. The three principal features which theologians agree in considering the essential characteristics of infused prayer, here stand revealed on every page: simple and intuitive vision of divine things, without multiplicity of concepts or discourse; the presence and action of God experienced in the soul; complete passivity in infused knowledge and love, which are given and withdrawn by God with sovereign independence of all our efforts. (Cited in Young, 1958, p. 200)

MYSTICAL EXPERIENCE

Ignatius' mysticism carries the stamp of his individuality. It is a mysticism of service based on love rather than a mysticism of loving union. It emphasizes both the Trinity and Christ's sacrifice in the eucharist. The Trinity is mentioned again and again in the *Diary*; among the passages marked for special emphasis, a dozen deal with visions of the Trinity, and four others with Christ in his role as mediator to the Trinity.[3] The trinitarian insights are diverse: on occasion Ignatius sees one or another of the persons of the Trinity without the others, or he is plunged into the bosom of the Trinity without any distinction among the three persons, or again he sees the Son and Spirit within the Father. Again he experiences the divine essence in its unity "without seeing the distinct persons as on the preceding days, but perceiving the one essence as in a lucid clarity." Again, his prayer "terminates in the Most Holy Trinity, without his having understandings or distinct visions of the three persons, but merely a simple attention to the Most Holy Trinity or a representation of it." At times his vision depicts Jesus as guide and companion, but without losing the sense of being in the presence of the Trinity and finds himself feeling even more united to the Trinity (De Guibert 1964; Stierli 1977). As Egan (1988) comments: "The Trinity bestowed upon him full participation in its life, especially through Ignatius' radical imitation of Christ's life, death, and resurrection. The triune God called Ignatius to the very depths of his spirit and beyond all narcissistic introversion to share fully in the divine life. Ignatius courageously risked everything and surrendered totally to the Trinity" (p. 20).

Ignatius' mysticism is also eucharistic, consistent with his long-standing devotion to Christ in the sacrifice of the Mass and his encouragement of daily communion. Much of his devotional life in later years centered around celebration of Mass, along with the preparations for it and its extensions into the rest of his day. He mentions graces received at Mass frequently in the *Diary*. De Guibert's (1964) judgment is that "the infused favors showered upon Ignatius were graces centered about Christ's Sacrifice of the Mass, and dominated by the Most Holy Trinity to whom this sacrifice gives us access" (p. 54).

Ignatius' mystical favors were both intellectual and affective. His visions carried with them profound understandings, but at the same time were accompanied by the most intense affective experiences—he was often moved to the point of tears by sentiments of great love and devotion. Preparing for Mass, he experienced "a deluge of tears and sobs, and a love so intense that it seemed to me to unite me with excessive closeness to the Trinity's own love—a love so luminous and sweet that I thought that this overpowering visit and love were outstanding and excellent among all other visits" (p. 54).

De Guibert (1964) draws attention to the absence in Ignatius' mysticism of any nuptial images of the mystical union—a significant aspect of the writings of other great mystics. Ignatius does mention the Church as the bride of Christ, but never the individual soul in such a role. His own sense of union with the Trinity or with Christ is expressed in the most loving and intimate of terms, but nowhere is it described as a spiritual marriage.[4] Ignatius will have none of the intense lyricism of John of the Cross, for example—"that burning aspiration toward an equality of love and toward a union consummated in the complete nudity of the spirit, that anticipation of the presence of the Well-beloved as one being approached through veils growing thinner and thinner, that advance toward clear vision" (De Guibert, 1964, p. 56). His relation to the Trinity and to Christ is consistently that of the humble and loving servant. As he wrote in the *Diary, Dadme humilidad amorosa,*—"Grant me a loving humility"—a sentiment that occupied the core of his spirituality (Rahner 1968). The thought of finding the grace to serve God, to seek and do his will, is uppermost in Ignatius' mind and prayer. Throughout his writings, even in his letters, the phrases recur with monotonous regularity: "the service and praise of His Divine Majesty," "the glory and service of God," "the service and praise of God."

Ignatius' mysticism is more kataphatic than apophatic.[5] In the apophatic tradition, the mystic advances through the passive prayer of quiet toward ecstatic union and finally transcendental life within the mystical marriage. In the kataphatic tradition, the focus is on "a progressive simplification of prayer, which culminates in the highest levels of sacramental contemplation. The increasing transparency of the mysteries, images, and symbols of salvation history guides the mystic along the contemplative journey to mystical transformation and spiritual fecundity" (Egan, 1984, p. 303). The *Exercises* would constitute a paradigm of an authentic kataphatic Christian mysticism.

CONSOLATION WITHOUT PREVIOUS CAUSE

One of most characteristic aspects of Ignatian mysticism is the concept of "consolation without previous cause." Ignatius describes this consolation in the *Exercises:* "It belongs to God alone to give consolation without previous cause, for it belongs to the Creator to enter into the soul, to leave it, and to act upon it, drawing it wholly to the love of His Divine Majesty. I say without previous cause, that is, without any previous perception or knowledge of any object from which such consolation might come to the soul through its own acts of intellect and will" (Exercises 330). The implication is that God alone can console in this way and that this is his way of consoling.[6]

The notion has been proposed as the high point of the movement of grace in the *Exercises* (Rahner 1976). It has been called the essence of the *Exercises* in that God holds sway over the soul and the soul responds with total surrender and self-depletion, thus realizing the profound unity between God and the soul in such consolation (Przywara 1938–1939; cited in Egan, 1976, pp. 9–10). Fessard (1956) sees this consolation as the measure of every other experience, the "immutable center of the Ignatian perspective." It is a movement in which the temporal and the eternal become one because of the divine initiative drawing the soul into loving union with the Father and the Son.

For Rahner (1976) this consolation serves as the primary principle in the "supernatural logic" of Ignatius' mystical experience and the standard against which all other mystical experiences can be measured. In itself, it can neither deceive nor be measured, carrying within itself its own indubitable evidence. It touches the subject's deepest core and draws him beyond all created objects into the infinity of God's love; it is "radical freedom, spirit supernaturally present to itself, hence a mystical, creative self-presence which leads the person into his own mysterious depths and into the Father's love" (Egan, 1976, p. 4). This basic form of consolation can be regarded as fundamental to the Ignatian method of discernment of spirits and central to his entire perspective on the spiritual life. The question is whether the Ignatian formula is meant to exclude all created causes. Can there be such a profound and meaningful psychological experience without conscious or unconscious motivation? We shall return to this issue later.

VISIONS

Among Ignatius' mystical experiences, his many and varied visions claim a prominent place. Various forms of vision can be described. Sensible visions, or apparitions, are primarily visual and consist in seeing an external object that others cannot see; auditory sensations may accompany the apparition. In imaginative visions, God is thought to influence the subject's imagination rather than sensory functions. The object is seen but is not sensed as externally present. In intellectual visions, the effect is on the understanding without sensory or imaginative components. These visionary experiences are usually of incomparable beauty, indescribable in human terms. They are regarded as the high point of infused contemplation.

Many of Ignatius' visions, especially early in his mystical career, have the quality of apparitions such as the image of the Virgin and Child at Loyola. Other experiences at Manresa are similar. Later experiences have more the stamp of imaginative visions. His visions of the Holy Trinity were especially compelling and meaningful (Rahner 1953). His account of one of these at Manresa bears repeating in this context:

> Now, one day, being about to recite the hours of our Lady on the steps of the Dominican monastery, his understanding began to be elevated. And it was as though he had seen the Holy Trinity under the form of three keys of an organ. And at this sight, he melted into tears until dinner. In the evening he spoke of nothing but the Holy Trinity. He could not keep from speaking of It; and he did so with an abundance of very different comparisons, his soul being filled all the while with

joy and consolation. And from this experience dates the feeling of great devotion he has felt all his life when praying to the Holy Trinity. (Vita 23)

The truth of this observation is amply borne out by the regularity with which his intimacy with the Holy Trinity appears in his *Spiritual Diary*.

The richness and frequency of these imaginative visions bear eloquent testimony to his inner spiritual life. They brought intense consolation and a deep sense of spiritual and intellectual enrichment which would last long after the vision had ended; Ignatius recalls how he would go through the day recalling the images of the Trinity to himself with great joy. The rules for discernment, which distinguish between the effects of God's action on the soul and the effects of human psychological reactions to it, are intended to cast light on the sources of the visions. Intellectual light and infused love come from God, the imaginative components that may accompany these experiences are human reactions—human psychology responding in its own terms to the divine influence. The ability of the human organism to respond is limited in affective responsiveness, in imaginative representation, and in linguistic communication. Ignatius often tries to communicate the nature of his experiences in sensory terms—warmth, color, taste, sweetness, and so on. The images and language are inadequate to convey the richness and intensity of the experience.

The visions at Manresa were many and varied: visions of meat when he was fasting, images of the Trinity "in the image of three keys of the keyboard," visions of how God created the world, apparitions of Our Lord and our Lady. Our Lord appears to him to help with his scruples, from which he is delivered. Or he sees clearly in a vision how Christ is present in the Blessed Sacrament. Frequently he sees in his mind's eye the humanity of Christ without distinct physical form. Similar visions of our Lady are recorded as well.

One of the most important visions having to do with Our Lord was the famous vision at La Storta. Ignatius, with Laynez and Faber, was on the way to Rome, where they hoped to establish a religious order. Rather than a single event, this vision seems to have evolved in stages. He prayed fervently to our Lady to place him with her Son. At first, there was a *loquela*-like[7] experience during the course of Mass in which Ignatius became aware of the inner words: "I will be favorable to you in Rome." Shortly thereafter the actual vision took place in the chapel at La Storta. He recalled: "It seemed to him that he saw Christ with his Cross on his shoulder and near him the Eternal Father who was saying, 'I want you to serve us.' " In the *Autobiography* he recalled, "And one day when he found himself in the church saying prayers—it was a few miles before arriving in Rome—he felt such a change in his soul and he saw so clearly that God the Father was uniting him with Christ His Son, that he would never dare doubt that God the Father had united him with His Son" (Vita 96). Whatever else one can say about such an experience, it seems clear that it served an important wish-fulfilling function on the brink of significant and uncertain adventures in the Holy City.[8]

DISCERNMENT OF SPIRITS

The flood of such mystical experiences created a problem for Ignatius: how could he know that these influences were from God? How could he be sure that they did not arise from some other source, even the evil one? How much was from God, how much from his own human nature? Ravier (1987) observes that the representational aspects of these imaginative visions were no more than psychological reactions to the deep emotion that had been stirred in Ignatius by the intensity of his experience.

But it is important to note the prevailing countercurrents in the Ignatian perspective on his mystical raptures. The first issue that pervaded his mystical life, as we have suggested, was the question of discernment of spirits. Ignatius was a gifted introspective observer of the inner movements of his psychic experience, who retained his capacity for self-observation and reflection throughout, and who was also a sensitive observer of psychic phenomena in others. The second element was his gradual retrenchment from his excessive and fanatical ascetical practices, often as a matter of expediency but always in the interest of furthering his mission of service to God's kingdom. Third, the distinctively Ignatian characteristic of drawing the fruits of mystical contemplation back to enrich his apostolic effectiveness. His earlier impulse was to scorn the world, to retreat into prayer and contemplation, to break utterly with the past and all attachments to human comfort. But as the years passed, he increasingly moved toward an integration of his ascetical life and mystical gifts with the demands of the life of service in the Society he founded and led.

The problem of discernment is dramatically displayed in the famous vision of the many-eyed serpent, which first appeared at Manresa.[9] Iñigo, ever the introspective psychologist, noticed that the apparition brought with it not only a feeling of delight but also doubts about his life of abnegation and following of Christ—how could he ever hope to continue for the full span of life? On the basis of his own rules for discernment, this was enough to convince Iñigo that the apparition was from the evil one and was a temptation.

MYSTICAL ILLUMINATIONS

Other manifestations had a more intellectual quality. Ignatius describes how, in these experiences, his understanding was deeply affected, but never without profound affect and emotion. At Manresa, he recalled to da Camara, "God dealt with him as a schoolmaster deals with a child whom he is instructing. Whether that was because of his inability and mental dullness, or because he had no one to instruct him, or because of the strong will to serve God which God Himself had given him, in any case it was and remained transparently clear to him that God was dealing with him in this manner. He would have thought it an offense against His Divine Majesty if he entertained a doubt about it" (Vita 27–31).

One form of this intellectual illumination would seem to be the interior and exterior loquelae he speaks of in the *Diary*. For example, he writes in the entry for 11 May 1544:

Tears before Mass and during it an abundance of them, and continued, together with the interior loquela during the Mass. It seems to me that it was given miraculously, as I had asked for it that same day, because in the whole week, I sometimes found the external loquela, and sometimes I did not, and the interior less, although last Saturday I was a little more purified. In the same way, in all the Masses of the week, although I was not granted tears, I felt greater peace and contentment throughout Mass because of the relish of the loquelas, together with the devotion I felt, than at other times when I shed tears in parts of the Mass. Those of today seemed to be much,

much different from those of former days, as they came more slowly, more interiorly, gently without noises or notable movements, coming apparently from within without my knowing how to explain them. In the interior and exterior loquela everything moved me to divine love and to the gift of the loquela divinely bestowed, with so much interior harmony in the interior loquela that I cannot explain it. (cited in Young, 1958, pp. 247–48)

Nowhere does Ignatius explain the meaning of these loquelae. Some further hints come from the entry of May 22:

In the greater part of the Mass, no tears, but much loquela, but I fell into some doubt about the relish and sweetness of the loquela for fear it might be from the evil spirit, thus causing the ceasing of the spiritual consolation of tears. Going on a little further, I thought that I took too much delight in the tone of the loquela, attending to the sound, without paying so much attention to the meaning of the words and of the loquela; and with this many tears, thinking that I was being taught how to proceed, with the hope of always finding further instruction as time went on. (Cited in Young, 1958, p. 249)

We are left in the dark as to the nature of these loquelae. Internal words are part of mystical experience, and this may be a similar phenomenon. The speaking takes place internally and comes from God, a form of infused knowledge. But why exterior and interior loquelae? Commentators have found these passages "obscure" and "strange" (De Guibert 1964; Ravier 1987). Egan (1976) connects them with the "consolations without previous cause" that carry the stamp of divine illumination.

One of the most significant of such illuminations was the famous episode on the banks of the Cardoner.[10] This extraordinary illumination was quickly followed by the vision of the many-eyed serpent. It is remarkable that, recounting the event some thirty years afterward, Ignatius still attributes such importance to it. These were direct infusions of spiritual knowledge—Ignatius emphasizes the elevation of his understanding and the breadth of his intellectual grasp. He was, therefore, experiencing the greatest mystical gifts even at Manresa (De Guibert 1964).

Many Jesuit spiritual writers, particularly Nadal, have attributed a central position to the illumination on the banks of the Cardoner, especially with respect to the quasi-divine origins of the Society.[11] But, as Silos (1964) points out, this does not fit with Ignatius' own account. Neither the *Autobiography* nor the *Exercises* contains any suggestion of such a connection. Also, for Laynez and Polanco, the Cardoner experience was no more than a turning point in Ignatius' spiritual development. The illumination contrasts with the prolonged struggle involved in the vision of the serpent, which seems to have been connected with the temptations against persevering in his spiritual path and led to agonizing scruples. Only by gradual discernment does Ignatius come to the conclusion that the serpent is from the devil. The great illumination, however, comes in a flash with unerring conviction and acceptance. This can be seen as a development in his capacity for discernment and increasing understanding of the importance of discernment in spiritual life. The experience at the Cardoner was a moment of realization in which the difficult lessons he had been learning were suddenly distilled into a principle that unified and gave meaning to the course of his experiences and confirmed him in the path he had chosen.

EXTRAORDINARY EXPERIENCES

Ignatius' mystical career also involved even more unusual manifestations. During his return visit to Azpeitia, he had to be hospitalized for a time, during which two of his nieces acted as nurses. One evening, they had retired a few moments after leaving Ignatius' room in darkness. A few moments later they heard him speaking in a loud voice and on returning found the room illuminated by a bright light. They retreated in troubled silence. When they asked him about it the next day, he forbade them to say anything about it. Other unusual events included his ability to read others' consciences; his accurate prediction of the course of events in Juan Pascual's life; his foretelling the deaths of Hocez, Codure, and Inés Pascual without any advance information about their illnesses; and his cures of Rodriguez, Le Jay, and Baroelo. His physician and Philip Neri once saw an aureola of light around his head, and when he had denied Father Kessel permission to visit him in Rome, he appeared to the good father soon after in his room some distance away. Even more extraordinary was the Pascuals' report that they saw Iñigo's body raised from the earth as he prayed, with his face aglow as though transfigured (Dudon 1949).

It is difficult to know what to make of such accounts, which have parallels in the accounts of the lives of other mystics from many religions and cultures.[12] They should be taken with a grain of salt as reflecting the hagiographic impulse in credulous and idealizing spectators. Such manifestations are the standard stuff of hagiographic enhancement of charismatic figures to transnatural levels; they were also the hallmarks of sanctity in the popular mind of the intensely supernaturally oriented and religiously pious culture of sixteenth-century Spain.

Even Ignatius did not put much credence in such extraordinary manifestations. During a visit to the professed house in Rome, one Fray Reginaldo, a prominent Dominican, told a story about a nun in Bologna who was in constant ecstasy and bore the stigmata. Ignatius commented that what was most commendable was the nun's obedience. When Ribadeneyra pursued the subject, Ignatius said, "It is for God alone to work in the interior of the soul; there the demon is powerless, but he has a way of deceiving through exterior phenomena that are plausible and false." When one of the fathers praised the prudence and holiness of the renowned ecstatic Magdalena de la Cruz, Ignatius reprimanded him: "A man of the Society ought not to talk like that, nor show so much esteem for things that are, after all, only exterior" (Dudon, 1949, pp. 225–26). Ignatius knew that such extraordinary phenomena occurred, but he also knew that they were ripe for illusion and deception. Delusion was the rule rather than the exception; and genuine mystical experience was the exception, never the rule (Rahner 1977).

He was often on his guard against illusion. He wrote to Adriaenssens, rector of the college in Louvain, that "to wait [before acting] for an interior movement to stir one, this does not seem to be proper, because [of the danger] of illusions and of tempting God." In 1554, advising the same religious superior about one of his tormented subjects, Ignatius wrote, "Don't be troubled, and don't get up because of these noises, or lose any sleep. The devil can do nothing without God's permission. If, however, some of these terrors are caused by a natural disposition inclined to melancholy, a doctor should be consulted" (Rahner, 1977, p. 101). As De Guibert (1964) comments: "This reserve sprang also from the fear of possible illusions in this matter. It is certain that St. Ignatius, complete mystic as he was and precisely because he was such an eminent mystic, stood in great fear of the illusions of the life of prayer"

(p. 563). We can add that his caution in this regard flowed out of his own experience and made the task of discernment even more central and weighty in his prayer life.

In Rome, his mystical life was private, even secret for the most part. His effort was consistently directed to modulating the enthusiasm and indiscreet fervor of his subjects. When Rodriguez wrote from Portugal about the "holy follies" of his overly zealous subjects, Ignatius urged moderation. He had to resist his own impulses to abandon himself completely to his mystical ecstasies and the folly of the Cross.[13] Discretion was never far from his mind.

TEARS

One of the most striking of Ignatius' mystical gifts was the so-called gift of tears. Especially during periods of prayer, when reciting the breviary or saying Mass, his devotion was so intense that his eyes would be bathed in tears. He often had to pause between phrases or words because his eyes were filled with tears and he could not see. Recitation of the office took an inordinate time, often the greater part of a day, as did saying Mass. After a while the constant tears began to affect his eyes, so that his disciples sought a papal dispensation from the obligation of the office, substituting a certain number of Our Fathers and Hail Marys for the office. But even these prayers brought their burden of consolation.

Prudence dictated other modifications in his prayer life in the interest of preserving his health (Dudon 1949; De Guibert 1964). In the *Spiritual Diary*, in the midst of intense and tearful devotion, he records: "Because of the violent pain that I felt in one eye as a result of the tears, this thought came to me: if I continue saying Mass I could lose this eye, whereas it is better to keep it." Reasonable discretion finds its way even into the mystical process. Late in his life he told Polanco: "Earlier I felt disconsolate if I could not weep three times during one Mass. But the doctor has forbidden me to weep, and I took that as a command of obedience. Since then, I experience much more consolation without tears." At times the physical ravages of his intense emotional reactions forced him to mitigate his ascetical and mystical practices: the tears and exacerbations of his "stomach" ailment were the primary problems. At times he did not celebrate Mass because of his fears of the visions and their aftermath. For a time he celebrated only on Sundays and feast days (Rahner 1977).

The experience of tears was usually accompanied by intense affects of sweetness, consolation, spiritual joy, and loving devotion. The experience of tears dominates the *Spiritual Diary*. He told Laynez that he had such experiences six or seven times a day (Young 1958). De Guibert (1964) comments that, although tears occur frequently in the accounts of other mystics, Ignatius has no rivals in the frequency and intensity of his tears. Yet he himself held tears in suspicion. In a letter to Nicholas of Gouda (Epistolae V, 713–715, cited in De Guibert 1964), he wrote:

The gift of tears should not be asked for in any absolute way. It is not necessary, and it is not good or profitable either absolutely or for all persons. . . . Some have the gift because their nature is such that in them the affections in the higher part of the soul have their reaction in the lower part, or because God sees that the gift would be profitable for them and grants it. But that does not cause them to have a greater charity, nor to do more good than others who do not have these tears, although their charity in the higher part of the soul is not less. . . . I tell Your Reverence that in the case of some persons, I would not grant this gift to them, even if it were in my power to give it, because these tears do not serve to increase charity in them, and are harmful to their body and head, and consequently impede many practices of charity. (p. 64)

De Guibert (1964) wonders, in the light of this mistrustful view of tears, why they dominate the *Spiritual Diary*. He answers that they are probably associated with the infused graces that were so precious to Ignatius. Ignatius wrote to Borgia distinguishing three kinds of tears: "Those that arise at the thought of one's own or others' sins, those arising from contemplation of the life of Christ, and those flowing from the love of the divine persons." (Epistolae II, 233–237 [Letter 466]; cited in De Guibert, 1964, pp. 64–65; also in Young 1959).

With this vast mystical panorama before us, we can only wonder at the power and spiritual richness, defying our experience and understanding. The next step will take us away from these lofty spiritual heights to the somewhat lower level of spiritual reality in Ignatius' ascetical and prayer life. The ascetical soil provided the matrix out of which his mystical life grew and continually drew its nourishment as he made his way toward his spiritual goal.

THE ASCETIC

XVII

The magnificent mystical edifice that arose in the spiritual life of Ignatius rested in part on an ascetical substructure that sustained his lofty mystical experiences. It is easier for us to grasp these more mundane expressions of Ignatius' spiritual life since they come much closer to our own experience. We turn our attention to Ignatius' life of prayer and penance to see what we may discern of the dynamic forces at work in the crusade of this intrepid knight of God.

THE LIFE OF PRAYER

From the first days of his conversion in the sick bed at Loyola, Iñigo devoted himself to prayer in imitation of the great saints he had read about in the *Flos Sanctorum*. This prayer gradually became more intense and extensive. Throughout his life, he would spend long hours at night gazing at the vast wonders of the heavens, lost in thought and prayer. He told da Camara that "the greatest consolation he received was to look upon the heavens and the stars; and that he did it frequently and for long periods" (Vita 11).

This devotional practice reached heroic proportions at Manresa. He assisted at Mass daily and attended vespers and compline in the local priory. When he moved into the Dominican priory he could also assist at matins. He knew no Latin, but the rhythms of the psalmody gave him great consolation. In private, he would then recite the hours of our Lady from the little book he brought from Loyola. As if this were not enough, he devoted himself to seven hours of prayer each day, usually on his knees. The rest of the day was given over to spiritual reading, especially the *Imitation of Christ*, but probably also the *Ejercitotario* of Cisneros and perhaps even the *Flos Sanctorum*. He constantly pored over the pages of notes and extracts he had made at Loyola and continued to add to them. This provided a sort of journal of spiritual reflections that was probably the basis for the *Spiritual Exercises* (Dudon 1949).

The intensity of his prayer life seems to have continued unabated after he left Manresa. In Barcelona, for example, he devoted most of the day and half the night to prayer. He attended Mass, vespers, and compline every day. He was frequently seen at prayer in the crypt of the chapel of St. Eulalia in the cathedral. He would kneel with arms outstretched or lie face down on the ground before the crucifix, uttering groans and prayers. At night, he would arise when others were asleep and spend the long hours of the night in prayer and ecstasy. Dudon (1949) sums up this life of continual prayer for us:

From the day of his conversion Ignatius of Loyola was a man of prayer. Daily Mass, the recitation of the Hours of our Lady, the rosary, visits to the most venerated sanctuaries of Manresa, long solitary prayers in the chapel of Villadordis and in the cave which thereafter took his name, were his familiar practice, and, as it were, a need of his heart. All through the ups and downs of Alcalá, Barcelona, Jerusalem, Salamanca, Paris, Azpeitia, and Venice, he changes his program only to enrich it. As the days follow one another and he walks toward his true destiny, Christ becomes more and more necessary and actual to him. Priest and Founder of an order, his spirit of prayer becomes purer and brighter to the point that he himself can remark to Laynez: "Manresa was but a beginning." (p. 365)

Even in his last years, when his ascetical excesses had begun to take their toll, he said Mass daily except when he was too ill. As his strength diminished, even this had to be limited, at first to Sundays and feasts, but gradually even more. Even when he could not celebrate it himself, he almost always attended Mass or would often have Mass celebrated for him in his private chapel. Da Camara recalls that he would recite the prayers designated for him as a substitute for the divine office, then go to the little chapel next to his room to say or hear Mass. After Mass he spent the next two hours lost in prayer—a time when he did not wish to be disturbed (De Guibert 1964).

There can be little doubt that prayer held a central place in Ignatius' spiritual life. He did not urge long hours of prayer on his followers but insisted on habitual recourse to and familiarity with God through prayer, even in the midst of work. He seems to have prayed for guidance with all his own problems and decisions of any import, turning to God for light and grace. As Ravier (1987) puts it, "No decision . . . was made except before God, or better, in God; it was preceded, 'enveloped,' prolonged by prayer" (p. 326). The formulas for this turning to God appear everywhere in the Constitutions and his letters—"to judge in the Lord," "to do what will seem best in Our Lord," "for the greater glory of God." At the end of his life, Ignatius wrote to Ramirez de Vergara, who was hesitant about entering the Society:

> The Holy Spirit will teach you better than anyone else the means for tasting with relish and for executing with sweetness that which reason dictates to be for the greater service and glory of God. Although it is true that for our pursuing the better and more perfect things the activity of the reason is sufficient, the other activity, that of the will, could easily follow this activity of the reason, even though this emotion in the will does not precede the decision and the execution, with God our Lord thus recompensing the confidence which one has placed in His providence, and recompensing too the abnegation of one's whole self, and the sacrifice of one's own comforts—indeed, with God compensating for these generous acts by much contentment and relish, and with an abundance of spiritual consolations which is the greater the less one has sought it, and has instead the more purely sought His glory and pleasure. (De Guibert, 1964, p. 97)

We can be fairly certain that Ignatius is telling us something about his own inner life of prayer.

DISCRETION

We previously noted Ignatius' discretion regarding mystical experiences and the extent to which he subordinated secondary mystical phenomena to the love and service of God. We should not be surprised to find the same discretion with regard to prayer. In 1548 he had to deal with two Spaniards, Oviedo and Onfroy, who wished to be allowed to retire into solitude for seven years in order to prepare for later apostolic labors by a life of prayer. They claimed that one or two hours a day was not sufficient and that more time should be given over to prayer. Ignatius sent a long instruction to Borgia refuting this "unsound teaching." According to Ignatius, long periods of time were not needed for effective prayer. Students must devote themselves to learning and need to preserve their strength for this purpose. Greater service can at times be given through other means than by prayer (De Guibert 1964; Stierli 1977; de Vries 1971).

He generally counseled moderation in prescribing the time spent on prayer by young scholastics during their studies. He was not slow to urge his followers to fervor and the seeking of perfection and exhorted the scholastics at Coimbra to greater heroism in God's service, but not without prudent discretion. Their studies were the work at hand for the greater glory of God—the way to balance the fervent devotion to prayer and the demands of God's service was through faithful obedience (Epistolae I, 496–510). In 1548 he learned that at Valencia and Gandia the practice of at least two hours of daily prayer had crept in, some even spending as much as eight hours at prayer. He at once wrote the provincial Araoz that this was an aberration and threatened to take action against them if they did not abandon this delusion. He even directed Araoz to set an example by reducing his own customary three hours of prayer to one (Epistolae II, 46–47). Similar directions were issued to Oviedo, the rector at Gandia (Epistolae II, 54–65).

In 1551, Antonio Brandao, a Portuguese Jesuit, raised doubts about the appropriate prayer life for those engaged in studies. Ignatius responded point by point: Mass on Sundays and feast days and twice during the week would suffice; unordained scholastics could devote an hour a day to prayer along with two daily examinations of conscience and recitation of the Little Office of the Blessed Virgin or similar prayers; ordained scholastics should be content with daily Mass, recitation of the breviary, two examinations of conscience, and another half hour for whatever special devotion they might have. Mental effort and study were their principal concern, but they should try to seek the presence of God in all things. Study performed out of love of God and offered to Him for his greater glory and service would be their best prayer. They can find as much devotion in works undertaken for the love of God and under holy obedience as in prayer (Dudon 1949).

For a time some uncertainty remained about whether the single hour of prayer Ignatius recommended was meant to include the examens and other prayers. The issue was decided when Ignatius corrected in his own hand the earlier rule in the Constitutions given to Nadal to promulgate in 1553: "In addition to daily Mass, those in studies were to have one hour. During it they will recite the Office of our Lady, and examine their consciences twice each day, and add other prayers according to the devotion of each one, until the hour mentioned above is filled out, in case it has not run its course. They are to do all this according to the arrangements and judgment of their superiors, whom they are obliged to obey as persons holding the place of Christ" (Constitutions 342).

Once Ignatius made his views on this subject quite clear, he did not change them. In 1553, the Spaniards complained to Nadal that they had only an hour each day for prayer and asked that the time be extended. Nadal brought the request to Ignatius, recommending that it be granted, but Ignatius reprimanded him and concluded, "For a truly mortified man, a quarter of an hour is enough to unite himself with God in prayer." At other times, he was heard to say, "Of a hundred persons making profession of lofty prayer, ninety at least are deluded." In general he felt that the methods of prayer outlined in the *Exercises* were enough for the prayerful formation of the scholastics, and that long hours of prayer were not necessary (Dudon 1949). We can guess that Ignatius was speaking from his own experience. During his study at the University of Paris he found it impossible to continue the long hours of prayer and penance that until then he had imposed on himself. During that seven-year period, he had moderated his ascetical practices and shortened the time he devoted to prayer, but we do not know by how much. During that time, discretion ruled over devotion. Shortly before his death, he wrote: "One should reflect that man does not serve God only when he prays. Otherwise all prayer would be too short that does not last twenty-four hours daily (if that were possible), since everyone indeed should give himself to God as completely as possible. But in reality, God is served better at certain times through other means than prayer or, a fortiori, if he shortens it" (Epistolae XII, 652).

SELF-ABNEGATION

Despite the extent and intensity of Ignatius' prayer life, it seems quite clear that prayer itself was subordinated in his mind, and in his practice as well, to self-denial and abnegation. Da Camara reports that when Ignatius reprimanded Nadal, "the Father said that his opinion, from which no one would ever move him, was that for the scholastics one hour of prayer is sufficient, it being supposed that they are practicing mortification and self-denial; and that such a one would easily accomplish more prayer in a quarter of an hour than another, who is not mortified, would do in two hours" (FN I, 676–677; Stierli, 1977, p. 146). This was the basic principle that governed Ignatius' spiritual journey and was embedded in his *Spiritual Exercises*. They are "Spiritual Exercises to conquer oneself and to order one's life without making a decision through any disordered attachment" (Exercises 21).

Uppermost in his mind was the necessity to eliminate inordinate attachments and control unruly passions by means of self-denial and the imitation of Christ. In his view, no one could vanquish the devil and preach to others until he had conquered himself. The fire of divine love and the ardent desire to serve God's kingdom could be aroused only by self-contempt and self-hatred; the path to spiritual growth lay in the denial of self out of love for the suffering and humiliated Christ. Contemplation of the events in Christ's life in the *Exercises* focuses on the lowliness, the poverty, and humiliations of the Savior. We are urged to imitate Christ in these aspects and to follow him in his impoverishment and tolerance of insults—"Let him desire and seek nothing except the greater praise and glory of God our Lord as the sum of all he does. For everyone must keep in mind that in all that concerns the spiritual life his progress will be in proportion to his surrender of self-love and of his own will and interests" (Exercises 189).

Self-abnegation, the essential condition of Christian perfection, is his constant theme, enjoined on his followers and practiced personally day in and day out. Overcoming self is the secret of all virtue, to be sought and achieved through the practice of poverty, chastity, and obedience to the will of God and His service (Dudon 1949). Ignatius' goal was the radical abnegation of self through the complete renunciation of comfort, honor, and especially one's own judgment (De Guibert 1964). In a letter to Fernandez on the qualities of candidates for admission to the Society, Polanco wrote: "With those who are received, I note that what the Father concerns himself most to make sure of, and what he thinks we must be most careful to secure, is obedience. . . . Individuals who are hard-headed, who upset and disturb others, even in slight things, he cannot put up with. In the matter of mortifications, I see that he wishes and esteems more those that touch one's sense of honor and self-esteem rather then those that make the flesh suffer, such as fasts, disciplines, and hair shirts" (Epistolae III, 501).

And again, he distills this teaching into the Summary of the Constitutions:

> Moreover, they must attentively consider and in the presence of our Creator and Lord hold it to be of the utmost importance as a help to progress in the spiritual life, to abhor completely and without exception all that the world loves and embraces, and to accept and desire with all their strength whatever Christ our Lord loved and embraced. For, as men of the world who follow the world love and very earnestly seek honors, distinctions and the reputation of a great name among men, as the world teaches them; so they who are making progress in the spiritual life, and are serious about following Christ our Lord, love and warmly desire the very opposite—to be clothed, in fact, in the same garments and wear the same attire as their Lord, out of love and reverence for Him: and this to such an extent, that if it could be done without offense to His Divine Majesty, or sin on the part of their neighbor, they should wish to suffer abuse, injustice, false accusations, and to be considered and treated as fools (without, however, giving occasion for such treatment), their whole desire being to resemble and in some way imitate our Creator and Lord Jesus Christ, by being clothed in His garments and raiment, since He first so clothed Himself for our spiritual benefit, and gave us an example to lead us to seek, as far as possible with God's grace, to imitate and follow Him, seeing that He is the true way that leads men to life. (Constitutions 101)

The ideal he proposes to his followers also appears in the Constitutions in the form of a portrait of the apostle of Christ:

> Men crucified to the world, and to whom the world itself is crucified, such would the rule of our life have us to be; new men, I say, who have put off their affections to put on Christ; dead to themselves to live to justice; who with St. Paul (2 Cor. 6: 5–8) in labors, in watchings, in fastings, in chastity, in knowledge, in long-suffering, in sweetness, in the Holy Spirit, in charity unfeigned, in the word of truth, show themselves ministers of God; and by the armor of justice in the right hand, and on the left by honor and dishonor, by evil report and good report, by good success finally and evil success, press forward with great strides toward their heavenly country. (Constitutions, Preface)

Ravier (1987) adds a final note to this perspective on Ignatian asceticism: "Let not these words and their austere reverberations hide the spiritual reality from us: abnegation, mortification, and the domination of the passions signify no more than total opening to the Spirit, a total availability to its action. From this interior 'nudity' the Ignatian prayer proceeds and in return is nourished and reinforced: it's a matter, in the last analysis, of the companions' immersing themselves with total Christian liberty in the love of God our Lord and in devotion to men" (p. 327).

PENANCES

Ignatius' teachings about self-denial, abnegation, and mortification came full blown from his own ascetical practice. He preached nothing that had not been implemented and realized fully in his own spiritual struggles. From the time he left Loyola, he practiced the most severe mortifications and penances with the two-fold aim of atoning for his past sins and demonstrating his love of God by imitating the austerities of the saints. The discipline became a nightly practice. Fasting became almost second nature to him, characteristic of the intensity with which he approached everything. He often did not eat for days on end, reducing his strength and even endangering his health. The long watches, penances, and fasts took their toll. Once at Villadordis, he collapsed while at prayer. Some pious women found him unconscious on the floor and were able to revive him and get him to a hospital where he could be cared for (Dudon 1949). His continued austerities at Manresa resulted in a stomach ailment that seemed to abate during his trip to Jerusalem. Once back in Barcelona, he resumed his austerities, and the ailment returned. For the most part during those years, he begged his food, gave the best part of his collections to the poor, and ate little himself.

He set out to eradicate all traces of his former dissolute life and inordinate attachments. His love of fine clothes was laid to rest by giving them to a beggar and donning the rough garb of the pilgrim. We know that for the rest of his pilgrim career he wore the most threadbare of garments. A thin and tattered cloak offered little warmth in the face of wintry winds and snow. In Barcelona he wore shoes without soles, even in the dead of winter. Instead of fine linen undergarments, he wore a hairshirt made of a heavy sack. Even during his days in Rome, the same fanatical ideal continued to hold its place in his mind, tempered only by prudence and moderation. Laynez tells us: "Ignatius is actually a despiser of the world. He told me that, if it depended on his own personal preference, he would be not in the least adverse to be considered insane as he would walk along with bare feet and with his deformed leg clearly in view or with horns on his head. But for the sake of souls he allowed none of this to become public knowledge" (FN I, 140; see also Rahner 1977).

He preferred poverty at all turns because he was intent on imitating Christ poor and humble. His conscience tormented him about the meager sum he had collected for his trip to Jerusalem; he resolved the conflict by giving the money away. When he and his companions finally abandoned their projected journey to Jerusalem, the two hundred scudi they had collected was returned to their benefactors. They lived instead on alms begged from day to day. Even during his Roman period, when he was head of the Society of Jesus, he continued a simple and poor life. Dudon (1949) describes the progression in his asceticism:

> In the beginning of his conversion he led a life of rugged penance, which left him broken in health for the rest of his days. At the time of his studies, his desire to carry the burden of intellectual labor without flinching led him to adopt a more moderate regimen. Later still, the pangs of illness and the sufferings of an early old age took the place of the fasts, the hair shirts, the bloody disciplines of Manresa. The flesh was conquered. The body had been reduced to impotence. Neither sleep nor food ever provided him with a temptation. He slept poorly, he ate little, and it made no difference what. (p. 372)

His room in the house facing the Piazza di Gesú was tiny, with only the simplest furniture. Dudon (1949) adds, "From the day when he broke with his worldly life, this man had never been able to surround himself with any conveniences. The mere word 'comfort' would have made him shudder" (p. 372).

The same sense of discretion that he urged on his followers in the matter of prayer also found expression with regard to ascetical practices. He wrote at one point to the scholastics at Coimbra: "Yet I would not have you conclude from this that I am displeased, or at all disapprove of what has been written me on the subject of some of the mortifications practiced among you. For these and other holy follies, I well know, have been used by the saints with great profit to their souls. They help one in the work of self-conquest, and progress in virtue, especially in the beginning of one's change of life. But when with God's grace you have gained some mastery over self-love, it is better, I take it, that you follow out what I have said in this letter on the necessity of discretion" (Epistolae I, 506; cited in Doncoeur, 1959, p. 37). In 1547, he wrote at length to Borgia in an effort to moderate the Duke's excessive penitential enthusiasm:

"With regard to fasting and abstinence, I would advise you for the love of God to guard and fortify your stomach and your other natural forces, and not to weaken them. For when the soul is disposed and firmly determined to die rather than commit the least deliberate offense against the Divine Majesty, and when besides it is not harassed by any particular temptation of the enemy, the world and the flesh, mortification is no longer so necessary. . . . we should care for the body and love it in proportion as it obeys and serves the soul more perfectly. On its part the soul finds in this obedient aid of the body more force and energy to serve and glorify our Creator and Lord. . . .

With regard to the chastisement of the body, instead of trying to shed a drop of blood, rather seek our Lord more closely in all things, I mean His holiest gifts: intensity of faith, hope and charity, joy and spiritual repose, tears and intense consolation, elevation of the spirit, divine illuminations and impressions, and all the other spiritual sweetness and feeling which flows from such gifts. . . . Of all these holy gifts, there is not one which should not be preferred to all bodily acts which are only good when they have for their aim the acquisition of these graces. . . . So, when the body finds herself in danger as a result of laborious exercises, the best thing is to seek these gifts by mental acts, or by other moderate exercises. For not only is the soul restored to serenity, but when a healthy mind is in a healthy body, all becomes healthy and fitted to a better service of God. (Epistolae II, 234; cited in Doncoeur, 1959, p. 37–39)

SCRUPULOSITY

Another striking aspect of Ignatius' ascetical practice was his persistent scrupulosity. This affliction apparently appeared for the first time as part of the crisis at Manresa in the form of agonizing doubts that he had adequately confessed and atoned for his former sins. He brought into play all his spiritual resources to gain victory—fasting, penances, long hours of prayer, repeated confessions, and consultations with his spiritual director. He devised the method of examination of conscience as part of the Spiritual Exercises and utilized it continually throughout his life. Laynez observed in 1547 that Ignatius took "so much care of his conscience that each day he compared week with week, month with month, day with day, seeking daily to advance" (De Guibert, 1964, pp. 39–40). Ribadeneyra adds: "He had always kept this habit of examining his conscience every hour, and of asking himself with careful attention how he had passed the hour. If at the end of it he happened upon some important matter, or a task that prevented this pious practice, he postponed the examen, but at the first free moment, or the following hour, he made up for this delay" (De Guibert, 1964, p. 66).

This practice was driven at least consciously by an obsession with sin and a fearful desire to root out any least semblance of fault. Ribadeneyra noted in 1554 an instance of extreme tenderness of conscience: "I heard from himself that he once had his confessor come to hear his confession for a single fault. It was for having made a certain father's fault known to three fathers, when to remedy his difficulties it would have sufficed to tell two. And yet these difficulties were numerous and not unknown to the third father, so that there was no danger of his conceiving a wrong idea of the father from this single communication" (De Guibert, 1964, p. 67). The result of this obsessional control was the appearance of complete dominion over his passions and impulses. Witnesses of his later years express amazement at the degree of this mastery and control over his affective expression—this in a man who was born with the full complement of Basque passion and affective vitality. De Guilbert summarizes this impression: "We should also add his examens, continued until his death with their incessant effort to keep his violent passions in check. The Diary of 1544 gives us a glimpse of their secret reawakenings, and he overcame them to such an extent that his most familiar witnesses remembered him only as one who had an absolute mastery over himself" (pp. 72–73).

ASCETICAL THEOLOGY

These aspects of Ignatius' life of prayer and penance and self-discipline reflect his intense devotion. The elements of this devotional life embraced love of God, familiarity with God, finding God in everything, and the preference for effective rather than affective[1] love expressing itself in the service of God above all. These elements are summarized in the Exercises in the Contemplation for Obtaining the Love of God and are distilled into the famous prayer from that contemplation, the *Suscipe*:

> Take, Lord, and receive all my liberty, my memory, my understanding, and my entire will, all that I have and possess. Thou hast given all to me. To Thee, O Lord, I return it. Dispose of it wholly according to Thy will. Give me Thy love and Thy grace, for this is sufficient for me. (Exercises 234)

The prayer expresses an ideal of self-abnegation for the love of God, which was also embedded in the third degree of humility in the Exercises and later in the eleventh and twelfth rules of the Summary of the Constitutions.

Ignatius' devotion was in the first instance trinitarian (De Guibert 1964; Egan 1976, 1984; Stierli 1977). He told da Camara about his devotion to the Trinity and his habit of prayer to the persons as well as to the Trinity as a whole. In his mystical transports, the Trinity is a dominating presence, while other figures, even Christ and the Blessed Mother, serve more as mediators to the Trinity than as direct objects of his prayer. The intense devotion to the Trinity that began at Manresa continued during the rest of his life; he told da Camara, "Throughout his whole life he had kept this impression of his having a great devotion when praying to the Trinity" (Vita 28). Nadal confirms this:

> Father Ignatius received from God the singular grace to contemplate freely all of the Most Holy Trinity, and to repose in this mystery. For, at times he was seized by the grace of contemplating the whole Trinity, and impelled towards It. He united himself with It wholeheartedly, with great feelings of devotion and spiritual relish. Sometimes he contemplated the Father, sometimes the Son, and sometimes the Holy Spirit. He always received the grace of this contemplation very frequently, but in an exceptional way during the last years of his earthly pilgrimage. (Epistolae Nadal, IV, 651ff; cited in Young, 1958, p. 201)

If Ignatius' devotion to his Lord and Master Jesus Christ takes second place to his devotion to the Trinity, the difference is difficult to discern. Christ is a central figure in the Exercises—he is the king who calls his followers to His service, the leader to whom the exercitant seeks to devote himself in total self-denial and dedication and to follow faithfully and fully. It is Christ's life and example that form the substance of the second, third, and fourth weeks: in the second week Christ's hidden and public life, in the third his suffering and death, in the fourth his resurrection and ascension to glory. The first companions were convinced that the essential parts of the Exercises derived from the vision at the Cardoner to which Ignatius himself ascribed such significance. In any case, there is little question that his theology and mysticism were centered on the figure of Christ (Rahner 1953). Service to God is translated into service to his Son, who is God incarnate. This service becomes a love of poverty and contempt with Christ poor and humiliated, the following of the spiritual standard taught by Christ rather than the riches, honors, and pride taught by the enemy.

Christ is above all the first and best of mediators (Egan 1976, 1984). In the colloquies of the *Exercises*, it is Christ as man who introduces the exercitant to the Trinity, who opens the way through his function as Son to the Father (Haas 1977). It is through the love, devotion, and following of Christ that the highest graces and mystical gifts are to be obtained. As De Guibert (1964) puts it, "From this love will be born the insatiable desire to serve, to give oneself, and to sacrifice oneself for Him, as well as the tender and unwearied effort for the souls whom He loved and redeemed" (p. 590). Thus, Ignatius' spirituality has been called "Christocentric" in the fullest sense. In the vision at La Storta it was Christ, bearing his cross, who said to him, "It is my wish that you should serve us" (Rahner 1953). As Egan (1976) puts it:

> The person of Jesus Christ became for Ignatius the very way in which and through which he grasped reality, his a priori stance, the very horizon against which and in which everything took its ultimate meaning. . . . When Ignatius says that the enlightened soul desires only Christ and Him Crucified, that Jesus Christ is the beginning, middle and end of all our good, that "all our wickedness shall be entirely consumed, when our souls shall be completely penetrated and possessed by Him," or that we should see all creatures as bathed in the blood of Christ, this is more than pious talk. It expresses Ignatius' emphatic Christocentrism, his appreciation of the christocentric dimension of all things. (p. 98)

THE BLESSED MOTHER

We should not overlook the unmistakable role of the Blessed Mother in Ignatius' devotional life. Mary was there at the beginning in the convalescing soldier's sick room. When he left Loyola, he carried with him a book of the hours of our Lady along with a picture of Our Lady of Sorrows. He lost no time in making his first nightly vigil at the shrine of Our Lady of Aranzazu on his way to Manresa. His second "vigil of arms" was spent before the altar of Our Lady of Montserrat, having divested himself of his fine clothes. The sword and dagger that had been his pride for all of his young manhood were hung in her chapel as an ex-voto as he left Montserrat; as a knight of God he had no need for worldly weapons. At Manresa, one of the great attractions for him was the plenitude of chapels to our Lady in the area. One of his favorite places for prayer was the chapel of Our Lady of Villadordis. When he left Manresa the picture of Our Lady of Sorrows was still with him (Dudon 1964).

We also note that important events were to take place on feasts of our Lady. The first vows of the companions in Paris were taken on the Assumption, August 15, and were renewed each year on that feast. Ignatius constantly turned to our Lady to intercede for him with her Son and his Father. In the colloquies of the *Exercises,* she is regularly invoked as one of the mediators; the progression often goes from Mary to her Son and finally to the Father. The vision of La Storta followed on his prayer of petition to her to place him with her Son. In the *Diary* he records how he petitioned her to intercede for him with the Father and at Mass that day had a vision of our Lady presenting his request to the Father:

> Later, on going out to say Mass, when beginning the prayer, I saw a likeness of our Lady, and realized how serious had been my fault of the other day, not without some interior movement and tears, thinking that the Blessed Virgin felt ashamed at asking for me so often after my many failings, so much so, that our Lady hid herself from me, and I found no devotion either in her or from on high. After this, as I did not find our Lady, I sought comfort on high, and there came upon me great movement of tears and sobbing with a certain assurance that the Heavenly Father was showing Himself favorable and kindly, so much so, that He gave a sign that it would be pleasing to Him to be asked through our Lady, whom I could not see.

While preparing the altar, and after vesting, and during the Mass, very intense interior movements, and many and intense tears and sobbing, with frequent loss of speech, and also after the end of Mass, and for long periods during the Mass, preparing and afterwards, the clear view of our Lady, very propitious before the Father, to such an extent, that in the prayers to the Father, to the Son, and at the consecration, I could not help feeling and seeing her, as though she were a part, or the doorway, of all the grace I felt in my soul. At the consecration she showed that her flesh was in that of her Son, with such great light that I cannot write about it. (Young, 1958, p. 211; De Guibert, 1964, pp. 52–53)

There are other passages in which Mary served this mediating function. The same sentiment is often found in his letters; he wrote to Inés Pascual, "May it please our Lady, to stand between us, poor sinners, and her Son and Lord. May she obtain for us the grace that in the midst of our sorrows and trials, she may make our cowardly and sad spirits strong and joyous to praise Him" (Epistolae I, 72; cited in Doncoeur, 1959, p. 36).

Ignatius' devotion to our Lady was by no means unique. Marian devotion had grown through the medieval period and had achieved great popular force. By the sixteenth century, her image had acquired almost divine attributes derived more from the Trinity than from goddesses of antiquity. The role of Mary in the economy of salvation was a point of controversy between Catholics and the Reformers. One view of the development of this devotion held that as the idea of God was progressively masculinized, the image of Mary as the feminine and maternal principle emerged with increasing emphasis. The quality of mercy and loving concern for poor sinners was entrusted to the figure of Mary, who could bring a mother's love and understanding to the inadequacies and failings of her children and plead their case before the seat of divine judgment (Johnson 1989). She became in this sense the idealized image of maternal perfection, of loving forgiveness and maternal concern (Saunders 1989).

PSYCHOANALYTIC IMPLICATIONS

What impressions does the mystical and spiritual life of Ignatius of Loyola make on the psychologist and psychoanalyst? There is no question that we are dealing with phenomena that defy simple explanation or reductive conceptualization. There is no question that many of the phenomena Ignatius experienced border on the pathological. But Ignatius' experiences cannot simply be reduced to the pathological, even those that most closely mimic pathological expressions, as we shall see. The ultimate question for the psychoanalyst is whether or not these experiences can be located within some intelligible framework that allows us to find psychological meaning and purpose in them.

Our effort is further frustrated by the complex nature and functioning of Ignatius' personality. Whatever one might say about his mystical and ecstatic experiences, there are two basic facts that require inclusion and explanation in any psychological account—his capacity to bring such intensely affective and regressively disruptive experiences under rational control and his capacity to perform on the highest level as leader, spiritual director, organizer, legislator, superior, guide, and practical administrator. Whatever the nature and quality of the dynamic psychological forces unleashed in Ignatius' mystical transports, they took place in an otherwise well-functioning, capable, and effective human being. This summary points us toward the next phase of our investigation—what psychiatric, psychological, and psychoanalytic insight can be brought to bear in understanding these phenomena? Or are we faced by an unbridgeable chasm between the supernatural and the natural, the spiritual and the psychological, the mystical and the psychic?

MYSTICISM
Psychopathology

XVIII

Confronted with the extraordinary richness and variety of the ecstatic experiences of Ignatius of Loyola, how can the psychoanalyst interpret it in meaningful terms that help us to understand this exceptional range of human experience? It is worth reminding ourselves that we can deal with these phenomena only from a limited perspective. The scope of our inquiry is dictated by the scientific methods proper to our psychological, psychiatric, and psychoanalytic approach. We must deal with these experiences as phenomena somehow related to the natural capacities of the human organism. We will have nothing to say, can have nothing to say, about their ultimate cause. The question of whether divine action exercised an extraordinary effect on the soul of Ignatius through grace does not fall within this purview—it is a matter for theological and faith-derived reflection.

MYSTICAL PHENOMENA

To focus the psychological dimensions of mystical experience, there is probably no better point of departure than William James' description of mystical states of consciousness. James (1902) described four marks or qualities that characterize these states:

1. *Ineffability*: Ineffability implies that the subject cannot find words adequate to describe his experience. It cannot be transmitted so that others can grasp it; it can only be experienced directly and personally. James comments that this aspect seems to emphasize the affective rather than intellective quality of the experience. One cannot explain it to another who has not had the experience himself. He says: "One must have musical ears to know the value of a symphony; one must have been in love one's self to understand a lover's state of mind.

Lacking the heart or ear, we cannot interpret the musician or the lover justly, and we are even likely to consider him weak-minded or absurd. The mystic finds that most of us accord to his experiences an equally incompetent treatment" (p. 300).

2. *Noetic quality*: While the affective aspect predominates, mystical states are also cognitive insofar as they seem to provide deep insight into truths that escape the grasp of discursive reasoning and logic. These illuminations and revelations are of particular significance and importance to the mystic, even though they remain diffuse and in-articulate.

3. *Transiency*: The mystical state lasts for only minutes or at most hours. Longer duration is most exceptional. But recurrence of the same state is common in mystical experience, often with a sense of continuity between episodes and of deepening richness and impor-tance of the experience or the content of the illumination.

4. *Passivity*: The mystical state may be induced by the voluntary activity of the mystic, such as exercises of concentration, bodily pos-tures, or—in Ignatian terms—spiritual exercises, but when the mysti-cal state sets in it carries with it a sense of powerlessness, loss of all control, total passivity, as though the mystic were in the grasp of another power against which he possessed no will of his own. James points out the parallel with such other paranormal phenomena as prophetic speech, automatic writing, and trance states found in cer-tain mediums or even to an extent in hypnosis. These states usually result in a lack of memory of the experience, but in mystical states some memory always remains along with a profound sense of the importance of the experience and subsequent modification of the sub-ject's inner life.

All these characteristics were present in Ignatius' mystical experi-ence. It is important here to maintain the distinction between primary and secondary mystical phenomena. As far as I can see, James' marks would qualify as primary dimensions of the mystical state. In this re-gard Ignatius was a mystic in the primary sense—certainly James thought so. This point has been elaborated by Egan (1988) who writes:

The word "mysticism" is commonly associated with the unreal, the otherworldly, the vague, the parapsychological, the occult, the "spooky," the poetic, or with altered states of consciousness brought about by meditation techniques or psychedelic means. Ignatius' mysticism has absolutely nothing in common with these.

Some scholars contend that the essence of mysticism is found in visions, locutions, the stigmata, levitations, and isolated instances of irresistible raptures and ecstasies. To be sure, one does find many of these *secondary* mystical phenomena in Ignatius' mystical life. Secondary mystical phenomena, however, do not disclose what mysticism is in its primary and strict sense—in the full sense that makes Ignatius one of the greatest mystics in Christian history. (p. 21)

From a psychoanalytic perspective, psychic process and psychodynamic influence are present in both primary and secondary manifestations of the mystical state. From the theological perspective, it is understandable that commentators would take care to distance the mystical experience from secondary phenomena, but the fact remains that these manifestations are frequent companions of the primary aspects and are found in the careers of all great mystics.

Such secondary phenomena may prove to be an aid or a hindrance to the mystic's progress. As Egan notes: "Ecstasies, raptures, visions, locutions, revelations, the stigmata, levitations, and other phenomena frequently occur with the primary phenomenon of *infused contemplation*, or God's experienced loving self-communication. If past studies tended to overemphasize these unusual phenomena at the expense of the essential mystical phenomenon, that is, infused contemplation, contemporary studies seem to dissociate them too sharply" (1984, p. 305). Theologians teach that secondary phenomena are suspect since they may not originate as a result of divine influence—they may come from the devil or from the self. They should not be sought for themselves, and even if they seem to come from God they should not be valued at the expense of more central spiritual concerns. This was certainly the attitude of Ignatius regarding such extraordinary manifestations and his continued emphasis on self-abnegation and obedience.

My purpose here is to evaluate these secondary phenomena from a psychiatric perspective and specifically to focus on the potential overlap between these experiences and psychotic forms of experience. To varying degrees, the mystic detaches himself from the real world, either by attributing greater reality to his inner world and experience or by believing in a transcendent or supernatural world. Although this seems to resemble states of schizophrenic detachment, it differs in that detachment for the mystic is deliberate and to some degree under subjective control; for the schizophrenic it is not. Although the mystic devalues certain aspects of the real world, he may also attribute greater significance or value to other aspects. Moreover, the goal of mystical union is the highest reality, next to which all events of daily life pale in comparison. The mystic is driven by a supernatural love transcending all human love. The metaphors of mystical language are often sexual, but the relation between this consuming divine love and the more familiar object love and/or narcissism remains in question.

In discussing the varieties of mystical experience, I am following Egan's (1984) detailed catalog of secondary mystical and charismatic phenomena but will focus on those that apply to Ignatius:

Ecstasy and Rapture: Religious ecstasy involves a narrowing of the field of conscious awareness; the mystic becomes intensely focused on and absorbed in God as the object of contemplation and withdrawn from everything else. In the process, all extraneous thoughts and feelings and all patterns of normal reasoning are eliminated until the unitive experience is reached; at that point the mystic's mind is empty, a blank screen. Through meditation he concentrates his thought on one aspect of his belief system and thus induces a state of altered consciousness. He achieves an awareness of the supernatural while maintaining a sense of distinctness and self-identity. In the contemplative state, the mystic is caught up in the transcendent reality of the numinous, the "wholly other." The immanence of divine presence is experienced as joyful, intimate, and transforming. In prayer the mystic strives for this state of total concentration on God, but in the ecstatic process the focus on the object cannot be resisted. Bodily processes—heart rate, respiratory rate, body temperature, and other metabolic functions—may be affected. Ecstasy is equally a trance state. Ecstatic states suggest a state of psychic union in which all inner psychic processes are absorbed in the experience of blissful merger with the object of sublime love. The mystic is transfixed, unable to move or speak, caught up in a state of inexpressible tranquillity and lucidity. The experience is intensely affective and at its fullest results in a state of mystical union.

Raptures have a somewhat different quality: they are ecstatic states that are sudden, involuntary, even violent in onset. Unlike the usual prayerful ecstasy, which has an induced character, the rapture is abrupt and uncontrollable and may intrude on the person's normal state of consciousness. There seems little doubt that Ignatius frequently experienced ecstatic states of consciousness as a regular accompaniment to his prayer life. Some of these experiences seem to have had a rapturous quality as well.

Visions: Visions may be sensible or corporeal visions or apparitions, in which the mystic sees an object that others do not, or they may be imaginative visions, in which the primary quality is the eliciting of dream-like images during sleep or during ecstatic states. Usually apparitions take the form of some religiously significant figure—the Blessed Mother appeared to Ignatius at Loyola, and various other apparitions of Christ and our Lady were repeatedly part of his prayer experience. Ignatius also had a variety of imaginative visions, such as the image of the Trinity in the form of three organ keys and other images of Christ in the eucharist. Visions can also be intellectual, without any sensory or imaginative content. This seems to me to be equivalent to the illuminations of the understanding of which Ignatius speaks quite frequently. His experience by the Cardoner seems to have been such an experience, but obviously there were others, recorded in the *Autobiography* and the *Diary*.

Loquelae: Mystical words or auditions—what Ignatius refers to as *loquelae*—may take an external, sensory form in which the mystic hears words spoken from outside. This is analogous to auditory hallucinations. Words may also be experienced as though coming from within or taking place in the depths of the understanding without any sensory or imaginative component. For Ignatius both exterior and interior loquelae were like divine music accompanied by a sense of sweetness and a profound feeling of love of God. The affect was so overwhelming that he complained that he could not pay attention to the meaning of the words. Consequently, he was suspicious of this affective component.

Revelations. These are visions or loquelae that carry informational content pertaining to the past, present, or future, usually something for the good of the church or the individual. These revelations are private and usually convey a deeper awareness or understanding of revealed truths or mysteries. Such revelations, or illuminations, abound in Ignatius' accounts of his mystical experience, especially during the Manresa period, but continued ever more profoundly to the end of his life. There are also suggestions that Ignatius had prophetic revelations that permitted him to foretell certain events, astonishing his contemporaries. We should be aware of the hagiographic impulse in evaluating such stories.

Touches, Tastes, and Smells: The mystics frequently report experiences of divine touches, smells, and tastes to some extent analogous to actual sensory phenomena. It is often difficult to disentangle metaphoric or poetic expressions from sensory experience. Ignatius urged the use of the senses as a technique for facilitating meditation—that is, seeing, hearing our Lord, imagining the smells and sounds,[1] and so on— to draw on the imagination to make the meditative experience as vivid and real as possible. For Ignatius, the application of senses was part of the process leading to mystical experience. He agrees along with other authentic Christian mystics that actual sensory experiences in the mystical state itself are suspect. As Egan (1984) notes, most mystics hold such phenomena to be highly dubious, and in fact, few authentic Christian mystics ever experienced them. There is no indication that Ignatius ever had such experiences.

DISCERNMENT

A constant problem that plagued the mystics (and their commentators) is that of discernment—that is, distinguishing the degree to which specific mystical experiences are authentic and come from the influence of God on the soul as opposed to influences that come from elsewhere and are therefore not authentic parts of the mystical state. In the late medieval context of Ignatius' life the devil was the leading alien influence. From today's more psychoanalytic perspective, we are more likely to appeal to the individual's own psychic processes. It is precisely from this concern that Ignatius' rules for the discernment of spirits play such a central role in his spiritual outlook and constitute an essential aspect of his *Spiritual Exercises.* We also know that he applied these rules assiduously not only in his own spiritual life but in his efforts to help others discern God's will in their own lives and spiritual experience.

Most mystics and their commentators agree that intellectual influences of any kind, unlike sensory or other psychosomatic reverberations, are an authentic aspect of divine self-communication and an expression of infused contemplation. But there is a question as to whether purely intellective infusions ever take place without some imaginative or sensory aftereffects. God's influence is assumed to affect the mystic's soul to such a degree and depth that his total organism must adjust to this radical and compelling input. Consequently, secondary manifestations may represent an integral part of the overall experience, the core of which is intellective and spiritual. Thus, secondary and charismatic mystic phenomena may be signals of God's mystical presence that reveal a more intimate and more meaningful infused contemplation. Egan (1984) expresses the tension between these more authentic expressions and other forces at work in the mystic's experience:

Genuine secondary mystical and charismatic phenomena never occur alone. The mystic or charismatic normally experiences genuine, pathological, and diabolical phenomena during the course of his mystical ascent or charismatic life. These phenomena will reveal not only his God-induced psychosomatic integration, but also his brokenness and the presence of the demonic. Taken together, therefore, these phenomena manifest God's presence, the devil's presence, and the Christian's own healthy and pathological accommodations and resistances to both the divine and the demonic presence.

Furthermore, it is not surprising that some of these phenomena reflect the Christian's infantile dreams, inordinate desires, immature projections, and pathological hallucinations. Others, however, counter directly the Christian's physically, psychologically, and morally pernicious tendencies. Conversion, renewed energy, strength, courage, authority, and peace accompany them. They bestow insight, knowledge, and wisdom, while deepening faith, hope, and love. (p. 330)

This, then, in the theological perspective, is the touchstone for evaluating the authenticity of such secondary experiences. Influences from God are marked by a trail of increased faith, hope, love, humility, and peace. Influences that derive from internal drives, conflicts, or frustrated desires leave the subject feeling arid, empty, frustrated, anxious, and experiencing greater degrees of pride, narcissistic enhancement, shame, guilt, or bitterness. Genuine ecstasies, which come from God, bring a sense of humility, inner peace, and a greater readiness to embrace the cross as the means for mystical ascent. They are life-enhancing, whereas pathological states lead toward psychic disintegration and destruction. Ignatius was suspicious of the sweetness of his experiences of loquelae because they distracted him from the meaning of the words that he thought came from God. This was analogous to his distrust of his ecstatic experiences at prayer, which distracted him from his studies; he saw the studies as God's will for him at the time, so that the spiritual rewards had to be the work of the devil.

PATHOLOGY

What can be said about such mystical experiences from the psychiatric perspective? I shall first discuss aspects of psychopathology as they may impinge on mystical states and then take up the rather sticky question of possible organic factors. The association between psychosis and religious experience has a venerable history—even Socrates regarded madness as a divine gift (Dodds 1951). The similarity between psychotic symptoms and mystical experiences has also been noted (James 1902; Bowers and Freedman 1966; Arieti 1967, 1976; Buckley 1981). Common features include the feeling of being transported beyond the self, a heightened state of awareness, loss of self-object boundaries, distortion of one's sense of time (especially time dilation), perceptual changes including synesthesia[2] and the intensifying or weakening of perceptions, frank hallucinations often more visual than auditory, and sensations of seeing and being enveloped in light (Buckley 1981).

A diagnostic set of categories has recently been suggested to deal with the apparent overlap between psychosis as such and mystical experiences: "mystical experiences with psychotic features" and "psychotic disorders with mystical features" (Lukoff 1985). Many argue that short-term psychotic episodes, in contrast to more chronic conditions, can have constructive outcomes. Boisen (1962), basing his view on the transformative aspects of his own psychosis, spoke of "problem-solving schizophrenia." Ellenberger (1970) has advanced the concept of "creative illness." Such experiences are by no means rare and occur in almost every variety of religious setting and even in nonreligious settings (Lukoff 1985). Differential diagnosis between mysticism and psychosis is not always easy, especially when the unusual experiences are positively regarded by the individual experiencing them. The beginning of a psychotic episode may be introduced by anxiety or confusion that is suddenly replaced by a feeling of understanding the "meaning" of the experience. The understanding often includes a sense of having been chosen as God's agent, or as the messiah, and having special hidden knowledge (gnosis). This may be associated with feelings of joy and exultation and a sense of communion or union with God.[3]

The phenomenology of psychotic experiences is similar to dreams, hallucinogenic experiences, certain forms of conversions, even shamanic[4] experiences. But the bizarre or fantastic content of such episodes is not sufficient to determine the presence of psychosis. Such content may be adaptive within a specific cultural or psychosocial context. Individuals can have unusual perceptual experiences, hallucinations, even strange delusions without being psychotic. Other significant indicators are the quality of the individual's object relations and his ability to maintain a level of reasonable functioning in other areas of his life. Aspects of mystical experience resembling psychosis might include ecstatic mood changes, the sense of gaining new and secret knowledge, perceptual alterations, especially auditory and visual hallucinations, or delusional content related to a specific theological perspective. Mythic content is common in psychotic delusions: death and rebirth, encounters with spirits, participation in cosmic conflicts (good versus evil), possession of magical powers, themes of radical social change (new world, world peace, utopias), and union or marriage with a divine figure such as Christ or with Mary and so forth. If such delusional content is believed without adequate reality testing, the border of psychosis has been crossed. Also essential to the diagnosis of psychosis is the presence of a thought disorder; evidence of thought disorganization or disruption, incoherence, and blocking are not components of mystical experience. Mystical experiences also tend to be self-limited and brief, characteristics that also differentiate them from psychosis.

Arieti (1967) maintains a firm distinction between psychotic and religious mystical states. He lists the following characteristics found in mystical states and not in psychotic states:

1. Religious hallucinations are predominantly visual, not auditory. Most of the time they have the aspect of apparitions. If there is an auditory component, it is as a rule secondary to the visual.

2. In their content they often involve old people, parent substitutes; but they are benevolent parents who guide the person to whom they appear.

3. Their content is gratifying in a manifest way.

4. The individual who experiences them has a marked rise in self-esteem and a sense of his being or becoming a worthwhile and very active person. He has been given a mission or a special insight, and from now on he must be on the move doing something important— more important than his own life. Although the message is experienced as an order, the subject does not feel that he is the victim of tyranny or a passive agent, but that he has been chosen to perform something of stupendous proportions. (p. 426)

Arieti adds:

The whole personalities and behavior of the people who experience religious hallucinations are not such as to warrant the diagnosis of psychosis. Mystics are fanatic, but not in the same way as the paranoid. They lack the bitterness and resentment or the calm resignation and disdain of the unjustly accused. They show instead a serene optimism, like that of people who have been blessed by the love of a good mother. Moreover, the hallucinatory and delusional experiences of the schizophrenic are generally accompanied by a more or less apparent disintegration of the whole person. Religious and mystical experiences seem instead to result in a strengthening and enriching of the personality. (pp. 426–427)

Even when a diagnosis of psychosis is likely, certain elements can be predictive of a positive outcome. Such elements would include:

1. Good premorbid functioning (before the onset of symptoms) as indicated by an absence of previous psychotic episodes, reasonable social history, intimate relations with the opposite sex, and vocational or career success (Goldstein 1970; Rappaport, Hopkins, and Hall 1978; Valliant 1964).
2. Acute onset of symptoms (Robins and Guze 1970; Sartorius, Jablenski, and Shapiro 1978).
3. An acute precipitant, such as a death in the family, divorce, loss of job, illness, or even positive life changes such as marriage, new job, and so on. Developmental crises, such as the transition from adolescence to adulthood, can also be precipitants (Stephens et al. 1966; Valliant 1964).
4. Positive attitude toward the psychotic experience, which can facilitate integration of the experience as meaningful, revelatory, and

growth-enhancing in postpsychotic life (McGlashan and Carpenter 1981).

Psychiatrists, however, have not hesitated to call mystical phenomena psychotic. Lenz (1979), for example, regards the numinous, inexpressible, or incomprehensible as irrational. Religiously based phenomena such as faith, inspiration, and many mystical experiences have the same quality as psychotic delusions: psychotic delusions often have the same quality of bursting in on the individual, changing him in some way, and delivering him up to a higher power outside himself. Lenz describes a series of such delusions:

1. Certain events or objects acquire abnormal importance. Things take on new meaning, new doors seem to open, and the individual begins to experience himself and the world in a new way.

2. Pseudo-hallucinations. These are not actual hallucinations but experiences expressed in vague terms, such as "It felt like . . . ," or "I had the feeling that . . . ," "It was as if . . ." Only the meaning of the experience seems clear, while the concrete elements never are. Such experiences are often related to visions or apparitions and seem to reflect the workings of the imagination.

3. The suddenness and passivity of the experience. The person feels "attacked," overwhelmed by a powerful force outside himself such that his ego is transformed.

4. The feeling of mission. The delusion almost always includes a call to do or not do something, to carry out some mission or action—to become an apostle, to make sacrifices for a cause, to do penance, and so on. Failure to carry out the mission brings a sense of shame and sinfulness.

5. Polarity of moods. Without apparent reason moods can shift often rapidly and radically—from joy to guilt, from a sense of possessing the truth to suicide, and so on.

6. A lack of awareness of time and space.

7. Shame. This feeling often prevents the individual from sharing or communicating his experience; it belongs to a personal "holy" sphere that is in some sense taboo and must be protected from prying eyes.

Lenz attributes all these phenomena except the last two to Ignatius. Certainly both the content and the ego state of the trance experience can be interpreted as reflecting a form of infantile regression symbolizing the gratification of desires for union with the idealized parent— especially the mother. In this view, part of the motivation behind mystical states can be restitutive and defensive—restoring a sense of self-cohesion and integrity and defending against repressed libidinal or aggressive strivings.

We also have to remind ourselves that these experiences are always culturally embedded. The period in which Ignatius lived was only beginning to draw away from the medieval mentality. Behaviors that might be regarded as pathological in our time and culture were often regarded in the Middle Ages as aspects of religious or transcendental experience—perhaps aberrant, but not pathological. Such behaviors were clearly distinguished from insanity. Visions in particular are vehicles of cultural determination and expression (Bourgignon 1976).

In reviewing a series of visionary experiences culled from medieval mystics, Kroll and Bachrach (1982) described five categories of such visions. In the first, no unusual circumstances or mental states were involved, and there were no indications of stress or abnormal physiological conditions. The second group of visions was produced by fasting and starvation, usually undertaken as a form of penance. The third category was related to stressful circumstances or stress-related syndromes; several took place during the seige of Jerusalem in 1098 and could be regarded as mass psychic phenomena. A fourth category was related to illness and death, usually in the form of an apparition of a saint or beloved religious superior coming to take the mystic to heaven. The final category was related to mental illness or alcoholism, associated with possible episodes of schizophrenia or psychotic depression. Only four of the hundred-and-thirty-four visions examined fell into this fifth category. The authors caution:

> There is a temptation to overexplain or overdiagnose all or most visionary experiences, since we live in a time when altered states of consciousness and transcendental experiences are suspect. . . . If visions have the transcendent significance which the visionary accepts, then it is gratuitous to think that a medical or psychological description explains anything other than the mechanical or efficient cause of such an experience. Such explanations tend to be overpersonalized with simplified dynamics, ignore the milieu in which the

experiences occur, and impose modern biases upon a very different society. (p. 47)

In his review of this subject, Buckley (1981), commenting on the similarity in the symptoms of psychotic and mystical states, concludes that they may share no more than "simply an ecstatic affective charge which imbues perception with an increased intensity" (p. 520). More chronic schizophrenic conditions are quite different from mystical states: thought disorders and disturbance of language and speech are not found in mystical states. There is no flatness of affect, and hallucinations tend to be visual rather than auditory—the opposite pattern to schizophrenia. The wide range of contexts in which such heightened consciousness can occur and the variety of factors that can initiate it suggest that an innate capacity of the human mind is involved. This may simply provide a final common path for mystical experience and certain forms of acute psychotic reaction (Bowers and Freedman 1966; Buckley 1981).

Even when there is an identifiable overlap between mystical experience and psychopathology, we run the risk of reducing a life of spiritual struggle to a pathological case history. Two systems of thought and analysis, observation and explanation, come into conjunction, as in the case of the thirteenth-century visionary Beatrice of Nazareth. In concluding their analysis of her case, Kroll and De Ganck (1986) ask:

Is there a way to encompass both systems of observation and explanation, in which each system provides different levels of understanding which are often not contradictory and at times may even be complementary? Beatrice is both a mystic and a manic-depressive with some colorful personality traits. . . . Thus one resolution to the problem of different level of analysis is the hypothesis that Beatrice's spiritual struggle involved precisely the struggle to overcome her depressive nature and stormy personality. Her painful episodes of despair and loss of faith, on the one hand, and her witness in relation to her own self-mortification and her demands for God's grace, on the other, were the twin enemies against which Beatrice had to struggle, just as in others a lustful nature, grasping after money or glory, a propensity for alcohol, or a long demoralizing illness are the enemies which must be overcome in order to attain spiritual perfection. (p. 755)

THE CASE OF IGNATIUS

Was Ignatius psychotic? We are not without reasons to think so. If we take his hypothetical psychosis as reflected in his mystical and ascetical experience (nothing else in his life story would support such a diagnosis), there was an acute precipitant—the life-threatening injury at Pamplona and the subsequent surgical torment and convalescence, which brought about a severe narcissistic crisis. In this context Iñigo began to experience the extraordinary phenomena that characterized his mystical career. We can then point to the clearly regressive crisis at Manresa, which had all the marks of a severely pathological episode in which he at least came close to psychosis, avoiding a catastrophic suicidal resolution by the narrowest of margins. The crisis of Manresa was resolved by the illumination at the Cardoner, and Iñigo was launched on his mystical journey. One could reasonably hypothesize that all this amounts to a form of psychotic regression that was resolved and encapsulated in a socially and culturally acceptable life of mystical elevation. For the rest of his life, Ignatius would have lived within this sublimated psychotic cocoon—a psychic resolution that would have satisfied basic narcissistic needs and found adequate reinforcement and support in his religious mission, in the adulation and collaboration of his followers and companions, and in his continued practice of ascetical heroism.

This hypothesis is enticing, but there are certain aspects of Ignatius' personality and experience that are difficult to integrate in such a picture. Clearly Iñigo de Loyola was an exceptional person even before his conversion. He was a courageous, forceful leader and operated at a high level of competence. His performance at Pamplona reveals his force of character, his determination, his refusal to accept defeat or discouragement even in the face of overwhelming odds. He carried those same qualities into his postconversion life. He did not wait to be carried up the spiritual mountain; he took it by storm. His ascetic practices speak of a relentless and determined crusade to win God's grace and become a spiritual hero in place of the military hero's role that fate had denied him. His early ascetical career had a quality of excess and fanatical intensity that was abnormal, if not pathological. But from circumstance and necessity, he gradually moderated these practices and brought them into more reasonable compass. He was assiduous in cultivating a sense of prudence and discretion in his spiritual followers; having learned bitter lessons from his own fervent excesses. The theme of discernment that runs throughout his mystical experience bespeaks the constant exercise of judgment, discrimination, and discretion, even during his mystical elevations. The integrity of his ego was such that in the face of powerful intrapsychic impulses he was able to reassert and maintain reasonable control and execution.

In the transformation from Iñigo to Ignatius, he remained a leader. He gathered around him at several stages of his career devoted followers who enthusiastically joined his crusade. Among these extraordinary men, Ignatius was clearly the leader, the guide, the one who gave purpose, meaning, and direction to their efforts. They could consider no one else for the first Father General. In that position, he once again demonstrated his extraordinary capacity for organization and inspiration. This is far from the picture of a psychotic. William James (1902) summed up the contradiction when he commented, "Saint Ignatius was a mystic, but his mysticism made him assuredly one of the most powerfully practical human engines that ever lived" (p. 324).

So what is the verdict? If Ignatius' psychosis was sufficiently encapsulated and his narcissistic equilibrium was adequately maintained, as it seems clearly to have been, by the ongoing current of religiously gratifying mystical experiences and by the course of events that allowed him to feel that he was doing God's will and doing his utmost to advance the kingdom of Christ in this world, it might conceivably have cleared the way for his residual ego functions to operate in more effective and secondary process ways.[5] If we were to accept this assumption, Ignatius would have to be regarded as psychotic in a different and unique sense— one that psychiatric science has yet to acknowledge or explain. It may be less prejudicial and more accurate to say that Ignatius' mystical life represented a form of extraordinary experience at the limits of human capacity. This would leave us with the further problem of trying to understand the nature of this experience in psychological or psychoanalytic terms. There is also the gnawing question—if Ignatius was in some sense psychotic, what does this imply in the wider arena of human history and human religious experience?

ORGANIC FACTORS

There is a further complicating question. Might there also have been an organic component to the basic phenomenology we have been discussing? Could some seizure disorder have had influenced Ignatius' intra-psychic experience? One possibility is a form of temporal lobe epilepsy that we now call a complex partial seizure disorder. The syndrome lacks clear definition but seems to present a reasonably consistent picture (Waxman and Geschwind 1975; Murray 1981; Hermann and Whitman 1984; Fedio 1986; Stevens 1988). The ictal manifestations (related to the seizure discharge itself) include paroxysmal expressions of hallucination and illusions, déjà vu or jamais vu, fear, depersonalization, as well as intensified affective and psychosensory[6] experiences. The interictal manifestations (between discharges) are less clearly defined, and investigators disagree as to whether they constitute a dispositional change in personality or a form of specific personality organization. The characteristics usually associated with this syndrome include a tendency to anger and aggressive behavior, including episodic dyscontrol, irritability, hostility, and quarrelsome behavior; altered sexuality, including global hyposexuality[7] and sexual hypoactivity[8]; hypergraphia, perhaps expressed by keeping a detailed diary or personal notes, extensive letter writing, or frequently writing about religious and philosophical themes of an intense emotional nature; inclinations toward contemplative, religious, or philosophical thought, sustained interest in spiritual activities, hypermoralism, mysticism; a tendency to circumstantiality[9] and pedantic speech; and finally, in the extreme stages of the syndrome, a schizophreniform[10] psychosis with depression, anxiety, paranoid thoughts, dissociative states, and pseudomanic episodes.

There is also fairly good evidence of a correlation between such temporal lobe disturbances and the occurrence of paranormal, religious, and mystical experiences. These manifestations may reflect more or less normal functioning of the temporal lobes, so that we all fit somewhere on a continuum of temporal lobe stability or lability. Seizures can take place within limbic circuits without any external motor expression, often even without disturbance of surface patterns of brain activity as recorded from the scalp electrodes of the usual EEG. Precipitating factors include fatigue, social isolation, musical stimuli, smells (incense), hypochondria from fasting, asphyxiation, certain psychedelic drugs, and intense pain. Such transient stimulating events can further be conditioned to become a form of learned microseizure. Individuals with this syndrome often experience multiple conversions and protracted periods of religious and mystical experience (Persinger 1983).

Religious and mystical phenomena are common in populations of temporal lobe patients (Slater and Beard 1963). Experiences of intense personal communication and sudden revelations and deep "knowing" are common features. Transient seizure patterns have been detected in peak experiences in transcendental meditation and glossolalia (Persinger 1984b). In addition, there is a certain overlap between paranormal experiences and temporal lobe signs, even in apparently normal populations (Persinger 1984a; Makarec and Persinger 1985; Persinger and Valliant 1985).

To what extent does this profile fit Ignatius? There is no good evidence that he ever suffered frank seizures in any form. There were occasional episodes, for example the collapse at Villadordis, but this may well have been the result of excessive fasting and penances. His experiences of apparitions and visions, however, as well as states of mystical elevation and ecstasy, with their intense and physically wrenching affective reactions, may well have been provoked by such limbic seizures. There were some outbursts of anger and aggression, for example his impulse to do in the Moor who insulted our Lady. Episodes of temper and irritability usually in some appropriate disciplinary context, were observed even in his later years. Hyposexuality is a prominent aspect of his postconversion experience, marked by the sudden renunciation of sexuality after his vision of the Blessed Mother at Loyola.

The evidence for hypergraphia is compelling—for years Ignatius kept elaborate notebooks recording his spiritual impressions and insights and sections copied from religious books. Later he carried on an extensive correspondence that encompassed thousands of letters, many of considerable length. Although there may often have been the best of reasons, the fact remains that circumstance may not explain all. There is no suggestion of psychotic deterioration, although we might be suspicious of the progressive intensification of his mystical experience, usually described in terms of his increasingly affecting and frequent experiences of mystical transport. On the hypothesis of some underlying limbic disorder, this progression may reflect an intensification of the limbic epilepsy, perhaps on the basis of a kindling[11] phenomenon. His continued ascetic practices, particularly the excessive fasting and denial of natural needs for sleep, warmth, and so on, may have contributed to the lowering of the seizure threshold.

CONCLUSIONS

We are left with a somewhat ambiguous picture. I have little doubt that if a modern psychiatrist had had the opportunity to examine Iñigo de Loyola during the period of postconversion turmoil and the severe crisis at Manresa, he might have diagnosed him as psychotic, possibly with qualifications. Another possibility would be to see him as some form of borderline disorder, caught in the throes of stressful and disruptive events and resolving the regressive borderline state by religious conversion and commitment. Possibly. This kind of retrospective historical reconstruction can be no more than sophisticated guesswork. If that same psychiatrist had the opportunity to consult the patient again in his later years, when he was General of the Society of Jesus, governing its world-wide operations and complex and difficult relations with royalty and the papal court, he might have formed a different impression. Certainly he would hardly have thought of psychosis, but would more likely have been impressed, as so many of Ignatius' contemporaries were, by the composure and power of this extraordinary man. The psychiatrist would not have been privy to the long hours of intense prayer and devotion, the mystical transports and ecstasies of his inner psychic and spiritual life.

We observers from the distance of half a millenium have no such privileged access and can only make our conjectures on the basis of the material before us. To our chagrin we can reach no definite conclusion. But let us suppose for the moment that Ignatius was suffering from some form of psychotic process that expressed itself in his religious and mystical experience. Let us suppose even further that a major contributing factor in the phenomenology of his illness was a form of limbic epilepsy or complex partial seizures. What then? Would these suppositions, if true, undermine and destroy the religious significance of Ignatius' personal experience and the meaning and import of his career for subsequent religious history and the history of salvation?

The answer can only be given in terms of the religious assumptions (or lack thereof) with which we approach the question. If we respond with an exclusionary and reductionist mind-set, the answer is that the whole picture is no more than a pathological aberration, a delusional portrait that has no more validity or value than a pipe dream. Such would have been the verdict of the German psychiatrists and psychologists earlier in this century and of many more skeptical and reductionistically minded in our own day. They would see it as a fabric of illusion that could have been cured by appropriate antipsychotic or possibly antiepileptic medications.

But we might also approach the question from within the conceptual framework of faith. Does the presence of psychosis or the effect of subliminal seizure discharges in the limbic structures of the central nervous system preclude the workings of divine grace in the soul of Ignatius? I think the answer would have to be no. If we accept the possibility of a psychology of grace based on the assumption of a loving communication of himself by God to the human soul through grace, and if we believe that such communication influences the natural capacities and functions of the human psyche (Meissner 1986)—*gratia perficit naturam*—none of these pathological factors, whether functional or organic, would stand in the way of God's influence over the soul. They can just as easily become the vehicles of divine influence as preclude it. Consequently, within this faith-based perspective, even if we accept the possibility of pathogenic influences in Ignatius' spiritual life, they would not necessarily diminish its religious significance and the import of his mystical life and his religious mission. His pathology, if such it was, would in no way diminish the historic significance and impact of the Society of Jesus on the stage of history, particularly in the crisis of the Counter-Reformation, and continuing after his death to the present day.

MYSTICISM
Psychoanalytic View

XIX

Whatever else can be said of Ignatius' mystical experiences, they took place within a human psyche and thus were subject to psychological influences and reflect the basic forces of human motivation. This fundamental fact gives the psychoanalyst license to examine the data and apply the resources of his scientific view to these otherwise transcendental experiences. The usual cautions must be observed—the psychoanalyst views these phenomena within the constraints of his own methodology and theory. This means not only that he has nothing to say about the religious or theological dimensions of these experiences, but that the orientation of his approach is toward the latent as opposed to the manifest content of the experiences, and toward the unconscious rather than the conscious dimensions. As one distinguished commentator on Jewish kabbalistic mysticism has written:

> It is my conviction that psychological or psychoanalytic approaches to mystical texts must be employed with care, given the reductionist tendency inherent in their hermeneutical techniques. The chance of success in reconstructing the nature of a mystical experience from written texts is close to nil. As the components of this experience— the human psyche, the external and inner conditions, and the divine aspects that enter the experience—are either fluid or incomprehensible, or both, any reconstruction is mostly an approximation based more on the presuppositions and tendencies of the scholar than on recombination of the authentic components of the original experience. (Idel, 1988, pp. 35–36)

Keeping this caution in mind, we can begin by accepting the idea that mysticism is a universal phenomenon, occurring in all religious systems, in all cultures. We can therefore take it to reflect a basic human capacity for ecstatic experience and altered states of consciousness. We can accept Buckley's (1981) conclusion that psychotic and mystical states may share no more than "simply an ecstatic affective charge which imbues perception with an increased intensity" (p. 520), an innate capacity of the human mind.

INFANTILE CORRELATES

In assessing the nature of this affective and cognitive state in Ignatius' experience, we first of all note the intense affective quality of all his descriptions and the often diffuse, undifferentiated, obscure, and vague nature of the experiences. Psychoanalysts are usually attuned to the quality of any psychic experience that resonates with infantile experience, since so much of what is psychically significant originates in infancy. These descriptions of Ignatius' mystical states call to mind the experience of the infant, in which sensory experience is relatively diffuse and disorganized and the distinction between affect and cognition is blurred, if not absent. The infant's experience is, to a much greater degree than the adult's, coenesthetic—that is, reflecting a relatively unorganized mixture of stimuli, among them proprioceptive,[1] thermal, equilibrial, tactile, vibratory, rhythmic, and auditory, and others. The line between biological and psychological functioning is difficult to draw. As Ross (1975) puts it, "The feeling is the thought, and the thought the feeling" (p. 86). Developmentally, this state probably extends to the point where self-awareness starts to emerge and enter into tension with the sense of fusion with the external world—that is, with the mother.

This state of affective-cognitive diffusion is analogous to the "oceanic feeling" that Freud described as the basic religious emotion. In 1923, Romain Rolland, the French writer and mystic, responded to a letter from Freud that initiated a correspondence focused on religious themes. The exchange led to a meeting between the two in 1924. Having read Freud's *Future of an Illusion* (1927), Rolland proposed the oceanic feeling as a counterpoise to Freud's critique of religion, basing his claims on the occurrence of such a state in Oriental mystics, especially the Hindu prophets. Freud made his effort to analyze the oceanic feeling in *Civilization and Its Discontents* (1930). For Rolland, the oceanic feeling was a sensation of the infinite, unbounded, limitless—a subjective fact that was the basis for religious belief and conviction. Freud does not challenge the occurrence of this feeling state, since he had experienced it himself. When he analyzes his own experience on the Acropolis, it reduces to a piece of unresolved oedipal conflict (Freud 1936; Meissner 1984). He doubts that it can bear the weight of being the *fons et origo* of the whole religious impulse and ascribes it to a primary ego-feeling reflecting earlier infantile bonds between the ego and the surrounding world. It involves a sense of "limitlessness and of a bond with the universe." It is probably not the source of religious needs, which Freud sees as derived from the child's sense of helplessness and dependence on adult caretakers. For Freud, the oceanic feeling together with all religious sentiment and faith were regressive recourses to states of infantile dependence (Werman 1977). Thus, without doubt Freud put his stamp on the psychoanalytic view of mystical phenomena as regressive and infantile.

Ross (1975) argues that the mystical state represents a condition of intense affective arousal and heightened cognitive conviction together with feelings of passivity, loss of discursive reasoning, and the sense of merging with a pervasive object. He sees such states as regressions to a stage of symbiotic union with the mother. The regression is essentially in the service of the ego and takes place with retention of a sense of identity. Thus the mystical state is not a true symbiosis. The transient nature of the experience further reflects a defensive operation of the ego preventing further regression to a state of total disorganization.

In his ecstatic experience, the mystic enters an "altered state of consciousness" which has certain similarities to infantile states. The similarity to Mahler's (1975) concept of the symbiotic phase, with its intensification of narcissistic features, is striking. The ineffability of the experience may also reflect the extent of the regression to pre-verbal levels of infantile experience. The depth of regression carries its own perils, specifically the threat of uncontrolled regression into the depths of schizophrenic disorganization. Ross (1975) points to mystical ecstasies as frequent prologues to schizophrenic deterioration—possibly "a last desperate attempt to cling to the object world by restoring the ancient symbiotic union with the mother" (p. 91). The strength and intactness of the mystic's ego preserve him from such a fate.

ALTERED CONSCIOUSNESS

The mystical propensity, so widespread in humankind, may reflect a basic unfulfilled yearning of the self for union with and immersion in something outside itself. Losing self-consciousness while retaining a sense of identity is not altogether uncommon in states of trance-like absorption or intense concentration, for example in a book, or a piece of music, an idea, a poem, a scientific problem. Individuals sometimes lose all awareness of the passage of time and become relatively oblivious to their environment. There is often a subtle alteration of consciousness in such immersions without disturbing the sense of self or identity. There is, on the contrary, often a sense of enrichment or self-enhancement. The striving for a sense of wholeness, for transcendence of the ordinary human condition and its limits, for union with an omnipotent deity, derives from forms of grandiose fantasy. As Bach (1977) remarks:

> Whether such fantasies are viewed as defensive regressions or as creative expressions depends not only on whether one consults a psychiatrist or a guru, but also on the meaning of this experience in the context of the person's life, a complicated issue which forms part of an as yet scarcely begun psychology of creative and mystical states. But perhaps we may assume that every narcissistic fantasy, omnipotent and transcendent as it may be, expresses in some distorted form an attainable human possibility as well as an unattainable divine one. (p. 287)

Psychoanalysts, following Freud's view of mystical states as regressive, have often emphasized the infantile and oral dimension of the mystical experience. The model for narcissistic union is the mother-child symbiosis (Bach 1977). Lewin (1950), for example, emphasizes the orality of mystical experience. He quotes a description by St. Francis de Sales cited by William James (1902): "In this state the soul is like a little babe, still at the breast, whose mother, to caress him whilst he is still in her arms, makes her milk distill into his mouth without his even moving his lips. . . . infants united to the breasts of their nursing mothers . . . from time to time . . . press themselves closer by little starts to which the pleasure of sucking prompts them. Even so, during its orison the heart united to its God oftentimes makes attempts at closer union by movements during which it presses closer upon the divine sweetness" (p. 28).

Ignatius' mystical ecstasies would certainly be congruent with these formulations. Again and again he returns to the theme of ecstatic union with God and the sweetness and joy of that experience. The psychoanalytic investigator is not interested simply in the manifest phenomenology of such experiences but seeks to discern the hidden elements that might reflect more basic infantile motivations. Since we know so little about Ignatius' early life experience and without confirmation from the object of our investigation, we can hope for no more than a plausible reconstruction.

We recall that Iñigo's mother died very soon after his birth, possibly in childbirth, but more likely within the period in which he still required nursing. Was the effect of this loss a continual yearning and unconscious seeking for the lost mother? Was this a determining element in his relationships with women more generally? Did this frustrated yearning provide the driving force behind his mystical ascent? Was it the strength of this yearning, continuing to exercise its influence in unconscious channels, carrying with it the threat of regressive engulfment in the embrace of the mother, which would have threatened a loss of self and psychic annihilation, that precipitated the massive repression of all sexual desires? The questions are easy; the answers harder to come by.

PATERNAL YEARNING

Another aspect of Ignatius' mystical experience that deserves comment is the major emphasis in his mystical orientation toward God the Father. His yearning for communication with and from the Father carried the major burden of the trinitarian thrust of his mystical impulse. The Father was inaccessible, remote, shrouded in mystery. Ignatius constantly appeals to the Blessed Virgin or to Christ to intercede for him with the Father. Is it possible that we are hearing here the echoes of the family constellation at the castle of Loyola? The first important element is that Iñigo lost his father early. Beltrán probably died in 1507, when Iñigo would have been about sixteen. But the picture of Beltrán in the years of Iñigo's growing up was of a remote, authoritarian, and highly paternalistic lord of the manor. That was when he was around; much of the time he was away on some campaign or adventure or other. Beltrán, we might conjecture, was not much of a family man. His focus was the struggle for power and influence in the world outside his castle. What transpired within its walls was the domain of the women. Even his libidinal interest was directed outside the walls of Loyola as well as within, to judge from the acknowledged record of his illegitimate children. In short, Beltrán was not merely the lord of Loyola, but close to a god for his youngest son. Does the quality of Ignatius' relation to his God mirror in some respects his relation to the remote and mysterious Beltrán? The yearning of the son for the attention, love, and approval of such a father is not easily satisfied. All hopes of fulfilling that longing were dashed when Beltrán died. The yearning in the heart of Iñigo had to remain unsatisfied and frustrated. Perhaps it found some satisfaction in Iñigo's mystical ecstasies.

This hypothesis does not necessarily conflict with the hypothesis of maternal symbiosis. God is neither male nor female; to the human psyche God can evoke the imagery of male or female, or both. Both components may have operated within the heart of Ignatius, fulfilling basic infantile needs and desires that remained unconscious but found sublimated expression in his mystical drive. The dual current would have to be taken to reflect opposing libidinal drives in Iñigo's psyche. The heterosexual oedipal yearning for symbiotic closeness to the maternal object must have entered into tension and interpenetration with the homosexual paternal current—and both found their respective sublimatory resolution. This duality in his psychic make-up would also reflect the internal structuring of his psyche based on contrasting patterns of identification—both paternal and maternal, masculine and feminine.

INTERNALIZED MOTHER

We might suspect that these dimensions of the motivational system underlying Ignatius' mystical experience were not without tension and conflict. Moloney (1954) postulates a basic conflict with the internalized image of the mother as a contributory component of mystical phenomena. As a result of infantile trauma and disturbance of the early mother-child relationship, the infant introjects[2] the frustrating or denying mother and thus creates an internal maternal demand system that he must constantly rebel against and struggle to escape. His own strivings for self-expression constantly conflict with the maternal demands embedded in his superego. If this inner struggle is relaxed, if the armed neutrality between the self-system and the mother-system is given up, the result may be a theophany, a flash of inspiration that seems to resolve the internal conflicts. Self-strivings are surrendered, and he submits to the maternal authority he had previously struggled to defeat and destroy. The corrective forces within seek regression back to the developmental point when the disturbance between the self-system and the mother-system began. From that juncture, the path toward real maturity and self-determination might possibly be recovered.

In the effort to gain domination of the self-system over the mother-system, there may be an appearance of pseudomaturity that masks continuing rebellion against authoritarian domination. According to Greenacre (1947), "Mastery is attempted by . . . the development of severely binding super-ego reaction-formations of goodness which are supplemented by or converted into lofty ideals" (p. 177). When the point of exhaustion is reached, a startling realignment of the tension between the self- and mother-systems may occur that results in the sudden theophany or inspiration. The pseudomature elements of the self-system are drawn back regressively to the period of infantile dependence on the mother. There may be flashes of light, bright aureoles, even visual hallucinations.

Might Ignatius' conversion experience have involved some part of this dynamic struggle? Possibly. Even though his own mother had died, his early years were dominated by other women of Loyola, the domestic authorities were female rather than male. The men of Loyola were occupied with both warring and libidinal conquest. The conflict between the self-system of the phallic narcissistic hidalgo, who dreamed of heroic exploits and libidinal triumphs, and the internalized prohibitive maternal system, which would have been permeated by profound religious and moral values, may have set the stage for the inner struggle and transformation that characterized his conversion experience, with its sudden illumination and vision of the Blessed Mother. Had Iñigo's phallic and narcissistic self-system capitulated to the maternal-feminine superego and embraced the path of religious inspiration, rejecting the masculine and paternal values that had dominated his life to that point? Had the recourse to powerful phallic drives and exploits served up to that point as a form of pseudomature defensive organization countering the powerful and threatening maternal influences? Was the tension between these internal systems upset by his wound and its traumatic aftermath? After all, when the fallen warrior was carried on his pallet back to Loyola, it was a journey away from the masculine and phallic fields of conquest into the bosom of feminine care and nurturance. It was the women of Loyola who nursed, tended, fed, and cared for the wounded man. He was placed in a position of extreme helplessness and dependence on their ministrations. Does his conversion reflect the binding of superego reaction formations in the construction of new and lofty ideals of religious perfection and the imitation of Christ? Moloney (1954) cites the case of Ignatius in support of his thesis.

AGGRESSION

Another dimension of these phenomena is their relation to aggression. Hartocollis (1976) argues that "those attracted to mystical movements are likely to be individuals who, sensitized by the violence around them, become preoccupied with their own potential for violence, which they find too threatening to express and are unable to neutralize within the available family and social context. Followers of mystical movements wish to cancel the aggression of the world in order to do away with their own" (p. 214). The peacefulness and sense of blissful union of the mystical state, whether induced by prayer and ascetical exercises, by psychedelic drugs, or by spontaneous conversion experiences, are identified as inspirational or transcendental and carry with them a sense of conviction analogous to delusional states, being in love, and vivid dreams. The experience requires no explanation but is taken as self-evident. As Bertrand Russell (1929) observed, "The mystic insight begins with the sense of a mystery unveiled, of a hidden wisdom now suddenly become certain beyond the possibility of a doubt. The sense of certainty and revelation comes earlier than any definite belief" (p. 9). The yearning for such enlightenment, along with the sense of undifferentiated unity, is usually regarded psychoanalytically as regression to preverbal levels that may be either objectless—a form of limitless narcissism connected with the oceanic feeling (Freud 1930)—or a fusion between the self and the maternal object, specifically the maternal breast (Lewin 1950).

The fantasy of such blissful and seamless fusion can correspond to the fantasy of escape from inner aggressive drives and their consequences in the form of anger, fear, anxiety, and despair. The escape may be a reaction to the sense of one's own violent potential generally or more specifically to the sense of inner evil and destructiveness embedded in introjective configurations stemming from the aggressive and feared father on the oedipal level and at a deeper level from the frustrating or over-exciting mother of infancy (Hartocollis 1976; Meissner 1978). The success or failure of the attempt at union is a function of the degree of aggressive contamination. Jacobson (1964) observes:

> Since normal experiences of ecstasy do not aim at destruction but are founded on a fantasy of libidinal union between self and object world, they result in a transitory sense of self-expression and the feeling that the self and the world are rich. Such experiences of merging, which may briefly retransform the images of the self and the object world into a fantasy unit vested with libidinal forces, permit an immediate reestablishment of the boundaries between them. By contrast, pathological regressive fusions caused by severe aggression may result in an irreparable breakdown of these boundaries and hence of the self and object representations. (p. 69)

In this formulation, when the libidinal charge is freed from all aggressive contamination, union can take the blissful and satisfying form that is the common experience of mystics. Hartocollis (1976) adds:

> What, in turn, motivates the search for a mystical experience is the emergence into consciousness of one's own potential for violence and the fear that his hidden aggression may destroy the internalized "good" objects. . . . This emergent awareness of potential inner violence is the result of exposure to an environment where violence is prevalent but random, avoidable but non-negotiable; seen as a product of a "sinful," materialistic, and exploitative civilization rather than as a means to an end, a necessary evil in the service of some personal or group ideology. (p. 224)

There is little doubt that Iñigo de Loyola was an aggressive, violent man. He was cut from the stuff of the Loyolas, whose family tradition was based on physical prowess and conquest. Iñigo was well on his way to cutting his own swath of violence when he was struck down at Pamplona. The essence of his conversion experience was his revulsion at his former manner of life and his turning toward a life of total and uncompromising opposition to everything it involved. The psychoanalyst cannot help but see the forces of conflict and defense at work. Iñigo's conversion and subsequent ascetical life were in effect a turning of his powerful aggressive drives against himself in the form of self-conquest. It is at least plausible that the interior struggles of his early postconversion experience and the torments at Manresa to a large extent reflected the as-yet unresolved aggressive residues at war within him. The bliss of mystical ecstasy had to wait for resolution of these basic and powerful conflicts. His struggle to follow in the footsteps of Christ can be seen as driven in part by his need to escape from and overcome the sense of inner violence, evil, and destructiveness buried in his introjective configuration.[3] The Christ he followed was the humble, suffering Christ—the model of victimization, the radical opposite of aggressive power and destructiveness.

NARCISSISM

I have hinted in passing at the narcissistic aspects of mystical experience. The mystical immersion rides on a grandiose fantasy of union with an omnipotent and infinite love object. This fantasy serves as the fulfillment of narcissistic needs. We have seen the basically narcissistic substructure of Ignatius' personality displayed dramatically on the heroic stage of his courtly and military career. From a psychoanalytic perspective, we can assume that these components did not disappear when his hopes of becoming a heroic warrior were struck down but turned in a new direction. He determined to become a hero in the spiritual realm like the spiritual heroes—the saints. His ambition was to become like them, paragons of self-sacrifice and self-denial. If he could not seek glory in the service of a worldly king, he would seek even greater glory in the service of another and greater king. The meditations on the Kingdom and the Two Standards in the *Exercises* bear eloquent testimony to this aspect of his narcissism.[4]

In this vein, his mystical experiences universally have the quality of wish-fulfillments—like dream experiences that satisfy unconscious desires. In his visions, in particular, his narcissistically driven wishes find satisfaction. He wants to be favored by our Lady and so she appears to him in an apparition. He hopes to be chosen for the service of Christ, his Lord and Master; the wish is realized in the vision at La Storta. In these experiences he achieves the most complete fulfillment of his postconversion ego ideal. As Chasseguet-Smirgel (1976) observes, "Mysticism follows the pattern of the fusion of the ego and its ideal. . . .

It promises fusion with the primary object—even when on the conscious level it is identified with a God-Father, who in the end is equivalent to the mother before defusion" (p. 367).

MYSTICAL TEARS

There is no other mystic in whom the phenomenon of mystical tears is so marked. Can analysis contribute anything to the understanding of this condition? Not directly, but the phenomenon of tearfulness has been studied in the analytic setting (Wood and Wood 1984). Although the data come from a more mundane context, the implications may have some bearing on mystical tears. In general, tears were found to express emotional impotence, inadequacy, the feeling of being overwhelmed, failure, angry frustration, or fear. Often tears served a more positive cathartic function, even being accompanied by feelings of hopefulness. Generally tears seemed to reflect a condition of affective excess due to intrapsychic conflict or need compromise.

Other researchers regard tears as connected with the infant's reflex cry, which later develops into a more purposive cry for help, and with the further development of object relations is associated with object loss, separation anxiety, and grief reactions (Sadoff 1966). In this sense, weeping can expel painful affects from the body or even bad internal objects or introjects—those derived, for example, from a punitive or rejecting parent. Others see weeping as a form of projection of painful affects in the interest of regaining emotional equilibrium (Peto 1946; Heilbrunn 1955). This discharge function may have a special connection to the discharge of unresolved aggressive energies (Lofgren 1966).

Greenacre (1965) summarizes and supports this thesis:

Lofgren was particularly concerned with the relation of weeping to aggression, and postulated the central thesis that "weeping is an act whereby aggressive energy is dissipated by secretory behavior." He sees the secretion of tears as the essential neutralizing process dissipating the internalized aggression occurring after a loss, which the sufferer has been unable to discharge in any direct way, or through a motor storm in which he regresses to a quasi-helpless state and beats himself in lieu of beating a real or hypothetical enemy. It seems to me that this may be substantially true, and certainly that weeping oc-

curs most frequently associated with some internal change in psychic attitudes coincident with a beginning change from hostile aggression to the use of its energy in a positive and nondestructive way.
(p. 250)

Greenacre makes the point that such affective distress is most commonly associated with the loss, by death or alienation, of someone to
whom the weeper has been closely attached. The first reaction may be
anger and a wish to attack the one who has deserted or anyone who can
be blamed for the loss. It is after the anger is spent or has proved futile
that weeping sets in. The eye plays a central role in the resolution of
such loss. As Greenacre observes:

> The weeper weeps because he does not see the person or the object
> which he has lost and must gradually accept the fact that his looking
> is in vain. The steps of establishing the reality of his loss must then
> be gone through as a kind of retracing of the steps originally involved
> in establishing the reality of the separate object. The eye is the most
> important sensory object in establishing a loss, though other senses
> participate according to the nature of the life contact which has
> preceded. (1965, p. 253)

The disappointed eye produces the same physiological response to the
failure to find the lost object as the irritated or traumatized eye. The
Woods (1984) summarize their findings:

> In our view, the tearful feeling state is occasioned by the ego tem-
> porarily threatened with being inundated by complex memories and
> affects. . . . The tearful feeling, a step in the direction of overt weep-
> ing, primitively expresses the frustration of an early wish for relief
> from pain, the pain of the imbalance of a complex conflict. The
> tearful feeling both expresses the wish for relief of pain and, at the
> same time, interrupts current verbal expression until the needed
> defense operations reduce the threat of ego disruption by working
> through old conflicts once again. (pp. 134–35)

Thus, weeping supports the important functions of both reparation and
communication.

Does any of this shed any light on Ignatius' mystical tears? Possibly.
There seems little doubt that his ecstasies were intense and wrenching

emotional experiences, with overwhelming affect. From the spiritual perspective, this might be seen as the result of God's making himself present with such overwhelming and loving self-communication that Ignatius' psyche could not encompass or contain it. The psychoanalyst, without gainsaying that view, would want to look further. What underlying motivations might there be in this transcendent experience that could have contributed to the tearfulness? Were there any dynamic configurations at work in producing this remarkable effect?

We can take full advantage of the license to conjecture at this point. If the mystical union was responding to basic emotional needs in Ignatius, we can hypothesize that among them were the infantile need for union with a loving mother and father that Iñigo had been deprived of in his early years. That yearning may have been generously satisfied in the mystical union, but not without tapping into the residues of infantile conflict that lay embedded in Ignatius' heart and mind. We can only guess at the unconscious levels of frustrated desire, libidinal wishes, denied object needs, separation fears, and the countercurrents of ambivalent aggressive impulses that were distilled into Ignatius' tearful outpourings. Were the tears a kind of projective riddance or purging of the deep inner conflicts and the aggressive tendencies that he labored so heroically to contain and defeat all through his spiritual career (Knapp 1967)? The fact that he found it necessary to continue this crusade of self-conquest suggests that they had not in any decisive sense left him. They were present even in his loftiest flights of mystical elevation. The mystical tears, then, may be the outpouring of intense infantile conflicts and needs based in unresolved mourning of the loss of his mother and frustrated yearning for love and intimacy with his unavailable father. These yearnings were satisfied and profoundly fulfilled in the mystical union with the divine love object. In this sense, the manifest content of the Trinity or God the Father masked the deeper psychic significance of symbiotic maternal reunion and loving fulfillment.

THE VISION OF THE SERPENT

I would like to turn for a moment to the question of Ignatius' visions. Particularly interesting is the vision of the serpent of the many eyes, which first occurred at Manresa and remained with him for many years. This can be taken as a symbolic representative of the libido, particularly in its phallic expression. In the earlier phases of evolution within the pilgrim's ego, this vision appeared as beautiful and consoling. But in fact the symbol was a thinly disguised representation of instinctual forces striving for expression. From the perspective of the elevated position of the pilgrim's ego after his illumination at the Cardoner, the vision no longer seemed beautiful. His intuition penetrated to the inner meaning of the symbol, and his ego came forth with renewed energy to slay what he now saw as a dragon. The experience of these visions thus reflects the dynamism of his deep psychic conflicts in the cave of Manresa.

We should note first the largely visual character of Ignatius' mystical experience. Throughout his mystical journey, visual apparitions reoccur with striking regularity. His conversion was centered dramatically around the apparition of the Blessed Mother, his ecstasies at Manresa have a remarkably visual and symbolic quality—visions of the Trinity in the form of organ keys, the wonderful serpent, and other remarkable phenomena. At Jerusalem the vision of Christ leading him on his way was prominent, and again at Vincenza he recounts his many visions.

To this catalog we can add the frequent visual emphasis in the *Spiritual Exercises*—in his imaginative reconstructions of scenes in hell, in the many compositions of place that introduce the meditations, in the repeated directives to see the scene, to watch our Lord acting in certain ways, and so on. We can add his gift of tears—so impressive an aspect of his mystical experience. Even in the preconversion framework, his imaginative representations of his deeds of daring and gallantry in the service of his lady have a largely visual quality. All this adds up to an impression that his visual function had become endowed with special importance in his psychic life and that this played a vital role in his mystical life.

The special investment in the visual function is a form of focal symbiosis (Greenacre 1959) in which a certain bodily organ or area is selected to express the union between the needs of the child and the projected pathology of the parent, usually the mother. Where the normal pattern of infantile mirroring is lacking, as it might be in the case of a narcissistic or absent mother, the result may be a heightened investment of the eyes or indirectly, a cathexis from the mouth and/or genitals displaced to the eyes. The primacy of the visual function may be partially determined by early deprivation and frustration, but can be abetted by subsequent primal scene exposure, castration anxiety, or even outright sexual abuse. The outcome in many patients may be a form of scopophilia[5] or hyperacuity with or without perversion. In Iñigo's case, there is evidence to support this speculation—the early maternal deprivation in conjunction with other possible factors that we can only imagine. Even the role of primal scene exposure is plausible if we take into account the living conditions in the blacksmith's cottage in which young Iñigo was raised. In the tiny peasant cottage, the blacksmith and his wife probably slept in the same room as the children and opportunities for primal scene exposure would have been ample.

We can only guess at the determinants of the snake symbolism, but they undoubtedly reflect the influence of castration anxiety and phallic narcissistic drive derivatives. The unusual conjunction of phallic derivatives with the visual component (represented in the many eyes) points toward the interlocking of phallic themes with a degree of presumptive optical focal symbiosis.[6] Clinically the scopophilic emphasis often connects with ophidiophobia, the fear of snakes—but in Iñigo's case, with a fixation on and fascination with the serpent imagery. Here speculation can run rampant. What experiences might have played a role that time and history conceal from us? Could the infant, deprived of mother and the intimacy of maternal mirroring, have been confronted with the potentially stimulating vision of adult copulation or anxiety-producing exposure to the phallic and genital endowment of the blacksmith? And with what effect?

Mahony (1989) argues that in at least one of his patients, a snake phobia was derived from the negative oedipal complex along with elements of prior, essentially preoedipal visual experiences and fantasies that had a primarily traumatic impact. Thus the core of the snake symptom was an accumulative symbol. He writes:

> Pandemic in mythology, religion, folklore, and dreams, the serpent symbolizes the phallus although it occasionally bears significance for the female genitalia. In the Gnostic biblical tradition, moreover, it underwent splitting so that Eve was impregnated by the bad serpent, and Mary by the good one (Hassal 1919; Fortune 1926). This notwithstanding, the pregenital meaning of a snake might better explain its worship as the most prevalent of all early religious practices. The snake's shape as a gut and a devouring mouth or as a *bolus*

fecalis makes it eminently suitable to represent early aggressive impulses of the late oral and anal stages. Indeed, the phallic interpretation of the Fall of Man has obscured the pregenital meaning of the
serpent's punishment, namely, to be deprived of its limbs and to
crawl despisedly on its belly in the dirt. Seeing the serpent may stir
up the uncanny feeling of the return of the repressed and the expelled
hostile excrement as fully alive. (pp. 393–394)

The vision of the many-eyed snake continued to plague Ignatius for
about fifteen years—at least until he was situated in Rome (Tylenda
1985). I would speculate that the vision of the serpent was done in once
and for all only after the dramatic and narcissistically enhancing vision
of the Father and the Son at La Storta, on the threshold of Rome. That
vision, in which Ignatius was placed under the special care and protection of God the Father and his Son, must have contributed powerfully to
the resolution of the conflictual and ambiguous dynamic forces that
found expression in the eerie serpentine apparition. Only when these
conflictual elements and their attendant anxieties had found resolution
in the promise of divine guidance—either from the powerful phallic and
omnipotent father or possibly also from the implicit promise of maternal presence—were the bases for the serpent vision finally disengaged.

DIVINE AND/OR
PSYCHIC CAUSALITY?

XX

THE ETIOLOGICAL QUESTION

In what sense can the mystical phenomena in Ignatius' life be explained by the exercise of divine causality, and to what extent do they reflect human motivational forces? The dual question can be sharply delineated by addressing the question of the discernment of consolation without previous cause (CSCP). According to Ignatius, "It belongs to God alone to give consolation without previous cause, for it belongs to the Creator to enter into the soul, to leave it, and to act upon it, drawing it wholly to the love of his Divine Majesty. I say without previous cause, that is, without any previous perception or knowledge of object from which such consolation might come to the soul through its own acts of intellect and will" (Exercises 330).

The argument among subsequent commentators centers on whether "without previous cause" is intended to mean without any previous cause of any kind—that the only possible causality in question was that of God himself—or whether Ignatius had in mind causes in the natural order that would involve conscious human actions, since he refers to acts of perception, the knowledge of objects, or acts of intellect and will (Egan 1976). Does this latter view leave room for the operation of unconscious determinants, as the psychoanalyst would argue? When the Ignatian exercitant experiences this apparently unmotivated consolation, what is the immediate cause—God or the unconscious? The question bears on the understanding of mystical experience since the primary form of mystical experience is so-called infused contemplation. Consolation without previous cause is the Ignatian equivalent of infused contemplation.

THEOLOGICAL VERSUS PSYCHOANALYTIC PERSPECTIVE

I will follow here Egan's (1976) careful exposition and analysis of the problem of causality. The important aspect for the exercitant is the religious significance of his experience in the context of his spiritual progression. Ignatius' rules for discernment are concerned only with the religious meaning of the experience, not with its causality as such. If it has this kind of religious significance, Egan—whose view is representative of perhaps the majority of commentators—seems to feel that unconscious dynamics are thereby excluded. Ignatius made the reading of moods the centerpiece of his discernment method, so that the quality of the affective experience is the touchstone of the origin of the feeling state. Egan marshals his objections to such an explanation in terms of unconscious dynamics; I will summarize and comment on his individual points in order:

1. Explanations in terms of unconscious dynamics exceed the limits of empirical psychology. "The Christian position that a personal God of love communicates Himself immediately and directly must not be tacitly assumed to be impossible. Mysticism and the life of faith in general mean a greater or lesser awareness of creation's graced situation." (p. 59)

This objection touches on a central issue, namely one's understanding of the operations of grace in psychic terms, and seems to suggest that grace can exercise its effects independently of any psychological considerations. I have in the past (Meissner 1964, 1966, 1987) proposed an approach to the psychology of grace based on an understanding of the effects of grace as working in and through man's psychic potentialities. On the assumption that *gratia perficit naturam*, I would argue that, insofar as divine causality is exercised through grace in the soul, it operates in and through natural psychic capacities and functions. By implication, then, Ignatius' mystical experience did not occur without grace, but it did not take place without his free psychic response and in terms codetermined by the dynamic forces operating within his heart and mind. There is no "either-or" here, but "both-and."

2. The term "unconscious" has "become an all too often imprecise, catch-all term to avoid the issue of God's personal communication of Himself." (p. 59)

I would concede that reference to the unconscious has been made often enough in these terms and with this consequence. It should be clear that this outcome is neither necessary nor advisable. The question is whether or not "God's personal communication of Himself" takes place in exclusion of unconscious dynamics. The insistence on transcendental influence on human experience and behavior to the exclusion of human faculties and capacities seems excessively spiritualizing to me. Even when God blesses man, he does not violate man's nature.

3. "Ignatius definitely thought that he was dealing with God and not merely with religious meaning alone." (p. 59)

A key issue. What Ignatius thought was happening may have little or no bearing on the question. This points to a critical difference between a theological approach and a psychoanalytic one: the theologian would hold that one can know the origin of certain feeling states—that is, whether or not they come from God. This assumption is built into Ignatius' rules for discernment. The psychoanalyst would maintain that no such knowledge or discrimination is possible. There is no given state of mind or affective experience, even Ignatius' most elevated mystical experiences, that could not be produced by psychic mechanisms alone. There is simply no way to validate the causality of any given experience. We are left with plausibility—based on certain assumptions. On the assumption of God's graceful intervention, one might conclude that certain outcomes would be consistent with divine action. Ignatius did so in formulating his rules for discernment, which do no more than state the conditions that are consistent with the assumption. They do not permit the conclusion that the effects were actually due to the influence of grace. Presumption is not proof. The same holds true for the psychic dimensions of the experience. On the presumption that the effects of grace are realized through psychic potentialities, we can draw conclusions that would be consistent and plausible, as long as we accept the assumption. It would be difficult to persuade the psychoanalytic observer that the behaviors and psychic experiences Ignatius described did not involve psychic mechanisms in all phases.

4. "Most mystics, including Ignatius, did err on occasion with respect to the origin and meaning of their religious experiences. If one assumes, however, that they were always wrong in claiming that God

Himself was then acting in a special way, the limits of truly objective, scientific methodology are once more exceeded." (p. 59)

All of Ignatius' spiritual experiences, including his mystical states, may or may not have been induced by divine influence. Ignatius devised his rules in order to make this discrimination. There were times when his discernment was undoubtedly correct and times when it was not. The point at issue is that there is no way he could tell the difference. When his discernment concluded that the vision of the many-eyed serpent was from the evil one, how could he be sure this conclusion was correct? He would have to make a presumption about the effects of divine influence and assume at least that the observed effects were consistent with that presumption. The psychoanalyst has no resource for making that discrimination either, but he has clear evidence of psychic processes at work. The issue for him is not whether Ignatius' psyche was involved in his psychic experiences but whether and to what extent divine action was involved at any given point. If we make certain theological and faith-based assumptions, there is ample room for the hand of the Lord. But the psychoanalyst can go no further than to conclude that the results are consistent with the assumption of divine action.

5. "It is naive to presuppose that Ignatius and much of the Christian mystical tradition had no knowledge of the unconscious and hidden motivation. They were very much aware of inordinate attachments, deep and hidden self-love, the different levels and dimensions of the one person, and of what often springs from a person's own habits and reflection. . . . Furthermore, Ignatius *discerned* the various movements in his soul. For example, one may dispute the actual origin of Ignatius' meat vision and snake-like vision, but the fact remains that he accepted the first as from God and the second as a demonic temptation only after very careful discernment. Ignatius hardly attributed to God every psychic twitch he experienced." (p. 59)

This objection has to be met head-on. Ignatius and the men of his age had no knowledge of unconscious processes and their implication. The experience of inordinate attachments, self-love, levels of psychic functioning, effects of habits, and so on are all conscious phenomena. They were certainly conscious at the point Ignatius was aware of them so that they could enter into his discernment. They may not always have been immediately available in awareness and to that extent would qualify for what Freud called the preconscious—meaning psychic elements that were not necessarily conscious at any given moment but could become conscious if attention were directed to them. Such elements were preconscious rather than unconscious. The Freudian unconscious is the so-called systematic unconscious involving elements hidden under a veil of repression and requiring certain repression-lifting techniques to allow them to become available to consciousness. Ignatius would have remained completely unaware of the unconscious dynamics and influences involved in his snake vision. The conclusion that the vision was brought about by the devil translates in twentieth-century terms into a decision that the experience arose out of his own soul rather than as a result of God's influence. There is no implication of knowledge of the unconscious in this. Freud's discovery of the unconscious, after all, followed Ignatius' birth by roughly four centuries; even then Freud's theories won only gradual and grudging acceptance, which is by no means universal even today.

6. "One must not tacitly presuppose that the unconscious is a primordial cesspool which often degrades consciousness. J. Marechal, among others, has shown the continuity between consciousness and the unconscious and stressed the riches and resources of this dimension." (p. 59)

This objection requires almost no response. It is precisely the goal of psychoanalytic treatment to reduce the areas of intrapsychic conflict and create the conditions in which a more harmonious integration of instinctual derivatives and relatively autonomous ego and superego functions becomes possible. I would argue that among the effects of grace, this form of psychic integration is one possibility. The facilitation and reinforcement of creative potentialities within the psyche is a possible channel for the development of spiritually elevating mystical experiences.

7. "Precisely because this area [the unconscious] of the person is profound, rich and often unexplored, its irruption into consciousness could strike the person as strange and mysterious. The unconscious,

however, is merely one dimension of the one person, and what comes from that dimension will bear the marks of that person. An adequate egocentric metaphysics, a metaphysics of self-appropriation, indicates that every person has at least an implicit, personal, holistic, non-reflexive knowledge of all that he is. This means, however, that the unconscious could never be experienced *intrinsically* as a foreign element. For extrinsic reasons, of course, the unconscious and its irruptions are often experienced as 'mystical,' 'divine,' 'angelic,' or 'demonic.' This may be true psychologically and extrinsically, but not metaphysically and intrinsically. Intrinsically, spirit means active self-identity and radical self-presence achieved in and through matter. Every person's deepest awareness is a global, holistic awareness of all that he is, and this includes the unconscious." (pp. 59–60)

This objection seems to come from a phenomenological perspective that finds the notion of the unconscious offensive and troublesome. Phenomenology began as a philosophy of conscious experience and only gradually has modified its stance with regard to psychoanalysis. For the philosophical mind, the notion of the unconscious or of unconscious actions poses difficulties, raising the question of what it means to say that there are mental processes that operate outside of conscious awareness, that the mind in its psychic functioning is at least at times deprived of the very quality that seems most essentially to define it— namely, consciousness. For example, one of the central themes of modern phenomenology is the doctrine of intentionality, which proposes, to simplify a bit, that every act of the mind is essentially directed toward an "other." Intentionality is thus a characteristic of all mental acts, including not only cognitive acts such as perceiving, imagining, and judging but affective acts as well. From a phenomenological perspective, then, every act of the mind intends an object, and it is by virtue of this act of intending that objects are rendered present and take on meaning for the subject.

The act of intending is simultaneously an act of conferring meaning on the object. In these terms, as, for example, in the philosophy of Husserl, reflection on the structure of the mind and reflection on the structure of its intentional acts become synonymous, in that the mind is defined in relation to intentionality. The reflection on intentionality is usually carried out in reference to conscious acts as an absolutely necessary point of departure. But the theory of intentional analysis also presupposes a crucial distinction between explicit or thematic intentionality and a nonthematic but exercised intentionality. Nonthematic intentionality is lived and experienced but not reflectively expressed. Phenomenology sets itself the task of making explicit and thematic what was previously only implicit and lived.

Phenomenology has developed in the direction of formulating a view that considers the meaning of man's existence as determined by and expressive of the significant relationships he establishes between himself and others, both in the immediate world of his experience and beyond (including God). Addressing the problem of the unconscious, de Waelhens (1959) writes:

> It is clear that if the unconscious must be [considered] as made up of an agglomeration of contents—dynamic or not—shot through and manipulated by biological forces radically heterogeneous to consciousness, we end up with the exact contrary of what psychoanalytic experience—obstinately and for more than half a century—proves with an evidence as blinding as the light of the sun: that is, that our actions, beneath their manifest meaning, have a meaning, and one which it is possible to elucidate, even at the level of the unconsciousness of the one who poses them. But it is precisely this which becomes absurd if the unconscious is defined as that which is radically other than the conscious and meaningful or—it comes to the same thing—if one holds consciousness and life to be "realities" of simply different kinds. (p. 222)

Thus, the phenomenological approach radically reverses the psychoanalytic dichotomy between conscious and unconscious mental processes. Phenomenology sets itself against the proposition that the unconscious is the true reality and that conscious acts can be explained or understood only when reduced to parallel unconscious processes. Rather, the conscious and the unconscious are seen as participating in the same order of reality and significance. Intentionality rather than consciousness becomes the defining characteristic of psychic life. Further, the distinction between intentionality as lived and as explicitly thematized gives rise to a view of consciousness and its absence as existing on a continuum, so that human mental processes are not necessarily exclusively conscious or unconscious.

Such a view is consonant both with actual clinical experience and with Freud's many statements concerning the nature of neurotic symptoms as expressing meaning, as well as with his view of dream processes and other unconscious psychic manifestations. Even the general theory of instinctual drives offers reinforcement to this view—even where Freud seems to be thinking in biological and reductionistic terms. Freud (1915) defined "instinct" as "a concept on the frontier between the mental and the somatic, as the psychical representative of the stimuli originating from within the organism and reaching the mind, as a measure of the demand made upon the mind for work in consequence of its connection with the body" (pp. 121–122). It is clear that in this context Freud was not drawing a hard and fast line between instinct as biological derivative and as psychic representation.

In Freud's view, then, instinctual drives originate in the body but translate into a psychological order in the form of felt impulses or needs directed toward specifiable goals. The linking of instinctual drives to the notions of purposive action and goal orientation introduces an element of finality and purposeful meaning into the very concept of drive itself. Thus, the Freudian concept of instinctual drives expresses a fundamental fact about the human condition; namely, that man is driven even as he is self-directing, that he is subject to powerful psychic forces which he also has the capacity to use for his own ends. The basic instinctual drives in their psychoanalytic sense are characterized by an inherent psychic intentionality as well as by an economic-quantitative[1] aspect. In this sense, the energic is dynamically transformed into a significance.

In phenomenological terms, what was once lived and experienced is now past and has ceased to be. But this does not mean that it has lost its intentionality or its capacity to influence behavior. From a psychoanalytic view, the lived past results in a concretization, a distillation of meaning, that is located within man's animated body. Moreover, it is through his body that man exists in the world, and this fact provides the basis for the profound historicity of human experience. This point has been argued forcefully by Merleau-Ponty (1962). The psychoanalytic methodology is nothing less than an approach to the discovery of such concrete realizations and derivatives of man's individual history as a means of gaining insight into his lived and experienced intentionality.

The essential discovery of both phenomenology and psychoanalysis, then, is that the basic intentionality of psychic life and its penetration with meaning are fundamental characteristics of human mental life, and that such intentionality is defined in terms that are at the same time dynamic and historic. Within this general frame of reference, the existence of unconscious mental activity plays a central role.

The distinction between extrinsic and intrinsic would seem to imply some experiential differentiation that psychoanalysts would have difficulty endorsing. The extrinsic is associated with the psychological and the intrinsic with the metaphysical, but the translation into terms of global and total self-awareness contravenes clinical and common experience. Aspects of psychic functioning involving unconscious determinants can be experienced as ego-dystonic, and in that sense extrinsic, as, for example, in experiences of superego criticism, or in experience of conflictual and unintegrated introjective formations. But unconscious determinants can exercise their influence and be experienced as totally ego-syntonic. The role of unconscious drive determinants in character formation, for example, is well known, but unconscious factors enter into a wide range of everyday experiences. It is typical for patients in analysis to begin to experience transference reactions as quite syntonic. If we were to take Egan's objection literally, there would be no room for the unconscious at all.

8. "We agree with those Ignatian commentators who stress that the exclusively divine CSCP does not rule out human preparation, emotional undercurrents, concepts, and reflection. To stress a consolation without previous cause, a consolation in which God is immediately present, does not exclude mediation, nor an immediacy in context. The mediated immediacy of the CSCP is analogous to the mediated immediacy of an act of human freedom. Both occur in context, in and through other factors, but not from or because of those factors. The CSCP may break forth from the deepest dimensions of the human spirit, from that mysterious point in the human spirit prior to its division into intellect and will, from man's faculty of mystery where only God can come and go as He pleases. This does not mean, however, that the CSCP can occur without a context, adequate preparation or the concomitant involvement of the other dimensions and faculties of the one person." (p. 60)

There is no difficulty here. The human preparations in question are the heart of the Ignatian method and the *Spiritual Exercises*; I would add only that the "deepest dimensions of the human spirit" or "that mysterious point in the human spirit prior to its division into intellect and will," "man's faculty of mystery where only God can come and go as He pleases," might include aspects of man's deepest level of psychic functioning, including the dynamic influences of his unconscious. Far be it from me to spiritualize the human unconscious, but I would not exclude it from possible divine influence. If God acts on the soul, his action is not restricted to any particular aspect—his action is total, encompassing, and presumably influential on all dimensions of the psyche, insofar as that action has psychological effects of whatever kind.[2] If consolation without previous cause does not rule out human preparation, neither does it rule out human motivation.

9. We maintain that the unconscious cannot adequately account for the CSCP, because this experience draws the person *entirely* into God's love. Any movement capable of excluding all inordinate affections and unifying the entire person can come only from the person's radical principle of unity, the human spirit. (p. 61)

This objection seems to suggest that the unconscious is not part of the human spirit. On the contrary, whatever involves the human spirit involves the human unconscious in some manner. The experience of consolation without previous cause, which draws the person into God's love, does not take place without involving unconscious libidinal forces that are inextricably involved in all human loving, even of a divine object. Insofar as libidinal forces are involved in all human loving, the dynamic and motivational aspects of such drive determinants are also involved.

10. "Although any movement which unites the entire person must also include the unconscious, the unconscious alone cannot account for the exercitant's experience of wholeness, totality and self-presence. Ignatius expects the exercitant to be rid of *all* sadness." (p. 61)

The unconscious itself can never account for anything. The unconscious exercises its influence only through the functioning of other psychic agencies—the ego and superego. Even dreaming, with its unique access to the unconscious, does not take place without the collaboration of other structures.

11. The CSCP is the supreme case of Ignatian *sentire*, that felt-knowledge which flows from the unification and harmony of all of the person's faculties. Although we basically agree with K. Rahner (1964) that this is not "feeling," "instinct" (p. 94, n. 9), but "an intellectual knowledge which is ultimately grounded in the simple presence to itself of the intrinsically intelligible subject which in the very accomplishment of its act has knowledge of itself, without that contrast of knower and known" (pp. 94–95, n. 9), we prefer to stress the holistic, body-person nature of the CSCP. Beginning in the presence of spirit to itself, the CSCP, however, can be explained only through the interior harmony and unity which results when the total body-person has become connatural to grace, when God's love has penetrated all of the layers and dimensions of the one person and unified this person to his very roots. (pp. 61–62)

Besides the fact that such total unification and interior harmony seem idealistic, the deepest roots of the human person must include the core elements of his human personality, including his unconscious. From a psychoanalytic perspective, it would seem somewhat naive to call for such inner harmony. Even in the best of circumstances, elements of conflict remain buried in the unconscious and are not only susceptible to activation, given the right eliciting conditions, but continue to exercise their influence even when there is no conscious awareness of their presence or activity. The findings in this study would seem to indicate that this was in fact the case for Ignatius of Loyola.

12. A. Brunner (1949) has called attention to the "superconscious" (*Überbewusstsein*), or beyond-the-conceptual aspect of human consciousness. This aspect of human consciousness is often confused with the unconscious, because it concerns the person's deepest interiority and horizon of consciousness. This "superconsciousness" is what we mean by the human spirit's presence to itself in radical active self-identity. During the CSCP, the exercitant becomes more explicitly aware of his supernaturally and Christ-affected active self-identity. This special form of Ignatian self-knowledge transcends discursive reasoning and is a type of "superconsciousness." For this reason, it may look like an irruption from the unconscious. (p. 62)

If the "superconsciousness" is not integrated with the functions and capacities of the human organism, it violates the nature of that organism and all norms for human experience. If it operates in conjunction with natural capacities, it does not thereby exclude the unconscious. The notion of an "irruption from the unconscious" does not make psychoanalytic sense. Any expression of unconscious dynamics is motivated and involves some involvement and integration with the functional capacity of other psychic structures. The notion of a superconscious state would presumably reflect a condition of integration of psychic structures in such a fashion as to create a unique state of altered consciousness that transcends the limits of ordinary human experience. The psychoanalytic perspective would insist only that such an extraordinary integration would involve the participation of pre-existing psychic potential and capacities.

13. Lastly, we readily admit that the unconscious can, should and does play a role in consolation or desolation. We maintain, however, that the unconscious alone cannot draw the person totally into God's love. Precisely because the CSCP is the basic unifying experience of the one body-person, the unconscious is involved, but not vice versa. We do accept, however, the unconscious as a source of CCCP [consolation with previous cause]. A consolation which had its roots in the unconscious would have to be splashed against the horizon of meaning, totality and wholeness supplied by the basic, "superconscious" consolation, the CSCP. (p. 62)

The phrase "unconscious alone" sticks out. The formulation, as I have suggested, is not psychoanalytically intelligible. To accept the role of the unconscious in the experience of consolation with previous cause— that is, when the consolation is consistent with the desire and intention of the one meditating—says no more than that unconscious factors can enter into conscious experiences. The consolation with previous cause addresses itself to conscious aspects of the meditative experience, and we would argue that unconscious factors are inexorably involved in the entire experience. To exclude unconscious factors from the experience of consolation without previous cause is to say that grace operates independently and exclusively of psychic functions. This would imply that such grace operates independently of man's capacity for freedom and has no psychic effects. Neither conclusion would seem to be consistent with Ignatian principles.

I hope that this dialogue between divergent orientations toward the understanding of Ignatius' mystical experience helps to bring the transcendent and mystical aspects of Ignatius' experience into contact with the dynamic understanding of his human experience and the dimensions of his human personality. I would urge that his mystical life is continuous with the rest of his experience and that it not only expresses profoundly meaningful motivations but also bears the stamp of his unique personality. We cannot hope to encompass the full scope of his spiritual life and doctrine without articulating them with what we can piece together of his inner psychic life. His spiritual life under grace had a profound effect on his psychic life, but I maintain that his psychic life had its own influence on the pattern and content of his spiritual and mystical ascent of the mystical mountain.

A PSYCHOANALYTIC PORTRAIT

6

DEVELOPMENT AND CONVERSION

XXI

The time has come to try to assemble the scattered fragments of an analysis of Ignatius' personality and psychic experience into a coherent picture. In a sense, this task brings us full circle, back to the place where our inquiry began. In bringing this study to a close, we are faced with the same limitations and hesitations with which we first set out. If the pieces fit together we shall have achieved an account that carries its own weight of plausibility. As Freud observed, when we are able to fit the last piece of a jigsaw puzzle into its appropriate place, we have before our eyes the conclusive evidence that we have successfully reconstructed the puzzle picture. But the fragments we are dealing with here lack the definitive shape and texture that allows each piece of the puzzle only one place in the whole. Consequently, the picture that emerges from this synthesis may bear some plausible relation to the real person of Ignatius, but the links are uncertain and the result no more than conjectural and probable at best. The reader must be the judge as to whether the portrait of Ignatius prescribed here carries any conviction and substantiation. I will present this hypothetical reconstruction under five headings—the developmental influences and the conversion experience in this chapter, the personality of the postconversion Ignatius (chapter 22), his mystical experiences, and finally the transvaluation of identity that all these aspects reflect (chapter 23).

DEVELOPMENTAL INFLUENCES

The pitfalls in any attempt to reconstruct the infant Iñigo's developmental career are considerable. The first important fact that emerges is the early loss of his mother. The problems here are rife. If his mother died early, how old was Iñigo? What were the circumstances surrounding the event? How salient are the elements of loss and abandonment? What were the living conditions in the peasant hut of the Garins? These are all factors that would qualify the impact of this early traumatic loss on Ignatius' infantile development. Particularly, we would like to know how his mother's death affected the process of separation and individuation that would lay the foundations for the process of development on which his evolving personality structure would build. The age at which this separation occurred makes a considerable difference in how the trauma is integrated or defended against and what long term sequelae it might induce.

My hypothesis is that these events had a pathogenic impact, which set up the conditions for continued reworking and mastery of the effects of loss, in Ignatius' more mature years as well as in childhood. The loss of his mother would have left him with a deep-seated unconscious wish for reunion with her, specifically through death. Correlative with this wish, we could infer unconscious fantasies, formed at an infantile level in his mind, of rejoining his mother in the heavenly kingdom, where mother and son could be reunited in eternal bliss. A consequence of this dynamic would be an essentially depressive core to his personality organization, rooted in his sense of abandonment, intolerable and inexpressible rage at the abandoning mother, and a devalued sense of himself as a child who was not worthy of his mother's love and fidelity.

The other side of this psychic coin is an idealization of the lost mother, whose image would embrace the highest and purest virtue. The perfection of this unconscious image would be proportional to the imperfection and lack of worth of his own self-image—a sense of inferiority and worthlessness that could be redeemed only by the longed-for reunion with the idealized mother. These dynamic processes were synthesized into an identification with the mother, particularly with the image of her as patient, long-suffering, deeply religious and faithful, and the paragon of feminine virtues. These elements of his maternal identification would determine a variety of important patterns and experiences that would shape and direct his later life. I will return to these developments later.

An interesting parallel to these dynamics can be found in the case of Ignatius' contemporary Michelangelo Buonarroti. Because of the illness of his repeatedly pregnant and probably chronically ailing mother, Michelangelo, like Iñigo, was put out to nurse soon after birth. The future artist's maternal deprivation was complicated by the loss of his nurse when he returned to his family and finally by the death of his mother when he was just six years of age (Liebert 1982; Oremland 1978, 1980). Analysis of his madonnas and pietàs suggests that Michelangelo struggled with the effects of maternal loss throughout his artistic life. The embrace of Jesus' dead body by the madonna-mother of Michelangelo's masterpiece in St. Peter's suggests both his deep-seated identification with Christ, particularly the suffering and dying Christ, and his frustrated yearning for reunion with the mother he had lost. Throughout his life, the dominant fantasy that came to such consummate expression in his works revealed the unresolved yearning for blissful and uninterrupted reunion with the idealized image of the maternal figures he had lost in childhood (Oremland 1989).

The parallels with Ignatius are striking, but for Ignatius the creative resolution of deep-seated unconscious conflict and its related fantasy took the form of mystical ecstasy rather than artistic externalization. The God-representation in his inner world became the restitutive substitute for the lost mother and fulfilled part of the deeper longing. The pattern of similarity between Ignatius and Michelangelo extends even to an identification with the lost mother that underlies the apparent maternal qualities of both men. For Michelangelo, this resolution took a homosexual form that led to his adopting a maternal role with beautiful young men in sexual liaisons that were equivalently efforts to master the effects of early maternal deprivation (Liebert 1982; Oremland 1989). For Ignatius, this aspect of the resolution took the more sublimated form of a religiously tinged paternity and an Eriksonian generativity permeated by the nurturant and maternal qualities derived from his identification with the lost mother.

The other important developmental influence in Ignatius' life took the form of a powerful identification with the image of his father as strong, masculine, phallic, aggressive—the image of the dominant, authoritarian warrior and leader, characterized by effectiveness of action and will and by sexual potency and prowess. Of the two important determinants of this pattern of identification with the phallic narcissistic father image, the first is more manifest and culturally reinforced. There is little question that the culture of late fifteenth- and early sixteenth-century Spain was male-dominated. This hypermasculinity seems to dominate Mediterranean cultures as well as Hispanic cultures elsewhere, and is manifested in patterns of physical and sexual aggressiveness (see Gilmore and Gilmore 1979). In present-day Spain, this seems to take the form of sexual aggression rather than physical prowess and toughness. This brand of machismo can be seen not as an assertion of secure masculine identity but as a defensively motivated attempt to resolve deeper conflicts between masculine and feminine identities, as a reaction formation against unresolved bisexuality. The Gilmores (1979) argue with regard to this Andalusian brand of machismo

> that boys identify pre-oedipally with nurturing parents, with mothers, and not, as Freud assumed, with fathers. Consequently, in matrifocal or father-absent societies, or where males (but not females) of certain social classes experience infantilizing economic and political dependency on more powerful external figures, the lack of a suitable adult male role model makes the necessary post-oedipal transition to male gender identification very difficult. It is postulated here that lower-class Andalusian machismo represents a post-oedipal mechanism by which dominated males seek to "disidentify" from the powerful Andalusian mother figure and thereby to resolve intrapsychic gender identity conflict. (p. 283)[1]

This pattern obtains in the strongly matriarchal lower-class family of Andalusia. But what about the pattern in the upper-class family of sixteenth-century Spanish nobility? The castle of Loyola was dominated by an authoritarian patriarchy. Beltrán was the lord and master of his castle and its domains. But he was in all likelihood a more or less absent father-figure, much taken up with fighting, contending for the rights of name and family, defending the honor of the king, extending his power and influence. It is thus possible that Beltrán was more of a remote figure for his youngest son. He would have been totally absent in the years that Iñigo spent outside the castle. When Iñigo was brought back, he was placed under the care and tutelage of Doña Magdalena. Thus he was enmeshed in the female sphere of influence both as an infant and as a young child.

My argument is that these cultural factors would have reinforced more specifically psychodynamic factors that influenced Iñigo's emerging identification with his father. The issue here is the lifelong struggle in the male to establish and maintain a masculine identity in the face of passive and dependent yearnings that exert an often powerful psychic pull toward the feminine. The male begins life in a state of dependence and attachment to the mother; the regressive pull toward that early and idealized infantile dependence is the force he must struggle against to preserve his sense of masculinity. Rochlin (1980) puts the argument in the following terms:

> It is the human condition to evolve inner defenses against our private, often ill-defined, emotional conflicts, and men, even as boys, are prone to particular defenses in regard to their masculinity. The most persistent, disturbing, and anxiety-provoking are those associated with the never-ending need to prove one's masculinity in the face of doubts as to its degree. Thus, we find at all stages of manhood—young boys, whose defenses of masculinity are developing; youths, whose masculinity is being tested in reality; and men, whose masculinity needs a constant reaffirmation—alarming fears that return in varying forms in even more distressing wishes. Principal among these are the fears and wishes to be feminine or to engage in what once may have been associated with notions of femininity. Such reverses of the "normal" conscious imperative of masculine striving, set off by the eruption of unconscious rooted desires, call out vigorous defenses: most commonly striving to be and to seem more "masculine." (p. 4)

These unconscious fears and wishes, along with their associated defenses, are the lot of all normal males but would have been complicated by special conditions for Iñigo. The loss of his mother provided an additional unconscious pull toward the feminine—a wish that would have been repugnant to his culture and the world he lived in. The unconscious theme of return to the feminine and reunion with the lost mother would have played itself out in this context of his struggle to achieve adult masculinity. The model for this process was, of course, the powerful phallic and narcissistic figure of Beltrán.

These conflicting identifications, with the phallic, narcissistic, and aggressive figure of his father on the one hand, and the passive, self-sacrificing, pious, virtuous, humble, and self-effacing image of his mother, elevated to the status of an idealized and sublime object through death, on the other were to contend for the intrapsychic hegemony of his inner world throughout Iñigo's life. This deep-seated conflict would never be fully resolved.

THE CONVERSION

A traumatic series of events led to Iñigo's conversion experience: his physical wounds, the humiliating experience of defeat, the long and painful journey back to Loyola to recuperate, the frustration of physical immobility (not an inconsiderable burden for this man of action) compounded by the enforced passivity and dependence on his caretakers, the added trauma of the failure of the bones to knit properly, followed by the agony of refracturing the leg without anesthesia, leading to more months of immobility and dependence, and his life-threatening illness, probably due to infection related to the wounds and the subsequent surgery. The final blow was the disappointing outcome of the second attempt to set the bone properly, which left him with a deformed leg and a noticeable limp.

All these details compose a picture of severe narcissistic trauma and depletion, the outcome of which could be nothing less than a profound depression. We need to recall his largely narcissistic and phallic personality structure and the inherent vulnerabilities of such character structures. The physical trauma was a castration-like experience that shattered his image of himself as a dashing, gallant ladies' man and romantic knight and soldier. His dreams of glory and conquest, both sexual and aggressive, were dashed. The effect had to be extreme narcissistic depletion, a depressive reaction, and a regressive dynamic that left him vulnerable to a host of drive-derivative and impulse-based influences, and possibly even to a regressive loss of a sense of self-cohesion, resulting in a degree of self-fragmentation. The narcissistic disequilibrium required redress and rebalancing—this much seems obvious.

But I would also suggest that his faltering ego may have been assaulted by a surge of libidinal pressures threatening in the extreme, both because of the taboo against any form of sexual expression toward the beautiful and nurturing Magdalena and, at a deeper and more unconscious level, because of the incestuous urges stirred by the figure of Magdalena. She was, after all, his third mother,[2] and the unconscious links between her and his lost mother of infancy would have tapped into forbidden oedipal and preoedipal wishes for the lost and yearned-for mother, infantile wishes that were reactivated and intensified in his regressive condition. We recall that Ignatius later in his life had to cover the picture of our Lady so that his libidinal wishes would not be stirred, precisely because the picture so resembled Magdalena. The same instinctual urges that could arise so readily and intensely in his later years were presumably also active in the sickroom of Loyola.

All these troublesome issues were resolved by the conversion experience. The basic elements of that experience were a hallucinatory vision of the Blessed Mother with the child Jesus, followed by the massive repression of all libidinal desires. The details can be telling. When Magdalena came to Loyola as the betrothed of Martín García, she brought with her as a royal gift a painting of Our Lady. We can wonder whether Iñigo's vision cast in the image of this portrait, so intimately associated with the figure of Magdalena?

The resolution of this narcissistic crisis took the form of abandoning the phallic narcissistic ego ideal of the past and replacing it with a new ego ideal based on spiritual values and cast in a mold of highly religious ambitions and desires. If his deformity and crippling injury had deprived him of following the ideal of the romantic knight and achieving fame and glory by his physical prowess and skill at arms, he could substitute another powerful ambition—to become a warrior in the service of a heavenly king rather than a mere earthly one. The resolution has all the earmarks of a manic defense—like Oedipus at Colonus, Iñigo "turns to omnipotence and is able to defeat his inner despair by becoming a holy man. It is a manic triumph which frightens us by its power and ruthlessness, and which impresses us through its grandeur" (Steiner, 1990, p. 230). As this renewal of narcissistic investment was taking place, is it any wonder that the models that he so fervently embraced were found in the books provided by Magdalena?

CONFLICTING IDENTIFICATIONS

Taking all these components into account, I would offer the more general hypothesis that in his conversion experience Iñigo abandoned the identification with his phallic, powerful, narcissistic, authoritarian, and domineering father and turned to an equally powerful identification with his passive, vulnerable, pious, religious, and idealized mother. I have already argued that the pattern of phallic narcissistic masculine identification was in some degree motivated by the need to counter and deny the unconscious but decidedly threatening feminine identification. The tension between these internalized configurations in his internal psychic world had been maintained in large part by a powerful narcissistic cathexis. When this structure was shaken by the severe narcissistic trauma of his defeat and injury, the masculine pattern of identification could no longer be maintained adequately; some effective substitute had to be found. No surprise that the narcissistic resolution was purchased at the cost of a feminine identification and the substitution of a masochistically tinged submission to the power and will of God. The reward would have taken the form of divine benevolence and caretaking, replacing the lost phallic narcissistic power with the grandiosity of divine allegiance and favor. As Steiner comments:

> Turning to omnipotence is a mechanism resorted to only in extreme situations when something has gone radically wrong in the individual's relationship with primary objects. If these objects are destroyed, and the guilt becomes unbearable, self-mutilating attacks on the perceiving ego may be resorted to. The resulting damage, to both the object and the ego, leaves a disability which can only be patched over by means of omnipotence since ordinary human figures are too weak to be of help. The individual is then possessed by monstrous forces which serve as suitable receptacles into which omnipotent parts of the self are projected. . . . When they take on a paranoid grandiosity . . . they seem to function primarily as a defence against disintegration and fragmentation. (1990, p. 234)

We should also remind ourselves that the conversion experience was extended and reworked during the more prolonged crisis in the cave of Manresa, so that these same elements also contributed to his emotional, psychological, and spiritual struggles and conflicts throughout that period.

THE PERSONALITY OF IGNATIUS

XXII

Psychoanalytic understanding generally emphasizes the continuity of the adult personality with developmental influences, especially the role of preoedipal and oedipal determinants, and the evolution of personality structures as the individual advances through the life cycle.

I will formulate my view of Ignatius' postconversion personality under a half-dozen headings: superego organization and functioning, obsessional character structure, libidinal conflicts, aggressive conflicts, narcissism and the ego ideal, and finally authoritarian characteristics. The strategy has its advantages, but also its drawbacks. It allows me to consider certain aspects of Ignatius' personality more clearly and systematically, although it runs the risk of dividing up what is essentially an integrated whole. It is necessary to keep in mind that the parts cannot be considered without reference to the whole, a complete and functional human being. In this instance as in so many others, the whole will be greater than sum of the parts.

SUPEREGO SEVERITY

We have noted the dominant role of aggression in the preconversion personality of Iñigo de Loyola. In the conversion experience he turned from the model of phallic aggression to one of passive receptivity, to defensive reaction formation directed against persistent aggressive impulses. This intrapsychic conversion was put in the service of his emerging ego ideal, patterned after the model of the saintly lives in the *Flos Sanctorum*.

The regression that followed the dissolution of the pilgrim's psychic structure, most notably at Manresa, was accompanied by a more direct expression of powerful instincts. In this more primitive state, the aggressive drives became aggregated to the superego. The superego was originally introduced by Freud as a psychic agency that watches the ego, compares it with an ideal standard—the ego ideal—and serves as the agency of repression of those instinctual impulses not in conformity with the standards of the ideal. It is a sort of structural precipitate within the ego that comes into existence at the time of the resolution of the oedipal conflict. As a derivative of parental and other identifications, it represents the child's relation to parents and society and functions as the vehicle of morality—primarily the moral values of the parents. Freud also stressed that the superego was itself a channel for powerful drives. The aggressive drives in particular can be diverted by the superego against the self. Freud described this by saying, "The ego forms its superego out of the id." Thus, the greater the control of aggressive impulses against external objects, the more tyrannical the superego becomes. And this tyranny is manifested in a sense of guilt or worthlessness or in other self-punitive postures.

When its external outlets are forestalled, as Freud (1923) pointed out, aggression turns inward and is channeled through the superego, thus increasing the severity of superego aggression directed against the self. Iñigo's capacity to manage and regulate his aggressive impulses was not very good at the beginning of his pilgrim years—the episode of the Moor who was saved by Iñigo's mule is a case in point. The aggressive residues of the hidalgo, the impulse to fight, to defend the honor of his lady, and even to kill, were coiled and ready to leap into consciousness.

But the modifications in his superego increasingly took the form of extreme self-punitive penitential and ascetic practices. At a conscious level the motivations involved guilt for past transgressions (as I have argued, there was probably plenty to feel guilty about!) and lifelong shame for his failure to live up to his religious and moral ideals. Iñigo's conscience would have been formed in the intense Catholicism of the Iberian peninsula, a form of religious praxis that tended to absolutes and moral rigidity, and under the influence of Magdalena, whose piety and religious devotion were noteworthy. Guilt and shame would have provided the motivating affects for his severe self-punishment, which was also an atonement for the past and, in a more positive vein, a more or less creative expression of his drive toward shaping a new identity congruent with his spiritual ego ideal. It is probably safe to say, therefore, that the pilgrim's extreme self-denial and penances were in large part motivated by the need to satisfy the demands of this newly formed narcissistically invested ego ideal. The superego was the instrument of execution of this intrapsychic drama, the motivating force behind Ignatius' guilt, depression, scrupulosity, suicidal impulses, and masochism.

The pilgrim's systematic throttling of the expression of the pleasure principle contributed to the dissolution of the old ego ideal, which had served as a major mechanism for the fusion of libidinal and aggressive drives and thus provided the motivating power for the constructive demands of development and mature adaptation (Hartmann 1958). Destruction of the previous romantic-heroic ego ideal served to unleash these energies in their primitive and deneutralized form so that they suffused the pilgrim's psychic structure and had to be diverted into other channels. An alternative means of expression was provided by the affinity of the superego to these basic energies. The pilgrim passed through a period of agonizing doubt, tormenting scruples, paroxysms of guilt, and feelings of worthlessness. His superego, feeding on its new-found aggression, not only tormented him with self-punitive impulses but drove his floundering ego to seek relief from the inner punishment by severe physical penances and infliction of pain. This torrent of superego rage reached its apogee in the temptation to commit suicide—the ultimate masochistic gesture.

The picture of the pilgrim at this phase of his journey is that of a man buffeted by uncontrollable forces. He had unwittingly unleashed something that he could no longer control. It is interesting to recall that he began with attempts at penitential self-punishment. The originating impulse was in some degree deliberate (coming from the ego) and religiously motivated but necessarily had some degree of superego involvement. The effort was penitential in intent, but its effect went beyond contrition. It unleashed destructive impulses that were much more readily enlisted in the service of the superego than they might have been in that of the ego. The superego came to dominate the conflict, and penance became to that extent masochistic. The rational was turned into the irrational. There is no surprise in this from a psychodynamic point of view. The inner life of Iñigo had always been, and was always to be, a process of dealing with powerful instinctual forces. The regression at Manresa merely allowed these forces their most unbridled display.

The mention of masochism raises a difficult question—to what extent can the pilgrim's penances be regarded as masochistic? In my opinion, Iñigo's severe penances were a form of masochistic perversion in that they reflected the degree of intrapsychic conflict he endured with regard to his instinctual life. These conflicts, which were recognizably libidinal, aggressive, and narcissistic, were extreme in the early years of his pilgrimage, and it was only over time that his suffering gradually, and only partially, freed him from these conflicts. However, these conflicts required vigilance and strong repressive and other defensive countermeasures until the end of his life. His penances seemed to have been mitigated only in the face of severe and even life-threatening self-injury. But if we base our analysis on a masochistic dynamism, we will not have adequately understood or explained Ignatius' ascetical life.

Psychoanalytically speaking, masochism is a complex phenomenon (Berliner 1947). The sexual perversion of masochism is usually distinguished from moral masochism[1] in that the perversion involves sexual gratification derived from suffering. Freud regarded masochism as the turning of aggression against the self. Masochism was linked to sadism, and the two served as opposite sides of the same coin. Often the sado-masochistic pattern takes place in an interpersonal context in which one person takes the role of sadist and the other that of masochist. Many unhappily married couples fall into this pattern—and it is not at all unusual for the members of the pair to exchange places, the masochist acting out a sadistic role and the sadist becoming the suffering victim. In these cases, the masochist role usually serves as a defense against aggressive drives—it is better to suffer the aggression of another than to become the hostile and destructive agent oneself. In intrapsychic structural terms, this takes the form of a struggle between aggressive and victim configurations (introjects) that contribute part of the core of the individual's personality structure (Meissner 1978) and reflect underlying conflicts over aggression. In Iñigo's case, his need to seek the role of suffering victim in his penitential practices served as an effective defense against his severe aggressive conflicts. Ignatius' colloquy at the conclusion of the meditation on the Two Standards in the second week of the *Spiritual Exercises* makes this clear:

A colloquy should be addressed to our Lady, asking her to obtain for me from her Son and Lord the grace to be received under His standard, first in the highest spiritual poverty, and should the Divine Majesty be pleased thereby, and deign to choose and accept me, even in actual poverty; secondly, in bearing insults and wrongs, thereby to imitate

Him better, provided only I can suffer these without sin on the part of another, and without offense of the Divine Majesty. (Exercises 147)

This masochistic stand aims at countering the wish for wealth and pride—presumably desires that stirred in some form in the breast of the pilgrim and against which he had to exercise continuing vigilance. The self-denial has the purpose of seeking love and approval from a divine object rather than a human one.

In the sphere of the sacred, the masochistic stance is articulated with a religious ego ideal and is often placed in the service of a spiritual set of values and objectives. We should not automatically assume that such religiously motivated masochism is pathological—it may or may not be. The masochism of the ascetic may elicit admiration or contempt; it may reflect psychic weakness or strength; it may be a vehicle for seeking or for expressing love. The masochistic surrender to God may serve as a way of avoiding reality, or the suffering and submission of the saint may serve as a vehicle for discovering increasingly meaningful levels of personal commitment and love of God. The mortification of the ascetic may reflect a profound love of God, it may alleviate guilt and expiate sin, it may be put to developmental uses—for example, growth in chastity and purity of mind and heart—or it may express a perversion that finds gratification in pain (Charmé 1983).

I think it is safe to say that Ignatius suffered from a rather extreme degree of moral masochism, but it was in many ways sublimated and adapted to a program of spiritual growth through the seeking of grace and an increasing love of God. Ignatius' penances were thus transformed into acts of love, driven more by seeking God's approval than by guilt or the need for punishment. If this is masochism, it is not simply the masochism of the neurotic or the moral masochist; it is masochism suffused with love and placed in the service of a highly narcissistically invested ego ideal, an ideal that is itself imbued with the highest spiritual aims.

OBSESSIONAL CHARACTER STRUCTURE

A salient aspect of Ignatius' personality is his obsessionality. Psychoanalysts would understand this aspect of his character as derived from the excessive severity of his superego—the need for obsessional control is based on the threat of breakthrough of instinctual impulses. The leakage of such impulses into consciousness is accompanied, in the classic Freudian model, by guilt from both libidinal (incestuous) and aggressive wishes. In Ignatius' case I think we can add narcissistic impulses, which may result in shame more than guilt.

The obsessiveness is striking in his own spiritual practice and in his direction of the spiritual lives of his followers. His examination of his conscience, carried on almost hourly and always with obsessive intensity, even to the point of compulsion, is notable. His spiritual teaching and direction, as evidenced in the *Spiritual Exercises*, for example, are highly structured and organized to the point that many have found them repellent and difficult to emulate. To the extent that this obsessional pattern reflects Ignatius' own spiritual experience, it offers us some insight into his character.

As we study Ignatius' postconversion life, we get a sense of discipline, tenacity to the point of stubbornness or obstinacy, and a pattern of behavior impressive for its consistent degree of control—especially emotional control. There is evidence of defense mechanisms—isolation, intellectualization, and reaction formation, among others. We have also seen the breakthrough of obsessional doubts, frequently taking the form of intense scruples. That these scrupulous doubts plagued him, not only in the early years of his pilgrimage, but even into his advanced years as General of the Society in Rome seems an established fact.

The last note of his Rules for Thinking with the Church in the *Exercises* carries with it a peculiar resonance. Ignatius writes:

> When such good soul wants to speak or do something within the Church, within the understanding of our Superiors, and which should be for the glory of God our Lord, and there comes to him a thought or temptation from without that he should neither say nor do that thing—bringing to him apparent reasons of vainglory or of another thing, etc.,—then he ought to raise his understanding to his Creator and Lord, and if he sees that it is His due service, or at the least not contrary to it, he ought to act diametrically against such temptation, according to St. Bernard, answering the same: "Neither for thee did I begin, nor for thee will I stop." (351)

I would associate this sage advice to several contexts. Might it not speak to the ambivalence and conflict that Iñigo felt when he violated the order of the Franciscan superior in Jerusalem by revisiting some of the holy places? Or when he was accused by the Inquisition and was confronted with the choice of defending his cause before the tribunal or capitulating and accepting their judgment? Or when he decided to address that fateful letter of protest to the irascible and future Pope and then head of the Theatines, Gian Pietro Carafa? These were all possible instances of obsessional doubt rooted in ambivalence that to some degree reflect the underlying conflicts over authority and obedience that preoccupied Ignatius as General and may have served as a focus for his scrupulous afflictions. Such a line of reasoning may have helped him to resolve his ambivalence in these and other instances, whether the outcome was advantageous or not. We might think that often enough in his brilliant career, especially with respect to the founding and advancement of the Society of Jesus, this approach had served him well.

These behavioral reflections give us some hint of the conflictual struggles that permeated his inner life and powered the rigid self-discipline that characterized him in later years. One might argue as well that this need for inner control spilled over into his style of governing the Society, with his passion for establishing regulations (reflected in his obsessional immersion in the writing of the Constitutions) and his insistence on unquestioning blind obedience from his followers—no doubt related to his authoritarian conflicts and character. It is worth noting in this context that the one area of his experience that seemed exempt from this consuming obsession was his prayer life and mysticism.

LIBIDINAL CONFLICTS

Iñigo's libidinal conflicts were considerable, as we have seen, and impinged on his psychic development almost from the beginning. The early trauma of the loss of his mother played a central role in his subsequent libidinal development and in his lifelong relations with women. In this connection we can note a hysterical tendency in the mature postconversion personality of Ignatius. The specific incidents that reflect this hysterical element are the massive repression of libidinal impulses at the critical juncture of his conversion experience (after the vision of the Blessed Mother and her Son), the breakthrough of conversion symptoms (that is, the development of pain in his hand after touching the plague victim and putting the hand in his mouth), the emergence of phobic symptoms (en route to rescue the Spaniard who had cheated him), and possibly his ecstatic experiences. These experiences all reveal an underlying sexual and libidinal conflict that on occasion broke through the repressive barriers and defenses in the form of symptoms.[2]

I have argued that the massive repression (with elements of denial) that he mobilized to defend against erotic and incestuous impulses (derived from infantile strata of sexual attachment to the mother image) was only partially successful. Even after his conversion, after the transformation in the cave of Manresa, his libidinal and sexual conflicts continued to cause him inner torments. The struggles between his unconscious (and at times conscious) sexual and erotic impulses and the severity of his superego condemnation, permeated with affective resonances of guilt and shame, powered his intense scrupulosity and in part his asceticism. To the end of his life, this saint had to guard against his impulses constantly and unrelentingly. When the struggle was not conscious, it carried on unabated on the unconscious level.

This permeable nature of his repression took various forms. One was the sublimation of his sexual drives in his preaching to and devoted concern for the spiritual welfare of women in all walks of life. The reform of convents and commitment to save the prostitutes and concubines of Azpeitia and Rome were major apostolic efforts. All these charitable and spiritual works were nobly motivated, but I would argue that mingled with these lofty spiritual goals were elements of aim-inhibited[3] and sublimated sexuality. This observation is in no sense intended to disparage these admirable and saintly endeavors, but even the noblest human purposes are never free of more basically human and instinctual drive-derivatives.

A second effect of Ignatius' relative repression of libidinal urges was the aura of charm that drew so many female admirers to seek spiritual guidance from him. For many of these women, the attachment to Ignatius was in no sense casual or trivial but quite intense, deeply affective, and in some measure erotic. The attraction of affectively starved and often sexually deprived women to this noble, handsome, kindly, fatherly, and responsive man of God—who listened so unstintingly to their tales of woe and anguish and spent long hours conversing with them about intimate spiritual and personal matters—requires little explanation. In a number of cases, these women proved to be excessively clinging and demanding; Ignatius frequently seemed to find himself embroiled in an emotional morass from which he could extract himself only with considerable distress, not only for the women involved but for himself. This speaks to the psychoanalytic ear of unresolved sexuality and conflictual libidinal drives in both parties. I would argue that the same relatively intense libidinal drives in the young hidalgo persisted in the pilgrim and saint, but that in later years they continued to be the object of unrelenting ascetic attack and, at an unconscious level, of drive-defense conflicts and compromises. I would also argue that among the areas of compromise and sublimation, Ignatius' dedication to the spiritual welfare of women—queens, duchesses, noblewomen, shopkeepers, courtesans, concubines, and prostitutes—has to be granted a lofty ranking.

The last and perhaps most difficult area of displaced and sublimated libidinal expression is in Ignatius' ecstatic mystical experiences. The libidinal components of those intensely affective experiences would reflect powerful currents of preoedipal fixation and desire deriving from the loss-and-restitution, the union or perhaps better reunion with the nurturing and soothing maternal object of early infancy.

AGGRESSION

The preconversion Iñigo was a forceful personality, vigorous, testy, pugnacious. What happened to this aggression during his conversion and in the shaping of his postconversion personality? Despite the occasional breakthrough, the major outcome of his conversion experience was a turning away from his aggressive impulses—certainly from the bellicose model presented by his father and brothers and from his interior identification with these phallic and aggressive objects.

His struggles to overcome the evil inclinations of the past and to seek out a new and spiritual identity markedly expressed his underlying aggressive conflicts. The impulse to do in the poor Moor on the road to Montserrat was one example. But in the cave at Manresa, the hostile force was physically and mentally turned against himself in the form of severe penances and deprivations, as well as in the form of the superego severity. The apogee of this turning of aggression against the self came in his suicidal ruminations. These aggressive derivatives also played a role in the masochistic dynamics that underlay his severe asceticism. It is also likely that the need to deny and defend against aggressive drives contributed significantly to his mystical experience.

NARCISSISM AND THE EGO IDEAL

Narcissistic issues run like a broad river across the landscape of Ignatius' intrapsychic world. It is in the vicissitudes and transformations of that narcissism that much of his psychology is played out.

No other psychological concept lends itself to greater misuse and greater misunderstanding. In its fundamental meaning, narcissism is an expression of libidinal drives. In *Group Psychology and the Analysis of the Ego* (1921), Freud wrote:

Libido is an expression taken from the theory of the emotions. . . . of those instincts which have to do with all that may be comprised under the word "love." The nucleus of what we mean by love naturally consists (and this is what is commonly called love, and what the poets sing of) in sexual love with sexual union as its aim. But we do not separate from this—what in any case has a share in the name "love"—on the one hand, self-love, and on the other, love for parents and children, friendship and love for humanity in general, and also devotion to concrete objects and to abstract ideas. (p. 90)

In Freud's view, the infant cannot love another prior to the development of the capacity to differentiate self from object. Life, therefore, begins in a state of primary narcissism in which libido resides in the as-yet undifferentiated self. Differentiation of self from the external world brings with it the capacity to direct libido to external objects or conversely to the self as an object. The primary love object is normally the mother. Freud also postulated that love directed toward objects could be again transformed into narcissistic energy by making the object part of the ego (we would now say self) through identification. This gave rise to secondary narcissism, implying that libido was redirected toward the self.

In his essay "On Narcissism," Freud (1914) sought to explain repression by an appeal to the ego ideal:

Repression, as we have said, proceeds from the ego; we might say with greater precision that it proceeds from the self-respect of the ego. The same impressions, experiences, impulses and desires that one man indulges or at least works over consciously will be rejected with the utmost indignation by another, or even stifled before they enter consciousness. The difference between the two, which contains the conditioning factor of repression, can easily be expressed in terms which enable it to be explained by the libido theory. We can say that the one man has set up an ideal in himself by which he measures his actual ego, while the other has no such ideal. For the ego the formation of an ideal would be the conditioning factor of repression. (1914, pp. 93–94)

The ego ideal was in Freud's view the heir of the original infantile self-love that the child enjoyed. The success of the struggle for identity depends in part on the satisfactory transfer of this original narcissism into a self-sufficient ego and its ideal (Murray 1964). The residues of infantile narcissism are therefore distilled into the ideal, which thus comes to possess every perfection that is of value.

The ego ideal thus becomes a repository of secondary narcissism and the inheritor of primary narcissism. Freud (1914) explains.

This ideal ego is now the target of the self-love which was enjoyed in childhood by the actual ego. The subject's narcissism makes its appearance displaced on to this new ideal ego, which, like the infantile ego, finds itself possessed of every perfection that is of value. As always where the libido is concerned, man has here again shown himself incapable of giving up a satisfaction he had once enjoyed. He is not willing to forgo the narcissistic perfection of his childhood; and when, as he grows up, he is disturbed by the admonitions of others and by the awakening of his own critical judgment, so that he can no longer retain that perfection, he seeks to recover it in the new form of an ego-ideal. What he projects before him as his ideal is the substitute for the lost narcissism of his childhood in which he was his own ideal. (p. 94)

This formulation was one of Freud's fundamental contributions to the understanding of the development and functioning of the human personality. The importance of this transformation cannot be overestimated. Murray (1964) has commented: "This transformation and socialization of narcissism would then consist in directing it toward an aim other than the egoistic pregenital one, in deflecting its expression and satisfaction to the area of idealistic, personal, and social values, and in striving to create realistically a world appropriate and suitable for such a highly regarded ego to live in" (p. 501). The mature ego ideal is thus a significant factor in the maintenance of the psychic integrity and mature balance between the expression of libidinal impulses and legitimate restraints, which is fundamental to the sense of identity. The implications of the deployment of narcissistic libido in the organization of many aspects of the mature psychic structure have not been settled even today.[4]

The recovery of lost infantile narcissism serves as the basis for the constitution of an ego ideal in adult life. The loss of infantile narcissism, when in a sense the child is his own ideal, results from disruption of the sense of primary fusion between the child and the mother. The result of this disruption is that the child is forced to begin to recognize the existence of the "not-me" world. But the desire to re-experience and regain the sense of fusion with the mother, with its implications of omnipotence and total satisfaction, continues to have residues. Subsequently, incestuous wishes emerging during the oedipal period and directed, for example, by the male child toward the mother ride on an underlying current of these narcissistic motivations. The corresponding wish of the male child to become like the father also reflects an incestuous current in that, to the extent that the child becomes like the father, the mother can be attained as a libidinal object and the desired reunion achieved through an incestuous genital relationship.

Ferenczi (1924) had even contended that the wish to return to the mother's womb was a fundamental human motivation expressed derivatively and achieved through coitus. The wish to return to the mother's womb is equivalently a reflection of archaic narcissistic impulses to return to a primal phase of undifferentiation, where there is no distinction between self and nonself. Consequently, the projection of narcissistic wishes into the developmental future serves as a basis for advancement to more mature and more adaptive and realistic levels. In any case, we will have occasion to return to the role of infantile, narcissistic, and symbiotic wishes in the psychology of Ignatius.

The ego ideal is a kind of internalized standard by which the ego measures itself and which sets the norms of personal perfection toward which the ego constantly strives. Freud called it a precipitate of the old idea of the parents, the powerful and omniscient beings of the child's early experience, and it undoubtedly reflects the child's admiring attitude toward them—Kohut's (1971) "idealized parental imago." The ideal arises by way of identification, through which the child's object-directed love is again redirected to himself and becomes focused in the internalized ideal he sets up in his own ego. While this ego ideal is derived primarily and originally from parental imagos, there is an accretion of other identifications and idealized elements which enlarge and modify the ego ideal as it evolves (Chasseguet-Smirgel 1973).

As far as we have been able to discern, the parental imagos provided to the growing Iñigo were powerful and positive. There was a strong identification with his father which left him with a firm sense of masculine identity, virility, chivalry, courage, high honor, and bold action. He was an aristocrat with a sense of family position and honor, a proud, vain, bold, audacious, fiery, and impetuous youth. If we recall Ribadeneyra's portrait of the dashing young Iñigo, it is impossible to ignore the libidinal and narcissistic elements. The ego ideal of the young Iñigo was cast in the image of the courageous soldier dedicated to the noble ideals of chivalry. The narcissistic investment, however, was in the service of lofty values and standards of behavior which were reinforced in the culture at large. Iñigo's ego ideal displayed itself on a canvas of history and contemporary events in such a way that ideal and reality are difficult to disentangle. We are undoubtedly dealing with a forceful narcissism, which operated in the service of a vigorous personality.

It is also in terms of the ego ideal that libidinal instincts are successfully sublimated. Not only was Iñigo's highly romanticized and chivalrous ideal imbued with sexual overtones, but we have some assurance that his sexual activity was not altogether inhibited in the reality. There can be no question that the ego ideal of the preconversion Loyola was not only the vehicle of narcissistic libido but served to legitimize object-libidinal as well as aggressive instincts. Iñigo's admitted fantasies of bold deeds for love of a fair maid and his yearnings for the lovely Doña Catherina are more or less direct expressions of object love. But they were legitimized and made acceptable by their consonance with his ego ideal. Freud speaks of three components of self-regard, which we can also discern in Iñigo. One part is primary, the residue of infantile narcissism, another arises from the fulfillment of the ego ideal, and a third part proceeds from the satisfaction of object-libido (Freud 1914). Besides Iñigo's infantile narcissism, which must be presumed, we have clear evidence of a highly invested ego ideal and strong libidinal object-investments.

Aggressive impulses also became acceptable by reference to this ideal. His courageous stand at Pamplona was aggression wearing the cloak of valor. Examples could be easily multiplied. Clearly, basic instinctive forces can be adapted to the demands of the ego ideal so that they not only become legitimate but even valued to the extent that they reinforce and support the ideal. Further, it is clear that the ideal of Iñigo did indeed serve this function. In fact, the ego ideal provides the ego with one of its most important ways of utilizing the energizing power of the basic instincts. The degree to which the ego is capable of accomplishing this integration with instinctual energies is a mark of its inherent strength.

It is clear, however, that the ego requires a fund of narcissism both for its normal development and for its continued functioning (Grunberger 1971). Narcissism embraces a spectrum of states that are normal complements of mature functioning. Narcissism is the libidinal aspect of comfort, gratification, self-regard, self-confidence, peace of soul, inner tranquility, self-respect, balance. Enjoyment of simple pleasures, whether in the satisfaction of basic drives like hunger, a good pipe, good music, gratifying sexual relations, or whatever, carries a component of narcissistic gratification. Dreaming is a form of regression to narcissistic satisfaction. This is not to deny that pathological forms of narcissism exist; in fact, the original formulations of narcissism were based on pathological manifestations in schizophrenia and autism. But narcissism must be considered as a natural resource rooted in basic instincts which can be diverted to serve and support man's best interests.

There is a tendency to think of narcissism in its aberrations rather than in its diffusion into all aspects of human activity and life. One can distinguish between normal and pathological forms. Federn (1952) provided a classic treatment of this question, summarizing the characteristics that distinguish healthy from pathological narcissism. First of all, healthy narcissism does not interfere with or replace libido directed to objects. Where narcissism begins to substitute, by way of fantasy or otherwise, for the investment in real objects or the capacity for investment in objects, the picture begins to look pathological. In normal narcissism the ego boundaries remain intact and the ego maintains its stability. Both of these aspects are due to the reinforcement of ego structures by narcissistic investment and the adequacy of narcissistic countercathexes.[5] In normal narcissism, the level of satisfaction resulting from narcissistic cathexis is moderate, not excessive. Further, satisfaction derived from conscious and unconscious fantasies depends in part on the capacity to achieve real libidinal discharge through real object relations. Real satisfaction predominates, whereas in pathological narcissism the satisfaction of narcissistic fantasy is primary. In addition, the fantasy material of normal narcissism is more reality oriented, less infantile, and much less a vehicle for perverse infantile sexual desires.

The further vicissitudes of narcissism in the course of development are complex and often quite perplexing. On the one hand, we have to reckon with the relation between narcissism and the ego ideal, the inheritor of infantile narcissism. On the other hand, there is the complex relationship between the ego ideal and the superego.[6] These relationships have not been adequately conceptualized or clarified since Freud introduced the notions over three-quarters of a century ago, but our interest here is not in the details of theoretical analysis. We are concerned rather to deepen our understanding of what Iñigo endured.

The world fell in ruins about Iñigo in the fortress of Pamplona—and in some further sense his ideal was dealt a crushing blow as well, for the crunch of the cannonball was the first of a series of providential episodes that led the pilgrim to Manresa and beyond. The convalescence in the castle of Loyola represents the initial phase of the erosion of the ego ideal and its inherent values. Iñigo had to face further ordeals of body and spirit, the threat of death and excruciating pain.

The ideal, of course, demanded fortitude in suffering, even as it demanded courage and daring in the face of overwhelming odds. It was no more possible for him to surrender to the French than to give in to physical hardship. At the same time, we should not overlook the less apparent aspects of his ordeal. To begin with, his injury brought him to the brink of death and thus elicited basic anxieties associated with the fear of death and drove him to religious resignation. In these circumstances, he was forced to examine his conscience and confess his sins, to look into his soul, and find there what was good and what was evil in the light of his religious belief. What reflections and realizations obtained in the inner recesses of his psyche we can only conjecture. But it seems likely that the inventory must have had far-reaching effects. The additional fact that he recovered in such dramatic fashion, saved as he fantasied by his patron saint, further underlined the religious impact of his experience.

There was also his sickness and suffering. Pain has a debilitating effect on the psychic organization, causing regression, infantile dependence, anxiety, and a general deterioration of psychic functioning. There seems to be little doubt that the courageous Iñigo could bear pain. But that is not the point. The utter dependence, the infantile reliance on others about him—probably most notably the women of the house—for the care of the most basic bodily needs and the debilitating effects of pain itself violated the demands of his ego ideal and undermined the defenses by which he had been able to protect and support it. His dependence on the women of Loyola must have been difficult in this regard, it would have re-awakened deeply repressed preoedipal wishes for union with the mothering object and powerful regressive pulls toward symbiotic dependence. Nor does it seem to square with the image of the vigorous and dashing man-at-arms.

It seems reasonable to conclude, therefore, that Iñigo's ego ideal suffered severe stress during his extended convalescence. Whatever the effect of the combined influences, it is clear that the old ideal hung on. Iñigo's willingness to undergo additional surgery on his leg for the sake of a more handsome appearance testifies to its vigor. Clearly the character structure of a lifetime was not going to change overnight.

At the same time, it seems reasonable to suggest that the ego ideal underwent a series of effects that left it less secure, overall less endowed with narcissistic cathexis, more questioned and tenuous. The signs of dissolution were revealed in Iñigo's capacity to fantasize alternative roles—idealized, of course—for himself as saint and penitent. The newly fantasied roles were themselves narcissistically endowed, but they carried within them a quite different set of values than those inherent in the old ideal. The ideals of saintliness and heroic asceticism, detailed in the *Flos Sanctorum*, were easily identifiable in the Catholic culture of sixteenth-century Spain. There is little doubt that Iñigo had drunk deep of the faithful heritage of the house of Loyola, but the religious motifs had not yet become dominant in his consciousness. He saw himself, interestingly enough, in these fantasied roles as performing "heroic deeds" in the same narcissistic style as before. The fact that the deeds were done in the name of Christ and his virgin mother is less impressive than their narcissistic style. There is continuity in change.

Iñigo was experiencing a form of regression which loosened the structure of his ego ideal, resulting in the increased availability of energies tied up in the maintenance of the structure. The ego ideal effectively binds large amounts of narcissistic potential, and the regressive loosening of the chivalrous ideal made available such narcissistic elements as could be diverted into other idealizing fantasies. It is curious, of course, that the religious motif should come to the fore under the pressure of sickness, pain, and death.

The process that began at Loyola continued and grew to nearly overwhelming proportions at Manresa. I am suggesting that Iñigo's ego ideal went through a series of radical alterations which involved the dissolution and transformation of a prior system of values. The vicissitudes of Manresa involved the dismantling of the old ego ideal and its replacement by a new one. What is most perplexing is how this transformation came about.

The dissolution of such an important structure in the psychic economy inevitably releases powerful instinctive forces which the ego ideal has served to integrate. This can be described in terms of regression or defusion of instincts, or as redistribution of energy, or, in more encompassing terms, as a restructuring of the self-organization. The essential element is that these basic potentials become diffusely available to other aspects of the psyche and begin to manifest themselves in more primitive, less modified, less differentiated, and less integrated ways (Chasseguet-Smirgel 1973). One result may be an increase in the experience of more direct and insistent expression of sexual fantasies and desires.

Aggressive impulses likewise may come increasingly to the fore. In the thematic development of the inner life of his old ego ideal, these instinctive forces had achieved some degree of acceptable expression and integration in fantasies of brave deeds in the service of some fair maiden. The chivalric code is a striking example of the sublimation of libidinal and aggressive drives in the service of a culturally determined ideal.

The pilgrim set a strategy of attack in which he systematically eliminated all manifestations of his worldly ego ideal. It was essentially an attack on the pleasure principle and on narcissism in all its guises. He denied himself every gratification—sleep, food, warmth, comfort, human companionship—many of them formerly sanctioned by his ego ideal. What comes through with great clarity is the struggle with powerful drives—libidinal, narcissistic, and aggressive.

This process involved an immense degree of inner conflict and turmoil. All the forces of psychic life were in play. The pilgrim consciously set about confronting his instinctual life and brought to bear incredible amounts of relatively effective energy. The picture the ego thus presents is far different from the early psychoanalytic views of the ego as a weak part of the psychic apparatus, dependent in large measure on the forces stemming from id or superego. We can take the liberty of translating the pilgrim's intuition in terms something like this. The ego ideal survives by virtue of its capacity for narcissistic gratification. That capacity must relate to the operation of the pleasure principle in some basic sense. If, therefore, all gratification is rooted out, the ego ideal cannot survive. To the pilgrim, his impulse under grace was to find the will of God—or, more to the point, to find God. It was in that quest that he hoped to fulfill his new found spiritual ideal.

AUTHORITARIANISM

I have discussed the issue of Ignatius' authoritarianism at length;[7] my purpose here is merely to fit this piece into the overall puzzle. There is no escaping the contradictions and conflicts in this aspect of his personality. His submissiveness and resignation to authorities, especially within the church, were prominent in his postconversion spiritually oriented demeanor. He tended to rationalize such directives as the will of God—the same will of God that he sought to come to know and follow as a central theme of his own spirituality. But this profession of submissive obedience has to be considered side-by-side with his stubborn and almost willful pursuit of his objectives regardless of opposition, his unwillingness to accept any lawful decision or order of ecclesiastical or royal superiors without bending every effort to have things turn out as he wished and mobilizing every resource to mold the decision or order to suit his purposes. Ignatius evidently played the cards on both sides of the game.

If we detect a certain disparity between his thinking and rhetoric about the exercise of authority and obedience on the one hand, and some of his actions on the other, there is also some suggestion of ambivalence about having and using power and authority. He was reluctant to accept the role of General, even though he was the obvious and universal choice; he remained ambivalent about continuing to carry the burdens of office and even tried unsuccessfully to resign. In the light of these factors, we would be hard pressed to avoid the impression that Ignatius had to deal with significant conflicts over the issue of authority.

I suggest that these conflicts were underlain by the basic conflict of identification at the very foundation of his inner psychic life. The ideal of submission, self-denial, and the complete commitment of self to the will of another in holy obedience would in this view reflect the maternal identification that played a dominant part in shaping his postconversion ego ideal and personality. The image of the authority figure, the possessor of power and influence, the one who commands and is obeyed, reverberates with the masculine and paternal identification that remained as the persistent residue of the image of Beltrán de Loyola.

These two powerful sources of internalized structure played out their conflictual and ambiguous roles in the heart and mind of Ignatius. Try as he might, he was never able to resolve or integrate these warring factions. The dominance of one or the other, as well as the precarious balance between them, found various expressions in his relationships with fellow Jesuits, in his governance of the Society, in his relationships with authority figures in the church and the body politic, and even in his mystical life.

THE SPIRITUAL ASCENT

XXIII

MYSTICAL EXPERIENCE

I have discussed Ignatius' mysticism at length and will add a few unifying observations here. I have emphasized the shifts in his core identifications and the role they played in his mystical experience. To a large extent, the feminine aspects of his character play the dominant role in his mysticism, reflected in his yearning for love, his intense affectivity, his passivity and submissive yielding to the divine embrace, and the overwhelming experience of copious tears to the point of physical disability. I have suggested that at some level, his mystical absorption may have its psychic roots in the yearning of the abandoned child for its lost mother. The repeated floods of tears would stem from the joy of reunion with the lost mother. I would not want to insist too emphatically on the hypothesis; nonetheless, it does fit with the rest of the psychological portrait of the saint.

The interplay between Ignatius' mystical life and his narcissism provides somewhat firmer ground for psychoanalytic speculation. Viewed through the psychoanalytic lens, his mysticism can be seen as the major locus of sublimation for his narcissism. It is an unequivocal expression of grandiosity. At crucial points along the troubled path of the pilgrim, we are told of divine apparitions that confirm, support, encourage, and reinforce his conviction and heroic efforts. Taken simply as an expression of psychic needs and processes, for example, the vision at La Storta is as powerful an expression of grandiosity as any clinician could imagine. If the account were not cloaked in the language of religious impulse and divine intervention, we would have to regard it as delusional. The extent to which these episodes served to reinforce his newly structured ego ideal and his resolution and sense of himself as the chosen servant of his king and Lord remains a matter of conjecture. My guess is that they played a significant part in maintaining his newfound narcissistic equilibrium.

Psychoanalytic theorists have repeatedly associated mystical states with early infantile states of symbiotic union or merging. Ernest Jones (1913) was the first to associate the "God-complex" with narcissism, or with what he later termed an unconscious fantasy of complete identification with God. He also identified the unitive ecstasy of mystical experience with the merger of the ego with the ego ideal in a regression to a primitive form of narcissism (Jones 1923). Chasseguet-Smirgel (1975) sees the ego ideal as the repository of primary narcissism with which the individual seeks to achieve reunion that can be experienced in the loftiest mystical experiences as a "reunion with the mother prior to the loss of fusion" (p. 217). This may have different connotations from the more traditional notion of a regression to primary narcissism in mystical states (Epstein 1990).

The fact that these experiences took place in states of altered consciousness and in a realm removed from everyday human psychic experience brings into consideration the issues of the nature of the God-representation in these contexts and how we are to understand the peculiar nature of the mystical episode itself. The experience of God as an object in the psychic representational world of every human being is a product of a host of developmental factors that contribute to the distillation and integration of those experiences in the form of a special and unique mental representation (Rizzuto 1979).

The God-representation in the mind of Ignatius undoubtedly derives in large part from the images of his father and mother—perhaps more from the mother, as the source of affective acceptance and love, than from the image of his father, but certainly involving some balance of the influence of both. The imagery is also cast in terms of majesty, infinite power, wisdom, and strength. The Divine Majesty of whom Ignatius speaks so constantly is a representation of the earthly majesties of Ignatius' experience, magnified to the immensity and transcendent glory of the divine. The images of the *Spiritual Exercises* in particular express the elements of this internal representation.

But the God-representation is not an object-representation[1] like any other. The most useful formulation I have found for thinking about transcendent experiences of this kind is the notion of transitional experience (Meissner 1978, 1984, 1990). The essential aspect of transitional experience is that it straddles subjective and objective realms of experience and thus partakes simultaneously of both. The model derives from Winnicott's notion of the transitional object (Winnicott 1953)—the doll or blanket or whatever other object that acts as the substitute for the mother, a sort of bridge between the infant's symbiotic attachment to the mother and the beginnings of investment in reality. In this view, the infant creates the mother that he requires in order to satisfy basic needs in the same context in which the real mother responds optimally to the child's expressed needs. The mother-object is thus created even as it is experienced. The experience itself is at one and the same time subjective and objective. Winnicott extends this analysis to transitional phenomena that constitute the realm of illusion. It is the basic human capacity for this kind of experience that lies at the root of all cultural experience, including religion. Reading a poem or immersing oneself in music or painting, for example, takes place in the intermediate realm of illusion, in which the esthetic experience is neither subjective nor objective but something of both.

The issue brought into focus by this analysis is the role of creativity in Ignatius' religious and especially his mystical experience. The role of creativity in religious experience parallels or is at least analogous to that in artistic experience. As Oremland (1989) has written:

Creative people seem to be developmentally those singular few individuals who maintain an extraordinary kinship to or maintain continuances of transitional phenomena. Pressing this developmental perspective, these perpetuators of transitional phenomena continue the ongoing capacity to explore the external and the internal anew and to invent, play with, and enact symbols akin to the initial discovering we all experienced as the differentiation of self from nonself progressed. . . . The emphasis on the transitional object closely parallels Emile Durkheim's (1915) description of the capacity to endow things with meaning as being the fundamental element of all religions, primitive and sophisticated alike. Pressing this developmental perspective, the transitional object links the art object and the religious object to the beginning of relatedness, a compelling parallel to the historical linkage between art and religion. Just as a historical commonality exists between the idolmaker and the artist, a developmental commonality seems to exist among the child playing, the primitive idolmaker, and the artist. (pp. 27–28)

For the artist as for the mystic, the creative urge is driven by the unconscious search for the primal object. Oremland (1989) continues: "creating is a reestablishing of primal union at a variety of levels with the primal object. . . . Like object relatedness, creativity seeks a version of the primal object out of which evolves the creation of a new object that is a version of the primal object. Creative individuals repeatedly 'find' their mothers, themselves, and the world anew" (p. 29).

I would submit that in his periods of prayer and mystical ecstasy Ignatius entered such a realm of transitional experience. His mystical experiences were forms of illusion, in Winnicott's sense,[2] that were expressions of his inner subjective psychic life, with its complex needs and determinants—infantile, narcissistic, libidinal, and otherwise—as they intersected with an external reality that can be described in theological terms as divine presence, grace, infused contemplation, and other transcendental manifestations. If one accepts the validity of such a conceptual device it becomes possible, even within the limitations of a psychoanalytic understanding, to speak of the influence of drives, needs, psychic representations (the God-representation), and the whole range of dynamic and adaptational considerations that might impinge on the mystical experience, without passing judgment on the objective reality or unreality of the experience itself. That issue is not for psychoanalysis to decide. It can do no more than reach its own understanding, in terms that do no violence to the objective dimensions of our human efforts to fathom such transcendent experiences that take place at the limits, or the horizons, of human capacity.

TRANSFORMATION AND TRANSVALUATION

We have looked into the face of Iñigo, soldier and courtier, and watched as it changed into the countenance of Ignatius, mystic and saint. We have sketched some of the dynamic aspects of that transformation, but our understanding remains incomplete and fragmented.

It is apparent that Ignatius was dominated by an idealized value-system. The rubric of this system was "the will of God" or as stated formally in the motto of the Society, *ad majorem Dei gloriam:* to the greater glory of God. This is what separates him from the dynamic and courageous Iñigo. What I see, however, in the face of Ignatius is an as-yet poorly understood transformation of the idealism, courage, chivalry, and vanity of the bold Iñigo.

Iñigo's ego ideal embraced a set of values whose significance should

not be overlooked. Values are important constituents of psychic organization in that they are the internalized normative standards in ac-
cordance with which the ego evaluates, judges, organizes, and directs
behavior. Values are thus action- and goal-oriented aspects of the self.[3]
When the ego is functioning more or less maturely and stably in its own
right, that is, when it is functioning more by virtue of its inherent
strength rather than in defensive response to instinctual forces of libido
or aggression, values are salient components of its activity. This is not
to say that the value system can not serve an integrative function for
basically instinctual forces in various forms of compromise formation.
That it does so and how it does so are difficult and perhaps undecidable
matters, but I feel certain that such diversion of instinctual, including
narcissistic, energies is an important aspect of the value system.

Iñigo de Loyola came to his mature years with a strongly formed system of values, which contributed in no small fashion to the strength of
his personality. Under the impact of the experiences at Pamplona, at
Loyola, and at Manresa, there was a marked metamorphosis in that
personality and in that system of values. Along with the change there
was a redistribution of the narcissistic investment that gave the ideal of
Iñigo its force and vitality. Adherence to values of that ego ideal carried
with it the narcissistic gratification and ego enhancement associated
with ambition fulfilled, ideals realized, or goals attained.

The value system, then, can be regarded as significant in the integration of narcissistic libido and ego and superego activity in a coherent
and well-functioning self-structure. Narcissistic sustenance of the
ego ideal and its inherent values strengthens and reinforces the value
system. The same investment increases the self-esteem essential for
mature ego- and self-functioning. The value system thereby serves an
integrative function within the self. That the value system embedded in
the chivalric ideal was a source of strength and ego enhancement for
Iñigo is more than likely. The motivations that in part drove him to
extremes in action at Pamplona were indeed love of country and devotion to a cause, but in a more profound sense there lies the narcissistic
need to serve an ego ideal and observe its inherent values. To have acted
otherwise would have meant the depreciation of self-esteem and the
depressive anxiety of guilt and/or shame.

We have traced the dissolution of Iñigo's ego ideal to the sickbed at
Loyola. That dissolution was initially partial and superficial, prompted

by the external circumstances of sickness, proximity to death, physical deformity, and so on. While this destructive process was taking place, there was also a constructive process at work, without which the struggle at Manresa would have ended in disaster. The extension of this process supplied the psychologically organizing and self-structuring dimension of the future course of the pilgrim. There was a metamorphosis in values which marked the *terminus a quo* and its transition to the *terminus ad quem*. The constructive intrapsychic developments can probably best be traced in terms of the display of these value-transformations.

Along with the beginnings of the negative dissolution, there arose positive promptings. These first appeared as fantasies of heroic deeds after the manner of the saints, highly colored by the residues of the old ego ideal—cast in an almost chivalrous mode. But they introduced an essential new element, the love of God, which was to become in time the overriding consideration in the pilgrim's course. There was, in other words, introduced at that early point a new set of values—at first no more than implicit—different from his own inner value system. Not that his perception of the values inherent in the lives of the saints was utterly new. Rather, it was exquisitely prepared by his family's religious tradition, his education, the strong religious culture of Catholic Spain. But the significant point is that these spiritual values, inherent in the reality, both social and cultural, of Iñigo's world, had never been assimilated as operative parts of his functioning value system.

Iñigo's perception of these spiritual values forces us to realize that values can indeed be spiritual values. It is important to clarify what is implied in this notion. If one accepts, as men of religious conviction do, the existence of God and an order of spiritual realities, that order has an inherent structure and value dimension that characterizes it and distinguishes it from other orders of reality. The existence of such an order of reality and its inherent values is a vital determinant in the lives of the saints which Iñigo made the subject of his reflections. The nature of the spiritual order is the burden of revelation, and the formulation and understanding of its implications and the values it implies are the work of systematic theology.

In Iñigo's case, the values inherent in the lives of the saints were first assimilated to his old ego ideal. He saw the heroic deeds of the saints as projections of heroic chivalry to the level of the service of God rather than to the service of a human lord. He bears testimony to this assimilation when he tells that later, after his departure from Loyola, "He continued his way to Montserrat, thinking as usual of the great deeds he was going to do for the love of God. As his mind was filled with the adventures of Amadis of Gaul and such books, thoughts corresponding to these adventures came to his mind" (Vita 17). Plainly, then, the initial mechanism involved an ego orientation and perception of an order of values, followed by assimilation of these perceived values to a preexistent internalized value system. The impulses he felt stirring within him were still cast in the frame of his phallic narcissistic preconversion ego ideal. It is immediately apparent that these sets of values are so radically different that they could not coexist in a coherent value-system. The conflict had to come to light sooner or later, and its intensity would be determined by the extent to which the respective values had been effectively internalized.

The significant point, then, is that the transformation taking place in Iñigo at this time did not consist in the substitution of one value system for another. The value system that had sustained Iñigo over the years and stirred him to noble and heroic deeds was too solidly established to collapse without a struggle. Iñigo hints at the beginnings of this conflict when he observes that he began to feel dry and dissatisfied with fantasies of worldly glory, but when he thought of the heroics of the saints he felt cheerful and satisfied. The integration of these value-systems had to be the work of the ego in its synthetic function.

It seems that at first Iñigo's ego sought to reconcile these divergent value-systems by assimilating the newly perceived spiritual values to the older and more evidently narcissistic system. But as his understanding of the dimensions of the new value-system deepened, he was gradually compelled to face the impossibility of reconciliation. But this realization and understanding took time, and during that time the only partially grasped values inherent in the spiritual orientation were more or less adherent to the older structure. Eventually they would achieve greater autonomy and precipitate the crisis of Manresa.

So it was that Iñigo de Loyola, as he lay on his convalescent bed, began to experience the transformation of his own inner values. He found himself shifting from a narrower, narcissistic, even juvenile ideal and set of values to a broader, nobler, more spiritual orientation. The shift somehow implied that the order of spiritual realities, which his religion had taught him, gradually entered into a new relation in which there was borne in on him the actuality of its existence and its pertinence to himself. This realization and the process by which it became operative in him were fundamentally an activity of the ego, accepting and internalizing this segment of reality. This implied a new awareness and a deepened understanding. It implied also an initial and possibly hesitant commitment of himself to the values that slowly became apparent to him.

The degree to which the old values dominated Iñigo's ideal as he set forth from the castle of Loyola is reflected in his meeting with the Moor. Here was the old Iñigo, hand ready to sword, aggression ready to leap forth to the defense of a somewhat libidinized relation to a woman. That the fair lady in question was the mother of Christ in itself bears the burden of multiple determinants and implications. But the incident has richer overtones. The impulse to pursue the demands of the old ideal brought with it conflict and uncertainty. Iñigo was, in fact, like Buriden's donkey standing between two bundles of values, uncertain which to follow in order to reach some degree of narcissistic satisfaction.

The vigil before the altar of our Lady gives us another clue. Iñigo dedicated himself as a knight might to the service of his Lady. The gesture is a magnificent compromise between the ingrained demands of the old ideal and the incipient promptings of the new, religiously oriented and motivated scheme of values. Iñigo here remains a knight, in the ideal of chivalry, but he tries to bring that ideal to the service of the Mother of God. This attempt to cling to the remains of the old ideal is doomed to failure. The old ideal and the new values could not tolerate compromise. The old would have to be uprooted to make room for the new.

These episodes reveal the increasing insistence of the new set of values for acceptance. They also reveal Iñigo's effort of to come to grips with the conflict in these value systems. The conflict was not to be resolved so easily, however, but only at the cost of tremendous upheaval and struggle. It was perhaps some inner sense that guided Iñigo to the cave of Manresa, where the struggle could be waged in earnest. There he had to work through the full fury of superego aggression, as we have seen; but the resources for meeting that onslaught had to be derived from other sources within the psychic economy.

The constructive and synthetic process through which the pilgrim had to pass can be envisioned as consisting in the reorganization of an ego ideal, in which narcissistic dynamisms could be meaningfully invested in a new and internally realized system of values. This reorganization of the ego ideal was an essential step toward reconstituting the balance of psychic forces, which had been so badly disturbed. In terms of a reconstituted ego ideal, it became possible once again for aggressive impulses to be integrated with libidinal energies.

The necessary leverage for this reorganization derived from the internalized value system which the pilgrim came to embrace as a vital part of his existence. The value system, a schema of Christian and spiritual standards, already existed and was culturally determined. In this sense, it had to be assimilated and internalized. But in a deeper sense, the process cannot be limited to the mere acceptance of a prior set of values. To internalize such standards and norms means to personalize them, to make them a functioning part of one's inner psychic reality. In the process of internalization, such values are modified, changed, given a uniqueness as specific as the personality of which they are a part. They must become an integral and functional part of the person, sharing generalized meaning with his fellow men, but also with a meaning uniquely related and relevant to himself.

The work of assimilation and integration implicit in internalization is proper to the ego, but to an ego working in harmony with the superego and at each phase subject to its continuing influence. Values must be perceived, recognized, however implicitly, considered, and accepted. Cognitive functions of the ego play an essential role. The reality, maturity, and viability of such values depend in great measure on the ego's capacity for reality-testing and orientation. The ego's basic capacity to relate to the real can be distorted by influences stemming from id or from superego. The value structures themselves are permeated by ideals that necessarily involve superego derivatives—with specific reference to the ego ideal and an ideal self. By the same token, values can be eroded by deneutralized instinctual influences which flood the ego with aggressive, or libidinal impulses or distorted more subtly by the defensive or drive-dependent demands of the superego.

The distortion of values by superego influences is the more likely prospect in general because the superego has a role in the formation of values. The integration of values into the psychic structure demands a compromise with the unconscious demands of the superego. Anna

Freud (1936) has observed that the division of functions between ego and superego is apparent only when they are in conflict; when they are functioning normally without conflict, superego and ego act as one. The fluctuating alignment and division of these psychic agencies make it all the more difficult to draw a clear line of demarcation between them. Values are assimilated and internalized primarily by the ego, but only under the influence of and in concert with the superego.

The ego ideal in this context can be viewed as that part of the superego which sets up the standards by which the ego maintains its own sense of narcissistic enhancement. If the ego fails to live up to the ego ideal, the superego punishes the ego. The measure of conformity to the ego ideal is ego enhancement; the measure of deviance is ego deflation, guilt or shame. Where the ego deviates from the demands of ego ideal and superego, conflict arises between ego and superego. However, the agency of change and modification is the ego, for it is the ego that carries its face open to the world and reality and is subject to the modifying influences of that reality.

Internalization of values and the corresponding modification of the ego ideal must be engineered by the ego, but they cannot be accomplished without superego compliance. Carrying as it does the unconscious residues of infantile experience, particularly those derived from parental identifications, the superego along with its expression in the ego ideal is not easy to change. Consequently the ego can meet tremendous superego resistance, as was Iñigo's experience.

One cannot think of the process in any mechanical sense. The ego does not assimilate a set of values and then present them to the superego. Rather, the complex apprehension of the ego initiates a process that issues into value formation only in so far as the functioning of ego and superego are conjoined in it. Values are not internalized without superego compliance and conjoined activity. The ego ideal lies at the interface of ego and superego and is profoundly affected by both sets of functions. For values to be incorporated into it requires the activity of ego as well as the permissive endorsement of superego. To this extent, superego itself is modified.

Thus the experience of Iñigo, from the initial promptings to the crucial resolution of his inner struggle on the banks of the Cardoner, was a dramatic dialogue between ego and superego. While the crucial and decisive events took place there, the issue was not closed. Values are never completely internalized. They are constantly in process, with varying degrees of security, always in a sense being internalized. Even though the crisis of Manresa had been left behind, we can often sense the disciplined effort of the mature Ignatius to reinforce and secure what had been won. No man can root out the past.

The man of Loyola was endowed with strong passions, powerful libidinal, narcissistic, and aggressive drives. The whole of his inner life in a sense evolved out of the need to adapt to and master those drives. In his later life, we cannot fail to be impressed with the rigor of his efforts to maintain that mastery. Long hours of prayer, frequent and repeated self-examination, exercises of penance and mortification, were all part of the continuing effort of his ego to preserve and deepen the sense of internalization and realization of the spiritual values he had made his own. For it was in the reaffirmation of these values and in the renewed effort to live and act in accord with their standards that greater degrees of psychic integration were achieved, greater mastery of instinctual forces was guaranteed, and through the progressive fusion of instincts richer resources of neutralized energy were made available for constructive ego efforts.

What I have been describing in metapsychological terms I have chosen to call "transvaluation." The transformation of Iñigo the hidalgo to Ignatius the saint was wrought through such a transvaluation. Transvaluation is primarily a function of the ego operating in conjunction with superego in the active creation of a system of values inherent in the ego ideal which modifies the preexistent value schema of the ideal. From a theologically informed and spiritually oriented perspective, one might conclude that the primary, underived source of psychic power available to the ego as the primary agency of this process is the energizing action of grace. In these terms, the remarkable transvaluation of Iñigo de Loyola can be regarded as an effect of grace that found expression through powerful and dynamic psychological processes.

One of the central and determining aspects of this process of transvaluation had to be Iñigo's deep-seated and strongly motivated identification with Christ, his Lord and Master. It was this core identification, operating at an unconscious level, that provided the substance of his postconversion ego ideal. It drew to itself all of the narcissistic libido unleashed in his conversion crisis and regression. If there had been messianic strains in his preconversion self, these narcissistically determined elements could come to rich fruition and focus around the Christ-identification. It answered his narcissistic needs most effectively—to be like Christ would be to fulfill his most ardent wishes to be singled out as one of God's heroes, one of God's chosen saints—like the heroic and self-sacrificing images of Francis and Dominic and Onofrius that had so stirred his imagination on the sickbed of Loyola.

That identification also solved his conflicts over aggression, since it was the suffering Christ that he followed and wished to imitate, the Christ who wandered the earth without a place to lay his head, who was poor and had to beg for his daily bread, the Christ who ultimately was rejected, humiliated, tortured, and crucified. Any occasion in which Ignatius had to suffer painful afflictions became a reason to glory in his infirmities and suffering, for through them he was walking in the path of the Savior. The identification with Christ, in other words, became the vehicle of masochistic fulfillment and gratification, all in the service of a narcissistic and religious ideal. The same identification enabled his psyche to consolidate the resolution of the libidinal conflicts that had so consumed and later tormented him and that were so strikingly resolved in his vision of the Blessed Mother at Loyola. The dramatic and massive repression that took place on that occasion could find powerful reinforcement by putting himself in the place of Christ, who was pure and chaste beyond any question or reproach.

So it seems that the identification with Christ, operating in the unconscious depths of his mind and reflected more superficially in his acting out of the imitation of Christ, was overdetermined[4] and served multiple functions in his psychic economy. In the beginning the focus fell fervently and simplistically on imitating the behavior and manner of the life of Christ. Only gradually did it evolve into a more spiritually meaningful and mature internalization of the spiritual values inherent in the Christian ideal. In particular it integrated the derivatives of his powerful narcissism, his stifled and conflicted aggression, and his repressed but rebellious sexual and libidinal drives in a way that was consistent with his ego ideal and formed the basis for the articulation of his saintly psychic and spiritual identity. The integration took place on several levels. If the identification with Christ could serve these multiple functions in helping to resolve conflictual and drive-related compromises in the integration of Ignatius' personality structure, it also encompassed the internalization of spiritual values that were embedded in the figure and teaching of Christ. These values were gradually internalized and consolidated to become a central component of Ignatius' ego ideal, and the centerpiece of his revitalized and transformed spiritual identity.

The substantive effect of this process was internal growth within the ego itself. Solely from the point of view of the psychology of the ego, that growth is achieved through increasing integration within the ego and between ego and superego and by the progressive integration of instincts and the resultant availability of psychic potential to the ego for its conflict-free synthetic and integrative functions. The correlate of this growth is an enrichment and deepening of the sense of identity. Identity is linked to the internalization of a value system and its integration in a cohesive self-structure. To speak of one is to imply the other. What the pilgrim experienced, then, pari passu, was growth in his own sense of identity—more fully realized as he grew in internal realization of a fuller, more realistic, and more spiritual system of values.

LETTER FROM IGNATIUS
TO ARCHBISHOP
GIAN PIETRO CARAFA (1536)

APPENDIX A

The life and everlasting happiness which we all desire so much is founded in an interior and genuine love of God our Creator and Lord. And this life that we desire binds us all together in a firm bond of sincere, true, and unfeigned affection in the same Lord, who desires to save us if it were not for our weakness, our faults, and our accumulated misery. These reflections led me to make up my mind to write this letter. One will not find in it the bombastic style affected by so many, and which I do not condemn if it is well ordered in our Lord. I realize that, when one has left the world and cast aside its dignities and fleeting honors, we can easily believe that he has no longer any relish for the empty honor and esteem of mere words. For he will understand that he who makes himself less in this world will be greater in the next. Every consideration, therefore, being set aside which might incite to disturb or undo true interior and enduring peace, I ask, by the love and reverence of Christ our Creator, Redeemer, and Lord, that this letter be read in the same spirit of affection in which it is written. So true is this affection that I beg and beseech His infinite goodness with all the strength that He has so graciously given me to bestow on you both in this life and in the next as many blessings both for body and soul as He will bestow on me in the most holy service which we are bound to render Him.

With a purpose, therefore, that is prompt and ready to be of service to all those whom I know to be servants of my Lord, I will touch upon three points, and I will be as simple and sincere as perfect candor and frankness require. Not that I wish to lay down an opinion or offer advice, but it is my purpose to persuade and urge that we take care always to lay our petitions before our Lord, from whom comes all enlightened opinion and sound counsel.

In the first place I think I have sufficient reason, founded on arguments that are sound and conjectures that are sufficiently probable, to be afraid of even entertaining the thought of loosening in any way the bonds of the community which God has given you. In speaking thus I am moved by a feeling of true peace, love, and charity. I think it would be for the greater praise and service of God our Lord for it to remain even more firmly compact. Indeed, I do not give full expression to my thought on this point. I wondered what might be the source of this feeling of assurance; and after commending the matter earnestly and often to God our Lord, I thought I would write as lesser people do with those in higher station if they can be of service in giving good advice in something which concerns the service of God our Lord. The chances are that they will not make use of any direct or indirect occasion of doing so.

Secondly, I am not scandalized or disedified when a person in such a position as yours makes his noble origin or the dignity of his station in life a reason for indulging greater elegance in dress or the furnishings of his apartment, especially if he does so with a thought of those externs who may come to deal with him. For even this can be done with a view to one's needs or the circumstances of time and place. And yet we should keep before our mind only that which is perfect. And for this reason I think it would be the part of wisdom to call to mind saints like the blessed Francis and Dominic and others of the long ago, and consider especially their manner of life in dealing with their associates and the example they gave at the time they were forming their orders. We should have recourse to the true and sovereign Wisdom to ask for greater light and to obtain that clearness of vision which will order everything to His greater service and praise. Many things are lawful which are not expedient, as St. Paul says of himself; and we must not give others the occasion of indulging a weakness but should serve as an example for their advancement, especially those of our own household, whose eyes and ears are more attentive to the words and actions of their superior.

Thirdly, I hold it as an established truth that God our Lord has created everything in this present life for the service and good of men, and this is true with all the greater reason in regard to those men who are more perfect. Now, since your pious and holy congregation is a way to perfection—in fact, is the state of perfection—I have no doubt, indeed I firmly believe, that even though they do not preach or engage in any of the corporal works of mercy, they are justified in expecting food and clothing according to the order of divine charity. They are leading a blameless life under obedience, and have, therefore, more time for occupations that are more spiritual and more important. They can thus accept this support which will help them to increase their praise and service of their true Creator and Lord. It seems, therefore, to be very good and a much safer procedure to place everything in the hands of Christ our Lord, for whose sake we do everything for the greater edification of all, and because this will be the best way of preserving and enlarging the pious and holy community which you have already begun.

But we must weigh well the reasons which others who are not so courageous or who find themselves in greater solicitude for the things of this world or the necessities of life may allege in an opposite sense, and who base their stand on apparently solid arguments. They assert that it would be very difficult for them to continue for any length of time in such an order for three reasons which stand out very clearly. First, they are without the bare necessities of life, and yet they do not beg; second, they do not preach; and third, they do not practice the corporal works of mercy, such as burying the dead, saying Mass for the dead, and so on. Even if they did not beg, as I have said, but performed some of their works in public, such as preaching and so on, they would awaken an interest in other members of the clergy, moving some to repentance and others to help them to preserve and increase their numbers. If they had neither facilities nor opportunities for such works, they should take the trouble to ask some parishes to call upon them for help in burying the dead and in praying for them and offering Masses gratis. I should think that, if they were thus to serve our Lord in pious works, the people would feel more inclined to support them with great charity. I might say that, even though they did no begging but put all their trust in the Supreme Goodness, this would be enough to guarantee their support. Men of weaker faith, or those who bear the responsibilities of authority, might object to this and say that St. Francis and others of the blessed who thought they had as much confidence and trust in God did not for this reason neglect to take proper means to see that their houses were preserved and grew in number for the greater service and praise of the Divine Majesty. To do otherwise would have seemed to them rather to tempt the Lord they aimed at serving and to act in a way that would not be in keeping with His service.

I omit other reasons of greater moment, as I do not wish to commit them to writing, since they were not conceived by me originally but were raised and suggested by others. It is enough for me to offer you these reasons which I have weighed and examined, and do this with perfect candor and frankness. Instead of harm, only profit can result from always having recourse to God our Lord, to ask that in His infinite and sovereign goodness He grant new remedies for new ills. May He be pleased in His usual kindness and sovereign grace to lay His most holy hand on all, so that all will turn out to His greater service and praise, just as I desire, and always pray and beseech Him in the interest of my own undertakings.

(Epistolae I, 114–118 [Letter 11]; in Young, 1959, pp. 28–31)

WRITINGS OF IGNATIUS
CONCERNING HOLY OBEDIENCE

APPENDIX B

LETTER TO THE MEMBERS OF THE SOCIETY
IN PORTUGAL ON PERFECT OBEDIENCE

May the perfect grace and everlasting love of Christ our Lord greet and visit you with his most holy gifts and spiritual graces.

1. Obedience Is To Be the Characteristic Virtue of the Society

It gives me great consolation, my dear brothers in our Lord Jesus Christ, when I learn of the lively and earnest desires for perfection in His divine service and glory which He gives you, who by His mercy has called you to this Society and preserves you in it and directs you to the blessed end at which His chosen ones arrive.

And though I wish you all perfection in every virtue and spiritual gift, it is true (as you have heard from me on other occasions), that it is in obedience, more than in any other virtue, that God our Lord gives me the desire to see you signalize yourselves. And that, not only because of the singular good there is in it, so much emphasized by word and example in Holy Scripture in both Old and New Testaments, but because, as Saint Gregory says: "Obedience is the only virtue which plants all the other virtues in the mind, and preserves them once they are planted." And insofar as this virtue flourishes, all the other virtues will flourish and bring forth the fruit which I desire in your souls, and which He claims who, by His obedience, redeemed the world after it had been destroyed by the lack of it, *becoming obedient unto death, even death on a cross* [Phil. 2:8].

We may allow ourselves to be surpassed by other religious orders in fasts, watchings, and other austerities, which each one following its institute holily observes. But in the purity and perfection of obedience together with the true resignation of our wills and the abnegation of our understanding, I am very desirous, my dear brothers, that they who serve God in this Society should be conspicuous, so that by this virtue its true sons may be recognized as men who regard not the person whom they obey, but in him Christ our Lord, for whose sake they obey.

2. The Foundation of Obedience

The superior is to be obeyed not because he is prudent, or good, or qualified by any other gift of God, but because he holds the place and the authority of God, as Eternal Truth has said: *He who hears you, hears me; and he who rejects you, rejects me* [Luke 10:16]. Nor on the contrary, should he lack prudence, is he to be the less obeyed in that in which he is superior, since he represents Him who is infallible wisdom, and who will supply what is wanting in His minister, nor, should he lack goodness or other desirable qualities, since Christ our Lord, having said, *the scribes and the Pharisees sit on the chair of Moses, adds, therefore, whatever they shall tell you, observe and do; but do not act according to their works* [Matt. 23:2–3].

Therefore I should wish that all of you would train yourselves to recognize Christ our Lord in any superior, and with all devotion, reverence and obey His Divine Majesty in him. This will appear less strange to you if you keep in mind that Saint Paul, writing to the Ephesians, bids us obey even temporal and pagan superiors as Christ, from whom all well-ordered authority descends: *Slaves, obey those who are your lords according to the flesh, with fear and trembling, in singleness of heart, as to Christ, not serving to the eye as pleasers of men, but as the slaves of Christ doing the will of God from your heart, giving your service with good will as to the Lord and not to men* [Eph. 6:5–7]. From this you can judge, when a religious is taken not only as superior, but expressly in the place of Christ our Lord, to serve as director and guide in the divine service, what rank he ought to hold in the mind of the inferior, and whether he ought to be looked upon as man or rather as the vicar of Christ our Lord.

3. Degrees of Obedience
Obedience of Execution and of the Will

I also desire that this be firmly fixed in your minds, that the first degree of obedience is very low, which consists in the execution of what is commanded, and that it does not deserve the name of obedience, since it does not attain to the worth of this virtue unless it rises to the second degree, which is to make the superior's will one's own in such a way that there is not merely the effectual execution of the command, but an interior conformity, whether willing or not willing the same. Hence it is said in Scripture, *obedience is better than sacrifice* [1 Sam. 15:22]. For, according to Saint Gregory, "In victims the flesh of another is slain, but in obedience our own will is sacrificed."

Now because this disposition of will in man is of so great worth, so also is the offering of it, when by obedience it is offered to his Creator and Lord. How great a deception it is, and how dangerous for those who think it lawful to withdraw from the will of their superior, I do not say only in those things pertaining to flesh and blood, but even in those which of their nature are spiritual and holy, such as fasts, prayers, and other pious works! Let them hear Cassian's comment in the Conference of Daniel the Abbot: "It is one and the selfsame kind of disobedience, whether in earnestness of labor, or the desire of ease, one breaks the command of the superior, and as harmful to go against the statutes of the monastery out of sloth as out of watchfulness; and finally, it is as bad to transgress the precept of the abbot to read as to contemn it to sleep." Holy was the activity of Martha, holy the contemplation of Magdalene, and holy the penitence and tears with which she bathed the feet of Christ our Lord; but all this was to be done in Bethany, which is interpreted to mean, the house of obedience. It would seem, therefore, that Christ our Lord would give us to understand, as Saint Bernard remarks, "that neither the activity of good works, nor the leisure of contemplation, nor the tears of the penitent would have pleased Him out of Bethany."

And thus my dear brothers, try to make the surrender of your wills entire. Offer freely to God through his ministers the liberty He has bestowed on you. Do not think it a slight advantage of your free will that you are able to restore it wholly in obedience to Him who gave it to you. In this you do not lose it, but rather perfect it in conforming your will wholly with the most certain rule of all rectitude, which is the divine will, the interpreter of which is the superior who governs you in place of God.

For this reason you must never try to draw the will of the superior (which you should consider the will of God) to your own will. This would not be making the divine will the rule of your own, but your own the rule of the divine, and so distorting the order of His wisdom. It is a great delusion in those whose understanding has been darkened by self-love, to think that there is any obedience in the subject who tries to draw the superior to what he wishes. Listen to Saint Bernard, who had much experience in this matter. "Whoever endeavors either openly or covertly to have his spiritual father enjoin him what he himself desires, deceives himself if he flatters himself as a true follower of obedience. For in that he does not obey his superior, but rather the superior obeys him." And so he concludes that he who wishes to rise to the virtue of obedience must rise to the second degree, which, over and above the execution, consists in making the superior's will one's own, or rather putting off his own will to clothe himself with the divine will interpreted by the superior.

Obedience of the Understanding

But he who aims at making an entire and perfect oblation of himself, in addition to his will, must offer his understanding, which is a further and the highest degree of obedience. He must not only will, but he must think the same as the superior, submitting his own judgment to that of the superior, so far as a devout will can bend the understanding.

For although this faculty has not the freedom of the will, and naturally gives its assent to what is presented to it as true, there are, however, many instances where the evidence of the known truth is not coercive and it can, with the help of the will, favor one side or the other. When this happens every truly obedient man should conform his thought to the thought of the superior.

And this is certain, since obedience is a holocaust in which the whole man without the slightest reserve is offered in the fire of charity to his Creator and Lord through the hands of His minister. And since it is a complete surrender of himself by which a man dispossesses himself to be possessed and governed by divine providence through his superiors, it cannot be held that obedience consists merely in the execution, by carrying the command into effect and in the will's acquiescence, but also in the judgment, which must approve the superior's command, insofar, as has been said, as it can, through the energy of the will bring itself to this.

Would to God that this obedience of the understanding were as much understood and practiced as it is necessary to anyone living in religion, and acceptable to God our Lord. I say necessary, for as in the celestial bodies, if the lower is to receive movement and influence from the higher it must be subject and subordinate, the one body being ordered and adjusted to the other, so when one rational creature is moved by another, as takes place in obedience, the one that is moved must be subject and subordinated to the one by whom he is moved, if he is to receive influence and energy from him. And, this subjection and subordination cannot be had unless the understanding and the will of the inferior is in conformity with that of the superior.

Now, if we regard the end of obedience, as our will so our understanding may be mistaken as to what is good for us. Therefore, we think it expedient to conform our will with that of the superior to keep it from going astray, so also the understanding ought to be conformed with his to keep it from going astray. *Rely not on your own prudence* [Prov. 3:5], says Scripture.

Thus, they who are wise judge it to be true prudence not to rely on their own judgment even in other affairs of life, and especially when personal interests are at stake, in which men, as a rule, because of their lack of self-control, are not good judges.

This being so, we ought to follow the judgment of another (even when he is not our superior) rather than our own in matters concerning ourselves. How much more, then, the judgment of the superior whom we have taken as a guide to stand in the place of God and to interpret the divine will for us?

And it is certain that this guidance is all the more necessary in men and matters spiritual, as the danger in the spiritual life is great when one advances rapidly in it without the bridle of discretion. Hence Cassian says in the Conference of the Abbot Moses: "By no other vice does the devil draw a monk headlong, and bring him to death sooner, than by persuading him to neglect the counsel of the elders, and trust to his own judgment and determination."

On the other hand, without this obedience of the understanding it is impossible that the obedience of will and execution be what they should be. For the appetitive powers of the soul naturally follow the apprehensive and, in the long run, the will cannot obey without violence against one's judgment. When for some time it does obey, misled by the common apprehension that it must obey, even when commanded amiss, it cannot do so for any length of time. And so perseverance fails, or if not this, at least the perfection of obedience which consists in obeying with love and cheerfulness. But when one acts in opposition to one's judgment, one cannot obey lovingly and cheerfully as long as such repugnance remains. Promptitude fails, and readiness, which are impossible without agreement of judgment, such as when one doubts whether it is good or not to do what is commanded. That renowned simplicity of blind obedience fails, when we call into question the justice of the command, or even condemn the superior because he bids us do something that is not pleasing. Humility fails, for although on the one hand we submit, on the other we prefer ourselves to the superior. Fortitude in difficult tasks fails, and in a word, all the perfections of this virtue.

On the other hand, when one obeys without submitting one's judgment, there arise dissatisfaction, pain, reluctance, slackness, murmurings, excuses, and other imperfections and obstacles of no small moment which strip obedience of its value and merit. Wherefore Saint Bernard, speaking of those who take it ill when commanded to do things that are unpleasant, says with reason: "If you begin to grieve at this, to judge your superior, to murmur in your heart, although outwardly you fulfill what is commanded, this is not the true virtue of patience, but a cloak for your malice."

Indeed, if we look to the peace and quiet of mind of him who obeys, it is certain that he will never achieve it who has within himself the cause of his disquiet and unrest, that is, a judgment of his own opposed to what obedience lays upon him.

Therefore, to maintain that union which is the bond of every society, Saint Paul earnestly exhorts all *to think and say the same thing* [1 Cor. 1:10], because it is by the union of judgment and will that they shall be preserved. Now, if head and members must think the selfsame, it is easy to see whether the head should agree with the members, or the members with the head. Thus, from what has been said, we can see how necessary is obedience of the understanding.

But how perfect it is in itself, and how pleasing to God, can be seen from the value of this most noble offering which is made of the most worthy part of man; in this way the obedient man becomes a living holocaust most pleasing to His Divine Majesty, keeping nothing whatever to himself; and also because of the difficulty overcome for love of Him in going against the natural inclination which all men have of following their own judgment. It follows that obedience, though it is a perfection proper to the will (which it makes ready to fulfill the will of the superior), yet, it must also, as has been said, extend to the understanding, inclining it to agree with the thought of the superior, for it is thus that we proceed with the full strength of the soul—of will and understanding—to a prompt and perfect execution.

4. General Means for Attaining Obedience

I seem to hear some of you say, most dear brothers, that you see the importance of this virtue, but that you would like to see how you can attain to its perfection. To this I answer with Pope Saint Leo, "Nothing is difficult to the humble, and nothing hard to the meek." Be humble and meek, therefore, and God our Lord will bestow His grace which will enable you to maintain sweetly and lovingly the offering that you have made to Him.

5. Particular Means for Attaining Obedience

In addition to these means, I will place before you three especially which will give you great assistance in attaining this perfection of obedience.

Seeing God in the Superior

The first is, as I said at the beginning, you do not behold in the person of your superior a man subject to errors and miseries, but rather him whom you obey in man, Christ, the highest wisdom, immeasurable goodness, and infinite charity, who, you know, cannot be deceived and does not wish to deceive you. And because you are certain that you have set upon your own shoulders this yoke of obedience for the love of God, submitting yourself to the will of the superior in order to be more comformable to the divine will, be assured that His most faithful charity will ever direct you by the means you yourselves have chosen. Therefore, do not look upon the voice of the superior, as far as he commands you, otherwise than as the voice of Christ, in keeping with Saint Paul's advice to the Colossians, where he exhorts subjects to obey their superiors: *Whatever you do, do it from the heart, as serving the Lord, and not men, knowing that you will receive from the Lord the inheritance as your reward. Serve the Lord Christ* [3:23–24]. And Saint Bernard: "whether God or man, his substitute, commands anything, we must obey with equal diligence, and perform it with like reverence, when however man commands nothing that is contrary to God." Thus, if you do not look upon man with the eyes of the body, but upon God with those of the soul, you will find no difficulty in conforming your will and judgment with the rule of action which you yourselves have chosen.

Seeking Reasons to Support the Superior's Command

The second means is that you be quick to look for reasons to defend what the superior commands, or to what he is inclined, rather than to disapprove of it. A help toward this will be to love whatever obedience shall enjoin. From this will come a cheerful obedience without any trouble, for as Saint Leo says: "It is not hard to serve when we love that which is commanded."

Blind Obedience

The third means to subject the understanding which is even easier and surer, and in use among the Holy Fathers, is to presuppose and believe, very much as we are accustomed to do in matters of faith, that what the superior enjoins is the command of God our Lord and His holy will. Then to proceed blindly, without inquiry of any kind, to the carrying out of the command, with the prompt impulse of the will to obey. So we are to think Abraham did when commanded to sacrifice his son Isaac [Gen. 22:2–3]. Likewise, under the new covenant, some of the holy Fathers to whom Cassian refers, as the Abbot John, who did not question whether what he was commanded was profitable or not, as when with such great labor he watered a dry stick throughout a year. Or whether it was possible or not, when he tried so earnestly at the command of his superior to move a rock which a large number of men would not have been able to move.

We see that God our Lord sometimes confirmed this kind of obedience with miracles, as when Maurus, Saint Benedict's disciple, going into a lake at the command of his superior, did not sink. Or in the instance of another, who being told to bring back a lioness, took hold of her and brought her to his superior. And you are acquainted with others. What I mean is that this manner of subjecting one's own judgment, without further inquiry, supposing that the command is holy and in conformity with God's will, is in use among the saints and ought to be imitated by any one who wishes to obey perfectly in all things, where manifestly there appears no sin.

6. Representation

But this does not mean that you should not feel free to propose a difficulty, should something occur to you different from his opinion, provided you pray over it, and it seems to you in God's presence that you ought to make the representation to the superior. If you wish to proceed in this matter without suspicion of attachment to your own judgment, you must maintain indifference both before and after making this representation, not only as to undertaking or relinquishing the matter in question, but you must even go so far as to be better satisfied with, and to consider as better, whatever the superior shall ordain.

7. Final Observations

Now, what I have said of obedience is not only to be understood of individuals with reference to their immediate superiors, but also of rectors and local superiors with reference to provincials, and of provincials with reference to the general, and of the general toward him whom God our Lord has given as superior, his vicar on earth. In this way complete subordination will be observed and, consequently, union and charity, without which the welfare and government of the Society or of any other congregation would be impossible.

It is by this means that Divine Providence gently disposes all things, bringing to their appointed end the lowest by the middlemost, and the middlemost by the highest. Even in the angels there is the subordination of one hierarchy to another, and in the heavens, and all the bodies that are moved, the lowest by the highest and the highest in their turn unto the Supreme Mover of all.

We see the same on earth in well-governed states, and in the hierarchy of the Church, the members of which render their obedience to the one universal vicar of Christ our Lord. And the better this subordination is kept, the better the government. But when it is lacking everyone can see what outstanding faults ensue. Therefore, in this congregation, in which our Lord has given me some charge, I desire that this virtue be as perfect as if the whole welfare of the Society depended on it.

8. Final Exhortation

Not wishing to go beyond the limits set at the beginning of this letter, I will end by begging you for the love of Christ our Lord, who not only gave us the precept of obedience, but added His example, to make every effort to attain it by a glorious victory over yourselves, vanquishing the loftiest and most difficult part of yourselves, your will and understanding, because in this way the true knowledge and love of God our Lord will possess you wholly and direct your souls throughout the course of this pilgrimage, until at length He leads you and many others through you to the last and most happy end of bliss everlasting.

From Rome, March 26, 1553.
The servant of all in our Lord,
Ignatius

(Epistolae IV, 669–681 [Letter 3304]; in Tylenda, 1985, pp. 72–83)

SECTIONS ON OBEDIENCE FROM THE
CONSTITUTIONS OF THE SOCIETY OF JESUS

Part VI, "The personal life of those already admitted or incorporated into the Society"

Chapter 1
"What pertains to obedience."

[547] 1. In order that those already admitted to profession or to membership among the formed coadjutors may be able to apply themselves more fruitfully according to our Institute in the service of God and the aid of their fellowmen, they themselves ought to observe certain things. Although the most important of these are reduced to their vows which they offer to God our Creator and Lord in conformity with the apostolic letters, nevertheless, in order that these points may be further explained and commended, they will be treated in this present Part VI. . . .[1]

All should keep their resolution firm to observe obedience and to distinguish themselves in it, not only in the matters of obligation but also in the others, even though nothing else is perceived except the indication of the superior's will without an expressed command. They should keep in view God our Creator and Lord, for whom such obedience is practiced, and they should endeavor to proceed in a spirit of love and not as men troubled by fear. Hence all of us should exert ourselves not to miss any point of perfection which we can with God's grace attain in the observance of all the Constitutions [A][2] and in our manner of proceeding in our Lord, by applying all our energies with very special care to the virtue of obedience shown first to the sovereign pontiff and then to the superiors of the Society.

Consequently, in all the things into which obedience can with charity be extended [B], we should be ready to receive its command just as if it were coming from Christ our Savior, since we are practicing the obedience to one in His place and because of love and reverence for Him. Therefore we should be ready to leave unfinished any letter or anything else of ours which has been begun and to apply our whole mind and all the energy we have in the Lord of all that our obedience may be perfect in every detail [C], in regard to the execution, the willing, and the understanding. We should perform with great alacrity, spiritual joy, and perseverance whatever has been commanded to us, persuading ourselves that everything is just and renouncing with blind obedience any contrary opinion and judgment of our own in all things which the superior commands and in which . . . some species of sin cannot be judged to be present. We ought to be firmly convinced that everyone of those who live under obedience ought to allow himself to be carried and directed by Divine Providence through the agency of the superior as if he were a lifeless body which allows itself to be carried to any place and to be treated in any manner desired, or as if he were an old man's staff which serves in any place and in any manner whatsoever in which the holder wishes to use it. For in this way the obedient man ought joyfully to devote himself to any task whatsoever in which the superior desires to employ him to aid the whole body of the religious Institute; and he ought to hold it as certain that by this procedure he is conforming himself with the divine will more than by anything else he could do while following his own will and different judgment.

[548] A. These first Declarations which are published along with the Constitutions bind with the same authority as the Constitutions. Therefore in the observance, equal care should be bestowed upon the Declarations and the Constitutions.

[549] B. Such things are all those in which some sin is not manifest.

[550] C. The command of obedience is fulfilled in regard to the execution when the thing commanded is done; in regard to the willing when the one who obeys wills the same thing as the one who commands; in regard to the understanding when he forms the same judgment as the one commanding and regards what he is commanded as good. And that obedience is imperfect in which there does not exist, in addition to the execution, also that agreement in willing and judging between him who commands and him who obeys.

[551] 2. Likewise, it should be strongly recommended to all that they should have and show great reverence, especially interior reverence, to their superiors, by considering reverencing Jesus Christ in them; and from their hearts they should warmly love their superiors as fathers in Him. Thus in everything they should proceed in a spirit of charity, keeping nothing exterior or interior hidden from the superiors and desiring them to be informed about everything, in order that the superiors may be the better able to direct them in everything along the path of salvation and perfection. For that reason, once a year and as many times more as their superior thinks good, all the professed and formed coadjutors should be ready to manifest their consciences to him, in confession, or secret, or in another manner, for the sake of the great profit this practice contains. . . . Thus too they should be ready to make a general confession, from the last one they made, to the one whom the superior thinks it wise to designate in his place.

[552] 3. All should have recourse to the superior for the things which they happen to desire; and without his permission and approval no individual should directly or indirectly request, or cause to be requested, any favor from the sovereign pontiff or from another person outside the Society, either for himself or for someone else. He should be convinced that if he does not get that which he desires from the hands of the superior or with his approval, it is not useful to him for the divine service; and that if it is useful for that service, that he will get it with the consent of the superior, as from the one who holds the place of Christ our Lord for him.

LETTER FROM IGNATIUS TO SISTER TERESA REJADELLA (18 JUNE 1536)

APPENDIX C

When I received your letter a few days ago, it gave me much joy in the Lord whom you serve and desire to serve better, to whom we ought to attribute all the good we find in creatures. As you said he would in your letter, Caceres has informed me at length about your affairs, and not only about them, but also about the suggestions or guidance he gave you for each particular case. On reading what he says to me, I find nothing else he need have written, although I should have preferred to have the information in a letter from you, for no one can describe sufferings so well as the one who actually experiences them.

You ask me to take charge of you for the love of God our Lord. It is true that, for many years now, his divine Majesty has given me the desire, without any merit on my part, to do everything I possibly can for all men and women who walk in the path of his good will and pleasure, and, in addition, to serve those who work in his holy service. Since I do not doubt that you are one of these, I am pleased to find myself in the position of being able to put what I say into practice.

You also beg me to write to you what the Lord says to me and that I should say freely what I think. What I feel in the Lord I will tell you frankly with a right good will and if I should appear to be harsh in anything, I shall be more so against him who is trying to upset you than against you. The enemy is troubling you in two ways, but not so as to make you fall into the guilt of sin which would separate you from God's greater service and your own greater peace of soul. The first thing is that he sets before you and persuades you to cultivate a false humility; the second that he strives to instill into you an excessive fear of God with which you are too much taken up and occupied.

As to the first point the general course which the enemy follows with those who love and begin to serve God our Lord is to set hindrances and obstacles in their way. This is the first weapon with which he tries to wound them—by suggesting "How will you be able to live in such penance all your life without the enjoyment of parents, friends and possessions and in so solitary a life, without even some slight relief? In another way of life you could save yourself without such great dangers." He thus gives us to understand that we have to live a life which is longer, on account of the trials which he sets before us, than that of any man who ever lived, whereas he hides from us the many and great comforts and consolations which the Lord is wont to give to such souls, if the man who has newly embraced the Lord's service breaks through all these difficulties, choosing to want to suffer with his Creator and Lord.

Then the enemy tries his second weapon, namely, boasting or vainglory, giving the soul to understand that there is much goodness or holiness in it and setting it in a higher place than it deserves. If the servant of the Lord resists these darts with humility and lowers himself, not consenting to be what the enemy would persuade him to be, he brings out the third weapon which is that of false humility. That is, when he sees the servant of the Lord so good and humble that, when he does what the Lord commands, he thinks it all valueless and looks at his own shortcomings, not at any glory for himself, the enemy puts it into his mind that if he discovers any particular blessing given him by God our Lord, any good deed done, or good intention or desire, he is sinning by another kind of vainglory, because he speaks in his own favour. Thus the enemy strives that he should not speak of the blessings received from his Lord, so that there shall be no fruit either in others or in the person himself, for the recognition of what one has received is always a stimulus to greater things, although such speaking must be practised with restraint and motivated by the greater profit both of others and of the man himself, as opportunity provides and when others are likely to believe what we say and profit by it. When, however, we make ourselves humble, he tries to draw us into false humility, that is, into humility which is exaggerated and corrupt. Of this your words are clear evidence, for after you relate certain weaknesses and fears which are true of you, you say, "I am a poor nun, desirous, it seems to me, of serving Christ our Lord"—but you still do not dare to say: "I am desirous of serving Christ our Lord" or: "The Lord gives me desires to serve him," but you say: "I seem to be desirous." If you look closely, you will easily see that those desires of serving Christ our Lord do not come from you, but are given you by our Lord. Thus when you say: "The Lord has given me increased desires to serve him," you praise him, because you make his gift known and you glory in him, not in yourself, since you do not attribute that grace to yourself.

Thus we ought to be very circumspect and if the enemy lifts us up, humble ourselves, going over our sins and wretchedness. If he casts us down and dejects us, we ought to look upwards with true faith and hope in the Lord, going over the benefits we have received and considering with how much love and kindness he waits for us to be saved, whereas the enemy does not care whether he speaks the truth or lies, but only that he may overcome us. Ponder well how the martyrs, standing before their idolatrous judges, declared themselves Christ's servants. So you, standing before the enemy of the whole human race and tempted in this way by him, when he wants to deprive you of the strength the Lord gives you and wants to make you weak and full of fear with his snares and deceits, do not merely say that you are desirous of serving our Lord— rather you have to say and confess without fear that you are his servant and that you would rather die than separate yourself from his service. If he represents God's justice to me, I bring up his mercy; if he puts God's mercy before me, I reply with his justice. If we would avoid trouble, this is the way wherein we should walk, that the deceiver may in turn be deceived, applying to ourselves the teaching of Holy Scripture which says: "Beware that thou be not so humble that in excessive humility thou be led into folly" [cf. Eccles. 13:11].

Coming to the second point, as the enemy has placed in us a certain fear under the cloak of a humility which is false, and so suggests that we should not speak even of good, holy and profitable things, so he brings in its train another, much worse fear, namely whether we may not be separated and cut off from our Lord as outcasts—in great measure on account of our past lives. For just as through the first fear the enemy attained victory, so he finds it easy to tempt us with this other. To explain this in some measure, I will bring up another device the enemy has. If he finds a person with a lax conscience who passes over sins without adverting to them, he does his best to make venial sin seem nothing, mortal sin venial and very grave mortal sin of small account— so that he turns the defect he finds in us, that of too lax a conscience, to account. If he finds some other person with an overtender conscience—

a tender conscience is no fault—and sees that such a person casts far from him mortal sin and as far as possible venial sin—for it is not in us to avoid all—and even tries to cast away from himself every semblance even of small sin, imperfection or defect, then the enemy tries to throw that good conscience into confusion, suggesting sin where there is no sin and defect where there is perfection, so that he may disturb and trouble us. In many instances where he cannot induce a soul to sin and has no hope of ever bringing that about, at least he tries to trouble it.

In order to explain more clearly how fear is caused, I shall speak, although briefly, of two lessons which the Lord usually gives or permits. The one he grants, the other he permits. That which he gives is interior consolation, which casts out all trouble and brings one to the full love of our Lord. To such souls as he enlightens with this consolation, he reveals many secrets, both at the time and later. In short, with this divine consolation, all trials are a pleasure and all weariness rest. In the case of him who walks in this fervour, warmth and interior consolation, there is no burden so great that it does not seem light to him, no penance or other trial so severe that it does not seem sweet. This shows and lays open to us the way we ought to follow, fleeing from the contrary. This consolation does not always remain with us—it follows its due seasons according to the divine ordinance. All this is to our profit, for when we are left without this divine consolation, then comes the other lesson, which is this—our old enemy now puts before us all possible obstacles to turn us aside from what we have begun, and he harasses us unceasingly, everything being the contrary of the first lesson. He often makes us sad, without our knowing why we are sad, nor can we pray with any devotion, contemplate or even speak of or listen to the things of God our Lord with relish or any interior delight. Not only this, but if he finds us to be weak and much dejected by these harmful thoughts, he suggests that we are entirely forgotten by God our Lord and we come to imagine that we are separated from God in everything and that however much we have done and however much we want to do, it is of no value whatsoever. Thus he strives to bring us into distrust of everything and we shall see that our great fear and weakness is caused in this way, for we then make too much of our miseries and are too passive in the face of his false arguments. It is necessary, therefore, that he who fights should look to what condition he is in. If it is consolation we should be humble and lowly and think that afterwards the test of temptation will come. If temptation, darkness or sadness comes, we must withstand it without any irritation and wait with patience for the Lord's consolation which will shatter all troubles and darkness coming from without.

It now remains for me to say something of what we feel when we read about God our Lord, how we must understand what we read and, when it is understood, learn to profit by it. It often happens that our Lord moves and impels our soul to one particular course or another by laying it open—that is, speaking within it without the sound of any voice, raising it all to his divine love, without our being able to resist what he suggests, even if we wanted to do so. In accepting such suggestions, we must of necessity be in conformity with the Commandments, the precepts of the Church, obedient to our superiors and full of complete humility, for the same divine Spirit is in all. Where we can frequently deceive ourselves is that after this consolation or inspiration, while the soul remains in bliss, the enemy creeps in under cover of joy and an appearance that is good, to make us exaggerate what we have felt from God our Lord, so as to make us disturbed and upset in everything.

At other times he makes us undervalue the lesson received, making us disturbed and ill at ease, because we cannot perfectly carry out all that has been shown to us. More prudence is necessary here than in any other matter. Many times we must restrain our great desire to speak of the things of God our Lord. At other times we must speak more than the desire or movement we have in us prompted—for in this it is necessary to think more of the good of others than of our own desires. When the enemy thus strives to increase or diminish the good impression received, we must go forward trying to help others, like someone crossing a ford. If he finds a good passage, that is, if he confidently hopes that some good will follow, he goes forward. If the ford is muddy, that is, if others would take scandal at his good words, then he always draws rein, seeking a more suitable time and hour to speak.

(Epistolae I, 99–107 [Letter 7]; in Rahner, 1960, pp. 331–5; also in Young, 1959, pp. 18–23)

ON SOURCES AND VERSIONS
OF THE *SPIRITUAL EXERCISES*

APPENDIX D

While it seems certain that Iñigo based his formulations in the *Exercises* on his own experiences, we have very little idea of where and when these observations were set down. The locale may have been the cave, the hospital, the Dominican priory, Villadordis, or anywhere else in the area of Manresa. We also have limited knowledge of the sources for Iñigo's notes. His confessor at Montserrat, the kindly monk Dom Chanon, had given him a copy of Cisneros' *Ejercitatorio de la vida espiritual* (in Latin *Exercitatorium Spirituale*), a manual of spiritual practice that was printed in Castilian and Latin in 1500. Cisneros' work may have served as an important basis for the *Exercises* (Leturia 1941, 1949). The overall framework, the division into "weeks," the organization of some subjects of meditation on the basis of the life and death of Christ, and certain of the annotations are probably derived from the earlier work. Both Ignatius and Cisneros were influenced by the Brothers of the Common Life, a Dutch order founded by Gerard Groote to promote the *Devotio moderna*, whom Ignatius would have encountered in Paris (after 1528) if not before (Buonaiuti 1968). We also know that Ignatius was influenced by the *Devotio moderna* and was especially devoted to the *Imitatio Christi* (Leturia 1941; O'Malley 1982; Boyle 1983).

Expert opinion, of course, differs considerably. Some argue that the *Exercises* were essentially written before he left Manresa, completed except for such sections as the Rules for Thinking with the Church (Codina 1926). Codina (1938) argues convincingly that the *Exercises* were the fruit of the Manresa experience and were not written prior to that time. Others hold that the experiences reflected in the teachings of the *Exercises* must extend over more than the few months of Iñigo's conversion. Certainly, the book as we now know it was complete by 1541. On Ignatius' own testimony, the book derived from the Manresa experience in 1522. Consequently, we can assume that the essential parts of the *Exercises* were written in the context of the Manresa experience, but that other elements may have been added during the following years (Dudon 1949; Leturia 1941; Pinard de la Boullaye 1950).

In the course of writing the autobiography, Gonsalvez da Camara asked Ignatius about the composition of the *Exercises*. "He answered that the *Exercises* were not composed all at one time, but things that he had observed in his own soul and found useful and which he thought would be useful to others, he put into writing—the examination of conscience, for example, with the idea of lines of different lengths, etc. The forms of election in particular, he told me, came from that variety of movement of spirits and thoughts which he experienced at Loyola, while he was still convalescing from his shattered leg" (Vita 99).

Further testimony comes from a letter from Laynez to Polanco in June 1547, which recounts that at Manresa Ignatius made a general confession of his whole life and began those meditations which were included in the *Exercises*. Polanco himself tells us that Ignatius had begun to formulate his ideas about the *Exercises* from the beginning of his conversion experience and during the course of his first experiment at Manresa, but that subsequently his own practice and experience had helped him to perfect this first effort. Nadal, arguing in 1553 against the charge that the *Exercises* had been composed by an uneducated man, wrote:

When for the first time Ignatius wrote a good part of the *Exercises*, he had not yet begun to study for when, after his departure from the country . . . he prepared to wipe out his sins by contrition and general confession, he wrote down in a notebook the meditations which helped him the most for this. Then, when he was meditating on the life of Jesus Christ he did the same, but in such a manner that he showed his confessor . . . not only what he wrote then, but all the thoughts which seemed to be (inspirations from) the spirit. Once he had finished his studies, he gathered together these first sketches of the Exercises, added many things, put them all into order, and gave them to the Apostolic See to be examined and judged. (Epistolae IV, 826)

The consensus view is that Ignatius revised his notes for the *Spiritual Exercises* in the light of his Paris experience, probably around 1535. Larrañaga (1956) argues from the testimony of the first companions and from internal evidence that further revisions may have been made during the Roman period, from 1538 to 1541, prior to the issuance of the *Versio Prima*.

It seems, therefore, that the essentials of the *Exercises* were already written down at Manresa. Moreover, at the trials at Alcalà in 1526–1527 (see chapter 8), the pilgrim was able to provide his examiners with at least the substance of the first week, and later at Salamanca he was able to give Bachelor Frías a copy of the *Exercises*. The same was true in 1535, when a copy of the *Exercises* was handed over to the Inquisitor Valentin Lievan.

The original version was written in Spanish, Iñigo's native tongue, and is preserved in the so-called autograph, which is actually a transcription by a copyist with corrections of a number of errors in Iñigo's handwriting. There are three principal Latin translations of this text. The oldest, the *Versio Prima*, is contained in a manuscript of 1541 and may well date to Ignatius' sojourn in Paris (1528–1535); it is not impossible that he himself could have translated it. Whoever wrote the translation knew little Latin and provided a quite literal translation of the original Spanish. In 1546–1547 the *Versio Vulgata* was made under Ignatius' direction by André des Freux, an accomplished Latinist. At the time, it was thought expedient to provide a more polished text before offering the slim volume to the Holy See for approval. The Vulgate version is certainly more elegant, but also less literal. Both Latin versions were handed over to the censors appointed by Paul III and were approved in the papal brief of 31 July 1548. The Vulgate version of des Freux became the official text. It was not until 1919 that the *Versio Prima* was also printed in the critical edition of the *Monumenta Historica Societatis Jesu*.

Because of the liberties in the Vulgate version as compared with the rough but often more expressive text of the *Versio Prima*, in 1835 the General of the Society of Jesus, John Roothaan, published a new Latin translation. This third version has largely replaced the Vulgate in practical use, but the older versions retain their prestige in that they have been solemnly approved by the Church, and during the last eight years of his life Ignatius himself used the Vulgate version in giving the Exercises.

NOTES

Introduction
Psychohistory, Psychobiography, and Psychoanalysis

1. The pitfalls were amply demonstrated in Freud's ventures into psychobiography, especially his attempt to analyze Leonardo da Vinci (Freud 1910) and his ill-fated participation in the Woodrow Wilson biography (Bullitt and Freud 1966).

2. Countertransference includes those reactions and attitudes experienced by the analyst insofar as they are rooted in his own unconscious—whether they are elicited by the patient's transference or derive in some other way from the analyst's inner world. In the context of psychobiography, these unconscious attitudes would arise in the biographer with regard to the subject of study and would affect the assessment and attitudes of the psychobiographer without his being aware of it.

3. This monumental series, consisting of nearly a hundred volumes, was begun in 1894 and continues to the present. In 1929 the project was moved from Madrid to Rome, where it is published under the auspices of the Institutum Historicum Societatis Jesu. Most of the material in these volumes is based on manuscripts kept in the Archives of the Society of Jesus in Rome.

4. The material pertaining to Ignatius' life and work is contained in the Monumenta Historica Societatis Jesu (MHSJ), in a series of volumes designated the Monumenta Ignatiana (MI). The Spiritual Exercises are found in MI series 2, vol. 1 (1919).

5. Bertrand counts some 6,815 such letters.

6. As Silos (1964) indicates, the *Autobiography* was not a simple straightforward narration, but rather a discerned account. "The author of the rules of discernment is at work sifting, interpreting, controlling, confirming the events, the thoughts, the motions in his soul from the fateful day when a cannonball ended a career and initiated the pilgrimage which began at Pamplona and was to end in Rome. The Autobiography is not a simple narration of a life. It is the history of God's actions in a soul—discerned" (pp. 7–8). Moreover, the mind-set of the narrator is that every step along the way, every episode, every action and reaction, was dictated and guided by the hand of the Lord, drawing him along the predestined path of spiritual growth and glory.

7. The uncritical acceptance of whatever appears in the autobiography as accurate and reliable has been scored as "Jesuit fundamentalism" (Endean 1987). Endean emphasizes that the available documents provide us with no more than a history filtered through the fallible memories and biases of a small group of

witnesses. As a result of this retrospective distortion, our knowledge of the events of Ignatius' life is severely limited.

Chapter 1
Origins

1. *Compendio historical de Guipúzcoa*, quoted in Dudon, 1949, p. 13.

2. The citation is from the fifteenth-century historian Lope García de Salazar.

3. The extent of the wealth and land holdings of the Loyolas in 1536–1539 is detailed by Dalmases (1980).

4. The actual date of Iñigo's birth is a matter of uncertainty and conjecture. There is no trace remaining of any birth or baptismal certificate, and Ignatius himself was apparently uncertain of his precise age. The possible range of his birth year is anywhere from 1491 to 1495. The position of Iñigo as the last of the children born to Marina rests on the testimony of the people of Azpeitia, which was collated in 1595. Ignatius' own remarks made 1493 the probable date, but when this was proposed to his old nurse at the time of his death in 1556, she seemed quite sure that he was two years older than that. Thus, 1491 was the date used by Ribadeneyra, Ignatius' first biographer, in 1572. It remained the accepted date until recent times when the question was reopened and Dudon (1949), the most prominent of modern-era biographers, finally opted with some misgivings for 1493. He notes that it is only by deduction that 1493 can be assigned as the probable year of Iñigo's birth. However, the subsequent discovery of a legal deed drawn up by the official notary of Azpeitia and witnessed in 1505 by Iñigo de Loyola lends support to the 1491 date, since Castilian and Basque law would not allow a male to act as a juridical witness until he had passed his fourteenth birthday. Consequently, at this reading, 1491 would seem to be the most likely date for Iñigo's birth.

5. The custom of wet-nursing was quite common in even late medieval times, especially among the aristocracy. More often than not, the wet nurse took the baby to her own home and raised the child, often for several years. The extended period of separation in Iñigo's case might have been due to conditions in the castle, where there seems to have been no woman of the house until the arrival of Magdalena de Araoz in 1498. In such cases, alienation was unavoidable. In a sermon, a certain Fra Bernardino told his parishioners: "You give your child to be suckled by a sow where he picks up the habits of his nurse. . . . And when he comes home you cry, 'I know not whom you are like; this is no son of ours!'" (Gies and Gies, 1987, p. 285).

6. Anaclitic depression is a condition in young children resembling the clinical expression of adult depression; it is seen in children who have been deprived of their mothers after having developed a relatively normal relationship with her

during the first six months of life. Hospitalism is a form of anaclitic depression, involving both somatic and psychic features, that is seen in infants under eighteen months of age who are subjected to prolonged stays in a hospital or similar institution and are thus deprived of maternal care for that period. Marasmus is a condition of extreme emaciation in young children, usually not due to any obvious or specific cause.

7. The terms "object relation" and "object relationship" refer to the manner in which the person relates to the world around him, especially to other human beings. The capacity for mature object relationships reflects the vicissitudes of a child's developmental experience and can be influenced by fixations, conflicts, and developmental failures.

8. The most noteworthy sequela of early parental deprivation is the tendency to depression that can afflict the individual throughout life, especially when it evolves into a factor in the individual's character structure. The unresolved mourning for the lost mother can also influence relationships with women and make forming mutually satisfying love relationships problematic. There may be long-term narcissistic difficulties involving issues of self-esteem regulation and the prolongation of infantile narcissistic grandiosity. The combination of identification with the lost mother and the wish for reunion may contribute to the unconscious motivation underlying suicidal impulses.

9. The effects of early parental loss may depend on the age and level of development of the child as well as the availability of proper support for facilitating the mourning process (see Furman 1964, 1968, and Furman and Furman 1974). Some findings suggest that a critical factor in determining whether childhood parental loss contributes to the later development of adult depression is the lack of care, defined more in terms of neglect than hostility and more often found after the death of the mother than after the death of the father (see Harris et al. 1986).

10. Aries's thesis, that childhood was not a functional category in the medieval mind or in medieval society owing to the high rate of infant mortality, has had a strong influence on the history of childhood. Shorter (1975) characterized the medieval attitude toward children as "maternal indifference." DeMause (1974) gives this thesis even more extreme and destructive emphasis: "The history of childhood is a nightmare from which we have only recently begun to awaken. The further back in history one goes, the lower the level of child care, and the more likely children are to be killed, abandoned, beaten, terrorized, and sexually abused." This negative and pessimistic view of childhood in the medieval world is challenged by Frances and Joseph Gies (1987).

11. No doubt the youngest son of the Loyolas would have made the rounds of many of these shrines and local sights with his father or brothers. Iparraguirre traces some of these early travels (1957).

Chapter 2
Satin and Sword

1. Nadal remarks in his dialogues that Iñigo "though educated with distinction as a noble at his home, . . . did not devote himself to studies, but moved by a generous ardor, dedicated himself, in conformity with the traditions of the nobility of Spain, to win the favor of the King and of the grandees, and to signalize himself in military glory" (Leturia 1949).

2. Here again assigning exact years is not easy. The dates range from 1496, when Iñigo would have been only five, to 1507, the year of Beltrán's death. Dalmases (1985, p. 29) says that the best conjecture is sometime between 1504 and 1507. Iñigo's tenure at the court of Arévalo lasted over ten years, until the death of Velázquez in 1517. This dating is supported by Martin (1980).

3. Velázquez' wealth, the extent of his holdings, and the opulence of his court are detailed in Martin (1980).

4. His horizons expanded geographically as well—Iparraguirre (1957) recounts the many trips to various towns of Castile that he would have undertaken as a member of the entourage of Velázquez.

5. Ignatius' script has been described in the following terms: "Ignace utilise une écriture calligraphique de copiste, nous voyons déjà une heureuse harmonie entre l'écriture humanistique et la gothique, où se marient les formes les plus anciennes de l'écriture caroline. Une extraordinaire richesse se dégage de ces alliances de formes si diverses: c'est comme si toutes les tendances, toutes les possibilités, toutes les douleurs et toutes les joies, tous les antagonismes avec leurs luttes et leurs espoirs s'étaient rassemblés dans les diverses structures de la psyché." See Affholder, 1960, p. 390. There is an interesting sideline to the study of Ignatius' character in the form of a graphological analysis of several autographs from the years 1536–1556. Among the qualities deduced from this analysis were: remarkable self-possession, autonomy, a sense of interior harmony among drives and functions, tenacity, and sensitivity and compassion. His thought processes are well-organized, . . . clear and methodical, not without a certain rigidity, at times manifesting a degree of obsessional control, but penetrating, and marked by a unique capacity for concentration. His capacity for judgment and discernment was both nuanced and firm, conveying a sense of vigilant control over powerful instinctual and emotional forces. . . . Interior crises of sadness, despair, suffering, inner agony and anxiety can be detected, suggesting an ongoing inner tension and struggle that was overcome by firmness of will and a transforming determination. Certain features also indicate the presence of both masculine and feminine traits, brought into conjunction and more or less harmonious integration. See Affholder (1960). Many points made in this analysis are congruent with some of the conclusions reached in the present study.

6. Phallic narcissism stems from the period of development in which the penis in males prototypically becomes invested with narcissistic libido and thus becomes highly valued and prized. This is the so-called phallic stage of development, usually occurring around the third to fifth year—also known as the oedipal phase. Along with this investment in the penis or its symbolic equivalents comes the threat of its loss in the form of castration anxiety. Phallic narcissistic qualities can be found in females as well as males but take different forms. Qualities associated with this narcissistic configuration are pride in phallic prowess and performance, the search for admiration especially of skill or mastery, a sense of daring, counterphobic behaviors, unwillingness to accept defeat, omnipotence in the face of seemingly impossible obstacles, exhibitionism, assertiveness, and self-aggrandizement. The underlying themes are the wish for admiration of the phallic accomplishment and the need to defend against anxiety from castration fears and vulnerability. Individuals with these character traits tend to be self-centered, independent, difficult to intimidate, often fearless, ready to spring into action—strong personalities that step readily and willingly into positions of leadership (Freud 1931). Reich (1949) described them as "self-confident, often arrogant, elastic, vigorous and often impressive. . . . The outspoken types tend to achieve leading positions in life and resent subordination" (p. 201). To this Kernberg (1979) adds, "Because narcissistic personalities are often driven by intense needs for power and prestige to assume positions of authority and leadership, individuals with such characteristics are found rather frequently in top leadership positions" (p. 33). The narcissistic need in such a personality compels him to take risks and undertake arduous tasks for the sake of winning a narcissistic prize and gaining a position of power and grandiose satisfaction. Moreover, the capacity to maintain self-esteem and integral psychic functioning depends on gaining the required narcissistic gratifications.

7. Behaviors or mental phenomena are drive-determined to the extent that they reflect the influence of basic drives, usually limited to libidinal, narcissistic, and aggressive drives. Defense mechanisms are usually brought into play to limit, channel, regulate, modify, or otherwise modulate drive influences. Identifications can be defensive—defending, for example, against the pain of loss of a loved one—or drive-determined—as, for example, identifications that involve narcissistic determinants. Iñigo's identification with his mother would have been based on the need to defend against the loss; his identification with his father would have involved the integration of phallic narcissism.

8. Dalmases (1985, pp. 36–37) notes that Iñigo was never really a soldier, but, like his father and older brother Martín, was a gentleman in the service of the duke who served in a military capacity when occasion required. For Iñigo, success at arms was his ticket to fame and fortune; the machismo culture of

sixteenth-century Spain required valor and skill at arms for a successful worldly career.

Chapter 3
Pamplona

1. Ignatius' recollection of time seems uncertain. By this account he would have been born in 1495. Later he would say that in 1555 he was 62, putting his birth in 1493. The consensus of historians, as we have noted, is that the best date is 1491. See Tylenda (1985).

2. "Objects" here is used in the psychoanalytic sense as including other persons toward whom libido can be directed in object-cathexis. Objects, therefore, are opposed to ego and, correlatively, object-libido is contrasted with narcissism.

Chapter 4
Conflict and Conversion

1. The rules for discernment of spirits, that is for discriminating between the influence of the good spirit versus the evil spirit, are found in the *Spiritual Exercises* [313–336].

2. St. Francis of Assisi was known as "Il Poverello" because of his love of poverty which he instilled in the Franciscan Order he founded.

3. The psychoanalytic view of the dynamics and consequences of loss have been detailed by Rochlin (1965) in terms of the "loss complex" and by Pollock (1989) in terms of the "mourning-liberation process."

4. Iñigo's obsession with Jerusalem may have been triggered by the introduction to Ludolph's life of Christ, in which the joy and devotion gained from visiting the Holy Land are highly praised. See Tylenda (1985, p. 15).

5. The place of the Virgin Mary as a cultural symbol of these ideals, particularly in southern European cultures, has been traced by Saunders (1981). These dynamics, which I infer were active in Ignatius' time, have remained part of these cultures and in a way determine the character of masculine and feminine gender roles and sustain an ambivalent view of the nature of woman, as madonna and whore. As Saunders argues, the son's erotic tie to the mother results in an idealization that implicitly connects her with the madonna, so that any woman who will have sex with him is automatically associated with the whore.

6. Epigenetic development refers to the pattern of human psychic development emphasized by Erikson (1950, 1959) in which stages of development follow a sequence in which subsequent stages incorporate and build on the accomplishments or lack of accomplishment in preceding stages.

7. Ego-syntonic describes the situation when mental contents or processes are

acceptable to the person's sense of self, particularly with reference to the demands of his sense of integrity, beliefs, and values. The theoretical point for such acceptance was considered to be the ego, but more recent developments would suggest that the self, including its ideals and values, would be more appropriate.

8. If we can rely on our hypothesis of the effects of his early maternal deprivation, this detail may have deeper significance. The mother he had lost in death was in a sense a mother of sorrows. His lingering attachment may have become displaced to the sorrowing Blessed Mother—a devotion that would stay with him until the end of his life.

9. The dark visage of Mary at Montserrat was redolent with ancient associations and unconscious meanings. The cult of the Blessed Mother extends back to the worship of Isis and Diana (see Festugière 1949). Johnson (1989) comments on the iconography of our Lady: "Artistic symbols of the goddess [Diana] accrued to Mary: her dark blue cloak, turreted crown, link with the moon and the stars, with water and wind. The iconography of Mary seated on a royal throne presenting her child to the world was patterned on the pose of Isis with Horus. Similarly, the still-venerated statues of the Black Madonna at Le Puy, Montserrat, and elsewhere derived from ancient black stones connected with the fertility power of maternal deities, black being the beneficent color of subterranean and uterine fecundity" (p. 506).

Chapter 5
Manresa

1. For the function of this mechanism in the context of the Exercises, see Meissner (1963).

2. Object-cathexis refers to the attachment of libido to objects—what Ignatius refers to in the *Exercises* as "inordinate attachment." In psychoanalytic usage, the term most often refers to attachment to other persons, but it can also have the more general connotation of investment in nonhuman objects or their equivalents. The pilgrim's crusade of self-denial was directed to rooting out such inordinate attachments and narcissistic investments.

3. Scruples are a form of obsessional self-doubt and self-criticism that condemn the subject to an unremitting feeling of having done wrong, of having sinned, even when there is no objective data to support that judgment. They are an effect of a harsh superego persistently criticizing the subject and subjecting him to constant self-doubt and guilt. Ignatius suffered mightily from scruples and left a set of rules in the *Exercises* [345–351] for dealing with them.

4. As a general rule, all psychic functions require an optimal degree of exercise in order to maintain effective integration and performance. In principle, this is no different than other organic functions—if muscles are not exercised they

atrophy, if the eye does not receive sufficient visual input (in both intensity and variety of stimulus patterns), vision suffers, and so on. The nature of the stimulus required is different and specific for each system.

5. The term "de-automatization" refers to the loss of autonomy of any given psychic function, usually as a result of some form of regression that shifts the level of functioning from a relatively autonomous one to one that is relatively drive-determined.

6. The vision of the Holy Trinity had a profound effect and remained an important influence for the rest of his life as the record of his *Spiritual Journal* amply attests. See Chapter 15.

Chapter 6
The Spiritual Exercises

1. Discussion of the origins and versions of the *Spiritual Exercises* is found in Appendix D. The version used here is the literal translation from the Spanish by Elder Mullan, S.J., which is based primarily on the original autograph text of Ignatius and is included with commentary in Fleming (1978).

2. A model for this approach to the text is provided by Freud's *Interpretation of Dreams* (1900). On the assumption (fairly well established) that the dreams were for the most part Freud's own, biographers infer that the content and analysis of the dream material offer a basis for inferences about Freud's own psychic life. See Gay (1989).

3. Leturia (1948) discusses the origins and variations of this traditional prayer, as well as the Minor Hours, or Office of the Blessed Virgin Mary, and their numerous influences on the *Spiritual Exercises*.

4. Numbers in brackets [ ] refer to numbered paragraphs in the original autograph text of the *Exercises*.

5. The particular examen was a method devised by Ignatius for the regular daily examination of conscience. He recommended that it be practiced three times daily—on rising in the morning, after dinner, and again after supper. The particular examen was intended as a means for self-betterment and the correction of faults. In contrast, the general examination of conscience was concerned with acknowledging one's sins for the purpose of confessing them and receiving absolution.

6. The general confession was a confession that included all the sins one committed or might have committed during the course of his past life. Such general confessions would be infrequent; Ignatius frequently made such confessions, however, presumably because of his scrupulosity. A general confession was recommended when anyone made the Exercises. See Calveras (1948) for a discussion of the influence of extant confessional manuals not only on the confessional practice reflected in these texts but on the methods of prayer, particularly

the first method. The three methods of prayer are proposed to the exercitant as part of the Spiritual Exercises [238–260].

7. See chapter 5, note 3, for a description of scruples.

8. Ignatius' military mentality is central to the view of his personality advanced by Huonder (1932). But this attribute must be considered in the context of his tact, diplomacy, sensitivity, empathy, and particularly his intensely affective and ecstatic mystical experience—a point made by Leturia (1933) in his critique of Huonder's work. See also Nicolau (1957).

9. For the meaning of transvaluation, see the discussion in chapter 5. Also see chapters 22 and 23 for discussion of various aspects of the modification of narcissism and the ego ideal that may be associated with such transvaluation. As used in the present context, the concept has nothing to do with Nietzsche, who spoke of the transvaluation of all values—but the term has a very different meaning in his vocabulary.

10. Leturia (1941) also points to the influence of both the *Flos* and the *Vita Christi* on the Exercises, particularly in the meditations on the King and the Two Standards.

11. An essential part of Freud's view of the mind and how it works concerns the effects of basic unconscious motivational drives, specifically libido and aggression, as they impact on the mind. One of the ways the mind regulates and controls these drives is by setting up defenses—regression, denial, projection, rationalization, and so on—which determine the extent and the manner in which drive influences are experienced on the conscious level. The drive-and-defense model is only one among the psychoanalytic models of mental functioning, but one that is well suited to the understanding of conflict and its resolution.

12. Compromise formation takes place when the tension between drive and defense reach a point at which drive-derivatives gain access to consciousness—in some modified or distorted form that makes the unconscious repressed material acceptable to the conscious mind. This "return of the repressed" may become conscious in dreams, symptoms, conscious fantasies, misperceptions, and so on. In the compromise both the unconscious desire and the requirements of defense find a degree of satisfaction.

13. See Part V, "Mystical and Spiritual Life."

Chapter 7
The Pilgrim

1. It was a common practice in plague-torn Europe to refuse strangers admittance to the city without a certificate attesting to their good health. See Tylenda (1985).

2. The identity of this lady remains uncertain. If the city was Fondi, she may

have been Beatrice Appiani, wife of Vespesiano Colonna; if Paliano, she was probably Joanna of Aragon, wife of Asconio Colonna. The argument that since Iñigo spoke Spanish, the lady would have to be conversant in that language is persuasive, but not compelling.

3. Dudon (1949) recounts this episode so as to suggest the role of divine providence in Iñigo's adventures: "One night Marc-Antonio Trevisano heard a voice saying to him in his sleep: 'Thou, thou art well sheltered in thy house, and my servant remains outside.' Trevisano was a good man; wherever he lived, at Cyprus, at Venice, he was called the 'Saint.' He arose, went straight to the poor pilgrim, brought him to his home, as though he were bringing in the trophies of conquest. Another time, a rich Spaniard met Iñigo and asked him who he was. Hearing his design of going to Jerusalem, he carried him off to dine with him, and kept him several days, in fact, until the moment of his departure" (p. 76). Hagiographic transference is well demonstrated here. See Meissner (1991).

4. The pilgrim ship carried the German and Dutch pilgrims, the *Negrona* the Spanish and Swiss and a crew of thirty-two. One of the Swiss pilgrims, Peter Fussli, kept a diary of the voyage. See Tylenda (1985).

5. The rock has been an object of simple devotion for centuries; the supposed imprint of the feet can still be seen, although the left impression has been worn away by the kisses of countless pilgrims over the centuries. St. Jerome apparently worshipped there. The rock is analogous to the rock in the Dome of the Rock, from which Mohammed is said to have made his ascension.

6. As he tells the story: "He did not, however, follow their advice, but continuing straight on his way, came upon a town that had been burned and destroyed, and until nightfall met with no one who gave him anything to eat. But at sunset he came to a walled town where the sentries took him into custody, thinking that he was a spy. They put him in a hut close to the gate, and began to examine him, as they usually do with suspects. To all their questions he answered that he knew nothing. They stripped him and searched him even to his shoes, overlooking no part of his person, to see whether he was carrying any letters. But as they could in no wise learn anything from him, they were angry with him and led him to their captain. 'He would make him speak.' When he told them that they had taken away all his covering with his clothes, they would not return it to him, and led him away clad only in his breeches and jacket, as above described.

"While they were on their way, the pilgrim remembered how Christ was led away, although there was no vision here as on other occasions. He was led through three main streets. He went without any sadness, rather with joy and satisfaction. He kept it as a practice to address anyone he met in the direct form of 'you,' finding devotion in the fact that Christ and the Apostles so spoke. As they went along the streets, he fancied that it would be good to give up that custom for the moment, and use the more elevated form of addressing the captain, with some lurking fear of the torture they might inflict on him. But he recognized this as temptation, and told himself that he would not use the courtly manner of speech, not show any reverence, nor even take off his cap. Arriving at the captain's palace, they left the pilgrim in one of the lower rooms, and there the captain spoke to him for a while. But he answered without giving any sign of courtesy, in a few words, with a considerable pause between one and the next. The captain thought he was crazy, and said so to those who had brought him in: 'This fellow has no brains. Give him his things and throw him out!' As he left the palace, he fell in with a Spaniard who was living there, who brought him home, and gave him something with which to break his fast and what was necessary for that night. He left in the morning, and walked until towards evening two soldiers caught sight of him from a tower, and came down to examine him. They brought him to their captain, who was French and who asked him, among other things, where he came from. Learning that he was from Guipúzcoa, he said: 'I am from nearby there,'—probably from the neighborhood of Bayonne—and then went on:'Take him along, give him something to eat, and treat him well.'

"On this journey from Ferrara to Genoa many other things of less importance befell him. He finally reached Genoa, where he was recognized by a Viscayan named Portundo, who on other occasions had spoken to him when he was in the service of the Catholic King. He helped to find him a ship bound for Barcelona, which ran great risk of being taken by Andrea Doria, who gave them chase, as he was then in the service of the French" [Vita 52–53].

Chapter 8
Barcelona, Alcalá, and Salamanca

1. The practice was not at all unfamiliar in the fifteenth and sixteenth centuries, when distinctions of grades by age and level of learning were not as well established as they would be in the seventeenth and eighteenth centuries. See Ariès (1962).

2. The good monk was probably Alfonso de Guerreto (Dudon 1949).

3. The texts studied were Alexandre de Ville-Dieu's *Doctrinale Peurorum*, the *Disticha Moralia* of Cato, Antonio Nebrija's *Introductiones in Latinam Grammaticam*, and finally Virgil's *Aeneid*. See Dalmases (1941).

4. A neurologist might suspect more than devotion on the basis of this information. Organic factors are discussed further in chapter 18.

5. The role of the Beghards and Beguines in medieval spirituality and their relation to the earlier heretical Free Spirit movement are traced in Cohn (1970). The *alumbrados* were the objects of intense prosecution by the Holy Office throughout Castile. They were suspect for their quasi-mystical beliefs and often accused of being secretly Lutherans, probably because they believed prayer alone

could lead to spiritual perfection. They were known for their mystical practices and spiritual trances (Kagan 1990; see also Elliott 1977).

6. Iñigo encouraged frequent communion, a somewhat revolutionary practice that would have brought further suspicion on himself and his companions. Years later he wrote to the community in Azpeitia: "In the early Church members of both sexes received Communion daily as soon as they were old enough. But soon devotion began to cool and Communion became weekly. Then, after a considerable interval of time, as devotion became cooler still, Communion was received on only three of the principal feasts of the year, each one being left to his own choice and devotion to receive oftener, either every three days or every eight days or once a month. And finally, because of our weakness and coldness, we have ended with once a year. You would think that we are Christian only in name if you can calmly and quietly contemplate the condition to which the greater part of the world has come.

"Let it be our glory, then, out of love for so good a Lord and because of the immense benefit to our souls, to restore and renew in some way the holy practices of our forefathers; if not entirely, at least in part, to the extent of monthly confession and Communion, as I have already suggested. Should one wish to go oftener than this, there is no doubt that he would be acting in conformity with the wish of our Creator and Lord, as St. Augustine and other holy doctors assure us. For, after saying 'I neither praise nor condemn daily Communion,' he added, 'but I do exhort you to communicate every Sunday'" (Epistolae I, 161–165; in Young, 1959, pp. 42–45).

7. The questions seem curious. This one seems to have been intended to determine whether Iñigo was a Jewish convert, since many such converts in Spain secretly continued to practice their native religion. To this Iñigo replied, "I spend my Saturdays in devotion to our Lady, and I have no other observances. Furthermore, in my country there are no Jews" (FN I, 174). The question may also have been prompted by the fact that a number of Jewish converts were known to have joined the alumbrados.

8. The mother was María del Vado and the daughter Luisa Velázquez (Dudon 1949; Tylenda 1985; Dalmases 1985).

9. Figueroa apparently believed Iñigo's story, but could not release him until the women returned to corroborate it.

10. In 1545, for example, in connection with some of the false accusations that had been brought against him in Rome and might have affected the work of the Society in Portugal, Ignatius wrote to John III of Portugal an account of his trials before the Inquisition. He reassured the king, "And if your highness wishes to know why there was so much indignant investigation of my case, you should be advised that there was never any question of being involved with schismatics or

Lutherans or Illuminati, for I never knew any of them or had anything to do with them" (Epistolae I, 296–298 [Letter 81]; in Young 1959).

11. See also chapter 14.

12. The view that the subprior was none other than the famed Dominican theologian Petrus de Soto has been challenged by Dominican scholars, who claim that he was never subprior at St. Stephen's and that the supposed encounter with Ignatius never took place. Review of the evidence concludes that our knowledge of the event rests on Ignatius' account and that there is no good reason to question it. The identity of the subprior is unknown. See Codina (1935).

13. Ignatius' account in the Autobiography leaves many questions about his judges in Salamanca unanswered. Early efforts to clarify their identities were marred by a lack of documentation. "Bachelor Frías" is not Martín de Frías, who received a master's degree in 1503, but can only be Sancho de Frías, the vicar general for the bishop of Salamanca. But he did not hold that office during Iñigo's stay there. The vicar general in the summer and autumn of 1527 was Alonso Gómez de Paradinas; it was probably he whom Ignatius called "Paravinhas." The tribunal examining Iñigo was thus composed of Paradinas as judge and three counselors: Francisco de Frías, Hernán Rodríguez de San Isídro, and Sancho de Frías. See Montes (1983).

Chapter 9
Paris

1. In Rabelais' *History of Gargantua and Pantagruel* (1955), Erasmus (under the pseudonym Salsamentarius) discusses conditions at Montaigue in one of his Colloquia with one Lanio, who says, "There, I hear, the very walls reek of theology." Salsamentarius answers, "You are quite right but I brought away from the place nothing except an infected body and a vast collection of lice. . . . the beds were so hard, the food so scanty and unappetizing, and the vigils and labours so heavy, that within a single year many youths of excellent quality and promise died, or went blind or mad, or became infected with leprosy" (cited in Brodrick, 1956, p. 217).

2. Peters (1956) conjectures that Iñigo would have visited Syon Monastery, near Ilseworth on the south bank of the Thames, about two hours' walk from London, where he would have encountered Richard Whitford, a former student at the University of Paris and a friend of both Erasmus and Thomas More. The contact was probably through Vives, whom Iñigo had met in Bruges. Whitford was a widely respected theologian, ascetical writer, and spiritual director. The similarities between his views and those of Ignatius are striking.

3. The translation is from Brodrick (1956, pp. 226–227). The whole question of Ignatius' antipathy to Erasmus and his writings has undergone some revision.

Ribadeneyra had reported a comment by Ignatius that Erasmus' *Enchiridion* cooled his devotion and that he had forbidden the reading of Erasmus in the schools of the Society. Recent study (Olin 1979; O'Reilly 1974, 1979) has challenged this report and shown that no record of such a prohibition of the reading of Erasmus can be found. Ignatius probably knew little of Erasmus and may have been prejudiced by antithetical attitudes toward northern humanism, but their views on many issues were not so disparate. See O'Malley (1982). In Alcalá, Iñigo was frequently in the company of adherents of Erasmus, especially Juan de Vergara. The influence of Erasmus on the *Exercises*, especially on the discernment of spirits, has even been suggested (see Boyle 1983). One can guess at the reasons for Ignatius' lukewarm attitude toward Erasmus. Erasmus' approach to spiritual matters was more moderate, intellectualized, and tempered by the classical learning of the humanist movement. This would not have appealed to the passionate drive of Ignatius' spirituality that insisted on total self-abnegation and unstinting devotion to the will of God in all things. The issue was summarized by Huizinga (1952): "In that robust sixteenth century it seems as if the oaken strength of Luther was necessary, the steely edge of Calvin, the white heat of Loyola: not the velvet softness of Erasmus . . . ; his piety is too even for them, too limp" (p. 189). Similar conclusions regarding Erasmus' ambivalence, vacillation, and need to seek approval and acceptance on all sides were reached by Minnich and Meissner (1978).

4. Dr. Fragus was Jeronimo Frago y Garces, a professor of scripture at the Sorbonne who had befriended Iñigo. He was also from the diocese of Pamplona.

5. It is not clear from his account what the ailment was, since the references to "stomach pains" are rather nonspecific; but kidney stones or gallstones would have been a plausible conjecture. No accurate diagnosis was ever made during Ignatius' life, but these pains afflicted him until his death.

6. The story is recounted in Brodrick (1956, p. 292), who notes that it probably comes from Peralta, who may have gotten it from the student himself. In any case—si non e vero, e ben trovato!

7. The story is from Ribadeneyra based on an eyewitness account; in Brodrick (1956, pp. 292–294). A hagiographic account might envision this episode as reflecting the prowess of the Holy Spirit with the billiard cue. A more mundane consideration is that this spiritual hustler might have spent a few hours in the game room at Arévalo—perhaps even at the billiard table.

8. A brief account of Faber's life and involvement with Ignatius can be found in Ravier (1987, pp. 62–64). See also Bangert (1959). See the account of Xavier's life in Ravier (1987, pp. 64–67). See also Brodrick (1952) and Schurhammer (1973).

9. A brief account of Laynez's life can be found in Ravier (1987, pp. 68–69). A note on Salmerón appears in Ravier (1987, p. 69). See also Bangert (1985).

10. An account of Bobadilla's life can be found in Ravier (1987, pp. 69–70).

11. An account of Rodriguez' life is in Ravier (1987, pp. 67–68).

12. Brief accounts of the three companions' lives are in Ravier (1987, pp. 78–79). A further account of Le Jay can be found in Bangert (1985).

13. The whole business may have been precipitated by the so-called "affair of the placards" which had inflamed anti-Catholic feeling and put the Inquisition on guard. See Wilkens (1978, pp. 197–198). The Protestants, particularly Zwinglian extremist reformers, who were anxious to demonstrate their strength in Paris, put up posters all over the city on the morning of 18 October 1534 attacking the sacrifice of the Mass. The Catholic reaction was strong, and the city was thrown into an uproar. A procession of atonement held the following 21 January precipitated the persecution of heretics—to the point of burnings and tortures. Francis I was one of the instigators of these repressive measures.

14. The Contarinis were a prominent Venetian family; Pietro later became a bishop in Cyprus.

15. Brodrick (1956) recalls one exception—a letter in Spanish to an old friend in Spain in 1546. After that, only "Ignatius." The origins and variations on the name Iñigo are detailed by Verd (1976). Verd concludes that Iñigo himself signed himself "Ynigo" after the custom of the time, but that the proper usage for our own time is "Iñigo."

Chapter 10
Azpeitia

1. His letter reads in part: "I will do all I can to give him a start in his studies, and see that he applies himself and keeps away from bad company. You write: 'If you decide that he is to live where you are, please let me know about what it will cost a year. If you can be of any help to me in this matter of expense, I will see that you are repaid when opportunity offers.' I believe that I understand the literal meaning of your words, if there has been no slip of the pen. You mean that you will appreciate it if your son studies here and that I should do all I can to relieve you of all expense. I do not know what makes you say that or what you mean by it. If it serves any purpose, make your meaning clear. As far as justice and reason are concerned, I do not think that God will permit me to be wanting, since all I seek is His most holy service, your comfort in Him, and your son's progress, in the event you make up your mind to send him here.

"You say that you are delighted to see that I have taken to writing again after so long a period of neglect. Don't be surprised. A man with a serious wound begins by applying one ointment, and then in the course of its healing another, and at the end still another. Thus, in the beginning of my way one kind of remedy was necessary; a little later a different one does me no harm. If I saw that it did, I would not look for a second or a third. . . .

"But to come to the point. I should have written you more frequently during the last five or six years but for two reasons. The first, my studies and my constant association with others, which, however, had nothing to do with temporal interests. The second was that I did not have sufficient reason for thinking that my letters would resound to the praise and service of God our Lord or so comfort my kindred according to the flesh as to make us kindred according to the spirit and to help us both in the things that last forever. The truth is, I can love a person in this life only so far as he strives to advance in the service and praise of God our Lord; for he who loves anything for itself and not for God does not love God with his whole heart. If two persons serve God equally, and one of them is a relative of mine, God wishes us to cherish a greater affection for our natural father than for another. He would have us prefer a benefactor and a relative to one who is neither; a friend and acquaintance to one who is unknown to us" (Epistolae I, 77–83; in Young, 1959, pp. 5–8).

2. Apparently a local custom.

3. Dalmases (1949) notes that the antipathy between the Anchietas and the Loyolas was bitter and longstanding. The rector's proposal that he resign and turn his office over to his nephew García would have eroded the established rights of the patron. The outcome was the assassination of the nephew by adherents of the Loyolas. For earlier details of this controversy, see chapter 3.

4. The letter reads in part: "I well remember the time I spent with you and the determination of the people to carry out certain proposals after they had been laudably and holily drawn up into constitutions. The ringing of bells, for example, for those in mortal sin; that there should be no poor who have to go begging but that all should receive the help they need; the doing away with card playing and forbidding the sale of playing cards; the wiping out of the abuse of women wearing the headdress of the married when they were unwed and offending God. I recall that the observance of these holy rules and constitutions was begun and continued during all the time I spent with you, and that with no little grace and blessing from God to help you in carrying out such salutary designs. But here I cannot be certain of your perseverance, seeing that your constancy may weaken in undertakings that are so upright and so pleasing to the infinite and supreme Goodness" (Epistolae I, 161–165; in Young, 1959, pp. 42–45).

5. He wrote in a postscript: "It seems to me in our Lord that this undertaking which I am going to explain should more properly be yours. There are many reasons; and once you have weighed and considered them, you will find them to be sound. I remember that, when I was at Loyola with you, you begged me to let you know something of the Society which I was hoping to begin. I also believe that God our Lord was waiting for you to take a prominent part in it, so that you could leave behind you a greater memory than others of the family have left. To come to the point, I have tried in spite of my unworthiness to lay with God's grace a firm foundation for this Society of Jesus. We have given it this name with

the pope's approval. It devolves on me, therefore, to exhort you again and again to build on the foundations thus laid, for you will have no less merit in the super-structure than I in the foundation, and all by the hand of God our Lord. I mean, of course, when the opportunity offers, and circumstances seem right and just to you, and His Divine Majesty gives you His most holy grace for it.

"I am writing in the same vein to Doña Mary de Vicuña, as I think that she can be of some help in this matter. Share this letter with my sister, Doña Magdalene, and the lord of Ozaeta, as in my letter to them I have referred them to you. If you know of any others who would be willing to help, they will be doing it for the Lord, who well knows how to repay them with interest. My deepest respects to the lady of the house. She should consider this letter as addressed to her" (Epis-tolae I, 148–151; in Young, 1959, pp. 39–41).

Chapter 11
The Band of Brothers

1. Ignatius recounts Bachelor Hocez's transformation: "During those days in Venice he spent some time giving the Exercises and in other spiritual associations. The more important people to whom he gave them were Masters Peter Contarini and Gaspar De Doctis, and a Spaniard called Rojas. There was also another Spaniard who was called the Bachelor Hocez, who had a good deal to do with the pilgrim and also with the bishop of Ceuta. Although he [Hocez] had some desire to make the Exercises he never carried it into execution. Finally, however, he made up his mind to make them, and after the third or fourth day, opened his mind to the pilgrim to tell him that he had been afraid that some wicked doctrine was taught in the Exercises. Someone in fact had told him as much. It was for this reason that he had brought with him certain books which he could use as protection, if he happened to want to impose these doctrines on him. He found great help in the Exercises, and when they were over he resolved to follow the pilgrim's way of life. He was also the first to die" (Vita 92).

2. Ignatius' letter can be found in Appendix A.

3. Mass stipends are free-will offerings of the faithful for masses to be said for personal intentions. Such stipends have often been an important source of income for poor priests.

4. I will follow here the argument developed by Quinn (1981).

5. See chapter 9.

6. Ignatius postponed celebration of his first mass until 25 December 1538, in the church of St. Mary Major in Rome.

7. Leturia (1940) contends that this date should be a year later, 1538.

8. See the discussion of Ignatius' mystical visions in chapter 16.

9. The documentation from this process has been collected by del Piazzo and Dalmases (1969).

10. Cited in Ravier (1987, p. 95). See the discussion of this question in Ravier, pp. 94–97.

11. One motive for this decision was to preserve and extend the bond of union that had grown up among them. This motif recurs in the Constitutions (VIII, c. I, n. 3, and X, n. 9) where obedience is proposed as an essential means for preserving unity in the Society. See Blet (1956).

12. The essence of the deliberations is summarized by Ravier (1987, pp. 81–94). The discussions and their implications are treated more fully in Toner (1974) and in Futrell (1970). The document was retitled the *Prima Societatis Jesu Instituti Summa* (First Summary of the Institute of the Society of Jesus) by the editors of the Monumenta (MHSJ). The text was reproduced almost completely in the papal bull establishing the Society. See Ravier (1987, pp. 101–107).

13. The source of this inspired tradition was Nadal, who seems to have thought that the entire detailed inspiration for the founding of the Society was implanted in Ignatius during his profound illumination on the banks of the Cardoner. See Calveras (1956).

14. The Franciscans of the Strict Observance form one of the branches of the original Franciscan Order founded by Assisi.

15. See also Castellani (1941). The discrepancy between 1541 and 1542 relates to the varying interpretations of the sources—see the discussion in Leturia (1940).

Chapter 12
The General

1. The early years of Ignatius' generalate and the rapid growth of the Society are detailed in Dudon (1949) and Dalmases (1985), the standard biographies. An especially useful account is presented in Ravier (1989).

2. In addition to his many letters, Ignatius was in the habit of sending "instructiones" to his followers. These more formal documents usually addressed an administrative or spiritual topic in Jesuit life or interpreted some aspect of the General's view on a particular subject. The instructiones tended to be more like treatises, longer and more systematically organized than the letters.

3. One recent commentary describes Ignatius in the following terms: "He came across as a forbidding personality, icily chaste, intellectually certain beyond challenge, preoccupied with obedience and endowed with iron-willed self-control" (Tetlow, 1989, pp. 9–10).

4. The radiance of Ignatius' face was commented on by others, including Philip Neri (Scripta II, 425–426, 428, 488, 491, 499, 559, 1010) and Isabel Roser (FN IV, 145). See Wulf (1977).

5. See my discussion of Ignatius' authoritarian conflicts in chapter 13.

6. Bertrand (1985), adding up the various categories of such documents, reaches the figure of 6,815. See p. 73 et passim.

7. Ravier (1987, p. 265) lists the Roman *Exhortations* (1557), Nadal's *Biographical Essays* (1554–1567), and the lives by Ribadeneyra (1567–1569) and Maffei (1579).

8. Dudon (1949) counted seventy-six houses at the time of Ignatius' death—distributed in twelve provinces spread throughout Europe, Brazil, Japan, and the Indies.

9. Cited in Ganss (1970, p. 309). The idea was espoused by Ribadeneyra as well; see Becher (1977). The reference to Jean Gerson as the author of the *Imitation of Christ* reflects the knowledge of the time. The authorship was long uncertain and frequently attributed to Gerson who wrote other spiritual works. Modern scholarship attributes the *Imitations* to Thomas à Kempis.

10. A specimen of Ignatius' method is available in his *Spiritual Diary*, in the account of his decision regarding the nature of the poverty of the Society, made between 2 February 1544 and 27 February 1545. The decision overturned the previous resolution of this matter made in 1541 by the first companions and approved by Paul III's bull.

11. Ravier (1987) notes that one reason for this was the juridical requirement in some countries that religious superiors be "professed" in order to accept donations, make contracts, and so on. The legal meaning of profession and its implications for the Society were not synonymous; the easiest way to avoid difficulties was to profess superiors in such circumstances.

12. The professed houses were part of Ignatius' ideal vision of the Society. The professed were to live apart in separate communities in which the prescriptions of the Institute and the Constitutions were to be observed with special care and devotion. The professed fathers were to live entirely on alms and were to dedicate themselves to apostolic labors.

13. The Sacred Penitentiary, one of the major tribunals of the Holy See, has jurisdiction over sacramental matters.

14. See the discussion in chapter 13.

Chapter 13
The Constitutions

1. Coemans (1932) concluded that Ignatius and the companions had intended to create formal constitutions from the time they decided to establish a religious order. See also de Aldama (1973).

2. See chapter 12.

3. The account of conscience was the manifestation by the subject to his superior of his mind and heart not only for his own spiritual progress but to enable his superior to better guide and direct him in his apostolic work. Ignatius made this a regular practice in the Society.

4. The term "capitular system" refers to the practice in older religious orders for the community to gather regularly to hear a reading of a chapter of the rules of

the order—thus being referred to as the "chapter." Ignatius did not want to confine his men by imposing the obligation of chapter.

5. Ganss' translation will be followed throughout and referred to henceforth as Constitutions.

6. See the discussion of this portrait of the Superior General in chapter 12.

7. Blet (1956) points out that the two currents in Ignatius' views on obedience—one reflecting the monastic tradition, the other an ideal of religious and apostolic perfection—reflect the dual end of the Society: personal perfection and salvation of others.

8. The letter reads in part: "According to information coming to us from Doctor Torres, whom I sent to the province of Portugal as my representative and visitor in the Lord, I understand that there is a notable failing, among not a few of Ours, in that virtue which is more necessary and essential in the Society than anywhere else, and in which the vicar of Christ, in the bulls of our Institute, most carefully recommends that we distinguish ourselves. I mean the respect, reverence, and perfect obedience to our superiors who hold the place of Christ our Lord, even of His Divine Majesty. . . .

"I command you in virtue of holy obedience to take the following step with regard to the safeguarding of that virtue. If there is anyone who is unwilling to obey you—and I say this, not to you alone but to all superiors or local rectors in Portugal—do one of two things: either dismiss him from the Society, or send him here to Rome if you think that a particular individual can, by such a change, be helped to become a true servant of Christ our Lord. If necessary, keep their highnesses informed, who I doubt will make any objections, in keeping with the spirit and holy good will which God our Lord has bestowed upon them. To retain one who is not a true son of obedience does no good for the kingdom. Nor is there any reason for thinking that such a person, his own soul being so destitute, can help other souls, or that God our Lord would wish to accept him as an instrument for His service and glory.

"We see from experience that men, not only with average talents but even less than average, can often be the instruments of uncommon supernatural fruit, because they are completely obedient and through this virtue allow themselves to be affected and moved by the powerful hand of the author of all good. On the other hand, great talent may be seen exerting great labor with less than ordinary fruit, because being themselves the source of their activity, that is, their own self-love, or at least not allowing themselves to be moved by God our Lord through obedience to their superiors, they do not produce results proportionate to the almighty hand of God our Lord, who does not accept them as His instruments. They achieve results proportioned to their own weak and feeble hands. . . . And while we have enough to do here without burdening ourselves with this additional task from Portugal, we will not decline the added burden because of the special charity which God our Lord causes us to feel toward Portugal" (Epistolae IV, 559–563 [Letter 3105]; in Tylenda, 1985, pp. 65–67).

9. The sections on obedience from the Constitutions are included in Appendix B.

10. Ignatius' views remain totally consistent and unwavering throughout his years as General; the same motifs found in his more formal statements on obedience are scattered generously throughout the letters he wrote as General. The maintenance of unity (Epistolae I, 558), the impossibility of maintaining social order and effective functioning in the Society without strict obedience (I, 599, 688; IV, 560), the necessity for proper authority to direct the work of the Society as in any well-ordered government (I, 553, 560; II, 55, 56), a harsh and rigid attitude toward any disobedience (IV, 561). The supernaturalization of the authority hierarchy (the idea that the will of the superior was the will of God and that the superior gave his orders in loco Christi) appears repeatedly in the Constitutions (General Examen, c. IV, n. 29, 30; IV, c. X, n. 5, 8; VI, c. I, n. 1; VII, c. I, n. 1; c. III, n. 1; VIII, c. I, D; c. VI, n. 6) as well as in the letters (Epistolae I, 561, 689, 691; II, 56; IV, 671, 672), along with the insistence on blind obedience (I, 228; XII, 662). In citations from the Constitutions, notations refer to the part of the Constitutions, the chapter (c.), and the paragraph number (n).

11. This passage is cited in the letter on perfect obedience, Epistolae IV, 669–681. See Appendix B.

12. My translation. The original reads: "Les circonstances qui ont motivé la *Lettre sur l'obéissance* et, aussi bien, tous les autres documents epistolaires qui en traitent, sont dans leur structure toujours les mêmes. *Il ne s'agit jamais defendre le pouvoir central, mais de susciter ou de soutenir le pouvoir périphérique, soit sur le plan local, soit à l'echelon de grandes aires nationales.* Il y a la une constante qui ne souffre aucune exception, au moins du vivant de saint Ignace."

13. See the letter to Miro above, p. 444.

Chapter 14
Women

1. Sexual exposure and particularly the primal scene experience, that is witnessing the parents in intercourse, can be excessively stimulating for an oedipal age child, to the point of trauma. The oedipal dynamics include conflicting libidinal desires, guilt induced by them, and the fear of castration as punishment for them. If the inhabitants lived in such close quarters in the peasant hut, these influences would have been unavoidable.

2. Such a connection is hinted at by Wilkens (1978, pp. 29–31).

3. See chapter 2.

4. The Infanta Catherina was the most likely candidate for the role of the object of Iñigo's amorous fantasies—see Leturia (1936). In the article on Cath-

erina in the *Diccionario de Historia de España*, she is designated as the "suspected" romantic object of Iñigo's fantasies. But she is actually only one of a number of candidates for the place of honor in Iñigo's erotic fantasies. Others would include Germaine de Foix, niece of Louis XII of France and second wife of Ferdinand of Castile, and Leonor, sister of the Emperor Charles and Catherina. Germaine de Foix was a few years older than Iñigo and not that attractive; she was also married, first to the Marquis of Brandenburg in 1518 and, after his death, to the Duke of Calabria in 1526. Doña Leonor, Catherina's older sister, is a possibility. She came to Spain with Charles in 1517, then married Manuel the Fortunate in Portugal in 1519. He died two years later, after which she entered a convent. At the time of Iñigo's recuperation, she was still a young widow. She afterwards married Francis I in 1547 and died in 1558. Nonetheless, Catherina remains the primary candidate in the judgment of Leturia and Rahner. The actual identity of the object of Iñigo's desire remains Ignatius' secret.

5. See my discussion of these dynamics in chapter 4.

6. He recounted: "He was very attentively cared for, and many prominent ladies of the town came to watch over him at night out of the devotion they felt for him. But even after his recovery from this illness, he remained quite weak with frequent stomach pains. For this reason, and also because the winter was very severe, they insisted that he dress properly, wear shoes and a hat, two dark gray jackets of a rough sort of cloth, with a headpiece that was half bonnet and half cap" (Vita 34).

7. See chapter 8.

8. It is one of the ironies of history that as Iñigo was being dragged to jail, he passed the escort of Francis Borgia who was passing through Alcalá to pay his respects to Charles V at Valladolid. Borgia would later succeed Ignatius as General of the Society and saint.

9. The role of libidinal derivatives in these interactions is recognized by de Vries (1971).

10. See also Rahner (1960, p. 176) and Brodrick (1956, pp. 122–123).

11. The incident is recounted in chapter 8.

12. See also Dudon (1949, p. 143); the letter is in Rahner (1960, pp. 182–183) and in Young (1959, pp. 12–13). Rahner (1960) provides a catalog of these women.

13. Rahner (1960) provides a list of the names of these women. See pp. 13–14.

14. The correspondence with Philip covers the years 1545–1548 and 1551–1554 when Philip was regent of Spain, and again in 1556 when Philip ascended the throne after the abdication of Charles V. The Jesuits later fell into disfavor with Philip, probably because the office of General passed to non-Spaniards. Philip's encounters with Father Aquaviva over governance of the Society seemed calculated to draw the control of the Society away from Rome and the Pope. See

Bangert (1986). This all took place after Ignatius had passed from the scene.

15. Juana's father, Charles V, was the son of Juana the Mad.

16. The letter appears in Appendix C.

17. Rahner cites March (1942).

18. Part of the letter reads: "In your third letter you tell me of all the malice, jealousy and false accusations that have been levelled against you from all sides. Nothing of this surprises me, nor even would it do so if it were much more, for from the moment when you give yourself to God our Lord, desiring and striving for his glory, honour and service, you are already embarked on warfare against the world, are setting up your standards against it, and disposing yourself to struggle against what is exalted by embracing what is lowly, resolved to accept indifferently things both high and low—honour and dishonour, riches or poverty, to be loved or hated, welcomed or rejected, in short the world's glory or its abuse. So long as they do not go beyond words, we shall not be able to count the insults of this life as much, for all of them together cannot destroy one single hair of our head" (Rahner, 1960, pp. 264–265, 266).

19. Cited in Rahner, 1960, p. 282. The testimony is that of an elderly nun of the Jerusalem convent in Barcelona during the beatification hearings in 1606.

20. Ignatius sent a letter to Miguel de Torres from Rome on 3 May 1547 (MI I, i, 488–90), dealing with the settlement of the dispute with Isabel Roser. There are many additions, erasures, and corrections in Ignatius' own hand (in brackets), intended with the help of special signs to make it easier for the secretary to write the good copy. In the first part of the letter Ignatius described to Torres the court of arbitration before which Isabel and her nephews had called Ignatius because of their demands for money. The judges were sympathetic to Isabel, and one was deeply affected by her tears. Ignatius comments: "At the sight of Senora Roser's tears he was [at first] favourably disposed [toward her], but now he recognizes that we are in the right. But that you may [see and judge what] credit those persons deserve who talk thus so readily, I will relate what a mean and low thing happened at the judicial enquiry. One day Dr. Ferrer, Senora Roser's nephew, brought up [against me] [against Master Ignatius] and against our house many evil accusations, in the presence of the same judge and of Master Gasparo (de Dotti) and our Father Don Silvestro (Landini). Don Silvestro retorted that he did indeed remember what that man had said, namely that he was right in bringing the action. He [Ferrer, after much beating about the bush] became frightened [and took everything back] and confessed twice [before the same witnesses] that he had lied [was lying erased] in what he had said. Having regard to the obligation of charity that we have towards all our neighbours, we would not have you [say anything] [show this erased] to anyone, unless it were in two cases: firstly, if anyone should be scandalized at us; and secondly, in defence of

the truth, having regard [always] the greater service of God our Lord in all things" (cited in Rahner, 1960, pp. xxi–xxii).

Chapter 15
Death

1. Menninger (1938) refers to such phenomena as "suicidal equivalents." See also Meissner (1977a, 1977b, 1986).

2. The diagnosis of biliary lithiasis and hepatic cirrhosis was confirmed by the Roman specialist Alessandro Ganezza in his re-examination of the data in 1922 (FN I, 769). Further confirmation is added by Marañón (1956).

3. The two Jesuits were joined in their elevation to sainthood by Philip Neri and Teresa of Avila.

Chapter 16
The Mystic

1. Spiritual relish is a descriptive term referring to an affective state of savoring and delight in spiritual experiences. Interior and exterior locutions are discussed later in this chapter.

2. See chapter 5.

3. Ricard (1956) points out that devotion to the Trinity was widespread in the Iberian peninsula at the time.

4. Ricard (1956) suggests that one reason for this is the massive repression of sexuality that accompanied his conversion and was reinforced by a vow of absolute chastity on his way to Montserrat.

5. The kataphatic and apophatic are different forms of mystical experience and relate to different mystical traditions. The distinction is described by Egan (1984): "The apophatic tradition, the *via negativa*, emphasizes the radical difference between God and creatures. God is best reached, therefore, by negation, forgetting, and unknowing, in a darkness of mind without the support of concepts, images, and symbols. . . . Kataphatic mysticism, the *via affirmativa*, emphasizes the similarity that exists between God and creatures. Because God can be found in all things, the affirmative way recommends the use of concepts, images, and symbols as a way of contemplating God" (p. 31). Ignatius and Teresa of Avila would belong in the kataphatic tradition, John of the Cross to the apophatic.

6. As Egan (1976) puts it, "The CSCP [consolation without previous cause], therefore, is not simply one consolation among many, but the God-given consolation. Only God, and He alone, can and does console in this precise way" (p. 33).

7. The *loquelae* or locutions are discussed later in this chapter.

8. The interpretations of the impact of this vision on Ignatius and the founding of the Society have been varied. See Baumann (1958).

9. Discussed in chapter 5.

10. This profound illumination has been discussed in chapter 5 above.

11. The oft-quoted passage from Nadal's *Scholia* reads: "Cum de instituti ratione rogaretur, solebat causam referre ad eximiam illam mentis illustrationem, quam ipsi Deus gratificatus est Manresa . . . quasi illuc omnia accepisset a Domino, quasi in spiritu quodam sapientiae architectonico." (When he [Ignatius] was asked about the basis for the institute [Society of Jesus], he used to refer to that extraordinary illumination of his mind that God granted him at Manresa . . . as though there he had received everything from God, as in a sort of architectonic spirit of wisdom) Original cited in Silos 1964, my translation.

12. Similar accounts of such transnatural manifestations that seem to exceed the laws of nature can be found, for example, in the history of Sabbatai Sevi, the self-proclaimed messiah of seventeenth-century Jewish kabbalistic mysticism. See Scholem (1973). For a more specifically psychological analysis of Sabbatai's messianic mission see Falk (1982) and Meissner (forthcoming).

13. The "folly of the cross" refers to the internal contradiction of the subjection of the Son of God to the indignities and suffering of the crucifixion. The folly in ascetical terms was the excessive and unnecessary indulgence in penitential practices.

Chapter 17
The Ascetic

1. Affective love is an emotional phenomenon—feelings of love, affection, and devotion—but confined to the realm of affective experience. Effective love shifts the emphasis away from the feeling state to the realm of action. Love is effective when it does that which is for the good of the loved one. Parents may experience an affection of love for their children, but unless their love is effective they can do their children great harm. Ignatius expresses this point with particular poignancy in the contemplation for obtaining divine love, where he gives a classic statement about effective love: "First it is well to remark two things: the first is that love ought to be put more in deeds than in words. The second, love consists in interchange between two parties, that is to say in the lover's giving and communicating to the beloved what he has or out of what he has or can; and so, on the contrary, the beloved to the lover. So that if one has knowledge, he gives to the one who has it not. The same of honors, of riches; and so the one to the other" (Exercises 230–231).

Chapter 18
Mysticism: Psychopathology

1. In the *Exercises* this technique is known as the "application of the senses." Ignatius writes: "it is helpful to pass the five senses of the imagination through the . . . contemplation in the following way:

"First Point. The first point is to see the persons with the sight of the imagination, meditating and contemplating in particular the details about them and drawing some profit from the sight.

"Second Point. The second, to hear with the hearing what they are, or might be, talking about and, reflecting on oneself, to draw some profit from it.

"Third Point. The third, to smell and to taste with the smell and the taste the infinite fragrance and sweetness of the Divinity, of the soul, and of its virtues, and of all, according to the person who is being contemplated, reflecting on oneself and drawing profit from it.

"Fourth Point. The fourth, to touch with the touch, as for instance, to embrace and kiss the places where such persons put their feet and sit, always seeing to my drawing profit from it" (Exercises 121–125).

2. Synesthesia refers to a condition in which a sensory stimulus elicits not only its proper sensory experience, it also gives rise to a subjective sensation in another sensory modality—color-hearing or color-taste would be examples.

3. See the case of Sabbatai Sevi, the "mystical messiah" of the seventeenth century, extensively documented in Scholem (1973); see also Falk (1982) and Meissner (forthcoming).

4. The experience of the shaman is often descriptively close to both secondary mystical phenomena and certain forms of psychotic experience. The role of the shaman, the cultic healer, is built into a cultural and religious context that gives credence and acceptability to his unique experience. His trance states usually come into play in highly ritualized situations of religious healing. Eliade (1964) refers to the shaman's "mystical vocation."

5. Secondary process is one of two modes of mental functioning described by Freud. Secondary process menation was conscious or preconscious and followed rules of logical and reality-oriented organization.

6. Psychosensory refers to the subjective dimension of sensory experience.

7. Diminished sexual drive and interest.

8. Diminished sexual activity.

9. A tendency to focus on minor, often irrelevant details.

10. A partial or incomplete form of schizophrenia manifesting some symptoms and signs of schizophrenia but not the full-blown syndrome. Schizophreniform attacks may be transient and episodic.

11. Kindling refers to the progressive lowering on the seizure threshold under the influence of toxic stimulants or as the result of repeated seizure discharges. The lowering of the threshold increases the frequency and intensity of seizure episodes.

Chapter 19
Mysticism: Psychoanalytic View

1. Stimuli arising from muscles, tendons, and other organic tissues of the body.

2. A technical term indicating a form of internalization that is in some degree drive-determined and defensive so that what is internalized remains in the service of defense. Introjects tend to be poorly integrated and can remain vulnerable to regression and other defensive vicissitudes—among them projection. See Meissner (1981).

3. The introjects assume a certain configuration, depending on the circumstances of internalization and the drive vicissitudes involved. Internalized aggression can be built into the introjective configuration, and this gives rise to affects, fantasies, and defenses whose purpose is to constrain, hide, transform, or disengage the aggressive components. The elements of Ignatius' aggressive sense of himself had to be denied, repressed, counteracted—especially by imitation of and identification with the victimized Christ.

4. See the discussion of the meditations on the Kingdom and the Two Standards in chapter 6.

5. Scopophilia is a form of perversion in which sexual pleasure is derived from looking.

6. The focal symbiosis reflecting the conjunction of infantile needs and parental pathology is here centered in the visual function. See Greenacre (1959).

Chapter 20
Divine and/or Psychic Causality?

1. Freud's early instinctual theory was cast in an energic model that stressed quantitative and economic considerations. Later developments of the theory have emphasized hermeneutic aspects concerned more with meaning and motive. These perspectives may not be exclusive, an argument that has been eloquently presented by Ricoeur.

2. See my discussion of the psychological effects of grace in Meissner (1987).

Chapter 21
Development and Conversion

1. On disidentification, see Greenson (1968).

2. See chapter 1.

Chapter 22
The Personality of Ignatius

1. Masochism is a perversion that finds pleasure or gratification in humiliation or suffering. Moral masochism is a derivative form which seeks victimization or the position of victim primarily out of an unconscious sense of guilt; sexual pleasure is not necessarily, or only indirectly, involved.

2. The essential elements of hysteria are an instinctual conflict, usually libidinal, repression of instinctual impulses, return of the repressed in some distorted, displaced, or otherwise disguised expression. One form of such displacement is from the mind to the body in the form of a conversion symptom—hysterical

paralysis, hysterical blindness, and so on. I would regard the symptoms described by Ignatius as expressions of an hysterical component in his personality makeup.

3. An instinctual drive is said to be aim-inhibited when it fails to achieve its direct mode of satisfaction, whether because of external or internal obstacles. Such aim-inhibited drives may gain some degree of attenuated satisfaction from activity or relationships that may be related to or more or less removed from the original source of satisfaction. Ignatius' mission to women would have provided such attenuated substitute satisfaction.

4. Opinions regarding the nature of the ego ideal and its relation to narcissism are still somewhat diverse and unsettled in psychoanalytic circles. See the discussion in Milrod (1990).

5. Countercathexis involves direction of energies mobilized by the ego to counter or regulate instinctual drive derivatives, usually resulting in some form of compromise. Such countercathexes presumably contribute to the stability of psychic structures and can become aspects of enduring character structures.

6. One view of the relation between ego ideal and superego regards the ego ideal as narcissistic in origin and leading to the dynamics of narcissistic vulnerability and shame, while the superego derives from the oedipal situation and leads to the complex of drive-superego-castration anxiety-guilt. See Grunberger (1989). Chasseguet-Smirgel (1973), following Grunberger's lead, writes: "There exists a fundamental difference between the ego ideal, heir to primary narcissism, and the superego, heir to the Oedipus complex. The first represents—at the outset at least—an attempt at recovering lost omnipotence. The second, in a Freudian perspective, is a production of the castration complex. The first tends to reinstate illusion, the second to promote reality. The superego comes between the child and the mother, the ego ideal . . . pushes him toward fusion" (p. 76).

7. See the discussion of Ignatius' authoritarian traits in chapter 13.

Chapter 23
The Spiritual Ascent

1. An object-representation is a mental representation of an external object—usually referring to persons as objects.

2. "Illusion" in this context has a specific meaning that requires careful exposition. See Meissner (1984). In brief terms, Winnicott's notion of illusion stands in opposition to Freud's. For Freud, illusions were defined by their role as wish-fulfillments. If the illusion contradicted reality, it was for him a delusion. For Winnicott, the illusion is an intermediate form of experience in which wishes and fantasies can touch reality, in which the subjective and the objective can find common ground, and in which neither the reality of the objects of desire are denied nor the experience of wishes and fantasies ignored. A painting, for

example, is an objective reality, but the experience of painting involves not just the reality but the subjective complex of feelings and meanings brought to it by the viewer. In Ignatius' raptures, there is an objective reality, the presence of God, but the experience of that presence is conditioned by a rich complex of subjective personality factors, some of which we have tried to illuminate.

3. See the section on values and their psychoanalytic meaning in Meissner (1987).

4. Overdetermination refers to the fact that psychic formation (symptoms, dreams, character traits, and so on) can be influenced by multiple determining factors — either in the sense that it is the resultant of multiple causes, or in the sense that it is open to different levels of meaning and interpretation.

Appendix B
Writings of Ignatius Concerning Holy Obedience

1. The omitted paragraph deals with the vow of chastity.

2. These "Declarations," designated by capital letters in the manner of a footnote, were additional and often more detailed expositions of particular points developed by Ignatius, and only later integrated with the text of the Constitutions. These have the same authoritative standing as the rest of the Constitutions. The texts of the Declarations follow the relevant sections of the Constitutions.

REFERENCES

Abse, D. W., and R. B. Ulman. 1977. Charismatic political leadership and collective regression. In *Psychopathology and political leadership,* ed. R. S. Robins. Tulane Studies in Political Science, vol. 16. New Orleans: Tulane University Press.

Adorno, T. W., E. Frenkel-Brunswik, D. J. Levinson, and R. N. Sanford. 1950. *The authoritarian personality.* New York: Harper.

Affholder, C. M. 1960. Saint Ignace dans son écriture. *Archivum Historicum Societatis Jesu* 29: 381–398.

Allport, G. W. 1955. *Becoming.* New Haven: Yale University Press.

Aries, P. 1962. *Centuries of childhood.* New York: Vintage Books.

Arieti, S. 1967. *The intrapsychic self: Feeling, cognition, and creativity in health and mental illness.* New York: Basic Books.

———. 1976. *Creativity: The magic synthesis.* New York: Basic Books.

Bach, S. 1977. On narcissistic fantasies. *International Review of Psychoanalysis* 4: 281–293.

Bangert, S.J., W. V. 1959. *To the other towns: A life of Blessed Peter Favre, first companion of Saint Ignatius.* Westminster, Md.: Newman Press.

Bangert, S.J., W. V. 1985. *Claude Jay and Alfonso Salmeron: Two early Jesuits.* Chicago: Loyola University Press.

Barnes, D. F. 1978. Charisma and religious leadership: an historical analysis. *Journal for the Scientific Study of Religion* 17: 1–18.

Barzun, J. 1974. *Clio and the doctors: Psycho-history, quanto-history and history.* Chicago: University of Chicago Press.

Baumann, S.J., T. 1958. Die Berichte Über die Vision des heiligen Ignatius bei La Storta. *Archivum Historicum Societatis Jesu* 27: 181–208.

Becher, S.J., H. 1977. Ignatius as seen by his contemporaries. In Wulf 1977, 69–96.

Begg, E. 1985. *The cult of the Black Virgin.* London: Arkana.

Berliner, B. 1947. On some psychodynamics of masochism. *Psychoanalytic Quarterly* 16: 459–471.

Bertrand, S.J., D. 1985. *La politique de S. Ignace de Loyola.* Paris: Les Editions du Cerf.

Birtchnell, J. 1969. The possible consequences of early parental death. *British Journal of Medical Psychology* 42: 1–12.

Birtchnell, J., I. C. Wilson, O. Bratfos, et al. 1973. *Effects of early parent death.* New York: MSS.

Blet, S.J., P. 1956. Les fondements de l'obéissance Ignatienne. *Archivum Historicum Societatis Jesu* 25: 514–538.

Boisen, A. T. 1936. *The exploration of the inner world.* New York: Harper and Bros., 1962.

Bottereau, S.J., G. 1975. La "lettre" d'Ignace de Loyola à Gian Pietro Carafa. *Archivum Historicum Societatis Jesu* 44: 139–152.

Bourgignon, E. 1976. Cross-cultural perspectives on the religious uses of altered states of consciousness. In *Religious movements in contemporary America,* ed. I. I. Zaretsky and M. P. Leone, 228–243. Princeton: Princeton University Press.

Bowers, M. B., and D. X. Freedman. 1966. "Psychedelic experiences" in acute psychoses. *Archives of General Psychiatry* 15: 240–248.

Boyle, M. O. 1983. Angels black and white: Loyola's spiritual discernment in historical perspective. *Theological Studies* 44: 241–257.

Bradley, S.J. 1979. The relationship of early maternal separation to borderline personality in children and adolescents: a pilot study. *American Journal of Psychiatry* 136: 424–426.

Breier, A., J. R. Kelsoe, Jr., P. D. Kirwin, S. A. Beller, O. M. Wolkowitz, and D. Pickar. 1988. Early parental loss and development of adult psychopathology. *Archives of General Psychiatry* 45: 987–993.

Brodrick, S.J., J. 1940. *The origin of the Jesuits.* New York: Longmans Green.

———. 1952. *Saint Francis Xavier.* London: Burns, Oates. Reprint. Garden City, N.Y.: Doubleday, 1957.

———. 1956. *St. Ignatius Loyola: The pilgrim years.* London: Burns and Oates.

Brunner, A. 1949. Philosophisches zur Tiefenpsychologie und Psychotherapie. *Stimmen der Zeit* 144: 92.

Buckley, P. 1981. Mystical experience and schizophrenia. *Schizophrenia Bulletin* 7: 516–521.

Bullitt, W. D., and S. Freud. 1966. *Thomas Woodrow Wilson: A psychological study.* Boston: Houghton Mifflin.

Buonaiuti, E. 1968. Symbols and rites in the religious life of certain monastic orders. In *The mystic vision: Papers from the Eranos yearbooks,* ed. J. Campbell, 168–209. Princeton: Princeton University Press.

Calveras, S.J., J. 1948. Los "confesionales" y los ejercicios de San Ignacio. *Archivum Historicum Societatis Jesu* 17: 51–101.

———. 1956. La ilustración del Cardoner y el instituto de la compañia de Jesús según el P. Nadal. *Archivum Historicum Societatis Jesu* 25: 27–54.

Castellani, S.J., G. 1941. La solenne professione de S. Ignazio di Loiola e di cinque dei primi compagni in San Paola fuori le Mura (22 Aprile 1541). *Archivum Historicum Societatis Jesu* 10: 1–16.

Charmé, S. L. 1983. Religion and the theory of masochism. *Journal of Religion and Health* 22: 221–233.

Chasseguet-Smirgel, J. 1975. *The ego ideal.* New York: Norton, 1985.

———. 1976. Some thoughts on the ego ideal: a contribution to the study of the "illness of ideality." *Psychoanalytic Quarterly* 45: 345–373.

Christensen, C. W. 1963. Religious conversion. *Archives of General Psychiatry* 9: 207–216.

Clancy, S.J., T. H. 1978. *The conversational Word of God: A commentary on the doctrine of St. Ignatius of Loyola concerning spiritual conversation, with four early Jesuit texts.* St. Louis: Institute of Jesuit Sources.

Cocks, G., and T. L. Crosby, eds. 1987. *Psycho/History: Readings in the method of psychology, psychoanalysis, and history.* New Haven: Yale University Press.

Codina, S.J., A. 1926. *Los origenes de los Ejercicios Espirituales de San Ignacio de Loyola.* Barcelona: Balmes. 5–72.

———. 1935. La estancia de S. Ignacio en el convento de S. Esteban O.P. de Salamanca. *Archivum Historicum Societatis Jesu* 4: 111–123.

———. 1938. Sant Ignasi a Montserrat. *Archivum Historicum Societatis Jesu* 7: 104–117, 257–267.

Coe, G. A. 1916. *The psychology of religion.* Chicago: University of Chicago Press.

Coemans, S.J., A. 1932. Quandonam S. Ignatius decrevit leges scriptas dare Societati: utrum iam ab initio an solum post aliquot annos? *Archivum Historicum Societatis Jesu* 1: 304–306.

Cohn, N. 1970. *The pursuit of the millennium.* New York: Oxford University Press.

Coles, R. 1975. On psychohistory. In *The mind's fate: Ways of seeing psychiatry and psychoanalysis.* Boston: Little, Brown.

Conn, W. 1986. *Christian conversion: A developmental interpretation of autonomy and surrender.* New York: Paulist Press.

Dalmases, S.J., C. de. 1941. Los estudios de S. Ignacio en Barcelona (1524–1526). *Archivum Historicum Societatis Jesu* 10: 283–293.

———. 1980. El patrimonio de los señores de Loyola. *Archivum Historicum Societatis Jesu* 49: 113–134.

———. 1985. *Ignatius of Loyola: Founder of the Jesuits.* St. Louis: The Institute of Jesuit Sources.

de Aldama, S.J., A. M. 1973. La composición de las Constituciones de la Comañpia de Jesús. *Archivum Historicum Societatis Jesu* 42: 201–245.

De Guibert, S.J., J. 1964. *The Jesuits: Their spiritual doctrine and practice.* Chicago: Institute of Jesuit Studies, Loyola University Press.

Deikman, A. 1966. De-automatization and the mystical experience. *Psychiatry* 29: 329–343.

del Piazzo, M., and C. de Dalmases, S.J. 1969. Il processo sull'ortodossia di S. Ignazio e dei suoi compagni svoltosi a Roma nel 1538. *Archivum Historicum Societatis Jesu* 38: 431–453.

DeMause, L. 1974. The evolution of childhood. *History of Childhood Quarterly* 1: 503–606.

Deutsch, H. 1937. The absence of grief. In *Neuroses and character types*, 226–236. New York: International Universities Press.

de Vries, S.J., P. P. 1971. Protestants and other spirituals: Ignatius' vision and why he took this position. *Archivum Historicum Societatis Jesu* 40: 463–483.

de Waelhens, A. 1959. Réflexions sur une problématique husserlienne. In *Edmund Husserl, 1859–1959*. The Hague: Nijhoff.

Directory to the Spiritual Exercises of Our Holy Father Ignatius. 1925. London: Manresa Press.

Dodds, E. R. 1951. *The Greeks and the irrational.* Berkeley: University of California Press.

Doncoeur, S.J., P. 1959. *The heart of Ignatius.* Baltimore: Helicon Press.

Ducasse, C. J. 1953. *A philosophical scrutiny of religion.* New York: Ronald Press.

Dudon, S.J., P. 1949. *St. Ignatius of Loyola.* Milwaukee: Bruce.

Durkheim, E. 1915. *The elementary forms of the religious life.* New York: Free Press, 1965.

Earle, A. M., and B. V. Earle. 1961. Early maternal deprivation and later psychiatric illness. *American Journal of Orthopsychiatry* 31: 181–186.

Egan, S.J., H. D. 1976. *The Spiritual Exercises and the Ignatian mystical horizon.* St. Louis: Institute of Jesuit Sources.

———. 1984. *Christian mysticism: The future of a tradition.* New York: Pueblo.

———. 1987. *Ignatius Loyola the mystic.* Wilmington, Del.: Michael Glazier.

Ellenberger, H. F. 1970. *The discovery of the unconscious.* New York: Basic Books.

Elliott, J. H. 1977. *Imperial Spain, 1469–1716.* New York: New American Library.

Endean, S.J., P. E. 1987. Who do you say Ignatius is? Jesuit fundamentalism and beyond. *Studies in the spirituality of Jesuits.* St. Louis: Seminar on Jesuit Spirituality.

Epistolae et Instructiones Sancti Ignatii (Monumenta Ignatiana). MHSJ, MI Series I. 12 vols. Madrid: 1903–1911. [Epistolae]

Epstein, M. 1990. Beyond the oceanic feeling: psychoanalytic study of Buddhist meditation. *International Review of Psychoanalysis* 17: 159–166.

Erikson, E. H. 1950. *Childhood and society.* New York: Norton.

———. 1958. *Young man Luther.* New York: Norton.

————. 1959. *Identity and the life cycle*. Psychological Monograph Series, no. 1. New York: International Universities Press.

————. 1975. On the nature of psychohistorical evidence: in search of Gandhi. In *Life history and history*. New York: Norton.

Falk, A. 1982. The messiah and the qelippoth: on the mental illness of Sabbatai Sevi. *Journal of Psychology and Judaism* 7: 5–29.

Federn, P. 1952. On the distinction between healthy and pathological narcissism. In *Ego psychology and the psychoses*. New York: Basic Books.

Fedio, P. 1986. Behavioral characteristics of patients with temporal lobe epilepsy. *Psychiatric Clinics of North America* 9: 267–281.

Ferenczi, S. 1924. *Sex in psychoanalysis*. New York: Norton, 1956.

Fessard, G. 1956. *La dialectique des Exercices Spirituels de Saint Ignace de Loyola*. Paris: Aubier.

Festugière, A. J. 1949. A propos des aretalogies d'Isis. *Harvard Theological Review* 42: 209–234.

Fleming, S.J., D. L. 1978. *The Spiritual Exercises of St. Ignatius: A literal translation and a contemporary reading*. St. Louis: The Institute of Jesuit Sources.

Fleming, J., and S. Altschul. 1963. Activation of mourning and growth by psychoanalysis. *International Journal of Psychoanalysis* 44: 419–432.

Fontes Narrativi. MHSJ, MI Series 4. 4 vols. Revised ed. Rome, 1943–1960. [FN]

Fortune, R. 1926. The symbolism of the serpent. *International Journal of Psychoanalysis* 7: 237–243.

Freud, A. 1936. *The ego and the mechanisms of defense*. New York: International Universities Press, 1946.

Freud, S. 1953–74. *Standard edition of the complete psychological works*. London: Hogarth.

1908. Creative writers and day-dreaming, 9: 141–153.

1910. Leonardo da Vinci and a memory of his childhood, vol. 11: 59–137.

1914. On narcissism, vol. 14: 67–102.

1915a. Instincts and their vicissitudes, vol. 14: 117–140.

1915b. Repression, vol. 14: 141–158.

1917a. A difficulty in the path of psychoanalysis, vol. 17: 135–144.

1917b. Mourning and melancholia, vol. 14: 237–258.

1921. Group psychology and the analysis of the ego, vol. 18: 65–143.

1923a. *The ego and the id*, vol. 19: 1–66.

1923b. Remarks on the theory and practice of dream-interpretation, vol. 19: 107–121.

1927. *The future of an illusion*, vol. 21: 5–56.

1930a. *Civilization and its discontents*, vol. 21: 57–145.

1930b. The Goethe prize, vol. 21: 205–214.

1931. Libidinal types, vol. 21: 217–220.

1936. A disturbance of memory on the Acropolis, vol. 22: 239–248.

Fromm, E. 1941. *The escape from freedom*. Reprint. New York: Avon, 1965.

Frosch, J. 1977. The morning ruminative state—the flash phenomenon. *International Journal of Psychoanalysis* 58: 301–309.

Furman, R. 1964. Death and the young child: some preliminary considerations. *Psychoanalytic Study of the Child* 19: 321–333.

———. 1968. Additional remarks on mourning and the young child. *Bulletin of the Philadelphia Association for Psychoanalysis* 18: 51–64.

Furman, E., and R. Furman. 1974. *The child's parent dies*. New Haven: Yale University Press.

Futrell, S.J., J. C. 1970. *Making an apostolic community of love: The role of the superior according to St. Ignatius of Loyola*. St. Louis: Institute of Jesuit Sources.

Ganss, S.J., G. E., ed. 1970. *The Constitutions of the Society of Jesus*. MHSJ, MI Series 3, 4 vols. Rome: 1934–1948 [Constitutions]. St. Louis: Institute of Jesuit Sources.

Gay, P. 1989. *Freud: A life for our time*. New York: Norton.

Gies, F., and J. Gies. 1987. *Marriage and the family in the Middle Ages*. New York: Harper and Row.

Gilmore, M. M., and D. D. Gilmore. 1979. "Machismo": a psychodynamic approach. *Journal of Psychoanalytic Anthropology* 2: 281–299.

Goldstein, M. 1970. Premorbid adjustment, paranoid status, and patterns of response to phenothiazine in acute schizophrenia. *Schizophrenia Bulletin* 1 (3): 24–37.

Greenacre, P. 1947. Vision, headache, and the halo. *Psychoanalytic Quarterly* 16: 177–194.

———. 1959. On focal symbiosis. In *Emotional growth*, vol. 1. New York: International Universities Press, 145–161.

———. 1965. On the development and function of tears. In *Emotional growth*, vol. 1. , 249–259.

Greenson, R. R. 1968. Dis-identifying from the mother: its special importance for the boy. *International Journal of Psychoanalysis* 49: 370–389.

Gregory, I. 1985. Studies of parental deprivation in psychiatric patients. *American Journal of Psychiatry* 115: 432–442.

Grunberger, B. 1971. *Narcissism*. New York: International Universities Press, 1979.

Haas, S.J., A. 1977. The mysticism of St. Ignatius according to his Spiritual Diary. In Wulf 1977, 164–199.

Harris, T., G. W. Brown, and A. Bifulco. 1986. Loss of parent in childhood and adult psychiatric disorder: the role of lack of adequate parental care. *Psychological Medicine* 16: 641–659.

Hartmann, H. 1958. *Ego psychology and the problem of adaptation*. New York: International Universities Press.

———. 1964. Comments on the psychoanalytic theory of the ego. In *Essays on ego psychology*. New York: International Universities Press.

———. 1964. Psychoanalysis and the concept of health. In *Essays on ego psychology*. New York: International Universities Press, 3–18.

Hartmann, H., and R. M. Loewenstein. 1962. Notes on the superego. *Psychoanalytic Study of the Child* 17: 42–81.

Hartocollis, P. 1976. Aggression and mysticism. *Contemporary Psychoanalysis* 12: 214–226.

Hassal, J. 1919. The serpent as a symbol. *Psychoanalytic Review* 6: 295–305.

Heilbrunn, G. 1955. On weeping. *Psychoanalytic Quarterly* 24: 245–255.

Hermann, B. P., and S. Whitman. 1984. Behavioral and personality correlates of epilepsy: a review, methodological critique, and conceptual model. *Psychological Bulletin* 95: 451–497.

Huizinga, J. 1952. *Erasmus of Rotterdam*. London: Phaidon Press.

Huonder, S.J., A. 1932. *Ignatius von Loyola. Beiträge zu seinem Charakterbild*. Köln: Katholische Tat-Verlag.

Ignatius. *Autobiography*. Fontes Narrativi, MHSJ, MI series 4: vol. 1. Rome, 1943.

———. 1956. *St. Ignatius' own story*. Trans. W. J. Young, S.J. Chicago: Regnery. [Vita]

———. 1959. *Letters of St. Ignatius Loyola*. Trans. W. J. Young, S.J. Chicago: Loyola University Press.

Iparraquirre, S.J., I. 1955. *A key to the study of the Spiritual Exercises*. Calcutta: Hibernian Press.

———. 1957. Viajes de Iñigo de Loyola anteriores a 1518. *Archivum Historicum Societatis Jesu* 26: 230–251.

Jacobson, E. 1964. *The self and the object world*. New York: International Universities Press.

James, W. 1902. *The varieties of religious experience*. New York: Collier Books, 1961.

Johnson, C.S.J., E. A. 1989. Mary and the female face of God. *Theological Studies* 50: 500–526.

Jones, E. 1913. The God complex. In *Essays in Applied Psychoanalysis*, vol. 2. London: Hogarth Press, 1951.

———. 1923. The nature of auto-suggestion. In *Papers on Psychoanalysis*. Boston: Beacon Press, 1948.

Jung, C. G. 1956. *Symbols of transformation*. New York: Harper and Bros.

Kagan, R. L. 1990. *Lucrecia's dreams: Politics and prophesy in sixteenth-century Spain*. Berkeley: University of California Press.

Kelly, H. A. 1965. Demonology and diabolical temptation. *Thought* 40: 165–194.

Kernberg, O. F. 1979. Regression in organizational leadership. *Psychiatry* 42: 29–39.

Kets de Vries, M. F. R., and D. Miller. 1985. Narcissism and leadership: an object relations perspective. *Human Relations* 38: 583–601.

Kohut, H. 1971. *The analysis of the self*. New York: International Universities Press.

Knapp, P. H. 1967. Some riddles of riddance. *Archives of General Psychiatry* 16: 586–602.

Kris, E. 1952. *Psychoanalytic explorations in art*. New York: International Universities Press.

Kroll, J., and B. Bachrach. 1982. Visions and psychopathology in the middle ages. *Journal of Nervous and Mental Disease* 170: 41–49.

Kroll, J., and R. De Ganck. 1986. The adolescence of a thirteenth-century visionary nun. *Psychological Medicine* 16: 745–756.

Krueger, D. W. 1983. Childhood parent loss: developmental impact and adult psychopathology. *American Journal of Psychotherapy* 37: 582–592.

Küng, H. 1990. *Freud and the problem of God*. Enlarged edition. New Haven: Yale University Press.

Langer, W. C. 1972. *The mind of Adolf Hitler*. New York: Basic Books.

Langer, W. L. 1958. The next assignment. *American Historical Review* 63: 283–304.

Larrañaga, S.J., V. 1956. La revisión total de los ejercicios por San Ignacio: en París, o en Roma? *Archivum Historicum Societatis Jesu* 25: 396–415.

Lenz, H. 1979. The element of the irrational at the beginning and during the course of delusion. *Confinia Psychiatrica* 22: 183–190.

Leturia, S.J., P. 1933. A propósito del "Ignatius von Loyola" del P. Huonder. *Archivum Historicum Societatis Jesu* 2: 310–316.

———. 1936. La conversión de S. Ignacio: nuevos datos y ensayo de síntesis. *Archivum Historicum Societatis Jesu* 5: 1–35.

———. 1936. Notas criticas sobre la dama del Capitán Loyola. *Archivum Historicum Societatis Jesu* 5: 84–92.

———. 1940. Importancia del año 1538 en el cumplimiento del "voto del Montmartre." *Archivum Historicum Societatis Jesu* 9: 188–207.

———. 1941. Genesis de los Ejercicios de S. Ignacio y su influjo en la fundación de la Compañía de Jesús (1521–1540). *Archivum Historicum Societatis Jesu* 10: 16–59.

———. 1949. Damas vascas en la formacion y transformacion de Iñigo de Loyola. *Revista Internacional de Estudios Vascos* 9: 7–24.

———. 1948. Libros de horas, anima Christi y ejercicios espirituales de S. Ignacio. *Archivum Historicum Societatis Jesu* 17: 3–50.

———. 1949. *Iñigo de Loyola*. Syracuse: Le Moyne College Press.

Leturia, S.J., P., and M. Batllori, S.J. 1956. Documenta duo Vaticana de familia Loyola atque de Sancto Ignatio. *Archivum Historicum Societatis Jesu* 25: 15–26.

Lewin, B. D. 1937. A type of neurotic hypomanic reaction. *Archives of Neurology and Psychiatry* 37: 868–873.

———. 1950. *The psychoanalysis of elation*. New York: Norton.

Liebert, R. S. 1982. *Michelangelo*. New Haven: Yale University Press.

Lifton, R. J. 1974. On psychohistory. In *Explorations in Psychohistory: The Wellfleet Papers*, ed. R. J. Lifton and E. Olson, 21–41. New York: Simon and Schuster.

Lofgren, L. 1966. On weeping. *International Journal of Psychoanalysis* 47: 375–381.

Lombillo, J. R. 1973. The soldier saint—a psychological analysis of the conversion of Ignatius of Loyola. *Psychiatric Quarterly* 47: 386–418.

Longhurst, J. E. 1957. Saint Ignatius at Alcalá. *Archivum Historicum Societatis Jesu* 26: 252–256.

Lukoff, D. 1985. The diagnosis of mystical experiences with psychotic features. *Journal of Transpersonal Psychology* 17: 155–181.

McGlashan, T., and W. Carpenter. 1981. Does attitude toward psychosis relate to outcome? *American Journal of Psychiatry* 138: 797–801.

Mack, J. E. 1971. Psychoanalysis and historical biography. *Journal of the American Psychoanalytic Association* 19: 143–179.

Mahler, M. S., F. Pine, and A. Bergman. 1975. *The psychological birth of the human infant*. New York: Basic Books.

Mahony, P. J. 1989. Aspects on nonperverse scopophilia within an analysis. *Journal of the American Psychoanalytic Association* 37: 365–399.

Makarec, K., and M. A. Persinger. 1985. Temporal lobe signs: electroencephalographic validity and enhanced scores in special populations. *Perceptual and Motor Skills* 60: 831–842.

Marañón, G. 1956. Notas sobre la vida y la muerte de San Ignacio de Loyola. *Archivum Historicum Societatis Jesu* 25: 134–153.

March, J. M. 1942. El Aya del Rey D. Felipe II y del Principe D. Carlos, Doña Leonor Mascarenas. Su vida y obras virtuosas. Relacion de una religiosa su contemporanea. *Boletin de la Sociedad Espanola de Excursiones, Arte, Arqueologia, Historia* 46: 12.

Martin, S.J., F. M. 1975. Un episodio desconocido de la juventud de Ignacio de Loyola. *Archivum Historicum Societatis Jesu* 44: 131–138.

Martin, S.J., L. F. 1980. El hogar donde Iñigo de Loyola se hizo hombre. *Archivum Historicum Societatis Jesu* 49: 21–94.

Martini, S.J., A. 1949. Di chi fu ospite S. Ignazio a Venezia nel 1536? *Archivum Historicum Societatis Jesu* 18: 253–260.

Mazlish, B. 1968. Group psychology and the problems of contemporary history. In Cocks and Crosby (1987), 225–236.

Meissner, S.J., W. W. 1963–64. Psychological notes on the *Spiritual Exercises*. *Woodstock Letters* 92 (1963): 349–366; 93 (1964): 31–58, 165–191.

———. 1964. Prolegomena to a psychology of grace. *Journal of Religion and Health* 3: 209–240.

———. 1966. *Foundations for a psychology of grace.* New York: Paulist Press.

———. 1971. *The assault on authority: dialogue or dilemma?* New York: Orbis Books.

———. 1977a. The individual: Suicide. In *Human life: Problems of birth, of living, and of dying*, ed. W. C. Bier, S.J, 229–251. New York: Fordham University Press.

———. 1977b. Psychoanalytic notes on suicide. *International Journal of Psychoanalytic Psychotherapy* 6: 415–447.

———. 1978a. *The paranoid process.* New York: Aronson.

———. 1978b. Psychoanalytic aspects of religious experience. *Annual of Psychoanalysis* 6: 103–141.

———. 1979. Narcissistic personalities and borderline conditions: a differential diagnosis. *Annual of Psychoanalysis* 7: 171–202.

———. 1981. *Internalization in Psychoanalysis.* Psychological Issues Monograph Series, no. 50. New York: International Universities Press.

———. 1984. *Psychoanalysis and religious experience.* New Haven: Yale University Press.

———. 1986. *Psychotherapy and the paranoid process.* Northvale, N.J.: Jason Aronson, 301–334.

———. 1990. The role of transitional conceptualization in religious thought. In *Psychoanalysis and Religion.* ed. J. H. Smith and S. A. Handelman, 95–116. Psychiatry and the Humanities, vol. 11. Baltimore: Johns Hopkins University Press.

———. 1991. Psychoanalytic hagiography: the case of Ignatius of Loyola. *Theological Studies* 52: 3–33.

———. n.d. Medieval messianism and Sabbatianism. *Psychoanalytic Study of Society*, forthcoming.

Menninger, K. A. 1938. *Man against himself.* New York: Harcourt Brace.

Merleau-Ponty, M. 1962. *Phenomenology of Perception.* London: Routledge and Paul.

Milrod, D. 1990. The ego ideal. *Psychoanalytic Study of the Child* 45: 43–60.

Miller, J. B. M. 1971. Children's reactions to the death of a parent: a review of the psychoanalytic literature. *Journal of the American Psychoanalytic Association* 19: 697–719.

Minnich, N. H., and W. W. Meissner. 1978. The character of Erasmus. *American Historical Review* 83: 598–624.

Mintz, I. 1971. The anniversary reaction: a response to the unconscious sense of time. *Journal of the American Psychoanalytic Association* 19: 720–735.

Moloney, J. C. 1954. Mother, god and superego. *Journal of the American Psychoanalytic Association* 2: 120–151.

Montaigne, M. de. 1958. *Complete Essays*. Trans. Donald M. Frame. Stanford, Calif.: Stanford University Press.

Montes, S.J., B. H. 1983. Identidad de los personajes que juzgaron a San Ignacio en Salamanca: problemas historicos suscitadoes por las primeras fuentes. *Archivum Historicum Societatis Jesu* 52: 3–51.

Monumenta Historica Societatis Jesu (MHSJ). Rome: Institutum Historicum Societatis Jesu, 1894–.

Murray, G. B. 1981. Complex partial seizures. In *Psychiatric Medicine Update: Massachusetts General Hospital Reviews for Physicians*, ed. T. C. Manschreck, 103–118. New York: Elsevier.

Murray, J. M. 1964. Narcissism and the ego ideal. *Journal of the American Psychoanalytic Association* 12: 477–511.

Neumann, E. 1954. *The origins and history of consciousness*. New York: Harper.

Nicolau, S.J., M. 1957. Fisonomía de San Ignacio según sus primeros compañeros. *Archivum Historicum Societatis Jesu* 26: 257–269.

Olin, J. 1979. *Six essays on Erasmus*. New York: Fordham University Press.

O'Malley, S.J., J. W. 1982. The Jesuits, St. Ignatius, and the Counter Reformation: some recent studies and their implications for today. *Studies in the Spirituality of Jesuits*. St. Louis: American Assistancy Seminar on Jesuit Spirituality.

O'Reilly, T. 1974. Saint Ignatius Loyola and Spanish Erasmianism. *Archivum Historicum Societatis Jesu* 43: 301–331.

———. 1979. Erasmus, Ignatius Loyola, and orthodoxy. *Journal of Theological Studies* 30: 115–127.

Oremland, J. D. 1978. Michelangelo's Pietàs. *Psychoanalytic Study of the Child* 33: 563–591.

———. 1980. Mourning and its effect on Michelangelo's art. *Annual of Psychoanalysis* 8: 317–351.

———. 1989. *Michelangelo's Sistine Ceiling: A psychoanalytic study of creativity*. Madison, Conn.: International Universities Press.

Orsy, S.J., L. 1973. Toward a theological evaluation of communal discernment.

Studies in the Spirituality of the Jesuits. St. Louis: American Assistancy Seminar on Jesuit Spirituality.

Ortiz, L. M., V. Agusti, M. Lecina, A. Macia, A. Codina, D. Fernandez, and D. Restrepo, eds. 1918. *Scripta de Sancto Ignatio.* 2 vols. Madrid.

Persinger, M. A. 1983. Religious and mystical experiences as artifacts of temporal lobe function: a general hypothesis. *Perceptual and Motor Skills* 57: 1255–1262.

———. 1984a. Propensity to report paranormal experiences is correlated with temporal lobe signs. *Perceptual and Motor Skills* 59: 583–586.

———. 1984b. Striking EEG profiles from single episodes of glossolalia and transcendental meditation. *Perceptual and Motor Skills* 58: 127–133.

Persinger, M. A., and P. M. Valliant. 1985. Temporal lobe signs and reports of subjective paranormal experiences in a normal population: a replication. *Perceptual and Motor Skills* 60: 903–909.

Peters, S.J., W. A. M. 1956. Richard Whitford and St. Ignatius' visit to England. *Archivum Historicum Societatis Jesu* 25: 328–350.

Peto, E. 1946. Weeping and laughing. *International Journal of Psychoanalysis* 27: 129–133.

Pinard de la Boullaye, S.J., H. 1950. *Les étapes de rédaction des Exercises de S. Ignace.* 7th ed. rev. Paris: Beauchesne.

Polanco, S.J., J. A. de. *Chronicon Societatis Iesu.* 6 vols. Madrid, 1894–1898.

Pollock, G. 1970. Anniversary reactions, trauma, and mourning. *Psychoanalytic Quarterly* 34: 347–371.

———. 1989. *The mourning-liberation process.* 2 vols. Madison, Conn.: International Universities Press.

Post, J. M. 1986. Narcissism and the charismatic leader-follower relationship. *Political Psychology* 7: 675–688.

Przywara, E. 1938–9. *Deus Semper Maior.* 3 vols. Freiburg.

Puhl, S.J., L. J. 1963. *The Spiritual Exercises of Saint Ignatius.* Westminster, Md.: Newman Press. Original in MI, series 2, vol. 1. Madrid, 1919.

Quinn, P. A. 1981. Ignatius Loyola and Gian Pietro Carafa: Catholic reformers at odds. *Catholic Historical Review* 67: 386–400.

Rabelais, F. 1955. *The histories of Gargantua and Pantagruel.* Trans. with intro. by J. M. Cohen. Baltimore: Penguin Books.

Rahner, S.J., H. 1953. *The spirituality of St. Ignatius Loyola.* Westminster, Md.: Newman Press.

———. 1956. Notes on the Spiritual Exercises. *Woodstock Letters* 85: 281–336.

———. 1960. *St. Ignatius Loyola: Letters to women.* New York: Herder and Herder.

———. 1968. *Ignatius the theologian.* New York: Herder and Herder.

———. 1977. Ignatius of Loyola and Philip Neri. In Wulf 1977, 45–68.

Rahner, S.J., K. 1964. *The dynamic element in the Church.* New York: Herder and Herder.

———. 1976. Foreword. In Egan, 1976, xii–xvii.

Rapaport, D. 1951. The autonomy of the ego. In *The Collected Papers of David Rapaport,* ed. M. M. Gill, 357–367. New York: Basic Books, 1967.

———. 1958. The theory of ego autonomy. In *The Collected Papers of David Rapaport,* ed. M. M. Gill, 722–744. New York: Basic Books, 1967.

Rappaport, M., H. Hopkins, and K. Hall. 1978. Are there schizophrenics for whom drugs may be unnecessary or contraindicated? *International Pharmacopsychiatry* 134: 100–111.

Ravier, S.J., A. 1987. *Ignatius of Loyola and the founding of the Society of Jesus.* San Francisco: Ignatius Press.

Reich, W. 1949. *Character analysis.* New York: Farrar, Straus and Giroux, 1972.

Ricard, R. 1956. Deux traits de l'expérience mystique de Saint Ignace. *Archivum Historicum Societatis Jesu* 25: 431–436.

Ricoeur, P. 1970. *Freud and philosophy.* New Haven: Yale University Press.

Rizzuto, A.-M. 1979. *The birth of the living God: A psychoanalytic study.* Chicago: University of Chicago Press.

Robins, E., and S. B. Guze. 1970. Establishment of diagnostic validity in psychiatric illness: its application to schizophrenia. *American Journal of Psychiatry* 126: 983–987.

Rochlin, G. 1965. *Griefs and discontents: The forces of change.* Boston: Little, Brown.

———. 1980. *The masculine dilemma: A psychology of masculinity.* Boston: Little, Brown.

Ross, N. 1975. Affect as cognition: with observations on the meanings of mystical states. *International Review of Psychoanalysis* 2: 79–93.

Russell, B. 1929. *Mysticism and logic.* London: Allen and Unwin.

Sadoff, R. 1966. On the nature of crying and weeping. *Psychiatric Quarterly* 40: 490–503.

Sartorius, N. A., A. Jablenski, and R. Shapiro. 1978. Cross-cultural differences in the short term prognosis of schizophrenic psychoses. *Schizophrenia Bulletin* 4: 102–113.

Saunders, G. R. 1981. Men and women in southern Europe: a review of some aspects of cultural complexity. *Journal of Psychoanalytic Anthropology* 4: 435–466.

Scholem, G. 1973. *Sabbatai Sevi: The mystical messiah.* Princeton: Princeton University Press.

Schurhammer, S.J., G. 1973. *Francis Xavier: His life, his times.* 4 vols. Rome: Jesuit Historical Institute.

Shore M. F. 1972. Henry VIII and the crisis of generativity. *Journal of Inter-disciplinary History* 2: 359–390.

Shorter, E. 1975. *The making of the modern family*. New York: Basic Books.

Silos, S.J., L. 1964. Cardoner in the life of Saint Ignatius of Loyola. *Archivum Historicum Societatis Jesu* 33: 3–43.

Slater, E., and A. W. Beard. 1963. The schizophrenic-like psychosis of epilepsy. *British Journal of Psychiatry* 109: 95–150.

Solnit, A. J. 1970. A study of object loss in infancy. *Psychoanalytic Study of the Child* 25: 257–272.

Spitz, R. A. 1945. Hospitalism. *Psychoanalytic Study of the Child* 1: 53–74.

———. 1946. Hospitalism: a follow-up report. *Psychoanalytic Study of the Child* 2: 113–117.

———. 1951. The psychogenic diseases in infancy. *Psychoanalytic Study of the Child* 6: 255–275.

———. 1965. *The first year of life*. New York: International Universities Press.

Starbuck, E. D. 1903. *Psychology of religion*. New York: Scribner's.

Steiner, J. 1990. The retreat from truth to omnipotence in Sophocles' "Oedipus at Colonus." *International Review of Psychoanalysis* 17: 227–237.

Stephens, J., C. Astrup, and J. Mangrum. 1966. Prognostic factors in recovered and deteriorated schizophrenics. *American Journal of Psychiatry* 122: 1116–1121.

Stevens, J. R. 1988. Psychiatric aspects of epilepsy. *Journal of Clinical Psychiatry* 49 (4, Suppl.): 49–57.

Stierli, S.J., J. 1977. Ignatian prayer: seeking God in all things. In Wulf, 1977, 135–163.

Tetlow, S.J., J. A. 1989. The fundamentum: creation in the principle and foundation. *Studies in the Spirituality of the Jesuits* 21/4, 9–10.

Toner, S.J., J. L. 1974. The deliberation that started the Jesuits. *Studies in the Spirituality of Jesuits*. St. Louis: American Assistancy Seminar on Jesuit Spirituality.

Tylenda, S.J., J. N. 1985. *A pilgrim's journey: The autobiography of Ignatius of Loyola*. Wilmington, Del.: Michael Glazier.

Valliant, G. 1964. Prospective prediction of schizophrenic remission. *Archives of General Psychiatry* 11: 509–518.

Verd, S.J., G. M. 1976. El "Iñigo" de San Ignacio de Loyola. *Archivum Historicum Societatis Jesu* 45: 95–128.

Volkan, V.D. 1988. *The need to have enemies and allies*. Northvale, N.J.: Jason Aronson.

von Matt, L., and H. Rahner, S.J. 1956. *Saint Ignatius Loyola: A pictorial biography*. Chicago: Regnery.

Waxman, S. G., and N. Geschwind. 1975. The interictal behavior syndrome of temporal lobe epilepsy. *Archives of General Psychiatry* 32: 1580–1588.

Weber, M. 1947. *The theory of social and economic organizations.* New York: Oxford University Press.

Werman, D. S. 1977. Sigmund Freud and Romain Rolland. *International Review of Psychoanalysis* 4: 225–242.

Wickham, John F. 1954. The worldly ideal of Iñigo Loyola. *Thought* 29: 209–236.

Wilkens, G. 1978. *Compagnons de Jesus: La genese de l'orde des Jesuites.* Roma: Centrum Ignatianum Spiritualitatis.

Wilner, A. R. 1984. *The spellbinders.* New Haven: Yale University Press.

Winnicott, D. W. 1953. Transitional objects and transitional phenomena. In *Playing and reality.* New York: Basic Books, 1971.

Wolfenstein, M. 1966. How is mourning possible? *Psychoanalytic Study of the Child* 21: 93–123.

———. 1969. Loss, rage, and repetition. *Psychoanalytic Study of the Child* 2: 432–460.

Wood, E. C., and C. D. Wood. 1984. Tearfulness: a psychoanalytic interpretation. *Journal of the American Psychoanalytic Association* 32: 117–136.

Woods, J. M. 1974. Some considerations on psycho-history. In Cocks and Crosby (1987), 109–120.

Wulf, S.J., F. 1977. Ignatius as a spiritual guide. In Wulf, 1977, 7–44.

Wulf, S.J., F., ed. 1977. *Ignatius of Loyola: His personality and spiritual heritage, 1556–1956.* St. Louis: Institute of Jesuit Sources.

Young, S.J., W. J. 1958. Spiritual journal of Ignatius Loyola. *Woodstock Letters* 87: 195–267. Original in MHSJ, MI Series IV, Vol. I. Rome, 1934.

Zaleznik, A. 1984. Charismatic and consensus leaders: a psychological comparison. In *The Irrational Executive*, ed. M. F. R. Kets de Vries, 112–132. New York: International Universities Press.

INDEX

CREDITS FOR ILLUSTRATIONS

Figures 1–6, 11–13, 19, and 20 reprinted by permission of Regnery Gateway. *St. Ignatius of Loyola: A Pictorial Biography* by von Matt, L. and Ratner, H., S.J., transl. by John Murray, S.J., Chicago: H. Regnery Co., 1956.

Figures 7, 8, and 9 reprinted courtesy of Rev. Richard Müller, S.J., of the Institut für Kommunikation und Medien an der Hochschule für Philosophie München.

Figures 10, 14, and 18 reprinted by permission of Verlag Herder, Freiburg.

Figure 15 reprinted by permission of the Museo del Prado, Madrid.

Figure 16 reprinted by permission of the Archivum Historicum Societatus Jesu, Rome.

Figure 17 reprinted by permission of Staatliche Museen zu Berlin, Preussischer Kulturbesitz Gemäldegalerie.

Maps of the province of Guipúzcoa (page 6) and of northern Spain (page 30) reprinted from J. Broderick, S.J., *St. Ignatius of Loyola: The Pilgrim Years* (Tunbridge Wells, Kent: Burns and Oates, Limited, 1956), pp. 360 and 361.

Map of Spain 1212–1492 (page 32) reprinted from W.R. Shepherd, *Historical Atlas*, 7th ed. (New York: Henry Holt, 1929).

DATE DUE

ILL			
BOOK			
6/2/99			
JA 19 '00			
DE 02 '05			

WITHDRAWN

Demco, Inc. 38-293